A Brand New Ballgame

A Brand New Ballgame

Branch Rickey, Bill Veeck, Walter O'Malley and the Transformation of Baseball, 1945–1962

G. Scott Thomas

McFarland & Company, Inc., Publishers
Jefferson, North Carolina

ISBN (print) 978-1-4766-8656-1
ISBN (ebook) 978-1-4766-4426-4

Library of Congress and British Library
cataloguing data are available

Library of Congress Control Number 2021050457

© 2022 G. Scott Thomas. All rights reserved

No part of this book may be reproduced or transmitted in any form or by any means, electronic or mechanical, including photocopying or recording, or by any information storage and retrieval system, without permission in writing from the publisher.

Walter O'Malley in front of an almost-completed Dodger Stadium in 1962 (Los Angeles Public Library)

Printed in the United States of America

*McFarland & Company, Inc., Publishers
Box 611, Jefferson, North Carolina 28640
www.mcfarlandpub.com*

To Barry Machado,
who taught me history
(and certainly knew his baseball)

"Baseball people—and that includes myself—are slow to change and accept new ideas."
—Branch Rickey

"Baseball, in general, is that way. It never does anything until the roof caves in."
—Phil Wrigley

Table of Contents

Preface 1
Prologue: Inertia 5

Part One: 1945–1952

1. MacPhail. 17
   HEADLINES: 1945 24
2. Rickey 25
3. Labor. 33
   HEADLINES: 1946 42
4. Pacific. 44
   HEADLINES: 1947 51
5. Veeck. 53
   HEADLINES: 1948 60
6. Clouds 61
   HEADLINES: 1949 69
7. Freefall 70
   HEADLINES: 1950 77
8. O'Malley. 79
9. Unhappy. 87
   HEADLINES: 1951 94
10. Celler 95
11. Shrinking 104
    HEADLINES: 1952 111

Part Two: 1953–1957

12. Milwaukee 113
    HEADLINES: 1953 121
13. Disruption 122
14. Toolson. 129
    HEADLINES: 1954 135
15. Philadelphia. 137
16. Wrigley. 144
    HEADLINES: 1955 150
17. Moses 152
18. Stoneham 161
    HEADLINES: 1956 168
19. Griffith 169
20. Showdown. 177
    HEADLINES: 1957 184

Part Three: 1958–1962

21. California 187
22. Shea. 196
23. Kefauver. 202
    HEADLINES: 1958 209
24. Chavez 211
25. Continental 218
26. Comeback 226
    HEADLINES: 1959 231
27. Outlaws 233
    HEADLINES: 1960 240
28. Uncertainty 242
29. Expansion 249
    HEADLINES: 1961 256
30. Twilight 258
    HEADLINES: 1962 264

Epilogue: Beyond 267
Chapter Notes. 279
Bibliography 313
Index. 321

Preface

Thomas Dewey was a successful politician who won three terms as governor of New York, though he is remembered today for his greatest failure.

Dewey was the odds-on favorite to unseat Harry Truman in the 1948 presidential election. Pollsters universally agreed that Dewey held a comfortable lead that autumn. *Newsweek* surveyed fifty political experts shortly before election day. All fifty predicted that Dewey would win.

Yet he lost.

Dewey affected a public attitude of nonchalance, but the defeat stunned and demoralized him. He had never enjoyed the daily grind of political campaigns—the speeches, the handshaking, the fundraising, "being dragged from pillar to post, with no time to think," and the sense that he was merely a player in a quadrennial diversion for the masses. He declared that he would have "to be touched with madness" to ever run for president again.

"I have learned from bitter experience," Dewey concluded, "that Americans somehow regard a political campaign as a sporting event."[1]

It works the opposite way, too, as this book will show.

Baseball and other professional sports are political to their very core. Teams compete fiercely with each other, but also cooperate as partners. They strive individually for championships, yet also work collectively to advance the interests of their sport.

The baseball executives who wield the greatest power in such a conflicted environment might disdain any comparison to Tom Dewey and his ilk, though they would be mistaken. Three of Dewey's contemporaries—Branch Rickey, Bill Veeck, and Walter O'Malley—could have been political kingpins if they had preferred that vocation. They were as adept at self-promotion and backroom machinations as any governor, senator, or president.

This book tells how these three Hall of Famers and several lesser lights pushed their own visions of baseball's future during a period of unprecedented change from 1945 to 1962. Six teams relocated to new cities, capped by the coast-to-coast moves of the Brooklyn Dodgers and New York Giants. Four expansion franchises were created from thin air. Dozens of black stars emerged after Jackie Robinson broke the color barrier. Higher salaries eventually materialized after the players created a union.

This eighteen-year span transformed baseball from a musty relic to the modern sport we recognize today, yet the metamorphosis was far from smooth. Rickey, Veeck, and O'Malley pursued their own ends, sometimes for personal gain, sometimes for broader purposes. Others sought to block them. "Baseball people—and that includes myself—are slow to change and accept new ideas," Rickey admitted.[2] He worked as strenuously as anyone to propel the sport into the modern era, though he suffered several defeats along the way.

Baseball's future course, as it turned out, would be determined as much by the powerful forces of fear, greed, and incompetence as by the well-laid plans of Rickey and his fellow giants. Any member of Congress or delegate to a presidential convention would have understood.

That's why this book is concerned as much with political maneuvers as with baseball—and why it delves into demography, technology, and several other factors that affect every business from coast to coast. (But don't worry. The game itself is always present. Annual summaries of on-the-field action are tucked between the longer chapters.) The experiences and lessons scattered across these pages are universal.

I pieced together this history through research in archival materials from the Library of Congress, the National Baseball Hall of Fame and Museum, and several universities from New York to California. My sources included the personal papers of commissioners, owners, players, and politicians; league and team documents; more than fifty oral histories; transcripts of congressional hearings and court trials; and decades of American and Canadian census reports. I also consulted scores of executives' and players' memoirs, as well as a wide range of contemporaneous newspapers and magazines.

The resulting mosaic features a multitude of stories that have been buried in manila folders, filing cabinets, and obscurity for decades. Consider a dozen that are examined at length in the pages to come:

- The postwar landscape of the major leagues would have been dramatically altered if the St. Louis Browns had moved to Los Angeles back in 1942. The shift was quietly added to the agenda for an American League meeting on December 8, 1941. It became moot after the Japanese attack on Pearl Harbor the day before.
- A secret 1946 study warned the owners against racial integration, which the report said "could conceivably threaten the value" of major-league franchises. Commissioner Happy Chandler later scoffed that several owners "predicted race riots and all sorts of dire occurrences" if blacks took the field.[3]
- Rickey insisted that morality guided his signing of Robinson as the first black major leaguer. Manager Leo Durocher remembered Rickey offering a different rationale: "Leo, it is my great ambition to win a pennant for Brooklyn. I aim to use anybody who can help me do it, be he white, green, blue, or black."[4]
- A majority of the Pittsburgh Pirates voted to strike in June 1946, seeking recognition for their new union. But veteran Rip Sewell turned the tide. "I'm going out and pitch if I have to go out there by myself," Sewell barked. "You can come if you want to." His teammates sullenly followed. A players' union would not be established for another eight years.[5]
- The Pacific Coast League, a prominent minor league, repeatedly sought elevation to the status of America's third major league in the 1940s and 1950s. "We are grown up, we are adults now, and you fellows have just got to vote us in," begged Charlie Graham, the owner of the PCL's San Francisco team. The existing big leagues always refused.[6]

- Cable television wouldn't gain a foothold until the 1980s, but O'Malley predicted as early as 1953 that pay TV would become a key revenue stream for baseball. He envisioned a coin-operated system: "A fellow who wants to see a ballgame drops in a quarter, which seems reasonable enough for two or three hours of entertainment for everybody in the room."[7]
- The first franchise shift occurred in 1953, when Lou Perini took his Braves from poverty in his hometown of Boston to prosperity in Milwaukee. Perini, who would later portray himself as a fearless pioneer, chose to forget his initial unhappiness. "It's unfortunate in a way," he said when announcing the move. "Maybe Milwaukee isn't a major-league city. I'm sure I don't know."[8]
- Fans of the Brooklyn Dodgers have been mistakenly immortalized for their passion and devotion. The truth is that Brooklyn's attendance plummeted from 1.81 million in 1947 to a paltry 1.02 million in 1954, even though the team was an annual contender. "Where is everybody?" asked *Brooklyn Eagle* columnist Dave Anderson.[9]
- The Washington Senators had the first shot at Los Angeles in 1956, as local officials ardently wooed owner Calvin Griffith. If he had simply given the word, the nation's third-biggest market would have been his. But Griffith waffled, and O'Malley seized the prize a year later.
- The Dodgers' shift to Los Angeles is commonly depicted as an intricate plot. It actually was so haphazard that O'Malley even failed to line up a stadium before arriving in California. "The move was about as well thought-out as a panty raid by a bunch of college freshmen who'd had too many beers," admitted Harold Parrott, the ticket manager for the Dodgers.[10]
- Congress showed unusual interest in baseball in the late 1950s, threatening to impose tight limits on the number of players a franchise could control. Joe Cronin, the American League's president, moaned that the bill was "certain to decimate all of baseball." It was defeated by the narrow margin of four votes in the Senate.[11]
- The now-forgotten Continental League emerged in 1959, vowing to become the third major league. Its success, promised its president, the ubiquitous Rickey, was "as inevitable as tomorrow morning." The Continental League never played a game, but its specter forced the majors to expand in 1960.[12]

These seminal events and larger-than-life personalities come together to create a fascinating saga—the story of baseball's monumental evolution between World War II and the early 1960s, a tale that unfolds in the pages ahead. The game would never be the same.

Prologue: Inertia

There could not have been a worse time to amass a personal fortune than the early and mid–1930s. The sudden collapse of the stock market in October 1929 had vaporized the financial holdings and bank accounts of millions of Americans, rich and poor alike. The market's heartbeat, the Dow Jones Industrial Average, plummeted 87 percent to its nadir in 1932 before beginning a fitful, unpromising recovery. The Dow still held less than half its 1929 value when the first day of trading dawned in 1936.[1]

Yet Donald Barnes somehow defied the odds. The energetic native of Springfield, Illinois, had relocated to the nearest big city, St. Louis, and established the American Investment Company, capitalizing on the nation's automotive mania during the Roaring Twenties. AIC financed installment payments, enabling thousands of people to buy their first cars. Business remained sufficiently strong into the gloomy 1930s to make Barnes a millionaire.

But the money wasn't enough. Barnes was young—just forty-two in 1936—and increasingly restless. He began to seek a new field that might bring greater joy than the arcane intricacies of automotive finance. One option emerged above others in his mind—a challenge of impressive dimensions that would indulge his love of sports. He cobbled together a group of investors and purchased the most hapless of the sixteen franchises in baseball's major leagues, the St. Louis Browns.[2]

The Browns had not won a single American League pennant since their creation in 1902, nor had they finished higher than fifth in the eight-team AL since 1929. It was their great misfortune to share St. Louis with the wildly successful Cardinals, winners of five National League championships and three World Series titles in the past eleven seasons. Local fans were cognizant of the disparity. The Cardinals drew an annual average of 419,000 fans to their home games between 1930 and 1936—a respectable figure during the Depression—but the Browns attracted only 117,000 per season, fewer than 2,000 per game.

None of this mattered to Don Barnes, who confided a pair of goals to his closest friends. The Browns hadn't drawn a sellout crowd to their home field, Sportsman's Park, since the early 1920s, and they had never played in a World Series, two shortcomings that he vowed to correct. He publicly pledged that he would elevate his new team to championship caliber by 1941.[3]

He could not have been more mistaken. Barnes swung into action—making dozens of trades, launching new promotional campaigns—but nothing seemed to work. The Browns lost 487 games between 1937 and 1941. Their home attendance was the worst in the majors in four of those seasons.[4] "We kept struggling and struggling," recalled Barnes's second-in-command, Bill DeWitt, Sr. "We borrowed money, and Don Barnes loaned the club money."[5] The team's losses reportedly exceeded $100,000 a year, the equivalent of $1.75 million in 2020.[6]

It slowly dawned on Barnes that St. Louis was the problem. The sixteen major-league teams had been frozen in place since 1903, bunched in ten cities across the Northeast and Midwest. Five cities fielded teams in both leagues, led by the nation's three largest urban centers, New York, Chicago, and Philadelphia, each with a population greater than 1.9 million as of the 1940 census. But the other multi-franchise cities were tiny by comparison. St. Louis and Boston had eight hundred thousand residents apiece.[7]

Larger virgin territories were available. A California lawyer had approached Barnes in 1940, hinting that Los Angeles investors might be willing to spend five million dollars to buy the Browns for their city. Barnes insisted that his team was not for sale, yet he wavered for a moment. "For five million dollars, I could do a lot of listening," he admitted.[8]

The 1940 census tallied more than 1.5 million people in Los Angeles, making it the fifth-most-populous city in the nation, by far the largest without a big-league team. Civic leaders had been trying to lure the majors westward since 1932, the year that Los Angeles hosted the Summer Olympics, but transportation was an impediment.[9] It took three days to ride from New York to the opposite coast by train. Transcontinental flights did not exist, and most Americans still considered air travel to be dangerous, no matter how short the trip.[10] "Los Angeles will never get a franchise in the American League," declared AL president Will Harridge in 1939. "It's all right for a few of us to fly around the country, but it would never do to transport complete ballclubs regularly in the air."[11]

Don Barnes wasn't so sure. He headed west from St. Louis in the summer of 1941 on a reconnaissance mission. The welcome in Los Angeles exceeded his expectations. The chamber of commerce promised to guarantee annual attendance of five hundred thousand for five seasons, and the president of the Bank of America pledged to buy a stake in the Los Angeles Browns. Only two barriers remained. Barnes needed to secure the territorial rights to the city and a place for his team to play. Both were controlled by Phil Wrigley, the owner of the Chicago Cubs and the minor-league Los Angeles Angels.[12]

"Phil made me a wonderful proposition," Barnes would recall.[13] Wrigley offered to sell the Angels and their stadium, Wrigley Field (namesake of the Cubs' Chicago ballpark), for $250,000 down and annual installments of $30,000 over the next 25 years. Visions of massive profits danced in Barnes's head. He hustled back to St. Louis, determined to launch the first relocation of a major-league franchise in 39 years.

Secrecy was the byword. Barnes confided only in DeWitt. The pair somehow convinced the Cardinals' owner, the notoriously frugal Sam Breadon, to chip in $350,000 to speed the Browns out of town. They met with officials from Trans World Airlines, who suggested that any team traveling to Los Angeles could ensure its safety by booking players on several flights in a single day, no more than six men per plane. And they helped American League officials devise a new schedule for 1942.[14] "We'd try it this way and that way, trying to work it out so the other clubs could get out to the coast and get back again," said DeWitt.[15]

Everything was in place, and not a single word had leaked to the press. Formal approval of the Browns' move was slated for the American League's winter meeting in Chicago on Monday, December 8, 1941. Barnes and DeWitt journeyed up from St. Louis on the seventh and bought tickets for a game between Chicago's two National Football League teams, the Bears and Cardinals. It was there in Comiskey Park that they heard the fateful news. "Somebody came up to me and said the Japanese just bombed Pearl Harbor," said DeWitt. "And Jesus, there goes the Browns."[16]

Relocation was suddenly out of the question. Restrictions on domestic travel were certain to follow America's entrance into World War II, dashing the schedule that Barnes and DeWitt had so carefully constructed. It also seemed likely that the Japanese might attack the Pacific Coast, maybe even Los Angeles itself. The American League voted unanimously to keep the Browns in St. Louis.

That's when the story finally hit the papers. Barnes obscured his own role when reporters came calling. "Certain interests of Los Angeles have approached me with reference to the possibility of moving the St. Louis Browns out there," was all he would say publicly.[17] But he did not mask his unhappiness in private, curtly informing his partners that the Browns had burned through all of their working capital. Expenses would have to be cut to the bone. All of the team's scouts were immediately laid off.

Barnes anticipated enormous losses for untold years to come, muting the solace offered by the *Sporting News*, the self-proclaimed "Bible of Baseball." Its editors praised Barnes for targeting the Los Angeles market, hailing him for "some looking-forward that might well be cultivated throughout the game." Baseball would break out of its geographic straitjacket when the war ended, the paper predicted, and the Browns would then be free to head westward. "Capital of the movie industry, center of styles, a city of some million and one-half," said the *Sporting News*, "Los Angeles cannot be denied its place in the sun."[18]

* * *

The distribution of major-league franchises, illogical though it might have seemed by 1941, had made perfect sense at the start of the twentieth century.

The American League sprang forth in 1901 as a fresh rival for the National League, which was then celebrating its twenty-fifth birthday. Each circuit consisted of eight teams scattered between the Atlantic Ocean and Mississippi River. The AL made a pair of early shuffles—transforming the Milwaukee Brewers into the St. Louis Browns in 1902 and the Baltimore Orioles into the New York Highlanders (soon to be the Yankees) in 1903—but the lineups of both leagues remained stable thereafter.

The dominant city in the 1900 census, New York, boasted three of the majors' sixteen teams once the Highlanders arrived. The Giants and Dodgers had been coexisting in the National League since 1890, the Giants ostensibly representing all of New York, the Dodgers belonging solely to the borough of Brooklyn. The next four cities in 1900's population rankings (Chicago, Philadelphia, St. Louis, and Boston) could not match New York's economic power, yet were sufficiently large and affluent to be coveted by both leagues, and thereby secured a team in each.

Just one other U.S. city had more than five hundred thousand residents as of 1900, sixth-rated Baltimore, which found itself bereft after the Orioles' departure.

The remaining big-league franchises were dispersed among five communities that ranged from seventh place (Cleveland) to fifteenth (Washington) in the population standings. The only cities among the top fifteen to be barred from the majors were those that had already been found wanting (Baltimore and Milwaukee), were too distant from the majors' geographic footprint (New Orleans and San Francisco), or were simply unlucky (Buffalo).[19] The latter was the sole omission that might be questioned. Buffalo was not only America's eighth-largest city, but also was an emerging high-tech hub, the Silicon Valley of its era, thanks to the recent harnessing of hydroelectric power in nearby Niagara Falls.

But no franchise would be granted to Buffalo in the decades to come, nor to any other city on the outside. Baseball much preferred the status quo. It clung tenaciously to its turn-of-the-century scaffolding into the 1940s—the same two leagues, the same sixteen teams—even as modes of transportation improved and the country experienced a demographic metamorphosis.

America changed dramatically during this forty-year period. The nation's population soared 74 percent from 76 million in 1900 to 132 million in 1940, an increase of 56 million people. Millions of families left their farms in the process, lured by the steady paychecks being dangled by rapidly expanding factories. Sixty percent of Americans lived in rural areas when the century began, but urban communities held a comfortable majority of 57 percent a year before the attack on Pearl Harbor.[20]

The 1940 census identified fourteen communities with populations larger than five hundred thousand and two others that fell only a few thousand short of that threshold. Nearly half of these metropolises—seven of sixteen—lacked big-league ball. The most glittering prize, the one that had so dazzled Don Barnes, was Los Angeles with its 1.5 million citizens. But Baltimore, San Francisco, Milwaukee, Buffalo, New Orleans, and Minneapolis also appeared to be large enough for the majors, as did two sizable cities just over the Canadian border (thereby absent from the U.S. census), Montreal and Toronto.

All of these places were more substantial than the tiniest member of the major leagues, Cincinnati (population: 455,610), and all, at one time or other, had expressed their eagerness to join baseball's exclusive fraternity. Yet they remained outside its doors as the 1940s slowly unreeled, with no reason to hope that an invitation would be coming soon.[21]

* * *

The owners of all sixteen big-league teams were capitalists, no question of that. They moaned about players' paychecks—this at a time when the heftiest salary was thirty-five thousand dollars for Detroit slugger Hank Greenberg—and they constantly schemed to cut expenses.[22] Some even confessed doubts about the value of winning a championship. "The best thing for a team financially is to be in the running and finish second," said Connie Mack, the tall, straitlaced owner/manager of the Philadelphia Athletics. "If you win, the players all expect raises."[23]

Expansion could have been a reliable source of additional cash for these harried executives. The United States and Canada were clearly capable of supporting twenty-four major-league teams, maybe more. The AL and NL might have added four franchises apiece, or perhaps a third eight-team league could have been created. New cities would have paid dearly to join the majors under either plan, as Don Barnes had learned to his delight in Los Angeles. These extra teams, in turn, would have spurred greater interest in baseball, generating more money for everybody. Capitalism at its best.

So why did the owners consistently refuse to admit new members? The only reasonable answer is that, on the whole, they were conservative, fearful, and not especially bright.

There were a few exceptions, but most owners belonged to one of two camps. The bigger group encompassed an array of inheritors—those who acquired a team upon a father's death (such as the New York Giants' boozily convivial Horace Stoneham), succeeded a dead husband (brisk, businesslike Grace Comiskey of the Chicago White Sox), bought a franchise with family money (shy, unassuming Tom Yawkey of the Boston Red Sox), inherited a massive corporation with a team attached (chewing-gum heir Wrigley), or received a franchise as an outright gift (twenty-eight-year-old Robert Carpenter, Jr., whose dad would hand him the Philadelphia Phillies in 1943).[24]

The second band consisted of men who clawed their way up from the field to the ownership suite, notably Mack of the Athletics and the irascible Clark Griffith of the Washington Senators. Both had attained Hall of Fame prominence as players and managers before acquiring controlling interest in their respective teams.

These people—inheritors and lifers alike—were not disposed to make waves. They revered baseball's intricate web of mysterious traditions and unwritten rules. Their lodestar was the status quo. One can imagine their intense dread as the roll-call vote approached for Barnes's relocation of the Browns—moving all the way to the *West Coast*? teams traveling there by *air*?—and their overpowering relief when the Japanese yanked the question from the agenda.

Emanuel Celler, the longtime chairman of the House Judiciary Committee, tangled with several baseball owners during his half-century on Capitol Hill. He came to believe that they were motivated primarily by greed. "They are usually out for all the dough they can amass," he said. "They squeeze and squeeze every ounce of the sport out of baseball."[25]

But there was more to it than that, as Leslie O'Connor noted at one of Celler's congressional hearings. O'Connor had observed the owners up close for more than two decades as the right-hand man to baseball's dour, omnipotent commissioner, Kenesaw Mountain Landis. The core truth, O'Connor told Celler, was that the game's leaders preferred to avoid action whenever possible:

> **CELLER:** Do you think there is inertia in connection with the thinking of the baseball owners? Do you think they are loathe to make any changes and want to maintain the status quo?
> **O'CONNOR:** I am obliged to say that I think the baseball owners, particularly in the majors, are ultraconservative.
> **CELLER:** What is meant by ultraconservative?
> **O'CONNOR:** I say they resist changes.[26]

The exemplar of this antediluvian philosophy was Clark Griffith, a dedicated opponent of change in any form. The Cincinnati Reds staged the first night game in big-league history in May 1935, inspiring other franchises to install lights, yet Griffith stood firm. "The Lord made baseball for the daytime," he barked.[27] Night ball, in his opinion, was "bush-league stuff and just a step above dog racing."[28] Several teams assembled massive farm systems to develop their own players in the minor leagues, but he dismissed such planning as a pointless exercise. "You can only play nine players at a time, anyway," he said.[29] Griffith reserved his greatest anger for visionary proposals, such as the idea that American and National League teams might play each other during the regular season. "We are not going in for any hippodrome stuff," he spat.[30]

Fellow owners sometimes wondered about Griffith's mental acuity. The Old Fox, as he was commonly known, had turned seventy in 1939 and no longer seemed able to compete effectively. His Senators hadn't won a World Series since 1924 and played about as poorly as the Browns. The team's finances became so shaky that Griffith unhappily capitulated in 1941 and purchased lights. The Senators soon were playing after dark more frequently than any other team in the majors, but their owner (and most of his big-league colleagues) remained steadfastly opposed to other innovations.[31]

Fear was the key factor behind their cautious approach—fear of failure, fear of the future, fear of the unknown. The most egregious of baseball's unwritten rules was its prohibition against black players. Several owners, including Griffith, privately conceded that integration was coming, but they declined to speed its arrival. "They were afraid to make a move," Ford Frick, then the president of the National League, admitted decades later. "They were afraid of upsetting the status quo."[32]

Many also lacked confidence and executive skill. The few owners with real-world business experience were often horrified by the way the major leagues operated. Lou Perini, who bought a share of the Boston Braves during the war, was president of one of the nation's largest contracting firms. Most teams, he thought, were run by men "who act like a bunch of kids."[33] His dismay was shared by the Cubs' Phil Wrigley, who ruled his family's gum empire. Wrigley was the rare inheritor who dared to deviate from baseball dogma on occasion, though his quiet personality prevented him from asserting himself. He understood the need to branch into new markets. Expansion sold more chewing gum; it ought to do the same for baseball. But Wrigley also knew that his counterparts did not agree.

"The heads of organized ball move slowly," he sighed. "Getting the major leagues to take action like this is a slow and tedious process."[34]

* * *

Only one man had the power to dispel the inertia enveloping the national pastime. Commissioner Landis began his third decade as the sport's supreme ruler in January 1941, the same year that brought his seventy-fifth birthday. The owners had invested him with absolute authority, and he evinced no desire to surrender his sovereignty for retirement.

Landis had grown to be synonymous with baseball in the mind of the average American. The commissioner was instantly recognizable in newspaper and magazine photographs, typically featuring his sour expression and distinctive mane of white hair. He was often pictured with one hand cupping his chin, as if his head were too heavy for his neck to support, his brain densely packed with shrewd insights and judicial precedents.

Landis had been elevated to the national stage by Theodore Roosevelt, who appointed the Chicago lawyer to a federal judgeship in 1905. Subordinates henceforth called him "Judge," even after he left the bench for the commissionership. Nobody used his peculiar given name of Kenesaw, which had been bestowed by his father, a Union Army soldier wounded at the Battle of Kennesaw Mountain. (The omission of the second N from his son's name would never be explained.) It would have been unthinkable to look directly into Landis's steely eyes and call him Ken.[35]

The new judge ran a lively, erratic courtroom. He vaulted into the headlines in 1907, when he fined Standard Oil Company of Indiana $29.2 million (the equivalent of $808 million in 2020) for violating the Sherman Antitrust Act. He again sprang to widespread attention in the superheated atmosphere of World War I. Landis issued a summons to Kaiser Wilhelm II, demanding that the German ruler answer personally for the sinking of the *Lusitania*. He later sentenced a prominent socialist, Victor Berger, to twenty years in prison for criticizing the American war effort.[36] "The law should have enabled me to have had him lined up against a wall and shot," Landis snapped.[37]

Legions of supporters hailed the judge's exuberance, though a smaller band of critics condemned his lack of restraint. The latter pointed out that Landis's major decisions rarely stuck. "Judge Landis will be dead a long time before this fine is paid," John D. Rockefeller snarled after losing the Standard Oil case, and he was right.[38] The ruling eventually was overturned by a higher court, and for that matter, the kaiser never traveled to Chicago and the unshot Berger was set free on appeal.[39]

This spotty record was of no concern to the owners of major-league teams, who had two reasons to hold Landis in high regard. They knew the judge as a devoted baseball fan often seen at Chicago's ballparks and, much more importantly, they had come to view him as the savior of the game.

Their warm feelings dated to 1915, when Landis was assigned an antitrust case filed by the Federal League, a renegade organization that billed itself as the third major league. The FL had launched operations the year before, brandishing lucrative offers that attracted more than two hundred defecting players from the American and National Leagues and the top minor leagues. The ensuing battle drove up the average salary 133 percent from twelve hundred dollars per player in 1914 to twenty-eight hundred the following season. Owners panicked as red ink flowed through the sport, and their fears rose further when the Federal League filed its lawsuit, accusing the older leagues of conspiring to drive it out of business.[40]

The assignment of Landis to the case only made the situation worse, or so it seemed. Everybody knew that the wiry, volatile judge was enamored of theatrical decisions and enormous fines. What would happen if he ruled in favor of the upstart league?

Such worries proved to be unwarranted. Landis tipped his hand early in the January 1915 proceedings. He admonished the Federal League's attorney: "Do you realize that a decision in this case may tear down the very foundations of this game, so loved by thousands?"[41] He interrupted again when a lawyer referred to players as workers. "As a result of thirty years of observation," Landis said, "I am shocked because you call baseball 'labor.'"[42] He wrapped up the trial in four days.

And then he did nothing.

Landis remained silent as the 1915 season played out. *Baseball Magazine* complained, "Judge Landis, for reasons best known to himself, has elected to delay the rendering of his classic decision to a point where all interest in that decision has expired of old age."[43] All three leagues continued to hemorrhage money, the Federal League most of all. The latter had been counting on an infusion of cash from Landis's ruling, but now saw no alternative but to sue for peace. A modest cash settlement and other inducements convinced the FL to disappear.

It was only then—in February 1916—that Landis reconvened the parties in his courtroom. He essentially admitted that his only proper course would have been to rule in favor of the Federal League. But "an appropriate order," he went on, "would have been, if not destructive, vitally injurious" to the game itself. Hence: "I decided that this court had a right—if not a right, a discretion—to postpone the announcement of any such order."[44] He had stalled until the Federal League died.

This unexpected favor was recalled by major-league owners in their great hour of need in 1920, when it was revealed that eight Chicago White Sox players—the infamous Black Sox—had been bribed by gamblers to deliberately lose the 1919 World Series. The resulting damage to baseball's image was extensive and potentially mortal. The owners sought a new commissioner to put the sport back on the right track, an incorruptible man whose love of baseball was beyond question.

They turned to Kenesaw Mountain Landis, who demanded untrammeled authority. He was granted the power to fine, suspend, or remove anyone from baseball whose actions were "detrimental to the game," a phrase that meant whatever he wished. He swiftly barred the Black Sox for life, moved with similar dispatch against

Kenesaw Mountain Landis became commissioner in 1920 and served for more than two decades. Sportswriter John Lardner described baseball's supreme boss as "a sort of combination reformer, hangman, and symbol of integrity" [Library of Congress].

some (though not all) of the other players suspected of gambling ties, and warned everybody else not to stray from the righteous path. The greatest star of that or any other era, Babe Ruth, defied Landis's 1921 ban on postseason barnstorming.[45] "What has that long-haired old goat got to do with me?" sneered Ruth.[46] The commissioner suspended him for the first quarter of the 1922 season.

These early moves cemented Landis's reputation. He would be regarded for the rest of his life, in John Lardner's phrase, as "a sort of combination reformer, hangman, and symbol of integrity."[47] Yet the praise was overblown. The years passed, and the commissioner made no effort to improve baseball's administration or expand its audience. Owners often asked for guidance on complicated issues. "Do it, and I'll rule on it," he invariably replied. He still thought of himself as a judge, not a leader.[48]

Casual baseball fans assumed that the all-powerful Landis could take any action he wished. If he believed that something was in the best interests of baseball—geographic expansion, for instance—he could simply decree it. But the owners doubted he would seize the moment. Many feared the old man, and all were wary of his volcanic temper, yet they were confident that he would not be launching any bold initiatives. He lacked both the inclination and the energy. The sport's course after World War II—whenever it finally came to a close—would be determined not by the elderly commissioner, but by the owners themselves.

Political leaders, newspaper columnists, and financial pundits were already warning that the looming postwar era would be tumultuous. Industries and other institutions would be forced to adapt to survive. Success would belong to the foresighted and the nimble. But a majority of baseball's hidebound owners shared a disinterest in preparing for the future or altering their tactics. They preferred to march blindly into this brave new world, driven by their fears, motivated by their greed, and hindered by their frequent incompetence.

* * *

The quality of the game itself—the competition within the basepaths—inevitably eroded as the war dragged on. A slight decline became evident in 1942 and 1943 as the first players enlisted or were drafted into the armed services, but the blow was cushioned by the lingering presence of several prewar stars. The flow of men to Europe and the Pacific attained full force by 1944, siphoning off most of the other stars and journeymen. The remaining mélange of 4-F's, teenagers, and old men staged a version of minor-league baseball in big-city ballparks before spectators who paid major-league prices.

Teams became so desperate for talent that they reached out to the extremely young and the partially disabled. The Cincinnati Reds called up a fifteen-year-old pitcher, Joe Nuxhall, on June 10, 1944, just four days after Allied troops stormed the beaches of Normandy on D-Day. The Cardinals rattled Nuxhall for five runs in his only appearance that year, which lasted only two-thirds of an inning. The St. Louis Browns pressed outfielder Pete Gray into service the following season. Gray, who had lost his right arm in a childhood accident, somehow batted .218 and struck out just 11 times in 253 at-bats.[49]

But the surest sign of baseball's great decline was the sudden emergence of the hapless Browns as a pennant contender. Other American League teams were decimated by the military draft, but St. Louis lost none of its players in 1943 and only one the next year, a stroke of good fortune that transformed the Browns into a temporary powerhouse. They defeated the Yankees, 5–2, on the final day of the 1944 season, clinching an improbable AL title before a home crowd of 35,518, the sellout that Don Barnes had long dreamed of.[50]

The Browns entered the World Series as steep underdogs against (who else?) the Cardinals, who indeed sent them packing in six games, but the positive vibes lingered. What everybody in St. Louis remembered was the final game of the regular season and the wild celebration, the unrestrained joy, that broke loose in Sportsman's Park when the Yankees' last batter popped up. Browns manager Luke Sewell would never forget the image of Barnes racing onto the field. "I looked at him, and he was crying, tears just running down his cheeks," Sewell recalled. "I never came as near crying myself on a baseball field."[51]

Barnes had achieved both of his dreams—a sold-out house and a World Series berth—on the same day. Yet the future remained cloudy. The Browns and Cardinals, champions of their respective leagues, attracted only 971,000 fans in 1944, a combined total that barely topped what the Detroit Tigers had drawn on their own. "It is not exactly a secret that St. Louis cannot support two major-league clubs," concluded Branch Rickey, the president of the Brooklyn Dodgers.[52] Rickey possessed special knowledge of the market's inadequacies, having spent three decades as a player, manager, and general manager for both St. Louis clubs.

Sam Breadon, the gravel-voiced owner of the Cardinals, had toyed as early as 1932 with relocating his franchise to Montreal or Detroit. He rejected the former after closer inspection, but the latter seemed an exciting possibility.[53] "Detroit is a large, prosperous city. It can stand continuous baseball," Breadon declared in 1935.[54] The Tigers, who had no intention of sharing their booming market, quickly vetoed the Cardinals' proposed move.

Breadon eventually concluded that he held the upper hand in St. Louis, leaving it to Barnes to seek a geographic solution. The war, of course, made that impossible. So the two men reached a compromise in the midst of their magical season of 1944. They appealed to Commissioner Landis and the other owners during a joint meeting of the two leagues in July:

> **Breadon:** Judge, before everybody leaves, I would like to move that a joint committee be appointed to go into the St. Louis situation to see what can be done about it, because I think that is the most important thing.
> **Barnes:** Second the motion.
> **Landis:** All in favor of the motion, say aye. Opposed, nay. It is carried.
> **Breadon:** I would like to have that kept quiet, though.[55]

It stayed very, very quiet. The two league presidents appointed executives from several teams to the new panel, some against their will. "From the looks of things, there is nothing any outsider can do to relieve the St. Louis situation," groused one unhappy member, Detroit general manager Jack Zeller.[56] If the committee ever issued a report—or indeed ever conducted a meeting—it left no record in the vast archives of the National Baseball Hall of Fame.

Not that it mattered. Don Barnes would always recall the Browns' 1944 American League pennant, not the American Investment Company, as his "greatest success in life."[57] But he felt no urgency to keep pushing for a World Series championship or to revive the transfer to Los Angeles. "I feel my purpose has been accomplished," he told reporters. He sold the Browns to a St. Louis businessman, Richard Muckerman, on August 10, 1945, the same day that the Japanese announced their willingness to surrender.[58]

The irony was inescapable.

Part One: 1945–1952

1

MacPhail

Harbingers of an eventual Allied victory emerged a year in advance of Japan's capitulation. American and British troops began their drive toward Berlin in the summer of 1944, while their Pacific counterparts island-hopped closer and closer to Tokyo. Nobody knew when World War II would end—the final battles in Germany and Japan were expected to be long and bloody—but it finally seemed reasonable to believe in the ultimate arrival of peace.

Business executives across America did the prudent thing under the circumstances. They began to plan for the postwar era, which promised to confront them with challenges of enormous proportions. Jobs would have to be made available to the millions of soldiers and sailors who streamed back home. Industrial plants would need to pivot quickly from the manufacture of military hardware to the production of consumer goods. If these goals were not attained, if the national reconversion were somehow botched, the price would be extreme. Various economists envisioned massive unemployment, superheated inflation, or perhaps even a rebirth of the Depression.

Kenesaw Mountain Landis harbored no doubts about the best man to lead baseball through the anticipated chaos. His term as commissioner was due to expire two years hence in 1946, though he had already indicated his desire for a contract extension. He could be counted upon to maintain a steady hand on the tiller, hewing to the same course he had been following since 1921.

The owners saw no reason to deviate. Baseball had survived the war in unexpectedly good shape. Major-league attendance initially plummeted from 9.69 million in 1941, the final prewar season, to 7.47 million two years later. But it rebounded strongly to 8.77 million in 1944, even as the on-field product deteriorated to an alarming degree. That last total was better than the attendance for any season during the heart of the Depression. The inevitable conclusion, in the opinion of *New York Times* columnist Arthur Daley, was that baseball was indestructible. "If the war couldn't kill it," Daley suggested, "nothing will."[1]

Landis received much of the credit for this surprising prosperity, and he was confident that future successes lay ahead. He still went to the office every day, always attended the All-Star Game and World Series, and spent much of his free time puttering about his garden in a Chicago suburb. "Here I am, still going strong, and where are the men who put me into office?" he asked a visitor in 1944. "Nearly all the men who elected me [in 1921] were younger than I, but only Griffith, Breadon, and I survive, and I'll soon be seventy-eight."[2]

No alarm sounded when Landis was admitted to the hospital on October 2,

1944, two days before the World Series opened in St. Louis. The commissioner's office issued a brief statement that his illness was "not serious," elaborating a few days later that he been waylaid by a cold, nothing more. Never before in his tenure had he missed a World Series game, but he was absent from all six in 1944. He listened to the Browns and Cardinals on a bedside radio.[3]

Reassuring bulletins were dispatched from St. Luke's Hospital every few days. The patient remained incommunicado as weeks passed, yet the newspapers maintained their flow of cheery updates. The sports editor of the *Chicago Times*, Gene Kessler, was among the few to suspect that the old man might be in worse shape than advertised. Kessler asked if he could send a photographer to snap a simple picture of Landis sitting up in bed. The commissioner had never been known to reject a photo opportunity, but the hospital surprised Kessler by brusquely refusing his request. "Can you imagine Judge Landis too ill to pose for pictures?" he asked colleagues.[4]

The owners did not share his concern. A special committee of American and National League executives met in Chicago on November 17 and unanimously recommended that Landis be retained as baseball's supreme leader until 1953. "The action ended all speculation concerning the office of commissioner," the *Sporting News* reassured its readers.[5] Final approval of his contract extension—a mere formality—was slated for the winter meetings in mid-December, where Landis himself was expected to wield the gavel.

This tranquility lasted a mere eight days, shattered by Landis's fatal coronary thrombosis in the predawn hours of November 25, 1944, five days after his seventy-eighth birthday. The death of the bedridden warhorse somehow came as a shock to the baseball world, which paid tribute with effusive praise. The *Sporting News* led the way: "Landis lifted the sport to the highest plane it has ever achieved and built for himself a monument that will endure as long as the game itself."[6] Even the perpetually cranky Clark Griffith was deeply affected by the loss. "We are beholden to him for so much," Griffith said.[7]

The owners spoke more candidly in private, agreeing that Landis's cold demeanor, erratic temper, and dictatorial behavior would not be missed. Reporters were already predicting that the next commissioner would be a Landis clone, most likely a hard-edged egomaniac like Douglas MacArthur, the army general in command of the Pacific theater, or J. Edgar Hoover, the director of the Federal Bureau of Investigation. A collective shudder vibrated through the game's leaders. They couldn't imagine a worse outcome, and they resolved to prevent it.[8]

The bylaws of the major leagues dictated that a simple majority—nine of sixteen teams—sufficed to elect a commissioner. The threshold was quietly raised to a supermajority of twelve votes in February 1945, guaranteeing that any unacceptable contender could be easily rejected. A four-man committee then began to assemble a long list of possibilities, eventually collecting more than a hundred names. The panel sought a candidate who combined a national profile with a pleasant, pliable personality. Such a man was not easily found.[9]

The owners convened in Cleveland on April 24, 1945, to discuss their desultory search. The commissioner's office had already been vacant for five months, but committee chairman Alva Bradley, the president of the Cleveland Indians, asked for additional time to find a man "who would have the respect and confidence of the public, the ballplayers, and the club owners." He proposed the appointment of a temporary commissioner, with the election of a permanent replacement later in the year.[10]

The meeting went into executive session—only one representative per team, no records kept—to ponder this request. Bradley set the stage by pulling out "a quite heavy file," as Branch Rickey described it. He reeled off the names of possible candidates, including such prominent figures as MacArthur, Hoover, and New York governor Thomas Dewey, an array of lesser politicians, and a handful of baseball men. Bradley even mentioned the play-by-play announcer for the Brooklyn Dodgers, Red Barber. An aimless discussion ensued.[11]

Larry MacPhail, the fiery, bombastic president of the New York Yankees, listened with growing frustration. His patience, never known for its durability, finally exploded in exasperation. "Gentlemen," MacPhail barked. "I am astonished at the weakness of the list submitted to us." He loudly announced, to absolutely no one's surprise, that he believed he could do better.[12]

* * *

It's safe to assume that MacPhail commanded the room on that April afternoon at the Hotel Cleveland. He inevitably took charge of any meeting—charming his colleagues one minute, berating them the next, and dazzling them throughout with his ceaseless stream of ideas. It was impossible to doze through a MacPhail presentation, which was typically delivered at an intense decibel level by a "raspy and carrying" voice that the *New Yorker* once compared to "the call of an adult male moose."[13]

MacPhail's intelligence and skill were beyond dispute. "He was imaginative, enterprising, a first-rate promoter. He was way ahead of most other owners," said Red Smith, the famed New York sportswriter.[14] Smith's assessment was echoed by none other than Branch Rickey, commonly believed to be the shrewdest executive in the game. "That fellow always had more ideas than a dog has fleas," Rickey said admiringly.[15]

But there was a dark side to MacPhail's genius, as Smith also recalled: "He was a good scotch destroyer. He drank heavily. And when he got loaded, he was outrageous."[16] His mood changed so dramatically under the influence that he seemed to be schizophrenic. "Sober, he was as sweet a fellow as I ever saw," said Albert "Happy" Chandler, then a senator from Kentucky. "Drunk, he was as mean as he could be."[17] Leo Durocher, who managed under MacPhail for four seasons, admired him greatly, yet also recalled several times when the boss fired him in a drunken rage, only to rehire him the following morning. MacPhail, in Durocher's opinion, "was a wild man."[18]

His bold, erratic personality was already on display in early adulthood, when MacPhail and seven fellow officers celebrated the end of World War I by attempting to kidnap Germany's kaiser, who had fled to the Netherlands. They failed in this decidedly unauthorized mission, though MacPhail did make off with one of the kaiser's ashtrays, emblazoned with the imperial coat of arms. The heavy brass tray, by far his favorite war trophy, was always displayed in MacPhail's office.[19]

And there were to be many offices. MacPhail had lived in Michigan, Illinois, and Tennessee before the war, but he settled in Columbus, Ohio, upon his return, working simultaneously as a lawyer, entrepreneur, and Big Ten football referee. His various interests coalesced in 1930, when he and several partners bought the city's minor-league baseball franchise, which was mired in debt. MacPhail energetically grabbed the reins of the Columbus Red Birds, tripling their attendance by 1932 and transforming them into a profitable concern, no small feat during the Depression. He sold the team along the way to Rickey's St. Louis Cardinals, who were assembling baseball's first farm system.[20]

Rickey retained MacPhail as president of the Red Birds, but the two men were direct opposites in temperament, and MacPhail was inevitably shown the door. He always insisted that Rickey refused to explain the dismissal. Yet his period of unemployment would be brief.[21] A local bank, which found itself owning the bankrupt Cincinnati Reds in 1933, asked MacPhail to run the franchise. National League approval was required for this arrangement, and it was Rickey who convinced the executives of other NL teams to vote yes. "He is a fast learner," Rickey told them. "He has a lot of aptitude, a lot of enthusiasm, a lot of industry."[22]

MacPhail revitalized the Reds in short order. His greatest innovation was staging the first night game in big-league history. President Franklin Roosevelt threw a switch in the White House on the evening of May 24, 1935, to illuminate Crosley Field 410 miles away, a typical MacPhail touch. His introduction of seven night games per season, combined with his gradual improvement of a team that had finished last in

Larry MacPhail brought a bombastic, energetic style to the front offices of the Reds, Dodgers, and Yankees. "That fellow always had more ideas than a dog has fleas," said Branch Rickey [National Baseball Hall of Fame and Museum].

the National League four consecutive years, sent the Reds' attendance soaring from 218,000 in 1933 to 466,000 in 1936.

Yet MacPhail quickly tired of the routine in Cincinnati, another trait that would repeatedly manifest itself. He abruptly resigned as general manager at the end of the 1936 season. "If I stay around here much longer, I'll have a nervous breakdown," he said vaguely, fleeing to the safe haven of his family's business in Michigan.[23]

History recycled itself in 1938. The Brooklyn Trust Company, which had seized control of the Brooklyn Dodgers, sought a savior for the bankrupt franchise. Why not Larry MacPhail, who had worked such magic in Cincinnati? He insisted on total control, and it was granted.[24] The Dodgers' play-by-play man came to believe that MacPhail possessed the ideal personality to succeed in Brooklyn. "He was loud," said Red Barber. "He was truculent. He was mad. He hated the Giants. He didn't like the Yankees." And Barber cited one last quality, the most essential of all: "He did things."[25]

That he did. MacPhail installed lights at Ebbets Field, broadcast all of the Dodgers' games on the radio (making them the first New York team with blanket coverage), hired Durocher as his manager, and overhauled a roster that had lost ninety-one games in 1937. A National League pennant flew over Brooklyn by 1941, the first for the Dodgers since 1920. Attendance shot up to 1.2 million that season, a quarter-million more than the world-champion Yankees drew across town and 450,000 more than anybody else in the majors.[26]

Yet success did not calm the turbulence in MacPhail's soul. He fired Durocher after a heated dispute on the eve of the 1941 World Series, only to rehire him hours before the first pitch. "That's the way the man was, so emotional that he could drive you to distraction and twist his own destiny into hairpin turns," Durocher recalled. "And when you rode with him, your life went dizzy, too."[27]

MacPhail would leave Brooklyn less than a year after the Dodgers fell to the Yankees in five games. America entered World War II during the offseason, and he felt himself drawn back to the army, the institution that had given him his first taste of glory. "Hell, there's a war going on. I figure they can use me somewhere," he told friends.[28] He enlisted after the 1942 season at fifty-two years of age, specifying combat duty as his preference, though he was assigned to the office of Robert Patterson, the undersecretary of war.

MacPhail's stint as Patterson's aide would ease his return to baseball. It brought him into contact with an up-and-coming Arizona contractor, Del Webb, who was constructing army bases in several Western states. And it renewed his acquaintance with Dan Topping, a captain at the nearby marine base in Quantico, Virginia. Topping was an heir to the Anaconda copper fortune and the owner of Brooklyn's National Football League team, yet he was most commonly known as the husband of Sonja Henie, the reigning Olympic ice-skating champion and an occasional actress.[29]

The three men shared a passion for sports and a craving for status, so it made perfect sense for them to join forces in January 1945 to purchase the most fabled franchise in baseball, the Yankees, from Edward Barrow and the heirs of Jacob Ruppert. The price tag was $2.8 million, the equivalent of $40 million in 2020. The new owners divided the stock in equal thirds, but Colonel MacPhail made it clear from the start that he was the man in charge. Webb and Topping consented.[30]

The rest of the baseball world found it difficult to comprehend. Volatile, mercurial Larry MacPhail running the staid, tradition-bound Yankees? It was a completely logical marriage, he told reporters, and he predicted it would be highly successful, too. "We purchased the Yankees because we know the war won't last very much longer in Europe," MacPhail said. "And once the Nazis are out of the way, we will be able to concentrate on wiping out the Japs, and in 1946, send baseball into the greatest boom in its history."[31]

* * *

It was up to the sixteen team representatives sequestered in the Hotel Cleveland to decide who would be placed in charge of baseball's transition to postwar prosperity.

Alva Bradley conceded that his panel had plucked a few favorites from its list of more than 100 candidates—anywhere from a half to a full dozen—but it hadn't approached any of them to ascertain their interest. Nor had it investigated their backgrounds. Several owners abruptly demanded the names of these finalists. Bradley glanced nervously at the other members of the search committee before he offered eleven possibilities, including Dewey, Hoover, federal price regulator Fred Vinson, Ohio governor Frank Lausche, and two chairmen of the Democratic National Committee, incumbent Robert Hannegan and predecessor James Farley.[32]

It was then that MacPhail erupted in dismay. He insisted that a name be added to the list: "I refer to Senator Chandler of Kentucky."[33]

Everybody in the room knew Albert Chandler, an amiable politician renowned for his swift upward mobility. He had been elected governor at the age of thirty-seven, rising to the Senate four years later. His legislative record in Washington was anything but distinguished, yet he had won his constituents' hearts with a folksy, back-slapping style that earned him the nickname of "Happy."[34] Chandler possessed an infectious laugh, and he laughed frequently. "I have not been unhappy—never—and I sort of take things in stride," he said.[35]

Chandler had proven to be a steadfast friend of baseball, standing up against critics who implored the major leagues to cease play for the duration of the war. "It's foolish to discount the value of baseball as a morale factor," he said. A tour of war zones in early 1945 convinced him, or so he told reporters, that a love of baseball was motivating American troops to bring the war to a speedy conclusion.[36] "When they return," he said, "they want to be able to enjoy the sports and other pleasures that no other land can produce save ours."[37]

Bradley responded agreeably to MacPhail's impromptu nomination, adding Chandler to the informal list of finalists, which now contained twelve names. The meeting proceeded without structure, as owners flitted from candidate to candidate, discussing their pros and cons. Several contenders encountered strong resistance and fell to the wayside.[38]

Warren Giles, the general manager of the Reds, did his best to sink Chandler's nascent candidacy. He knew all about Happy, he told his colleagues, reminding them that Kentucky was directly across the Ohio River from Cincinnati. Giles bemoaned the senator's "singing proclivities and the fact that in his political campaigns he had his children singing from the platform." He implied that Chandler was somewhat of a clown.[39]

But MacPhail had also lived in Cincinnati, and his was a different story. He depicted Chandler as a skilled and intelligent lawyer who had attended Harvard Law

School, a master promoter who had won several statewide elections, and an experienced legislator who had forged strong Washington connections. The bonus, of course, was his sunny disposition. Kenesaw Mountain Landis had never been described, let alone nicknamed, as happy.

Evening was approaching. Most owners were still leaning toward the appointment of a temporary commissioner, but they consented to a test vote, just to see where things stood. Secret ballots were quickly distributed, collected, and tabulated. The frontrunner, to the surprise of many, was Larry MacPhail's candidate. Chandler received five first-place and six second-place votes. Hannegan and Lausche were the runners-up.

It suddenly seemed logical to push forward. There was more discussion, then another test vote. Chandler now emerged as the clear leader, with eight firsts and five seconds.[40] "Gentlemen, it seems that we have reached a situation in which it is, after all, possible to elect a new commissioner," Sam Breadon said excitedly.[41] A third tally—a real election this time—secured the necessary twelve votes for Chandler. The owners dissolved the executive session at five-twenty, hastily reconvened their regular meeting, confirmed Chandler unanimously, and then marveled at what they had done.[42]

Nobody had anticipated that a new commissioner would be named in Cleveland—it was difficult to envision the owners suddenly awakening from their five-month slumber—so the reporters lounging outside the meeting room were stunned when informed of Chandler's election. They assumed, with good reason, that he had been picked because he was so agreeable, so good-humored, so unlike Landis. "He wants to please, and he knows that it pays off to please," an *Esquire* profile would say of him that summer.[43]

But there was more to it than that. The election of Happy Chandler stamped Larry MacPhail as one of baseball's power brokers, perhaps the most powerful of them all. He had recently taken charge of the most lucrative franchise in American sports, and now he had installed his personal favorite as commissioner. Chandler readily conceded that he owed his fancy new title to MacPhail: "He had the dominant role. He was a very dominating fellow. Whatever he was for, he was *for*."[44]

The new commissioner also suspected that a few owners had been swayed by his conservative Southern heritage. The game had remained lily-white throughout Landis's tenure, and it seemed unlikely that a senator from Kentucky would countenance integration. "They knew I was a Southerner, they knew I had Confederate leanings, and that was all true," Chandler later said. "And they thought I'd be the last fellow that would agree to let a black boy play."[45]

This variety of factors—Chandler's amiability and conservatism, coupled with MacPhail's emphatic endorsement—convinced the owners that they had stumbled into the right man. They hoped that the new commissioner would prove to be a five-star salesman, a splendid ambassador for baseball—and perhaps just a bit of a pushover.

Newspapermen was more concerned about Chandler's ability to measure up to the Judge's towering image. Some had their doubts. Tom Meany complained in *PM*, a New York daily, that a politician, "even one nicknamed 'Happy,' should have a little more dignity."[46] Ed McAuley told readers of the *Cleveland News* that Landis "would have died a decade sooner or refused to die at all" if he had known his successor's identity.[47]

None of this mattered to Happy Chandler, who endured the furor with his habitual smile. He had no doubt that he would be a supremely successful commissioner in his own right. "I knew Old Man Landis," Chandler later explained. "I knew him well. He was a nice old man—but nothing special."[48]

Headlines: 1945

ONE-ARMED OUTFIELDER HAS FIELD DAY FOR BROWNS

Browns left fielder Pete Gray enjoyed the brightest day of his brief big-league career on May 20, reaching base five times and driving in two runs in a doubleheader sweep of the Yankees. Gray also handled nine chances cleanly in the field, despite having only one arm. "He's a fine ballplayer, fast, courageous, and he can hit," said Manager Luke Sewell.[49]

GREENBERG COMES BACK FROM ARMY IN STYLE

More than forty-seven thousand fans jammed into Briggs Stadium on July 1 for the return of Tigers slugger Hank Greenberg, who had been serving in the army since 1941. Greenberg thrilled the crowd by launching a home run into the left-center-field seats in the eighth inning, helping Detroit beat Philadelphia, 9–5. Manager Steve O'Neill couldn't stop grinning. "He was great out there, wasn't he?" O'Neill kept asking reporters.[50]

FELLER WHIFFS A DOZEN IN FIRST START SINCE '41

Fireballer Bob Feller, who won ninety-three games for Cleveland from 1938 to 1941, enjoyed a triumphant homecoming from the navy on August 24. A headline in a Cleveland newspaper screamed: THIS IS WHAT WE'VE BEEN WAITING FOR. Fans placed so many calls for tickets that the Indians' switchboard broke down. Feller struck out twelve Tigers and allowed only four hits in his first start in four seasons.[51]

TIGERS ROAR BACK TO WIN WORLD SERIES

The Chicago Cubs were installed as slight favorites in the World Series after seizing the National League title with a record of 98–56. The American League champs, the Tigers, finished with only eighty-eight wins. But both squads had been depleted by military call-ups. "Neither contender is a super team," wrote Fred Lieb in a *Sporting News* preview. The Cubs knotted the series with a dramatic twelve-inning victory in Game Six, but the Tigers roared back, 9–3, on October 10 to win their first world championship since 1935.[52]

2

Rickey

No discerning critic would have called Dan Daniel a journalistic stylist. His prose was saturated with clichés and bizarre synonyms. Pitching was "slinging" or "hurling." Hustling ballplayers were "earnest strivers." Managers didn't protest, they "vehemed." Inside information came to "your correspondent" by way of the "grapevine."

The clunky quotes in Daniel's stories sounded as if they were uttered by robots. Reds manager Bill McKechnie angrily accused Dodgers pitcher Rube Melton of throwing at his batters. "I do not regard Melton as a fit person for pitching in the National League," McKechnie primly told Daniel, or so the latter reported.[1] Thirty-five-year-old pitcher Joe Bowman, fighting to stay in the big leagues at his advanced age, supposedly said, "I can show you plenty of pitchers my senior in both circuits."[2] Did anybody speak that way?

But Daniel knew his stuff. The esteemed columnist for the *New York World-Telegram* and the *Sporting News* had a plethora of well-connected sources on his grapevine. His stories may have been awkwardly worded, but they offered an insider's view of the behind-the-scenes maneuvers of baseball executives. So it was noteworthy when Daniel informed his readers in 1946 that the sport's balance of power had shifted.

"The writer is led to believe that Col. Larry MacPhail has become the No. 1 magnate of the major leagues," Daniel declared in a front-page story in the *Sporting News*. Only a year had passed since Happy Chandler's election as commissioner, yet his patron had swiftly accumulated influence and power. Daniel wrote that "many shrewd critics" agreed with his assertion that "the president of the Yankees has become the top man in the whole game."[3]

But the vote wasn't unanimous. The president of the Brooklyn Dodgers, Branch Rickey, had several adherents.

Hall of Famer Rogers Hornsby, an ornery old-timer who disliked almost everyone he ever met, mellowed when Rickey was the subject. "He is the smartest baseball man in the country," Hornsby said, the highest possible praise from him.[4] Buzzie Bavasi, a big-league executive for nearly four decades, knew MacPhail and the other owners of that era, but he considered Rickey their superior: "He was the finest baseball man I ever met. Everyone who knew him will tell you the same thing."[5] The immortal boss of the Athletics, Connie Mack, suggested "from my long years of intimate acquaintance with Rickey and knowing his great ability" that he would make an ideal president of the United States.[6]

Rickey had turned sixty-four the week prior to Christmas 1945. He was eight years older than MacPhail, and his baseball experience was considerably more extensive. He had arrived in the big leagues in 1905 as a catcher for the St. Louis Browns, renowned for his strong throwing arm.[7] But an offseason injury neutralized that awesome weapon in 1907, earning him an unhappy entry in the official record book. The Washington Senators stole thirteen bases off of him, the most a catcher ever allowed in a single game. "They all ran down as soon as they got on," he remembered sadly.[8]

The injury dropped the curtain on Rickey's big-league career. He earned a law degree from the University of Michigan and established a practice in, of all places, Boise, Idaho. But the winters were rough, business was slow, and baseball was impossible to forget. He jumped happily when the Browns called with the offer of a front-office position in 1912.[9]

Rickey would remain in St. Louis for thirty years, filling a variety of roles. He was pushed into service as the Browns' field manager to finish the 1913 season, stayed in the dugout the next two years, and then returned to the executive suite. But Rickey fell out with the team's new owner, the abrasive Philip Ball, and fled in 1917 to become general manager of the Cardinals. It wasn't a sound move financially. The Browns possessed the deeper pockets in St. Louis in those days. The Cardinals, who were badly in debt, struggled to meet their payroll.[10]

Rickey's new employer lacked two essential ingredients—money and competent players—so he set out to find both. One of the investors he recruited, auto dealer Sam Breadon, would emerge as the Cardinals' savior, eventually acquiring 80 percent of the franchise. Breadon and Rickey would form a successful duo after an initial rocky patch, the former holding the title of president, the latter overseeing the day-to-day operations.[11]

Improving the product on the field proved to be more difficult. Rickey grabbed the manager's reins after the Cardinals finished last in the National League in 1918. He kept the job for six seasons, cajoling the team as high as third place in 1921 and 1922, but no higher. Breadon angered Rickey by yanking him back into the front office full time in 1925, a command that Rickey still condemned years later as "brutal" and "callous." He was forty-three when the order came, and he considered himself a failure. His baseball career was summed up by two mediocre numbers: a .239 batting average and a .473 managerial winning percentage.[12]

Yet Breadon's decree proved to be a godsend. "He's the kind of man who should be a general manager," Hornsby said, and Rickey now confirmed his assessment.[13] Minor-league teams operated independently at that time, generating income by selling their better players to the majors. Rickey's brainstorm was to seize control of the production process. If the Cardinals directly signed and trained hundreds of young ballplayers, they could guarantee a steady stream of talent. He put this theory into practice by buying minor-league teams in Syracuse, Houston, and Fort Smith, Arkansas. Many more were to follow.[14]

Rickey was fond of saying that quantity would lead to quality. "Don't be finicky," he exhorted his scouts.[15] His "farm system," as it became known, corralled 203 ballplayers onto 7 minor-league squads by 1928, numbers that ballooned to 600 players on 32 farm clubs a dozen years later. Critics accused him of creating a monopoly that was uncompetitive and un–American.[16] "The farm system," Rickey said in defense, "is the only vehicle that a poor club has available to it to use to mount into respectability."[17]

Admirers and critics agreed that Branch Rickey was intelligent, devious, and stunningly loquacious. "For a life's work," said Pirates owner John Galbreath, "he should have been a Shakespearean actor" [Library of Congress].

There was no doubt of its success in that regard. The Cardinals would win four world championships and six National League pennants between 1926 and 1942, finishing in second place five other times during the seventeen-year span. This streak inspired sportswriter Tom Meany to bestow on Rickey the enduring nickname of Mahatma. The St. Louis general manager, in Meany's opinion, demonstrated the same mystic wisdom and overarching superiority that characterized the famed mahatma of India, Mohandas Gandhi.[18]

Yet Rickey's brainchild also sowed the seeds of his destruction in St. Louis. Kenesaw Mountain Landis hated everything about the farm system, which he condemned as "the octopus of common ownership," though there was little he could do to retard its growth.[19] The commissioner spotted a rare opportunity to intervene in 1938. He accused Rickey of controlling players on two teams in the same minor league, an arrangement prohibited under baseball's rules. Landis swiftly set seventy-four of the Cardinals' farmhands free, declaring them to be free agents.

Rickey denied guilt. He demanded that Breadon file suit against Landis, but the Cardinals' convivial owner had no desire to oppose the baseball establishment. The commissioner's censure had brought Breadon considerable embarrassment. His relationship with Rickey began to cool.[20]

The two men also were driven apart by money. Very few players in the St. Louis farm system climbed all the way to the big-league club. Those with less promise were sold to other teams, enriching the Cardinals' coffers by more than two million dollars during Rickey's tenure. The Mahatma had a special incentive to swing as many of these deals as possible, since his contract allowed him to pocket 10 percent of the proceeds from all player sales. This unusually generous provision applied as long as the Cardinals generated a profit, which was virtually an annual occurrence.[21]

The parsimonious Breadon eventually wearied of making large payouts to his controversial, freewheeling general manager—$88,000 in 1941 alone, the equivalent of $1.5 million in 2020. He also grew tired of seeing Rickey receive full credit for the Cardinals' prolonged success. The inevitable parting of the ways occurred in 1942, when Breadon quietly informed Rickey that his contract would not be renewed at the end of the season.[22]

Many men would have been discouraged by the prospect of a fresh job search so late in life, but Rickey remained characteristically upbeat when rumors of his dismissal finally surfaced. "I cannot say now what I will be doing next year," he told reporters in September 1942. They asked if he had reached the end of the line. Would they see him again in 1943? Rickey grinned. "There certainly is a possibility," he said slowly, "that I will continue to be associated with baseball."[23]

* * *

Branch Rickey had ample reason to smile as the final days of the 1942 season slipped away. Larry MacPhail's pursuit of military glory had suddenly and unexpectedly presented him with a golden career opportunity.

MacPhail resigned as president of the Dodgers on September 23, 1942, to re-enlist in the army. His departure from Brooklyn dovetailed nicely with Rickey's pending unemployment, and the Mahatma wasted no time in notifying the Dodgers of his availability. Only two men were seriously considered as MacPhail's replacement: Rickey and George Weiss, the Yankees' coldly efficient farm director.

Rickey seemed to be the logical choice, given his string of championships in St. Louis, but a countervailing argument could be made for Weiss, an impersonal, humorless man who was best known for his attention to the smallest of details.[24] Weiss was once asked to characterize his management style. "I guess I am ultra-conservative," he replied.[25] There was no danger that he would deviate from the wishes of the Dodgers' board of directors, a pleasant thought in the wake of MacPhail's tumultuous half-decade.

Rickey, on the other hand, was accustomed to giving orders, not taking them. His powerful, multifaceted personality contrasted sharply with Weiss's bland demeanor. The Dodgers' board had good cause to wonder if he might be difficult to work with, perhaps even more so than the blustery MacPhail.

Admirers insisted that Rickey possessed unusual strength of character. Critics derided him as stubborn. This quality, whatever it might be called, was evident in his unwavering adherence to his religious beliefs. Rickey's mother had asked him never to set foot in a ballpark on Sunday, a request he obeyed as a player, manager, and executive, no matter how much his absence angered his bosses. Neither a direct order nor a personal request could entice him to lift this self-imposed ban.[26] "Sunday to me," he said, "has always been a day apart."[27] He did not gamble or drink, two of the most popular activities of baseball men in his or any other time. And he never swore. The strongest exclamation to pass from his lips was "Judas Priest."[28]

Rickey's vocabulary was so extensive that he had no need for profanity. Profiles in newspapers and magazines commonly called him loquacious or voluble. He could hold forth on almost any topic—the dangers of communism, the condition of the postwar economy, the proper way to lay down a bunt—for as long as someone would listen. Reporters joked that any room where Rickey held a press conference should be renamed the Cave of the Winds.

Yet he had an undeniable presence. His bushy eyebrows, perpetually rumpled suit, and wire-rimmed glasses gave him the appearance of a slightly scruffy professor at a small Midwestern college. But his strength was verbal, not visual.[29] Rickey's baritone voice and evangelical fervor could engulf any crowd, sending a spark through his listeners. Red Barber recalled his first encounter with this phenomenon. "From the moment he began speaking, he captivated me," Barber said. "There was a strength. There was a magnetism. There was a depth. There was great art."[30] John Galbreath, the owner of the Pittsburgh Pirates, was equally mesmerized. "For a life's work," said Galbreath, "he should have been a Shakespearean actor."[31]

These impressive thespian skills made Rickey an influential force in the baseball world, but they were accompanied by two traits that should have given the Dodgers pause. Rickey was not the most straightforward of men, and he was exceedingly fond of money.

"He was a devious fellow," Happy Chandler once said with a laugh, and few would have disagreed.[32] Rickey did not often lie, but he frequently used his linguistic skills to confuse an issue. "He was so good at evasion, at circumlocution, that he didn't have to lie," said sportswriter Red Smith.[33] Leo Durocher, who played and managed for Rickey, found it maddeningly difficult to coax a straight answer to any question. "The only trouble with Branch," he said, "is that if he was going from Minneapolis to St. Paul, he'd take the night train to Kansas City."[34]

Rickey's talent for indirection gave him a tremendous advantage when negotiating with his employees. He always drove the hardest financial bargain possible. "He had both players and money, and he didn't like to see the two of them mix," joked Chuck Connors, a journeyman first baseman who later became an actor.[35] But Rickey's own salary was a different matter. He valued his skills highly and insisted on being compensated accordingly. Hall of Famer Al Lopez, who played against Rickey's teams for eighteen seasons, considered the old man's priorities to be crystal clear. "He was for *Rickey*," said Lopez. "He made a lot of money for *Rickey*."[36]

Sam Breadon could have warned the Dodgers—and perhaps he did—that it would cost them dearly to hire the Mahatma.

*   *   *

Brooklyn's brain trust interviewed both candidates, weighed the risks, and offered the presidency to Rickey in October 1942. He insisted on a five-year contract, which reportedly stipulated an annual salary between forty thousand and fifty thousand dollars, along with bonuses tied to attendance and profits. It was an impressive haul, dwarfing the peak salary for any player in the coming season, the twenty-seven thousand paid to Joe Cronin of the Red Sox.[37]

Rickey insisted that he would be worth every penny. "If our aim is to make Brooklyn the baseball capital of America," he declared, "by Judas Priest, we'll do it!"[38] He began to overhaul the roster, unloading such popular and accomplished veterans as Dolph Camilli and Joe Medwick. Camilli had been voted the National League's Most Valuable Player in 1941, while Medwick had batted .306 since joining the Dodgers in 1940, but both were on the wrong side of thirty. Rickey valued youth above all.

"We're on an elevator here in Brooklyn," he said, "and we will go down before we go up, until the youngsters learn."[39]

The team's supporters were outraged. The Dodgers had been wonderfully good in 1942, amassing 104 victories, the most in franchise history. (It was their misfortune that St. Louis had set its own team record with 106 wins, taking the National League crown.) Brooklyn slipped to third place after Rickey's housecleaning in 1943, then plummeted to seventh a year later. Fans expressed their displeasure through the protest signs they carted to Ebbets Field. "We Want MacPhail," said many of the placards.[40]

Rickey paid no attention to the critics—self-doubt had never been a personal weakness—and he refused to deviate from his plan as the losses piled up. His immediate goal was to solidify his own position, to guarantee that no future Sam Breadon could deprive him of his livelihood. Twenty-five percent of the franchise came up for sale in 1944, and the Dodgers' attorney, an aspiring plutocrat named Walter O'Malley, suggested that Rickey join him and a third partner in the purchase. Rickey was not a rich man, his enormous salary notwithstanding, but he seized the opportunity. He tapped into his life insurance and sold his stock holdings to raise the money.[41]

An additional 50 percent hit the market the following year, and O'Malley and Rickey again obtained the necessary funds. They and John Smith, president of the Charles Pfizer & Co. pharmaceutical firm, now owned three-quarters of the Dodgers. The three men agreed to act in unison. If two of them favored a particular action, the third was contractually obligated to fall into line. Yet the likelihood of such a situation seemed remote. O'Malley busied himself with financial and legal matters in the front office, and Smith appeared content to be a silent partner. Both deferred to Rickey, who had finally secured absolute control of a big-league ballclub.[42]

Rickey had begun beefing up the Dodgers' farm system from the day he arrived in Brooklyn, yet he knew it would be impossible to duplicate his St. Louis success. The Cardinals' minor-league network had been unequaled in the 1920s and early 1930s, conferring a tremendous advantage over the rest of the National League, but times had changed. Most major-league teams had assembled their own farm systems by the 1940s. George Weiss became a finalist for the Brooklyn presidency primarily because of the skill with which he had imitated the Cardinals' model.

So Rickey began searching for a different idea, a fresh innovation that would vault Brooklyn to the top of the major leagues. He eventually settled on the boldest step of all. He decided to integrate the national pastime.[43]

Black players were confined to a segregated backwater collectively known as the Negro Leagues, though it was an open secret that many (if not most) were of big-league caliber. Dizzy Dean, a white pitcher whose Hall of Fame skills were matched only by his braggadocio, had barnstormed with a legendary black pitcher, Satchel Paige, after the 1934 and 1935 seasons. "My fastball looks like a change of pace alongside that pistol bullet old Satch shoots up to the plate," Dean conceded with rare humility, adding that Paige had "the greatest stuff I ever saw."[44] Another Hall of Fame pitcher who barnstormed in the 1940s, Bob Lemon, was more general in his admiration. "Everybody knew they could play," he later said. "I played against a lot of good colored players."[45]

It was an incontrovertible fact that blacks had been barred from the majors since 1884, despite Judge Landis's vehement denials. "There is no rule, formal or informal, or any understanding—unwritten, subterranean, or sub-anything—against the hiring of Negro players," Landis insisted as late as 1942.[46] But the commissioner wasn't telling the truth, and Larry MacPhail admitted as much. "There has been an unwritten law tantamount to an agreement between major-league clubs on the subject of the racial issue," MacPhail conceded.[47]

Rickey would later contend that he shattered this time-honored barrier for moral reasons, harkening back to a college game in 1904 between Ohio Wesleyan, where he was the baseball coach, and Notre Dame. Rickey's team checked in at its hotel in South Bend, Indiana, but the desk clerk barred the sole black player, catcher Charlie Thomas. Rickey somehow convinced the hotel manager to allow Thomas to sleep on a cot in the coach's room. This incident, he often said, motivated him to challenge racial injustice.[48]

Perhaps he was telling the truth; perhaps Charlie Thomas was a factor. But Rickey, who was deep into his thirty-third year as a big-league executive in 1945, had not previously challenged the professional color line. The Browns and Cardinals fielded all-white teams throughout his tenure in St. Louis, and a city ordinance confined black fans to a small portion of the bleachers at Sportsman's Park. "I would have changed that, had it been up to me," he said of the latter arrangement, but he spoke only after moving to Brooklyn.[49]

Contemporaries remembered a different motivation behind Rickey's crusade for integration. Harold Parrott, a former sportswriter who served as the Dodgers' traveling secretary, quoted the Mahatma's excited explanation: "Son, the greatest untapped reservoir of raw material in the history of our game is the black race!"[50] Durocher, the Dodgers' manager since 1939, recalled a similar exclamation: "Leo, it is my great ambition to win a pennant for Brooklyn. I aim to use anybody who can help me do it, be he white, green, blue, or black."[51] Rickey's right-hand man, Arthur Mann, agreed that his boss was primarily interested in gaining a competitive advantage. "He had firm beliefs about the equality of man," Mann said, "but they were never a factor in his decision."[52]

Rickey maintained absolute secrecy. He secured the approval of the Dodgers' board of directors in 1943, then assigned scout Tom Greenwade to comb the Negro Leagues for talent. He cautioned Greenwade "to work quietly without any newspaper publicity whatever."[53] It was a sensible admonition in the prevailing social climate. Most institutions, including the military, were still rigidly segregated in the mid-1940s, and public attitudes were firmly entrenched. Only 42 percent of white respondents agreed that blacks were as intelligent as whites, according to a comprehensive 1942 survey by the National Opinion Research Center, and just 30 percent believed that children of both races should attend the same schools.[54]

These numbers confirmed the prejudices of big-league owners, a conservative and fearful bunch. An internal report in 1946 warned that the introduction of black players might attract swarms of black fans to "parks such as the Yankee Stadium, the Polo Grounds, and Comiskey Park [and] could conceivably threaten the value of the major-league franchises owned by these clubs."[55] Happy Chandler, long into his retirement, vividly recalled the panic that ensued whenever owners discussed the dangers of integration. "They predicted race riots and all sorts of dire occurrences and consequences," he said. "They did everything they could to throw cold water on the thing."[56]

But Branch Rickey would not be deterred. The first team to sign black players, he believed, would gain an enormous jump on the competition. He intended to make his decisive move as soon as World War II was won.

Greenwade eventually focused on a shortstop with the premier team in the Negro Leagues, the Kansas City Monarchs. Jackie Robinson was not among the biggest names in black baseball, but he was young (twenty-six), college-educated (UCLA), extremely athletic (a star in football, basketball, and track), and a solid hitter (.340 in 1945). These qualities gave him a fighting chance not only of making the majors, but also of surviving the inevitable furor that would accompany his quest.[57] Greenwade had only one concern. He doubted that Robinson's arm was strong enough for his current position. "Maybe he'd make a first baseman or second baseman, but never a shortstop, I told Mr. Rickey," the scout recalled.[58]

The Mahatma would be the final judge. He and Robinson met at the Dodgers' offices on August 28, 1945, less than two weeks after the announcement of Japan's surrender. Rickey painted a grim picture of the difficult months and years that lay ahead—fans spewing racial epithets whenever Robinson stepped out of the dugout, opposing players spiking him on the basepaths and challenging him to fight, members of his own team freezing him out with the silent treatment. Rickey told Robinson that it was important—*it was absolutely essential*—that he not retaliate in any way. Their next exchange would pass into legend:

"Mr. Rickey, do you want a ballplayer who's afraid to fight back?"
"I want a ballplayer with guts enough not to fight back."[59]

The two men reached an agreement that very day in August, but Rickey maintained secrecy until the 1945 season ended. Robinson didn't sign his contract until October 23, and then not in Brooklyn, but in Montreal, home of the Dodgers' top minor-league club. The boss was nowhere to be seen. He dispatched his farm director, son Branch Jr., to preside at the brief ceremony.

The younger Rickey, known to baseball acquaintances as Twig, explained that the newest Dodger wasn't ready to play in the major leagues. Robinson would gain the necessary seasoning in Montreal. But the assembled reporters were already speculating about the step that might follow. Weren't the Dodgers worried about the consequences of breaking the racial barrier? Weren't they frightened that their own players might revolt?

Twig acknowledged the latter danger. "Some players now with us may even quit," he admitted. Then he brightened, as if such a serious matter would be of no lasting concern. "But they'll be back in baseball," he said, "after they work a year or two in a cotton mill."[60]

3

Labor

Danny Gardella always seemed a bit out of place. The typical ballplayer in the 1940s sought to be a model employee, to be quiet and colorless, to hew to the line. Not Gardella. He burst into song in hushed hotel hallways. He slept in baggage racks on trains. He debated philosophy with gusto, employing an unexpectedly broad vocabulary. And he roamed left field for the New York Giants with notable zeal, though with distinctly average skill.

A punctured eardrum kept Gardella out of World War II, allowing him to rise to the Giants' roster by 1944. He became a semi-regular the following year, appearing in 121 games, swatting 18 home runs, and batting .272. It was a decent season, albeit against wartime's diminished competition.[1]

But the money wasn't so decent. Gardella, like most ballplayers, required a second job in the offseason, and the position he landed in late 1945 perfectly suited his needs. The muscular 160-pounder, a fanatic about physical fitness, became a trainer at Roon's Health Club in Manhattan. The job allowed the gregarious Gardella to interact with people all day, while giving him the means to stay in shape. He loved it.[2]

Roon's was where he met Jorge Pasquel, a wealthy Mexican who visited New York for three weeks in January 1946. Pasquel, who never missed his daily workout, was assigned Gardella as his trainer. The two men hit it off, thanks to their common passion for baseball. The businessman owned two franchises in the Mexican League and also served as league president.[3]

Pasquel had been trying since 1940 to improve his league's quality of play. The necessary funds were available, since he and his four brothers controlled a family fortune valued at $60 million (the equivalent of $790 million in 2020).[4] His most successful strategy had been to import Negro Leaguers from the United States. "Color didn't mean anything to him," said Monte Irvin, one of his recruits. Sixteen black Americans populated Mexican League rosters in 1945. Many had become stars.[5]

It stood to reason that white U.S. players could enjoy similar success in Mexico, and Pasquel was preparing to recruit them. He discussed his plan with Gardella and suggested that his new friend might lead the southward migration. The latter politely declined the offer. He was determined to land a spot on the Giants' postwar roster.

But that was before the free-spirited Gardella spurned a five-thousand-dollar contract offer, sparked a verbal altercation with a team official, and otherwise ran afoul of Manager Mel Ott during spring training.[6] "This fellow," Ott told reporters, "apparently has to be taught that players of his type are no longer of great importance in the major leagues, now that the war is over." Ott threatened to ship the miscreant to the minors.[7]

His impending demotion caused Gardella to suddenly remember his pal from Roon's. "I do not intend to let the New York Giants enrich themselves any further at my expense by selling me to a minor-league club," he announced in his flowery patois. "So I have now decided to take my gifted talents to Mexico."[8] Pasquel hiked his salary to eight thousand dollars and sweetened it with a five-thousand-dollar bonus.[9]

The signing of Danny Gardella was the opening shot in what would become known as the Mexican raids. Pasquel and his agents enticed twenty-three major leaguers to head south of the border in 1946. Most were of no particular consequence—they were marginal big leaguers like Gardella—but Vern Stephens was an exception. The shortstop for the St. Louis Browns had paced the American League in home runs the previous season, finishing sixth in the balloting for Most Valuable Player. He accepted a 5-year, $175,000 offer from Pasquel on March 30, a monstrous contract that shook the very foundations of the game.[10]

Stephens drove in the winning run for Veracruz in his Mexican debut, though he was quickly awash in regret.[11] "I decided that while Mexico might be good for the songwriters, it was not good for ballplayers like Vern Stephens," he would say. The Browns assisted him in a clandestine escape, capped by his use of a borrowed overcoat and hat to conceal his identity at the border.[12]

The most prominent players who jumped to Mexico and didn't immediately flee were catcher Mickey Owen, a four-time All-Star for the Dodgers, and pitcher Max Lanier, winner of seventeen games for the Cardinals in 1944. Both soon tired of the adventure. Owen received letters from players back home, eagerly seeking his assessment of the Mexican League. "I didn't answer," he said, "because I didn't want to [say] what I really believed at the time, which is that I had made the mistake of my life."[13] Lanier endured persistent stomach trouble. "The food was brutal," he recalled. "I was sick half the time."[14]

Jorge Pasquel set his sights higher, targeting a quartet of future Hall of Famers. "As far as baseball is concerned, we have the atomic bomb in our hands," he bragged of his supposedly unlimited funds.[15] But Bob Feller, Ted Williams, Stan Musial, and Phil Rizzuto spurned hundreds of thousands of dollars.[16] Jorge's brother, Alfonso, met Musial in a St. Louis hotel suite. Alfonso tossed Musial's signing bonus, five cashier's checks totaling fifty thousand dollars, onto a bed. "My eyes bugged out at the sight of so much money," recalled Musial, whose 1946 salary with the Cardinals was $13,500. But he said no.[17]

Happy Chandler seemed unconcerned by the Pasquels' initial incursions during spring training. "I wonder," he chuckled, "how much they'd pay a good baseball commissioner?"[18] But the owners demanded a firm response, perhaps a one- or two-year suspension for all jumpers. Chandler, having seen the light, scrambled to prove he could be harsher than that. "A fellow could take a chance for two years," he reasoned. "But five years, they couldn't take a chance."[19] Stephens had returned to the fold prior to opening day, so Chandler issued him a reprieve. The others were banned from major- and minor-league ball for half a decade.

That stopped the exodus, but it didn't end the controversy. Disillusioned jumpers began drifting back to the United States as early as the summer of 1946, only to find their chosen field off-limits. Mickey Owen applied to Chandler for reinstatement upon his return in August.[20] "I thought I was going to be reinstated. I really did," he recalled.[21] The commissioner sternly pointed Owen back to his farm in Missouri.

Danny Gardella was one of the few Americans who thrived in Mexico. He hit a home run on opening day, slugged a pair of homers in the Mexican League All-Star Game, and batted a solid .275 for the season.[22] But Chandler's five-year ban stuck in his craw. "It was baseball which was wrong," he concluded, "so undemocratic for an institution that was supposed to represent American freedom and democracy." He began to think about filing a lawsuit.[23]

* * *

The Mexican raids provoked the devout Branch Rickey to an astonishing display of vigor and profanity. One of Jorge Pasquel's agents surfaced at the Dodgers' training camp in Florida, only to be chased off by the sixty-four-year-old club president. "Don't you know these boys are under contract?" Rickey thundered.[24] Bystanders claimed he tossed in a few obscenities for good measure. "I didn't dream Mr. Rickey knew all those cusswords," marveled Babe Hamberger, a longtime Dodgers employee.[25]

Rickey's outburst accurately described most of the players lured away by Pasquel. They had indeed affixed their signatures to major-league contracts for 1946, putting them in breach. That was not true of Gardella, who had rejected his offer, yet the Giants still had recourse. They charged him with violating baseball's reserve clause, which stipulated that anybody under contract for a previous season (as Gardella had been in 1945) remained the property of his team in perpetuity, with or without a signed agreement, until the club chose to trade or cut him. (A release required just ten days' notice.[26]) The clause specified that a player could not take the field for any team "otherwise than for [his] club."[27]

The baseball establishment hailed the reserve clause as the keystone of big-league ball—its stabilizing force—and few players or reporters dared to dissent. "Without the reserve clause, the structure collapses," asserted *New York Times* columnist Arthur Daley.[28] Any critic who questioned this gospel drew the unremitting wrath of the sport's leaders. Rickey accused the clause's opponents of "avowed communist tendencies," and Commissioner Chandler swore that they hoped "to kill baseball in the United States."[29]

Why such intensity? Supporters of the reserve clause warned that its elimination would destroy the competitive balance of the major leagues. If players were allowed to become free agents, teams in small markets would suffer an erosion of talent. Stars would inevitably migrate to the best and richest clubs, primarily the three New York franchises.

But this argument defied reality. Baseball, despite the reputed perfection of the reserve clause, actually was wildly imbalanced. A quick glance at the previous decade told the tale. New York's teams won six of the ten World Series between 1930 and 1939, and the Dodgers, Giants, and Yankees posted a combined ten-year winning percentage of .562, compared to .486 for the other thirteen teams. "Clearly," wrote economist Simon Rottenberg, "there has been [an] unequal distribution of talent."[30]

History revealed the true motivation behind the reserve clause. Ballplayers had been unfettered in the 1870s, free to hop from team to team in search of the best deal. Ballclubs sought to outbid their opponents for talent, which inflated the pay scale. "The financial results of the [1879] season prove that salaries must come down," groaned William Hulbert, the president of the National League.[31] He proposed that each team be allowed to "reserve" five players for the coming year, thereby removing them from the open market.[32]

Hulbert's idea worked perfectly. It destroyed the bargaining power of baseball's best players, binding them to their current teams. Rosters were stabilized, salaries were reduced, and happiness reigned, at least among the owners. They increased the number of reserved players in subsequent years, finally opting to go whole hog in 1887. That's when they inserted the reserve clause into the standard National League contract.

John Montgomery Ward, a shortstop with the Giants, was unusually well-qualified to grasp the significance of this move. Not only was Ward a future Hall of Famer, but he also held a degree from Columbia Law School. "Like a fugitive-slave law," he wrote in 1887, "the reserve rule denies [the player] a harbor or a livelihood, and carries him back, bound and shackled, to the club from which he attempted to escape."[33] That was precisely the idea.

Ward questioned the legality of the reserve clause, an issue that would eventually confront judges in several states. New leagues popped up every decade or so—the Players League in 1890, American League in 1901, Federal League in 1914—and these fledglings invariably stole players from the National League. The NL and its teams, in turn, filed lawsuits to get their employees back.

Most courts were unimpressed by the reserve clause. Ward jumped from the

Hall of Famer John Montgomery Ward was multitalented. He was a lawyer, as well as one of the greatest shortstops of his era. Ward attacked the reserve clause as early as 1887, saying it kept players "bound and shackled" [Library of Congress].

Giants to the Brooklyn franchise of the Players League in 1890, and the New York State Supreme Court simply let him go.[34] "We have the spectacle presented of a contract which binds one party for a series of years and the other party for ten days," the judge sniffed. He dismissed the clause as vague, unenforceable, and lopsided in favor of the owners.[35]

The Players League vanished after a single season, but the American League proved to be of hardier stock. It enticed more than 100 National League players in 1901 and 1902, triggering several lawsuits. Most judges followed the Ward precedent and ignored the reserve clause. The notable exception involved star second baseman Napoleon Lajoie, who switched from the NL's Philadelphia Phillies to the Athletics, the AL franchise in the same city. A state court ruled that Lajoie could play only for the Phillies within the boundaries of Pennsylvania, a decision that the American League circumvented by shipping him to Cleveland.[36]

The young manager of the Athletics, Connie Mack, masterminded the Lajoie signing, and pitcher Clark Griffith, who had ditched one Chicago team for another, emerged as the AL's chief recruiter.[37] Griffith bragged that he had targeted forty National League players and netted all but one. The holdout was the Pirates' great infielder, Honus Wagner, who supposedly locked the door when he saw Griffith coming up the walk. "Go away, you," Wagner shouted out the window. "If I let you talk to me, I'll jump the Pirates sure!"[38]

Mack and Griffith changed their minds by 1914, the year of the Federal League's birth. The two men had become part-owners—Mack of the A's, Griffith of the Senators—and they now saw considerable merit in the reserve clause, which the American League had accepted in its 1903 peace agreement with the NL. Eighty-one players jumped from the two established leagues to the Federals in 1914 and 1915, and the A's were especially hard hit.[39] "I didn't get a nickel for them," Mack moaned of the players who left. "This was like being struck by a hurricane."[40] Griffith denied any parallel between the Federal League jumpers, whom he considered criminals, and his own youthful leap in 1901, which he dismissed as insignificant. "You know," he said lamely, "they did not pay any attention to it much in those days."[41]

That wasn't true, of course. The baseball establishment had valued the reserve clause as highly in 1901 as it did in 1914. But the courts continued to disagree. The latest blow came in the case of Hal Chase, a slick-fielding first baseman who deserted the Chicago White Sox for the Federal League's Buffalo team in the midst of the 1914 season. The New York State Supreme Court likened the clause to "peonage" as it ruled in favor of Chase.[42]

The reserve clause was thoroughly discredited by this point, having been rejected by a string of courts in several states. But it survived. Only a ruling from the United States Supreme Court could kill it for good, and no relevant case had reached its chambers in Washington. The death of the Federal League in late 1915, meanwhile, deprived players of an alternate outlet. If they wished to call themselves major leaguers, they once again had no option but to sign the standard contract.

The status of the reserve clause would finally be resolved, ironically enough, because of a ghostly remnant of the Federal League. The owners of the late Baltimore Terrapins filed suit against the American and National Leagues, charging them with conspiring to destroy the Federals, thereby violating the Sherman Antitrust Act. The case, formally known as *Federal Baseball Club v. National League*, wound its way ever so slowly to the Supreme Court, which ruled unanimously in favor of the established leagues on May 29, 1922. The decision was written by Justice Oliver Wendell Holmes, who asserted that major-league baseball was not engaged in interstate commerce, and hence was not subject to federal antitrust regulations.[43]

It was a strange verdict, contrary to common sense and simple observation. Teams clearly crossed state lines to play games in other cities, yet Holmes insisted that such transportation "is a mere incident, not the essential thing." He also implied that major-league baseball really wasn't a business at all: "The exhibition, although made for money, would not be called trade or commerce in the commonly accepted use of those words."[44]

The *Federal Baseball* decision had a powerful impact, giving the owners *carte blanche* to do almost anything without judicial interference, and legitimizing many long-standing practices that previously had seemed questionable. It would have been laughable—not to mention illegal—for a group of plumbers to restrict New York to three plumbing firms, or for newspapers in Cleveland and St. Louis to trade reporters without their consent, or for the banking industry to draft college graduates and assign them to jobs at specific banks. But baseball now had the Supreme Court's permission to do all of those things.

It also had the undisputed right to force players to abide by the reserve clause. This privilege would make it possible for the owners to tighten the financial screws in the decades that followed. Player salaries accounted for 35 percent of team expenses in 1929, a share that dropped to 32 percent by 1939, then would plummet to 22 percent by 1950.[45]

The Mexican League threatened to ruin this idyllic situation for the owners. Jorge Pasquel offered players an alternative that had been missing since the death of the Federal League. His inflated bids to the game's stars couldn't help but drive all salaries higher, and they were already giving players like Danny Gardella crazy ideas about going to court.

The latter was the bigger of the two dangers. Baseball had blossomed into a much bigger business in the quarter-century since Holmes's decision. What if a new case inspired the Supreme Court to change its mind and remove the antitrust exemption? Many of the sport's leaders, including Dodgers attorney and co-owner Walter O'Malley, sensed doom ahead. "My persistent view," O'Malley advised Branch Rickey, "is that this situation should not be in the courts."[46]

Happy Chandler readily agreed. The commissioner promised the owners he would do his best to protect their interests by keeping the lid on the judicial system. "They didn't want to upset the applecart," he recalled, "and going to court would always give somebody an opportunity to open the thing up again."[47]

* * *

Americans had set aside their lives for four years to fight the Germans and the Japanese. Millions were dispatched overseas to do battle with the enemy; tens of millions stayed home to toil in war plants. All endured the strictures of rationing.

Now they insisted on making up for lost time. They demanded higher wages and better benefits, and they were willing to strike to get them.

The nation's steelworkers, eight hundred thousand strong, hit the picket lines in January 1946, initiating the most powerful wave of labor walkouts in American history. Autoworkers, telephone operators, glassmakers, meatpackers, electric workers, railroad engineers, and coal miners followed the steelworkers' lead. Nearly five million employees went on strike in the first year after World War II. A total of 107 million man-days of work were lost.[48]

Baseball was not immune from this discontent, as Robert Murphy discovered during that turbulent winter. The thirty-five-year-old Harvard graduate had served as a hearing officer for the National Labor Relations Board, yet he remained an athlete at heart. He had boxed and run track in college, and a few of his current friends played for the Boston Braves. The depth of their unhappiness with their contracts surprised him.[49] "I heard a lot of gripes," said Murphy, who offhandedly suggested that the players should form a union.[50]

There had been four previous attempts to unionize big-league players, dating as far back as John Montgomery Ward in 1885, but the organizers always wilted under pressure. The Fraternity of Professional Baseball Players of America issued the sternest challenge, even hinting at a strike in the spring of 1917. The owners calmly replied that replacements would be easy to find. "If the players want to strike, let them go ahead," said American League president Ban Johnson. "There will be baseball just the same this summer." The union backed down, soon to disappear.[51]

Murphy sensed that a different outcome might be possible in 1946, thanks to New Deal legislation that had gone on the books a decade earlier. "Back in the old days, there was no National Labor Relations Act," he said. "Today, we have the law behind us."[52] The more he pondered creation of a union, the more he liked the idea. He registered the American Baseball Guild as a labor organization in April.[53]

"The days of baseball serfdom will soon be over," Murphy declared.[54] He laid out his demands: a minimum salary of $7,500 for major leaguers ($99,000 in 2020 dollars), mandatory arbitration of salary disputes, and a sizable payment to any player who was sold to another team.[55] "The code of the slave trader says that if a slave grows big and strong and more valuable, he can sell him and pocket a nice profit. But the slave himself gains nothing," Murphy said. "Is this, in any way, different from the professional baseball setup?"[56]

Such rhetoric was certain to infuriate any stalwart capitalist, and the baseball establishment, almost to a man, was suitably enraged. Larry MacPhail and Happy Chandler stood out as rare executives who seemed unconcerned.[57] A union probably would be harmless, Chandler said, though he couldn't understand why the players were bothering to start one. "I didn't figure they needed it," he said, "because they had a commissioner who was sympathetic with their interests."[58] But Clark Griffith spoke for most owners when he condemned Murphy as an unprincipled rabble-rouser who was creating a vaguely communistic organization. "Such a move would destroy the reserve clause," the Senators owner sputtered. "It would wreck baseball, knock it flat on its face."[59]

Griffith was spared an immediate confrontation with this devil. Murphy sought a test case to establish his union, and he figured a pro-labor city would be the ideal locale. He traveled to Pittsburgh, headquarters of the powerful United Steelworkers Union, where he made his pitch to the Pirates.[60] Most of his listeners were impressed. "Rather than being a slick Eastern lawyer in an expensive suit, he was a forthright guy," recalled future Hall of Famer Ralph Kiner, a Pittsburgh rookie in 1946. The players voted to join the union, setting the stage for a dramatic confrontation.[61]

Murphy demanded that Pirates president William Benswanger recognize the American Baseball Guild as the official bargaining unit for his players. If not, Murphy said, they would take a strike vote on June 7. Other unions ratcheted up the pressure, warning Benswanger not to hire replacements. "No red-blooded American man or woman carrying a union card will go to a ballgame while there is a strike of players," pledged Anthony Federoff, a regional director of the Congress of Industrial Organizations. It was a meaningful threat in such a heavily unionized city.[62]

Talks between Benswanger and Murphy did not go well—"tempers were sharp and excitement was tense," reported the *Pittsburgh Press*—and June 7 arrived without an agreement.[63] Manager Frankie Frisch admitted that he had no clue of what lay ahead. "I'm going to be in uniform," he told reporters. "If nine players report, we'll play the Giants."[64]

Frisch knew he could count on several of his men to defy the union. Pitcher Rip Sewell and infielder Jimmy Brown were among the few Pirates whose salaries topped ten thousand dollars, and both disliked Murphy.[65] "He tried to get me to go to his meetings," Sewell recalled. "I said, 'Stay away from me. I want no part of you.'"[66] And some of the pro-union players began to waver as the strike vote neared. "There should be a way for the Guild to get an agreement and avoid such an unpleasant thing," grumbled right fielder Bob Elliott.[67]

The doors to the clubhouse were locked at six o'clock. Players gathered inside to discuss their options, while Murphy hovered in the concourse, nervously puffing a cigar. Veteran catcher Al Lopez made the case for unionization, then Sewell jumped on a bench to argue the other side.[68] "I'm going out and pitch if I have to go out there by myself," he barked. "You can come if you want to."[69] The Pirates were carrying a bloated roster of thirty-six players due to federal regulations that protected the jobs of military veterans. Twenty voted to strike—a clear majority—but Sewell had persuaded his teammates prior to the election to establish twenty-four as the threshold for action.

The doors finally swung open at 7:15, twenty-five minutes after the Pirates should have taken the field for batting practice. Farm director Bob Rice, who had been summoned to the clubhouse in the midst of the meeting, was the first man to emerge. "No strike!" he boomed to the waiting reporters.[70] The players silently trudged out behind him. Many were somber. "We played the game rather than make history," Kiner said.[71]

Murphy wandered to the grandstand, where he watched the Pirates break a three-game losing streak in convincing fashion. They lashed the Giants, 10–5, seemingly unaffected by the pregame drama. Reporters who trooped up to Murphy's seat found him in a curious mood, both glum and defiant. "We have lost the first round," he said quietly. "You can be sure this is not the end of the Guild."[72]

* * *

The old guard—Clark Griffith and his ilk—craved a battle to the death with Murphy. "Baseball can't exist without the reserve clause," Griffith roared, "and when a union wants to tear that from our game, I'll continue to speak."[73] But younger owners—men like Larry MacPhail, Bob Carpenter of the Phillies, and Lou Perini of the Braves—thought it was time to cool the rhetoric. And the new commissioner agreed.[74]

Happy Chandler announced the creation of a special committee during the 1946 All-Star break, charging it to study "the outstanding problems now before the majors." The two worst headaches, as everybody knew, were the Mexican League and the American Baseball Guild. The panel's assignment was to counteract both—and to do it quickly.[75]

MacPhail, a member of the six-man committee, took charge with predictable speed. He believed that the relationship between labor and management had descended to its nadir—"the morale of our players was not high at that particular time; the players had a lot of gripes"—and he implored his colleagues to conceive imaginative solutions. They met with representatives of the players before the end of July and promised to unveil their recommendations the following month.[76]

Murphy, who was still in Pittsburgh, knew precisely what was happening. "It is obvious," he told reporters, "that efforts of the Guild to correct injustices to the player are in a large measure responsible for this action by the baseball barons."[77] He fine-tuned his strategy to prepare for what seemed likely to be a lengthy battle. No longer would he push the Pirates to call an immediate strike. He now asked the Pennsylvania Labor Relations Board to conduct an election, which would allow Pittsburgh's players to formally designate the Guild as their permanent bargaining agent.

Murphy had come a long way in a short time. "He made amazing progress for a chap who didn't seem to have a whole lot of credentials when he began this," said Shirley Povich, longtime sports editor of the *Washington Post*.[78] But the Guild's leader also made plenty of mistakes. His choice of targets, for instance, seemed dubious to many. MacPhail and the commissioner privately agreed that Murphy should have launched the union not in Pittsburgh, but in the minors.[79] "I think he might have succeeded [with minor leaguers] because they were not well-treated," Chandler said.[80] And Murphy's vote-counting skills were questionable at best. He had rushed the strike vote without accurately understanding his level of support.

The next misstep came on August 20, a week before the owners were scheduled to meet. Stories were already circulating about management concessions, perhaps a minimum salary and a pension plan. Many players now believed that the battle could be won without creating a union. Yet Murphy insisted on forging ahead with the unionization election. Only eighteen Pirates participated, and fifteen voted against the Guild. Murphy sputtered, "This fight has just begun."[81] But it had essentially reached the end.

MacPhail's committee swooped in on August 27 with a twenty-five-page secret report, written entirely by its chairman. It was blatant about its goals—"to frustrate Murphy and protect ourselves against raids on players from the outside"—but some of its language was too extreme for most owners.[82] They especially objected to MacPhail's prediction that the courts would never uphold the reserve clause because of its "unreasonable restraint upon the player." The owners first demanded that this section be removed, then that all copies of the report be collected at the end of the meeting and destroyed. (The destruction was incomplete. Copies of MacPhail's draft would surface five years later, much to everyone's embarrassment.)[83]

Of more immediate importance were the actions that stemmed from the report. The owners approved a minimum salary of five thousand dollars, a weekly allowance of twenty-five dollars during spring training, and a pension plan that would pay an ex-player between fifty and one hundred dollars a month, depending on years of service, beginning at age fifty. Players throughout the major leagues greeted these modest reforms ecstatically.[84]

The spring-training stipend would be known for decades as "Murphy money," an homage to the man who had forced the owners to bend. But Murphy himself was unimpressed. "The players have been offered an apple," he said, "but they could have had an orchard."[85] He drifted away from baseball after 1946, talking vaguely about his desire "to do something for hockey players," though nothing came of it.[86] "Murphy rather mysteriously faded from the scene," Chandler mused in retirement. "I often wondered whatever became of him."[87]

The Mexican League disappeared almost as quickly. It piled up four hundred thousand dollars in losses in 1946, much to the irritation of Jorge Pasquel, who slashed the salaries of his players, Americans and Mexicans alike.[88] He spoke bitterly of unnamed employees who "come here, sit down with money in their pockets, and either turn out failures or leave without thanks."[89] He would conduct no more raids for American talent. The Mexican League dwindled to four teams by 1948, and Pasquel would resign as president at the end of that season. "We're not helping anyone but ourselves," resolved brother Bernardo.[90]

Relief flooded through America's baseball establishment. The owners hadn't conceded much—a comfortably low floor for salaries, a bare-bones pension plan—and they believed they had ensured labor peace for a generation. Unions and rogue leagues would trouble them no longer.

It fell to a sportswriter for the *Brooklyn Eagle*, Paul Gould, to disturb their reverie. Gould, writing in the *New Republic* in August 1946, conceded that Murphy's "premature, poorly conceived offensive" had set back the cause of organized labor. But he envisioned a day when "the newer generation of intelligent, non-subservient players" would be open to joining a union, and it would be a union with muscle. "It will take players who recognize that their greatest weapon is the strike," Gould predicted, "and who will not hesitate to employ it if they must."[91]

Headlines: 1946

ROBINSON MAKES SMASHING MINOR-LEAGUE DEBUT

Branch Rickey downplayed the significance of Jackie Robinson's April 18 debut with Montreal, the top team in the Dodgers' farm system. "He is not now major-league stuff," said Rickey, implying that Robinson might be years away from breaking the majors' racial barrier. Robinson began dispelling doubts in his very first game, going four for five with a home run. He would hit a robust .349 in Montreal.[92]

FELLER DEFIES SKEPTICS BY NO-HITTING YANKEES

Something seemed wrong with Bob Feller, who lost two of his first three starts for the Indians. Columnists dared to suggest that the hard-throwing righty was fading, but Feller responded by no-hitting the Yankees on April 30. "I think it was only human for me to want to answer these questions about whether I had lost my fastball," he said. Feller would lead the majors in 1946 with 348 strikeouts.[93]

Cardinals hunt down Dodgers and win playoff

The Dodgers roared to a 7-game lead over the rest of the National League by July 4, but they couldn't hold off the hard-charging Cardinals, who won 41 of their final 60 games. The two teams finished the season tied for the pennant, necessitating the NL's first tiebreaker playoff, which started October 1. The Cards remained red hot, sweeping the best-of-three series, 4–2 and 8–4.[94]

Slaughter's dash brings title to St. Louis

The World Series matched batting skill against pitching prowess. The 1946 Red Sox led the majors in batting average (.271), while the Cardinals posted the best earned run average (3.01). They split the first six games, setting the stage for a dramatic showdown on October 15. Enos Slaughter secured the 4–3 win for St. Louis, dashing all the way home from first base on Harry Walker's two-out double in the eighth inning.[95]

4

Pacific

Most of baseball's owners were old enough to remember the rocky aftermath of World War I. A brief spell of economic euphoria in 1919 gave way within a year to a painful recession, slashing attendance at big-league games by 6 percent. The turnstiles in America's ballparks spun at a sluggish pace until the middle of the 1920s.

An array of politicians, economists, and commentators warned of similar difficulties in the wake of World War II. Secretary of Commerce Jesse Jones called on business leaders to expend every effort "to avoid another postwar depression."[1] Leo Cherne, who was both an economist and a commentator, predicted that hungry, unemployed veterans would soon be roaming a devastated country. "An occasional soldier will be seen on a street corner selling a Welcome Home sign," he wrote. "Others will start house-to-house canvassing in their uniforms."[2]

A worried, confused public didn't know what to expect. The Gallup Poll started asking as early as 1942 about the likely condition of the postwar economy. Respondents were almost equally divided: 45 percent envisioned prosperity whenever the guns stopped firing, 43 percent anticipated another depression. Pessimism gained the upper hand by January 1945, when Gallup asked workers to forecast the size of their paychecks after the cessation of hostilities. Seventy-one percent expected their incomes to fall.[3]

Consumers were understandably cautious in such an environment, disdaining frivolous purchases and speculative investments. The Dow Jones Industrial Average plummeted 11 percent in 1946, then treaded water for two subsequent years, long after it became clear that the Great Depression would not be returning.[4] The chairman of the Federal Reserve Board, Thomas McCabe, bemoaned this new aversion to risk-taking. "Security, rather than opportunity, recently has become more and more a part of our national philosophy," he said sadly.[5]

Security was defined by returning veterans as a string of simple nouns—job, wife, family, home—and they raced to acquire all four as quickly as possible. The typical bridegroom in prewar 1940 had been 24.3 years old, a benchmark that fell by 1950 to 22.8, the youngest median age of first marriage in American history. Millions of newlyweds rapidly added to their households as the birth rate accelerated into overdrive: 2.86 million babies in 1945, 3.41 million in 1946, 3.82 million in 1947. It was the start of a demographic wave that would be immortalized as the baby boom.[6]

The baseball establishment was troubled by these new tendencies—the economic caution, the young marriages, the millions of babies—even as it enjoyed the very best of times. Attendance at big-league stadiums skyrocketed by 71 percent in 1946 to 18.5 million fans, obliterating the single-season record of 10.8 million, yet most owners doubted the upswing would be permanent. They wrote it off as a brief postwar frenzy. "Some people were foolish enough to believe that was the new normal," National League president Warren Giles said from the vantage point of 1951. "But I never kidded myself. I knew it couldn't last."[7]

It had long been an article of faith among the game's leaders—unsupported by any known research—that young, unmarried men formed the backbone of baseball's fan base. But now these stalwarts were getting hitched at an unprecedented rate, supposedly a prescription for box-office disaster. "Once they are married, they are deeply in debt for house furnishings, etc., soon followed by children, so that they are under such financial strain that they have little left for sports or amusements," whined Cubs owner Phil Wrigley.[8]

Enhancing the gloom was the Census Bureau's insistence that America's rapid expansion was a temporary phenomenon. "The outlook after 1950 is for a continuation of the longtime decline in population growth," said a 1947 report, which wrongly predicted "a sharp decrease" in the birth rate within a year or two. The United States would add fewer than eight million residents during the 1950s, according to the bureau's demographers, and the nation's population would actually start to shrink by 1990.[9]

The owners therefore faced the prospect—or so they believed in 1947—of coping with a declining fan base and a decelerating economy. They also had cause to worry about the cities where they had done business for so long. The Depression and World War II had brought a virtual halt to construction for fifteen years, leaving America's urban centers bedraggled and dilapidated.[10] "A visitor touring downtown St. Louis is amazed at the desolation and desertion characterizing scores of blocks in the business district," wrote *Forum and Century* as early as 1939.[11] Another magazine, the *Saturday Evening Post,* ran a series of articles on urban decay in 1946, decrying the conditions in places such as Cincinnati ("the city is smeared with soot") and Pittsburgh ("a fruitful, filthy monster").[12]

Later generations would be taught that America's cities weathered the war in fine shape, only to be swamped by a postwar suburban tsunami. But that wasn't the case at all. Four of the ten cities with big-league teams had begun losing population during the 1930s, and three others had stagnated. Their residents were already trickling out to newly sprouting suburban communities. The city of Cleveland, for example, slipped by 2.5 percent between 1930 and 1940, while adjacent suburbs grew by 11.4 percent. The splits were similar for other hubs, such as St. Louis (city down 0.7 percent, suburbs up 11.9 percent) and Philadelphia (urban loss of 1.0 percent, suburban gain of 7.6 percent).[13]

The stage was set for a postwar explosion, despite the contrary predictions of naysayers. Millions of veterans demanded homes of their own, and the construction industry complied. The number of new houses shot up from 114,000 built in 1944 to 937,000 in 1946, then vaulted past 1.2 million in 1947. Subdivisions sprouted on open land distant from urban centers, most notably in a fifteen-hundred-acre potato field on Long Island, where William Levitt created a massive suburb from scratch. A new home was completed every sixteen minutes in Levittown, which became the prototype for the frenetic suburban development that would characterize the decade to come.[14]

Baseball's owners were distressed by this trend. They watched helplessly as hundreds of thousands of white veterans and their families eagerly abandoned major cities—and the ballparks within—for spacious suburbia. Even worse, from the owners' perspective, was the influx of blacks who filled the urban void, attracted by industrial jobs that paid more than they earned in their native South. The impact of these demographic forces on Chicago was typical. The city's white population declined by 3,000 during the 1940s, while its number of black residents ballooned by 214,500. The infusion of minorities drove Chicago's population higher by 6.6 percent for the decade—seemingly a healthy gain—yet the nearby suburbs ballooned at a rate that was five times greater.[15]

Big-league attendance remained strong in 1947, but the baseball establishment was increasingly nervous. Owners quietly agreed that their white audience was slipping away, and there was no suitable replacement on the horizon. Any thought of reaching out to the newest urban dwellers, the black migrants from the South, was rejected as contrary to the entrenched customs of the major leagues. Another decade would pass before Horace Stoneham, the affable owner of the Giants, would dare to voice this secret fear to a congressional subcommittee. "The baseball population," Stoneham would say with sadness, "has moved to the suburbs."[16]

* * *

Most of the owners ignored a coincident trend of monumental importance, though they would soon be forced to confront it.

The federal government had poured more than sixty billion dollars into the Western states during World War II, subsidizing aircraft, shipbuilding, and munitions plants and constructing a vast array of military bases. This massive investment attracted millions of workers, soldiers, and sailors from other parts of the country. A substantial number decided to remain in their new homes after the war ended.[17]

The West boasted seven of America's ten fastest-growing states during the 1940s, paced by California's dizzying increase of 53 percent in ten years. Longtime residents could still remember the sparsely settled California of 1900, whose population of 1.5 million was smaller than the totals for twenty states. But the postwar behemoth overflowed with 9.3 million people in late 1945, vaulting it ahead of every state but New York.

The nation's balance of power was tilting. Major-league teams were concentrated in seven Northeastern and Midwestern states and the District of Columbia, which collectively added just twenty-six thousand people between 1931 and 1945, an anemic increase of 0.1 percent. The other forty-one states—those without big-league ball—picked up 8.4 million residents, a gain of 11.4 percent.[18] Branch Rickey, as usual, was quicker than his colleagues to comprehend the implications for baseball. "Circumstances will push from the top and the bottom," he said, "to force recognition of the fact that the center of population in this country has shifted."[19]

Rickey's insight was shared by Dan Reeves, the thirty-three-year-old owner of the National Football League's Cleveland Rams. Reeves should have been on top of the world in December 1945. His team had just eked out its first NFL title, defeating the Washington Redskins in any icy championship game, 15–14. But Reeves was distracted by the Rams' massive financial losses. The only solution, he believed, was to move his franchise to a bigger, more affluent market, and Los Angeles was his choice. He filed a formal request in January 1946.[20]

The other NFL owners brusquely rejected his application. The thought of moving to the Pacific Coast seemed frighteningly bold. But the exasperated Reeves would not be denied, bursting out, "And you call this a *national* league?" He sputtered that he would fold the Rams rather than stay in Cleveland. The owners reluctantly agreed to take a second vote, this time granting permission. The Los Angeles Rams would become the first major-league sports team based in the Pacific time zone.[21]

Yet the Rams would not be alone. Actor Don Ameche had been seeking an NFL expansion franchise since the early 1940s, proposing that his new team play in Buffalo until the end of World War II, then shift to Los Angeles. Ameche had enlisted the support of a well-connected friend, *Chicago Tribune* sports editor Arch Ward, who fancied himself a man of influence, not a mere journalist.[22] "You can buy a writer for one hundred dollars a week," Ward liked to say. "It's the people with ideas who are hard to find."[23] He guaranteed Ameche that the Buffalo-Los Angeles concept would fly.

The NFL, in no mood to expand during a war, shot it down. "Arch was furious. His fury was to prove costly," recalled George Halas, the owner and coach of the Chicago Bears.[24] A new idea soon popped into Ward's head. He would establish a competing league to teach the NFL a lesson. His revenge, the All-America Football Conference, would begin play in 1946 with eight teams, including franchises in San Francisco and Los Angeles. The latter, appropriately nicknamed the Dons, would be owned by Ameche. Ward promised to wage unrestricted war. The AAFC, he said, would "engage in a battle of dollars with the National Football League, if necessary."[25]

Fans in California happily greeted their three new professional teams. Yet football remained a secondary sport in 1946, a mere diversion during the national pastime's offseason. It was baseball that truly mattered, and baseball still evinced no interest in the West Coast, half a decade after Donald Barnes's brief flirtation with Los Angeles. Bill Leiser, the sports editor of the *San Francisco Chronicle*, allowed his bitterness to seep through when writing about the World Series. "Only that part of the world between the Mississippi and the Atlantic Seaboard is involved," he noted caustically. "Not even the Pacific Coast is considered as being part of the world."[26]

The best baseball in the West was played in the Pacific Coast League, one of three minor leagues that carried the highest classification of AA through 1945, AAA thereafter. The PCL was considered a step above its counterparts at this top level. It played a longer schedule, 183 games, compared to 154 in the American Association and International League (and, for that matter, in the major leagues). It outdrew either of the other AAA leagues by almost two million fans per year. And it enjoyed a storied history. Joe DiMaggio and Ted Williams had refined their precocious talents in the PCL before departing for big-league stardom, while older players extended their careers by returning after stints in the majors.[27] "The weather was perfect for those aging arms, and they loved it out here," said California native Bill Rigney, who played the infield for the PCL's Oakland Oaks, as well as the New York Giants.[28]

The PCL's president, Clarence "Pants" Rowland, had deep connections to the major leagues. He managed the White Sox to a World Series title in 1917, made an unusual pivot to umpiring in the 1920s, and then worked for the Cubs as a scout and farm director. If the majors wouldn't come to the Pacific Coast, he eventually decided, the Pacific Coast would go to the majors. Rowland proposed that his entire league—all eight teams from Seattle to San Diego—be elevated to big-league status simultaneously. He envisioned the PCL as America's third major league.[29]

The Los Angeles and San Francisco-Oakland metropolitan areas, each with a pair of PCL franchises, were clearly big enough. The 1950 census would show the Los Angeles area with 4.4 million residents, San Francisco-Oakland with 2.2 million. But none of the other PCL markets had a population higher than 750,000, with Sacramento the baby at 277,000. The latter was smaller than fifty-three metros outside the major leagues, including such unlikely prospects as Wheeling, West Virginia; Harrisburg, Pennsylvania; and Utica, New York.[30]

Yet Rowland was determined. He led a delegation to baseball's winter meetings

White Sox manager Pants Rowland (right) and pitcher Eddie Cicotte went different ways after this 1917 photograph. Rowland eventually became the president of the Pacific Coast League, while Cicotte went down in infamy as one of the Black Sox [Library of Congress].

in Chicago in December 1945, where Charlie Graham, the owner of the San Francisco Seals, made the formal pitch. "We are grown up, we are adults now, and you fellows have just got to vote us in," he said. Graham took a hat-in-hand approach, almost obsequious in tone. He stressed that the PCL in no way saw itself as a competitor to the American and National Leagues. "We are a country of our own," he said, "with a climate of our own out there."[31]

The Pacific Coast League's request for major-league status was curtly rejected by fourteen of the sixteen owners. Horace Stoneham of the Giants cast the only vote in favor of the PCL, while Phil Wrigley abstained, citing his unique situation as proprietor of both the Chicago Cubs and the PCL's Los Angeles Angels. But Wrigley cautioned his colleagues that they would soon have no choice but to address the geographic issue. "I think you ought to face the fact," he said, "that you are going to have a major league out there either with our blessing or without it."[32]

Rowland was angered by the smug intransigence that he encountered at the winter meetings. "The men who control major-league baseball are merely postponing the inevitable," he said, pledging to continue the fight.[33] His league enjoyed another strong year in 1946, paced by San Francisco's home attendance of 670,563, a single-season minor-league record that would endure until 1982.[34] The PCL trooped to the 1946 winter meetings with renewed confidence, and Charlie Graham again made the presentation: "We feel now that with the advance that we have made this year—a greatly increased attendance, a great increase in our salaries, the enlargement of our ballparks, and so on—that we are now ready again." The major-league owners felt otherwise.[35]

The subsequent year, 1947, was even better. The Pacific Coast League attracted more than four million fans, setting a record for an eight-team minor league. The Angels scaled their all-time peak of 622,485, and every single PCL franchise outdrew the American League's St. Louis Browns.[36]

And yet the pattern recurred. Rowland and Graham once again bowed before their big-league overlords during the All-Star break and asked to be admitted to their exclusive circle. The owners rebuffed them unanimously. Even Horace Stoneham, uncomfortable with playing the rebel, now stood in opposition. "At the present time," said a resolution approved by the owners, "there appears to be no minor league which, as a league unit, justifies major-league classification."[37]

The status quo remained safely undisturbed.

* * *

The National Football League's owners had been as reluctant as their baseball brethren to head west, but Dan Reeves left them with no alternative. If George Halas and his colleagues hadn't reconsidered their negative vote, Reeves insisted that he would have disbanded the Cleveland Rams. The All-America Football Conference would have had California all to itself.

"How fortunate that was," Halas later said of Reeves's firmness. "Had we stayed with [a] no [vote], the West Coast would have become a monopoly of the new league. Californians took to pro football."[38]

That was an understatement. The Los Angeles Rams stunned East Coast chauvinists by finishing third in NFL attendance in their inaugural season of 1946, outdrawing everyone but the New York Giants and Chicago Bears. Only six pro-football franchises would draw more than 200,000 fans per season between 1946 and 1949, with all three California teams (the Rams, Los Angeles Dons, and San Francisco 49ers) belonging to that elite group. Nobody could plausibly deny the West Coast's ability to support major-league sports.[39]

Baseball was intrigued by football's western experiment, though it remained unconvinced. There was no Dan Reeves among baseball's owners, nobody with the necessary determination (or desperation) to force the geographic issue. The NFL had been unable to resist internal pressure to expand westward, but the sources of baseball's pressure were external—Pants Rowland and his pesky PCL colleagues—and it was remarkably easy to turn them down.

But how much longer could baseball cling to its traditional alignment? There was a growing sense that time was running out, that the demographic trends violently sweeping America could not be ignored. Phil Wrigley's warning hung in the air—"you are going to have a major league out there"—and a few of his fellow owners began to concede its truth.[40]

The National League decided to take western soundings in the summer of 1947, tapping NL president Ford Frick and Pirates owner Frank McKinney as its Lewis and Clark. The pair would tour Rowland's domain and prepare a report on "the Pacific Coast and its baseball potentialities."[41] Their expedition was supposed to be hush-hush, but Happy Chandler decided to tag along, which elevated its profile. "We are going to ascertain the facts," the commissioner declared to all who would listen. "We want to make a fair decision."[42]

Frick and McKinney headed west in late August, with the voluble Chandler in tow. They targeted all six Pacific Coast League markets. "The potential drawing power of each suggested club was studied," Frick said.[43] He and his partner reached the inevitable conclusion that Los Angeles "undoubtedly has major-league possibilities," perhaps for two teams, though they felt its ballparks were inadequate. Local promoters pointed to the cavernous Los Angeles Memorial Coliseum, the ninety-three-thousand-seat home of the Rams and Dons, but Frick and McKinney disdained its oval playing field as "not suitable to baseball."[44]

San Francisco also received a qualified thumbs-up. The city "offers rich opportunity for major-league expansion," said the pair, though they rejected Seals Stadium as too small. Neighboring Oakland, a bridge away on the eastern shore of San Francisco Bay, intrigued them. "From a major-league standpoint," Frick and McKinney asserted, "an Oakland-San Francisco set-up would induce much the same rivalry that now exists between New York and Brooklyn."[45]

But those were the only bright spots. The other four PCL markets were dismissed out of hand. Seattle was "not yet ready" for the big leagues. Portland had "not the potentialities of Seattle." Sacramento was "entirely too small." And San Diego was "utterly unready for major-league status." Frick and McKinney noted ominously of the latter city: "At the moment, the population has a high percentage of Negroes and Mexicans."[46]

These verdicts were not for general consumption. They would be conveyed to the owners in a secret report after the 1947 World Series. Baseball's public face was milder and less judgmental. The commissioner portrayed the Frick-McKinney expedition as a positive development for the PCL, a crucial step toward its major-league dreams. "Don't be impatient if it takes a few more years," he advised.[47]

The West Coast trip convinced Chandler of two things. Expansion was inevitable, he now believed, but the Pacific Coast League was the wrong vehicle. He began to think about adding two teams to each of the existing major leagues, perhaps divvying up the PCL's franchises in Los Angeles, Hollywood, San Francisco, and Oakland.[48] He floated this concept at the 1947 winter meetings, where the National League was surprisingly enthusiastic. But the American League said no, and Pants Rowland vowed defiance when he learned what was going on. "Over my dead body," he thundered.[49]

Chandler went public with his idea in 1948, suggesting that each league should expand to ten teams as soon as feasible. "If it works," he said, "then expand to twelve teams and then, perhaps, split the twenty-four teams into three major leagues."[50]

Baseball's old guard was shocked by the commissioner's heresy. "There will never be a third major league," scoffed eighty-five-year-old Connie Mack. "Major-league baseball can never be profitable if it extends from New York to Los Angeles."[51] But some of the younger executives were more receptive. Boston Braves president Lou Perini, roughly half Mack's age at forty-four, had a broader frame of reference. Perini owned a massive construction firm that built bridges, dams, tunnels, airports, and housing developments from coast to coast, a business that gave him a firm understanding of the nation's changing demographics.[52]

"Should we penalize the fans of San Francisco and Los Angeles by preventing them from seeing major-league baseball?" Perini asked in 1948. He mentioned other cities that he believed were ready for expansion—Baltimore, Houston, Montreal, Milwaukee—and then he ventured further afield: "Why shouldn't Cuba have a team in the major leagues? Why shouldn't Mexico City?"[53]

The best way to enter these new markets, Perini told a reporter, was to elevate eight AAA clubs to big-league status. Take the best PCL franchises and add a few from the International League and American Association. The sportswriter interjected an alternative. A few of the current major-league teams were struggling at the box office. Why not move them to some of these open cities, just as Don Barnes had envisioned in 1941? Perini wrinkled his nose at that idea. "That would be more difficult than most folks think," he said hesitantly.[54] Even the most innovative spirits in baseball, it seemed, had their limits.

Headlines: 1947

Robinson breaks big-league color barrier

It seemed an inauspicious game for Jackie Robinson—oh-for-three with a double-play groundout—yet his April 15 debut with the Dodgers was a landmark in baseball history. The first black major leaguer of the twentieth century promised better days ahead. "Will I hit? I hope I'll hit. I believe I'll hit. I'm sure I'll hit," he told reporters. Robinson rapped seven singles, a double, and a home run in his next five starts.[55]

Dean flashes old form against White Sox

Future Hall of Famer Dizzy Dean retired in 1941, joining the hapless St. Louis Browns as their radio announcer. He didn't like what he saw. "I swear, I could beat nine out of ten of the guys that call themselves pitchers nowadays," he groaned. The Browns finally gave him a chance to prove it, activating him on September 28. Dean responded with four innings of shutout ball against the White Sox.[56]

Yankees hold off Dodgers in World Series

Bill Bevens pitched poorly in 1947, losing thirteen of twenty decisions for the Yankees. But he was outstanding in Game Four of the World Series, carrying a no-hitter into the ninth inning. Cookie Lavagetto's double simultaneously ruined Bevens's masterpiece, won the game for the Dodgers, and knotted the series at two victories apiece. Was it an omen of Brooklyn's first world championship? No. The Yankees triumphed in Game Seven, 5–2.[57]

Williams wins Triple Crown, loses MVP

Boston's Ted Williams cruised to his second Triple Crown in 1947, leading the American League in batting average (.343), home runs (32), and runs batted in (114), dominating New York's Joe DiMaggio (.315, 20, 97) in the process. But relations between Williams and reporters were strained—the star mocked them as "knights of the keyboard"—so the writers struck back. They inexplicably chose DiMaggio as the AL's Most Valuable Player.[58]

5

Veeck

It seemed a futile gesture at the time, an ineffectual expression of liberal outrage. Several picketers paced outside Yankee Stadium on 1945's opening day, demanding the racial integration of major-league baseball. One of their placards alluded to the hundreds of thousands of black soldiers involved in the American war effort. "If We Can Stop Bullets," it asked, "Why Not Balls?"[1]

Nobody in the majors deigned to answer. New York mayor Fiorello La Guardia, an outspoken advocate of integration, glumly conceded that several years might pass before a black player took the field. "While everybody is interested," he said in August 1945, "nothing is being done."[2]

The mayor's political antennae, finely tuned on most issues, worked poorly in this instance. It was Branch Rickey, not La Guardia, who correctly surmised that the civil-rights movement was gathering momentum beneath the surface, and it was Rickey who acted accordingly. The president of the Dodgers secretly finalized his agreement with Jackie Robinson that same August, the very month in which La Guardia was bemoaning the lack of racial progress.

A handful of politicians shared Rickey's insight, realizing that the flood of new black residents to Northern cities—the influx that scared most baseball owners—actually presented an opportunity, not a threat. Clark Clifford, an aide to the new American president, stressed this view in a 1947 memo. "Unless there are new and real efforts," Clifford warned Harry Truman, "the Negro bloc, which, certainly in Illinois and probably in New York and Ohio, does hold the balance of power, will go Republican." Democrat Truman heeded the advice. His unexpected announcement of a comprehensive civil-rights program energized the North's new black voters, enabling him to score an upset victory in the 1948 election.[3]

Truman's flexibility stood in contrast to the rigidity of most baseball owners. An infusion of black talent could have invigorated the woeful Washington Senators on the field and at the box office, yet crusty Clark Griffith held firmly to the color line. "Didn't he see how good [that blacks] could play? Didn't he like money?" asked Monte Irvin, an African American star who was destined for the Hall of Fame.[4] But Griffith insisted that black players should remain confined to the Negro Leagues "in which colored people of this country have faith and confidence."[5] Left unspoken was his own financial dependence on segregation. The black Homestead Grays played at Griffith Stadium whenever the Senators went on the road, paying as much as fifty thousand dollars in annual rent.[6]

Griffith's curmudgeonly opposition to integration was unsurprising, but even as kindly a gentleman as Connie Mack insisted on keeping the races separate. Several reporters were chatting with Mack in 1946 when Jackie Robinson's name came up. A writer speculated that the Dodgers might use the speedy minor leaguer in an upcoming spring-training game against the A's. Did Mack have any special strategy in mind? "I wouldn't play them," Mack blurted. "I used to have respect for Rickey. I don't anymore."[7] The stunned reporters agreed to protect the old man by keeping the interview off the record. (Mack's opinion of the newcomer would evolve by 1950, when he hailed Robinson as a future Hall of Famer.)[8]

Robinson's own team was not immune from racial prejudice, as Rickey had conceded in their initial meeting. Announcer Red Barber, who had been born in Mississippi and raised in Florida, was horrified when he learned of the Dodgers' plans for integration. "Why did I go straight home and tell my wife I was going to quit? Well, I said, I'm Southern," Barber later wrote. He eventually reconsidered and remained in the radio booth.[9]

Several of Brooklyn's key players came from the South, including the ace of the pitching staff, Kirby Higbe, who led the Dodgers in wins (17) and strikeouts (134) in 1946, and the best hitter, Fred Walker, who paced the team with a .319 batting average and 116 runs batted in. Higbe was an unrepentant South Carolinian who attributed his blazing fastball to a youthful habit of "throwing rocks at Negroes."[10] The allegiance of Walker, a Georgia native and Alabama resident, was signaled by his famous nickname, Dixie.

It was Walker who decided it was time to take a stand. The Dodgers had already signed four black players besides Robinson to minor-league deals, and there were rumors that as many as twenty-five others were under consideration. Walker proposed that he and his fellow Southerners sign a petition, beseeching Rickey to maintain the racial purity of the national pastime. If the owner failed to comply, there was an implied danger that his biggest stars might refuse to play.[11]

The Dodgers were crossing Panama on a spring-training tour when the team's feisty manager learned of this dissension. Leo Durocher rousted everybody out of bed for a snap meeting. He rejected the petition with five curt words—"wipe your ass with it"—and informed his players that Robinson was the forerunner of an inevitable black wave.[12] "From everything I hear, he's only the first," Durocher thundered. "*Only the first, boys.* There's many more coming right behind him, and they have the talent, and they're gonna come to play."[13]

Durocher seemed to be the perfect manager to handle such a touchy situation—fearless, profane, colorblind—but he failed to make it to Ebbets Field for Robinson's debut on April 15, 1947. Happy Chandler had suspended him six days earlier, banning him for the entire season for "conduct detrimental to baseball," an indictment that the commissioner never clarified.[14] Chandler was known to be annoyed by Durocher's marriage to actress Laraine Day immediately after her quickie Mexican divorce, his friendships with gamblers, and his inadequacy as a role model. "Leo was a general all-around bad actor," Chandler said toward the end of his life.[15]

The suspension evoked outrage in Brooklyn and among Durocher's pals throughout the game. "I don't think anybody in baseball thought that Leo should have been suspended," said Red Barber.[16] But the press and general public hailed this indication that Chandler—often ridiculed as a loquacious backslapper—actually had a spine. "Kicked around unmercifully, maligned, even libeled and slandered, Chandler took stock of himself," the *Sporting News* said approvingly. The new guy had shown that he could be as tough as Kenesaw Mountain Landis.[17]

And so Jackie Robinson began the longest year of his life without his closest protector. It unfolded as Branch Rickey had envisioned—angry fans, hostile opponents, mute teammates. There was abuse at every stop, though nowhere with more intensity than Philadelphia, where Tennessee native Ben Chapman managed the Phillies. "Hey, nigger, why don't you go back to the cotton field where you belong?" shouted Chapman. And: "They're waiting for you in the jungle, black boy!" Some of the Phillies pointed bats at Robinson as if they were rifles.[18]

But Durocher had been accurate with his prediction that the newest Dodger would emerge as "a real great ballplayer" despite the odds against him. Robinson pushed his batting average to .310 by the midpoint of the 1947 season, putting him on course to win the Rookie of the Year Award. And Rickey had been correct, too. Robinson was indeed instrumental in securing Brooklyn's first National League pennant in six seasons, with five more titles to come by 1956.[19]

Rickey was once again on top of the baseball world, hailed by colleagues and columnists for his innovative genius. But not everybody joined the applause. Owners of teams in the Negro Leagues were angered by Rickey's refusal to pay for Robinson and the other budding stars he signed. "Whether we get any recompense for Robinson may be considered beside the point. We want Jack to have a chance," said J.L. Wilkinson, who owned the Kansas City Monarchs.[20] But such charity was only for public consumption. "Rickey got a one-hundred-thousand-dollar ballplayer for nothing," Wilkinson said bitterly in private.[21]

There also was the matter of credit. "I kept getting the impression that Rickey felt he was God Almighty, and that he was somehow the savior of the black people," snapped Chandler, who knew that several big-league owners had been counting on him to block integration. The commissioner had quietly flashed the green light before Robinson was signed, and he wanted everybody to know. "Of course," he later wrote of Rickey, "he couldn't have done it without my approval."[22]

Yet it was also true that somebody had to take the first step, and only Rickey had possessed the courage to defy the status quo. Pitcher Don Newcombe, one of the black minor leaguers who signed with the Dodgers in 1946, found it difficult to imagine any other member of baseball's tight fraternity breaching the color barrier if Rickey had not acted. "Who would have been the owner to have changed things?" Newcombe once asked. Only one name occurred to him: "Would Bill Veeck have done it?"[23]

* * *

William Louis Veeck, Jr., was a neophyte as a big-league owner—he had acquired the Cleveland Indians in June 1946—yet his baseball pedigree was unimpeachable. His life's course had been established in December 1918, shortly before his fifth birthday, when his father, a longtime Chicago sportswriter, was summoned by William Wrigley, Jr., the owner of the Cubs.

Various stories would be told about their meeting. One version had Wrigley expressing admiration for the reporter's closely reasoned analysis of the Cubs' shortcomings. A second tale had him expressing frustration with Veeck's sharp-edged criticism. "If you think you can do a better job of running my ballclub," Wrigley supposedly sputtered, "why, go ahead!" The upshot was an astounding offer to become vice president of Chicago's National League franchise. The writer accepted and was promoted to the presidency within a year.[24]

The senior Veeck was mild-mannered and somewhat formal—"far too dignified a man to pull any promotional stunts," his son would admit—yet he proved to have a flair for baseball operations.[25] He staged a weekly Ladies' Day to attract female fans, encouraged play-by-play radio coverage in an era when most teams spurned the new medium, and spent whatever it took to keep Wrigley Field spotless. Veeck's actions were validated at the turnstiles. The Cubs drew more than 1 million fans in 1927, the first National League club to pass that benchmark, and they soared to 1.48 million by 1929.[26]

Veeck had high expectations for his only son, sending him to elite schools: Phillips Academy, The Ranch School at Los Alamos, Kenyon College. But young Bill loved Wrigley Field most of all. He began working for the Cubs at age fifteen and rotated around the ballpark in subsequent summers, lending a hand in the concession stands and on the grounds crew. He became determined to make baseball his life's work.[27]

Leukemia claimed his fifty-seven-year-old father in 1933, accelerating the son's timetable. "I returned to Kenyon to finish out the football season," Bill recalled, "then went to the Cubs' office and asked for a job." Phil Wrigley, who had inherited the franchise a year earlier, hired him for eighteen dollars a week.[28]

Veeck rose in the Cubs organization while studying accounting and business law in night school, eventually becoming the assistant to Boots Weber, the team's general manager. His great hope was to be promoted to GM upon Weber's resignation in 1940—an extremely ambitious goal for a twenty-six year old—but Wrigley took a page from his own father's book and again hired a sportswriter, James Gallagher.[29]

So Veeck resolved to set out on his own. He spied the perfect opportunity ninety miles to the north, where the minor-league Milwaukee Brewers teetered on the brink of bankruptcy. Veeck and Cubs coach Charlie Grimm agreed to assume the team's debts, a pledge sufficient to make them the Brewers' new owners in June 1941.[30] "We arrived at the Milwaukee station on a cold, drizzling Saturday afternoon with a grand total of eleven dollars between us," Veeck said. "Immediately, we crossed the street to a tavern and drank ten dollars of toasts to the glorious future that lay ahead." Then they headed to that night's game. Twenty-two fans were in attendance.[31]

Veeck was certain he could turn the moribund franchise around. "He had nothing to lose except money, which never worried Bill, especially when it wasn't his own," joked Grimm.[32] Veeck did not share his father's aversion to promotions, and he was willing to try anything to attract fans. He would award a fifty-pound cake of ice to one lucky fan, a stepladder to a second, and live lobsters to a third, delivering all prizes directly to their seats. He would reschedule evening games to the morning to accommodate night-shift workers. He would speak to any civic group that would listen.[33] "Arouse their curiosity," he said of fans, "and they'll come out in droves."[34]

That they did. The Brewers topped all minor-league teams in attendance in 1942, then outdrew the big-league Boston Braves and St. Louis Browns in 1943. The iconoclastic Veeck, who defied convention by steadfastly refusing to wear ties or hats, began to attract national attention for his unorthodox and highly successful ways. *Esquire* hailed him for running "the greatest baseball show on earth."[35]

Veeck always spoke fondly of his years with the Brewers—"Milwaukee was the great time of my life"—though most insiders believed he was destined for the majors.³⁶ He made a quiet attempt to rise in 1943, so he later claimed, only to be blocked by Commissioner Landis, who objected to Veeck's plans to stock the Philadelphia Phillies with stars from the Negro Leagues. Historians remain uncertain of his veracity.³⁷ "The major difficulty with this oft-told story is that it is not true," insisted David Jordan, Larry Gerlach, and John Rossi in 1998, though a subsequent study by Paul Dickson found Veeck's story to be plausible.³⁸

A different cause, in any event, would soon draw him away from Milwaukee. Veeck enlisted in the marines in November 1943 and was shipped to the South Pacific, where his right leg was crushed by the recoil of an antiaircraft gun. His right foot would be amputated in 1946, everything up to his knee would be taken in 1949, and the rest of his leg would slowly be whittled away by a series of thirty-six operations.³⁹ Yet his frenetic pace never slowed. "He could do more things on that one leg than a lot of people could do," marveled Roy Sievers, a slugger who played for him after the war. "He played handball. He'd go up a flight of stairs faster than anybody. He danced. He just enjoyed life."⁴⁰

The Cleveland Indians hit the market in 1946, and the thirty-two-year-old Veeck seized the opportunity. He lined up several investors, including movie and radio star Bob Hope, to help him raise the necessary two million dollars.⁴¹ "I am going to give the fans of Cleveland a lot of fun," he promised. "But I also plan to give them a pennant. That will come in time."⁴²

Cynics snickered. Veeck's stunts might have worked in a bush-league town like Milwaukee, but he was in the major leagues now. The Indians had never drawn more than 913,000 fans in a season, and they hadn't won a pennant since 1920. Their callow owner would soon be forced to scale back his expectations.

Veeck launched the same promotions—the giveaways, the circus acts, the fireworks shows—and spoke to more than five hundred community groups in his first year. His tactics proved to be even more successful in Cleveland than in Milwaukee. The Indians topped 1 million in attendance in 1946, then soared past 1.5 million a year later. "People are people," Veeck concluded. "Coca-Cola doesn't change its advertising from town to town. I don't change my promotion."⁴³

Bill Veeck became famous as baseball's greatest promoter, an owner who was willing to try anything to attract fans. "Arouse their curiosity," he said, "and they'll come out in droves" [National Baseball Hall of Fame and Museum].

His flashy gimmicks and highly publicized success had irritated his fellow owners back in the minors. Donie Bush, a former big-league shortstop who ran the Indianapolis team, once voiced his exasperation to Charlie Grimm. "You know I've always liked you, Charlie," Bush said. "And they didn't make them any better than old William Veeck. But tell me, Charlie, how could such a nice man ever have had such a so-and-so for a son?"[44]

The same question was now being asked around the American League. "My fellow club owners haven't exactly lavished their affection on me," Veeck admitted.[45] The truth was that they disliked almost everything about him—his boisterous promotions, his refusal to wear ties to league meetings, his unsolicited advice. Veeck earned the enmity of George Weiss by publicly suggesting that the Yankees general manager was shortchanging Joe DiMaggio. "If the Yankees don't want to pay him what he's worth," Veeck said, "well, I'll take him and pay him two hundred thousand dollars."[46]

His counterparts were especially displeased by Veeck's unilateral decision to integrate the American League. He signed outfielder Larry Doby from the Negro Leagues on July 3, 1947, purchasing his contract from the Newark Eagles.[47] "I understand that some of you said if a 'nigger' joins the club, you're leaving," Veeck told the white Indians in a clubhouse meeting. "Well, you can leave now because this guy is going to be a bigger star than any guy in this room."[48] Doby would bat .301 the following season, his first step toward induction in the Hall of Fame.

The signing of his new black star showed a different side of Bill Veeck. He was a master promoter, to be sure, but he was also a seasoned baseball man. He had built a pennant winner in Milwaukee, and he was determined to do the same with the Indians. "You can shoot off your fireworks, hire your clowns, pull off your stunts; all that is only the frosting on the cake," he once said. "The game of baseball is the thing on which, in the end, you will have to live or die."[49] Veeck had a sense, as he gazed toward the 1948 season, that everything was coming together in Cleveland. There was a possibility that his twin goals—a World Series crown and an all-time attendance record—might soon be attained.

* * *

Veeck was not alone in his success. Almost every club in the major leagues was riding a postwar wave of prosperity. Americans were determined to purge their memories of sacrifice and stoicism. They wished to consign the war to their rearview mirrors; they insisted on being entertained. "We had an amusement-hungry public after the war," said Cincinnati Reds general manager Warren Giles, "and some people were very free with their money."[50]

Television had not yet established its unbreakable grip on the American family—only eight thousand households owned TV sets in 1946—so other diversions flourished in its absence. People flocked to the movies, nightclubs, and racetracks. And they streamed into ballparks, boosting the majors to a series of annual attendance records: 18.5 million tickets sold in 1946, 19.9 million in 1947, the previously unimaginable total of 20.9 million in 1948.[51] No end seemed to be in sight. Connie Mack confidently predicted that big-league attendance would exceed thirty million by 1960.[52]

Individual teams aimed for the magic number of one million fans per season, a quaint figure by later standards, but then the benchmark for box-office excellence. Only four franchises crossed that threshold during the war's final season, 1945, but ten teams (even the hapless Washington Senators) reached the charmed circle a year later. This upswing of support had a dramatic impact on baseball's bottom line. Big-league teams luxuriated in a collective profit of nearly $4.9 million in 1946 (the equivalent of $64.7 million in 2020), dwarfing 1945's profit of $1.2 million.[53]

The game's wealthiest franchise led the charge into this brave new world. The New York Yankees drew 2.27 million fans in 1946—the first time a team had surpassed 2 million—and repeated the feat with 2.18 million in 1947. Veeck was determined to go them one better. His overriding goal was the establishment of a new single-season attendance mark, perhaps as soon as 1948, though the New Yorkers dismissed him as an insignificant pest.

The Yankees' bigger concern was the 1947 World Series. They cruised to the pennant that season, outdistancing the closest American League contender by twelve games. Their brain trust devised a two-pronged plan—first trounce the Brooklyn Dodgers for the world title, then announce an astonishing rearrangement of their front office. The mercurial Larry MacPhail had secretly agreed to sell his one-third interest in the team to partners Dan Topping and Del Webb, clearing the way to indulge his dream of becoming a horse breeder. Yet MacPhail had no intention of leaving New York. He had agreed to remain as president and general manager of the Yankees for the princely salary of fifty thousand dollars a year.[54]

Things did not go according to plan. The pesky Dodgers tied the series at two games apiece when Cookie Lavagetto ripped his famous double off Bill Bevens, and they knotted it again by winning Game Six. That set the stage for a nail-biter at Yankee Stadium on October 6. The Dodgers grabbed an early 2–0 lead, though the Yankees battled back.

MacPhail found it difficult to remain calm under the best of circumstances, and he came completely unglued after his team surged ahead, 5–2. The world championship that had eluded him in Cincinnati, Brooklyn, and his previous two seasons in the Bronx was tantalizingly close. He stood in the press snack bar with a group of writers during the ninth inning, vibrating with nervous energy. "That's it! That does it! That's my retirement!" he shouted when pitcher Joe Page induced a double play to clinch the title. "I mean it. I'm through. I got what I wanted, and I can't take any more of this." Tears streamed down his face.[55]

The reporters, who had no knowledge of the impending sale, were stunned. They were even more surprised when they gathered around MacPhail at the Yankees' victory party at the palatial Biltmore Hotel a few hours later.[56] "Stay away or get punched," he barked. It was the first volley in a night that would be immortalized as the "Battle of the Biltmore."

MacPhail verbally lashed any member of the Yankees organization who mistakenly crossed his path. He bumped into his farm director, Weiss, whom he immediately fired, and then he berated Topping: "You're just a guy who was born with a silver spoon in your mouth."[57] Topping finally decided to end the fireworks. "Dan went over to Larry and punched him in the nose," recalled Hazel Weiss, George's wife. "Anyone could have knocked him over, Larry was so drunk."[58]

The deal was off, at least the part about MacPhail sticking around. Topping and Webb announced their purchase of his share of the team the very next day, along with Weiss's promotion to GM.[59] Columnists chattered for days about MacPhail's breakdown, which they attributed to alcohol and overwork. The dynamic owner, so recently hailed as the most powerful man in the major leagues, retreated to his Maryland farm, never to work in baseball again.

"It was a damn fool thing to do," MacPhail would say a dozen years later, reflecting on his ignominious departure from the game he loved. "That was a happy occasion, and it belonged to the players. I should have kept my big mouth shut."[60]

The Yankees would roll on without him. Their record of 94–60 in the subsequent season of 1948 certainly wasn't bad—it would have been sufficient for the pennant a year earlier—though it dropped them to third place. But the slip was only momentary. Bigger prizes lay ahead.

Headlines: 1948

Cleveland sets new mark for one-day crowd

The Yankees had held the record for single-day attendance (81,841) since 1938, and Bill Veeck naturally wanted it. He heavily promoted a May 23 matchup with New York, but Cleveland fell short with 78,431 fans. Nothing special was planned for a June 20 date against the Athletics, yet 82,781 streamed into cavernous Municipal Stadium. Veeck made the announcement: "The attendance today is eighty-two thou…." The rest was drowned out by the crowd's gigantic roar.[61]

Durocher shocks baseball world by leaving Dodgers

Leo Durocher returned from his one-year suspension in April, yet the Dodgers played sluggishly. Brooklyn was mired in fourth place on July 16, when Durocher astounded everybody by jumping to the archrival New York Giants. He accepted their managerial offer after asking Branch Rickey if his job with the Dodgers was safe. "He chewed on his cigar," Durocher recalled. "He said nothing."[62]

Indians clinch AL title in playoff game

The Indians held first place in the American League for most of 1948—setting an annual attendance record of 2,620,627 along the way—yet a loss on the final day of the regular season left them tied with the Red Sox. Rookie Gene Bearden, Cleveland's starter in the October 4 tiebreaker, pitched a gem, winning 8–3. His knuckleball was perfect. "How are you going to beat a guy like that?" moaned Boston second baseman Bobby Doerr.[63]

Cleveland wins crown in six games

The World Series seemed almost anticlimactic after the hectic pennant race. The Indians lost Game One to the Boston Braves, 1–0, then stormed back to take four of the next five. A quarter of a million Clevelanders jammed the streets to salute their champions, yet the celebration was bittersweet for Veeck, who faced a divorce. "Do you know what the saddest thing in the world is?" he asked. "To go home to an empty apartment in a moment of triumph."[64]

6

Clouds

The *Sporting News* sounded a jarringly discordant note during the golden season of 1948, even as ballpark box offices teemed with customers and major-league coffers overflowed with profits.

"It is a fact that, outside of Cleveland, not another club in the Big Time has played up to its turnstile potential," contended an editorial in the June 2 edition. That undoubtedly came as news to the Yankees, Tigers, Red Sox, and Pirates, all on track to draw more than 1.5 million fans and set franchise attendance records. But the *Sporting News* insisted that "effervescent, ebullient, clever, acumen-loaded, publicity-conscious" Bill Veeck was the only executive who had unlocked the true potential of the national pastime. "Let the other magnates tear a page out of the Veeck book," it recommended, "and send already impressive big-league box-office figures soaring to empyrean heights."[1]

That sounded too much like work to most major-league owners, who did little more than open their gates on game days. Why run all over town giving speeches like that lunatic Veeck? Why waste energy plotting special promotions for every home date? They were prospering nicely as it was. Yet the *Sporting News* cautioned against such complacency. "Now is the time to build against a possible letdown at the gate," it warned.[2] But most owners found it impossible to envision a decline. Attendance had increased by more than 5 percent each season since 1943. Who could see any signs of a letdown?

There were a few killjoys, of course. Branch Rickey seemed unnaturally worried about the competitive potential of professional football. He had predicted as early as 1943 that football would emerge as a serious threat to baseball, though it was easy to wave off his concerns. The Gallup Poll reported in April 1948 that 39 percent of Americans considered baseball their favorite sport, dwarfing the 17 percent who opted for football.[3] *New York Times* columnist Arthur Daley spoke for the establishment on this issue, as on so many: "What challenge can a 20-game sport ever make to a 154-game one?"[4]

Football seemed to be a greater danger to itself than to any other sport. Its battlefield was littered with victims of the war between the National Football League and the All-America Football Conference. Only three teams turned profits in 1949—the NFL's Chicago Bears and Washington Redskins and the AAFC's Cleveland Browns—while the other fourteen franchises wallowed in red ink. Widespread desperation finally forced a truce in December 1949, resulting in a consolidated National-American Football League (a name soon stripped of its hyphenated adjective). The sport's road back to stability and prosperity appeared likely to be a long one.[5]

Yet Rickey would never deviate from his vision of football's destiny. His belief was so strong that it had led him to briefly link the Dodgers to the AAFC. "Brooklyn should be represented in professional football," he declared in 1948, though the borough's citizens would show little interest in the team he established.[6] The football Dodgers flopped so badly that their only option was to merge with the league's New York franchise a year later.

It's impossible to get a precise handle on Rickey's losses in the AAFC, but historians' estimates range as high as seven hundred thousand dollars.[7] Did this unhappy experience cause him to doubt football's potential power? Not in the least. His warnings would only grow louder as the 1950s progressed. "I am alarmed at the subtle invasion of professional football, which is gaining preeminence over baseball," he would conclude gloomily in 1959.[8]

* * *

Another simmering problem—ignored by most owners, yet nonetheless real—was the general deterioration of big-league ballparks.

The invention of reinforced concrete had inspired a stadium-construction spree during the first two decades of the twentieth century. Fourteen of the sixteen big-league teams still played in facilities that had been built between 1909 and 1915, ballparks that were thirty-four to forty years old by 1949. The younger exceptions were New York's Yankee Stadium and Cleveland's Municipal Stadium, which opened in 1923 and 1932, respectively.[9]

The Depression and World War II had virtually paralyzed America's construction sector for a generation. Building a new stadium—or even renovating an existing structure—would have been an unthinkable luxury during those emergencies. Next came the massive postwar housing shortage. Millions of returning veterans and their rapidly growing families were in urgent need of new homes, a requirement that clearly took precedence over frivolities such as baseball. The 1940s would go down in major-league history as the only decade in which no new ballparks were constructed.

That meant the national pastime was being played in aging stadiums that often were poorly maintained and usually were jammed into decaying urban neighborhoods or polluted industrial zones. Some of these facilities had lovable quirks—the wall (later known as the Green Monster) towering 37 feet above left field in Boston's Fenway Park, the ivy-covered fences adorning Chicago's Wrigley Field, the 258-foot porch looming behind right field in New York's Polo Grounds, the steep upward slope to the warning track in Cincinnati's Crosley Field. But the typical big-league ballpark was drab, dirty, and unappealing.[10]

Teams struggled to improve the ambience of their homes, though they generally failed. The Braves planted fir trees outside their bleak stadium, vainly attempting to hide the smoke billowing from the nearby yards of the Boston and Albany Railroad.[11] Nobody was fooled. "My first impression of Braves Field was that it was a big, cold cement arena," wrote third baseman Eddie Mathews. "Later, after I had played there awhile, I thought it was a big, cold cement arena."[12]

The White Sox initiated a perpetual maintenance program to keep Comiskey Park in service. "We repaint every year," said heir Chuck Comiskey, "and with a stadium as old as ours, we have to replace a lot of wiring and water lines each season."[13] But the ballpark was down on its heels, and its location on Chicago's South Side didn't help. "Comiskey Park was dim," recalled pitcher Billy Pierce. "The nearby stockyards were going full blast, and the aroma was terrible."[14]

Little could be done for Shibe Park in Philadelphia and Sportsman's Park in St. Louis. Each pulled double duty, serving as the home field for teams in both leagues. Off-days were rare for the two facilities, and their staffs fought a losing battle to keep the grandstands clean and the fields playable. "With the hot weather they had down there, the infield was like playing on a rockpile," Warren Giles said of the St. Louis park.[15] Browns catcher Les Moss suggested a different comparison that was equally unforgiving: "By the middle of July, most of the grass was gone, and it was like playing on a cement street."[16]

Only three hundred thousand automobiles were registered in the United States as of 1909, the year that Shibe Park opened its gates, inaugurating the binge of stadium construction. Most Americans still used public transit in those days, so it made sense to build ballparks in densely settled neighborhoods adjacent to streetcar lines. Stadium sites usually were constricted by thoroughfares, homes, and businesses, which forced the adoption of the abnormal outfield dimensions that distinguished Fenway Park, the Polo Grounds, and several of their counterparts. Parking was almost nonexistent.[17]

But times had changed by the late 1940s, with fans now more likely to drive to the ballpark than take a trolley. Baseball's customers increasingly came from outlying parts of the city or even from the suburbs. They found parking to be a hassle, and they felt uneasy about the urban disorder in the stadium's vicinity. This fear would be crystallized by a bizarre incident at the Polo Grounds in 1950. A New York Giants fan, Bernard Doyle, had just taken his seat when he was struck and killed by a stray bullet fired from a nearby apartment complex. The game went on as scheduled.[18]

Perhaps no ballpark epitomized the positive and negative traits of city stadiums more than Brooklyn's Ebbets Field. Dodgers owner Charles Ebbets spent three-quarters of a million dollars constructing the thirty-two-thousand-seat stadium in 1913. It was hailed as an architectural wonder, with its elaborate rotunda, white marble floor inlaid with the red stitches of a baseball, and bat-and-ball chandelier at the main entrance. It would attain the status of a holy shrine, the sacred home of the borough's cherished team.[19]

Ebbets Field was much smaller than New York's other big-league parks, Yankee Stadium and the Polo Grounds, and it was landlocked, which precluded future growth. There were only seven hundred parking spaces. Larry MacPhail and Branch Rickey did what they could to maintain the park throughout the 1940s, but its postwar deterioration became obvious. "MacPhail stuck a lot of paint on it and spruced it up," said Red Barber, "but it was still a dirty, stinking, old ballpark."[20]

Nobody was more concerned about the decline of Ebbets Field than Rickey's partner, Walter O'Malley. "Ballparks then were almost all old," he said decades later, his distaste still palpable. "They were built in the poorer section of the city. The toilets at most ballparks were a germ hazard that would have turned a bacteriologist gray."[21]

O'Malley offered a solution that apparently had not occurred to the owner of any other big-league franchise. The economy was starting to percolate, and attendance was booming, so why not build a new ballpark? He made his formal proposal at an October 1946 meeting of the Dodgers' board. "Mr. O'Malley also reported on the possibility of moving to a new site and erecting thereon a modern sports stadium,"

Dodgers owner Charles Ebbets said in 1913 that he expected his eponymous ballpark to last for thirty years. But an aging Ebbets Field remained in service long beyond its projected lifespan [National Baseball Hall of Fame and Museum].

read the minutes. One can imagine Rickey's annoyance with O'Malley's audacity—spending money on *a ballpark* rather than the farm system—as well as the rapidity of the Mahatma's response.

No discussion was noted in the minutes. Just a curt dismissal: "The board advised that the matter should be deferred for the time being, considering the limited resources of the corporation and the uncertainty as to future attendance."[22] Rickey had prevailed in the short term, though not necessarily for good. O'Malley would not be so easily deterred.

* * *

Owners generally seemed unconcerned about the clouds forming over their beloved game. Football didn't trouble them, at least not in its present weakened condition. Nor did their stadiums cause them worry—not much, anyway. But broadcasting was different. Radio and television absolutely terrified most big-league executives.

The big problem was the uncertainty. The initial broadcast of a regular-season game had occurred in 1921, just a year after the nation's first commercial radio station, KDKA, signed on from its Pittsburgh studios. But nobody knew if radio coverage would attract fans to the stadium or encourage them to stay home.[23] The *Sporting News* opted for the pessimistic view as early as 1922. "Mr. Radio," it warned, "is going to butt into the business of telling the world all about the ballgame without the world having to go to the ballpark to find out."[24] Most owners tended to agree. They rejected all play-by-play proposals from local broadcasters.

But William Wrigley, Jr., thought along different lines. His experience in the chewing-gum business had convinced him of the power of advertising, so he and the president of his Cubs, William Veeck, Sr., welcomed the new medium with open arms. Any radio outlet that wished to broadcast from Wrigley Field, they announced in 1925, could do so without charge. Seven stations scrambled to cover the Cubs, blanketing the local airwaves. It was no coincidence that Chicago led the National League in attendance every season between 1926 and 1932.[25]

Several other teams, especially those in the Midwest, eventually emulated the Cubs with positive results. The play-by-play man for the Detroit Tigers, Ty Tyson, was astonished to receive checks and money orders from residents of distant Michigan towns. They asked him to act as a ticket broker, reserving seats for their upcoming visits to Navin Field. "Radio has attracted these people to the ballpark," Tyson said in 1929, "and they admit it."[26] Only the three New York teams stood fast against the audio tide, making a pact to abstain from radio coverage. This gentleman's agreement was finally broken by Larry MacPhail—who else?—when the Dodgers began broadcasting their games on WOR in 1939.[27]

It was clear by then that something new—and much more powerful—was on the horizon. Engineers for General Electric, Radio Corporation of America (RCA), and Westinghouse had engaged in a quiet competition throughout the 1920s and 1930s, seeking the best method to transmit pictures along with sound. Their early systems produced grainy, low-resolution images with a greenish tint.[28] "Television has a long way to go to equal the movies in clarity," *New York Times* radio editor Orrin Dunlap, Jr., wrote sadly after a 1937 demonstration.[29] But subsequent refinements paved the way for TV's public debut before the decade's end.

The National Broadcasting Company, RCA's powerful radio network, was determined to extend its dominance into video. NBC operated an experimental television station, W2XBS, which could be viewed on two hundred or so "telesets" that its engineers had installed around the New York area. The network scored a coup by telecasting Franklin Roosevelt's speech at the opening ceremonies for the World's Fair on April 30, 1939. Its producers began searching for other events worthy of coverage.

They chose baseball. W2XBS dispatched a rudimentary mobile unit and a single camera to an inconsequential Ivy League game between Princeton and Columbia on May 17.[30] The cameraman, who was planted along the third-base line, had to pan whenever the ball was hit, often losing it completely. "We got so we were actually praying for all the batters to strike out," recalled announcer Bill Stern. "That was one thing we knew the camera could record."[31] Dunlap, again watching for the *Times*, wondered if baseball could ever be successfully captured by TV: "Where are the peanuts, the pop, the scorecards, hot dogs, and the mustard pot? They don't come through the air."[32]

NBC moved up to the big leagues on August 26, 1939, telecasting a game between the Reds and Dodgers at Ebbets Field. There were two cameras this time, and Dunlap was happier with the picture—"baseball becomes a natural for television"—yet plenty of skeptics remained, MacPhail among them.[33] Radio enticed fans to the ballpark, he told Phil Wrigley a few days later, but TV might make stadium visits unnecessary. "Your club may someday be playing in private in Wrigley Field," said

MacPhail, "while fans in Ottumwa, Iowa, and Kalamazoo, Michigan, are paying fifty cents to watch it in a theater."[34]

The war soon intervened, putting the full-scale development of commercial television on hold, though baseball executives never stopped debating its potential. Would TV become a reliable revenue source, they wondered nervously, or would it destroy the game by eliminating the incentive to buy tickets? "Everybody was afraid of it," recalled Bill DeWitt, Sr., then the general manager of the Browns.[35] The jury was still out in 1946, when Walter O'Malley advised Brooklyn's board of directors to calm down. "Television is not now considered to have great commercial value because of the limited number of sets," he said.[36] It was a sensible short-term verdict. Only four of every thousand U.S. households would purchase a TV prior to 1948.[37]

The long term? That was a much different story. Everybody expected television to generate buckets of money. The only question was when. Baseball had been selling the radio rights to the World Series since 1934, when the Ford Motor Company agreed to pay $100,000 per year ($1.9 million in 2020 dollars), a breathtaking sum at the time. Owners happily anticipated sizable payments from TV stations and networks in the future.[38]

The Yankees offered a hint of this windfall in 1947, becoming the first team to sell its local television rights. The going rate was seventy-five thousand dollars for the season. Other teams scrambled to make their own deals, temporarily forgetting their fears of reduced attendance. Only eleven TV stations operated in the United States that year. Nine forged deals to carry baseball games.[39]

The Dodgers were among the participants in 1947's gold rush, despite O'Malley's earlier reticence. They televised a substantial portion of their home schedule, yet still drew 1.81 million fans to Ebbets Field, a franchise record. It seemed that everybody's worries might have been unwarranted. "The board was unanimous that television has not adversely affected attendance," said the minutes of Brooklyn's postseason meeting, "and it has reason to believe that the additional publicity is a proper promotion for great attendance." Other factors behind the box-office spike, such as Jackie Robinson's debut and the National League pennant, were conveniently ignored.[40]

The Dodgers would henceforth be cited as Exhibit A in support of the unrestricted use of television. Their success helped to ease baseball's sense of dread, freeing teams to pursue TV money. Fifteen franchises—all but the Pirates—locked down television contracts by 1949. Nine of those teams offered all seventy-seven home games to local viewers, free of charge, a season later.[41]

These arrangements sprinkled varying amounts of cash throughout the major leagues—the actual sums depended on each team's fan appeal and the size of its market—and the potential for profit was even greater on the national scale. That point was driven home when Happy Chandler signed a contract in late 1950 with the Gillette Safety Razor Company and the Mutual Broadcasting System for telecasts of the World Series and the All-Star Game. The deal was so incredibly lucrative—six million dollars over six years—that baseball executives began to fret that their TV partners were being too generous. "It looks like a lot of money to me," Reds general manager Warren Giles said worriedly. "I hope they get their value out of it."[42]

* * *

6. Clouds

The national pastime also was bothered, as usual, by labor headaches. The owners found two issues especially annoying during the late 1940s—inflated prices for young talent and legal fallout from the Mexican League fiasco.

The Detroit Tigers were widely blamed for instigating the former problem in 1941, when they paid a signing bonus of $52,000 (the equivalent of $911,000 in 2020) to Dick Wakefield, a University of Michigan outfielder. The unprecedented enormity of his bonanza horrified the baseball establishment, though it initially seemed to be a prudent investment. Wakefield topped the American League with two hundred hits and thirty-eight doubles in 1943, but he faded after World War II and would be consigned to the bench by 1949.[43]

Spending on bonuses returned with a vengeance after the war. Five teams engaged in a 1946 battle for seventeen-year-old Tookie Gilbert, a New Orleans first baseman, who resorted to a lottery to make his decision. His mother drew a slip of paper from a hat, giving the lucky Giants the chance to fork over fifty thousand dollars. Gilbert would appear in only 183 games in the major leagues, batting an anemic .203.[44]

Gilbert's signing convinced the owners to take action in late 1946. They imposed restrictions on any new player who received more than six thousand dollars to sign. These "bonus babies" would be allowed to play just one season in the minors before being elevated to the majors or placed on waivers. It was hoped that this stark choice would discourage teams from casually tossing money at youngsters, yet it had no such effect. The Phillies anted up sixty-five thousand dollars for Curt Simmons in 1947, topped a year later by the Braves' seventy-five-thousand-dollar advance to Johnny Antonelli. Both were destined to become solid big-league pitchers.[45]

Their success brought no comfort to most owners, who feared that a one-hundred-thousand-dollar bonus loomed around the corner. Nobody was more upset than the old penny-pincher himself, Branch Rickey. "Why a bonus for a boy to learn his profession?" he sputtered. "A boy goes to medical school for eight years *at his own expense* to study to become a doctor."[46]

Rickey and his colleagues also remained angry at Jorge Pasquel, even though the czar of the Mexican League had been exposed by then as a small-time operator. "I am ready to compete with organized ball, dollar for dollar and peso for peso," Pasquel had bragged in 1946, though his words were hollow.[47] He allowed many of his high-priced American players to flee after that first season. Those who stuck around were clamped under a payroll cap in 1947, then pushed out the door when Pasquel threatened additional salary cuts.

Happy Chandler's suspensions were still intact, so the jumpers eked out a living as best they could. Sal Maglie, the only American who developed into a star in Mexico, grudgingly returned to his native Niagara Falls, New York, to work at a gas station. Mickey Owen unhappily tended his farm in Missouri. They and the others occasionally barnstormed or played in so-called "outlaw" leagues that were beyond the commissioner's reach.[48] Maglie wound up in Canada's Provincial League in 1949—"anything to get away from those pumps"—as did Danny Gardella, notorious by then for his willingness to fight baseball's power structure.[49]

Gardella had filed a federal lawsuit in September 1947, contending that his suspension (and consequently the reserve clause) violated federal antitrust laws. His attorney, Frederic Johnson, argued that Gardella had not signed a contract with the

Giants for the 1946 season, and hence could not be considered their employee. A federal district judge ruled against Gardella in July 1948, but the U.S. Court of Appeals reversed the decision seven months later.[50] Judge Jerome Frank asserted that the reserve clause "results in something resembling peonage of the baseball player."[51] He dismissed any suggestion that players were different from other workers because they were better paid. "No court," Frank wrote, "should strive to ingeniously legalize private (if benevolent) dictatorship."[52]

Chandler was apoplectic. He noted that every big leaguer was paid at least five thousand dollars per season, and a rare few were close to one hundred thousand. "If that's slavery or servitude," the commissioner said, "then there's a lot of us who would like to be in the same class."[53] But he was privately frightened. "I do not think the lawyers thought we could win the Gardella case," he would admit after leaving baseball.[54]

Chandler did what he could to relieve the pressure. His first step was to announce on June 5, 1949, that he was lifting the suspensions of all jumpers who had not sued baseball.[55] He phoned Mickey Owen as reporters listened. "Get your bag packed, boy, and get to your club right away," the commissioner barked.[56] Chandler would later insist that he acted out of a broad sense of compassion—"it is no fun punishing kids like that, a lot of good kids"—but his benevolence did not extend to the lone holdout.[57] The appellate court had remanded Gardella's case to federal district court, which was preparing for a November 1949 trial. Chandler himself was scheduled to be deposed in September.

Gardella's lawyer, Johnson, ratcheted up the pressure during the two-day deposition. He and Chandler, who had been classmates at Harvard Law School, were on a first-name basis, yet there was no denying the tension in the air. Johnson fired a lengthy series of questions about broadcasting rights, seeking to prove that baseball truly was a big business, contrary to Oliver Wendell Holmes's 1922 ruling.[58] Chandler conceded that the radio and television fees for the 1947 World Series had totaled $275,000, and Johnson pounced. "Organized baseball," he crowed, "is engaged in interstate commerce to the nth degree."[59]

Baseball had wandered into dangerous territory. If Johnson could persuade the judge to his point of view, everything that the owners held dear might be lost—the reserve clause, the antitrust exemption, the underpinnings of the game's whole financial structure. Chandler summoned Fred Saigh, who not only owned the St. Louis Cardinals, but was a lawyer himself. Settle the case, Chandler told him.[60] The two men would later disagree about the commissioner's state of mind. Chandler maintained that he made a simple request. Saigh contended that Chandler begged for help. "I saw a scared man who was not willing to stand up and fight," Saigh said.[61]

Gardella seemed an unlikely candidate for a settlement. He never missed an opportunity to insist on pushing all the way to the U.S. Supreme Court. "We'll fight it to the limit," he often said.[62] But the two-year battle had taken its toll on Gardella, who was earning just thirty-six dollars a week as an orderly at a Mount Vernon, New York, hospital. Saigh waved $60,000 ($650,000 in 2020 dollars) in front of him. He wavered, then surrendered.[63]

The owners emitted a collective sigh of relief, with the commissioner leading the chorus. "If I were a drinking man, I'd sure celebrate this," said the teetotaling Chandler, a huge grin on his face.[64] Reporters badgered him about the size of the settlement, which would not be made public for several years. He denied any knowledge, a peculiar stance for the game's supreme leader. "I didn't pay the money," Chandler said, "and purposely avoided learning what amount was paid."[65]

Gardella, for his part, initially expressed no doubts about his decision to drop the suit. "Being a poor man, I felt more or less justified," he said in 1961. "It wasn't like I had a lot of money and was being paid off."[66] But his mood changed as he aged. He began to sense that he had missed his chance to become a historic figure. "If you sue someone for something, why should money appease you?" he asked in 1980, when he was sixty years old. "It's like a Judas taking money and being bought off."

He chuckled ruefully. "So I'm bought off," he said. "Apparently, my lawyer thought it was all right."[67]

Headlines: 1949

WAITKUS WOUNDED IN BIZARRE INCIDENT

Phillies first baseman Eddie Waitkus received a puzzling note from a stranger on June 15. "It's extremely important that I see you as soon as possible," wrote Ruth Ann Steinhagen, who was staying in the same Chicago hotel. Waitkus went to her room, where she inexplicably shot him. The attack inspired Bernard Malamud's 1952 novel, *The Natural*, and the 1984 movie of the same name. Waitkus would recover and play six more seasons.[68]

NEW YORK EDGES BOSTON FOR AL CROWN

The Red Sox trailed the Yankees by twelve games on July 4. But Boston won sixty-one of its next eighty-one games, vaulting into the American League lead with two dates left. That's when its momentum vanished. The Sox lost both games—and the title—to the resurgent Yankees. Casey Stengel, New York's first-year manager, gave all the credit to his players. "Their guts did it," he yelled in a frenzied clubhouse.[69]

BROOKLYN SEIZES NL TITLE ON FINAL DAY

The first-place Cardinals lost six of their final nine games, opening the door for Brooklyn in the National League's pennant race. All the Dodgers needed was a victory over Philadelphia on October 2. They broke out to leads of 5–0 and 7–4, yet the Phillies battled back. Duke Snider and Luis Olmo finally settled the matter in the tenth inning, driving in a pair of runs to give Brooklyn its second NL title in three years.[70]

YANKEES EASILY TAME DODGERS IN WORLD SERIES

The Dodgers boasted a sublime blend of power and speed, pacing the majors in homers (152) and stolen bases (117) in 1949. Yet the Yankees shut them down with ease in the World Series, allowing only fourteen runs en route to a five-game triumph. Brooklyn third baseman Spider Jorgensen gave voice to his team's shock: "I was dumbfounded that they won it so easily."[71]

7

Freefall

Bill Veeck's attention span was extremely limited. Even his staunchest friends conceded that Veeck would dart from topic to topic like a hummingbird from flower to flower. "Once he accomplished what he wanted to—or if he couldn't, if he were stymied—he'd lose interest," admitted Rudie Schaffer, his right-hand man since the early days in Milwaukee.[1]

There were rumors in late 1948 that Veeck was bored in Cleveland. His Indians had just won the World Series, establishing a big-league attendance record in the process. What else was there to do? Local reporters asked Veeck if he had devised an exit strategy. They anticipated a denial, only to be surprised by his noncommittal response. "Anything is for sale," he said mildly. "For a price, of course."[2]

No purchase offers were forthcoming, so Veeck geared up for the 1949 season. The Indians performed reasonably well on the field (third place in the American League) and at the box office (2.23 million fans), though they fell short of both 1948 benchmarks. The reason was obvious to Veeck's new acolyte. "He had lost enthusiasm for the game," said Hank Greenberg, "and he wasn't able to instill the same spirit and determination into the entire organization."[3]

Greenberg, a slugger who attained fame with the Detroit Tigers, had been invited to spring training by the Indians a year earlier, though he eventually opted to retire. He had galvanized the nation with his 1938 pursuit of Babe Ruth's hallowed record of sixty home runs in a season, falling short by only two. Veeck initially envisioned Greenberg as a power hitter who might bring a pennant to Cleveland, but came to respect his intelligence and ability to weather adversity. The gregarious promoter invited the reserved, dignified ex-player to join his front office.[4]

Baseball insiders doubted that two men so dissimilar in personality could coexist, but Veeck and Greenberg became great friends. They shared a sense of being outsiders—Veeck as a thorn in the establishment's side, Greenberg as one of the few Jews to play big-league ball. "Sure, there was added pressure being Jewish," he admitted. "How the hell could you get up to home plate every day and have some son of a bitch call you a Jew bastard and a kike and a sheenie and get on your ass without feeling the pressure?"[5]

Daily contact with antisemitism caused Greenberg to sympathize with underdogs. He finished his career in Pittsburgh, where he was one of the few National League players to show outward support for the beleaguered Jackie Robinson in 1947. The two stars had a brief encounter when Robinson slashed a single against the Pirates. "Stick in there," said Greenberg, the first baseman for the Pirates. "You're doing fine. Keep your chin up." Robinson, accustomed to vicious abuse on the basepaths, never forgot the words of encouragement.[6]

Greenberg was equally supportive of Veeck, even though the maverick owner infuriated executives throughout the sport. "I was enchanted with him," Greenberg said. "His exuberance and his enthusiasm and knowledge of the game were extraordinary."[7] But Veeck's vaunted energy seemed to be in short supply as the 1949 season neared its close. Boredom was undoubtedly a factor, but Greenberg sensed a second reason for his lethargy: "It seems his imminent divorce had gotten him down."[8]

The divorce would be finalized in October 1949, and Veeck sold the Indians to local investors a month later. He needed the money, he said, to pay his ex-wife and support his children.[9] "For one minute," he recalled, "I held a check for one million dollars in my hands, made out in my name, the end product of the one dollar I had started out with in Milwaukee. That million dwindled fast."[10]

Veeck denied any interest in returning to baseball, though nobody believed him.[11] "Bill would like to come back to the Cubs," said Phil Wrigley. "But he wants to return only as the owner. And it so happens that I like the Cubs, too. I'm not selling."[12] The crosstown White Sox were also said to be of interest to the native Chicagoan, and some reports tied him to the woeful St. Louis Browns. The latter possibility was quickly dismissed by Franklin Lewis, sports editor of the *Cleveland Press*. "There is no future in St. Louis," Lewis said, "for a promoter of Veeck's verve and ambition."[13]

The Browns themselves seemed to lack a future. Richard Muckerman, who bought the team from Don Barnes in 1945, grew discouraged by his lack of progress. He bailed out in February 1949, selling the franchise to Bill and Charley DeWitt, who had been associated with the Browns since working as vendors at Sportsman's Park as teenagers. Bill had risen to become the team's general manager, Charley the traveling secretary.[14] "As long as we have anything to say about them," they said in a joint statement, "the Browns will stay in St. Louis."[15]

The DeWitts were full of brave words, though ominously short of cash, and their customers were few. The Browns drew only 271,000 fans to Sportsman's Park during the new proprietors' first season, while the Cardinals attracted 1.43 million to the same stadium. A persistent lack of funds plagued the Browns, no matter who owned the team. They averaged ninety-five losses per season between 1946 and 1950. "Every time we had a fairly good ballplayer develop, they had to sell him to make money to stay in the league," outfielder Roy Sievers recalled sadly.[16]

It was commonly assumed that the Browns would have to pack their bags someday. "There is no doubt that St. Louis can't support two major-league teams," Arthur Daley wrote in the *New York Times*. "That's presuming, of course, the Brownies are a major-league team."[17] The Cardinals clearly had the upper hand, even after legendary owner Sam Breadon decided to sell in 1947 at the age of seventy-one. "Every year I am less sufficient," Breadon explained, "and at my age, it's time to quit."[18]

Politician Robert Hannegan and lawyer Fred Saigh were introduced as the Cardinals' new owners. Hannegan was a truly powerful man—confidant of President Harry Truman, former chairman of the Democratic National Committee—and was assumed to be the dominant partner. Saigh possessed a rare ability to structure complex real-estate deals—he owned two of the largest buildings in downtown St. Louis—but otherwise operated in obscurity.[19] He was soft-spoken, unusually short (five-foot-four), and thin-skinned. Superstar Stan Musial would remember him as "a highly sensitive man."[20]

This touchiness motivated Saigh, who had no intention of being overshadowed by his partner. He moved quickly when the opportunity arose. A heart condition unexpectedly sidelined Hannegan in 1948, eventually compelling him to sell in January 1949. (He would die in October at the age of forty-six.) Saigh snapped up his shares and basked in his sudden celebrity.[21] "Saigh overnight became a well-known name and face, which is a heady experience when you've been an unknown, even a wealthy one," said Bob Broeg, who covered the Cardinals in that era for the *St. Louis Post-Dispatch*.[22]

Saigh now had the franchise all to himself, and he was determined to maintain his grip. "We'll win this year, and we'll win a lot more pennants," he crowed before the 1950 season. "And I'll be here to see them won. I'm in baseball to stay."[23]

* * *

The St. Louis Browns weren't the only team struggling to survive after World War II, despite the general prosperity that was washing over the major leagues. Franchises were also floundering in Boston, Philadelphia, and Washington.

The Boston Braves were a perennial doormat, never finishing higher than fourth place in the National League between 1917 and 1945. The crosstown Red Sox, who boasted future Hall of Famers Ted Williams and Bobby Doerr, outdrew the Braves by 3.2 million fans during the 1940s. The Braves were hampered not only by their weak on-field product, but also by their unwieldy management structure. Nearly a hundred men were listed as co-owners of the team. "It was hard to find a Bostonian who didn't know someone who owned the Braves," Al Hirshberg joked in the *Sporting News*.[24]

Sanity finally prevailed in 1944. A trio of Boston contractors, nicknamed by the press as the "Three Little Steamshovels," bought out dozens and dozens of fellow Braves owners. Forty-year-old Louis Perini, a son of Italian immigrants, emerged as the dominant Steamshovel. Perini had begun working for his father's construction firm as a water carrier at age six, moving up to the presidency at twenty-one upon the older man's death. He greatly expanded the small family business, transforming it into a multinational corporation.[25]

Lou Perini smiled easily and was well-liked by peers and underlings. Longtime Braves employee Donald Davidson was surprised by the new team president's openness to suggestions and willingness to experiment. The soft-spoken Perini wasn't an imposing boss, Davidson said, but "a kind, friendly man" and a "progressive thinker."[26]

Yet he was no pushover. Competition for construction contracts could be cutthroat, especially in a highly political state such as Massachusetts. Perini knew how the game was played. He and Joe Maney, a fellow Steamshovel, had pleaded guilty in the late 1930s to participating in an income-tax evasion scheme, funneling kickbacks to elected officials to secure a contract for a massive dam project. Perini and Maney were fined, but avoided jail time.[27] A separate trial in 1947 would produce evidence of Perini making under-the-table payments to labor leaders to facilitate a New York City water project, though he would not be charged with a crime.[28]

Perini promised to take a businesslike approach with the Braves. "As contractors, we are planners," he said, "and we know that good organization will accomplish wonders."[29] The first victim of this new efficiency was Casey Stengel, who had amassed a miserable 373–491 record in six seasons as manager. Perini was bothered not only by Stengel's losing, but also by his famously garbled syntax. "This man can't really know much about baseball if he isn't able to explain a simple play," said Perini, who handed Stengel his walking papers.[30]

Perini found his ideal manager two years later, luring Billy Southworth from the Cardinals for a base salary of thirty-five thousand dollars, plus a bonus of twenty thousand if he achieved the seemingly impossible goal of a National League pennant. Southworth possessed a self-righteous streak and a weakness for alcohol, but his managerial record was beyond reproach, capped by a pair of world championships in St. Louis.[31]

The ingredients for success were in place. Perini busied himself with promoting the Braves and bolstering their organization. He purchased Bill Veeck's old minor-league team in Milwaukee to serve as the keystone of a greatly expanded farm system, while predicting that bigger things lay ahead for Brewers fans.[32] "Milwaukee will be in a major league within five years and should get ready for it," he said in 1948.[33] Southworth, meanwhile, steadily directed the Braves upward in the National League standings—fourth in 1946, third in 1947, then a miracle pennant in 1948.

Lou Perini was the first fan to vault the railing at Braves Field on September 26, 1948, the day his team clinched its first NL title in thirty-four years. "I'm walking on air and tripping over clouds," he yelled to reporters in the delirious clubhouse.[34] It almost didn't matter that the Braves succumbed to the Indians in the World Series, or that even in their year of triumph, the Red Sox outdrew them at the box office.

The fall from the mountaintop would be shockingly rapid. Southworth's drinking worsened in 1949, and he took to boasting about his accomplishments. "We didn't have a good ballclub in 1948. They didn't win the pennant. I won it," the manager bragged within earshot of star pitcher Johnny Sain.[35] Dissension was rife by mid–August, when Perini granted Southworth a "leave of absence" that would last for the rest of the season. The defending National League champions finished twenty-two games behind first-place Brooklyn.[36]

Perini compounded his problems by televising most of his home games in 1949 and subsequent years. Fans no longer had much incentive to trek to gloomy, decaying Braves Field, so they either watched their TV sets or visited vibrant Fenway Park to root for the Red Sox instead. The Sox drew 4.25 million fans during the three-season span starting in 1949, compared to 2.51 million for the Braves.[37] This disparity worried Roland Hemond, a young Braves employee at the start of a long baseball career, but he also acknowledged the logic behind it. "There was more glamour and excitement at Fenway because the crowds were better, with Williams and Doerr and those guys being real attractions," he admitted.[38]

Lou Perini didn't know what to do. His team was no longer competitive on the field or at the gate. The Braves were losing hundreds of thousands of dollars per season, even with their new stream of television revenue. Their attendance was in freefall, plummeting 67 percent between 1948 and 1951. "I don't think we can ever bring them back," Perini said of the Braves' lost fans. "We can't take the town away from the Red Sox. The town belongs to them."[39]

* * *

The Philadelphia Athletics and Washington Senators had fielded profitable, championship-caliber teams as recently as the early years of the Depression. But both were tumbling toward insolvency and irrelevance by the end of the 1940s.

The two clubs were remarkably alike. Each was run by a Hall of Famer—Philadelphia's Connie Mack, Washington's Clark Griffith—who had grown up in rural America, fashioned a lengthy playing career, become a big-league manager, secured a small bit of stock in his franchise, and eventually emerged as its primary owner. And each team was paying the price for falling dangerously behind the times after World War II.

Cornelius McGillicuddy was born to Irish immigrants in East Brookfield, Massachusetts, a year after the outbreak of the Civil War. He seemed destined for a life of hard labor—working as a teen in a shoe factory and a cotton mill—until his ability as a catcher offered an escape. McGillicuddy spent eleven years in the major leagues, a serviceable player known not by his lengthy given name, but as Connie Mack, an alias that fit neatly into newspaper box scores.[40]

Griffith's story was even more bucolic. His parents traveled westward in a covered wagon after the Civil War, bound for Clear Creek, Missouri, where their son was born in a log cabin in 1869. Young Clark's childhood was highlighted (so he always claimed) by a chance meeting with legendary outlaw Jesse James. Griffith, like Mack, developed into a fine ballplayer with major-league talent. He reached his zenith between 1894 and 1900, notching 151 victories for the Chicago Colts (not yet known as the Cubs).[41] "Can you imagine," he mused five decades later, "what a pitcher of that type could command in the major-league market today?"[42]

It was a telling question, a hint that money was always in the forefront of Griffith's mind. The prospect of a better salary motivated him to jump in 1901 from the Colts to the fledgling American League, which welcomed him as the player-manager of the Chicago White Sox. He steered his new club to the AL's very first pennant, the only title he would ever win on a winding managerial path that took him to New York, Cincinnati, and Washington during the next nineteen years.

Mack, who also hitched his fortunes to the new league, enjoyed considerably greater rewards. He led the Athletics to six AL pennants and three World Series championships during his first fourteen seasons at the helm. Mack evolved into a baseball icon, instantly recognizable in his three-piece business suit and straw skimmer, never the uniform and cap worn by other managers. He usually clutched a rolled-up scorecard, which he waved to position his outfielders. Sportswriters dubbed him the Tall Tactician, a nod to his six-foot-two-inch height and his sagacity in the dugout.[43]

Mack's first dynasty was destroyed when the Federal League raided his roster. "Nothing could be more disastrous at this time than a salary war," he decreed.[44] He allowed his stars to seek bigger paychecks elsewhere, took his lumps (finishing last every season from 1915 to 1921), and slowly rebuilt the Athletics. His second dynasty went toe-to-toe with the immortal Yankees of Babe Ruth and Lou Gehrig, winning three straight American League titles, capped by consecutive world championships in 1929 and 1930. "Perhaps the 1927 Yankees were the greatest team of all time," said Shirley Povich, the longtime sports editor of the *Washington Post*. "But if there was a close second, perhaps an equal, it was those A's."[45]

Griffith enjoyed his own success during this era. He left the dugout for good in

1920, the year he secured control of the Senators with the help of William Richardson, a wealthy Philadelphia exporter who was introduced to him by Mack. The Senators defeated the New York Giants in a dramatic World Series four years later. A seemingly routine ground ball took a strange hop in the bottom of the twelfth inning of Game Seven, allowing Muddy Ruel to barrel home with the most famous run in Senators history, triggering pandemonium in Griffith Stadium. American League titles followed in 1925 and 1933.[46]

But that was the end of the line. Mack and Griffith would never win another championship. They stuck with their tried-and-true methods, scorning the innovations being embraced by other owners. They refused to build extensive farm systems, hire large scouting staffs, or pay bonuses of any size. "They were running a general store in a supermarket era," said Povich.[47]

Both men retrenched, not always unhappily, as the Depression dragged on. "The years I won pennants, I didn't make money because of increased expenses," Mack said. "The years I didn't win, I often made plenty of money."[48] Griffith adopted a simple strategy for contract negotiations with his players. "Start out tough," he said, "and stay tough."[49] The defeats piled up for both clubs, and their attendance correspondingly declined. The Senators drew only 548,300 fans per season between 1934 and 1950, while the Athletics averaged just 492,300. Yet they somehow stayed afloat.

Owner/managers Connie Mack (left) and Clark Griffith are all smiles on opening day in 1919, but darker times lay ahead. Mack's Athletics and Griffith's Senators would lose games and money with shocking regularity by the 1940s [Library of Congress].

Mack and Griffith were polar opposites in personality. The Philadelphia owner/manager, despite occasional flashes of anger and sarcasm, was usually depicted as a candidate for sainthood. "If you did something wrong, he'd never bawl you out on the bench or in the clubhouse," said Hall of Fame pitcher Stan Coveleski.[50] The tart-tongued Griffith unleashed his cantankerous fury on anyone and everyone, even close relatives. "His eyes could pierce right through you," recalled nephew Calvin Griffith in 1983, as he gazed at a photo of his uncle. "Look at those goddamn bushy eyebrows. When he got mad at you, it was like they were coming out and pointing at you."[51]

The common thread was their belief in family. Clark Griffith and his wife were childless, yet they raised two of her deceased brother's children, Calvin and Thelma Robertson. Slow-witted Calvin was groomed to eventually take charge of the Senators, while Thelma would marry one of the team's pitchers, Joe Haynes. Almost everybody in Washington's front office carried the last name of Griffith, Robertson, or Haynes. Calvin was never legally adopted, yet he changed his own surname to Griffith as an homage to his uncle.[52]

Bill Veeck once put Clark's family loyalty to a severe test. The Senators had sold Joe Haynes in 1941 to Chicago, where he proved to be a passable reliever and spot starter. But the White Sox put him on the market in late 1948, and Veeck snapped him up for the Indians. "To put it in the most delicate possible way," Veeck later wrote, "I had Joe Haynes stashed out in an abandoned mine shack, and I was holding him for ransom." Griffith was one of Veeck's most caustic critics. The thought of his niece's husband pitching for such an infidel enraged him, so a multi-player trade was quickly arranged. The aging, sore-armed Haynes returned to the safety of Washington, while future Hall of Famer Early Wynn headed to Cleveland.[53]

Mack also valued family—or in his case, families—above all else. His first wife gave birth to two sons and a daughter before her death in 1892. Mack's remarriage in 1910 yielded another boy and four girls. Connie angered his second wife by distributing Athletics stock to his three sons, ignoring his daughters. Their dispute grew so intense that the elderly couple actually separated for a few months in 1946, though Mack never did allocate any shares to the women.[54]

His two older sons were heavily involved in the team's daily operations—Roy as vice president, Earle as assistant manager—but neither was respected by the baseball establishment. They were commonly known as "the Mack boys," even though both were in their late fifties after the war.[55] "Connie Mack's sons became senile before Connie did," scoffed Philadelphia sportswriter James Isaminger.[56]

No matter. Mack aspired to permanent family control of the Athletics. "I have trained my sons to keep the tradition going," he wrote in 1950, "and I hope they will train their sons to follow in the path of their grandfather—and so on all through the Mack line." He hoped just as strongly to remain in the dugout for the rest of his life.[57]

"Give up the reins," Clark Griffith had advised him way back in 1939. "Let a younger fellow manage the club."

"Clark, the day I get off that bench I'm going to become an old man, and an old man dies," said Mack. "I'm going to stay on the bench as long as I humanly can."[58]

And that he did. Mack hung onto his job into 1950—even though he was eighty-seven years old, even though he had finished above .500 just three times since 1934, and even though Philadelphia's other team, the Phillies (on the way to an unexpected National League title), was crushing his woeful A's at the box office. Mack often seemed confused during games, summoning pinch hitters and relief pitchers who were no longer on the roster. "Young man, you look familiar. Do I know you?" he once asked Woody Wheaton, one of his outfielders.[59]

Mack's third son, Connie Jr., was more energetic than his older brothers. He had initially believed that the franchise could be revived, but he lost hope as the disastrous 1950 season unspooled. The A's would finish with the worst record (52–102) and second-worst attendance (309,805) in the majors. Connie Jr. urged his father to sell, much to the displeasure of Roy and Earle, who demanded an opportunity to purchase majority control. They stunned everyone by coming up with the necessary $1.74 million in August, slapping an enormous mortgage on Shibe Park in the process. Connie Jr. left for Florida to start a fishing business.[60]

An even bigger surprise came at the end of the season. Roy and Earle had publicly insisted that Connie Sr. could remain as manager as long as he wished, but they privately pressured him to make way for a younger man. The Tall Tactician relented at an October 18, 1950, press conference. "I'm not quitting because I'm too old, but because I think the people want me to," he said unhappily.[61]

There were a couple of consolations. The Athletics remained under his family's control, and Mack himself still served as the franchise's titular president. "So far, at least, I have managed to keep busy," he told a reporter a few days after his dramatic announcement. "There is still plenty to do."[62]

Headlines: 1950

Gardella makes final big-league appearance

Baseball faced a dilemma after settling with Danny Gardella. The Giants refused to take him back, but somebody had to offer a contract to create an illusion of fairness. Fred Saigh volunteered his Cardinals. Gardella batted just once for St. Louis, flying out to right on April 20. "It seems undesirable to give him his unconditional release," cautioned Louis Carroll, the National League's attorney. So Saigh shipped Gardella to the minors, then quietly cut him in June.[63]

Red Sox destroy Browns, 29–4

The Red Sox were relentless all season—batting .302 as a team—but never more so than on June 8, when they pounded the Browns, 29–4. Boston ripped twenty-eight hits, led by Bobby Doerr with three home runs and Ted Williams and Walt Dropo with a pair apiece. It stood as the worst rout in major-league history until the Texas Rangers pummeled the Baltimore Orioles, 30–3, on August 22, 2007.[64]

Phillies and Konstanty prevail in NL

Philadelphia hadn't won a National League championship since 1915, a drought that ended when Dick Sisler blasted a three-run homer in the tenth inning of the season-ending game on October 1. The Phillies' dramatic 4–1 victory over Brooklyn clinched a title that confounded the experts. Equally improbable was the selection of

Philadelphia's Jim Konstanty as the NL's Most Valuable Player, the first relief pitcher so honored by either league.[65]

Yankees win second straight championship

The vaunted Yankees repeated as world champs in 1950, but victory did not come easily. "We swept the Phillies in the World Series, so a lot of people assume they were overmatched. But that series was tight," said New York outfielder Gene Woodling. Each of the first three games was decided by one run. Rookie Whitey Ford then locked down a 5–2 win for the Yanks in Game Four.[66]

8

O'Malley

Everyone knew that America was changing rapidly, but the extent of the postwar metamorphosis didn't become clear until the federal government conducted its decennial census on April 1, 1950.

The results astounded the experts, who were still predicting an imminent decline in the birth rate. The nation's population had grown by 19 million since 1940, which was more than twice the increase a decade earlier, 8.9 million from 1930 to 1940. And the pace seemed to be accelerating. The Census Bureau's analysts detected a gain of 3.1 million residents between 1949 and 1950, the sharpest one-year upswing in the decade.[1]

The numbers seemed—on the surface, at least—to be positive for baseball. All ten major-league cities grew during the 1940s, with upticks ranging from a muted 0.8 percent in Pittsburgh to a robust 21.0 percent in Washington.[2] But the 1950 census also provided what a contemporary reporter described as "evidence of a mass-scale movement from the cities to the suburbs—to get more fresh air, cheaper land, lower taxes, more auto parking room."[3] And that was troubling indeed.

Baseball had always targeted a white, urban audience, but the unsteadiness of those twin demographic pillars was exposed by the new census. The population increases in Eastern and Midwestern cities were largely minority-driven, with Southern blacks streaming northward to seek factory jobs and escape the overt racism of their native region. Big-league cities added a total of 1.04 million black residents during the 1940s, 4 times larger than the number of new white inhabitants (257,000).

Relatively few blacks had lived in Northern cities prior to World War II—too few to wield significant clout—but that was no longer true by 1950. Blacks now accounted for 35 percent of the population in Washington, 18 percent in Philadelphia and St. Louis, 16 percent in Cleveland and Detroit, and 14 percent in Chicago.[4] Some whites did what they could—even resorting to violence—to resist the encroachment of these newcomers. Nine serious racial disturbances were reported in Chicago between 1945 and 1954, including one that stemmed from a black family's attempt to integrate an all-white housing project. The unfortunate pioneers fled after enduring nine months of rock tossing, window smashing, and arson.[5]

A greater number of whites opted not to fight, but to leave the city behind. Thirteen million new homes would be built between 1948 and 1958, with eleven million in suburbia. Race was not the sole motivation behind this land rush—the simple dream of homeownership was preeminent—but it was undoubtedly a factor.[6] William Levitt unapologetically inserted a whites-only clause in the standard contract for his model suburb on Long Island. "We can solve a housing problem, or we can try to solve a racial problem," he said. "But we cannot combine the two."[7]

Suburban growth rates between 1940 and 1950 easily outstripped the corresponding figures for adjacent cities, often by astonishing margins. The joint population of the bedroom communities encircling Cleveland soared by 41.6 percent, ten times greater than the city's increase of 4.2 percent. Suburbs grew seven times faster than the central city in the St. Louis area, six times faster in Washington, five times in Chicago, and four times in Detroit, New York City, and Philadelphia.[8]

Baseball's owners were baffled and saddened by these emerging trends. Historian Neil Sullivan reduced their concerns to a simple question: "If your job and home were no longer a short hop from the ballpark, then how would you get to the game, or who would take your place in the seat?"[9] Nobody knew the answer.

Politicians, retailers, and transportation planners also struggled to make sense of this brave new world. They wondered if the central city could retain its dominance as the local population expanded ever outward. Many were doubtful. "When people find it too much trouble to park downtown, they stop coming downtown," warned the Cleveland Planning Commission in 1951.[10] So cities began to fight back, scrambling to build parking lots and garages to accommodate suburban commuters and shoppers.

That begged a larger and more expensive question: How could these workers and customers be efficiently transported from their suburban homes to their urban parking places? Officials in two major cities believed they already had the answer. Los Angeles had opened the first urban expressway, the Arroyo Seco Parkway (later renamed the Pasadena Freeway), back in 1940, the same year that Chicago had unveiled its blueprints for a network of seven superhighways. Cities from coast to coast were following their lead by 1950, bulldozing through parks and neighborhoods as they built expressways of their own.[11]

It was taken as an article of faith that these new freeways would guarantee the continued viability of America's central cities and the businesses (including ballclubs) within them. Detroit mayor Albert Cobo echoed counterparts across the nation with his 1949 prediction that expressways would "retard the decentralization of business into suburban areas" by easing travel from distant communities to the city's hub.[12] (Time would reveal his basic miscalculation. Traffic on these modern highways, of course, flowed in both directions, funneling people away from downtown just as easily as toward it.)

The U.S. Bureau of the Budget took note of this frenzied activity—the vast migration to suburbia, the extensive campaign to sustain the central city, the new links between the two—and it devised a statistical concept in 1949 to reflect these changes. The "standard metropolitan area" was a zone that encompassed a given city and its surrounding suburbs, treating them as a single entity.[13]

The 1950 census was the first federal report to generate data for metropolitan areas. The New York City metro, with 12.9 million people, was far and away the largest, followed by Chicago at 5.5 million and Los Angeles at 4.4 million. Fourteen metropolitan areas—including every baseball hub but Cincinnati—contained more than one million residents. Marketers in other fields quickly grasped the value of the metropolitan concept, which offered a more accurate accounting of potential customers, but baseball steadfastly resisted. It would rely solely on city-based data for almost another decade.[14]

The sport's owners also turned a blind eye to a second finding of the 1950 census, its documentation of the West's rapid growth. The population of the San Francisco metro area expanded at an annual rate of 4.4 percent during the 1940s—not 4.4 percent *total*, but *per year*—and the Los Angeles metro came close at 4.1 percent. San Diego, smaller than its California brothers, was quickly gaining ground with a meteoric annual growth rate of 6.8 percent, almost five times faster than the national pace of 1.4 percent.[15]

These were breathtaking numbers, but baseball did nothing to capitalize on the California boom, just as it made no attempt to reach out to suburbia. Even the *Sporting News*, hidebound on so many issues, was exasperated by the lack of geographic initiative. "Everything else in the United States has changed, except baseball. The game remains static," it groaned in a May 1950 editorial. "Nothing is more certainly fatal than stand-pattism in a changing world."[16]

* * *

Newspaper reporters tended to describe suburbia as a recent invention, a postwar phenomenon, an entirely new way of life. But they were wrong. Historians traced the suburban impulse all the way to 1814, when ferry service initially linked Manhattan with the opposite shore of the East River. Merchants, clerks, and factory owners began moving to the Brooklyn side, where homes were cheaper and streets were less congested.[17] Thousands commuted by boat each morning, then back again at night, inspiring Charles Dickens to call Brooklyn "New York's dormitory."[18]

It would eventually attain a much greater status. Brooklyn grew rapidly as an independent community, rising to become America's fourth-largest city by 1890, when its population reached 806,000. Only New York City (then confined to Manhattan and part of the Bronx), Chicago, and Philadelphia were bigger. Brooklynites were fiercely proud of their city, which boasted its own daily newspapers, banks, and even a National League baseball team, all despite New York's lurking presence to the northwest.[19]

But there were reasons for concern. Brooklyn's water supply was undependable, and its municipal government was fiscally unsound. Business leaders, in their eagerness for future stability, began agitating for consolidation with their giant neighbor. The question was put to a referendum in November 1894 after a heated campaign. Three days of counting determined that a narrow majority had indeed chosen to merge Brooklyn with New York as of January 1, 1898.[20]

Not that its political elites—or even many of its citizens—were happy. Manhattan threw a raucous party in City Hall Park on New Year's Eve 1897, complete with fireworks, bands, choral groups, and a cacophony of boat whistles and church bells. Brooklyn staged a somber ceremony—almost a funeral—at its own City Hall.[21] Will Carleton read "The Passing of Brooklyn," a poem specially written for the occasion. He asked: "Why does a feeling of sadness surround us?/As when the blade of bereavement has found us?" He supplied the answer a few lines later: "We are aggrieved that this fair, comely maiden/At midnight must die."[22]

Brooklyn struggled to retain its identity in the coming decades, though with limited success. Author John Gunther wrote as late as 1948 that the borough (its post-city status) was still "a world in itself," but such characterizations came with a whiff of condescension.[23] "Brooklyn itself was on the margin of New York," recalled writer Pete Hamill, who was born there in 1935. "It was the butt of jokes in all those radio shows and war movies. There was always some dumb guy in the platoon who was from Brooklyn, and people would make fun of the way he talked."[24] The specter of their glamorous, powerful neighbor haunted Brooklynites, who resented their second-class status. "The great ocean liners docked in Manhattan," said Red Barber. "Brooklyn got the cargo ships."[25]

This inferiority complex was exacerbated by the postwar demographic trends. All five of New York's boroughs grew between 1940 and 1950, but Brooklyn's increase of 1.5 percent was by far the smallest—pitifully tiny next to the 19.5 percent gain in Queens, the adjacent borough to the east. It soon became clear that the new decade would be worse. Brooklyn would lose an average of 2,300 white residents each month during the 1950s, only partially countered by a monthly inflow of 1,350 blacks.[26]

"With the blacks moving in came a great fear," said journalist Jack Newfield, a Brooklyn native. "There was blockbusting. There was panic selling."[27] A steady stream of anxious whites fled to the suburbs on Long Island or in New Jersey, joined by fellow Brooklynites who simply dreamed of abandoning apartment life for a free-standing house with its own yard. "It was the desire to get away from the crowds, to get away from the cement," said radio announcer Marty Glickman.[28] *To get away* became a mantra for disaffected residents throughout Brooklyn.

But at least they still had the Dodgers.

The borough's beloved franchise, which dated back to 1884, had carried several names over the years—Atlantics, Grays, Bridegrooms, Superbas, Robins, Dodgers—but had rarely been successful. The team won only six pennants in its first fifty-seven seasons, until Larry MacPhail and Branch Rickey turned things around in the 1940s, delivering three National League titles. But the ultimate prize, a World Series championship, remained beyond Brooklyn's grasp.

Dodgers fans were rabid, impatient, and extremely vocal. "Poor performance was not appreciated in Brooklyn, and the fans let you know it," laughed pitcher Carl Erskine.[29] But they were also loyal. The Dodgers attracted 12.2 million paying customers to their ballpark during the 1940s. No other National League team topped 10 million for the decade.

The fans came despite the filth and general deterioration of Ebbets Field. "I want a structure that will fill all demands upon it for the next thirty years," owner Charles Ebbets had told his architects.[30] But the ballpark exceeded that lifespan—it would mark its fortieth anniversary in April 1953—and it was showing its age. "The grandstands were dirty and smelled of stale beer," recalled sportswriter Robert Creamer. "The clubhouse was so small and cluttered, even the Dodger clubhouse, it was like somebody's attic. And the visiting clubhouse was worse. It was like the Black Hole of Calcutta."[31] The players weren't the only ones who were uncomfortable. The fans suffered, too. "We had narrow seats, narrow aisles, and a lot of obstructed views," admitted club executive Buzzie Bavasi.[32]

It was a bewildering situation. Brooklyn and Ebbets Field were both on the decline, yet the Dodgers were somehow prospering. Could the good times be sustained? The team's traditional base of proud white Brooklynites was scattering to the suburbs. Would the fans keep coming if the Dodgers began losing? Would they remain loyal even though the ballpark was a lengthy drive from their new homes?

The latter question was difficult to answer, especially given the paucity of parking spaces around Ebbets Field. Co-owner Walter O'Malley couldn't envision suburbanites willingly fighting the traffic into Brooklyn, engaging in a lengthy (and perhaps fruitless) search for a parking spot, and climbing tight, steep stairways to sit in cramped, malodorous seats—all just to watch the Dodgers.

"Lack of parking accommodations, more than anything else, TV included, keeps people from coming to our games," O'Malley wrote, his impatience jumping from the page. "Ebbets Field was built in the trolley car era. There are no trolleys to speak of today, but there are automobiles and intelligently planned parkways."[33] His opinion hadn't changed a whit since 1946, when he had first raised the issue. He was certain that the Dodgers needed a new ballpark.

* * *

Walter O'Malley did not follow either of the well-trod paths to baseball's ownership ranks. He wasn't a wealthy inheritor who purchased a team as a hobby, nor was he a lifer who was devoid of outside interests. He more or less stumbled into the game, only gradually coming to believe that it could generate the personal wealth he so fervently desired. "O'Malley was not a baseball man. He was a bottom-line man," said Jim Murray, a Pulitzer Prize-winning columnist for the *Los Angeles Times*.[34]

His father was one of the innumerable cogs in Tammany Hall, the formidable Democratic Party machine that dominated New York City between the Civil War and the Depression. Tammany was known to play fast and loose with the public treasury, and Edwin O'Malley was not one to deviate from tradition. Mayor John Hylan named him the city's commissioner of public markets after World War I, and it wasn't long before state investigators began sniffing around. They accused O'Malley of receiving kickbacks, a scandal that played out on the front pages of the city's tabloids. New Yorkers waited for Hylan to toss O'Malley out of office, but the mayor stuck with his man, and the storm eventually passed.[35]

Walter did not follow his father into government. He picked up his law degree from Fordham in 1930, just a few months after the stock-market crash, a terrible time to launch a legal career. But he shrewdly decided to specialize in bankruptcies, a suddenly burgeoning field. "A lot of professional people were selling apples on street corners at the time," he recalled, "but I was fortunate in building up an active practice."[36]

O'Malley made important contacts in those early years, aided by his father's Tammany connections. Edwin introduced Walter to a former police commissioner, George McLaughlin, who was destined for the presidency of the Brooklyn Trust Company. The Depression had staggered many of the bank's clients, including the Dodgers, who borrowed frequently to meet their payroll and other obligations. McLaughlin asked his young friend in the late 1930s to see if anything could be done to stabilize the franchise.[37]

"The Dodgers were merely another client," O'Malley said later, and that was true at first.[38] He started by eliminating the team's bizarre habit of storing its concessions income in duffel bags—"the bags weren't sealed, and some of our employees were supplementing their income"—and then streamlined other front-office practices.[39] O'Malley slowly became hooked. Baseball was more interesting than bankruptcy law, and it seemed potentially lucrative. He officially committed himself to the Dodgers in 1942, becoming their in-house counsel, and then scraped together the cash in 1944 to purchase a portion of the team. He, Branch Rickey, and John Smith established themselves as the ruling triumvirate a year later.[40]

O'Malley couldn't have been more different from the pious, abstemious Rickey or the colorless Smith, a silent partner who concentrated on running his chemical firm. Batboy Steve Garvey, who would grow up to play first base for the Dodgers, was only a youngster when he first spotted O'Malley in spring training, but he never forgot the owner's magisterial presence: "a stout man, with wire-rimmed glasses and a unique gruff voice."[41] The overweight, cigar-smoking O'Malley looked like an editorial cartoonist's conception of a plutocrat, and his terse managerial style often matched the stereotype. "He dominated others more skillfully than anyone I have ever seen," marveled Bowie Kuhn, who would serve as commissioner from 1969 to 1984.[42]

Yet O'Malley had a fun side. "He could be a backslapper," wrote biographer Andy McCue. "He loved a drink and a party."[43] He also possessed an unexpectedly sharp sense of humor. Star catcher Roy Campanella went under the knife in his early years with the Dodgers, and the operation proved to be more extensive—and expensive—than anticipated. "It appears," O'Malley quipped to reporters, "that the doctor thought he was operating on Roy's bankroll instead of his hand."[44] Even author Roger Kahn, no fan of O'Malley, conceded his wit. "Walter had a sense of style," Kahn admitted. "He could tell a joke."[45]

He also loved to embellish. McCue discovered that O'Malley's biography in *Who's Who in America* was replete with errors and false claims, which could only have been submitted by the subject himself.[46] "Surely, you realize that only half the lies the Irish tell are true," O'Malley laughed, but others viewed his tall tales as a serious defect.[47] "O'Malley is a devious man, about the most devious man I ever met," said Dodgers play-by-play broadcaster Red Barber.[48] He was as flexible with his loyalty as with the truth, switching allegiance whenever it suited his purposes. "If he thought a guy was going to lose, he'd drop him," said Bill DeWitt, Sr. "If he thought he was going to win, he'd be on his side."[49]

O'Malley deferred to Rickey in the early years of their partnership—the Mahatma, after all, was a living legend—but the younger man's faith began to ebb. He became irritated by the teetotaling Rickey's sanctimonious pronouncements, and he took to privately deriding the Dodgers president as "a psalm-singing faker."[50] O'Malley was also troubled by the sizable losses incurred by Rickey's venture into pro football and, most of all, by the heftiness of his paycheck. Rickey was earning more than $200,000 a year in salary and bonuses by 1948 (the 2020 equivalent of $2.15 million), which tripled the top pay for any big-league player at the time, $65,000 for Joe DiMaggio and Ted Williams.[51]

"We had to get him out of there if the club was ever going to make money," O'Malley said.[52] The key to his strategy was John Smith, who steadfastly endorsed whatever Rickey chose to do with the Dodgers. O'Malley quietly went to work on Smith, finally convincing him in 1950 to jettison their partner and his spendthrift ways.[53]

All of this scheming was undone, though only momentarily, by Smith's unexpected death in July 1950. O'Malley moved swiftly to secure the proxy of his widow, Mary Louise.[54] "I leave the management and decisions to Mr. O'Malley," she said, thereby sealing Rickey's doom.[55] His contract as president was scheduled to expire at the end of the season, and there was no longer any chance of its renewal.

Rickey did not want to leave Brooklyn, not with a long-elusive World Series title seemingly within reach, but he also had no desire to remain a part-owner without untrammeled control of the franchise. O'Malley tried to lowball him, offering $346,667 for his Dodgers stock, precisely what Rickey had paid for it. But the old man played it cool, confirming his reputation as baseball's cleverest executive. He found an outside buyer, real-estate developer William Zeckendorf, who bid $1.05 million ($11.2 million in 2020 money) for his shares.[56]

That put the ball in the unhappy O'Malley's court—"it annoyed the hell out of me"—and he grumpily set out to raise the necessary funds.[57] His partnership agreement gave him the right to match any outside offer for Rickey's stock, but he hadn't expected to pay anywhere near this much. He suspected—correctly, as it turned out—that Zeckendorf's bid was somewhat of a bluff. It had been secretly solicited by Pirates owner John Galbreath, who wanted Rickey to assume the presidency of his franchise, an offer the Mahatma couldn't accept until his Dodgers stock was sold.[58]

Bluff or not, it didn't matter. O'Malley had no intention of sharing his Dodgers with a rich interloper, so he "liquidated everything" (his later words) to exercise his option.[59] His sour mood worsened when he learned the reason for the odd size of the enormous payment. Rickey had wanted one million dollars for his shares, a sum that Zeckendorf readily agreed to pay. But the developer, knowing that O'Malley would almost certainly match his bid, sought $50,000 for his trouble. Hence the final price of $1.05 million.[60]

Walter O'Malley had a sharp sense of humor. But he was deadly serious about the Dodgers, which is why he pushed Branch Rickey out as co-owner in 1950. "We had to get him out of there if the club was ever going to make money," O'Malley said [National Baseball Hall of Fame and Museum].

The two strong-willed Dodgers executives parted ways amicably—in public, at least. The sixty-eight-year-old Rickey insisted that he was simply "resigning." He winced when a different possibility was mentioned. "I don't want to retire, as I understand the word," he told reporters, though he was vague about his prospects.[61] O'Malley projected an aura of sadness. "I am terribly sorry and hurt personally that we now have to face this resignation," he said at a meeting of the team's board.[62]

Their real feelings surfaced in unguarded moments. Dodgers traveling secretary Harold Parrott encountered Rickey on the street a few minutes after his October 26 resignation announcement. "He was in tears, despite the million bucks in his pocket," Parrott wrote. "He did not want to leave this baseball juggernaut he had built, with all its fine, upcoming young stars."[63] Rickey was bound for Pittsburgh, which had finished dead last in the National League in 1950. Dark days lay ahead.

O'Malley held a series of press conferences as he consolidated control of the Dodgers during the coming weeks. They were upbeat, forward-looking affairs, though a note of bitterness occasionally seeped through. "You may be sure," O'Malley told sportswriters, "that for the next seven or eight years, Mr. Rickey will be credited with the victories of the Brooklyn ballclub and that its losses will be charged to somebody else."[64] His grievances against his former partner ran deep, and he had no desire to forget them. O'Malley soon added a newly framed item to his office wall—the canceled check that he had paid Branch Rickey (and William Zeckendorf) to leave him alone.[65]

9

Unhappy

Happy Chandler had reason for optimism as 1949 drew to a close. He was finally free of the headaches that had plagued his early years as commissioner. Robert Murphy's union had given up the ghost, Jorge Pasquel had stopped signing American players, four big-league teams had integrated without serious incident, and Danny Gardella's lawsuit had just been settled. The sun was shining brightly on the national pastime.

Chandler felt so good that he decided to seek a contract extension, even though his current pact wasn't scheduled to expire until April 1952. The dean of baseball writers, Dan Daniel, envisioned no opposition from the owners. "Chandler's able handling of all the issues has convinced the few doubters among the magnates," Daniel asserted in his typically grandiloquent style. He predicted that a new seven-year deal would be approved unanimously in December 1949.[1]

Chandler wasn't quite so naive. He was aware that a few owners weren't totally pleased with him, though he saw no cause for worry. The former governor and senator was famed for his political instincts—"I could count noses pretty accurately"—and he was confident that he had the necessary twelve votes lined up.[2]

Yet he didn't, at least not right away. The owners debated his request at length, eventually deciding it was premature. They tabled it for twelve months, promising to vote on a contract extension at their winter meetings in December 1950. Chandler saw nothing unusual in their reluctance. He still expected an affirmative vote in the end.[3]

But the ingredients for a negative decision were scattered about, like dry brush awaiting a spark.

Chandler was always giving speeches, always talking to reporters, always politicking. His verbosity contrasted sharply with Kenesaw Mountain Landis's austerity, and it privately annoyed some of the owners. "He was a completely uninhibited man," observed Shirley Povich, "and naturally developed enemies."[4] Several influential columnists, including Red Smith and Arthur Daley, were openly caustic about the commissioner's down-home ways, and they chipped away at his reputation. "They could see I was a Southern country fellow," Chandler said later, "and New York reporters look down their noses at Southern country fellows."[5]

But it wasn't all about style. A segment of the baseball establishment was dissatisfied with the commissioner's performance, indicting him on several counts: He had been slow to recognize the dangers posed by the Mexican League and the American Baseball Guild. He had failed to offer an adequate rationale for Leo Durocher's suspension. He had allowed Gardella's lawsuit to linger in the courts. And he had rolled out the welcome mat for Jackie Robinson. "A majority of [the owners]," said Chandler, "resented me helping break the color line."[6] They had hoped for a malleable figurehead as commissioner, but he had proven to be what they feared most, an outspoken, meddlesome politician.

Yet a powerful force—baseball's never-ending affection for the status quo—was aligned in his favor. Several owners remained strong supporters of the commissioner, and several more appeared indifferent. It seemed likely that they would collectively choose the path of least resistance, offering Chandler the seven-year contract he so fervently desired. Only two owners—Fred Saigh of the Cardinals and Del Webb of the Yankees—appeared to be vehemently opposed to such a deal.

Chandler had summoned Saigh in September 1949, asking him to fashion a settlement with Gardella, an experience that left sour memories. "I lost all respect for Chandler. I thought he was a weak sister," said Saigh, who favored harsh treatment for all Mexican League jumpers.[7] The two men also clashed over Saigh's desire to schedule games on Sunday nights (which Chandler prohibited) and Chandler's negotiations for network radio and television revenue (which Saigh mocked as inadequate).[8]

Their animosity reached such intensity that Chandler assigned a former FBI agent, Robert Boyle, to dig up dirt on the Cardinals owner.[9] Boyle turned in a biting seventeen-page report that demeaned Saigh's professional skills ("a mediocrity as a lawyer"), his personality ("a 'four-flusher' or 'phoney' of the first water"), and even his driving record ("thirty-two arrests, principally involving the operation of motor vehicles"). But the investigator relied heavily on conjecture and hearsay, and his report failed to produce any evidence to warrant Saigh's suspension.[10]

Saigh was determined to strike his own blow. He quietly began lobbying his fellow National League owners to deny Chandler an extension, and he put out feelers for an American League ally. "I told Del of the situation," he recalled, "and we cooperated in getting Chandler out."[11] It seemed an odd alliance, since Webb was commonly believed to be only a limited partner in the Yankees. The front man in New York was Dan Topping, highly visible heir to the Anaconda copper fortune, former husband of skater Sonja Henie, and renowned amateur golfer. Webb stayed in the background, focusing on his day job as a developer of office buildings, shopping plazas, housing projects, and hotels.[12]

It was easy—but dangerous—to underestimate Webb, a tall, slender man who wore glasses and spoke softly. His reticent demeanor masked a steely tenacity. Webb had dropped out of high school in his native Fresno in 1913 to make his way as an itinerant carpenter, eventually boosting his earnings to the grand sum of six dollars per day. His future seemed unpromising, especially after one of his employers skipped out on a sizable job, yet the resulting turmoil would be his big break. Webb took over the assignment—acquiring ten wheelbarrows and twenty shovels in the process—and thereby founded what would become one of America's largest contracting firms.[13]

World War II was a boon for the Del E. Webb Construction Company, which landed enormous government contracts to build military bases and Japanese-American internment camps throughout the West. Webb employed twenty-five thousand workers at the peak of his wartime prosperity, though he worried that his empire might collapse when peace returned and federal largesse dried up. He avoided such a dire fate by diversifying. His firm branched into such wide-ranging fields as hospital construction, oil exploration, movie production, and leather-goods manufacturing.[14]

And baseball, too. Webb bought into the Yankees with Topping and Larry MacPhail during the final months of the war. Newspapers reported that the six-foot-four-inch Webb had pitched in the Pacific Coast League in the 1920s, either for Oakland or Salt Lake City. (It was true that he had played semi-pro ball, but no records of a PCL career exist.)[15] Everybody naturally assumed that he was purchasing a big-league team for nostalgic reasons, though Webb scoffed at such sentimentality. "I invested in the Yankees strictly from a business standpoint," he insisted.[16]

His original intention was to be a silent partner, but he couldn't help himself. Webb's love of baseball was too great, and the void left by MacPhail's abrupt departure in 1947 was too large. So he began to work behind the scenes, serving on committees (often as chairman) to address some of the sport's most contentious issues. He rapidly accumulated clout, as *New York Journal-American* columnist Bill Corum would reveal to his unsuspecting readers in 1952. "I wouldn't be surprised," Corum wrote, "if Webb doesn't wield more real power in baseball than any other man in the game."[17]

This behind-the-scenes influence was the first reason why Fred Saigh approached Webb. The second was Webb's extreme distaste for Happy Chandler, spawned by their disagreement over the Flamingo Hotel in Las Vegas.

Mobster Bugsy Siegel had invested heavily in the Flamingo in late 1945, hoping that the massive casino would serve as a magnet for postwar consumers. But the project was plagued with cost overruns, and an unhappy Siegel went looking for a new contractor to finish the job. He hired Webb, who claimed to be ignorant of Bugsy's profession.[18] "The name didn't mean anything to me at the time," Webb said. "But I sure found out in a hurry." Siegel turned out to be a model client. Webb said that he always paid on time—a rare treat for a contractor—and he always paid in cash.[19]

The commissioner was angered by Webb's association with a known gangster—a link that increased in toxicity after Siegel's highly publicized assassination in June 1947—and he ordered the developer to cut any ties with the gambling industry. But rumors continued to float about Webb and Las Vegas, centering on his quiet involvement in a new casino-hotel complex, the Sahara, which was slated to open in 1952.[20]

Chandler would later be clear about his goal—"if I had remained commissioner, I would have banished both Del Webb and Fred Saigh"—but they beat him to the punch.[21] The sixteen owners took up the matter of his extension on December 11, 1950. Only nine voted in favor, falling three short of the required twelve.[22] Chandler was defiant after receiving the bad news. He persistently demanded a second chance, causing Webb to moan, "What's the matter with this guy? Doesn't he know he is out?"[23] The owners granted his wish on March 12, 1951, but the tally was precisely the same—nine yes, seven no.[24]

Chandler accepted the results the second time. His contract had another year to run, but he announced his resignation as of July 15. His stint as baseball's supreme leader would inspire a range of reminiscences for the rest of his life. He occasionally was philosophical: "After you have said no to people for six years or more, it doesn't endear you to a great many of them."[25] But he was more frequently bitter: "If I'd known the snakepit I was stepping into, I'd have passed."[26]

Webb and Saigh shared a single emotion. They were euphoric. Webb didn't expect outsiders to understand—"it might sound strange for me to call that exciting"—but he went so far as to describe the commissioner's ouster as his greatest thrill

"I have not been unhappy—never," said Albert "Happy" Chandler (left), shown here as a senator offering a gift of tobacco to Vice President John Nance Garner in 1940. But Chandler's mood darkened after he was denied a second term as baseball's commissioner in 1951 [Library of Congress].

in sports, even better than the world titles his Yankees had won.[27] "If I've never done anything else for baseball," he bragged, "I did it when I got rid of Chandler."[28]

* * *

The excitement didn't last long. Baseball's old guard was still savoring the dismissal of its overly energetic commissioner when another of its adversaries unexpectedly reappeared on July 5, 1951, ten days before Chandler's official departure.[29]

Bill Veeck, whom Chandler hailed as "one of the most knowledgeable fellows I ever saw," emerged from a year and a half of restless retirement to purchase the St. Louis Browns.[30] He brought along a new wife, Mary Frances, who was both charmed and amused by the iconoclastic tendencies of her well-educated husband. "Bill started out on the right side of the tracks," she once laughed, "and spent his whole life trying to get over to the other side."[31] Most of his fellow owners—Webb prominent among them—had sighed with relief when the pesky, outspoken Veeck sold the Indians in late 1949. They were not happy to see him return.

Veeck had chosen a daunting assignment. "The Brownies have no tradition and no hope," Arthur Daley wrote dismissively in the July 4 edition of the *New York Times*, and the stats bore him out.[32] St. Louis was mired in last place in the American League with a 21–49 record when Veeck took charge the following morning. The Browns hadn't drawn more than 10,400 fans to any game at Sportsman's Park so far in 1951, and their attendance had dipped below 3,000 on 12 occasions. The team's star pitcher, Ned Garver, contended that St. Louis was blessed with the politest fans in the AL. "The crowd didn't boo you," he said, "because we had them outnumbered."[33]

Veeck had given as many as five hundred speeches per year in Cleveland, and he began making the rounds in his new city. His opening line was always the same. "You're going to have to forgive me if I seem nervous," he would say. "I'm not used to seeing so many people."[34] He warned potential customers that it would take time to improve the Browns on the field, which meant a string of defeats in the immediate future. "Stay away unless you have a strong stomach," he joked, though he promised outstanding service for any fan who decided to buy a ticket against his advice.[35] Sportsman's Park, he said, "is the only park in the league where there is an usher and vendor for every paying customer."[36]

But Veeck was deadly serious on one point. Officials from Baltimore, Los Angeles, Milwaukee, and the New York borough of Queens immediately contacted the new owner, urging him to shift the Browns to their cities. He refused them all.[37] "When I say I have no plans to move the Browns, I mean just that. Not even long-range plans," he said.[38]

It was a curious stand. "This city is big enough to support two major-league teams," Veeck publicly insisted, though almost everybody in baseball disagreed.[39] The sagacious Branch Rickey, a veteran of the St. Louis baseball wars, had been saying since 1944 that one of the local teams would have to leave, and the prime candidate was obvious. The Browns had drawn only 1.7 million fans in the first five postwar seasons, 71 percent below the Cardinals' total of 5.9 million.

Veeck privately admitted that St. Louis was a one-team town. "That would seem to mean only one thing," he later wrote. "That I had come into St. Louis to try to run the Cardinals out of town. That was precisely what I had in mind." It was an audacious goal, almost absurd in its arrogance. The Cardinals possessed all of the advantages—a better team, an impressive treasury, an enormous radio network—but Veeck felt he had identified a key weakness, their owner. "As I saw it," he said, "Saigh didn't have the foggiest notion of what he was doing."[40]

Veeck developed a two-pronged strategy: He would outpromote the Cardinals, and he would steal their history. The first part of his plan bore fruit almost immediately, when the Browns sent Eddie Gaedel, a three-foot-seven-inch, sixty-five-pound midget, to the plate against the Detroit Tigers on August 19. A promotion for Falstaff's Beer had lured 18,000 fans to Sportsman's Park—the Browns' largest crowd in four years—and they were electrified when Gaedel unexpectedly popped out of the dugout, swinging three toy bats and wearing the fraction ⅛ on the back of his uniform.[41]

"What's going on here?" screamed Detroit manager Red Rolfe, who charged toward home plate. But Browns manager Zack Taylor was ready for him. "I played it nice and calm," Taylor chuckled, "like I had been sending up them little fellows every day."[42] He showed Gaedel's contract to umpire Ed Hurley, who waved baseball's smallest rookie into the batter's box after a fifteen-minute argument. Gaedel was under strict orders. "If you so much as look as if you're going to swing, I'm going to shoot you dead," Veeck told him.[43] He took four straight balls and walked into baseball history.

A photo of Gaedel in a deep crouch, with Detroit catcher Bob Swift low on his knees behind him, ran on the front pages of newspapers from coast to coast, even the austere *New York Times*. It would be the signature event of Veeck's Hall of Fame career.[44] "If I returned to baseball tomorrow, won ten straight pennants, and left all the old attendance records moldering in the dust," he conceded in 1962, "I would still be remembered, in the end, as the man who sent a midget up to bat."[45]

Yet he staged dozens of other promotions in those early months in St. Louis, notably Grandstand Managers Day, which occurred less than a week after Gaedel's appearance. Fans picked the Browns' starting lineup against the Athletics and then made all of the strategic decisions. Manager Taylor watched in civilian clothes from a rocking chair, while fans held up green or red cards in response to questions on signs displayed by a club official. St. Louis won, 5–3, then lost its next five games upon Taylor's return to the dugout.[46]

The baseball establishment was predictably outraged by such antics, though St. Louis fans began to pay attention. The Cardinals still outdrew the Browns decisively in 1951, but the trends were unmistakable. Attendance rose 19 percent for the Browns in comparison to 1950, while it dropped 7 percent for the Cards. "My first full year in St. Louis, I will maintain to the end of my life, was the best job of promoting I have ever done," Veeck wrote.[47]

The second part of his plan—pilfering the Cardinals' glorious history—had begun in a small way shortly after Veeck moved to St. Louis. Both teams played in Sportsman's Park, but the Browns held the mortgage, which made the Cardinals their tenants. Veeck repainted the stadium—all except the Cards' offices—and then decorated the ballpark with large murals of great St. Louis ballplayers, all of them former Browns. Fred Saigh was infuriated.[48]

His anger deepened after the season, when Veeck hired Rogers Hornsby as the new Browns manager. Hornsby, widely considered the greatest second baseman in baseball history, was most closely associated in the public mind with the Cardinals, for whom he had played 1,580 games. Veeck swooped in again a few weeks later after Saigh fired his own manager, Marty Marion. The Browns immediately snapped up Marion as a coach.[49]

Skeptics doubted that Veeck could make St. Louis fans forget the nine National League pennants the Cardinals had won since 1926, and they were especially dubious about the ebullient owner's chances of coexisting with the dour Hornsby. The new manager of the Browns was typically snappish at his introductory press conference. A reporter asked him to state his goals for 1951. "No midgets, no gimmicks, just good baseball," Hornsby shot back.[50]

Veeck's late father had fired Hornsby as manager of the Cubs in 1932 after his harsh, uncompromising personality alienated the entire team. Yet the son chose to ignore this particular history lesson. He was getting under Fred Saigh's skin; he was certain that his plan was working.[51]

A brief note from Veeck's mother arrived in the mail a few days after the hiring. She posed a single ominous question: "What makes you think you're smarter than your daddy was?"[52]

* * *

There remained the matter of choosing a new commissioner. The task was shuffled off to a four-man nominating committee, the same as after Landis's death, and several familiar candidates popped up once again in newspaper speculation. The imperious Douglas MacArthur, who had recently been dismissed from his Korean War command by President Truman, was widely trumpeted as a frontrunner.

But this search differed from the previous effort. Del Webb, who had been a new and quiet owner in 1945, was now one of the four committee members. He had no intention of hiring MacArthur, whose dictatorial ways made Chandler's style seem tame. The mood of the other owners had changed, too. They had ventured beyond baseball for the first two commissioners, but no longer felt the need.[53] "You wouldn't take your watch to a blacksmith for repairs, would you?" asked Phil Wrigley. "So why should baseball select an outsider?"[54]

The two leading candidates, National League president Ford Frick and Cincinnati Reds president Warren Giles, did not inspire great passion. Frick, an amiable ex-sportswriter, had spent the previous seventeen years in the league presidency, a largely ceremonial post with few duties. He passed his time in such aimless (and fruitless) pursuits as a campaign to curtail ballplayers' swearing.[55] Giles had won the favor of fellow executives over the years—he had warned them, after all, not to hire Chandler—but he was certainly no heavyweight. "I thought Warren was a jolly, kind of dumb guy," said Red Smith.[56]

It was difficult to choose between them. The owners went into executive session shortly before noon on September 20, 1951, and they remained behind closed doors ten hours later. Ballot after ballot was cast through the long afternoon and evening, with neither man ever getting more than ten votes, two short of the magic number. It was nearly ten o'clock when Giles asked to be admitted to the room. He made a short withdrawal speech, clearing the way for Frick's unanimous election.[57]

The new commissioner undeniably looked the part of a chief executive—trim in stature, with receding gray hair—but his high-powered image was deceiving. He had made his mark not in corporate boardrooms, but in press boxes and locker rooms as a sportswriter for the *New York American* in the 1920s and early 1930s.

The young Frick covered the Yankees for thirteen seasons, making no pretense of impartiality. He plainly worshiped Babe Ruth, an ardor that remained undiminished for the rest of his life. His blatant enthusiasm put extra money in his pocket, clinching a free-lance assignment to ghostwrite syndicated columns under the Babe's byline, often as many as three per week.[58]

Such robust productivity was Frick's greatest strength as a reporter. He became known not as a stylist or an investigative journalist, but as a beat man who churned out a prodigious stream of copy. "I was a hell of a typist," he admitted. "Maybe I wasn't a good writer, but I could type."[59] The best thing about Frick's stories, as far as baseball insiders were concerned, was their unfailingly upbeat and inoffensive tone.

This was the kind of commissioner the owners wanted, a friendly man who revered the game and its legends, abhorred controversy, and eagerly stayed in the background unless absolutely necessary. "I am not a monitor on high, ready to swing the big stick," Frick assured them after assuming office.[60] A reporter inquired about his philosophy a few months into his tenure. Frick reduced it to fourteen words: "Change the status quo only when there is a compelling reason for a change."[61]

This conservative doctrine drew praise from almost everybody associated with the game. A notable exception was Bill Veeck, who would experience several run-ins with the new commissioner. "Let us be fair," he once said. "Ford Frick does not try to do the wrong thing. Given the choice between doing something right or something wrong, Frick will usually begin by doing as little as possible."[62]

One of the few who agreed with Veeck's characterization—unsurprisingly so—was Happy Chandler, who remained bitter about the brusqueness of his dismissal. Chandler was frequently asked about his successor's performance, and he always offered a well-polished quip in response. "When the clubs pushed me out in 1951, they had a vacancy and decided to keep it," he liked to say. "So they named Ford Frick."[63]

Headlines: 1951

Rookies Mantle and Mays start slowly

Two all-time greats debuted in 1951 to massive acclaim unmatched by early production. "Mickey Mantle is the greatest prospect I can remember," said the immortal Joe DiMaggio. But Mantle rapped only eight hits in his first thirty-eight at-bats (.211) for the Yankees. Willie Mays fared even worse for the Giants, eking out a lone hit in his first twenty-six trips (.038). Both soon got untracked, and Mays went on to win the National League's Rookie of the Year Award.[64]

Giants overtake Dodgers for league crown

The NL race seemed over by August 11, with Brooklyn thirteen games ahead of second-place New York. But the Giants won thirty-seven of forty-four games down the stretch, forcing a best-of-three playoff with the Dodgers. New York again fell behind—trailing 4–1 in the ninth inning of October 3's deciding game—yet another miracle was in store. Bobby Thomson's legendary home run clinched a 5–4 victory—and the pennant—for the Giants.[65]

Yankees win third crown in a row

The Giants staggered into the World Series in a state of emotional exhaustion after their intense title drive. "Somebody said we needed a week's rest. I said that we needed a month's rest," said infielder Bill Rigney. The Yankees secured their third consecutive world championship with relative ease, dispatching their crosstown rivals in six games.[66]

DiMaggio calls it a career

Joe DiMaggio drove in five runs for the Yankees in the World Series, putting a bow on his distinguished thirteen-season career. He announced his retirement on December 11. "All the fun had gone out of playing the game," said the famed center fielder, whose legacy included two batting titles, three Most Valuable Player Awards, and a lifetime batting average of .325.[67]

10

Celler

The story would be told in different ways—sometimes Danny Gardella was the impressed onlooker, other times it was Max Lanier—but the gist was always the same. Ray Dandridge, a hard-hitting, smooth-fielding third baseman, was displaying his considerable abilities on a baseball diamond in Mexico, astonishing a former big leaguer who had never heard his name.

"Man, where did you come from?" Gardella/Lanier finally asked in amazement.

Dandridge paused for a moment and looked at him coolly. "Same country you did," he said.

Ray Dandridge's black skin was the only reason he was playing in virtual anonymity in the Mexican League in 1946, rather than drawing a big-league paycheck. Most white ballplayers had been blind to the existence of black stars like Dandridge, but Gardella, Lanier, and fellow jumpers had their eyes opened in Mexico. Major leaguers began to see the truth when Jackie Robinson landed in Brooklyn in 1947.

Six big-league teams were integrated by 1951, and three had already won league titles with blacks on their rosters. The quality of these new players was indisputable. Robinson became the first black winner of a Most Valuable Player Award in 1949, followed by Dodgers teammate Roy Campanella in 1951 and again in 1953. Every National League Rookie of the Year between 1949 and 1953 was black.

Dandridge would not be part of this infusion of talent. Scouts were fully aware of his ability—he would be elected to the Hall of Fame solely on the basis of his play in Negro and Mexican ball—but they were leery of his advanced age. He was thirty-five when the Giants signed him for their AAA club in Minneapolis in 1949. He batted a robust .362, but the call to the majors never came.[1] "They said he was too old," recalled fellow Hall of Famer Monte Irvin. "I asked what difference it made if he could play."[2]

The answer was that baseball's racial attitudes were evolving at a sluggish pace. Ten franchises still fielded lily-white rosters in 1951, while the six trailblazers were nervous about overextending themselves. It seemed too risky to add a relatively old black player who might see only part-time duty. Who could be sure how a team's white fans might react? "I know it was the old quota system," Irvin said sadly of Dandridge's exclusion.[3]

Yet it could not be denied that progress was being made. Baseball's racial status quo was slowly eroding by 1951, and the same was true of other long-standing prejudices, including the sport's refusal to expand to the West Coast and its reluctance to build new stadiums.

The Pacific Coast League had not abandoned its big-league dreams, though it did take a different tack in 1949. It no longer spoke boldly about becoming the third major league, instead emphasizing its desire to be excluded from baseball's annual draft, an autumn ritual that allowed each major-league club to purchase the AAA player of its choice for $10,000, provided that the player had spent at least four years in the minors.[4]

Big-league executives described the draft as a benevolent mechanism to rescue players from servitude. Minor-league owners who operated without major-league financial assistance—a group that included every PCL team but Los Angeles—took a much darker view. They relied heavily on the revenue generated by their offseason sales of prospects to big-league teams—sometimes for as much as one hundred thousand dollars—but the draft took their very best players for peanuts.[5] It was "out-and-out robbery," insisted Brick Laws, the owner of the Oakland Oaks.[6]

PCL owners hoped to maximize their profits, of course, but an ulterior motive lurked behind their anti-draft campaign. If they were allowed to hang onto their most promising young players, many would eventually develop into stars. The PCL's talent level would inevitably rise, more fans would be attracted to its games, and it would gradually—and naturally—evolve into the third major league.

Demographic trends—specifically the brisk growth rates reported by the 1950 census—were clearly running in the PCL's favor. So was a change in national attitudes. New York and the other great East Coast cities had always been economically and culturally dominant, but a new resistance was emerging. Ohio senator Robert Taft, a prominent presidential candidate in 1948 and 1952, condemned "the power of the New York financial interests."[7] Arizona's Barry Goldwater, a new senator elected in 1952, went even further. If somebody would "saw off the Eastern Seaboard and let it float out," he once said, "I sometimes think the country would be better off."[8]

Happy Chandler, still the commissioner in 1950, sensed that the West Coast was gaining momentum. He suggested that the PCL might be elevated to its own AAAA classification and given some form of draft relief, an idea that ran into immediate opposition.[9] One of Chandler's advisers, Graham Claytor, Jr., warned that "the Pacific Coast League without the draft is a blind alley from which a really good player has no possibility of escape," perhaps increasing the likelihood of a court challenge to the reserve clause.[10] Branch Rickey was more succinct. He read the latest anti-draft screed from PCL president Pants Rowland, then scrawled a single word—"Pooh"—in the margin.[11]

Rickey seemed publicly ambivalent about the Pacific Coast League, but he led the opposition behind closed doors. He contended that the PCL's proposals had always been short in specifics, rendering them unworthy of discussion. "I have never given it serious thought," he said of its request for major-league status. His fellow owners and club presidents fell in line at a joint meeting in Chicago in 1950, rejecting the PCL's request for the sixth straight year.[12] Rowland's frustration was near the boiling point. "We have made a lot of trips back east," he said, "but we don't seem to be getting anywhere."[13]

He was wrong. A growing number of owners were coming to share Chandler's views, even as they pushed the commissioner out the door. Phil Wrigley, uniquely situated as an owner of National League and PCL clubs, asserted in April 1951 that Los Angeles "is deserving of major-league ball," a claim he buttressed with a surprising declaration. "If I had to choose between selling the Chicago and Los Angeles franchises, I would sell the Cubs," he said. "Los Angeles, I believe, has a greater future."[14] Del Webb added his support for the West's largest city in particular and the PCL in general. "I don't think you can keep major-league ball out of Los Angeles," he said in May, then spoke more broadly in August: "The Coast League is deserving of some kind of relief."[15]

Support from such influential owners gave fresh hope to the oft-spurned PCL in 1951, while a new development in another AAA league offered a possible solution to baseball's stadium logjam.

Only one big-league ballpark had been built in the previous twenty-seven years—Cleveland's Municipal Stadium in 1932—and no new facilities were in the planning stage as of 1951. The only large baseball stadium under construction in America, oddly enough, was the future home of an American Association team, the Milwaukee Brewers, the AAA farm club of the Boston Braves.[16]

Local business leaders had joined forces in 1945, creating the Greater Milwaukee Committee to jump-start postwar planning. The group's members envisioned a rejuvenated city with a modern expressway network, an expanded library system, an updated airport, a new museum, a new zoo, and a new indoor arena. These were powerful men, and they applied pressure on government officials to convert their dreams into reality.[17]

At the very top of their extensive (and expensive) wish list was an outdoor stadium for the Brewers and football's Green Bay Packers, who annually played two games in Milwaukee. Ground was broken for Milwaukee County Stadium in October 1950, with completion expected for the 1952 baseball season. But the outbreak of the Korean War diverted necessary steel, and a labor strike slowed construction, pushing the timeline to 1953. The cost of the $1.6 million project kept spiraling upward.[18] "It'll be five million dollars before we get through," moaned a county supervisor, and he was proven right.[19]

The blueprints for County Stadium called for thirty-six thousand seats, an absurdly large capacity for minor-league baseball. But the Greater Milwaukee Committee made no secret of its true intentions. Its 1952 annual report called the stadium "a bargaining tool in the battle of major American cities for a place in the big leagues of sports and entertainment," a remarkably sophisticated concept.[20] PCL teams loudly demanded big-league status, yet did nothing to upgrade their cramped, decaying ballparks. Milwaukee decided to erect a modern stadium first, then use it to attract a major-league franchise.

The logical target was Lou Perini's Boston Braves, who owned the territorial rights to Milwaukee. It was bad enough that the Braves' attendance had skidded to 487,000 in 1951, but even worse that it plummeted to 281,000 the following year. Perini spoke admiringly of Milwaukee's rising stadium—"the finest I've seen"—but denied any plans to relocate there, even as his financial losses piled up.[21] He laughed when the *Boston Herald-Traveler* reported in July 1951 that a move was imminent. "The whole thing is utterly fantastic," he said. "The Braves will remain in Boston, which is where they belong."[22]

But Milwaukee had raised the stakes. Other cities with big-league aspirations began to consider drawing up their own stadium plans. Struggling major-league teams started to imagine the profits they might generate in a glistening new facility. Would Milwaukee's gambit pay off? Everybody waited to learn the answer.

* * *

Baseball's woes were compounded in April 1951 by the return of a formidable nemesis. Frederic Johnson, who had masterminded Danny Gardella's battle against the reserve clause, filed two new lawsuits to renew the challenge. Clients Jack Corbett, the ex-owner of a minor-league team in El Paso, and Jim Prendergast, a former pitcher for the AAA Syracuse Chiefs, had different reasons for heading to court, but their complaint was identical. Both men contended that the reserve clause constituted an illegal restraint of trade.[23]

Prendergast, who had pitched eleven seasons in the minors, refused to sign his 1951 contract after the Chiefs slashed his pay by 33 percent. No big-league organization or independent minor-league team would touch him, citing his supposed ties to Syracuse under the reserve clause. "It's a weapon used by the owners," he said angrily. "They can reach out, no matter where you play, and use the reserve clause to keep you from making your livelihood."[24]

A third legal challenge followed in a matter of days, this one without Johnson's assistance. Earl Toolson, a pitcher in the Yankees' farm system, had refused a 1950 demotion from AAA Newark to Class A Binghamton, seeking a job in the Pacific Coast League instead. But the Yankees asserted their property rights, and the PCL backed off. Toolson responded with a lawsuit on May 1, 1951.[25]

Emanuel Celler watched these filings with an appraising eye. The Brooklyn Democrat had been a fixture in the House of Representatives since Warren Harding's administration, slowly accumulating seniority that invested him with considerable clout. He chaired both the House Judiciary Committee and a subcommittee that investigated business monopolies. The latter had been Celler's vehicle for high-profile probes of the steel, aluminum, and newsprint industries.[26] He now saw an opportunity in baseball, announcing on May 4 that his subcommittee would hold extensive hearings. "In my opinion, baseball is now operating in violation of the antitrust laws," he said. "We should not permit matters to drift any longer."[27]

This was ominous news indeed. The sixty-three-year-old Celler was a fiery, vigorous legislator, one of the most powerful men on Capitol Hill. His genial personality, sometimes approaching shyness, could be greatly misleading. Celler became aggressive during committee hearings, relentlessly questioning witnesses and verbally lashing any executive he suspected of monopolistic practices.[28] His "capacity for righteous indignation knows no bounds," warned the *New York Times*.[29]

Celler staged an entertaining show in his committee room, and he knew it. His ferocity was motivated by a deep thirst for attention, a trait that dismayed John Paul Stevens, a young lawyer for his subcommittee. "His evaluation of the previous day's hearing seemed to depend on the amount of coverage that it had engendered in the press, rather than the significance of any particular evidentiary development," said Stevens, who would be named a Supreme Court justice in 1975.[30]

Celler was a dangerous political hybrid—part attack dog, part publicity hound—and the owners knew he would be difficult to fend off. They sought help from Paul Porter, a former chairman of the Federal Communications Commission who had become a partner in one of Washington's most powerful law firms. The amiable, back-slapping Porter initially seemed unsuited for the assignment—a colleague likened him to a teddy bear—but he was remarkably adept at maneuvering behind the scenes. He knew everyone who was anyone in Washington, and more importantly, he knew how to persuade them to his point of view.³¹

Porter advised the owners and their supporters to portray baseball as a treasure of inestimable value, their gift to a grateful nation. They were not to discuss profits unless asked. "Organized baseball is not 'big business' in the accepted sense of the term," Porter told them.³² He stressed this point in his communications with Celler, depicting major-league clubs as benevolent employers who doled out large salaries despite meager revenue. "Viewed solely from a business standpoint," Porter told the chairman, "baseball as a whole would seem to have little excuse for existence."³³

His ultimate goal was to defend the reserve clause, a process that began on July 30 with Celler's very first witness, Hall of Famer Ty Cobb. "Baseball has made it possible for hundreds of young men from small towns, like myself, to improve their lot in life," Cobb said patriotically. He insisted that the reserve clause was essential to the sport's existence, an assessment echoed by current players.³⁴ Tigers pitcher Fred Hutchinson called it "a necessary and reasonable provision," and Dodgers shortstop Pee Wee Reese went further. "Without the reserve clause," Reese testified, "I do not think that baseball could operate."³⁵

Emanuel Celler was genial in personal conversation, but fiery and aggressive as the chairman of the House Judiciary Committee. He pushed baseball to expand: "I can envisage the day when there will be four major leagues, not two" [Library of Congress].

Their blind faith annoyed Celler, and his frustration only increased when Ford Frick dismissed the clause as "a long-term contract, which is nothing unusual."³⁶ The chairman exploded. "You and your colleagues are so inflicted with the idea of status quo that you are like people who ride in railroad cars backwards," Celler lectured Frick. "You only see things after they have passed you by."³⁷

The hearings dragged on through August and into the fall. Most of the testimony was to Porter's liking, though Celler did expose weaknesses in baseball's supposedly solid front. A subcommittee staffer somehow obtained Larry MacPhail's blockbuster 1946 report—all copies were supposed to have been destroyed—and MacPhail was summoned to discuss its contents, in particular its assertion that the reserve clause "could not be enforced in an equity court."³⁸ The subcommittee's general counsel, Ernest Goldstein, led the questioning:

GOLDSTEIN: Would it be fair to say that your understanding of the reserve clause was that there was a doubt as to its enforcability as of 1945?
MACPHAIL: In my mind, certainly.
GOLDSTEIN: So this at least reflected your own personal doubt, if not the doubt of [baseball's] counsel?
MACPHAIL: That is correct.[39]

The baseball establishment downplayed MacPhail's testimony—he had been away from the game for four years—but it went speechless when a current owner deviated from Porter's script. Celler asked Phil Wrigley if the major leagues should be exempted from antitrust laws. "I don't see why anybody should be," was the surprising answer. The chairman hastily followed up, asking if the Cubs owner truly believed that baseball should be treated like any other business. "It is a very peculiar business," Wrigley said, "but it *is* a business."[40]

Celler was baffled that a pair of former and current executives could question the reserve clause, yet players were nearly unanimous in their support. He cited the miraculous performance by pitcher Ned Garver in 1951. Garver was credited with twenty of the Browns' fifty-two wins, exceeding the combined total of eighteen victories for the staff's other four starters. Garver also excelled at the plate, batting .305, twenty-three points better than any of the Browns' position players. Yet he was paid only $18,000 ($178,000 in 2020 dollars). If baseball were forced to comply with antitrust laws, Celler suggested, Garver might very easily be making $100,000 a year.[41]

Did such speculation inspire Garver and his fellow major leaguers to repudiate the reserve clause that restricted their earning power? Did it cause them to ponder the possible joys of free agency? Not at all. Garver simply laughed off his hypothetical pay hike. "I only wish that Congressman Celler owned a ballclub," he said. "I'd like to play for him, so I could earn that kind of salary." Then he happily accepted the Browns' offer of twenty-five thousand dollars for 1952.[42]

The reserve clause wasn't the sole topic addressed in Celler's hearings. The chairman was also curious why the majors continued to rebuff markets that were clamoring for baseball. "I can envisage the day when there will be four major leagues, not two. There would be more competition," Celler said, and several witnesses shared his vision.[43] Damon Miller, an executive with the San Francisco Seals, testified that the Pacific Coast League was ready to ascend to big-league status, but the American and National Leagues were doing their best to prevent it. "We've been brushed off," he said.[44] Happy Chandler, now an ex-commissioner, exhibited a sudden eagerness for expansion when he took the stand. "I would love to organize a third major league, or even a fourth," he said.[45]

But the old guard—led by the indomitable Clark Griffith—remained as stubborn as ever. The Senators owner belittled the PCL's prospects in his testimony, drawing the ire of Patrick Hillings, a young congressman from California:

GRIFFITH: Now, the Pacific Coast League might do that thing in time. They have not got the population to do it there. They brag a lot about it.
HILLINGS: Do you know the population of California, Mr. Griffith?
GRIFFITH: No. I understand it has grown pretty big. Or, at least, they talk like that.[46]

Further questioning established that Griffith had not visited the Pacific Coast since 1923, long before the boom that had vaulted California past every state but New

York in population. He was untroubled by his lack of firsthand information. "There was not much out there in 1923, I will say that much," Griffith said.[47]

The long parade of witnesses finally ended on October 24, 1951, leaving behind a transcript that ran 1,643 pages. The last man to speak was Paul Porter, who thanked the chairman for a "fair and impartial" investigation and offered his assistance "in trying to arrive at a solution on this very difficult problem."[48]

It was a disingenuous benediction. Porter had launched an extensive lobbying campaign even before Celler gaveled the hearings to order in July, and he now dialed up the pressure. The chairman and his subcommittee were working behind closed doors, debating whether to recommend elimination of baseball's antitrust exemption and, by extension, the reserve clause. Porter enlisted an army of volunteers to agitate for the status quo—from owners and player representatives to business leaders and newspaper columnists.

Celler had been in politics a long time, yet he was shocked by the strength of baseball's offensive. Not even the steel industry had reacted with such intensity to one of his investigations. "If I thought storms had broken furiously over my head before, I knew better when these hearings started," he later wrote of his baseball probe. "Never had such controversy raged."[49]

* * *

Celler agonized over his decision for seven months, weighing five courses of action. At one pole was baseball's greatest desire—codifying into law the antitrust exemption bestowed by Oliver Wendell Holmes in 1922. At the opposite extreme was baseball's greatest fear—nullifying the exemption and the reserve clause. In between were three milder alternatives—granting a limited exemption, creating a federal agency to monitor baseball's operations, or doing nothing.[50]

Celler surprised most pundits by choosing the final option. His subcommittee issued a 232-page report in May 1952 that left the reserve clause undisturbed. "Legislation is not necessary until the reasonableness of the reserve rules has been tested by the courts," it said.[51] The chairman had heatedly accused baseball of antitrust violations even before the hearings began, but he blandly passed the buck to the judicial system at the end. The Toolson, Prendergast, and Corbett cases were steaming toward the Supreme Court, affording Celler a welcome opportunity to wriggle off the hook. He admitted to reporters that there would have been "a tremendous outcry throughout the nation of undue interference if we changed the reserve clause."[52]

Yet Celler remained firm on the separate issue of franchise placement. "Organized baseball since World War II has not been without problems arising from the anachronistic distribution of clubs among the larger cities of the continent," said his report. It named several places that appeared to be ready for big-league ball, including Los Angeles, San Francisco, Baltimore, and Montreal, the latter a curious inclusion in a study by the United States Congress.[53] Celler promised to keep a close eye on the majors until they expanded into these promising markets. "It is high time such changes were effected," he said, a remark the Brooklyn congressman would have cause to regret.[54]

But the Pacific Coast League was no longer willing to confine itself to watching and waiting, not after six years of rejection. It had already rolled the dice a few months prior to the issuance of Celler's report, triggering a high-stakes confrontation with the big leagues. PCL owners met in San Francisco on August 29, 1951—as the subcommittee hearings entered a second month—and voted unanimously to withdraw from the National Association, the umbrella organization that oversaw the minor leagues. Their stated intention, in baseball parlance, was to "go outlaw" for the 1952 season.

Establishing itself as an independent league would benefit the PCL in a couple of ways. It would no longer be subject to the annual draft, and it could immediately proclaim itself to be the third major league. But Pants Rowland was clearly nervous when making the announcement, a sign that the PCL had no real stomach for outlaw action. Its true aim was to exploit Celler's hearings for leverage. Major-league owners, already facing intense pressure in Washington, were unlikely to desire a second front on the West Coast. The PCL was gambling that its threat to break away from organized baseball would yield a quick settlement.[55]

The bet paid off in November, when the new commissioner, Ford Frick, unveiled a minor-league classification plan similar to Happy Chandler's AAAA concept. The PCL would be designated as an Open league, a step above AAA. Any league in the Open category would be allowed to apply for major-league status as soon as it met five requirements, including an average annual attendance of 3.5 million and a minimum capacity of 25,000 seats in each stadium.[56] Dan Daniel smelled a rat—"the Open classification has been contrived with an eye to Congress"—but Frick denied any subterfuge.[57] "This has been charged," he said, "and this is untrue."[58]

Rowland was greatly relieved. "This gives us the assurance that the integrity of the Pacific Coast League will be recognized," he said happily.[59] His teams would still be subject to the annual draft, though fewer budding stars were likely to be snatched away. Frick raised the eligibility threshold from four to five years for players at the Open level, while hiking the price from ten thousand to fifteen thousand dollars. Rowland envisioned roster stability and a gradual improvement in the quality of the PCL's teams. "Granted five years to build them up, we could get ready to step into the major-league family," he predicted.[60]

Cities in other parts of North America also had reason for optimism in 1952. Big-league owners were ecstatic that Manny Celler had spared their precious reserve clause. It only made sense to stay on the chairman's good side by bowing to his geographic dictates. Nobody wished to incur his wrath and incite another round of hearings.

Frick consequently recommended a loosening of the rules that governed franchise shifts. The approval of both leagues was currently required for any move, but the commissioner recommended that any future vote be confined to the league directly involved in a transfer to an open market. This seemingly minor adjustment, which was approved by the owners on December 7, 1952, had significant ramifications. It reduced the red tape involved in a franchise shift, and it prevented one league from restraining the territorial ambitions of the other.[61] Walter O'Malley hailed it as the "most exciting" rule change in years.[62]

Rumors of imminent transfers—mostly involving the St. Louis Browns and Boston Braves—immediately began to fly. The *New York World-Telegram and Sun* reported on December 10 that Bill Veeck's Browns had a "75–25 chance" of moving to Milwaukee for the 1953 season.[63] The story elicited a hasty denial from Lou Perini, who retained territorial rights to the Wisconsin city. "Veeck not only won't be moving into Milwaukee for next April's opening," Perini said, "but he won't for 1954 either."[64]

What, then, about the Braves? Joe Barnes, the sports editor of New Hampshire's *Manchester Union Leader*, sent fifteen questions to Perini shortly before Christmas. A few dealt with trades or the team's prospects; others were about television or finances. The Braves owner mailed his responses on December 29. He answered all of Barnes's questions but the tenth: "In the event the fans do not turn out to support the Braves in the 1953 season, will you consider transferring the franchise to Milwaukee?"

Perini was uncharacteristically—and ominously—evasive in response. "I would like to pass on this question," he wrote.[65]

11

Shrinking

Wire contraptions began popping up on rooftops in the late 1940s—first on a house here or there, eventually on almost every home in sight. These strange-looking antennae captured television signals for a rapidly expanding array of receivers. Only nine hundred thousand U.S. households owned TV sets as of 1949, but the number would climb to fifteen million by 1952, then soar to forty-six million by the decade's end.[1]

Yet television's alteration of the skyline was nothing compared to its impact on society. The sudden and easy availability of visual entertainment encouraged people to stay home after dinner. "It is now possible for the first time to answer an inquiring foreign visitor as to what Americans do in the evening," wrote author Theodore White. "The answer is clear: They watch television."[2] Tex Schramm, then the general manager of football's Los Angeles Rams, viewed this phenomenon through a caustic lens. "The Fifties," he later said, "was a decade in which everybody became watchers instead of doers."[3]

Nostalgists would falsely remember the 1950s as the golden age of television. The truth was less inspiring. Budgets for most TV shows were minuscule, production facilities were primitive, and top-line stars were absent, preferring the glamour of the movies. TV programs were usually produced in cramped, inadequate studios. "There was little room for the visual sensations of car chases, shootouts, or even outdoor scenery," wrote historians David Marc and Robert Thompson. "The typical *mise-en-scene* consisted of a few talking heads in a crowded little room."[4]

Movie producers initially saw nothing to fear. "People will soon get tired of looking at a plywood box every night," Darryl Zanuck scoffed, but sales of TV sets accelerated.[5] Theater owners eventually decided to fight back, pooling their money for a national advertising campaign. Billboards proclaimed "Movies Are Better Than Ever" and asked "Why Not Go to a Movie Tonight?" But five thousand theaters succumbed to declining ticket sales, while attendance at surviving movie houses plummeted 20 to 40 percent.[6] "You can't charge for mediocrity anymore when everybody can get it at home for nothing," a theater operator sadly told the *New York Times*.[7]

Sports were a big draw on television from the very beginning, offering broadcasters the rare opportunity to break free of their claustrophobic studios. Boxing, wrestling, and roller derby were especially popular, largely because they were staged in confined spaces, were inexpensive to cover, and could be viewed easily on the era's tiny TV screens. Boxing became a Friday night fixture, and wrestling was carried on more than two hundred stations in the early 1950s.[8] Critics derided many of these purported athletic events as theater—and bad theater at that. "Roller derby is a sport," wrote John Lardner. "Defenestration is also a sport, for those who like it."[9]

Intense on-air rotation sapped the vitality of these television staples. Boxing faded badly by the late 1950s because of overexposure. The typical fight drew ten thousand spectators to Madison Square Garden in 1948, but average attendance dropped to twelve hundred by 1957. Roller derby and wrestling fared even worse, virtually disappearing from the airwaves by 1960.[10]

Baseball was more difficult to televise. Early TV cameras were stymied by its fast pitches and broad fields, and viewers were often frustrated by the resulting pictures, which were small and blurry. But baseball was America's most popular sport, boasting the legitimacy that roller derby and wrestling lacked. Television stations were eager to carry as many games as possible, and major-league teams happily accepted their checks.

A few baseball executives still denied any cause for concern about TV. The movies might be dying because of television's competitive strength, boxing might be struggling because of TV's overuse, but the national pastime would persevere. "We cannot imagine fans preferring TV to live baseball," said Buzzie Bavasi, the new vice president of the Dodgers.[11]

But there was mounting evidence to the contrary. Big-league attendance, which had peaked at 20.9 million in 1948, dived all the way to 14.6 million by 1952, a 30 percent fall in just 4 seasons. Fourteen of the sixteen franchises suffered declines during that period—the St. Louis Browns and Chicago White Sox were the exceptions—and some of the drops were horrific. Detroit fell 41 percent, Cleveland 45 percent, Pittsburgh 55 percent, and Lou Perini's Boston Braves 81 percent. "Television has definitely hurt baseball attendance," Perini conceded. "I mean television as a whole, not only the telecasting of baseball games. I know it has murdered the movies, and it might possibly do the same to baseball."[12]

The danger would intensify as TV grew more powerful. A network of coaxial cables and microwave relays connected New York and California on September 4, 1951, making nationwide telecasts possible for the first time. The initial coast-to-coast show was a high-minded affair, a speech by President Truman in San Francisco, but the implications for sports were obvious. Los Angeles viewers were able to see the exciting National League playoff a month later, watching live as Bobby Thomson's epochal home run soared over the left-field fence in the Polo Grounds.[13]

All sports executives faced the same question: How could they capture as much revenue from this behemoth as possible, while avoiding the risk of overexposure?

One possible answer was to confine the use of television to public venues, forcing viewers to buy tickets, just as they would at the ballpark. A group of theater owners bought exclusive rights to a boxing match between former heavyweight champ Joe Louis and Lee Savold on June 15, 1951, snatching it from the TV networks. The bout was shown in eight theaters in six cities, drawing twenty-two thousand paying customers. Albany's Palace Theater attracted the biggest crowd, four thousand fans who paid seventy-five cents apiece.[14]

The Louis-Savold fight carried "incredible implications for baseball," said Paul Jonas, the chief of sports telecasting for the Mutual Broadcasting System. Mutual already held the TV contract for the World Series, but Jonas envisioned vast additional revenue from theaters. "The major leagues," he said, "are face to face with a pot of gold."[15] His enthusiasm was not wholly shared by the owners. "I don't believe this will take television of baseball games out of homes," said Walter O'Malley, though he hedged: "We don't know until we see how this thing develops."[16]

O'Malley was more interested in the related concept of pay television. Competing systems were already being developed by Zenith, International Telemeter, and Skiatron. All three corporations proposed to transmit movies and sports to home TV sets through scrambled channels. Customers of Zenith's Phonevision system would dial a designated telephone number to unscramble the picture for a specific program, settling their accounts through a monthly bill. Telemeter planned to install a coin box on top of each TV. Skiatron opted for a punch-card reader.[17]

Zenith was first out of the box, wiring three hundred Chicago homes for a three-month test of Phonevision. The service debuted on New Year's Day 1951 with *April Showers*, a 1947 musical starring Jack Carson. The fee was one dollar.[18] "For ninety minutes, no one left the living room," wrote the radio-TV editor of the *Chicago Tribune*, Larry Wolters, who hosted a viewing party. "While pictures on a sixteen-inch screen are not comparable to theater-sized prints, the group was pretty well agreed that this is the way to see movies."[19] Final figures showed that the typical Phonevision family spent $1.73 a week ($17.14 in 2020 money). "Phonevision hits the spot," said another test subject, *Chicago Daily News* city editor Clem Lane. "It's the best thing that I know of."[20]

The others followed with their own tests—Telemeter in Los Angeles in 1952, Skiatron in New York in 1953—but an imposing hurdle remained. Approval for full-fledged pay-TV systems had to be obtained from the Federal Communications Commission, and the major networks vowed a no-holds-barred fight to prevent such permission.[21] NBC chairman David Sarnoff predicted that pay TV would "ultimately destroy the present system of television."[22] CBS president Frank Stanton insisted that FCC approval would be a "betrayal of the public."[23]

The owners of New York's two National League teams shook their heads at this impassioned rhetoric. Horace Stoneham's Giants had suffered a 33 percent attendance decline between 1948 and 1952, while O'Malley's Dodgers had fallen 22 percent. Both men were looking for new sources of revenue, and pay television seemed to fit the bill even better than theater TV.

Stoneham posed it as an issue of fairness—"there is no reason why stay-at-home fans should not pay some sort of nominal fee"—but O'Malley typically cut to the heart of the matter.[24] There were millions of TV households in Brooklyn and the New York metropolitan area, and he wanted as many as possible to contribute to his bottom line. "A fellow who wants to see a ballgame drops in a quarter," said O'Malley, "which seems reasonable enough for two or three hours of entertainment." He envisioned enormous financial returns.[25]

* * *

Baseball wasn't the only sport baffled by the paradox of television. The National Football League was equally entranced by the tube's promise of easy money, yet repelled by its depressing impact on attendance.

The Los Angeles Rams had enjoyed a banner season in 1949, winning the Western Division title, hosting the first NFL championship game played on the West Coast (which they lost to the Philadelphia Eagles), and leading the league in attendance.

Owner Dan Reeves dreamed of even greater success in 1950. The All-America Football Conference and its Los Angeles Dons had finally disappeared, leaving the nation's third-largest market solely to the Rams.

Reeves was especially excited about a new revenue source. The Admiral Corporation, a prominent manufacturer of television sets, purchased the TV rights to Rams home games in 1950, seemingly offering the best of both worlds. It was taken for granted that ticket sales would remain robust at the Los Angeles Coliseum. Eighty-six thousand fans had flocked to an October 1949 game with Chicago, and an even bigger crowd was anticipated for 1950's season opener against the very same Bears. The TV money was just a sweetener, an enhancement that might make 1950 the most lucrative season in Rams history.

Reeves began to have second thoughts on September 17, 1950, as he gazed out at a sparsely populated Coliseum. Only twenty-one thousand of the ninety-three thousand seats were occupied. Most Los Angeles fans—hundreds of thousands of them—had chosen to watch the Rams and Bears on TV. The same trend held all season. Attendance at the Coliseum plummeted 50 percent in 1950, even though the Rams once again made it to the league's championship game (losing this time to the Cleveland Browns).[26]

The only saving grace for Reeves was the fine print his lawyers had inserted in the TV contract, requiring Admiral to compensate the Rams for any decline in ticket revenue. The manufacturer handed over a check for $307,000 ($3.28 million in 2020 dollars) at season's end, then canceled any future plans to sponsor football on TV. The Rams had learned a valuable lesson. They immediately stopped telecasting home games, triggering a 95 percent upswing in attendance in 1951.[27]

The Rams-Admiral debacle proved to be an instructive, if costly, experiment. NFL commissioner Bert Bell came to believe that any owner who televised his home games would meet the same fate as Reeves, and he resolved to prevent such a disaster. Bell imposed a leaguewide blackout in 1951, decreeing that no NFL contest could be telecast within seventy-five miles of the stadium where it was being played. A fan could still see his team's road games on TV, but he had to buy a ticket for any game at home.[28]

Bell's uniform television policy stood in sharp contrast to the chaotic situation in baseball, where each franchise made its own decisions about when and where to appear on TV. Several baseball teams—including the Chicago Cubs and all three New York clubs—continued to telecast all of their home games, even as crowds dwindled.[29] Walter O'Malley admitted to reporters in 1951 that TV "definitely has hurt attendance," yet he was unable to resist the money that broadcasters waved in his face. "I feel this is a passing phase and that eventually television will build new baseball fans all over the country," he said lamely.[30]

The difference between football and baseball on this issue was explained by the differences between their commissioners.

Gravel-voiced Bert Bell wielded authority as if born to it, as indeed he had. His father had served as Pennsylvania's attorney general, and Bert (short for De Benneville) had been raised on Philadelphia's Main Line and educated in the Ivy League.[31] The younger Bell had no desire to follow his dad's career path—"all I ever wanted to be was a football man"—so he purchased the Philadelphia Eagles in 1933, his first step toward becoming commissioner in 1946. He naturally spoke the same language as the

National Football League commissioner Bert Bell (center) gives President Harry Truman a 1949 season pass, as Washington Redskins owner George Marshall looks on. Bell proved to be a more dynamic commissioner than his baseball counterpart in the 1950s, Ford Frick [Harry S. Truman Library and Museum].

NFL's owners, all of whom (even crusty George Halas) respected his dynamism and decisiveness.[32]

Ford Frick had been a sportswriter and National League president, two positions that rewarded subservience, not assertiveness. The owners made him commissioner not because of his independence or creativity—two qualities he lacked—but because he was milder and quieter than Happy Chandler. "Frick would never tell an owner what to do with his ballclub," wrote journalist Al Hirshberg. "Bell not only tells owners what to do with their clubs, but sometimes tells them what to do with their money as well."[33]

These divergent approaches yielded vastly different results. Baseball's attendance would rise 6 percent during Frick's first six years on the job, yet even this modest gain was misleading. Three franchises relocated during that span, boosting ticket sales by 233 percent in their new homes. The other thirteen teams—the ones who stayed put—actually suffered a collective attendance decline of 14 percent between 1951 and 1957.

The NFL, on the other hand, enjoyed a meteoric box-office gain of 48 percent over the same six years, with every team but Washington experiencing a sales increase. Bell's TV policy was given much of the credit. "Professional football's attendance has been going straight up in the same decade that baseball's attendance has been going straight down," Bill Veeck later wrote, "because Bert Bell gave the NFL such aggressive leadership."[34]

Yet it had not been a sure thing. Football did not enjoy the same antitrust exemption as baseball; Oliver Wendell Holmes had mentioned only the latter sport in his 1922 decision. Federal lawyers were convinced that Bell's blackout constituted an illegal restraint of trade, and they filed suit to prevent it. Most experts predicted the NFL's imminent defeat.

They—and Bell himself—were in for a surprise on November 12, 1953, when Judge Allan Grim ruled in the league's favor. Grim's twenty-one-page opinion was unexpectedly nimble, asserting that the blackout actually promoted competition by boosting ticket sales for weak teams. The judge allowed the seventy-five-mile radius to stand, and Bell happily claimed victory.[35] "The league's most vital need," he said, "is the protection of our home gate if we are to continue our existence."[36] Baseball owners knew exactly what he meant.

* * *

TV's new coaxial-microwave link brought America's two coasts closer together, offering simultaneous experiences that previously had been unavailable. Everyone could now watch President Truman or a famous comedian or a World Series game at exactly the same time. The nation somehow felt smaller, and baseball's rationale for excluding Los Angeles and San Francisco seemed weaker.

A second factor—a revolution in transportation—accelerated the shrinking of the continent. World War II had introduced millions of soldiers to air travel. Many of them, upon returning to civilian life, chose planes for business or pleasure trips. Only one of every fourteen Americans had taken an airline flight as of 1945, according to the Gallup Poll, but that ratio would balloon in the first postwar decade. Domestic air carriers, virtually an afterthought prior to the Pearl Harbor attack, would surpass Pullman trains in service mileage by 1953.[37]

The piston-engine, propeller-driven Douglas DC-6 and Lockheed Constellation were the commercial airplanes of choice in those years. They were more powerful and more comfortable than their prewar predecessors, and they were faster, too. Passengers were stunned by the unprecedented speed of the service launched by Trans World Airlines in May 1950. TWA's sleek Constellation zipped from Los Angeles to New York at a breathtaking three hundred miles per hour, covering the route in less than eleven hours, including a stop in Chicago.[38]

Bernard DeVoto was a Pulitzer Prize-winning historian who had written extensively about the Lewis and Clark expedition. He found it almost incomprehensible that a plane could rapidly cover a distance that had challenged intrepid explorers for eighteen months, so he booked a Washington-San Francisco trip to see for himself. The flight initially bored him—he pronounced it "the dullest mode of travel"—but his mood lightened after seeing vast Midwestern prairies and the sunset beyond the Rocky Mountains. "An airliner at night," he decided toward the end, "is one of the most beautiful, most peaceful, most comfortable of places."[39] But DeVoto fretted that airline executives would disrupt the contentment by chipping away at flight times. "I hope they never compress it further with jets," he wrote.[40]

That, of course, was precisely what the commercial carriers planned. The United

States had been late to sense the possibilities of jet travel. The National Bureau of Standards had decreed in 1923 that development of a jet engine was "practically impossible," causing U.S. research to lag for two decades.[41] Yet Germany and Great Britain were able to develop jet fighters after the outbreak of World War II, and America finally shook off its complacency with Britain's help, debuting the Lockheed P-80 Shooting Star in 1944. The production of military jets was given top priority for the rest of the decade, but airlines waited impatiently for the anticipated arrival of commercial jetliners in the 1950s.[42]

United Air Lines was not content with standing by. It started a "paper jet" program in November 1952, filing daily flight plans for two aircraft that did not yet exist. Engineers studied storms and wind patterns between New York and San Francisco to simulate trips in both directions. Estimated durations were less than six hours eastbound, six and a half hours westbound into prevailing winds. But nobody would know for sure until 1956, when Pan American World Airways had tentatively scheduled the first passenger-jet service for North America.[43]

Baseball, to absolutely nobody's surprise, reacted sluggishly to the rapid evolution of air travel. The train remained the preferred mode of travel for short jaunts (ninety-five miles from Philadelphia to Brooklyn) and long treks (twenty-three grueling hours from St. Louis to New York).[44] Executives and players extolled the coach car as an ideal laboratory for the improvement of team morale. "On trains, we played a little cards, talked baseball, got to know each other," said Red Sox third baseman Frank Malzone.[45] But they also endured boredom and other discomforts. "The train swayed and jerked along, stopping at every crossroad," Dodgers vice president Fresco Thompson said of one unhappy trip. "A stomach seemed upside down after the first fifty miles."[46]

Larry MacPhail, renowned for his innovative spirit, had been the logical pioneer to break baseball's railroad monopoly. He chartered two planes in June 1934 to carry his Reds from Cincinnati to Chicago. A coach and three players refused to board this inaugural flight; they traveled by train.[47] Next came the Red Sox in July 1936, escaping a steamily hot St. Louis for Chicago. "Let's get out of here as fast as we can," snapped owner Tom Yawkey. "See if the players will fly." All but five agreed. The laggards rode the rails with the team's luggage.[48]

But those were isolated incidents. MacPhail tried to book most of the Yankees' trips by air in 1946 and 1947, only to back down when several players complained. It wouldn't be until 1954 that a big-league team would take to the skies almost exclusively. Branch Rickey chartered a fifty-passenger plane to carry the Pittsburgh Pirates on all but their very shortest routes, such as Philadelphia to New York.[49] Going by air, he said, would "save time, eliminate travel fatigue, and provide the players with more personalized service." The parsimonious Rickey also noted happily that the Pirates would spend five thousand dollars less by plane than by rail.[50]

Twelve other teams were taking some trips by air at that point, though none as extensively as Pittsburgh. Most players consented, albeit with a distinct lack of pleasure. "When it took off, it sounded like a sewing machine. We knew we had to do it, but it was scary," said Braves pitcher Bob Buhl of a typical flight in the 1950s.[51] Bob Cerv, a slugging outfielder with the Yankees and Athletics, had similar memories. "If you sat behind the props," he recalled, "it about tore your ears out."[52]

The imminence of transcontinental jet travel opened new vistas for the major leagues, but the old guard vowed to resist as long as possible. Connie Mack, who turned ninety in 1952, ticked off the negatives of air travel—engine noise, cramped seats, stale air, and above all else, the ever-present danger of crashing. "It's too much like putting all your eggs in one basket," he said. If the majors one day expanded to the West Coast, he told reporters, he would make sure that his Athletics went there on a train.[53]

Headlines: 1952

PIRATES START SLOWLY, FINISH BADLY

Branch Rickey's Pirates floundered from the start in 1952. They were outscored 78–23 during ten straight losses in April, then suffered separate losing streaks of six and eight games in May. Pittsburgh, already a full twenty games behind first-place Brooklyn as of May 25, was destined to finish 42–112, the worst record for any big-league team from 1936 through 1961.[54]

WILLIAMS HOMERS IN POSSIBLE SWAN SONG

Ted Williams wrapped up his 1952 season—and possibly his career—with a game-winning home run off Detroit's Dizzy Trout on April 30. Fans at Fenway Park roared as the ball sailed into the right-field seats. The thirty-three-year-old Williams would report for a lengthy hitch with the marines two days later, raising doubts that he would ever play ball again. "How can I tell what will happen in the next seventeen months?" he asked querulously.[55]

MANTLE PROPELS YANKEES TO FOURTH TITLE

This finally seemed to be the year for Brooklyn. Duke Snider's eleventh-inning double plated Billy Cox with the winning run in Game Five of the World Series, leaving the Dodgers one victory away from their first championship. But Mickey Mantle blasted decisive home runs in the final two games, clinching the Yankees' fourth straight title. "Mantle beat us," said Jackie Robinson. "That kid was the difference between the two clubs."[56]

DODGERS FALL SHORT OF SELLOUT

A standing-room-only crowd was anticipated at Ebbets Field for Game Six of the World Series, with the Dodgers having an opportunity to secure a championship. But only 30,037 tickets were sold for the October 6 contest, roughly 2,000 below capacity. "Many fans believed they would have no chance to obtain ducats," explained the *Sporting News*, "and remained at home to watch the game on television." The empty seats did not amuse Walter O'Malley.[57]

PART TWO: 1953–1957

12

Milwaukee

Bill Veeck spoke to hundreds of civic groups, service clubs, and professional organizations over the winter of 1952, hustling to every corner of the St. Louis area to whip up enthusiasm for the Browns. His goal was nothing less than a capacity crowd for the April 18 season opener against Chicago, a vital step toward his objective of destroying the Cardinals.

Disappointment awaited. Only 12,573 fans passed through the turnstiles at Sportsman's Park, exceeding 1951's season-opening turnout by almost 7,000, yet falling 22,000 short of a full house. The day's only positive news came on the field. St. Louis trounced the White Sox, 7–1, and continued to play respectably for five weeks. Manager Rogers Hornsby had his team at .500 as late as May 18, unfamiliar territory for the lowly Browns.[1]

Hornsby seemed to be getting results with his no-nonsense approach. "If they've called me rough and hard-boiled and demanding," he once said, "it's because I love the game and wanted to give my best to it."[2] But his intensity was accompanied by a callousness that soon took its toll. Postwar players, especially those with military records, were accustomed to disciplinarians, but Hornsby was uniquely misanthropic. "I guess he'd wanted to be an army general, but never made it. So he tried running his ballclub like an army," said pitcher Satchel Paige.[3] Mild-mannered Hank Peters, assistant farm director for the Browns, failed in every attempt to engage Hornsby in conversation. "He just didn't like other people," said Peters, the future general manager of the Baltimore Orioles.[4]

The Browns, who were in virtual revolt against Hornsby by June 9, had fallen seven games below .500 and were sinking fast. Veeck flew to Boston the next day and fired his manager. "I saved Hornsby from getting whacked," he confided to a reporter.[5] The players expressed their gratitude by presenting the owner a twenty-four-inch silver trophy. "To Bill Veeck for the greatest play since the Emancipation Proclamation," read the engraving. Pitcher Ned Garver took credit for the trophy, though critics insisted it was a tasteless promotion masterminded by Veeck himself.[6] "When you work for a screwball," said Hornsby, "you've got to expect screwball tactics."[7]

The final verdict was handed down by Veeck's mother, who had been horrified when the manager was signed in October 1951. She sent her son a five-word telegram: "What did I tell you?"[8]

It was a moment for self-reflection. Veeck's two-pronged strategy—outpromoting the Cardinals and pilfering their history—was in disarray. The first part had failed to generate the desired attendance, and the second had produced the Hornsby debacle. Veeck's magic touch—the source of his massive success in Cleveland—seemed to have vanished. "St. Louis was the opposite. Everything turned out badly," he acknowledged.⁹ The question facing him in June 1952 was what to do next. "Things went from bad to worse until the middle of the season, when I got the idea to move the club out of St. Louis," he later said.¹⁰

Veeck's attention span wandered easily, as friends and critics agreed. Sidney Salomon, Jr., a wealthy St. Louis businessman who had invested in the Browns, watched it happen as 1952 dragged on. "He lost his interest in St. Louis," said Salomon. "I don't think he bought the team with the idea of moving it, but eventually he lost interest."¹¹ Veeck was clearly making progress. The Browns would boost their attendance by 77 percent in 1952, while the Cardinals would suffer a 10 percent drop. But the Cards still dominated the market, and the Browns weren't building momentum quickly enough. It was nothing like Cleveland, where Veeck had won the World Series and set the all-time attendance record in his third year.

Friends from Milwaukee called Veeck from time to time—people he knew from his days with the Brewers—and they implored him to move the Browns to their beautiful new ballpark. The answer was always negative until October 1952, when County Stadium manager Frederic Mendelson got in touch. Veeck expressed interest for the first time, though he warned that two problems had to be solved prior to a shift. The

Lou Perini (left) attends a game with Braves general manager John Quinn. Perini pledged to keep his team in Boston, though with a caveat. "I have no plans to move the Braves," he said. "But I'm not going to be stubborn about this thing" [Wisconsin Historical Society].

Browns needed to sell Sportsman's Park, and Lou Perini had to hand over his territorial rights to Milwaukee.[12]

The Cardinals were the logical buyers of the stadium that they shared with the Browns, though Veeck's feud with Fred Saigh promised to complicate the negotiations. Getting Perini to sell his rights seemed to be an easier task, since the Braves owner had pledged as recently as September 22 not to block a big-league team from moving to Milwaukee. "We couldn't stand in their way," he had said.[13] Perini's focus seemed to be entirely on Boston, where he was consolidating power by buying out the team's minority shareholders, a process he completed in late November.[14] "The way has been paved for the Braves to stay in Boston," the *Sporting News* reported. "Under [Perini's] new setup, they will be able to remain in this city as long as the owners desire."[15]

But Perini's ties to his hometown were fraying. The Braves lost $459,000 in 1952 (the equivalent of $4.45 million in 2020), severely taxing the owner's bank account and his patience.[16] He offered his ritualistic vow to remain in Boston after the final home game of the season, though acute observers noticed his first equivocation. "I have no plans to move the Braves," he said. "But I'm not going to be stubborn about this thing. I don't intend to spend ten years here when people don't want to see the Braves."[17]

Perini's private actions belied his public preference for Boston. He called an October staff meeting, revealing that a move to Milwaukee was likely, though in 1954, not 1953. "He told us the Braves couldn't be competitive in Boston, based on market surveys, and that the future there was bleak," recalled Chuck Patterson, Perini's personal assistant. "Then he told us not to say a word to anyone, not even our wives."[18] Perini later admitted that he made his decision before the end of the 1952 season. The Braves couldn't move prior to the next opening day—there wasn't enough time for that—but they would definitely pull up stakes the following year. "We had made up our mind that, regardless if we had won the pennant [in 1953], we would go to Milwaukee," he said.[19]

The next few months promised to be tricky. Perini needed to break his vow by blocking Veeck's Browns, yet without revealing his secret or alienating the people of Wisconsin. He hoped to transform his woeful Braves into Milwaukee's big-league heroes in 1954. If he blundered, Perini knew that a different fate awaited. He would be reviled as the villain who thwarted the city's dreams in 1953.

* * *

It was Veeck, not Perini, who committed the first error.

Baseball's bylaws required home teams to split ticket revenue with their visiting opponents. It was a logical arrangement. Both clubs were putting on a show for the public, so both deserved to be paid. The lion's share went to the home side, since it had the added expense of staging the game. Formulas varied by league and seat location, but visitors generally received twenty-seven to twenty-nine cents for each ticket sold.

The rules were different for radio and television revenue. Each team negotiated its own broadcast fees and kept whatever it collected. There was no split, which Veeck insisted was unjust.[20] He spoke of a hypothetical game at Yankee Stadium between St. Louis and New York. If the Yankees televised the game, fewer New Yorkers would come to the park, thereby reducing the Browns' share of the box-office take. "Who does it hurt? Only the visiting teams like mine, who don't televise," he said. "The Yankees, with their television revenue, wind up with more money despite an attendance decrease."[21]

Veeck called it a question of fairness—"we present half the show and don't get a dime out of it"—though his protest exuded a whiff of desperation.[22] He had ignored the disparity in broadcasting revenue while riding high in Cleveland. But losses of $330,000 in 1952 ($3.2 million in 2020 dollars) had altered his perspective.[23] "Ever since I took over the Browns," Veeck said, "I know just how the people who work in mines feel about the people up in the open air."[24]

His preferred solution was to pool the radio and TV money for all eight American League teams and divide it equally. But that idea, he knew, would never fly. So he formally recommended that home and road teams split broadcast revenue on a game-by-game basis. His proposal was added to the agenda for the league's winter meeting on December 4, 1952.[25]

There was no doubt where the baseball establishment stood. "That is a socialistic theory, pure and simple," Walter O'Malley snarled.[26] Tom Yawkey echoed the complaint, muttering that Veeck was a "goddamned socialist."[27] The Yankees' ruling triumvirate—Dan Topping, Del Webb, and George Weiss—quietly rolled into action to unite the opposition.

Veeck's proposal was rejected, seven to one, and he knew who to blame. "Whenever I offered any plan that would give the other teams a fighting chance against them," he said, "the Yankees always cried socialism, the first refuge of scoundrels."[28] He resolved to fight back. Each owner routinely signed reciprocal agreements over the winter, granting permission to the other franchises to televise games involving his team. Veeck announced that he would not sign his waivers for 1953. Teams that wanted to put games with the Browns on TV would not be allowed to do so.[29]

It was a quixotic gesture, guaranteed to annoy the powers that be. "Sooner or later, the pixielike Mr. Veeck will have to capitulate," predicted Arthur Daley in the *New York Times*.[30] The Yankees, Red Sox, and Indians soon ratcheted up the pressure, announcing that all of their home dates with the Browns in 1953 would be played in daylight, when the gate receipts would be weakest.[31] "While we might draw some fairly decent crowds at night, we had no chance of drawing anything on weekdays," Veeck wrote. "My choice was to sue or to throw in the towel."[32]

He chose the latter, though the damage was already done. Veeck's relationships with most American League owners—chilly in the best of times—had now been strained beyond repair. "It is fairly obvious—as these things are always obvious in retrospect—that since I knew very well that I might be asking permission to move shortly, I had not picked the best possible time to offend the Yankees," he later admitted.[33] The transfer rules had been loosened, but Veeck would still need six affirmative votes to shift the Browns to Milwaukee. It remained to be seen if he could get them.

* * *

A cloud of uncertainty hovered over Fred Saigh during and after the 1952 season. A federal grand jury had indicted him for income-tax evasion on April 22, 1952. He learned of the indictment while watching his Cardinals play at Cincinnati's Crosley Field. "I knew an investigation had been going on," he said nonchalantly, "but

I was of the opinion the case was in the process of settlement."[34] Saigh called it a misunderstanding over accounting procedures. He predicted he would be "completely vindicated."[35]

The case disappeared from the newspapers after an initial flurry. Saigh consulted with high-powered lawyers and politicians in advance of his January 28, 1953, court date—he later claimed to have spoken directly with Harry Truman—and they assured him that a prison sentence was highly unlikely. The only question was whether Ford Frick would impose his own punishment, perhaps suspending Saigh from baseball for his indiscretion.

"Under a promise from the president of the United States that I would get fined only," Saigh said, "I went in to plead *nolo contendere*," tacitly (but not formally) admitting guilt.[36] He expected leniency in return, yet Judge Roy Harper sentenced him to fifteen months in prison. "I think you have been very severe with me," Saigh complained. Harper bristled: "You're an attorney. You knew what you were pleading to."[37]

Saigh always maintained that he had been double-crossed. "Someone in Washington—and I know who—threw the book at me," he said in 1978.[38] He insisted that a vengeful Happy Chandler had used his Washington connections to initiate the Internal Revenue Service's investigation and dictate Harper's sentence. The ex-commissioner enjoyed Saigh's misery—he certainly made no effort to hide his satisfaction—but no evidence surfaced of his involvement in such a conspiracy.[39]

A felony sentence left Frick no choice. He ordered Saigh to sell the Cardinals or place them under a trusteeship no later than February 23. Potential buyers quickly called from Houston and Milwaukee. The Houston interests had begun sniffing around the Cardinals the previous fall, reportedly promising to build a fifty-five-thousand-seat stadium if Saigh would move his team to Texas. They now offered to buy the franchise outright. The president of the Miller Brewing Company, Frederick Miller, spearheaded the Milwaukee effort. Saigh told him that any bid below four million dollars would be unacceptable.[40]

The biggest shock was the total lack of concern within the local business community. Nobody in St. Louis stepped forward to save the Cardinals. Team employees, according to the *St. Louis Post-Dispatch*, were informed in early February that the franchise was most likely bound for Milwaukee. If they wished to keep their jobs, they would be compensated for their relocation expenses. Saigh scheduled a mid–February appointment with Frick in New York, presumably to discuss the transfer.[41]

Nobody was more surprised than Bill Veeck. His impossible dream was on the verge of coming true. The hapless Browns seemed likely to be the last big-league team standing in St. Louis.

Then August Busch, Jr., came on the scene.

Busch was the stocky, strong-willed, hot-tempered president of one of the nation's great breweries, Anheuser-Busch, which had been established by his grandfather. The family business meant everything to the younger Busch, known to one and all as Gussie.[42] He would never forget watching the first trucks roll out of the St. Louis brewery upon the end of Prohibition in 1933. "It was the greatest moment of my life," he said. "The greatest, I guess, that I ever will know."[43]

Busch's outside interests were decidedly lowbrow for a man of such vast wealth. He was an avid outdoorsman, a passionate poker player, and so devoted a fan of fighting that he installed a boxing ring in his mansion.[44] St. Louis broadcaster Harry Caray succinctly described him as "a booze-and-broads man."⁴⁵ Team sports, on the other hand, held no appeal for Busch, who hadn't attended a Cardinals game in years.

His aversion posed a difficulty for a pair of prominent St. Louis bankers, who approached Busch on February 13 about saving the city's National League franchise. "I told them that if anyone else could keep the Cardinals in St. Louis, we would not take any part in the situation," he recalled.⁴⁶ But the bankers persisted. They convinced Saigh to cancel his trip to see Frick, then brought him together with Busch. The brewer reluctantly agreed on February 20 to purchase the team for $3.75 million ($36 million as of 2020), more out of a sense of duty than any personal excitement.⁴⁷

St. Louis fans perceived no shades of gray in the transaction. They would remember Fred Saigh as a blundering, felonious owner who had nearly allowed the city's revered team to slip away. Gussie Busch would always be their hero, the knight in shining armor who had saved the Cardinals. Saigh angrily dissented, insisting that he had given a hesitant Busch a hometown discount. "I could have made between $700,000 and $750,000 more," Saigh sputtered. "But I wanted to leave the team in the city."⁴⁸ He would report to prison on May 4, muttering, "This is a terrible thing to happen to a guy who doesn't deserve it."⁴⁹

Saigh's fate was of no particular interest to the baseball establishment, which had weathered the St. Louis crisis unexpectedly well. Warren Giles dashed off a celebratory telegram to National League owners on February 21, promising them that they had passed safely through the worst of times. "I am sure the Cardinals are in good hands," he told them.⁵⁰ Any other problems could wait. It was time to head south for spring training. Opening day was just seven weeks away.

* * *

Bill Veeck had tried over the winter to lay the groundwork for a Milwaukee transfer, yet he made no headway. He placed an occasional call to Boston, asking Lou Perini about his territorial rights, but the Braves owner refused to be pinned down. Veeck spoke more frequently—two or three times a week—with the sports editor of the *Milwaukee Journal*, Russ Lynch, in the hope of stirring action in Wisconsin, though nothing resulted.⁵¹ "Veeck was scared stiff at the idea of publicity, said he might never come here if there was publicity," Lynch wrote.⁵²

But everything changed when the Cardinals were sold. Veeck was suddenly gripped by an urgent desire to escape St. Louis. He began to work the phones, starting with Browns manager Marty Marion. "Marty, this is a tough day. Anheuser-Busch just bought the ballclub from Fred Saigh," Veeck said. "You know what that means. We can't buck Anheuser-Busch."⁵³ He called Lynch, telling him to find somebody who could negotiate with Perini. Veeck offered to pay as much as $250,000 for the territorial rights. "If it costs more," he said, "you'll have to raise it in Milwaukee."⁵⁴ Then he dialed Gussie Busch, asking if baseball's newest owner wanted to buy Sportsman's Park.

Veeck no longer harbored delusions of vanquishing the Cardinals. A single season of competition with Busch's "full-bodied and well-foamed bankroll," he admitted, would probably consign the Browns to bankruptcy.⁵⁵ He couldn't afford to wait until the following winter, so he decided to flee St. Louis before the season opener on April 14.

The Greater Milwaukee Committee took the lead with Perini. It offered $250,000, then $500,000, only to be turned down both times. The committee's leaders accused Perini of thwarting Milwaukee's big-league ambitions. He denied it. Nobody had formally applied to move there, he said, which was technically true. And he expressed dissatisfaction with the potential landing places for his AAA Brewers, who would be forced to leave town for the Browns.[56] Toledo was a possibility, but Perini found it unimpressive. "We want another AAA franchise as good as Milwaukee," said a Braves official.[57]

The press was oblivious to these machinations. Lynch knew what was happening, yet he wrote nothing in the *Journal*. He functioned as a member of the bargaining team, not a reporter. Other newspapers remained in the dark until March 2, when the inevitable leak occurred. The *Chicago Tribune* breathlessly disclosed that negotiations to move the Browns to Milwaukee "were nearing a decisive stage."[58] The story was incorrect—any discussions had been brief and fruitless—but it triggered hysteria in Boston, St. Louis, and Milwaukee.

Fans in the latter city concluded that Perini was an obstructionist. Mayor Frank Zeidler predicted that the Brewers would face a "hostile citizenry" because of their owner's refusal to accommodate the Browns.[59] The Milwaukee County Board of Supervisors pondered cancellation of the Brewers' County Stadium lease on March 4, the Wisconsin State Senate formally condemned Perini on March 5, and a congressman from Milwaukee proposed a new antitrust investigation of baseball on March 6.[60]

Perini was frantic. "You don't know all the letters, telegrams, and telephone calls I've been getting on this thing from the Midwest," he moaned.[61] His worst nightmare was becoming reality. What if Milwaukee boycotted his Brewers in 1953? What if it spurned his Braves in 1954? It suddenly seemed possible that both teams could lose massive amounts of money in the years ahead.

Veeck realized that Milwaukee was no longer an option for the Browns. He quietly turned his attention to Baltimore, the only other minor-league city with a ballpark of major-league capacity, the renovated Memorial Stadium. He contacted local officials on March 3, then dispatched his lawyers to Maryland four days later to hammer out an agreement. Veeck was still so desirous of privacy that he assigned a code name, "Ashtray," to his hasty negotiations with Mayor Thomas D'Alesandro, Jr., and Jack Dunn, the owner of the AAA Baltimore Orioles.[62]

The secrecy held until March 12, when Baltimore reporters confronted D'Alesandro with rumors of a Browns move. "To say more at this time might jeopardize the whole venture," the mayor warned, but the story broke in the next morning's papers.[63]

This new development intensified Perini's stress. If Baltimore landed a big-league team and Milwaukee was shut out, Wisconsin's fans might never forgive him. He could rule out his plans for a move in 1954. Yet the only real alternative—staying in Boston—appeared less desirable by the day. Interest in the Braves was almost nonexistent. They had sold just 420 season tickets for 1953.[64]

Perini caved to the pressure on March 14, thirty days before the Braves were scheduled to open the season in Cincinnati. He announced at a Bradenton, Florida, press conference that he was moving his team to Milwaukee immediately, though he seemed strangely unhappy. "It's unfortunate in a way," he told reporters. "Maybe Milwaukee isn't a major-league city. I'm sure I don't know, but I feel it will become one."[65] A day's reflection only deepened his melancholy. "Maybe someday I'll be back there," the Massachusetts native mused on March 15. "Maybe someday Tom Yawkey will sell the Red Sox, and I'll buy them."[66]

Each transfer required league approval, which was considered a mere formality. Six affirmative votes were needed in the American League, eight in the National. Veeck had several enemies in the AL, but the profit motive appeared to have trumped animosity.[67] Everybody was tired of losing money in St. Louis. "As far as I know, no club will oppose the shift," said Senators vice president Calvin Griffith.[68] The well-liked Perini seemed a cinch to get the NL's green light.

The Browns were up first. American League owners gathered in Tampa on March 16. Veeck opened the meeting by outlining his problems in St. Louis and stressing his belief that Baltimore was "a more favorable objective." Then he sat down, anticipating a brief debate and a stamp of approval.[69]

"In less than five minutes, I knew that I had been had," Veeck said later.[70] Complaints were raised about the speed of the move and the quality of Baltimore's stadium. The general manager of the destitute Athletics, Art Ehlers, insisted (contrary to his own experience) that it was possible for both clubs to thrive in a two-team city. George Weiss urged caution. "We should not rush into any temporary solution," he said.[71] The discussion dragged on for five hours before ballots were distributed. The final tally was four nays, two ayes, one evasion (no for 1953, but yes for 1954), and one absence (Veeck had been asked to leave the room).[72]

The other owners dispersed, telling reporters that the timing simply hadn't been right. But everybody knew what had really happened. Veeck had been punished for his apostasy. "This was their chance to clobber him good, and they didn't muff it," Shirley Povich wrote in the *Washington Post*.[73] Another dreary, costly season lay ahead in St. Louis. "The only reasons anyone can give for voting against me are either silly or malicious," Veeck said angrily. "I prefer to think they're malicious."[74]

It was a different story on March 18, when everything went smoothly for Perini. "There was no real opposition," a smiling Warren Giles said as he left the conference room.[75] The first transfer of a major-league franchise since 1903 had been approved unanimously. Walter O'Malley, who made the formal motion to allow Perini to leave Boston, predicted that more shifts would be coming. "This is bound to start a chain reaction," he said.[76]

The Braves faced an immediate need to establish an office and sell tickets in their new city. General Manager John Quinn phoned a young staffer, Roland Hemond, and ordered him to catch the next plane to Milwaukee. "I weighed 130 pounds at the time he called me," Hemond said. "Six weeks later, I weighed 118 pounds. I was working around the clock."[77] The enthusiasm in Milwaukee far exceeded expectations. Advance tickets flew out of the box office almost as fast as they could be printed. "People were bringing cash," said Hemond, "and we didn't know where to stuff it."[78]

Eighty thousand people jammed Wisconsin Avenue when the team itself arrived on April 8. The players—the newly minted Milwaukee Braves—were astounded.[79] "They had a parade for us, just like we'd won the World Series," marveled pitcher Bob Buhl.[80] Third baseman Eddie Mathews echoed his shock: "The people were packed three or four deep and screaming and waving like we were heroes or something." Confetti rained down. Church bells rang. Factory whistles shrieked.[81]

Lou Perini had still been plagued with doubt when the Braves broke camp in Florida. Had he betrayed his friends in Boston? Was Milwaukee truly a big-league city? He didn't find peace until he saw the crowd awaiting the Braves. "This is marvelous, just marvelous," he kept saying. "There was never anything like this in Boston."

Perini rode in an open convertible with Frederick Miller of Miller Beer, smiling broadly and waving to his new fans. Miller leaned over at one point. "This could be the beginning of a championship. It's how they start," he shouted above the din. Perini took it all in, the enormous throng, the wild excitement, the sheer adulation. "This could lead to anything," he shouted back.[82]

Headlines: 1953

BRAVES SET NEW ATTENDANCE MARK

The Milwaukee Braves drew a full house of 34,357 to their April 14 home opener at County Stadium, which was still under construction. Center fielder Bill Bruton, normally a singles hitter, rapped a tenth-inning home run to clinch a 3–2 victory. "Bruton's homer, to me, set up all the wondrous years in Milwaukee's baseball story," Braves manager Charlie Grimm later wrote. Milwaukee's 1953 attendance of 1,826,397 would set a new National League record.[83]

MANTLE BLASTS TAPE-MEASURE HOME RUN

Mickey Mantle launched a titanic homer over Washington's left-center-field bleachers on April 17. The ball soared an estimated 565 feet, landing in a nearby backyard. Clark Griffith, who rarely spoke kindly of the younger generation, lauded the twenty-one-year-old Mantle. "No doubt about it," the Senators owner conceded. "That was the longest home run ever hit in the history of baseball."[84]

HOLLOMAN TOSSES NO-HITTER IN FIRST START

Alva Lee "Bobo" Holloman was toiling unhappily in the bullpen for the St. Louis Browns. "When you gonna start me?" he kept asking Manager Marty Marion. His demotion to the minors was imminent, so Marion threw him a bone on May 6. Bobo rose to the occasion, no-hitting the Athletics in the first start of his career. But the magic didn't last. Holloman ended the season with an earned run average of 5.23.[85]

YANKEES MAKE IT FIVE IN A ROW

The Dodgers entered the 1953 World Series with more regular-season wins than the Yankees (105 to 99), as well as a better batting average (.285 to .273) and more homers (208 to 139). "There was nobody on the Dodgers to knock. We respected all those guys," insisted Yankees outfielder Gene Woodling. But New York still managed to lock down its fifth consecutive title, defeating Brooklyn in six games.[86]

13

Disruption

Max Surkont was a New Englander through and through, a native son of Central Falls, Rhode Island, a tiny manufacturing town north of Providence. His great dream—one he shared with millions of American boys—was to pitch in the big leagues. He achieved his goal when the White Sox called him up as a reliever in 1949.

But the really exciting news came a year later. Chicago traded Surkont to the Braves, who immediately inserted him into the starting rotation. He would spend the next three seasons on the mound in Boston, just a forty-five-mile drive from his hometown.

Lou Perini disrupted this idyll with his abrupt decision to relocate the franchise. Surkont suddenly found himself in the heart of the Midwest, more than a thousand miles from home. He was apprehensive at first, but his new workplace won him over with its enthusiasm. "Boston has always meant home for me," he said. "But for baseball, it can't compare with Milwaukee. Every day is Christmas for us. Milwaukee is out of this world."[1]

The Boston Braves drew only two crowds larger than 10,000 in their terminal season. The Milwaukee Braves topped 30,000 on thirty-seven occasions in 1953. Fans flocked to County Stadium from all points of Wisconsin, many arriving on specially scheduled trains.[2] Mayor Frank Zeidler, an undemonstrative man, was as excited as his constituents. "Milwaukee has never had as much pure fun as it is having this summer," he said with a smile. An out-of-town reporter asked why the city had responded to the Braves with such passion. Zeidler credited baseball's ability to elevate an entire community to major-league status. "Our voice has not been heard in the land," he said. "This is a means of letting people know we exist."[3]

That was one explanation, but there were others. Perini's hard-earned knowledge of TV's power was a prominent factor. "The Milwaukee Braves are not going to permit the televising of their at-home games," he informed Walter O'Malley at the start of the season. "And in view of our experience in Boston, I doubt very much if we would even consider the televising back to Milwaukee of our games when we are away from home."[4] There was only one way to see the Braves—buying a ticket at the County Stadium box office.

It didn't hurt that Perini's team, anchored by young slugger Eddie Mathews and veteran pitcher Warren Spahn, improved with unexpected swiftness. The Braves had stumbled to seventh place in 1952, but they led the National League as late as June 27, 1953, and finished second to Brooklyn. "O, lucky Milwaukee, to win a pennant contender right off the bat," wailed *Boston Globe* columnist Harold Kaese.[5] But Perini thought the city itself deserved credit. "The enthusiasm of the ball fans here in

The Braves set a National League record by drawing 1,826,397 fans in 1953, their first season in Milwaukee County Stadium. "Every game is like a World Series game," marveled Lou Perini [Wisconsin Historical Society].

Milwaukee has really done something for the ballclub," he said. "Every game is like a World Series game."[6]

He showed his appreciation by raising his own rent. The Braves' contract with Milwaukee County stipulated an annual payment of one thousand dollars for use of the ballpark, but Perini sent a check for twenty-five thousand in June 1953. He imposed another voluntary hike a year later, paying a quarter of a million dollars. The county gratefully responded by expanding the stadium to forty-three thousand seats.[7]

Milwaukee's success story received coast-to-coast media coverage, in part because it ran counter to industry trends. The Braves' attendance soared at an incomprehensible rate—549 percent—from Boston's final count of 281,278 to a record-setting sum of 1,826,397. But thirteen of the other fifteen clubs suffered year-to-year declines. Major-league attendance dropped by 1.7 percent between 1952 and 1953. If Milwaukee was factored out of the equation, the decline accelerated to a frightening 12.5 percent.[8]

Other teams—and other cities without teams—took notice. "Ever since the Braves moved to Milwaukee, people in minor-league cities that are hoping for a major-league team have written and said they want the Dodgers," O'Malley revealed in August 1953. He dismissed this flurry of interest—"it isn't to be taken seriously"—though he admitted that some of the nation's biggest cities had contacted him. "Sure, Los Angeles wants the Dodgers," he said. "But I want them in Brooklyn."[9]

Kansas City also entered the hunt. Its city council voted in August to take steps to upgrade its minor-league ballpark to big-league standards. Its first target was the logical one, the team that so many cities coveted because of its obvious availability, the St. Louis Browns.[10]

Bill Veeck had surprised almost everybody by attending the traditional preseason luncheon honoring St. Louis's two ballclubs. It was an even greater surprise when he offered to speak, telling his audience that the Browns would be greatly improved in 1953 because of several offseason moves to acquire new players. "But," he added, "not all the moves we would have liked to make."[11] The crowd applauded his courage, though not his intentions. Fans boycotted Sportsman's Park as the Browns settled in for what Veeck called "a prison sentence, compliments of the American League."[12]

Veeck no longer owned the aging ballpark. Gussie Busch bought it for eight hundred thousand dollars in early April. His first impulse was to rechristen it as Budweiser Stadium in honor of Anheuser-Busch's signature product, but cooler heads convinced him that a blatantly commercial name would be inappropriate. So it became Busch Memorial Stadium.[13]

The Browns adopted a bunker mentality, abandoning their aggressive promotional strategy. Veeck no longer made public appearances. His second-in-command, Rudie Schaffer, stopped cajoling fans to come out to the park.[14] "We sold more tickets accidentally in Cleveland than we do by knocking them on the head here," Schaffer groused.[15] The Browns drew fewer than 3,000 people to eighteen home dates, bottoming out at 980 for an August 13 game with the Tigers. "It's a good thing I brought my car along," Veeck said on one such occasion. "I can drive all these folks home after the game."[16]

The Browns kept losing—they would finish in last place—and the red ink kept flowing. The team ran a 1953 deficit of $707,000 (the 2020 equivalent of $6.8 million).[17] "It was kind of a disastrous year," recalled Marty Marion. "You weren't winning. You had no support. Hell, it was just horrible."[18]

The sole goal was to survive the season. Perini's massive success had benefited everybody in the National League. Visiting teams were leaving Milwaukee with sizable box-office checks. The American League watched with envy, inspiring Veeck to push for reconsideration of his transfer request.[19] He stayed in touch with Baltimore officials, meeting on several occasions with Thomas D'Alesandro. The mayor sailed to London on the *Queen Mary* in June. Awaiting him in his cabin was a cryptic telegram from Veeck. "Bon voyage," it said. "Let nothing worry you from this end."[20]

The situation in St. Louis became so dire that the league acquiesced, promising another vote in late September, but only if Veeck thoroughly researched the possibilities and presented a report to a four-man committee. He caught a flight to California in midsummer, the start of a coast-to-coast fact-finding tour.[21] "Los Angeles is a major-league city in every respect," he said at his first stop. "But there appears to be no organized civic campaign for big-league baseball, not like there is in Baltimore."[22]

That remained the theme as he headed on to San Francisco, Kansas City, Minneapolis, and Toronto, and contacted officials in Houston and Montreal by phone. Veeck acknowledged each community's strengths, but his original commitment did not waver. "The only city we're really going to present is Baltimore," he said.[23] The American League committee listened to his report on September 16 and voted to recommend relocation of the Browns. A subdued Veeck offered only two words to waiting reporters—"I'm happy"—but his relief was evident. He had every reason to believe that the league's owners would approve his shift before the end of the month.[24]

* * *

Walter O'Malley was of two minds about Milwaukee. He was greatly impressed by the Braves' prosperity, which confirmed his belief that baseball could generate sizable profits, yet he would have been happier if the money had been his. Milwaukee drew 663,000 more fans than Brooklyn in 1953. Nine of the Dodgers' eleven games at County Stadium attracted crowds larger than thirty thousand. Only six of their home dates in Brooklyn reached that threshold the entire season.[25]

O'Malley became obsessed with Lou Perini's success, which caused him to view the future through an apocalyptic lens. "If that disparity between the two best draws in the league, Milwaukee and Brooklyn, were permitted to continue," he later explained, "it would be only a question of two, three, four, or five years before Milwaukee would be the Yankees of the National League and Brooklyn would be the Washington."[26]

O'Malley's vision was greatly exaggerated—the Dodgers had just won their fourth NL pennant in seven years—though he did have cause for concern.[27] It was true, on the one hand, that a lucrative television contract guaranteed the team an annual profit. "We were in the black before opening day, but we never told that to anybody," laughed Buzzie Bavasi. "You don't exactly advertise a gold strike, do you?"[28] But ticket revenue remained vitally important to the bottom line—the key to the fortune that O'Malley desired—and sales were steadily declining.

Brooklyn fans were mythologized as paragons of loyalty. "A lioness defending her young is a mild-mannered tabby compared to a Brooklynite defending his beloved Dodgers," Arthur Daley gushed in the *New York Times* in 1952.[29] But the legend simply wasn't true. The Dodgers won 662 games from 1947 through 1953–that was 62 more than any other National League club—yet their annual attendance plummeted 36 percent during that span. The memory of those empty seats at the 1952 World Series would never fade.

O'Malley had been sounding the alarm for years, even before the Braves struck it rich. He said this in 1951: "We've got to get the real customers back, the little fellows who really support baseball."[30] And 1952: "The fans quit on us. It is my job to win them back."[31] And 1953: "What the Brooklyn club needs most for 1953 is fans."[32]

The solution, he had always believed, was a new stadium. O'Malley did not mask his disdain for Ebbets Field: "Did you ever ask yourself why, in an electronic age, we play our games in a horse-and-buggy park?"[33] He commissioned a renowned industrial designer, Norman Bel Geddes, to devise a new facility in 1952. The renderings were startlingly futuristic. Bel Geddes envisioned a fifty-two-thousand-seat stadium with a retractable roof, artificial grass, and a seven-thousand-car garage. There was nothing like it anywhere in the world.[34]

But O'Malley lacked two essential ingredients for his dream stadium—land and money. He kept Bel Geddes's sketches in a desk drawer for more than a year, until Perini's success imparted a new sense of urgency. Reporters were summoned to the Dodgers' offices on December 10, 1953. "I am certain that we will have a new stadium within the next five years," O'Malley announced. "The Dodgers will own it, but it will be constructed to accommodate other enterprises." He said he had three sites in mind, making it sound as if work could begin as soon as he chose one.[35]

It wouldn't be that easy. O'Malley was sadly aware of the history of his current ballpark. Charlie Ebbets had labored for nearly four years to assemble the necessary land, even creating a shell corporation to purchase lots along Bedford Avenue. But word leaked out, and several property owners jacked up their prices before Ebbets broke ground in 1912. O'Malley resolved to avoid a corresponding waste of time and money. He intended to build his stadium with private funds, but he hoped to persuade a government agency to condemn the desired site, delivering it to the Dodgers as a unified parcel.[36]

The first steps toward this goal had been taken in great secrecy six months prior to the press conference. O'Malley approached New York's development czar, Robert Moses, in June 1953. "My problem is to get a new ballpark—one well located and with ample parking accommodations," he wrote. "This is a must if we are to keep our franchise in Brooklyn."[37] O'Malley's mentor, George McLaughlin, was a Moses ally, so the Dodgers owner contacted him, too. "We could not acquire land suitably located without the condemnation assistance of the government. Title I of the Federal Housing Act of 1949 would probably have to be used," O'Malley wrote.[38]

The answers were swiftly—and surprisingly—negative. McLaughlin, who had been instrumental in advancing O'Malley's career, now seemed reluctant to get involved. "I am not inclined to believe that Bob will go along with the idea," he jotted back.[39] Moses soon confirmed that impression, stressing that Title I was intended for slum clearance, not stadium construction.[40] O'Malley, ever the optimist, refused to be dissuaded. He wrote Moses again in October, expressing hope that "a way will be found for a new Dodger stadium."[41] Moses shut the door as emphatically as possible. "Neither the city nor any existing public agency," he replied, "has any power or right to acquire by eminent domain property for the purposes you outline." He suggested that O'Malley should follow Charlie Ebbets's lead and enter the real-estate market himself.[42]

A lesser man might have been discouraged, but O'Malley simply turned up the heat. He called his December press conference, where he stressed the need for a new stadium by 1958. And he infused his public statements and private correspondence with a sense of anxiety previously lacking. "We cannot long continue to operate in our present stadium," he wrote darkly to Frank Schroth, the publisher of the *Brooklyn Eagle*, in February 1954. "If I appear to be unreasonable, intemperate, or impatient, forgive me, but I cannot wait much longer. We have been on this project since 1947."[43] That was an exaggeration—O'Malley had gotten serious about his stadium project only during the past year or two—but there was no mistaking his desperation for a solution.

Weak box-office numbers dialed up the pressure even further. Attendance at Ebbets Field declined another 12 percent in 1954, barely topping a million at 1,020,531, the team's lowest count since World War II. A September 16 home date with the Reds attracted just 522 people, and a game against the Pirates eight days later drew only 751.[44]

Dave Anderson, a beat writer for the *Brooklyn Eagle*, was unable to reconcile this apathy with the borough's reputation for baseball fanaticism. The Dodgers finished a strong second in 1954, just five games behind the Giants, yet they drew fewer than seven thousand fans to fifteen home games. The baffled Anderson posed a blunt question to his readers: "Where is everybody?"[45]

* * *

The St. Louis Browns took the field on September 27, 1953, for what was billed as their farewell appearance. Only 3,174 fans wandered into Busch Memorial Stadium to watch. The Browns squandered an early lead over the White Sox, stretching the meaningless game into extra innings. Plate umpire Art Passarella called for a fresh batch of balls, only to be informed that the financially strapped team didn't have any left.[46] "The era of the Browns came to an end in St. Louis with nicked and dirty baseballs flying around," Bill Veeck recalled.[47] The symbolism wasn't lost on anyone. Chicago won in eleven innings, handing the Browns their one hundredth defeat of the season.

Not that it mattered. American League owners were meeting that very afternoon in New York, and Veeck fully expected them to stamp his passport for Baltimore this time, most likely by a unanimous vote. "The reasons assigned by the league in turning down Veeck's [March] request to pull out of St. Louis have all been removed," that morning's *Baltimore Sun* confidently reported.[48]

It would not be a short meeting. The league had decided to prove to Manny Celler and other critics that it was open to geographic expansion, so it invited groups from Kansas City, Los Angeles, Minneapolis, Montreal, and San Francisco to make presentations. They held forth for a couple of hours, stressing their immediate viability as big-league markets. The question at hand—the future of the Browns—wasn't addressed until late afternoon.[49]

Veeck was stunned when the old criticisms of Baltimore were rehashed at great length. Yankees co-owner Del Webb, whose connections to California were strong, insisted that the league could do better. "I am a Westerner," he said. "Therefore, I know better than any of the other owners what a great potential Los Angeles and San Francisco have."[50] Webb proposed a thirty-day delay to allow a study of alternative sites. Veeck refused, demanding a decision within twenty-four hours. Secret ballots were distributed shortly before 10 p.m.

A grinning Webb strode from the conference room after the tally. "The vote was four to four," he announced to the waiting reporters. "The application was denied."[51] Veeck straggled out a few minutes later, struggling to control his anger, anguish, and disbelief. "I have no plans to bring up the question of a shift again," he said. "What's the use?"[52]

But something had to be done. The Browns were teetering on the verge of bankruptcy. Veeck buttonholed other owners that evening, desperately seeking a way out. He even spoke briefly with the other owner of the Yankees, Dan Topping, who (as Veeck told it) freely admitted a conspiracy. "We're going to keep you in St. Louis and bankrupt you. Then we'll decide where the franchise is going to go," Topping supposedly said.[53]

The owners reconvened for emergency meetings the next two days, with Webb pushing for Los Angeles behind closed doors. "I have a bona fide offer for this franchise from a substantial man," he declared, eventually revealing that his mystery investor was Howard Hughes.[54] But no groundwork had been done for a move to California, no suitable stadium existed in Los Angeles, and nobody had contacted Phil

Wrigley, who held the city's territorial rights. Webb finally bowed to reality, asking his colleagues to approve a face-saving resolution that advocated the eventual expansion of the American League to ten clubs, which they did.[55]

The battle was essentially over. Veeck might have taken the league to court, but he lacked the time and money. He raised the white flag instead, hastily arranging a sale to Clarence Miles, the president of the Maryland Bar Association. Miles's group paid $2,475,000 for the Browns (roughly $23.8 million in 2020 money), and the league conveniently forgot its objections to Baltimore. The team's shift was approved unanimously.[56] "I am selling against my own desire," Veeck told the other owners. "Obviously, though, you want to get rid of me. All right, you have succeeded."[57] He made a small profit on the sale, but it couldn't outweigh the embarrassment the St. Louis debacle had caused. "What I take out isn't important." he told reporters. "The fact that I failed in this assignment, lost prestige as well, is important."[58]

The Browns, to no one's surprise, were renamed the Baltimore Orioles. Their new owner was Veeck's polar opposite, a wealthy lawyer whose patrician style seemed better suited for private clubs than public ballparks.[59] But Miles showed an unexpected flair for dramatic announcements. He pledged to spend "as much as we can" to make the Orioles an immediate contender, and he vowed to draw more than two million fans to Memorial Stadium in 1954.[60] The team's offseason ticket drive adopted an audacious slogan: "Let's Beat Milwaukee!"[61]

The goal would not be fulfilled. The Braves played in a brand new facility, but the Orioles were moving into thirty-two-year-old Memorial Stadium, which was undergoing a massive renovation. Hedges delineated the center-field boundary; there wouldn't even be a fence until June 1954.[62] Baltimore announcer Chuck Thompson spoke fondly of the park, though even he acknowledged major faults like "those huge concrete pillars that blocked the sight lines of so many fans."[63]

The loyalties of those fans were clearly divided. The National Football League had granted a new franchise to Baltimore in 1953, and the Colts proved to be unexpectedly popular, outdrawing six of the eleven established teams. "Baltimore was basically a football town," conceded third baseman Brooks Robinson, who would join the Orioles later in the decade.[64] The inferiority of the city's new baseball team didn't help matters. Milwaukee had embraced an instant contender, but Baltimore was saddled with a horrible club that finished fifty-seven games out of first place. "The trouble is that we were still the St. Louis Browns, although Baltimore was written on our uniforms," laughed pitcher Bob Turley.[65]

The Orioles' inaugural season could be interpreted in different ways, depending on the yardstick one chose. Baltimore welcomed 1,060,910 fans, a total that exceeded the Browns' all-time record (712,918 in 1922) and surpassed nine of the other fifteen big-league teams in 1954. But the turnout wasn't as strong as universally expected, falling 42 percent short of Milwaukee's performance the year before.[66]

"Baltimore's enthusiasm for its new baseball team has been, while deeply felt, more muted than that of Milwaukee," wrote Gilbert Millstein in the *New York Times*.[67] The Braves' wild success had inspired the owners to view franchise shifts as the ultimate remedy for the sport's ills, a panacea for any team in desperate financial straits. The Orioles' experience, however, was causing them to think again.

14

Toolson

The early 1950s challenged the equilibrium of major-league baseball in several ways, far beyond the uncertainty about franchise relocation. The labor woes that had troubled owners during the previous decade were still unresolved—and getting worse.

Teams continued to pay large bonuses to callow prospects. Branch Rickey's nightmare came to life on January 31, 1950, when the Pirates signed an eighteen-year-old pitcher, Paul Pettit, for one hundred thousand dollars, making him the first six-figure bonus baby.[1] The nation let out a collective gasp, though Pittsburgh general manager Roy Hamey played it cool. "We don't mind paying out big money if we feel we're getting value received," he said. "We've been told this boy can't miss."[2]

The numbers certainly predicted success. Pettit struck out an average of 15.5 batters per 9 innings in his California high-school league, once whiffing 27 in a 12-inning game. His blazing fastball produced six no-hitters. Rickey wasn't involved in Pettit's signing—the Mahatma was still running the Dodgers at the time—but they would become fellow employees of the Pirates organization before the end of the year. "There hasn't been a schoolboy pitcher like him for a long time," Rickey said excitedly. "He's the Bob Feller type, definitely. And maybe this time next year, a lot of people will know it."[3]

Pettit was assigned to the Pirates' farm club in New Orleans, where he remembered throwing 155 pitches in his first start. "I contracted a sore arm right away," he said, "and I wound up pitching with a bad arm all year."[4] Pettit was invited to spring training with the big-league club the following season, and Pittsburgh's best hitters eagerly awaited the chance to step in against the prodigy. "When he finally took the mound, everybody watched and waited," Ralph Kiner remembered. "Nothing happened. He didn't have anything on the ball." Pettit would pitch only twelve major-league games before giving up his dream.[5]

His story wasn't unusual. Bonus babies frequently failed to deliver. A few teams consequently kept their checkbooks closed—the parsimonious Athletics had a rule against any bonus larger than $150—though most clubs willingly defied the odds in their pursuit of the next great star. The only way to restrain their undisciplined spending was to legislate against it, which is precisely what the owners thought they had done in 1946. If a prospect received a bonus larger than six thousand dollars, his team was required to promote him to the big leagues or cut him loose after one season in the minors. The rule was designed to force a club to think twice before writing a bonus check. But the theory did not work in reality, as Pettit's case proved.[6]

A covey of disgusted owners revoked the ineffectual rule in December 1950, and then things truly got crazy. The chief instigator was Tom Yawkey, who started tossing money at young ballplayers, a mania that reached its peak in June 1952. The Red Sox owner spent $450,000 on prospects that month, capped by six-figure payouts to outfielder Marty Keough and pitcher Frank Baumann. The latter was a St. Louis phenom who tossed four no-hitters, including a pair of perfect games, in the 1952 Missouri high-school tournament.[7] Bill Veeck, then running the Browns, marveled that Baumann could "throw it past little kids, big kids, and also grown men."[8] But Veeck didn't have the money to sign the hometown hero, certainly not the $125,000 that Yawkey paid.

New regulations were inevitable. The owners agreed in December 1952 to impose a bonus barrier of four thousand dollars. Any prospect who crossed that financial threshold would be required to spend his first two seasons on the signing club's big-league roster.[9]

It was difficult to imagine that most teams would willingly fill their dugouts with inexperienced, unproductive teenagers, but the bonus signings continued.[10] Infielder Billy Consolo hooked up with the Red Sox for sixty thousand dollars in 1953. "I wish I could be sent out to the minors," he said, but a rule was a rule.[11] He sat on the bench. So did eighteen-year-old pitcher Tommy Qualters, who received forty thousand from the Phillies. He pitched one-third of an inning during the entire 1953 season, yielding six runs. "I had no business being in the major leagues," he later admitted.[12]

There were rare exceptions. Al Kaline joined the Tigers directly from high school in 1953, becoming the regular right fielder a year later. He would win the American League batting title in 1955 at age twenty. Third baseman Harmon Killebrew slowly evolved into a slugger for the Senators.[13] And Brooklyn signed a promising pitcher in 1954 after a workout that announcer Vin Scully happened to observe. "I never thought, wow, you're unbelievable. Nothing like that at all," Scully recalled.[14] But the Dodgers offered Sandy Koufax a bonus, anyway.

Success did not come easily to the future Hall of Famer. Koufax felt out of place on Brooklyn's veteran roster—"I am wearing the uniform, but I am contributing nothing"—and he would continue to struggle for six long years, posting a 36–40 record with an earned run average of 4.10 between 1955 and 1960.[15] Pirates executive Joe L. Brown considered him to be a victim of the bonus rule. "Had Koufax gone out where he could have gotten in 150 to 200 innings in minor-league competition," said Brown, "he probably would have been ready at least three years before he was to take his rightful place as a great pitcher."[16]

* * *

The players had won a rare concession when management established a pension fund in 1946. But theirs was no Cadillac plan. The payment structure was decidedly modest. A player who spent five years in the majors was slated to receive fifty dollars per month upon turning fifty. Such a sum was equal to $660 in 2020.

Postwar inflation greatly reduced the payout. The purchasing power of $50 shrank 27 percent between 1946 and 1953, slipping to the 2020 equivalent of $481 per month. Representatives elected by the players in both leagues—Allie Reynolds in the AL, Ralph Kiner in the NL—asked for an increase to redress the balance. They proposed a minimum monthly pension of eighty dollars, with payments beginning at age forty-five.[17] They also announced the hiring of a New York lawyer, J. Norman

Lewis, to help them get what they wanted. "After all," said Kiner, "we're just ballplayers and need some advice."[18]

The baseball establishment reacted with fury. It was hard to decide which was worse—players asking for more money or players hiring an outsider to represent their interests. What was next, a full-blown union? Lewis tried to quell the controversy. "There is absolutely no contemplation of a union," he told reporters. "The players don't want it, and I don't advise it."[19]

It didn't matter. Several owners were so enraged by September 1953 that they initiated private discussions about killing the pension plan. Ford Frick urged them to think deeply before acting, and they reluctantly delayed final action. The commissioner was uncommonly energetic as he sought a solution in the ensuing months, even summoning player representatives from all sixteen teams to a joint meeting in Atlanta in early December. But his activity went for naught. Reynolds and Kiner arrived at Frick's suite a few minutes early and requested permission to bring their lawyer to the talks. Frick refused, and the player reps voted to leave town immediately.[20]

That gave the owners the opening they sought. Walter O'Malley submitted a resolution on December 9 to investigate elimination of the pension fund, and his fellow owners gave their blessing. National League president Warren Giles made the announcement. The owners wanted to maintain the pension system, he said, "but the excessive demands by the players' representatives and their attorney have compelled the major-league clubs to consider the possible necessity of terminating the plan." Two executives—Pittsburgh's John Galbreath and Cleveland's Hank Greenberg—were deputized to work out a compromise if possible, but otherwise to make the necessary preparations for a shutdown.[21]

The forces of moderation prevailed by February 1954. Galbreath and Greenberg enjoyed good relationships with their workers—Greenberg was only six years removed from being a player himself—and they talked easily with Kiner, Reynolds, and even Lewis. Both sides agreed to stabilize the pension plan by providing a dedicated revenue source, setting aside 60 percent of the radio and TV proceeds from the World Series and the broadcasting and gate receipts from the All-Star Game. Discussion of a benefit hike was delayed until 1956, when a new television contract would be negotiated. Lewis predicted that the monthly payment for experienced players would exceed three hundred dollars.[22] (He was too optimistic. The deal in February 1957 would stipulate monthly payments ranging from $88 for 5 years of service up to $275 for 20 years.)[23]

The true importance of the pension crisis was not the settlement that was reached, but the seed that was planted. The players had stood up to the commissioner by refusing to attend his meeting without their lawyer, and they believed their solidarity had helped to achieve a deal. "It is a joke to me now to hear baseball officials take credit for the new pension plan," Indians fireballer Bob Feller would say in 1957. "We got it because of our own efforts in standing up to the owners for our rights."[24]

The next logical step was creation of a permanent organization, the Major League Baseball Players Association, which was founded by player representatives at a lengthy meeting during the 1954 All-Star break in Cleveland.[25] The *Sporting News* immediately detected "the framework for a union," but the mild-mannered Lewis called it a fraternal organization and an information clearinghouse.[26] "I'd prefer to think of it as a corporation, with the four hundred big-league players as the stockholders," he said.²⁷ The group wouldn't get around to electing a president until 1956. The militant Feller was chosen, but he also dismissed any talk of a union. "You cannot carry collective bargaining into baseball," he said.²⁸

Lewis had been retained as the group's legal counsel, so it fell to him to handle day-to-day operations. His biggest problem was simply getting anybody on the management side to pay attention, as he once explained to Emanuel Celler's subcommittee:

> **CELLER:** Don't you have periodic meetings with the owners?
> **LEWIS:** I found it rather difficult to arrange for those periodic meetings with the owners.
> **CELLER:** What is the difficulty?
> **LEWIS:** The difficulty is that they aren't, shall we say, cordial about arranging these meetings.

Julius Singman, the subcommittee's assistant counsel, leaned into the microphone with a follow-up question. "You mean they are not anxious to meet with the baseball player representatives?" he asked. Lewis smiled in response. "Well," he said, "they are not anxious to meet with *me*."²⁹

* * *

Baseball's overriding priority in the field of labor relations—more important than reducing bonuses or discouraging a union—was to protect the reserve clause. "Baseball can't exist without the reserve clause," barked Clark Griffith, and almost everybody in the game agreed.³⁰

Danny Gardella had caused them a few sleepless nights before succumbing to the lure of a sixty-thousand-dollar settlement in 1949. And Manny Celler had given them a scare in 1951 and 1952 before recommending congressional inaction. But baseball's leaders weren't out of the woods, as they well knew.

They had two reasons for concern. The first was rarely discussed, and then only behind closed doors. The titans of the sport, dating all the way back to Kenesaw Mountain Landis, stood foursquare behind the reserve clause in public, yet doubted its legality in private. "The judge, being a lawyer, knew that certain things we were doing in baseball were pretty doubtful, legally," Ford Frick conceded in retirement.³¹ Landis's right-hand man, Leslie O'Connor, confirmed his boss's fear of a judicial showdown. "Judge Landis and I," he said, "fought for twenty-four years to keep baseball out of the courts."³²

Branch Rickey, himself a lawyer, had alluded to this undercurrent of panic while testifying before Celler's subcommittee. Rickey acknowledged the possibility of "harmless illegality about the reserve clause," but suggested that any abnormality could be smoothed away. "If our basic and indispensable rules are technically illegal," he said, "then, for our country's sake, surely our Congress will wish to do something about it."³³

But Celler had opted to do nothing, relying on the judicial system to fill the void, which was the second reason for concern. The legal challenges filed by Earl Toolson and Jack Corbett in 1951 had been slowly progressing for two years, apparently destined for the highest court of all. "Organized baseball is sitting on a keg of dynamite," Celler noted with a touch of glee. "The impending Supreme Court cases will spell rule or ruin for baseball."³⁴

Toolson and Corbett were attacking the reserve clause from different angles—the former as a disgruntled Yankees farmhand, the latter as a minor-league club owner—but their contentions were identical. They insisted that the clause illegally restrained trade and restricted freedom of choice by binding a player to a single big-league organization. The same charge was leveled by another pair of minor leaguers in lawsuits of their own. Jim Prendergast had filed in the spring of 1951, about the same time as Toolson and Corbett, and Walter Kowalski had submitted his paperwork shortly thereafter.[35]

District and appellate courts ruled against the plaintiffs in all four cases, exhibiting a reluctance to overturn the antitrust exemption granted by Oliver Wendell Holmes in 1922. "If the Supreme Court was in error in its former opinion, or changed conditions warrant a different approach, the Supreme Court is the place to correct the error," wrote the district judge in Toolson's trial.[36] The final decision could be made nowhere else but Washington.

The Supreme Court agreed to hear three of the reserve-clause cases on October 13 and 14, 1953, consolidating them under the name of *Toolson v. New York Yankees Inc.* (Prendergast's lawsuit had stalled in a lower court, so he was excluded.) The thirty-one-year-old Toolson would go down in history as the primary plaintiff, with his surname serving as the shorthand reference to all three suits. He was to be represented by a young lawyer, Howard Parke, who had been born on May 29, 1922, the very day that Justice Holmes issued his fateful decision in the *Federal Baseball* case. Kowalski's attorney was Frederic Johnson, who had been awaiting this moment since acquiring Danny Gardella as a client six years earlier.[37]

Twenty-six-year-old Bowie Kuhn, destined to become commissioner in 1969, was a junior member of the legal team defending the reserve clause. "I worked on the *Toolson* case during its progress through the courts, counting myself fortunate to

Earl Toolson was a Yankees farmhand who filed a legal challenge against the reserve clause in 1951. "Organized baseball is sitting on a keg of dynamite," Emanuel Celler said gleefully as Toolson's case wound its way to the Supreme Court [**National Baseball Hall of Fame and Museum**].

be dealing with a matter of such critical importance to the game," he recalled.[38] Another young man bound for fame, future Chief Justice William Rehnquist, became entwined in the case as a law clerk for Justice Robert Jackson. Rehnquist advised his boss to reject Toolson's argument. "I feel instinctively that baseball, like other sports, is [unique], and not suitably regulated by a bunch of lawyers," he wrote.[39]

Each plaintiff was allocated an hour before the court, with Toolson in the leadoff spot. Parke started boldly, calling "every phase of baseball a monopoly" and charging that "men were treated like automobiles" under the reserve clause. But he faltered a bit when Justice Jackson interrupted:

> JACKSON: In other words, we have no way to decide this case but to override that Holmes decision?
> PARKE: Well, I must say I honestly believe it should be overruled. But, of course, I don't like to say that.
> JACKSON (SMILING): Oh, things like that happen around here all the time.[40]

Baseball officials watched glumly as the familiar arguments were batted back and forth. They sensed that the case was slipping away, that a costly era of free agency might soon be upon them. Warren Giles dispatched a cautionary memo to National League owners after attending the Supreme Court sessions. "I am not too optimistic about the decision, which is expected to be rendered soon," he warned. "The questions propounded by members of the court indicated that some of them were not sympathetic to our cause."[41]

The ruling came more rapidly than anybody expected, and the result was equally surprising. The court rejected the claims of Toolson, Corbett, and Kowalski on November 9 by a vote of seven to two.[42] Chief Justice Earl Warren read the majority decision in open court. "If there are evils in this field which now warrant application to it of the antitrust laws, it should be by legislation," he intoned.[43] Celler's subcommittee had kicked the issue to the Supreme Court, and the court was now kicking it back. The antitrust exemption and reserve clause would remain in effect.

Baseball officials were publicly ecstatic about the *Toolson* ruling. "Until this decision, baseball was in a fog of uncertainty," Ford Frick told reporters. "From now on, the responsibility is ours of modernizing baseball—of stepping from the past into the changing present."[44]

But the positive glow would fade in the months and years ahead, as the commissioner came to realize that *Toolson* had not dissipated the fog at all. Joseph O'Mahoney, a senator from Wyoming, once assured him that the Supreme Court's ruling had solved baseball's problems. "But *Toolson* can also be reversed, sir," Frick shot back.[45] He sounded a similar note when a Senate counsel, Paul Rand Dixon, suggested that *Toolson* "says you can do whatever you want to." Frick reared back. "Oh, no. It doesn't," he replied.[46]

The commissioner faced a conundrum. He could ask Congress to embed the antitrust exemption in a federal statute, permanently legalizing the reserve clause. But he had no hope of success without Manny Celler's support, and the Brooklyn congressman seemed to be in an ornery mood. Celler had blasted an appellate court's decision to uphold the exemption "as wrong as a two-foot yardstick."[47] If Congress turned Frick down, there was a danger that the courts might finally swoop in and declare the reserve clause unconstitutional. It seemed safer to do nothing for the time being, which is precisely what he did.

A growing number of players, however, were not satisfied with the status quo. They had experienced a modest victory in the pension crisis, and they were starting to dream of free agency. "I believe that after five, six years or so, that a player should have the right to express himself and perhaps go to some other club," Jackie Robinson proposed.[48]

Stan Musial would suggest much the same thing in 1957. "Limiting the reserve option to ten years," he said, "might eliminate outside criticism that baseball is bondage." Such a modification would undoubtedly push salaries higher, though Musial had no doubt the money was available. He reminded reporters that Gussie Busch had recently offered the Cubs five hundred thousand dollars in exchange for star shortstop Ernie Banks.

Musial grinned. "The Cubs turned down the offer because they couldn't play cash at short," he said. "But what do you think would have happened if there was no reserve clause, and if [Busch] could have offered that half-million to Banks himself?" The owners shuddered to imagine.[49]

Headlines: 1954

AARON MAKES PROMISING DEBUT FOR BRAVES

Charlie Grimm liked almost everything about twenty-year-old Milwaukee prospect Henry Aaron, except his glovework. "As a second baseman, Aaron is a very good hitter," the Braves manager laughed. "But we'll find a place for that bat." He converted the rookie into an outfielder. Aaron swatted the first homer of his career on April 23 against the Cardinals. Another 754 would follow.[50]

INDIANS SET TORRID PACE TO WIN AL TITLE

Nobody in 1954 could match the Indians' pitching depth. Their staff posted an earned run average of 2.78, the lowest ERA for any team in a decade. Cleveland secured its one hundredth victory on September 9—the first American League club to reach triple digits since the 1946 Red Sox—and finished with a 111–43 record, a comfortable eight games ahead of the second-place Yankees.[51]

GIANTS PULL SURPRISING WORLD SERIES SWEEP

The Indians entered the World Series as prohibitive favorites, but the Giants had Willie Mays, the National League's Most Valuable Player with a .345 average and forty-one homers. "He's the spark," said New York manager Leo Durocher. Mays repaid his faith with a sensational over-the-shoulder grab of a Vic Wertz blast in Game One, immortalized as one of the greatest catches of all time. The Giants went on to sweep the Indians.[52]

Orioles, Yankees swing biggest trade ever

Dour, intense Paul Richards had revived the moribund White Sox during a four-year stint as manager, inspiring the lowly Orioles to lure him away in mid–September. Richards engineered a seventeen-player trade with the Yankees on November 17, the biggest transaction in major-league history. "We got the best of it, as time will prove," he crowed. But New York actually prevailed, receiving a pair of future World Series MVPs from Baltimore, Don Larsen and Bob Turley.[53]

15

Philadelphia

Brooklyn's drive for a third straight National League pennant fell short in the end, but the Dodgers remained strongly competitive in 1954. They blasted 186 home runs (tied with the Giants for the major-league lead), batted .270 (better than every team but the Cardinals), and drew 634 walks (tops in the NL). Their fearsome attack displayed its full potency during an August 29 doubleheader in Milwaukee, which Brooklyn swept by the lopsided scores of 12–4 and 11–4.

But Walter O'Malley was more interested in a different pair of numbers: 45,922 and 1,841,666. The first was the capacity crowd at County Stadium on that Sunday afternoon; the second was the Braves' attendance for the year to date, a new National League record. Milwaukee would push the mark to 2,131,388 by the end of the season, more than doubling Brooklyn's total of 1,020,531.

This chasm would persist in coming years, simultaneously angering O'Malley and mystifying him. The Braves would attract 184 home crowds in excess of 30,000 fans between 1953 and 1957, while the Dodgers would draw only 18.[1] O'Malley once asked Lou Perini to explain his unprecedented success. "There's no secret formula," the Milwaukee owner replied. "It's just the terrific enthusiasm."[2]

It was more than that, of course. Novelty was a factor, as was the young, exciting roster that the Braves had assembled. Perini's strict policy against the use of television also boosted attendance. But it was true that no special promotions were required to motivate the enormous crowds that swarmed to County Stadium. The Braves simply had to print the tickets, open the turnstiles, and count their money.

The worries that had plagued Perini in the spring of 1953—"maybe Milwaukee isn't a major-league city"—were long forgotten by this point.[3] He now thought of himself as a trailblazer, a fearless pioneer who had led the major leagues to the promised land. "Moving," he said, "is one of the greatest contributions to modern baseball."[4] The shift had evolved in his mind from a mere business decision to a humanitarian gesture that exposed the sport to a new audience. "Wouldn't I have been selfish had I said, 'I can afford to lose whatever it takes to keep the Braves in Boston,' just because that's my home?" he asked.[5]

O'Malley wasn't the only owner to be jealous of Perini's box-office magic, but nobody had more cause for envy than Connie Mack's sons, who were struggling to keep the Philadelphia Athletics above water. The A's sold only 304,666 tickets in 1954—by far the worst attendance in the majors—and their future was bleak. The Phillies had stolen Philadelphia's heart with an unexpected pennant in 1950, and they outdrew the A's by 118 percent during the first five years of the decade.[6]

Earle and Roy Mack had saddled the Athletics with a sizable mortgage upon purchasing the franchise in 1950. Rent checks from their Shibe Park tenants, the Phillies and the football Eagles, helped them make their monthly payments, though they still relied on surreptitious infusions of cash from their concessionaire and the American League itself. Their deficit expanded steadily, leaving the A's perpetually strapped for cash, even unable to pay for the uniforms their players wore on opening day in 1954.[7] It was an unsustainable business model. "The last thing we want is to move the team out of Philadelphia," Roy said. "But we can't stand another year as bad as the last one."[8]

The previous season had indeed been miserable. "We had no money to plug holes, no bench strength," moaned Manager Jimmie Dykes. The 1953 version of the A's lost ninety-five games. The 1954 team was worse, staggering to a 9–22 record in May and suffering a 10-game losing streak in July en route to 103 defeats.[9] Philadelphia Mayor Joseph Clark, Jr., issued an impassioned call on July 8 for "a community-chest kind of drive" to save the team. He urged his constituents to buy as many tickets as possible. Only 5,625 showed up for the next night's game.[10]

The situation appeared hopeless even to the franchise's eternally optimistic patriarch, ninety-one-year-old Connie Mack. "We're washed up in Philadelphia," he told reporters in Chicago in August. "I want to sell. Earle does, but I can't understand why Roy doesn't. The club is through in Philadelphia. There is no more interest in the team there."[11]

Roy was indeed trying to line up financing—"I'm going to battle for all-out control of this club"—though nobody believed he had a chance.[12] "Roy talks big, but we don't have a dime," scoffed his brother.[13] The only viable option seemed to be a purchase offer, reportedly in the neighborhood of four million dollars, submitted in early August by Chicago businessman Arnold Johnson. "It's a case either of taking Johnson's offer or waiting for the sheriff," muttered White Sox general manager Frank Lane, who was voicing the conventional wisdom.[14]

The forty-eight-year-old Johnson was an exceptionally slick investor with an affinity for complex financial transactions. He first displayed his skills as a young employee of a Chicago bank, successfully reorganizing a bankrupt tile company during the heart of the Depression. He eventually branched into a variety of business roles—a part-owner of the Chicago Black Hawks hockey team, a director of twenty corporations (chairman of five), and a millionaire several times over.[15]

Johnson's passion for real estate inspired his interest in major-league baseball. He purchased Yankee Stadium on December 17, 1953, in one of the dizzyingly complicated deals that became his hallmark. Johnson bought the Yankees' ballpark for $6.5 million, granting the team a 70-year lease. He immediately sold the land under the stadium to the Knights of Columbus for $2.5 million, leasing it back for the same 70-year period. He obtained a pair of mortgages, one for $500,000 and the other for $2.9 million. The latter was secured by personal friends Dan Topping and Del Webb, the co-owners of the Yankees, who had sold him the stadium in the first place.[16]

It was enough to give a casual observer a headache. But the reasoning behind the chain of transactions gradually became evident: The Yankees reaped substantial tax benefits from the deal, and Arnold Johnson obtained a valuable piece of real estate without spending much of his own money. He may have put down as little as five hundred thousand dollars, according to an analysis by the *Saturday Evening Post*.[17]

The only problem, from Johnson's perspective, was that the Yankees' minor-league ballpark in Kansas City had been folded into the transaction, given an arbitrary value of $650,000, one-tenth of the overall $6.5 million. He had no desire to possess aging, dilapidated Blues Stadium, but Topping and Webb insisted on its inclusion.[18] An unhappy Johnson traveled to Kansas City to tour his newest property. He was accompanied by Ernest Mehl, the sports editor of the *Kansas City Star*, who contended that the ballpark could be transformed from a liability to an asset. Mehl encouraged the new owner to purchase a big-league team to play there. "Sounded good to me," Johnson later said.[19]

His motivation wasn't actually so straightforward. Johnson sensed an opportunity to unload his unwanted ballpark. The Kansas City government agreed to buy Blues Stadium for $650,000—allowing him to recoup his investment—provided that he attracted a major-league tenant. The city also pledged to increase its capacity from sixteen thousand to thirty-six thousand seats. Taxpayers would foot the entire three-million-dollar bill, yet Johnson would be allowed to choose the contractor. Nobody should have been surprised that he designated the Del E. Webb Construction Company to handle the job.[20]

Chicago businessman Arnold Johnson had no interest in owning a major-league team—not initially, at least. But a complicated real-estate transaction drew him into negotiations to buy the Philadelphia Athletics and move them to Kansas City [National Baseball Hall of Fame and Museum].

Arnold Johnson was known for his diligence and persistence, and he set out to lock up his deal with Kansas City. The Athletics were the obvious target. Johnson submitted his bid and gradually warmed to the idea of owning a big-league team. "I was inspired by the success of the Braves in Milwaukee," he said, "and a little investigation convinced me that Kansas City could become an even better baseball town."[21]

* * *

The stage was set for a tumultuous month. American League owners gathered in New York on September 28, 1954, anticipating an update on the Athletics' difficulties, and hoping for a quick resolution. They learned that Johnson's offer actually was $3,375,000—not the higher figure bandied about by the press—and that Roy Mack was determined not to sell. The league granted him two weeks to find a viable alternative.[22] "We haven't a chance," Earle Mack said. "I can't imagine why Roy insists upon trying."[23]

Several owners were quietly rooting for the elder Mack son. Philadelphia had been a disaster for two decades—they all agreed on that—but Kansas City seemed a poor replacement. The federal census counted 814,000 residents in the Kansas City metropolitan area, which was smaller than six North American markets currently outside the big-league structure.[24] "Toronto, St. Paul, or maybe some other city, I might go for. But Kansas City, never," said Detroit president Spike Briggs.[25] Cleveland general manager Hank Greenberg was more succinct in his opposition. "It simply doesn't have enough people," he said.[26]

Roy arrived late to the October 12 follow-up meeting in Chicago, though his tardiness was no indication of diligence at the negotiating table. Nothing had been settled. He suggested that a "young group" in Philadelphia might come up with the necessary money, or that "a man named Finley" might prove to be the franchise's savior. (This was baseball's introduction to Charles Finley, an Indiana insurance broker.) Roy was clear on only one point. "I am not going to sell my stock to anybody," he said defiantly.[27]

Johnson was summoned behind closed doors to tell his side. The owners were impressed by his stadium deal and the $1.5 million in commitments he had already received from prospective ticket holders in Kansas City.[28] Finley also spoke briefly. He pledged, unlike Johnson, to keep the Athletics in Philadelphia for one more year, though he wanted advance permission to move in 1955 if attendance failed to improve. "All I have is $450,000," Finley said, "and if I had the guarantee I just mentioned, we could bring in the balance."[29]

That was no better than Roy Mack's vague plans or the distasteful possibility of Bill Veeck's return. Veeck had been spotted in the Blackstone Hotel, where the meeting was being held, though he laughed it off as a mere coincidence. (A decade would pass before Veeck admitted that he had been secretly angling to buy the A's.) The sense of the meeting tipped toward Kansas City. Several of Roy's counterparts gathered around him during the dinner break, pressing him to sell. He agreed to consider it.[30]

The owners seized on this opening and voted at 11 p.m. to approve Johnson's purchase, provided that Roy and Earle gave their assent within six days. The minutes of the meeting, which wouldn't be made public for decades, were crystal clear about the conditional nature of the transaction.[31] But league officials were less precise in their conversations with reporters, who generally treated the move as a done deal. "Kansas City Goes Big League," screamed the next morning's headline in the *Kansas City Times*.[32]

Roy predictably backed away. "If he changes his mind, I suppose that is his prerogative," sighed American League president Will Harridge.[33] A group of eight Philadelphia business leaders soon added to the confusion by submitting a bid of four million dollars, promising to admit Roy as an equal partner.[34] "I can't understand it. I offered Roy a much better deal," sputtered Johnson, who threatened to file a lawsuit.[35] But Roy quickly accepted this newest overture. "I am very, very happy," he gushed.[36]

Another American League meeting—the third in a month—was scheduled for October 28 in New York to consider the latest Philadelphia proposal. There was every reason to believe the deal would be accepted, at least until Dan Topping weighed in.[37] "The American League will be making a grave mistake if it permits the Athletics to remain in Philadelphia," warned Topping, who was not only the co-owner of the

Yankees, but also Arnold Johnson's friend, tenant, and mortgagee.[38] Not even a personal appeal by the frail Connie Mack could sway the Yankees and their allies to permit the sale, which was rejected by a deadlocked vote of four to four. "Let's call it a 0–0 tie in thirteen innings," laughed Topping as he left.[39]

Only one option remained, as the senior Mack acknowledged in a bitter "open letter to Philadelphia fans" that he released the following day. His wife, Katherine, the likely author of the letter, read its contents to reporters. "No matter what the Macks say or do, the answer still will be Kansas City, of course," she read. Then she added her own comment: "New York wants this club to go to Kansas City, and when New York's in the back and pushing it, well, there's your answer."[40]

Arnold Johnson pleaded innocence. "All we are trying to do is get somebody to take our money," said his lawyer.[41] The opportunity finally came on November 4, when Connie Mack, propped up in his sickbed, affixed his signature to the document of sale. Representatives of the Philadelphia group, hoping to pitch yet another offer, were left to cool their heels in the lobby of Mack's apartment building. "There was nothing else we could do. Mr. Johnson is a nice man, and he won out," Katherine Mack told reporters in a tone of resignation. Earle Mack left the building in tears.[42]

American League owners trooped to another meeting on November 8 to unanimously approve the sale of the Athletics. The proposed transfer to Kansas City was a separate matter, requiring six affirmative votes. Cleveland and Washington were on record against moving to such a small market. Detroit's Briggs, who shared their unhappiness, also insisted that it was inappropriate for Johnson to own the ballpark where one of the Athletics' rivals played.[43]

Johnson bridled. "A piece of real estate is a piece of real estate, and has nothing to do with the play on the field. It makes no difference who owns Yankee Stadium," he said.[44] But he caved to the pressure, reluctantly agreeing to sell the New York park within ninety days. Only then did Briggs give his consent. He wasn't excited about adding Kansas City to the American League, but he decided it was more important to end the lengthy fiasco. "We were all starting to look stupid," Briggs said with a shrug. "You've got to go somewhere."[45]

* * *

Two moving vans pulled up to Philadelphia's ballpark on January 20, 1955. Workmen packed them with fifty-four years of memories—huge photographs of Home Run Baker, Jimmie Foxx, Lefty Grove, Rube Waddell, and other famous Athletics, twelve showcases of championship cups and trophies, and innumerable filing cabinets stuffed with financial records and scouting reports. The movers somehow found room for two large electric fans, a pair of crutches, and a cuspidor before slamming the doors shut.[46]

Roy Mack watched silently as a pair of drivers hopped into their cabs and slowly put their trucks in gear, bound for Kansas City. "They asked for everything," he said, "and there it goes."[47]

The stadium itself had already been discarded. Shibe Park, renamed Connie Mack Stadium in 1953, had served as the Athletics' home for forty-six seasons, the final seventeen with the Phillies as tenants. Renting had suited Bob Carpenter, the Phillies owner, who had no desire to purchase the gloomy, decaying facility. But Arnold Johnson insisted on selling, hinting at a steep rent increase if he didn't get his way.[48] "We will be under much more expense as owners than lessees," groaned Carpenter, though he wrote Johnson a check for $1,675,000 in mid–December.[49]

Stadium work in Kansas City was well underway by then. The winter of 1954–1955 was bitterly cold, but four hundred laborers worked diligently in the frigid, snowy conditions. They poured more than two hundred concrete footings and rebuilt what would henceforth be known as Municipal Stadium. Johnson capped the project by acquiring the old Braves Field scoreboard, which was disassembled and transported from Boston in four trailer trucks.[50]

The renovation was miraculously completed by April 12, when a crowd of 32,147 welcomed the Athletics to their new home. The A's defeated the Tigers, 6–2, inspiring a brief flurry of optimism. But they reverted to form by losing seven of their next eight games, including a 29–6 thrashing at the hands of the White Sox. "There have been times when I've suffered, times when the heart has stopped momentarily, times when it appeared as if we might have trouble winning another game," admitted Manager Lou Boudreau near the end of a ninety-one-loss season.[51]

Yet Kansas City fans steadfastly supported their flawed heroes, buying 1.39 million tickets. Only the Braves and Yankees did better at the box office in 1955. One of the team's strongest boosters was Connie Mack himself, unable to sever connections with the franchise he had founded five and a half decades earlier. Mack flew to Missouri for opening day, drove to Baltimore when the A's played there, and returned to Kansas City in July for a strange ceremony honoring great Philadelphia ballplayers. The latter proved to be the last hurrah for baseball's grand old man, who died on February 8, 1956, at the age of ninety-three.[52]

Johnson pledged to retool the inept team the Macks had bequeathed him—he promised "a pennant contender in five years"—but his attention was diverted from this lofty goal by a pair of controversies.[53]

The first involved his ownership of Yankee Stadium, which lingered past the American League's ninety-day deadline. Johnson finally announced on March 22, 1955, that he had sold the park to fellow Chicago businessman John Cox, whom he called "my closest friend." There was no sales contract, just five lines written on a piece of paper, followed by two sets of initials: "O.K." and "J.W.C."[54] The casual nature of such a large transaction seemed peculiar to Emanuel Celler, who raised the question at a 1957 hearing:

> **CELLER:** There was no other document beyond that?
> **JOHNSON:** No, sir.
> **CELLER:** No formal document, in any sense of the word?
> **JOHNSON:** No, sir.
> **CELLER:** Did it work out all right?
> **JOHNSON:** Yes, sir. It worked out fine.[55]

Cynics couldn't help but wonder if Johnson secretly remained the owner of Yankee Stadium. "Mr. Johnson is not that character of man," retorted his lawyer, though he never produced definitive proof of a sale. Celler's subcommittee chose to let the matter drop.[56]

The second controversy also involved the Yankees, specifically the tight relationship between the front offices in New York and Kansas City. The two teams would swing sixteen trades involving fifty-eight players during the first five years of Johnson's ownership, much to Boudreau's unhappiness.[57] "Too many of our good young players went," the manager said, "and we wound up with players the Yankees no longer wanted."[58]

Critics accused Johnson of converting the Athletics into a farm club for his former (and perhaps current) tenants, a charge that enraged him. "We are not anyone's country cousin," he snapped.[59] But the trades continued. The A's shipped out several players who would play key roles on championship teams in New York (Clete Boyer, Art Ditmar, Ryne Duren, Hector Lopez, Roger Maris, Bobby Shantz, and Ralph Terry), receiving such nonentities as Milt Graff, Dick Kryhoski, Al Pilarcik, Lou Sleater, and Marv Throneberry in return.[60] "The Yankees and Kansas City have faith in each other," explained New York general manager George Weiss, perhaps stifling a rare grin.[61]

The succession of lopsided trades prevented the Athletics from delivering on Johnson's promise of contention. They lost an average of ninety-one games per season between 1955 and 1959, never rising above sixth place. Fans quickly lost interest. Kansas City's attendance waned to 901,000 as early as 1957, falling behind all American League cities but Cleveland and Washington. Rumors began floating about Johnson's desire for a home that was bigger and brighter than Kansas City. He and his pal Del Webb reportedly made a scouting trip to Los Angeles.[62]

Yet Johnson denied it all. He remained defiant as he struggled through his fifth year in Municipal Stadium, again putting a losing team on the field and again failing to sell one million tickets. "We are perfectly satisfied to remain in Kansas City," he said in July 1959. "I hope the club is here for the next one hundred years."[63]

16

Wrigley

The lords of baseball yearned for a respite. Three franchises had switched cities in three years, a violent spasm of activity after a half-century of inertia. An owner with inherited wealth had triumphed in each instance—Tom Yawkey in Boston, Gussie Busch in St. Louis, Bob Carpenter in Philadelphia—forcing a financially strapped competitor to flee to virgin territory. The teams that changed locales had benefited, and so had those that remained in place.[1] "With the Braves moved to Milwaukee, the Browns to Baltimore, and the Athletics to Kansas City, there just aren't any obviously weak franchises left," wrote Arthur Daley in the *New York Times*.[2] It was time for a break.

But the pressure did not relent, thanks to a basic law of economics. Demand continued to outstrip supply. Several cities desperately wanted their own major-league teams, and they were large enough to make a case. The next decennial census would count 6.7 million residents in the Los Angeles metropolitan area and 2.8 million in the San Francisco region, dwarfing the population of Kansas City, the tiniest big-league metro in 1960 at 1,039,493. Seven other U.S. markets outside the majors would contain more than one million residents by the late 1950s—Minneapolis-St. Paul, Buffalo, Houston, Seattle, Dallas, San Diego, and Atlanta—as would the Canadian metros of Montreal and Toronto.[3]

The American League had endorsed Del Webb's expansion resolution in September 1953, though the vote was considered an empty gesture, a harmless way to placate the Yankees owner. But the demographic pressure did not abate, and Webb's colleagues realized by 1955 that resistance might soon become impossible. The AL privately crafted four hypothetical schedules adding a pair of new teams—Los Angeles and San Francisco in the first two cases, Houston and Minneapolis in another, Montreal and Toronto in the fourth.[4] Even Ford Frick, chief apostle of the status quo, acknowledged the emerging reality. "Expansion is inevitable, and it may be that two ten-team leagues would be an interim answer," he said. "Eventually, however, if not now, there will be enough population centers available to fill out a third eight-team major league."[5]

The Pacific Coast League, of course, had been pitching the latter scenario for a decade. Its dream of attaining big-league status—rebuffed for years by the American and National Leagues—had suddenly appeared attainable after its elevation to the Open classification prior to the 1952 season. Pants Rowland, the league's president, earnestly predicted that the PCL would evolve into America's third major league no later than 1957.[6]

But Rowland was unaware—he had no way of knowing—that the Pacific Coast

League had already passed its peak. Its eight clubs drew a combined average of 3.4 million fans per season between 1947 and 1951, an impressive figure indeed, yet the league was not immune to television and the other attendance-dampening pressures that were distressing the majors. The PCL's box-office count plummeted to 2.2 million in 1952, then slightly below 1.8 million the following year.[7] A stretch of anemic crowds in his city caused *Los Angeles Times* columnist Al Wolf to despair of the league's future. "It's high time to call the doctor," Wolf wrote, "and maybe start looking up the undertaker's number, as well."[8] The existing big leagues had never been eager to admit the eight West Coast teams as equal partners. They now felt justified in ignoring them.

It was at this point that Bill Veeck, still reeling from his St. Louis disaster, arrived in Los Angeles. Phil Wrigley, who owned both the NL's Cubs and the PCL's Angels, hired Veeck as a consultant on October 17, 1953. "Bill not only will help Los Angeles get a major-league club," announced Wrigley. "His job also is to go out and organize the effort so that Los Angeles—and possibly other PCL cities—can get top-flight baseball in an orderly and sensible way."[9]

The annual meeting of Pacific Coast League owners was scheduled for October 29, and Wrigley had resolved (with Veeck's help) to seize the opportunity to reenergize the drive for big-league status. Such a decision was out of character for the reclusive Wrigley, who was nothing like his effusive, back-slapping father.[10] *Fortune* once likened the late William Wrigley, Jr., to "a jolly bartender."[11] His son, who inherited his family's chewing-gum empire, the Cubs, and the Angels in 1932, valued his privacy above all else. "My ambition," he once said, "is to go live in a cave somewhere with no telephones and a big rock over the door."[12]

Yet Phil Wrigley was not actually a hermit. He, not his secretary, answered his office phone, even after he stepped up to the presidency of the Wrigley Company at the age of thirty-one. He flashed an unexpectedly sly sense of humor on that occasion—"I'm not sure I'm succeeding on my own merits"—as he took charge of the family business, making all of the major decisions and greatly increasing sales. Some of his moves diverged from standard corporate practices, such as the 10 percent pay raise that he

Cubs owner Phil Wrigley could have been one of baseball's dominant figures. He was rich, ran a large corporation, and hailed from a major market. But his habitual reticence generally kept him in the background [National Baseball Hall of Fame and Museum].

granted all Wrigley employees in 1932, the darkest year of the Depression. "I don't know," he shrugged, "maybe I'm a socialist or something."[13]

Phil had no great love of baseball, yet he considered the Cubs and Chicago's Wrigley Field to be sacrosanct. "The club and the park stand as memorials to my father," he said.[14] He saw no reason to attend games—"I can't hit or field or pitch"—so he listened on the radio while he tinkered in his home workshop. Wrigley was a master mechanic, happiest while rebuilding car engines. He personally did most of the repair work on his estate, and also did much of the yardwork. "There's a lot more exercise in handling a chain saw and working on logs than in playing a game of golf," he said.[15]

Wrigley did not display the same degree of involvement with his baseball clubs, only occasionally asserting his ownership powers. The notable exception was his absolute refusal to allow lights to be installed in Wrigley Field. The other fifteen teams had all succumbed to night ball—the Tigers being the last in 1948—but Wrigley held fast. He had wavered years earlier, purchasing lights in late 1941, only to cancel the order after the Pearl Harbor attack.[16] He never renewed it, nor did he offer a detailed explanation. "This night ball," Wrigley simply said, "is like a drug."[17]

He stood alone on that issue, yet he possessed the necessary characteristics to become a dominant force in the big leagues. Wrigley was a wealthy man, a corporate titan, an independent spirit who was capable of speaking bluntly behind closed doors. But his habitual reticence canceled out these attributes. He tended to stay in the background at National League meetings, confining himself to the rare pithy comment or trenchant observation. "He could have been very influential if he had tried," said Happy Chandler, "but he wouldn't try."[18]

The upcoming Pacific Coast League meeting, however, was going to be an exception. The Cubs owner had no intention of sitting in the shadows. He had decided to resuscitate the third major league.

* * *

Phil Wrigley had every reason to anticipate an enthusiastic audience at October 29's PCL gathering. The baseball establishment might snicker at the thought of big-league ball in Portland or Sacramento or San Diego, but Pants Rowland and his gang were adamant. "I have no doubt that Los Angeles and San Francisco are major-league cities, but so are the other six," Rowland had declared earlier in 1953. "We're all in this thing together."[19] If spunk were a prerequisite for success, the PCL—with Wrigley's help—might very well achieve its goal.

But attitude wasn't the determining factor. Two seasons had passed since its elevation to the Open classification, yet the Pacific Coast League had not really progressed. Its rosters had not grown noticeably stronger, despite the draft relief that had been granted in 1951. Nor had its stadiums been modernized or expanded, even though Ford Frick had mandated a minimum capacity of twenty-five thousand seats for big-league status. Oakland's Brick Laws was one of the PCL's toughest talkers, yet he had done the least. His eleven-thousand-seat ballpark was literally falling apart because of inadequate maintenance.[20]

The league's public rhetoric simply did not translate to private commitment, as Wrigley learned during a chat with Emil Sick of the Seattle Rainiers a few days before the meeting. The subject of Bill Veeck came up. Wrigley suggested that Veeck was the perfect man to reinvigorate the PCL, to really give it some pep. Sick did not seem convinced or inspired. "I hope he doesn't pep us right out of the business," he said.[21]

And so it went. Wrigley tried to fire up the other PCL owners. He stressed the need for improvement—better teams, better stadiums, better attendance—but his counterparts hesitated. They either didn't want to spend the money or simply didn't have it. That came as no real surprise to Wrigley, who then offered a drastic suggestion.[22] The PCL's all-or-nothing demand was clearly unrealistic, he said, so it should be dropped. "San Francisco certainly is major-league territory as much as Los Angeles is," he went on. "There might also be one or two other cities in the Coast League that could support big-league baseball."[23]

Wrigley proposed the creation of a hybrid major league. Los Angeles, San Francisco, and possibly Seattle would move upward, joined by five other minor-league teams from the Southwest and Midwest. There were several good candidates. Minneapolis–St. Paul, Kansas City (still a year away from landing the Athletics), Houston, Dallas, and Denver all ranked among the nation's twenty-six largest metropolitan areas. Two of the PCL's five remaining teams—San Diego and Portland—also were possibilities.[24]

This idea, despite its plausibility, failed to stir any enthusiasm. PCL owners did not want to pay the price for big-league ball, yet they were equally unenthusiastic about surrendering their slots to interlopers from the heartland. Wrigley wrapped up his presentation and headed back to Chicago. He grumbled to associates that he had wasted two perfectly good business days.[25]

The Pacific Coast League's pipe dream had been exposed. Wrigley soon announced that he was abandoning his efforts to bring the major leagues to multiple West Coast cities. "As a result of what has taken place," he said, "I will have a one-point program which Bill [Veeck] will present later."[26]

Wrigley's focus would henceforth be confined to his own property. He gave Veeck two assignments: Find a solution to the Angels' stadium dilemma—there still was no suitable big-league ballpark in Los Angeles—and determine the franchise's value on the open market. Reporters naturally assumed that Veeck was slyly working an angle, perhaps preparing to buy the Angels himself. He admitted that Los Angeles had been a temptation during his recent effort to relocate the Browns—"this is the move I'd have paid money to make"—but he denied any ulterior motives.[27] "I'm happy to be working for Mr. Wrigley," he said with a laugh. "In fact, I'm happy to be working for anybody."[28]

Veeck's first task was to prevent the conversion of football's Los Angeles Memorial Coliseum—the enormous oval where the Rams played—into a baseball park. Oil magnate Edwin Pauley, who had tried to buy the St. Louis Browns in 1948, contended that any necessary alterations could be made for less than five hundred thousand dollars. The foul lines could be extended to an adequate length, he said, by simply making two "pie cuts" into the grandstands.[29] Skeptics abounded. "The Coliseum is unfit for baseball," insisted *Los Angeles Times* columnist Al Wolf.[30] But Pauley's proposal was being actively considered.

Veeck countered in late November 1953 with his own plan to renovate and expand Wrigley Field, the twenty-two-thousand-seat bandbox built by William Wrigley, Jr., in South Los Angeles in 1925. Double-decked stands would encircle the field, inflating the Angels' home to a capacity of fifty thousand.[31] "The new Wrigley Field should be baseball's most modern park, with every convenience for the fans—escalators, nurseries, snack bars, powder room facilities, and restaurants," Veeck said grandly.[32] His enthusiasm was enhanced by the simplest of factors. Wrigley Field, unlike the Coliseum, was owned by his boss.

Yet the project would not be easy or inexpensive. Homes and businesses would have to be condemned to make way for the additional seats and ten thousand parking spaces. Veeck estimated the total cost at $7.5 million ($71.8 million as of 2020). Phil Wrigley certainly had no intention of footing such a large bill, and it was unclear if anybody would. But the short-term goal was achieved. The Coliseum Commission met three days after Veeck's press conference and killed Pauley's plan.[33]

Setting the franchise's value was next on the agenda. Wrigley conferred with Veeck, then announced on February 4, 1954, that he was prepared to sell the rights to Los Angeles for $3 million (the 2020 equivalent of $28.7 million).[34] "We've never had a direct offer for the Angels. Not even any nibbles," Wrigley told reporters. "But the Angels are on the market. So we feel they should bear a definite price tag."[35]

Veeck tried to scrape up the money, his denials notwithstanding. He was determined to own another big-league team, and what site could be better than the golden city of Los Angeles? "I thought there would be an expansion to ten clubs in each league," he later explained, "and then, maybe five years later, an increase to twelve clubs, followed by a split into four major leagues."[36] If he owned the baseball rights to America's biggest open market, he would be a cinch to land one of the new franchises. But there were too many uncertainties. How quickly would the first expansion take place? How much would it cost to operate the minor-league Angels in the interim? And who would pay to enlarge Wrigley Field? Veeck was never able to make the pieces fit.

Wrigley's change of heart also had an impact 350 miles to the northwest. San Francisco had been banking on the PCL to elevate its Seals to major-league status, but a new strategy was clearly in order. Local leaders created a committee to pursue existing clubs that might be willing to move west, and they proposed a five-million-dollar bond sale to pay for a new stadium.[37]

The bond issue was placed on November 1954's ballot as Proposition B. Supporters waged a vigorous campaign, lining up endorsements from a wide range of politicians and baseball figures.[38] Leo Durocher, manager of the reigning World Series champions, the New York Giants, was unusually candid during his visit on October 27. "I'd love to move the Giants out here," he told a surprised crowd of five hundred business executives. "The players would welcome the addition of San Francisco to the league."[39] Voters happily seconded Durocher's emotion a week later, approving Proposition B by a margin of nearly three to one. "It's possible we'll have big-league baseball in 1955," gushed Francis McCarty, a member of the San Francisco Board of Supervisors.[40]

His timetable may have been absurdly aggressive, but it was a reliable indicator of the city's newly optimistic spirit. Progress was finally being made. "The favorable vote enabled San Francisco to take a long stride ahead of Los Angeles in the race for a major-league franchise on the Coast," the *Sporting News* concluded at the time.[41]

The only pessimistic note was sounded on the continent's opposite shore. Reporters finally caught up with Horace Stoneham on November 14, as he returned to New York from a Puerto Rican trip. The Giants owner scoffed at Durocher's zeal.

"There is nothing, absolutely nothing to it," Stoneham said of the hypothetical move to San Francisco. His team's lease at the Polo Grounds still had seven years to run, and he expressed interest in buying the old ballpark outright, even though it wasn't in the best of shape.

The brief controversy clearly puzzled Stoneham, who had been born and raised in the New York area, and who had operated the Giants since 1936. "I'm not too well-informed about the prospects for major-league baseball in California," he said to the assembled press, "but why should the Giants be interested in moving there?"[42]

* * *

Pants Rowland raised the white flag after the 1954 season. Pacific Coast League attendance remained below 1.8 million for the second straight year—less than half of its 1947 peak of 4,068,432—and several franchises were struggling. A loan from the league was keeping the San Francisco Seals afloat. The Sacramento Solons were running on borrowed money, too. The owner of the Portland Beavers was ensnared in an Internal Revenue Service investigation. And the Oakland Oaks were in danger of having their ballpark condemned.[43]

The seventy-six-year-old Rowland no longer dreamed of running America's third major league. He resigned as the PCL's president on November 18, 1954, and returned to a site of past glory, Chicago, where he had managed the White Sox to a world championship thirty-seven years earlier.[44] Phil Wrigley evinced no guilt at hiring Rowland as executive vice president of the Cubs. "I stuck with the Coast League as long as I could," Wrigley said. "The PCL appeared to be going places until it won Open classification. Then it dropped by the wayside."[45]

Bill Veeck soon said his goodbyes. He submitted a comprehensive report to Wrigley the day after Rowland closed his PCL office. Numbered copies were sent to all National League owners. The report urged them to admit Los Angeles and San Francisco as quickly as possible, downplaying any concerns about scheduling or transportation costs.[46] Veeck warned that the American League was scheming to reach California ahead of the NL. "The plain fact," he wrote, "is that the league that gets to the Pacific Coast first will obviously maintain the edge of having a coast-to-coast set-up for a long time to come."[47]

Veeck left California three months later, bound for a forty-seven-thousand-acre ranch in New Mexico.[48] He extolled Los Angeles as "wonderful new territory," but questioned its willingness to make the necessary stadium improvements.[49] "I can't understand the lack of enthusiasm on the part of certain public officials," he said.[50] Wrigley praised Veeck's work. "Bill talked to all the important people, collected the facts, evolved a working plan, and lined up capital," he said. "Now it's up to somebody to do something."[51]

That, of course, was always the problem on the Pacific Coast. Californians had remained on the sidelines as Veeck, a Chicago native, did everything possible to bring them a big-league team. His efforts to buy the Angels had fallen short, a brief run at the San Francisco Seals had been fruitless, and his attempt to purchase the Athletics and move them to Los Angeles had never been realistic.[52] "I made the first passes at Milwaukee and Los Angeles, the two bonanzas of recent years, and lost out because my timing was bad and my finances were weak," he later wrote.[53] He headed unhappily into his New Mexican exile.

San Francisco's referendum and Veeck's criticism inspired a brief flurry of activity. Civic leaders in Los Angeles, fearful of being left behind, decided to float their own stadium bond issue, submitting it to voters on May 31, 1955. Baseball greats were again trotted out, the strategy that had worked so well in San Francisco.[54] "You can have a big-league team the minute you have a home for it," urged Yankees manager Casey Stengel.[55] The electorate was unconvinced. Two-thirds support was required for approval of the $4.5 million bond sale, but 55 percent checked the No box.

Del Webb had long been the foremost proponent of West Coast baseball—"I know better than any of the other owners what a great potential Los Angeles and San Francisco have"—and he had never missed an opportunity to advance the cause.[56] It was Webb who had tried to shunt the St. Louis Browns to Los Angeles, and Webb who had pushed for the American League's expansion resolution. But his enthusiasm had begun to wane even before the voters went to the polls. He, like Veeck, was baffled by the prevalent lethargy. "They are all talk and no money out there," he grumbled about Los Angeles on one occasion.[57] Webb had virtually given up by December 1954. "I can see no prospect of a definite nature in sight for going to California," he told reporters.[58] The defeat of the bond issue five months later seemed to be the final blow.

Headlines: 1955

HOWARD CROSSES YANKEES' COLOR LINE

Vic Power, an outspoken first baseman, envisioned himself as the first black Yankee after batting .331 in AAA ball. But New York kept him down on the farm. "I think they were waiting for my skin to turn white," Power said. The Yankees preferred quiet catcher/outfielder Elston Howard, who broke their color barrier on April 14. "He behaves on and off the field," columnist Dan Daniel wrote approvingly.[59]

KOUFAX LAUNCHES CAREER WITH DODGERS

Brooklyn shipped veteran Tommy Lasorda to the minors on June 8 to make way for nineteen-year-old pitcher Sandy Koufax. The bonus baby interspersed extreme wildness (eight walks on July 6) with flashes of greatness (fourteen strikeouts on August 27) in his rare outings. He pitched only twelve times in 1955. "I [was] with the team, but not of it," Koufax said of his rookie year.[60]

DODGERS WIN WORLD CHAMPIONSHIP AT LAST

"Wait till next year" was the rallying cry for Brooklyn fans, whose Dodgers failed in all seven trips to the World Series prior to 1955. Next year finally arrived on October 4 with a 2–0 victory over the Yankees in Game Seven. The borough exploded in celebration. "This night, Brooklyn, not Manhattan, was the center of the world," happily recalled author Doris Kearns Goodwin, then a twelve-year-old Dodgers diehard.[61]

Mahatma reaches end of the line in Pittsburgh

Branch Rickey's attempt to resuscitate the Pirates ended with his departure as general manager on October 19. His reign had begun with high expectations in 1951—"I aim to win a pennant for Pittsburgh by 1954, hopefully sooner"—but the Pirates stumbled to a 269–501 record during his five-year tenure. It was announced that the seventy-three-year-old Rickey was retiring, but he privately admitted being pushed out.[62]

17

Moses

Gussie Busch hopped a plane to St. Petersburg, Florida, after purchasing the St. Louis Cardinals in February 1953. His new employees were reporting for spring training, and he wanted to take a look.

Everything about the Cards' training camp was unfamiliar to Busch, who had never been much of a sports fan. He gazed quietly at the batting cages, the infield drills, the pepper games. But one omission seemed so peculiar that he was moved to speak. "Where are our black players?" Busch asked. A long silence ensued, finally broken by one of the coaches. "We don't have any," he said.

Busch stared in disbelief. "How can it be the great American game if blacks can't play?" he shot back. "Hell, we sell beer to everyone."[1] Anheuser-Busch's workforce was multiracial, and the new owner demanded the same of his baseball club. The arrival of first baseman Tom Alston on April 13, 1954, made the Cardinals the tenth major-league team to employ a black player. The Cincinnati Reds and Washington Senators would fall in line later that year, pushing the number to twelve.

The pace of integration was accelerating. Only eleven minority players had risen to the majors within three years of Jackie Robinson's debut. But blacks occupied 5 percent of all big-league roster slots by 1954, and the share would double to 10 percent within four years. The proportion of black stars was even larger, due to the owners' obvious reluctance to retain any marginal player who wasn't white. Nine of the National League's Most Valuable Player Awards between 1947 and 1960 were presented to blacks, just five to whites. The breakdown of NL Rookies of the Year was identical: nine minorities, five whites.

The American League was slower to integrate. It contained three of the four 1954 holdouts: the Boston Red Sox, Detroit Tigers, and New York Yankees, who would promote Elston Howard the following season. (The only National League team to resist racial equality after 1954 was the Philadelphia Phillies.) White players would win all fourteen of the league's MVP Awards during the 1947–1960 span.[2]

The consistent success of George Weiss's all-white Yankees enabled his intransigence. A variety of defiant quotes would be attributed to the New York general manager over the years. They included blunt declarations: "I will never allow a black man to wear a Yankee uniform."[3] And sociological explanations: "Box-seat customers from Westchester County don't want to sit with a lot of colored fans from Harlem."[4] And crude instructions to scouts: "I don't want you sneaking around down any back alleys and signing any niggers."[5] Weiss elevated Howard with great reluctance, bowing to the inevitability of integration and the catcher's obvious skill. Howard would be named the American League's first black MVP in 1963.

The Red Sox outlasted the Yankees by four years, fielding an all-white roster until July 1959, the last major-league team to do so.[6] Boston general manager Joe Cronin cited a curious form of reverse racism in his team's defense. "Pigment of the skin means nothing to us," he said. "We will not be pressured into signing a player merely because he is a Negro."[7] The refusal to recruit minority talent was a factor in Boston's inability to win an American League title after 1946, just as the AL's general recalcitrance contributed to its nine defeats in the thirteen All-Star Games between 1950 and 1960.

Brooklyn remained the driving force behind integration long after Branch Rickey signed Jackie Robinson. Other milestones for the Dodgers included the first black pitcher (Dan Bankhead) and black catcher (Roy Campanella) in baseball's modern era, the first black MVP (Robinson), and the first batting order with blacks in the majority (Robinson, Campanella, Jim Gilliam, Sandy Amoros, and Don Newcombe on July 17, 1954).[8] No other franchise, in Newcombe's opinion, could have enjoyed popular support for such decisive moves. "Brooklyn Dodger fans were the best there will ever be in baseball," he said. "They truly wanted Jackie, Roy, and me to do well."[9]

Teammates shared Newcombe's fondness for the denizens of Ebbets Field, praising their devotion and knowledge of the game. "If you were a ballplayer for the Dodgers, you were special. You were like a god," said Don Drysdale, a white pitcher who joined the club in 1956.[10] His admiration was echoed by John Roseboro, a black catcher who arrived in Brooklyn in 1957. "Baseball was a religion there," he said. "The Dodgers conducted a kind of church."[11]

But many of the pews remained unoccupied, as the team's attendance woes persisted into the mid–1950s. Brooklyn drew 4.43 million fans between 1953 and 1956, falling 26 percent below the Yankees' total of 5.99 million and 45 percent below Milwaukee's 8.01 million. The usual factors were blamed—television, a decaying stadium, a lack of parking.[12]

A detectable erosion of decorum complicated the problem. Rowdy fans in Ebbets Field's upper deck delighted in pouring beer and peanut shells on the people below. "To sit safely in the lower portion, it was almost necessary to wear raincoats on a day when the sun was shining brightest," recalled Dodgers vice president Fresco Thompson.[13] Phillies pitcher Jim Konstanty was hit square in the face by a tomato chucked from the stands, and other weapons were easily at hand. Groundskeepers found golf balls, a switchblade knife, and even a shotgun as they cleaned up after games in 1954.[14]

Walter O'Malley blamed the borough's changing demographics for the declining quantity and quality of attendance.[15] He summoned Buzzie Bavasi one day to his office on Montague Street, which faced the state and federal courthouses.

"Look down there," O'Malley commanded. "What do you see?"

The general manager peered out the window. "I see a long, long line of poor Puerto Rican people getting their welfare checks," he said.

Bavasi appended a clarification when offering this anecdote. "The Puerto Rican part did not bother Walter," he insisted. "What did bother him was the word 'poor.'"[16] Not everybody was so certain. Sportswriter Roger Kahn, who covered the Dodgers in the 1950s, conceded that any businessman might worry about the encroachment of local poverty, but he did not dismiss the racial component. "O'Malley was aware of everyone's ethnicity," Kahn said. "It is excessive to accuse him of bigotry, but he did harbor stereotypes."[17]

The neighborhoods around Ebbets Field had been monochromatic as recently as 1950: 99.5 percent white, according to the U.S. Census Bureau. But change was in the wind. The stadium, in Kahn's words, "stood in the path of the black advance." The proportion of white residents in the vicinity would slip to 92.3 percent by 1960, then plummet to 41.8 percent a decade after that.[18]

Longtime residents had always extolled Brooklyn as a special place—the borough's welcome signs still bragged of being the "fourth-largest city in America"—but their faith began to flag during this demographic upheaval. "It could still pretend to be a city," Branch Rickey said, "as long as it had its own sports team, its own newspaper, and other distinguishing characteristics."[19] But those hallmarks were disappearing. The last remaining daily paper, the *Brooklyn Eagle*, folded on January 28, 1955, and its publisher, Frank Schroth, blamed sinister forces on the opposite shore of the East River. "Again Brooklyn falls victim to the Manhattan pattern," he wrote darkly in his final editorial.[20]

Many Brooklynites sought to make light of the *Eagle's* demise, joking that theirs was the only city in America without a newspaper, a railroad station, or a decent left fielder.[21] But O'Malley did not join in the laughter. The loss of the *Eagle*, he believed, was an especially grim omen. "I can remember when there were four newspapers in Brooklyn," he said. "Now there are none worth mentioning. And if you don't think a newspaper is important to baseball, you don't know baseball."[22]

* * *

O'Malley accelerated his campaign for a new stadium in 1954 and 1955, though success remained elusive. The Dodgers owner knew precisely where he wanted his dream park to be built—two miles northwest of Ebbets Field at the intersection of Atlantic and Flatbush Avenues—and he worked vigorously to line up support. But every forward step seemed to be followed by a reverse. He didn't appear to be getting anywhere.

O'Malley dispatched a steady stream of notes, letters, and memorandums to business leaders and politicians. His early correspondence had a sunny, unhurried quality. "I thought you might like to thumb through it at your leisure," he wrote of a report that he sent a public official in 1953.[23] But a fresh urgency emerged in the years that followed. O'Malley's frustration spilled out in a private meeting with Brooklyn borough president John Cashmore in April 1955. "Unless a site can be found for such a stadium in Brooklyn," he said, "the Dodgers franchise will be transferred elsewhere."[24]

O'Malley had been adamant to that point about staying within the borough's boundaries. An intriguing proposal had surfaced in 1954 to build the new Dodgers stadium over a railroad yard. The site, however, was in Long Island City, a Queens neighborhood that was separated from Brooklyn by narrow Newtown Creek. Even that short distance—a few hundred feet—was too far for O'Malley, who declined to pursue the idea. "Brooklyn would lose its identity with the Dodgers and the Dodgers with Brooklyn," he said, though he conceded that the plan could be revisited under dire circumstances: "A move to Long Island City, however, would be preferred to a move to Los Angeles."[25]

Rumors about California began floating again after the 1954 season. The *New York Times* reported in November that a double play was secretly being discussed— the Dodgers to Los Angeles, the Reds to San Francisco.[26] O'Malley dismissed the story as laughable, yet he acknowledged the West Coast's golden appeal. "I would like to see the National League move into Los Angeles," he said. "I think you'd draw three million people a year out there if you had a pennant contender."[27] But he denied any personal interest. "He wanted to stay in Brooklyn, and to this day, no one can convince me otherwise," Buzzie Bavasi said decades later. "His roots were there, his family was there."[28]

Everything hinged on his plans for the corner of Atlantic and Flatbush. O'Malley had two very specific requirements. He wanted to erect the world's first domed stadium—"I am not interested in just building another baseball park"—and he wanted to own it himself.[29] His lobbying campaign gradually convinced Cashmore and other second-tier politicians that the Dodgers were unable to acquire the land without government help, but he failed to make headway with the only man who truly mattered. "I wish this were Bob Moses's idea and not mine," said O'Malley, "as he has the know-how and zeal to see it through."[30]

Brusque, arrogant Robert Moses, then in his mid-sixties, wielded unbridled power as the economic-development dictator of New York City. "He was, for the greatest city in the Western world, the city shaper, the *only* city shaper," asserted biographer Robert Caro.[31] Moses concurrently held several influential titles, including state parks chairman, city parks commissioner, city construction coordinator, city planning commissioner, city slum-clearance chairman, and Triborough Bridge and Tunnel Authority chairman. The latter sounded less impressive than the others, but actually afforded him the greatest clout. Triborough's tollbooths generated a massive stream of revenue, which Moses was able to channel to—or withhold from—local projects at his whim.[32]

The dimensions of his power were staggering. Moses was directly responsible for the construction of 7 major bridges, 15 expressways, 658 playgrounds, 20,000 acres of parks, and 148,000 apartments during his 44-year reign from 1924 to 1968. He retained control of these projects after their completion, melding them into a personal empire within the boundaries of New York. "He was the greatest builder in the history of America, perhaps in the history of the world," wrote Caro. He was also the most powerful municipal official the nation has ever seen.[33]

This record of unprecedented accomplishment was accompanied by a decidedly unpleasant personality. Moses possessed a rare intelligence—he had studied at Yale and Oxford and held a Ph.D. from Columbia University—and he never allowed mere mortals to forget his superiority.[34] "To me, he was the personification of a certain arrogance against the average man," said reporter Joseph Kahn, who covered him for the *New York Post*.[35] Moses initially desired a career in politics, but his hubris repelled the voters in his sole campaign, a landslide defeat for governor in 1934. He was content thereafter to manipulate other politicians, employing his unique blend of brainpower, bureaucratic skill, and Triborough's overflowing treasury.

One person theoretically possessed the authority to bring Moses under control. Robert Wagner, Jr., the son of a famous U.S. senator, had been elected mayor of New York in 1953, putting him above Moses on the city's organizational chart. But Wagner was a quiet man who abhorred confrontation.[36] "Some people like the dramatic," he said. "I'm just not built that way."[37] If he faced a difficult problem, he preferred to appoint a committee to study it, rather than be rushed into a decision. He often quoted his father's advice: "When in doubt, don't."[38]

Moses's ability to cultivate young politicians was one of the keys to his longevity, and he had briefly focused his selective charm on young Wagner in the late 1930s. He privately told the new state assemblyman to announce that a swimming pool would be built in his district. "He was going to build it anyway, I'm sure," Wagner said, "but he gave me an opportunity to tell my constituents that I had gotten it there. I was always very grateful to him for that."

New York mayor Robert Wagner, Jr. (left), and the city's economic-development czar, Robert Moses (right), tour a high-rise housing project. Wagner was as quiet as Moses was brusque. The two men were incapable of working together [Library of Congress].

Yet not grateful enough, as far as Moses was concerned. The older man comported himself as the czar of New York City—an informal title that best described his untrammeled authority—and he believed that Wagner was a "bubblehead" with an undesirable streak of independence, worthy only of the disdain that Moses conferred upon most elected officials.[39] Wagner would summon Moses to City Hall, and the latter would simply ignore the command. If an appearance could not be avoided—if, for example, Moses needed Wagner's signature on a form or resolution—the czar made certain to arrive late. There was nothing the mayor could do to control him.[40]

Surely this iron-willed colossus could open the necessary doors for Walter O'Malley. Robert Moses defied anybody he pleased, and he circumvented federal, state, and local regulations with impunity. It would be a simple matter for him to assemble the necessary land for the Atlantic-Flatbush ballpark.

O'Malley began dispatching a stream of entreaties to Moses in 1952. The Dodgers owner persistently contended that Title I of the Federal Housing Act of 1949 allowed the city to foreclose on the businesses and homes occupying the stadium site. Title I required that the land be used for a larger "public purpose," and Moses easily could have slipped a ballpark under that umbrella. But the czar was no fan of spectator sports, and he had other plans for Brooklyn that did not involve the Dodgers. He always said no.[41]

"Our Slum Clearance Committee cannot be used to encourage speculation in baseball enterprises," Moses wrote to O'Malley on one occasion.[42] A second letter advised O'Malley to proceed on his own: "You should shop around with the idea of purchasing land at reasonable cost."[43] And then the clincher: "Dear Walter, let me see if I can simplify this matter, no."[44]

Yet O'Malley made one more attempt, writing to Moses on August 10, 1955, again insisting on the Atlantic-Flatbush site and again proposing Title I as the vehicle. The blistering reply arrived five days later.[45] "I can only repeat what we have told you verbally and in writing," Moses wrote, "namely, that a new ball field for the Dodgers cannot be dressed up as a Title I project." He proposed that O'Malley explore other options, perhaps even selling the franchise. If that led to the team's departure, so be it. "In spite of any feeling I might have of the need for keeping as many attractions in Brooklyn as possible," Moses wrote, "I would have to agree that you would be strictly within your rights."[46]

* * *

O'Malley waited twenty-four hours before igniting a bomb. The Dodgers announced on August 16 that they would play seven home games in Jersey City, New Jersey, in each of the three upcoming seasons. The National League had secretly given its consent a month earlier, but O'Malley timed his explosion for maximum effect. Moses's latest letter inspired him to light the fuse.[47]

The Dodgers clearly weren't attracted to Jersey City by its ballpark. Roosevelt Stadium was a poor man's version of Ebbets Field—newer, yet smaller; blessed with better parking, yet plopped in an even less desirable neighborhood. The park had been built in 1937 over a landfill just east of Newark Bay, a breeding ground for fog and mosquitoes. Jersey City's minor-league team played there until 1951, when it fled to the Canadian capital of Ottawa. Roosevelt Stadium subsequently served as a venue for high-school football games and stock-car races. An asphalt track bisected what had previously been the outfield.[48]

So what did O'Malley hope to accomplish? Why would he shift a handful of games from one inadequate site to another? Contemporaries pondered his motivation at the time, and baseball historians have speculated ever since.

O'Malley sometimes referred to Jersey City as an experiment. "They had much greater parking facilities over there than we had in Brooklyn, and I frankly wanted to test how important this problem of parking was to attendance," he told a congressional subcommittee in 1957.[49] He occasionally stressed Roosevelt Stadium's value as an "insurance policy," a fallback site if Ebbets Field deteriorated to the point of being uninhabitable. He even raised the prospect of a full-scale move. "It's possible that our permanent home could be Jersey City," he said. "It might turn out to be a great spot. We won't know until we have tested the market."[50]

Cynics offered a different interpretation. They believed that O'Malley was asserting his independence, sending a subtle threat to Bob Wagner, Robert Moses, John Cashmore, and anybody else with leverage over the Brooklyn stadium project.[51] The Jersey City gambit demonstrated O'Malley's willingness to move the Dodgers outside their native borough if local officials refused the help he desired, an impression he reinforced a day later by announcing that Ebbets Field "must be sold by 1958."[52]

His message came through loud and clear. Wagner sprang into action without impaneling a committee. "I am very anxious to keep the Brooklyn Dodgers in New York City," said the mayor, who summoned O'Malley, Moses, and Cashmore to an emergency meeting on August 19. Hurricane Diane was pounding New York and Connecticut with torrential rain and intense winds, yet the stadium controversy received heavy play in that morning's papers. O'Malley delighted in the sudden attention. "If you wish," he told reporters, "you may call it Hurricane Dodger."[53]

O'Malley pressed his advantage, proposing Atlantic-Flatbush as the only acceptable site. Moses's response was predictably combative. "What you're saying," he snapped, "is that unless a way is found to make a home for the Dodgers in this location, you'll pick up your marbles and take them away." O'Malley stayed calm. "You, Mr. Moses, never got anything without fighting for it," he said. "If I go down, I want the record to show I went down swinging." O'Malley denied that Jersey City was his first stride out the door—"I don't want even to consider ever having the Dodgers leave New York"—yet he also insisted on a solution to his dilemma within three years. "It is serious, Mr. Mayor, very serious," he said.[54]

Wagner made a good-faith gesture, ordering an engineering study of the Atlantic-Flatbush site. The mayor set aside one hundred thousand dollars for the work.[55] It was a small step, yet O'Malley hailed it as a promising start. "I hope for prompt action on the study," he said.[56]

Cities without big-league ball had started to pay close attention to Brooklyn's stadium dilemma, sensing an opportunity to lure an established franchise. Several communities contacted O'Malley in the wake of his Jersey City announcement. Some were only a short drive away—the borough of Staten Island, the Long Island village of Patchogue—while the farthest was twenty-five hundred miles across the continent.[57] The Los Angeles City Council approved a resolution submitted on August 22 by its youngest member, Rosalind Wyman, to "discuss possibilities" with the Dodgers.[58]

Two factors made Wyman an unlikely leader of her city's baseball campaign—her age (just twenty-four) and her gender (the first woman elected to the council since 1915). Little had been expected of her after she unexpectedly defeated eight male candidates in 1953.[59] The *Los Angeles Times* patronized her as "an attractive brunette with a fine clear skin," and her new colleagues on the council ignored her.[60] "I was resented when I first got there—greatly," she said. "Most of the men were old enough to be my father and my grandfather."[61]

But Roz Wyman had grand aspirations. She believed that a city's prominence depended on the quality of its cultural and athletic attractions. Los Angeles, in her opinion, fell woefully short on both counts. Wyman's mother, an Illinois native, had passed a rooting interest in the Chicago Cubs to her daughter, who now set out to attract top-quality baseball to the West Coast.[62] "Pro football has been sensationally successful," she said of the Rams, "and I think a major-league team would be more of a moneymaker than football."[63]

Wyman sent O'Malley a telegram on the very day that her resolution was approved. She invited the Dodgers owner to visit Los Angeles "for a serious conference and inspection of our facilities." If he preferred to stay at home, she added that she and a fellow councilman, Edward Roybal, would be in New York on business in late September.[64] Ten long days passed without a response.

Tenacity was one of Wyman's strongest attributes—she had worn out thirteen pairs of shoes during her door-to-door campaign in 1953—so she tried again. She mailed a letter to O'Malley's office on Montague Street. "Councilman Roybal and I feel that, in time, major-league ball will be played here," she wrote. "We are merely desirous of speeding up the progress." She asked for a meeting.[65]

The great man stirred himself to reply on September 7, 1955—sixteen days after Wyman's initial contact—though not in a manner conducive to a lengthy relationship. Yes, O'Malley said, he had received Wyman's telegram, though he had set it aside as unworthy of an answer. "I assumed it was part of a publicity stunt," he wrote. Nor was he interested in getting together: "I doubt very much that I could see you during the period when you will be in New York." He exhibited no interest in Los Angeles whatsoever.[66]

Other teams, however, had reportedly become curious about the West Coast. The Boston Red Sox bought the San Francisco Seals of the Pacific Coast League in November 1955, sparking stories about a cross-country shift.[67] "Every time the Red Sox slump and their attendance falls off, you and I are going to get mighty tired being told that the turnstiles had better start spinning or the club will be moved to San Francisco," Harold Kaese, a *Boston Globe* columnist, warned his readers.[68] Red Sox owner Tom Yawkey insisted that he valued the Seals only as a farm club, not as a placeholder. "How many times do I have to deny this story?" he groaned.[69] Yet the rumors persisted for almost two years.

The Washington Senators were also peeking westward, an interest previously inconceivable. Longtime owner Clark Griffith had gone on record in 1951 with his dim opinion of the Pacific Coast's ability to support big-league ball—"they have not got the population to do it there"—but the Old Fox was no longer in the picture.[70] His heir, Calvin Griffith, assumed control upon Clark's death in October 1955. "We have no intention of moving out of Washington," Calvin quickly announced, though his franchise was clearly in trouble.[71] The Senators had drawn only 425,000 fans in 1955, the worst attendance in the majors, and the new president found only $25,000 in the team's bank account.[72]

Griffith explicitly denied rumors of a move to Los Angeles—"reports to the contrary are baseless"—but he was privately weighing his options.[73] The Pacific Coast intrigued him, as did Canada. Calvin would later insist that Clark, who was renowned for his steadfast loyalty to Washington, had actually planted the seed for a possible shift. "He told me if you really want to make it big, go to Toronto," Calvin later said, a recollection that strained credulity.[74] The new owner stayed put for the time being, delaying any decision until the end of the 1956 season.

None of this seemed to matter to O'Malley. Others might dream of Los Angeles, but his professed goal was a stadium in Brooklyn. The Dodgers established a one-man office in Jersey City in the autumn of 1955 to stimulate interest in the games there, simultaneously dialing up the pressure on officials in New York. Irving Rudd, who anointed himself "the first and only general manager of a major-league baseball team in the history of the great state of New Jersey," was assigned to coax capacity crowds to Roosevelt Stadium. He encountered a decided lack of interest in the Dodgers. "They know their baseball over in Jersey City," Rudd said, "only it is Giants baseball or New York Yankees baseball."[75]

The Atlantic-Flatbush engineering study was launched on November 1, 1955, less than a month after the Dodgers' miraculous World Series triumph. O'Malley had already leaped to the next step by then, meeting with famed architect Buckminster Fuller to discuss the stadium's design. Fuller built a model of a translucent dome that would soar 300 feet high.[76] "It would be the first thing to catch the eye as you approached New York Harbor by ship," O'Malley enthused, waving his cigar excitedly.[77]

He had good reason to be happy. The Dodgers had won their elusive world title, and his Jersey City maneuver had compelled Bob Wagner and Robert Moses to finally pay attention. "I don't see how anyone could want to see the Dodgers leaving Brooklyn," O'Malley told the press. "Certainly, we don't ever want to go anywhere else, and I am now more confident than ever that something will turn up which will enable us to build a new home befitting world champions."[78]

18

Stoneham

Walter O'Malley's Jersey City announcement not only stirred New York officials to action. It also awakened Horace Stoneham from a lengthy slumber.

Stoneham's New York Giants had been consistently competitive in recent seasons, winning a National League title in 1951, capturing a World Series crown in 1954, and finishing above .500 every year from 1947 through 1955. But their success on the field didn't carry over to the box office. The Giants drew only 1.16 million fans in their world-championship season and failed to reach 1 million any other year after 1951.[1]

The Giants' plight was easily as dire as that of the Dodgers. Stoneham's bizarrely shaped stadium, the Polo Grounds, was decaying as rapidly as Ebbets Field. The Giants' Manhattan neighborhood, which straddled the line between Washington Heights and Harlem, was experiencing a demographic decline every bit as profound as Brooklyn's. And parking spots were even more difficult to find in upper Manhattan than in the vicinity of the Dodgers' ballpark.

Yet Stoneham said nothing as O'Malley noisily maneuvered for a new stadium in the first half of the 1950s. He remained mute until August 18, 1955, two days after the Jersey City announcement. "We could certainly use a new field," Stoneham suddenly blurted out. "But instead of helping us, everything the civic fathers have done in recent years has been pointed at hurting us." He did not offer specifics. His loyal vice president, Charles Feeney, chimed in, "It's not just a Brooklyn problem, but an all-New York problem."[2]

Feeney wasn't entirely accurate. The city's third team, the Yankees, was leading the American League in attendance for the seventh straight year. But the Giants were in danger, as 1956's first series made clear. Only 12,790 fans showed up for opening-day ceremonies at the Polo Grounds, with 2,490 and 1,920 coming the next two days. Stoneham's team would draw only eight crowds larger than twenty thousand all season, falling short of five thousand on twenty-six occasions.[3] The Polo Grounds were eerily quiet during most games. "Sometimes all we heard was the sound of our own voices," recalled announcer Russ Hodges.[4] Outfielder Whitey Lockman likened the experience to "walking through a morgue."[5]

This apathy was especially troublesome for the fifty-three-year-old Stoneham because the Giants were all he had. He wasn't a lawyer like O'Malley or a chewing-gum executive like Phil Wrigley or a deep-pocketed, diversified capitalist like so many other owners. He was a pure baseball man with no outside business interests.[6]

The Giants had come to the Stoneham family in 1919, purchased by Horace's father, Charles, who was routinely (and genteelly) called a financier or stockbroker.

He actually was a free-wheeling buccaneer, described by sportswriter Frank Graham as "a sharp-witted and sometimes ruthless trader in the hurly-burly of the curb market," a gambler who equated Wall Street with an enormous casino.[7] Charles died in 1936, passing control of the Giants to his son, who had never been called sharp-witted or ruthless by anybody.

The elder Stoneham once had great aspirations for his offspring. He enrolled Horace at Fordham University, but the boy dropped out in less than a week. So Charles shipped him to a copper mine he owned in California, trusting the power of manual labor to accelerate his son's maturity.[8] "I don't exactly know what Pop expected to happen," Horace said, "but when it came to handling liquor, those boys in that camp really completed my education."[9] The only remaining option was to pull him back to New York to work for the ballclub.

Charles's death vaulted Horace into the executive suite. He enjoyed immediate success as the youngest owner in the major leagues—a pair of National League pennants in his first two seasons—but a lengthy drought followed that initial harvest. The Giants never climbed higher than third place between 1938 and 1950, twice finishing dead last. The Dodgers, who had long been a laughingstock, surpassed the Giants during this period, both on the field and in the countinghouse.

The blame landed on Horace, who was admittedly an easy target. The new owner was as shy and self-effacing as his father had been jovial and gregarious. He rarely gave interviews, and he interacted with the fans as infrequently as possible.[10] He watched games not from a box seat at the Polo Grounds, but from a small window in the center-field clubhouse. "I always liked it better up there," he said. "I don't like having people give me hell in the stands."[11] Stoneham surrounded himself with front-office cronies, often former players, who stayed with him for decades. He found it difficult to sever ties with anybody, even a seldom-used benchwarmer. "You always hate to see your players leave," he said. "Maybe I'm too much of a sentimentalist."[12]

Stoneham was heavily criticized for his nostalgia, especially his fondness for managers and executives (regardless of competence) who had once starred for the Giants. But his biggest problem, critics and supporters agreed, was his addiction to alcohol. "Horace Stoneham has only two occupations in life. He owns the Giants, and he drinks," joked Bill Veeck.[13] Leo Durocher, who managed the Giants for seven and a half seasons, saw his boss inebriated on hundreds of occasions. "To say that Horace can drink," he wrote, "is like saying that Sinatra can sing."[14]

All of these factors—the shyness, the isolation, the tight inner circle, the alcoholism—caused the baseball establishment to think of Horace Stoneham as a lightweight. This opinion was so prevalent that *The Sporting News* felt safe in making the following observation in 1952, when discussing the possibility of Durocher quitting the Giants: "*Even Horace is smart enough* not to let such a talented and valuable asset get away."[15] And that was in a news story, not an opinion piece. Durocher himself dissented after his eventual departure from New York—"there's no owner who knows more about the game than Stoneham, unless it might be Rickey"—but his was a voice in the wilderness.[16]

Stoneham's personality—and his image—almost predestined him to approach his stadium problem the way he did. It was just like him to stay mum for years, compelled by his reticence and sense of loyalty to retain the ballpark his father had known. But an eventual outburst, perhaps fueled by alcohol, was inevitable. Hence his abrupt cry for a new stadium in August 1955, without any of O'Malley's extensive preparatory work. Stoneham handled it badly, just as most of his fellow owners would have expected.

The Giants weren't losing money—not yet—but their arrow was definitely pointing in the wrong direction. Stoneham amassed a comfortable profit of $396,000 in the golden season of 1954. But his margin slipped in subsequent years to $151,000, then $81,000, and he was chilled by the realization that those tiny surpluses would have vanished without the sizable checks he received from local TV stations.[17]

Stoneham offered plenty of excuses for his predicament. He blamed the Giants' woes on demographic trends, the New York City government, urban congestion ("what a ballpark needs now is parking space more than anything else"), changes in leisure habits, the weak drawing power of some National League opponents, the local dominance of the Yankees, even the aura of the late Babe Ruth ("prior to his coming, the Yanks were just another team").[18]

He said nothing of his own complicity—his failure to promote the Giants energetically, his unwillingness to spend money on his current ballpark, his refusal to emulate O'Malley's campaign for a new stadium. "Stoneham had the best franchise in the National League," Bill Veeck later said. "He had, potentially, the best drawing card in Willie Mays. He was in New York, the center of the communications industry. What did he do about it?"[19] Row after row of empty seats in the Polo Grounds supplied the answer.

* * *

At least Stoneham still had a ballclub. Two of his high-profile contemporaries were withering on the sidelines as 1956 began. Branch Rickey was being paid $50,000 a year (equivalent to $474,000 in 2020) to serve the Pirates as a consultant, though nobody in the Pittsburgh organization seemed to want his advice. And Veeck was idling on his ranch in New Mexico, light-years removed from the major-league mainstream. The peace and quiet were driving him crazy.[20]

Rickey's dismissal as general manager in October 1955 closed the books on his greatest failure. "It will be very embarrassing if I don't live long enough to see this program through to a successful culmination," he had said upon taking the Pittsburgh job in 1950.[21] The ensuing nightmare was darker than he could have imagined. The Pirates had averaged 86.6 defeats in the five seasons prior to Rickey's hiring. They suffered 100.2 losses per year on his watch.

The Mahatma claimed to see light at the end of the tunnel by 1954, a long-awaited upturn that would vindicate his lengthy rebuilding program. He confessed his optimism to Fred Haney, asking if the Pittsburgh manager felt the same. "We have a lousy ballclub," Haney replied. Rickey thought for a moment and sighed. "I'm afraid you're correct," he said.[22] The Pirates would go 53–101 that year, then 60–94 in 1955, finishing last both times.

This uninterrupted streak of incompetence jarred the successful executive who had won eight National League titles and four World Series in St. Louis and Brooklyn. "My methods are the same, and my men are the same," Rickey told a Pittsburgh sportswriter.[23] He consequently expected his results to be the same, yet they deviated dramatically. The biggest problem was his failure to innovate. Rickey's invention of the farm system had propelled the Cardinals to the top of the standings; his pioneering role in integration had done the same for the Dodgers. But farm clubs and black stars were ubiquitous by the mid–1950s, and he was out of fresh ideas. A headline on the cover of *Sport* magazine dared to ask the question on everyone's mind: "Has Rickey Lost His Touch?"[24]

Rickey acquired a few budding stars who blossomed after his departure, notably Roberto Clemente, a flashy right fielder destined for the Hall of Fame. But the Mahatma's ability to identify young talent was no longer unassailable. He had once spurned bonus babies, but he signed several for the Pirates. Most vanished without a trace. He was especially excited about a fireballer whom he rated among the two greatest pitching prospects he had ever seen.[25] "One of those boys was Dizzy Dean," he said. "The other is Ron Necciai, and Necciai is harder to hit."[26] The early returns were brilliant—Necciai struck out twenty-seven batters in a nine-inning Class D game—but big-league fame was elusive. Necciai pitched only twelve games for the Pirates, accumulating more walks than strikeouts.

Pittsburgh's veterans, almost to a man, grew to dislike Rickey. They were repelled by his imperious tactics at the bargaining table. "If you demanded a raise from Rickey, he would scare you into thinking he would demote you, rather than pay," recalled pitcher Roy Face.[27] Some players, including outfielder Frank Thomas, came to hate him. "He might have been a great baseball man," said Thomas. "But as a human being, I had no respect for him."[28]

Rickey feuded with the Pirates' only star, Ralph Kiner, who led the National League in home runs every season from 1946 through 1952.[29] "We finished in last place with you. We can finish last without you," Rickey famously told the slugger.[30] The inevitable trade came on June 4, 1953, when Rickey shipped Kiner to the Cubs. Pittsburgh fans were outraged. Cecilia Raisdek, who rarely missed a home game, voiced the consensus. "I wish Rickey would fall out of his box and break his neck," she told a reporter.[31]

Rickey was approaching his seventy-fourth birthday when owner John Galbreath stripped him of the general manager's title after the 1955 season. "I did not bring Pittsburgh a winner," said the mortified legend, who called it "the biggest disappointment in my baseball life."[32]

Bill Veeck was more than a generation younger—turning forty-two in February 1956—but he shared Rickey's embarrassment. Veeck had failed repeatedly in the early 1950s. His Browns had fizzled at the box office, his move to Baltimore had been blocked twice, and his year in Los Angeles had yielded nothing. Veeck's second wife, Mary Frances, had married him in 1950, about the time his losing streak began. "If only she could have seen me in Cleveland when it was going good and I was riding high, and no matter where I turned, I was a big winner," he recalled thinking.[33]

Veeck dreamed of a big-league comeback. He would have traded places with Horace Stoneham in a heartbeat, regardless of the difficulties in New York.[34] "I wish I could get hold of the Giants," he mused. "But that's only an idle wish."[35] He stayed busy by helping a pair of friends who owned a AAA team in Miami. And he kept his eyes peeled for his next opportunity.

Detroit seemed the best possibility. The Tigers had been operated since 1935 by Walter Briggs, who died in 1952. His will transferred ownership to a trust, which benefited his four daughters and son Walter Jr. The latter, known as Spike, was expected to remain the team's president, a position he had assumed upon his father's death.[36]

That prospect failed to excite Tigers fans, who had grown weary of Spike's proclivity for speaking without thinking. They remembered his 1954 promise to win a pennant within two years. A reporter asked for an explanation when the Tigers stumbled to fifth place in 1956. "Did I say that?" the forty-four-year-old Briggs replied. "Well, I'll have to revise my timetable."[37]

Spike's reign was interrupted by the lawyer for his father's estate, who determined that a ballclub was not a prudent investment for a trust. The son's subsequent offer of three million dollars was rejected by his sisters, and the team was placed on the open market. Eight syndicates scrambled to submit bids by the deadline of July 3, 1956, including groups led by Veeck, Indiana insurance broker Charlie Finley, Toronto entrepreneur Jack Kent Cooke, and a tandem of Michigan radio-station owners, Fred Knorr and John Fetzer.[38]

The financial details were foggy, but Veeck reportedly entered the highest cash offer, $5.25 million, while Knorr and Fetzer proposed a combination of $4.6 million in cash and $900,000 in interest-bearing notes. The trust accepted the latter bid, which totaled $5.5 million, the highest price ever paid for a big-league franchise.[39]

Veeck angrily insisted that Knorr and Fetzer's hybrid offer violated the rules of the bidding process. "My wife told me I was stupid to come up here and bid. She was right," he snapped.[40] Nearly three years had passed since his forced sale of the Browns, yet he was certain that he was still being blackballed: "The Briggs sisters, I had good reason to believe, had been warned that if they sold the club to me, the American League would not approve the deal." He threatened to go to court, then thought better of it.[41]

Knorr and Fetzer declined to comment. Their immediate goals were to win the confidence of fans who had been alienated by Spike Briggs—and to make friends with the owners of other AL clubs. Their first announcement sought to do both at once. The new owners publicly pledged to give Detroit a "dignified" ballclub, with "no midgets, no farm nights, no roving musicians, nothing to distract the keen interest of the tie-and-jacket folk in the audience."[42] The baseball establishment couldn't have been happier.

* * *

Veeck had been correct about the New York Giants. It was pointless to dream of purchasing the franchise from Horace Stoneham, who intended to retain ownership until death. Stoneham's whole life was tied up in the Polo Grounds, the architectural monstrosity in the shadow of Coogan's Bluff that had been home to the Giants since 1911. He had spent his teen years hanging around his father's ballclub, then devoted his twenties and early thirties to learning the ropes.[43] "Bit by bit," he recalled, "I got into the running of the ballpark."[44]

It was the strangest of stadiums. The playing field was far from level, sloping eight feet downward from home plate to the outfield fence. A manager sitting in the dugout could see only the upper halves of his outfielders. The distances down the foul lines were absurdly small. The right-field fence hovered just 258 feet from the plate, and left field wasn't much farther at 280. Center field was a cow pasture by comparison, stretching 505 feet deep.

These bizarre dimensions cemented several reputations. Mel Ott powered the Giants with 511 homers in 22 seasons, ranking third at the time behind Babe Ruth and

Jimmie Foxx on the career home-run list. Nearly two-thirds of Ott's blasts, 323, came in the cozy Polo Grounds. Would he have reached the Hall of Fame if he had played in a more spacious stadium? Bobby Thomson's pennant-winning shot in 1951—"the Miracle of Coogan's Bluff"—sailed into the looming left-field stands. Would it simply have been a long out in Ebbets Field? Willie Mays dazzled the nation with his breathtaking catch of Vic Wertz's smash in the 1954 World Series. Would his fielding genius have been as obvious if the center-field fence were a hundred feet closer?[45]

The Polo Grounds were better suited for football's rectangular proportions. New York's National Football League team, also known as the Giants, had played there since Tim Mara founded the franchise in 1925. The presence of this namesake was crucial to Stoneham's survival. The Mara family paid him $75,000 ($721,000 in 2020 dollars) in annual rent. Football money had been the difference between profit and loss for Stoneham in 1955.[46]

That's why the news on January 27, 1956, hit with such force. The football Giants announced their departure for Yankee Stadium, signing a ten-year lease that would take effect in September.[47] President Jack Mara explained the move by alluding to the prospective demise of his club's longtime home. "We doubted that the Polo Grounds would remain available for any considerable period," he said.[48] Reporters immediately sought Stoneham's reaction. Was he determined to remain in his aging facility, or would he follow the football Giants out the door? "We may move, possibly to Yankee Stadium sometime in the future," he said, "but certainly not out of New York."[49]

It was commonly believed that Stoneham owned the Polo Grounds, an assumption that was only half-correct. The ballpark was indeed his, but the land underneath belonged to the estate of real-estate developer James Coogan. Stoneham had periodically tried to buy the property, only to be rebuffed. His current lease would expire in April 1962, and the Coogan family was talking vaguely about constructing an apartment complex on the site. Jack Mara was right. Time seemed to be running out.[50]

Manhattan borough president Hulan Jack was desperate to keep the baseball Giants from following their football brethren to the Bronx. He announced on March 4, 1956, that he was initiating a search for a stadium site. He proceeded with uncommon speed, choosing a location within twenty-four hours. Jack proposed on March 5 that a ballpark be constructed over the New York Central Railroad yards between Sixtieth and Seventy-Second Streets. He fleshed out his idea in the coming month, suggesting that a 110,000-seat domed stadium be built on stilts over the railroad tracks. Nobody asked why the Giants, who drew about ten thousand fans per game, needed such an enormous facility.[51]

Stoneham clambered on board, pronouncing himself "deeply interested" in Jack's proposal. Everything fell into place with amazing speed.[52] Preliminary plans for the stadium complex were unveiled on May 14, now including an office tower and a television studio. The total cost was pegged at seventy-five million dollars. A sum of that magnitude was bound to attract the attention of Mayor Robert Wagner, who summoned Jack and Stoneham to City Hall a week later.[53] He liked what he heard. "We are anxious to see this type of stadium in Manhattan as a home for the Giants," the mayor said excitedly.[54]

This sudden burst of energy had two points of inspiration, the football Giants'

Manhattan borough president Hulan Jack (right), takes part in a ceremony honoring famed publisher Joseph Pulitzer. Jack spearheaded a 1956 proposal to build a 110,000-seat domed stadium for the Giants. Also in the photograph are Carl Ackerman (left) of Columbia University and Anthony Donargo, the borough's chief engineer [Library of Congress].

flight from the borough being the obvious one. But Wagner and Jack were also motivated by developments a thousand miles to the northwest.

The Minneapolis Millers, who played in the Class AAA American Association, opened a new ballpark on April 24, 1956. Metropolitan Stadium seated only 21,600, but provisions had already been made for a quick expansion. This was of particular interest to New Yorkers because the owner of the Millers—and hence of the territorial rights to Minneapolis—was Horace Stoneham.[55] He attended the grand-opening ceremonies and declared the stadium to be "strictly big league."[56] It didn't escape his attention that the Millers drew 18,366 fans to their first game, roughly 5,600 more than the Giants had attracted to their opener a week earlier.

A New York columnist asked Stoneham the logical question: Had he ever thought about moving his team to Minnesota? Loyal, sentimental Horace, who had recently declared undying fealty to his hometown, fixed his gaze on the sportswriter. "We've been thinking of that for a year and a half, and I thought everybody knew it," he said. "It's no secret."

It was, of course, a bombshell. Stoneham had never spoken publicly about leaving New York. His openness to a shift came as a shock, especially since the stadium talks were gaining momentum back home. But he was adamant about this new option. "I am studying all angles," he said. "And if and when I do move, I will do what is best for my ballclub."[57]

Headlines: 1956

Mantle reaches apex of career

Mickey Mantle came within inches of being the first batter to slug a fair ball out of Yankee Stadium. His May 30 homer against the Senators struck the third deck 117 feet off the ground, a foot short of the roof. The prodigious blast heralded Mantle's greatest season, which he capped with the Triple Crown (.353 average, 52 homers, 130 RBIs) and the American League's Most Valuable Player Award.[58]

Dodgers hunt down Braves at the wire

Milwaukee entered the final weekend with a half-game lead over Brooklyn. But the Dodgers swept a doubleheader from Pittsburgh on September 29, while the Braves lost a twelve-inning heartbreaker to St. Louis, 2–1. Warren Spahn pitched a five-hit complete game for Milwaukee, yet took the loss. "We had every reason to win," he said, "but it was like it wasn't meant to be." Brooklyn's National League crown was its fourth in five years.[59]

Larsen achieves immortality with perfect game

Fun-loving Don Larsen stayed out past midnight prior to Game Five of the World Series. "Don't be surprised if I pitch a no-hitter," he jokingly told his companion as they reached the hotel. The Yankees pitcher actually fared even better against the Dodgers on October 8, tossing the only perfect game in postseason history. New York's series victory two days later seemed almost anticlimactic.[60]

Robinson retires after trade to Giants

An era ended when Brooklyn traded Jackie Robinson to the Giants on December 13. Robinson chose instead to retire. Walter O'Malley was happy to be rid of the combative Robinson, yet the Dodgers owner sent a conciliatory note. "The roads of life have a habit of recrossing," he wrote. "There could well be a future intersection." But relations between the two men remained frosty.[61]

19

Griffith

Walter O'Malley's campaign for a new Dodgers stadium gained momentum during the early months of 1956. Engineers completed the first phase of the Atlantic-Flatbush study in January, and their preliminary findings were positive. Robert Wagner and John Cashmore were emboldened to propose creation of a Brooklyn Sports Center Authority to oversee financing and construction. Their bill was submitted to the New York State Legislature on February 5, 1956.[1]

That wasn't O'Malley's preferred course. He wanted Wagner and Cashmore to condemn the land, sell it to him at market value, and then get out of his way. But forming an authority seemed better than doing nothing, so he publicly commended the bill's cosponsors for their "courage and intelligence." He spoke as if the legislation's passage in Albany were a sure thing. "It will be sad to see Ebbets Field demolished," he said, "but anyone familiar with its many limitations will understand that this fine old landmark has to go, and soon."[2]

It wouldn't be quite that simple. Lawmakers representing districts across Upstate New York, many of whom lived hundreds of miles from New York City, had no particular reason to help the Dodgers. Their disinterest was shared by a number of politicians closer to the action. Robert Barnes, a city councilman from Queens, imitated a public-address announcer in mocking the potentially expensive proposal. "Pitching for the Brooklyn Dodgers, the city administration," he intoned. "Catching, as usual, the people of the City of New York."[3]

But O'Malley had Governor Averell Harriman on his side, an alliance that would prove decisive in the short run. Harriman claimed to be a Dodgers fan, though his dedication never seemed particularly intense. Of greater relevance were the Democrat's plans to seek reelection in two years, motivating him to reach out to his party's base. Building a sparkling new ballpark seemed just the ticket, especially a park that would save the only big-league team in a heavily Democratic borough.

O'Malley jumped aboard as Harriman's legislative staff guided the stadium bill through the state capitol. The Dodgers owner did what he could to help. He promised to kick-start the Brooklyn Sports Center Authority by purchasing at least four million dollars of its bonds.[4] And he slyly offered to reduce the new agency's workload, suggesting that it sign the Dodgers to "a management contract for the operation of the premises for multi-purposes in addition to baseball." If O'Malley couldn't own the new ballpark, he could at least run it—for a sizable fee, of course.[5]

The bill passed safely through the Assembly and State Senate by springtime. Harriman carried the final version to Brooklyn for a signing ceremony on April 21. His signature terminated the lengthy stadium controversy and safeguarded Brooklyn's big-league status—or so it seemed at the time.⁶ "No one can imagine the Dodgers existing and retaining their quality—in short, being the Dodgers—anywhere but in New York City," sportswriter John Lardner had written a few weeks earlier. "They would not be the same team in Albany or Elmira. They cannot be transplanted, intact, to Los Angeles or Montreal."⁷

But the Dodgers could be moved—temporarily, at least—to Jersey City. The world champions had made their New Jersey debut on April 19, two days prior to Harriman's ceremony. They defeated the Phillies before a sparse gathering of 12,214, half the size of the turnout at Ebbets Field's season opener earlier in the week. The few fans who showed up were buffeted by frigid winds off Newark Bay.⁸

Crowds improved in tune with the weather, though not tremendously. The attendance for 1956's seven games at Roosevelt Stadium would average 21,196, well below the listed capacity of 24,500. O'Malley, who was clearly disappointed, no longer speculated about a full-scale relocation to New Jersey.⁹ "Jersey City must be considered in the Dodgers' future plans," he now said, "that is, in a limited sort of way."¹⁰

He was banking everything on the new stadium authority. An occasional rumor still popped up about a transfer to another city—supposedly the next logical step after the Dodgers' limited jump to Roosevelt Stadium—but O'Malley dismissed such talk as absurd. "Would you make a move to Los Angeles with a stop in Jersey City on the way?" he joked during a Manhattan speech early in the year.¹¹ He exuded confidence about the prospects for his dream ballpark.

But O'Malley's sunny optimism would fade as 1956 rolled along, largely because of Robert Moses's intractability. New York's development czar detested spectator sports—he once referred to fans as "oafs, hecklers, and bottle throwers"—and he disdained any project that lay beyond his dictatorial control.¹² Moses couldn't prevent creation of the Brooklyn Sports Center Authority, but he intended to do everything possible to render it powerless.

He began by ridiculing the scope of the stadium proposal, which now encompassed 108 city blocks, roughly 500 acres in the Atlantic-Flatbush area.¹³ "The more acreage you throw into this thing, the less chance it has of success," said the man who had conceived several projects of far greater magnitude. Moses suggested that nobody should "take this business of 500 acres too seriously."¹⁴ He privately advised Mayor Wagner that the new agency didn't need anything close to the $278,000 it had initially requested, and he publicly expressed doubt that its bonds would find any buyers.

The authority formally sprang to life in July 1956, when Wagner appointed three members to its board of directors. But Moses made certain that little happened after that.¹⁵ He urged Brooklynites to remain patient with the process—"let the critics with their ever-sharp harpoons lay off"—while he quietly orchestrated a slowdown.¹⁶ The authority received only twenty-five thousand dollars in funding—less than 10 percent of what it had requested—and even that paltry sum was delayed until late December. Chairman Charles Mylod blasted City Hall for its "failure to go forward with the program as originally contemplated." His discouragement was palpable.¹⁷

A detailed engineering study had been completed by then. It estimated that the Dodgers' new stadium would cost seven million dollars without a roof or nine million with a lid. Those prices weren't terribly shocking, falling in the 2020 range of sixty-five to eighty-five million dollars. But the project had ballooned far beyond a mere ballpark. The Brooklyn Sports Center Authority was also expected to coordinate with other public agencies and private developers to acquire property, realign streets, build parking garages, reconstruct rail lines, erect a new Long Island Rail Road station, and relocate an enormous wholesale meat market.

The overall cost of redeveloping the 500-acre site, according to the consultants, might be as high as $250 million in public and private money, the equivalent of $2.35 billion in 2020. Politicians and taxpayers bridled at this massive expense. Their unhappiness, coupled with the ongoing bureaucratic inertia, imperiled the proposed stadium. It became obvious by the end of 1956 that if the project were to survive, it had to be scaled down and speeded up.[18]

None of this came as a surprise to that master of governmental infighting, Robert Moses, who now offered another suggestion to further slow the gears. The authority's staff, he said, should conduct an economic feasibility study during the coming months, perhaps issuing a report by April 1957. If it concluded that the stadium would be truly viable, work could proceed. And if not? "Nothing will have been lost because it will then be possible for [the city government] to pick up the [development] problem where the Sports Center left off," Moses wrote in a memo to Wagner.[19] The czar had his own plans for Atlantic-Flatbush, and a ballpark was definitely not included.

* * *

Calvin Griffith was also displeased with his stadium situation, though Walter O'Malley found it impossible to sympathize. Griffith was demanding a modern ballpark for his Senators—"there will have to be a new stadium built in Washington if we stay"—and local officials were doing their best to accommodate him.[20]

It could be difficult to get things accomplished in the District of Columbia, where the city government was subject to strict congressional oversight. But the Democrats and Republicans on Capitol Hill came together in August 1956 to create the National Stadium Commission, a body empowered to pick a site and set a timetable.[21] President Dwight Eisenhower gave the project his wholehearted support, a sure sign that federal funding would be available when the time came. "I am all for an athletic program, and I don't see how it could be better symbolized than by a good, big stadium in this city," the president said.[22]

Griffith was blessed with everything that O'Malley lacked—enthusiastic local support, a stadium committee with clout, a guaranteed source of money—yet he still wasn't happy. He made a lengthy trip to California in mid–September, reportedly assessing the charms of Los Angeles and San Francisco.[23] The *Washington Post* revealed on October 4, 1956, that Griffith was eager to move his team westward, a story that Senators vice president Joe Haynes dismissed as "absolute nonsense and pure conjecture."[24] But Griffith publicly confirmed his interest twenty-four hours later.

The very thought of vacating the nation's capital horrified the baseball establishment, even though the Senators had ranked last in major-league attendance in 1955 and again in 1956. Manny Celler was already making noises about reopening his antitrust investigation. If Griffith left town, congressional hearings were certain to follow. American League president Will Harridge hastily dismissed all talk of moving the Senators as "silly." Commissioner Ford Frick chimed in that a shift would be "catastrophic."[25] Even the president expressed an opinion. "This is the first I have heard of it," Eisenhower said at his October 5 press conference. "But I will tell you one thing, I am 'agin' it."[26]

This united opposition meant absolutely nothing to Calvin Griffith, whose brief presidency of the Senators had been marked by extreme frugality and rock-ribbed stubbornness. "It's not just that he marches to his own drum," Bill Veeck once said. "I don't even think he hears anyone else's."[27] The forty-four-year-old Griffith had been associated with the Washington franchise ever since his 1922 debut as a batboy, and he equated the team's interests with his own. He had inherited control of the Senators in 1955, pledging to honor his uncle's legacy by staying in the District of Columbia, though his resolve was flagging.[28]

Clark Griffith, while still a young man, had been nicknamed the Old Fox because of his sly intelligence and cutting wit, a pair of traits that did not pass to the next generation. Calvin often seemed to be fighting a losing battle with the English language. He said on one occasion that a knee surgeon had removed his "cartridge." He expressed no concern about being booed: "I've been hung in apathy before." He once refused to reveal his next choice of a manager, promising only that "I won't do anything rational." And he dismissed the widespread ridicule of his front office, which was heavily staffed by family members. "I don't really know what the word nespotism [*sic*] means," he said.[29]

Many of his relatives/employees shook their heads in despair. "Sometimes he speaks without thinking. He's not that good at putting thoughts into words," said his sister, Thelma Haynes, the team's executive vice president.[30] Most baseball executives were not as charitable. They cursed the Old Fox for leaving such an important franchise in apparently incompetent hands, an anger leavened by occasional twinges of sympathy for the new owner. "Calvin always seemed so stupid," wrote Veeck, "that you almost felt sorry for him."[31]

Griffith's initial impulse was to shift the

Calvin Griffith began his career with the Washington Senators as a batboy in 1922. He grew up to inherit his uncle's club in 1955, then almost immediately began to contemplate its relocation [Library of Congress].

Senators north of the border—"we gave Toronto a lot of consideration"—but he worried about the legal ramifications of a transfer to a foreign country.[32] Several American cities seemed safer. Kenneth Hahn, a young member of the Los Angeles County Board of Supervisors, met twice with Griffith during the 1956 World Series in New York. Earl Warren pushed for San Francisco, which sat across the bay from the chief justice's home in Oakland. "I used to go up there and talk to him in his chambers [at the Supreme Court]. He was telling me I should go to California," Griffith recalled.[33] Minneapolis and Louisville also threw their hats in the ring. The campaign for the latter was coordinated by old pal Happy Chandler, once again the governor of Kentucky.[34]

Griffith's dalliances with these cities were splashed across the front pages of Washington's newspapers day after day in October 1956. He always stressed his passive role in the negotiations. "I have never approached any city about moving our franchise," he said. "They have all come to the Washington baseball club."[35] But there was no doubt about his eagerness to listen. "His head is spinning with dreams of fortune," *Washington Post* sports editor Shirley Povich wrote caustically, "and if, out of it, Washington spins off as a major-league city, well, it can have its memories, such as they are."[36]

Griffith summoned the Senators' board of directors on October 19. The decision should have been a formality, given that he and sister Thelma controlled a majority of the stock, but a complication had arisen.[37] "Everybody on the board has an open mind on the matter except one person," Calvin muttered.[38] The holdout was minority stockholder Gabriel Murphy, who had grown to dislike and distrust the new owner. Murphy threatened to "sue in every court in the land" if the team tried to leave town.[39]

Thirty-five reporters and photographers jammed an anteroom as the board meeting began at 10 a.m. They passed the time by setting up a pool. Fifty cents bought the right to pull a slip of paper from a hat, with all proceeds going to the person who drew the city where the Senators would play in 1957. The odds did not favor the first person in line, Morrie Siegel of the *Washington Daily News*. His slip said Waterloo, Iowa.[40]

The correct answer, to almost universal surprise, was Washington. Griffith emerged from the seven-hour meeting to declare that everything was fine. "We are very happy to be in Washington and hope we will stay here the rest of our lives," he said with unexpected excitement. The other cities had been dangling stadium plans and incentive packages, while Washington had not made any substantive commitment. A confused reporter asked which city had submitted the best offer. Griffith simply smiled. "Washington," he said, offering no further explanation.[41]

Joy reigned in the District of Columbia that night, and no one was happier than Clark Griffith's eighty-one-year-old widow. Ann Robertson Griffith had watched sadly as her nephew prepared to head to the West Coast. She broke into tears when she heard of the last-minute reprieve. "Clark put his lifeblood into that ballclub," she said. "He would have wanted it this way. He never would have moved."[42]

* * *

New York's two ballpark proposals traveled on parallel tracks in 1956. Hulan Jack's 110,000-seat stadium and the Brooklyn Sports Center Authority accelerated rapidly during the year's early months, fueled by initial excitement and unrestrained optimism. Preliminary plans were unveiled, government support was pledged, and detailed timetables were outlined.

But the pressure gauges for both projects began to lose steam by midyear. Jack's gigantic arena proved to be too costly at seventy-five million dollars—especially after he ruled out public funding—and his follow-through was slipshod. The Giants' new ballpark was supposed to be built on a twelve-block site owned by the New York Central, yet nobody ever bothered to contact the railroad.[43] The *New York Times* eventually judged the prospects for Jack's stadium to be "nebulous."[44] It was as good as dead by autumn.

Brooklyn's ballpark encountered similar problems. The euphoria inspired by Governor Harriman's April signing ceremony was dulled by subsequent months of inaction, largely the result of Robert Moses's dilatory tactics and the public's genuine concern about spiraling costs. It was evident by Labor Day that the project was in serious danger.

The owners of New York's two National League teams reacted differently as their dreams vaporized. Horace Stoneham stayed in character by doing absolutely nothing, but Walter O'Malley wasn't wired that way. The Dodgers owner fancied himself a shrewd operator, a master manipulator able to sway others to do as he wished. This self-image was dangerously inflated—as evidenced by his continuing inability to get his ballpark built—yet O'Malley decided it was time to unleash his vaunted skills.

He settled on two bold steps.

O'Malley, despite his public denials, had always held Los Angeles in his back pocket. The California city served as a handy threat to spur action in Brooklyn, as well as a viable alternative if moving ever became necessary. But Calvin Griffith's sudden lurch in October 1956 threatened to foreclose this alluring option. O'Malley was shocked to learn of Griffith's newfound interest in Los Angeles, and he was dismayed that the Senators owner was meeting with Kenneth Hahn right under his nose during the 1956 World Series.

Griffith and Hahn were sitting together in Ebbets Field when O'Malley made his first move. He scribbled a note on a napkin, summoned an usher, and told him to deliver the message to the Los Angeles politician. The exact wording has been lost to history, but the gist was unforgettable. Don't be hasty, the president of the Dodgers told Hahn. Don't make a deal with anybody before talking to me.[45]

O'Malley's second step, also taken surreptitiously, was equally dramatic. He initiated negotiations to sell Ebbets Field, an action he later attributed to his confidence in the Brooklyn Sports Center Authority.[46] "This show was on the road," he told a congressional subcommittee in 1957. "This was something where we were going to start throwing up steel overnight." He had pledged to buy the authority's bonds, O'Malley said, so he had to sell his current ballpark to raise the necessary funds.[47]

It was a disingenuous argument. The Brooklyn project was near death by October, as the Dodgers owner well knew. The authority didn't have a staff or any operating funds. It certainly wasn't preparing to throw up steel. O'Malley's obvious intention was to ratchet up the pressure on local officials.

Both of his steps quickly bore fruit. The Dodgers had previously scheduled a goodwill tour of Japan after the World Series, beginning with a layover in Los Angeles.[48] O'Malley freely admitted that he planned to meet a local official during the October 12 stop—"if Mr. Hahn would like to have breakfast with me in the morning, it will be a pleasure"—though he again denied any interest in moving the Dodgers.[49] Hahn would always insist that the two men shook hands on the transfer that very day, though such haste would have been uncharacteristic of O'Malley.[50]

The sale of Ebbets Field was announced less than three weeks later. Developer Marvin Kratter paid three million dollars for the decrepit ballpark on October 30, revealing his plans to eventually build a massive housing project on the site. He granted the ballclub a three-year lease in the interim.[51] "The Dodgers fully intend to stay in Brooklyn," said Red Patterson, the team's assistant general manager. "The lease insures us a home now until the new stadium can be built."[52]

O'Malley's maneuvers during the critical month of October 1956—his open flirtation with Los Angeles and the sale of his ballpark—tightened the screws on New York's political leaders. The same actions also signaled the erosion of his oft-expressed optimism.

Three letters to John Cashmore documented the change. O'Malley never pulled his punches in early letters to the Brooklyn borough president, nor did he make threats. "Our situation is really acute," he wrote in a typical note in January 1955, stressing his eagerness for a new stadium, but making no mention of the possibility of failure.[53] O'Malley still seemed calm on December 7, 1956, though he was now unable to resist a dark hint: "Let's be patient a bit longer, and if things do not seem to be working out, we will have to be practical and reluctantly go elsewhere."[54] Even this lingering tone of forbearance disappeared by January 11, 1957. "On the matter that you and I have been interested in for so many years," O'Malley wrote Cashmore, "it would appear to be in a critical state with little practical hope for a quick recovery."[55]

The latter note was sent upon O'Malley's return from another whirlwind trip to California. He purchased a forty-four-passenger Convair 440 in San Diego during the first week of 1957. "If any club should go to the West Coast, it would have to fly, and it would have to own an airplane," he admitted to reporters, though he also reiterated his devotion to Brooklyn.[56] He then squeezed in a visit to a potential stadium site in Los Angeles. "We just happened to be driving past Chavez Ravine," he joked, "and we thought we'd have a look."[57]

A move to California now seemed likely, though it was unclear if O'Malley truly wanted to go. He continued to stress his preference for Brooklyn—"I belong there; the team belongs there"—but it was obvious that his hardball tactics had failed to motivate New York's leaders.[58] Cashmore and Mayor Wagner had nothing new to offer, while Robert Moses was already developing plans for an Atlantic-Flatbush housing project. *The New York Times* concluded at the beginning of 1957 that prospects for a stadium had "neared the vanishing point."[59] O'Malley had backed himself into a corner. Los Angeles appeared to be his only remaining option.

So he pushed forward, escalating the stakes with a dramatic announcement on February 21, 1957. The Dodgers purchased the Los Angeles Angels of the Pacific Coast League for three million dollars—the price that Phil Wrigley had established three years earlier—and acquired the city's territorial rights in the process. The *Los Angeles Times* heralded the transaction with an eight-column, two-deck headline that dominated its front page, a massive display normally reserved for historic military victories.[60] O'Malley was defiant. "Many persons seem to have thought that in the moves I have made, such as playing games in Jersey City, I have been bluffing—trying to swing a big stick," he said. "I haven't been bluffing."[61]

Bob Wagner responded with a telegram, vaguely promising "all possible efforts to arrive at a satisfactory solution."[62] Wagner's counterpart, Los Angeles mayor Norris Poulson, reacted with greater vigor. He traveled to Florida to meet O'Malley at the Dodgers' training camp on March 6. Kenneth Hahn flew with him. Their enthusiasm was contagious. "They came down laden with all manner of colossal, gigantic, spectacular, and other Hollywood adjectives in their promises," recalled Dodgers vice president Fresco Thompson.[63] Mayor Poulson cut straight to the point. "Mr. O'Malley has a problem," he told reporters. "We believe we can solve it—and quick."[64]

That was too much for O'Malley, who abruptly called a halt to his joint press conference with the mayor. "That's the last question, boys," he said. "It's about time I reached the point to button up my lip on the matter until something develops."[65] But he was more forthcoming in his private correspondence, as in a March 11 letter to his friend Frank Schroth, the former publisher of the late, lamented *Brooklyn Eagle*. "The Los Angeles matter," O'Malley wrote, "is much firmer than the newspaper accounts would indicate."[66]

20

Showdown

Bill Radovich believed he had a solid legal case.

The 240-pound lineman had established himself as a key member of the Detroit Lions during his five years in the National Football League, even winning All-Pro honors in 1945. But his family was two thousand miles away in Los Angeles, and his father had been afflicted with bladder cancer. Radovich asked the Lions to trade him to the Rams so he could be closer to his dad. It seemed a simple request.

The Lions refused. The NFL's reserve clause was similar to baseball's, which normally would have left Radovich with two options—stay in Detroit or retire. But 1946 was an abnormal year. The All-America Football Conference had just been born, and it was only too happy to welcome somebody with Radovich's skills. He signed with the Los Angeles Dons.

There wasn't much the NFL could do about his defection—football was no more eager than baseball to test its reserve clause in the courts—though the league did slap Radovich onto its blacklist. The AAFC couldn't have cared less, but the sport's minor leagues were wary of offending the NFL, as Radovich learned upon his retirement in 1948. He accepted a coaching job with the San Francisco Clippers of football's Pacific Coast League, only to see the offer suddenly rescinded. The Clippers explained that they couldn't afford to hire anybody who had been blacklisted.[1]

Radovich countered with a restraint-of-trade lawsuit against the NFL. "I'm not out to wreck football," he said. "I wouldn't want to do anything like that. But I didn't like to have a man tell me I could play for one club and nobody else."[2] His hopes for swift justice, however, would be repeatedly frustrated. Radovich filed his paperwork in 1949—two years before Earl Toolson went to court against baseball's reserve clause—yet his case would still be snaking through the judicial pipeline long after the Supreme Court issued its *Toolson* ruling in 1953.

Legal experts were uncertain of Radovich's prospects. The *Toolson* decision had landed in baseball's favor, leaving the NFL hopeful of a similar victory. Yet other Supreme Court rulings during the mid–1950s tipped in the opposite direction. A pair of 1955 decisions specifically denied antitrust exemptions to boxing promoters and traveling theatrical companies, even though they shared much in common with baseball teams.[3] "*Toolson* is not authority for exempting other businesses," decreed Earl Warren in the boxing case.[4]

The chief justice's opinion confused almost everybody. A baseball team that crossed state lines to play a game was not participating in interstate commerce, according to the Supreme Court, yet a boxer or theatrical troupe that traversed the same borders was classified as a fully commercial venture. Baseball consequently fell outside the purview of the antitrust laws, but the latter two activities were completely covered.

What did this mean for football—and, by extension, for baseball? Emanuel Celler was getting riled up again, blasting the reserve clause as "barbarous" and threatening another congressional investigation of professional sports.[5] The boxing decision, as he saw it, hinted at a change in the Supreme Court's thinking. Celler suggested that the *Federal Baseball* and *Toolson* precedents might soon be overturned, exposing all sports—even baseball—to antitrust regulations. "At last, the Supreme Court is coming to its senses," he said. "I don't see how it can reconcile its argument that boxing is interstate commerce and baseball is not. It will have to eat its words sooner or later."[6]

The first chance to test the congressman's theory came on February 25, 1957, when the Supreme Court finally ruled in the case of *Radovich v. National Football League*. The 6–3 decision went precisely as Celler had predicted. The court ruled that pro football was indeed involved in interstate commerce, and hence was subject to all antitrust laws. It returned the case to an appellate court to determine Radovich's monetary award. (He eventually accepted a settlement of $42,500.)[7]

What was truly important about the *Radovich* decision—and what absolutely frightened the baseball establishment—was a sentence buried in the opinion written by Associate Justice Tom Clark, who acknowledged the absurdity of treating baseball and football differently: "If this ruling [on football] is unrealistic, inconsistent, or illogical, it is sufficient to answer … that, were we considering the question of baseball for the first time upon a clean slate, we would have no doubts." Clark contended that Oliver Wendell Holmes's 1922 grant of an antitrust exemption in *Federal Baseball* "was of dubious validity" and would not be approved by the current court. So why not simply declare it unconstitutional? "The orderly way to eliminate error or discrimination, if any there be, is by legislation, and not by court decision," Clark wrote.[8]

Ford Frick immediately advised baseball owners to keep their mouths shut. Nothing would be served by commenting on the *Radovich* decision. The commissioner's edict fueled Manny Celler's rage. "Frick wants to gag everyone," he spat. "Hasn't he heard of the First Amendment? He wants to be the poohbah—and the only one."[9]

Celler possessed a massive amount of power himself—certainly more than Ford Frick—and he began to lay plans to wield it. The Supreme Court had once again punted the antitrust issue back to Congress. Celler decided to field the kick.

* * *

Horace Stoneham affected a lack of interest in Brooklyn's stadium drama. "What the Dodgers do is their business," he said at the beginning of 1957. "As far as we're concerned, we like New York and plan to stay there."[10] He appeared to have forgotten his recent expression of interest in Minneapolis. Stoneham now denied any desire to move there, severely dashing hopes in Minnesota. "You are a big-league city, and you are going to make it eventually," he assured a reporter with the *Minneapolis Star*.[11]

But Stoneham's equanimity did not last. He was bragging by early March that he had received offers from several cities—"I certainly have; you can bet your life I have"—and the flurry seemed to have rekindled his wanderlust. "If the Dodgers should move to Los Angeles, our rivalry with them would suffer considerably," he said. "In that case, we would have to decide whether it would be better for us to move, too."[12]

It was difficult to follow Stoneham's logic. The Giants were currently pocketing annual radio-TV revenue of $730,000 ($6.7 million in 2020 dollars), a sum likely to soar if the other National League club vacated the New York market. Thousands of disenfranchised Dodgers fans could be expected to attend Giants games at the Polo Grounds, and Stoneham would suddenly be free to build a stadium anywhere in the city, even in Brooklyn, prior to the 1962 expiration of his lease.[13]

O'Malley was as confused as everybody else. Was Stoneham determined to remain in New York, or was he preparing to escape? The Dodgers owner asked for a meeting to clear the air, and the two men sat down in Clearwater, Florida, on March 22, 1957. They talked for three hours.[14]

Stoneham surprised his colleague by admitting that he had already decided to move to Minneapolis in 1958, despite his public denials. "We had a ballclub there, so I had the rights to the area, and it's a big city in itself," he later explained.[15] O'Malley suggested that an isolated market in the Upper Midwest might not be the best destination for the Giants. "I asked Mr. Stoneham if he had considered San Francisco, and he said he was not at all impressed by that location," O'Malley wrote in an internal memorandum the following day.[16]

That posed a challenge. "I wanted him in San Francisco, so I could turn our interborough feud into an intercity feud," O'Malley said two decades later.[17] The Dodgers owner offered to arrange a meeting between Stoneham and San Francisco mayor George Christopher. The ebullient Christopher was a natural salesman, eager to convince Stoneham of his city's demographic advantages (a metropolitan population of 2.8 million as opposed to 1.5 million in Minneapolis–St. Paul) and its rock-solid funding for a new ballpark (the $5 million bond issue that had been approved in 1954).[18]

"We like New York and plan to stay there," said Giants owner Horace Stoneham at the beginning of 1957. But he soon decided to move his franchise to Minneapolis. Walter O'Malley intervened to reroute Stoneham to San Francisco [National Baseball Hall of Fame and Museum].

O'Malley's own decision

was virtually set in stone. "I have about given up of ever getting the politicians and the saboteurs together," he wrote Frank Schroth on March 31. "My efforts from now on will be quite seriously in the direction of a move." Yet he was still intrigued by the possibility of striking a deal with Robert Moses, a dichotomy he could not easily explain. "Now you see the inconsistency of the Irish mind," he told Schroth in the same letter. "In one paragraph, I am sailing to a distant port, and in the last above one, I am still trying to keep my anchor in Brooklyn."[19]

Well, not quite Brooklyn. The Dodgers owner and the development czar met at Moses's Long Island home in early April 1957. The Atlantic-Flatbush site was a dead issue, Moses said, but he thought another location might be acceptable. He dug out a map of Queens and pointed to Flushing Meadow Park. "The site outlined on the map which we examined has possibilities," O'Malley conceded in an internal memo. The two men agreed to tour the park on April 15.[20]

There were reasons to greet Moses's new idea positively. Queens was expanding rapidly—adding 2,150 residents per month during the 1950s—in contrast to Brooklyn's average monthly loss of 920. And Queens was more accessible to the Long Island suburbs where most of those ex-Brooklynites were relocating. Adjacent Nassau County was growing at the mind-boggling pace of 5,200 persons per month.[21]

O'Malley did his best to appear interested as he and Moses tramped around Flushing Meadow, though his initial enthusiasm was already dwindling. Moses stressed that the seventy-eight-acre site would be roomy enough to park twelve thousand cars, meeting one of O'Malley's chief demands. The Dodgers owner countered with a complaint about inadequate public-transit connections. He also expressed doubt about the stability of the parkland itself, much of which had been reclaimed from nearby Flushing Bay.[22] It might be too risky, he mused, to build a triple-decked grandstand there. "By the Fourth of July, maybe I'd have only two decks above ground," he said. "And by Labor Day, a single deck."[23]

His biggest objection, of course, was the location in Queens, roughly thirteen miles northeast of Ebbets Field. "You would not be the Brooklyn Dodgers if you were not in Brooklyn," O'Malley said. "And as long as you're going to move, what difference does it make whether you move five miles or five thousand miles?"[24]

It was an absurd question. Brooklyn residents might be angered by a transfer to Flushing Meadow, but at least they could still attend games there, a privilege that would be foreclosed by a move to Los Angeles. And what about the hundreds of thousands of Dodgers rooters who lived outside the borough? Those in Queens and the Long Island suburbs would actually be closer to the new ballpark than to Ebbets Field, while fans who lived farther away were unlikely to care about a thirteen-mile shift. The Dodgers' radio network had nineteen affiliates across Upstate New York, Connecticut, Massachusetts, and Pennsylvania. Most listeners in that far-flung territory would have happily supported the New York Dodgers or Long Island Dodgers as easily as the Brooklyn Dodgers.[25]

Robert Moses, the master of delay, suddenly morphed into an advocate of action. "We in the Park Department can build a first-class, all-purpose sports center at Flushing Meadow in jig time if we are given the green light," he insisted.[26] But he found it impossible to get O'Malley's undivided attention. The Dodgers owner caught a flight to Los Angeles in late April, incongruously sporting a pin that said "Keep the Dodgers in Brooklyn."

O'Malley toured Wrigley Field and the Memorial Coliseum, then helicoptered over Chavez Ravine. He envisioned the first two as temporary homes for the Dodgers while his dream ballpark was erected on the latter site.[27] Chavez Ravine was a hilly tract north of downtown Los Angeles, inhabited by a small number of Mexican-Americans. Plans for a public-housing project—a West Coast version of one of Robert Moses's massive productions—had been announced for the area in 1950, only to be abandoned in the face of intense political pressure. Few Los Angeles voters wanted to build homes for poor people, especially those with darker skins. "Public housing follows the communist pattern," declared John Holland, a prominent city councilman. "These are the people who are trying to wreck America."[28]

Mayor Poulson tried to find another use for Chavez Ravine. "I talked to sponsors of the opera-house project, to zoo patrons, to horse-show enthusiasts, and others, but none was excited," he said.[29] And then O'Malley showed up, proclaiming the area an ideal site for a ballpark. Poulson happily tucked two million dollars into his upcoming budget to build access roads to the ravine, an added incentive for the Dodgers.[30]

O'Malley had returned to New York by then, arranging the first meeting between Horace Stoneham and George Christopher at the Hotel Lexington on May 10, 1957. Stoneham asked Christopher what type of stadium deal San Francisco would offer the Giants, but the mayor's response was vague. O'Malley quietly started writing on the back of an envelope, then showed his handiwork to both parties. They agreed it was an acceptable framework for a deal.[31]

It had been widely assumed that O'Malley and Stoneham would wait until October to disclose their plans and seek National League approval for any moves, but their recent maneuvers left them impatient for action. A league meeting was hastily called for May 28. Both men admitted behind closed doors that they were intrigued by California, though they refused to be pinned down. O'Malley suggested it would be helpful if the other owners indicated where they stood on the question of abandoning New York for Los Angeles and San Francisco. Unanimous support was quickly offered.[32]

"All I can say now is that this action opens the doors for exploration of further possibilities," said O'Malley after the vote was made public. Stoneham was equally noncommittal. "This permission merely gives us a further chance to examine the possibilities," he said.[33] But it meant much more than that, as everybody knew. The Dodgers and Giants were as good as gone.

Robert Wagner resolved to make a last stand, inviting O'Malley and Stoneham to City Hall on June 4 for what the newspapers extravagantly billed as a "showdown meeting." Nothing was accomplished.[34] The mayor was alternately supplicating and defiant—pledging to devote his full attention to the Dodgers' and Giants' stadium problems, yet insisting that he would "not be blackjacked into anything."[35] O'Malley was hazily agreeable. If the Wagner administration came up with a workable plan in the next few weeks, he said, "we will sit down with them, and our decision will be definite and final and correct."

But the Dodgers owner hastened to make one important adjustment to his position, officially withdrawing his 1956 pledge to invest in bonds issued by the Brooklyn Sports Center Authority. It seemed that all the money was gone. "Since then,"

O'Malley explained, "we have invested in Los Angeles real estate, and we no longer have the five million dollars."[36]

* * *

The contradictory nature of the *Radovich* ruling bothered several members of Congress. Patrick Hillings, a young representative from California, introduced a bill in February 1957, the very month of the Supreme Court decision. His proposal targeted baseball—Hillings called it the "horsehide cartel"—by subjecting it to the same antitrust obligations as football. Emanuel Celler, the chairman of the House Judiciary Committee, gave his blessing. "You can't call one [sport] a fish and the other a fowl," he said.[37]

But Hillings's bill languished in committee. Celler, despite his rhetoric, felt no motivation to push it. He dithered until the National League voted to allow his hometown Dodgers to flee to Los Angeles, which reignited his anger. Celler swiftly introduced his own bill to extend the antitrust laws to all sports, and he announced on June 1 that he would initiate subcommittee hearings in just two and a half weeks.[38]

The chairman made it clear that O'Malley and Stoneham were his targets. "In one breath, they say that baseball is a sport, not subject to antitrust regulations," he said angrily. "In another breath, they say they have the right to move franchises in the interest of dollars, selling to the highest bidder. If that isn't business, I'd like to know what it is."[39]

Celler had been relatively kind to baseball during his 1951 hearings—leaving the reserve clause undisturbed—but he was out for blood this time. He seemed to be motivated by pure contempt. "The owners indeed are like troglodytes. They live in caves and rarely see the light," Celler told an associate.[40] This was a bad omen for Ford Frick, who desired a harmonious relationship with Congress, unmarred by troublesome legislation.

The commissioner, though vested with supreme powers, had been dodging the controversy that the Dodgers and Giants had stirred up. Pesky reporters kept inquiring in June 1957 if he planned to intercede to force both teams to remain in New York. "That's a National League problem," he brusquely replied.[41] Frick later explained that he had sympathized with both sides. "As a fan, I was upset by the action," he wrote in his 1973 memoirs. "As commissioner, if I had the final decision and knowing the facts in the case, I would have approved the move with no reservations."[42] It seemed best to stand clear.

Celler had no intention of letting him off the hook. He summoned Frick as a witness on June 19, the second day of the hearings. The two men, along with Upstate New York congressman Kenneth Keating, quickly got to the heart of the matter:

> **CELLER:** I take it at this juncture you don't know what is going to happen with reference to Brooklyn and Los Angeles.
> **FRICK:** I do not know what is going to happen with reference to Brooklyn and Los Angeles and the Giants and San Francisco.
> **KEATING:** Aren't we going to have Mr. Stoneham and Mr. O'Malley here to testify? They would know probably more than you would about that.
> **FRICK:** If they don't, then I am sure we have no answers.
> **CELLER:** We have the commissioner of baseball here, and they apparently don't tell him.[43]

Frick admitted that he lacked the rhetorical gifts of Celler—"a man who can give me aces and spades and beat me at that sort of game"—but he managed to accomplish his primary mission.[44] The former sportswriter understood how to generate headlines, and he landed on the front page of the *New York Times* by predicting catastrophe if Celler's antitrust bill were enacted. "I see baseball set back fifty years," he said.[45]

But Frick was a mere sideshow in the chairman's eyes. The main event occurred seven days later. Celler wasted no time after O'Malley settled into the witness chair on June 26:

> **CELLER:** Now, Mr. O'Malley, I have to ask you the burning question. Can you tell the committee at this time whether or not the Dodgers will play in Los Angeles next year?
> **O'MALLEY:** I'm sorry, I cannot answer that question.
> **CELLER:** Why?
> **O'MALLEY:** I do not know the answer.[46]

They jousted for more than two hours, settling nothing. O'Malley portrayed himself as a faithful son of Brooklyn, a visionary who wished to build a beautiful ballpark in a decaying borough. "I am crazy enough to be willing to put five million dollars into an old place that I just happen to love," he said.[47] He blamed City Hall for sabotaging this simple dream, for stalling every attempt to commence the Atlantic-Flatbush project. "I have seen a lot of inaction," O'Malley told the committee. "I have seen a lot of divertisements and decoy propositions." The situation on the opposite coast, he said, was considerably different: "Things are moving very rapidly and very intelligently in Los Angeles."[48]

Celler was caustic in response. "If you think Brooklyn is so terrible, I'm surprised that you want to remain there," he told O'Malley.[49] Not that the chairman believed there was any possibility of the Dodgers staying put. "There's no question about it," Celler told the reporters who encircled him after the session. "I think Mr. O'Malley has his mind made up to go. It's all cut and dried."[50]

O'Malley had been a self-assured, vague, and conciliatory witness, the epitome of a seasoned lawyer. Horace Stoneham displayed none of these qualities when he appeared before the subcommittee on July 17. He exuded desperation, bluntly expressing an urgent desire to relocate to San Francisco. "If our club does not make an immediate move, we are confronted with diminishing income each year," he said.[51] He envisioned no prospects whatsoever for success in Manhattan: "In my thinking, the city of New York cannot support three clubs of major-league proportion."[52]

Stoneham offered an additional reason for a quick transfer to California. He anticipated an eventual windfall from pay television, even though the Federal Communications Commission had not approved any of the competing systems that had long been under development. Zenith, for instance, had been doggedly pushing its Phonevision concept ever since 1952. Yet the FCC's imprimatur remained elusive, primarily because TV networks and movie studios were lobbying strenuously in opposition.[53]

Subcommittee members pressed Stoneham for details. Couldn't he reap the same benefits from pay television if the Giants remained in New York? Local competition made it impossible, he replied. The Yankees and Dodgers were blanketing the market with free telecasts of their games. "It would not be very practical to attempt to charge in competition with free television," Stoneham said.⁵⁴ San Francisco was preferable because the Giants would have the region all to themselves.

But what about the FCC's inaction? Stoneham said that he was investing his hopes—and five thousand dollars of his personal funds—in Skiatron, a firm that had found a way to circumvent federal oversight. The FCC regulated all programming transmitted through the public airwaves—the method preferred by most pay-television systems—but Skiatron intended to string an extensive network of cables to provide its service. The company, in fact, was currently negotiating to spin its web throughout the San Francisco and Los Angeles areas. The FCC exercised no control over cable systems.⁵⁵

The Giants owner predicted that five or six hundred thousand San Francisco households might pay to watch a single Giants game on television. A subcommittee lawyer did some quick math in his head. "Your income from that would be about $125,000?" he asked. Stoneham just smiled. "That is right," he said.⁵⁶

Walter O'Malley remained coy as the final days of summer drifted away—maintaining that he was still assessing the relative merits of Brooklyn and Los Angeles—but Stoneham saw no need to play such games. He desperately wanted the new stadium and new income stream that awaited in San Francisco. "If we don't move now," he warned his stockholders, "there won't be any good cities left."⁵⁷

The board of directors of the National Exhibition Company, the Giants' legal parent, was bound to follow Stoneham's lead, given that he controlled a majority of its stock. The members gathered on August 19, 1957, and voted eight to one to shift the team westward. "It just tears my heart to see them go," said the only dissident, M. Donald Grant.⁵⁸

Horace Stoneham—the ultimate sentimentalist, the steadfast believer in loyalty—was emotional, too. "I had to do a helluva lot of soul-searching before I decided to take this move," he said.⁵⁹ His face was flushed; his voice was tremulous. A reporter asked about the children and teenagers whose heroes would be leaving town. Stoneham returned his gaze. "We're sorry to disappoint the kids of New York," he replied, "but we didn't see many of their parents out there at the Polo Grounds in recent years."⁶⁰

Headlines: 1957

Liner destroys career of budding star

Herb Score seemed to be the second coming of Bob Feller. The young fireballer led the major leagues in strikeouts in 1955 and 1956, inspiring the Red Sox to offer the Indians one million dollars for him in March 1957. Cleveland declined the offer. "I'm really very flattered," said Score. But hopes for a Hall of Fame career were extinguished on May 7, when a line drive struck Score in the eye. He would be gone from the major leagues before his twenty-ninth birthday.⁶¹

Reds fans stuff All-Star ballot box

The public was allowed to elect the starting lineups for the 1957 All-Star Game, an opportunity eagerly embraced by one National League city. Cincinnati voters generated a tsunami of five hundred thousand ballots, propelling seven Reds into the NL's batting order. Commissioner Ford Frick condemned the "terrible" election results, tossing out two Reds in favor of Willie Mays and Henry Aaron.[62]

Aaron's blast locks up NL crown for Braves

The Braves, who had fallen one game short of a National League pennant in 1956, ran away from the competition in 1957. Henry Aaron's eleventh-inning home run against the Cardinals on September 23 clinched Milwaukee's first title. *Time* magazine was moved to quote Exodus 8:17: "For Aaron stretched out his hand with his rod, and smote the dust of the earth."[63]

Milwaukee celebrates World Series triumph

The Braves kept rolling in the World Series, outdueling the Yankees in seven games. Lew Burdette tossed three complete games for Milwaukee and secured three wins, including a 5–0 triumph in Game Seven. One hundred thousand fans jammed the airport to welcome their heroes back from Yankee Stadium. "I was in New York on V-J night," said Braves traveling secretary Donald Davidson, "but I've never seen a city pitch a party to compare with Milwaukee's victory ball."[64]

PART THREE: 1958–1962

21

California

The Dodgers and Giants had fallen out of the pennant race by Labor Day 1957. Brooklyn was nine games behind Milwaukee; the Giants were twice as far back. Both teams were playing out the string, leaving plenty of time for Horace Stoneham to pay a quick visit to his adopted city, and for Walter O'Malley to conduct simultaneous negotiations on both coasts.[1]

Stoneham hustled in and out of San Francisco within twenty-four hours in late August. He inspected the proposed site for the Giants' new ballpark on Candlestick Point, met with Mayor George Christopher, and sparred with the local press. "Things are magnificent," he told the reporters.[2] They asked skeptically if he had spent much time at Candlestick, which was known for its stiff and chilly breezes. "Your native San Franciscan is used to this weather," Stoneham said dismissively.[3]

O'Malley, meanwhile, continued to play one city against the other. The Brooklyn Sports Center Authority was a dead letter—everybody agreed on that—so he revived his original plan. The Dodgers owner met with New York deputy mayor John Theobald on August 26, again proposing to build his own ballpark if the city would quickly condemn twelve acres at the intersection of Atlantic and Flatbush. He estimated that the stadium would cost the Dodgers $21.5 million ($197 million as of 2020).[4] City Hall's reaction was muted. "If Mr. O'Malley's offer aroused city officials here, it is not immediately apparent," wrote Bill Becker in the *New York Times*.[5]

Robert Wagner, who was up for reelection in November, had feared a huge outcry against the departure of the Giants and Dodgers, but New Yorkers were surprisingly apathetic. The anticipated flood of letters, phone calls, and telegrams never materialized. The mayor shrugged his shoulders when a reporter asked if the baseball issue seemed politically dangerous. "Not particularly," he said.[6] This nonchalance trickled down to his staff. "If we find that O'Malley and Stoneham are dead set about leaving New York," said William Peer, Wagner's executive secretary, "then we'll just have to pick up our marbles and go home."[7]

Robert Moses did not share this indifference. He reacted to the latest stadium proposal with an unalloyed blend of annoyance and contempt. O'Malley had once again stressed his love for Brooklyn, which greatly irritated Moses. "I have heard this speech over and over again *ad nauseum*," the czar moaned. "From time to time, Walter has embroidered it with shamrocks, harps, and wolfhounds, and has added the bouquet of liqueur Irish whiskey."[8] Moses's anger was accentuated by O'Malley's dismissal of the stadium site in Queens, which the latter considered unsafe. "What Walter says about foundation problems at Flushing Meadow is rubbish," Moses said.[9]

O'Malley was also negotiating with Los Angeles officials as August turned to

September, much to the displeasure of those closest to him. His wife and daughter emphatically opposed a coast-to-coast move, as did a majority of the Dodgers' front-office employees.[10] Buzzie Bavasi never forgot a staff meeting where O'Malley asked for a show of hands. "The vote was eight to one not to go to California," he said, "but the one vote was Walter's."[11]

Most of the men in uniform were unhappy, too. "If you'd have asked the players on the Dodgers to take a vote, it might have been 25–0 to stay in Brooklyn," pitcher Don Drysdale recalled in 1990.[12] Center fielder Duke Snider remembered two years earlier that he had been "heartsick" at the prospect of moving.[13] Their emotions were especially notable because both of these future Hall of Famers had been born in Los Angeles.

But Drysdale was wrong about unanimity. A third Dodger destined for Cooperstown, Brooklyn native Sandy Koufax, thought it might be fun to live somewhere different. "I have to confess that, Brooklyn boy or no, I was rather looking forward to another adventure," Koufax later wrote.[14] Contemporary newspaper accounts suggested that he wasn't alone. The *Los Angeles Times* reported in 1957 that Drysdale ("why all the stalling?") and Snider ("most of the fellows can hardly wait") were especially eager to head west, regardless of their memories three decades later.[15]

Yet their fates remained uncertain as O'Malley continued to prod New York officials and dicker with their Los Angeles counterparts. He seemed to be making no discernible progress until September 10, when tycoon Nelson Rockefeller unexpectedly declared his desire to save the Dodgers for New York. "Certainly the greatest city in the world should have two baseball teams," said Rockefeller. "It has proved that it can support them."[16]

This was a game changer. Rockefeller was one of the richest men in America, so wealthy that he could have paid for a stadium himself. The mayor of Los Angeles all but surrendered. "If it is true that Mr. Rockefeller has entered this picture, I'm very much afraid we don't have much of a chance to get the Dodgers," Norris Poulson said disconsolately.[17]

Rockefeller had never been a sports fan—he directed his passion toward his massive art collection—but it was an open secret that he intended to run for governor of New York in 1958. Professional politicians considered his plans absurd. How could such a blue blood possibly connect with the average voter? Rockefeller confided his political dreams to a former three-term governor, Thomas Dewey, who slapped him on the knee. "Nelson, you're a great guy," Dewey laughed, "but you couldn't get elected dogcatcher in New York."[18]

That's where the Dodgers came in. Rockefeller's chief aide, Frank Jamieson, pushed him to intervene. "Most politicians have to build themselves up. You've got to bring yourself down," Jamieson said.[19] Here was an opportunity to grab a few headlines and appeal to the workingmen who loved the Dodgers. "You don't have to buy the team," Jamieson said. "You just have to make a bid, to show your interest."[20]

The next nine days brought a whirlwind of publicity. Wagner, Rockefeller, and O'Malley huddled for more than two hours on September 18 to hammer out the final details of their secret proposal. O'Malley offered only three words—"it has merit"— to reporters who pushed for details.[21] But there was widespread dissent when the plan was unveiled the following day. Rockefeller wanted the city to condemn the Atlantic-Flatbush site, then sell the property to him for two million dollars. He, in

Nelson Rockefeller was no baseball fan, but he needed publicity to fuel his impending campaign for governor of New York. Aide Frank Jamieson convinced Rockefeller to try to save the Dodgers for Brooklyn. "You just have to make a bid, to show your interest," said Jamieson [Library of Congress].

turn, would lease the site to the Dodgers, rent-free, for twenty years. The team would have the right to buy the land at any time.[22]

James Lyons, the Bronx borough president, expressed the majority view. "There is no great need to subsidize the Dodgers," he said.[23] Rockefeller quietly exited the stage—his political profile having been greatly enhanced by all the front-page play—and the momentum shifted back to Los Angeles.

The time inexorably came for New York's teams to say goodbye. The fate of the Dodgers had not yet been announced, but it was assumed that their Tuesday night game against the Pirates on September 24 would be their farewell to Brooklyn. Only 6,702 fans bothered to show up. Ebbets Field organist Gladys Goodding played tunes appropriate for the occasion: "California, Here I Come," "After You're Gone," "Don't Ask Me Why I'm Leaving," "Thanks for the Memories," and "How Can You Say We're Through?" She capped the 2–0 victory over Pittsburgh with "Auld Lang Syne."[24]

The Giants wrapped up their forty-seven-year stay in the Polo Grounds five days later. Among the 11,606 in attendance was the widow of John McGraw, the team's Hall of Fame manager from 1902 to 1932. Blanche McGraw came to pay her respects despite her sadness—"New York can never be the same to me"—but Horace Stoneham was curiously absent.[25] "I couldn't go to the game," the owner explained. "I just didn't want to see it come to an end."[26] His Giants played listlessly, losing 9–1 to the Pirates, but most fans stayed till the bitter end. They cheered loudly as their favorite player, Willie Mays, came to bat in the bottom of the ninth. "I never felt so nervous," Mays said. "My hands were shaking. It was worse than any World Series game."

He swung wildly, hoping to salute the fans with a home run, but tapped back to the pitcher.[27]

All eyes now turned west. The National League had set a deadline of October 1 for resolution of the Dodgers' fate, yet O'Malley still lacked a firm offer from Los Angeles. Poulson was proposing to give 185 acres of Chavez Ravine to the Dodgers, while promising to help the team secure another 115 acres from private owners. He pledged that the City Council would vote on his package by October 7. The league unanimously granted O'Malley an extension.[28]

Poulson's proposal required two-thirds approval—ten of the fifteen council members—and he knew it would be a close call. The land deal was unpopular with conservative elements in Los Angeles, led by Councilman John Holland, who blasted it as "nothing but a steal and a giveaway."[29] The resulting meeting was predictably contentious and extremely long.

The marathon began as O'Malley watched Game Five of the World Series in Milwaukee—the very city that had inspired his desire to build a new stadium—and it droned on as he flew back to his home in Amityville on Long Island's southern shore.[30] A desperate Rosalind Wyman reached him by phone shortly after he walked in the front door. She pushed for a commitment that might help her to sway the council's recalcitrant members.

"I am going to the floor," Wyman said. "I would like to say you are coming."

But O'Malley would not tip his hand, not even at this late hour. "Mrs. Wyman, I am grateful for everything you have done," he said. "I am grateful for everything the mayor has done. But I have to tell you if I could get my deal in New York, I'd rather stay in New York."[31]

Wyman returned to the debate, saying nothing to her colleagues about the bewildering conversation. Had O'Malley made a secret arrangement in New York? Did he view Los Angeles as a mere bargaining chip? Or was he truly torn, unable to decide between his native city and the promised land? Wyman didn't know what to think. She cast an affirmative vote when the time finally came, and nine others joined her. The 10–4 vote barely met the threshold for approval.

O'Malley remained uncharacteristically quiet the following day. It fell to the assistant general manager of the Dodgers, Red Patterson, to post a fifty-two-word statement in the World Series press room at New York's Waldorf-Astoria.[32] The press release announced that the Dodgers would be taking "the necessary steps ... to draft the Los Angeles territory," a convoluted way of saying that they were heading west.[33]

The agonizing decision had finally been made, and O'Malley swiftly put Brooklyn behind him. He shot a telegram to Mayor Poulson: "Get your wheelbarrow and shovel. I'll meet you at Chavez Ravine."[34] And he summoned reporters from Los Angeles newspapers to his old office on Montague Street, eager to establish new relationships as quickly as he could. "Good teams and good attendance go hand in hand," he told them. "It takes money to build a winner. Witness Milwaukee's success. Well, the Braves can consider themselves challenged as of today."[35]

* * *

Robert Wagner appeared confident on the surface, yet no politician ever operates without fear. The mayor still wondered if the loss of both National League clubs might emerge as a last-minute issue in his reelection campaign. He hustled to preclude the possibility, declaring on September 26—twelve days prior to the Dodgers' official departure—that he would soon appoint a committee to secure a new NL team for New York.[36]

There was no particular reaction to his announcement. Millions of local fans were experiencing a mixture of anger, depression, and grief. Their gloom enveloped the city, inspiring Arthur Daley to write a remarkably pessimistic column in the *New York Times*. "Will there ever again be another National League club in New York?" Daley asked in mid–October. "The answer is a vehement no."[37] Individual action of any sort—even as simple as political retribution against the mayor—seemed pointless.

This lethargy worked in Wagner's favor. He crushed his Republican opponent, Robert Christenberry, by 924,000 votes on November 5. It was the largest margin of victory for any mayor since 1898's five-borough amalgamation, and it remains the biggest to this day. Wagner ran up an edge of 331,000 in Brooklyn alone, winning three-quarters of the borough's votes. The baseball issue had truly caused him no harm.[38]

But some owners worried that the sport itself would not be so lucky.[39] Phil Wrigley had loyally supported both moves—"Mr. Stoneham knows what he is doing, and what he is doing is strictly his own business"—yet he wasn't sure it was wise to vacate the nation's largest market.[40] He warned his colleagues that they might have opened the door for a third major league. "I mean an independent group competing with the present leagues. Why not?" Wrigley said.[41]

The president of the Class AAA International League was thinking along the same lines. Frank Shaughnessy announced on October 17 that the IL's Havana Sugar Kings would relocate to Jersey City in 1958. He hailed it as "the first big step in becoming a third major league" and speculated about adding a club in Brooklyn. "I don't know how long it will take," said Shaughnessy. "Maybe a year, two, or five. But we are on our way."[42]

Ford Frick had no intention of allowing a repeat of the protracted Pacific Coast League nightmare of the late 1940s and early 1950s. Some of the International League's markets seemed big enough for the majors—Buffalo, Miami, Montreal, Toronto—but others were way too small. The Rochester region had only 600,000 residents, Richmond just 400,000. The commissioner brusquely advised Shaughnessy to jettison his big-league dreams. The IL would not be putting a team anywhere in the New York metropolitan area—not in Jersey City and definitely not in Brooklyn.[43]

Frick had other headaches. If two of baseball's flagship franchises could abandon North America's largest market, why couldn't smaller teams indulge themselves? Calvin Griffith resumed his flirtations late in the 1957 season, even though President Eisenhower had just signed a bill authorizing a new fifty-thousand-seat stadium for the Senators.[44] Griffith greeted a delegation from Minneapolis—"I listened intently and was happy that I sat in on the session"—and visited the city's two-year-old ballpark after the World Series.[45] The two sides held eight meetings before Griffith pulled the plug on October 21.

The young owner promised to restrain his wandering eye in the future, proclaiming his loyalty in an op-ed piece in the *Washington Post*. "This is my home," Griffith wrote on January 15, 1958. "As long as I have any say in the matter, and I expect that I shall for a long, long time, the Washington Senators will stay here, too. Next year. The year after. Forever."[46] Frick applauded the sentiment, though he conceded that Washington could be a tough place to make money. "From the standpoint of baseball, it is not good to be leaving the nation's capital," the commissioner said. "But you have to think of the poor devil who is holding the franchise."[47]

It would have been unthinkable a decade earlier, but the Indians were also debating a move. Cleveland's 1957 attendance was only 722,256—falling 72 percent short of Bill Veeck's 1948 total of 2,620,627, still the big-league record. Hank Greenberg, who had remained in the front office after Veeck's departure, was now the general manager, and he had gone sour on Cleveland.[48] He privately urged the team's chairman, Bill Daley, to grab Minneapolis before Griffith changed his mind. "Our management was composed primarily of Clevelanders, and they were afraid to make the move. I was pushing for it," Greenberg later admitted.[49] Daley eventually had his fill of Greenberg's agitation, firing the GM in October 1957, then buying his share of the Indians a year later.

This turbulent state of affairs—the air of uncertainty that pervaded baseball—gave hope to Robert Wagner. He appointed four men to his baseball committee on November 29 and challenged them to lure a National League team to New York. He assumed it would be a simple task.

Three of Wagner's appointees were well-known. James Farley had been one of Franklin Roosevelt's closest aides. Bernard Gimbel was chairman of the renowned department store that bore his name. Clinton Blume had pitched for the Giants in 1922 and 1923, and then served as president of the Real Estate Board of New York. A somewhat obscure lawyer, William Shea, rounded out the panel.[50]

It came as a surprise when Shea was named the committee's chairman—and even more shocking when he emerged as the point man in New York's recruitment drive. "We are in competition with other cities now," Shea said confidently, "but I can't see certain National League teams resisting an offer which includes fourteen million people within thirty-five miles."[51]

The new chairman winnowed his list to three targets. The Braves, Cardinals, and Cubs were blessed with solid fan bases and stable ownership; they weren't moving anywhere. That left the Cincinnati Reds, Pittsburgh Pirates, and Philadelphia Phillies as possibilities. Shea approached each of them, dangling a short-term lease at Ebbets Field and the long-range prospect of a new ballpark. He believed that one of the three would shift to New York before 1958's opening day. "I started out to get a team, and it looked easy," he said later.[52]

The Board of Estimate, New York's preeminent legislative body, added weight to Shea's pitch in January 1958, voting to build a stadium on city-owned land. But the resolution wasn't quite as decisive as it originally appeared. It stipulated that absolutely no action would be taken until a National League club made a solid commitment. "You just can't build a stadium on a promise," Wagner explained, even though a city with fewer resources, Milwaukee, had succeeded by doing precisely that.[53]

It didn't matter in the end. The owners of the three targeted teams were unanimous in their refusal to relocate. Powel Crosley briefly feigned interest in leaving Cincinnati—"we are under no obligation to stay here"—in order to obtain more parking around his ballpark.[54] The city quickly caved, allocating two million dollars for an additional twenty-six hundred spaces near Crosley Field. Pittsburgh's John Galbreath refused to even discuss moving. "[I] won't even entertain any thoughts of it," he said.[55]

Philadelphia's Robert Carpenter, Jr., was similarly adamant. He politely sat down with New York's representative, then he firmly said no.[56]

This last meeting had the greatest impact on Shea, who was impressed by Carpenter's loyalty to his city. "I begin to see that I am placing myself in the position of asking him to do the very thing I would never do. Pull out of your own town. That cured me," Shea recalled.[57] He resolved to find a different solution to his problem, though he knew it would take more time than he had originally expected. The National League would not be playing ball in New York in 1958.

* * *

The Pacific Coast League had no choice but to accept the National League's invasion of its territory. Three franchises were affected. The Seals, who had been based in San Francisco since 1903, slipped off to Phoenix. The Angels, whose ties to Los Angeles dated back to 1892, shuffled nine hundred miles north to Spokane, Washington. And the second PCL club in L.A., the Hollywood Stars, crept inland to Salt Lake City.

The Dodgers and Giants agreed to pay an indemnity totaling $946,000 ($8.65 million in 2020 dollars) to be split equally by all PCL teams except Phoenix and Spokane, which were owned by the two big-league invaders. But the windfall was coupled with a demotion. The PCL was stripped of the Open classification that Pants Rowland had worked so hard to obtain in 1951.[58] Its return to the AAA level—triggered by the loss of its biggest markets—evoked no sympathy from the baseball establishment. "This change of the baseball map has been hanging over the Coast League's head for ten or twelve years," said Phil Wrigley, "but its owners never did a thing about it. Baseball, in general, is that way. It never does anything until the roof caves in."[59]

That was a perfect description of Horace Stoneham's management style over the years. Inaction was his preferred strategy, so he had naturally remained passive as his Giants deteriorated and the Polo Grounds crumbled. His decision to move to San Francisco shocked his fellow owners because of its uncharacteristically proactive nature. This new Stoneham—a man of surprising efficiency and resolve—remained in the forefront in the wake of the 1957 season. He swiftly made himself at home in San Francisco, accompanied by a moving van jammed with the club's equipment and office furniture.[60] "Personally, I'm not really missing Broadway and New York so much," he would insist after just a few months in California.[61]

Stoneham made progress on several fronts. He decreed that his club would remain the Giants—"we think it's a pretty good name"—even though local fans advocated a switch to the Seals.[62] He hammered out a deal for temporary use of tiny Seals Stadium, which had just 22,900 seats, and he approved the blueprints for his new ballpark on Candlestick Point. Contractors promised that it would be ready for opening day in 1959.[63]

There were a couple of hitches in this generally smooth transition. Stoneham's biggest failure in New York had been his unwillingness to promote the Giants. He sought to turn over a new leaf in San Francisco, even agreeing to speak at a baseball banquet that winter. It did not go well. Stoneham rambled incoherently, then abruptly stopped. "Some of us drink too much," he muttered, ending his experiment in public relations.[64] A more dispiriting episode involved the efforts of star center fielder Willie Mays to purchase a home. "I'd never get another job if I sold this house to that baseball player," said the recalcitrant builder, who carefully left out the fact that Mays was black. The sale was eventually consummated, but only after San Francisco's supposedly liberal orientation was laid open to question.[65]

Yet the Giants' move, taken all in all, appeared to be going well, inspiring the *San Francisco Chronicle* to brag in a January 1958 editorial. "In San Francisco, the city that knows how, the Giants are in business, flourishing and making friends like sixty," the paper crowed. "In Los Angeles, the city that never has known how, chaos and frustration are roomies."[66]

The *Chronicle's* jab contained a kernel of truth. Walter O'Malley and thirty Dodgers employees had landed in Los Angeles on October 23, 1957, greeted by several hundred excited fans at the airport. But the team's arrival was far from an unalloyed success. O'Malley was served with a subpoena shortly after stepping on the tarmac. A taxpayer group had filed suit against the Chavez Ravine land swap, charging that construction of a baseball stadium did not constitute a "public purpose," the very objection that Robert Moses had raised in New York.[67]

That first day foreshadowed the Dodgers' entire first winter in their new home. Every success, or so it seemed, was diluted by a subsequent failure. O'Malley stoked the enthusiasm of his new fan base—"we're not going to be second to Milwaukee in anything"—only to be inundated with bills for moving expenses, the PCL indemnity, and leases that remained in effect for Ebbets Field and Jersey City's Roosevelt Stadium.[68] He trumpeted his impressive ticket sales—pocketing a million dollars by late November—only to learn that eighty-five-thousand citizens had signed petitions demanding a referendum on the Chavez Ravine deal. "We never had such a thing in New York," sputtered O'Malley, who was stunned to learn that local voters would decide the fate of his dream ballpark in June 1958.[69]

His biggest problem was simply finding a place to play for the upcoming season. Sportswriters expected the Dodgers to settle into Wrigley Field, which O'Malley had acquired when he purchased the minor-league Angels. But he turned up his nose at its puny capacity, lack of parking, and general decrepitude. It reminded him of nowhere quite as much as Ebbets Field, and he cast his veto.[70]

Only two stadiums in Los Angeles were big enough for O'Malley. Both, however, were ovals that had been designed for football. He preferred the Los Angeles Memorial Coliseum, but its governing board deadlocked on the Dodgers' application, with four members voting in favor, four against. So he turned reluctantly in December to the Rose Bowl. It had all the seats he could possibly desire—slightly more than one hundred thousand—though its location was not ideal, ten miles northeast of downtown in suburban Pasadena.[71]

"The Rose Bowl will prove to be a happy stadium for our West Coast debut," O'Malley declared in early January, putting the best face on an unhappy situation.[72] But the two sides could not agree on a formal contract, and the Dodgers suddenly found themselves adrift again. O'Malley desperately gave Wrigley Field a second look, renewed contact with the Coliseum, and even floated a drastic possibility.[73] "If anything should happen to make it impossible for us to open in Los Angeles," he said, "we could still return to Brooklyn."[74]

The lengthy stadium debacle horrified Norris Poulson—"I'm sorry to say we are the laughingstock of the country"—and he finally intervened to force a solution.[75] The mayor brought O'Malley and the Coliseum Commission together on January 17, 1958, and they managed to reach an agreement. "This ended my longest losing streak," O'Malley joked lamely as he shook hands on the deal.[76] Only ninety-one days remained before the season opener, and there was plenty of work to be done. Dugouts and a press box had to be built in the Coliseum, the vast territory beyond right field had to be fenced off, and a gigantic 40-foot screen had to be erected above the left-field fence, which loomed just 250 feet from home plate.[77]

O'Malley was destined to pass into baseball mythology as the quintessential mastermind, a clever strategist who coolly planned every facet of his epic move from Brooklyn to Los Angeles. But his legend did not comport with reality. The Chavez Ravine transaction—the impetus for the Dodgers' relocation—had quickly become entangled in a lawsuit and a referendum, both of which had caught O'Malley off guard. And the team's temporary stadium was clearly inadequate, perhaps the most absurd ballpark in the history of the major leagues.

The task of filling the Dodgers' new home fell to Harold Parrott, the Ebbets Field ticket manager who had come west with the club. He considered the Coliseum to be a joke—he likened it to a "gigantic saucepan"—and he scoffed at any suggestion that O'Malley might be a genius.[78] The haphazard nature of the California shift caused him to think otherwise. "The move," he would later write, "was about as well thought-out as a panty raid by a bunch of college freshman who'd had too many beers."[79]

22

Shea

The Pacific Coast's new ballclubs assembled their 1958 rosters in markedly different fashions.

Walter O'Malley believed that star power was essential for success in the movie capital of the world, so the Dodgers brought their aging heroes to Los Angeles. First baseman Gil Hodges was thirty-four, right fielder Carl Furillo thirty-six, and shortstop Pee Wee Reese a creaky thirty-nine, yet all three were in the opening-day lineup. Thirty-six-year-old catcher Roy Campanella—the National League's Most Valuable Player in 1951, 1953, and 1955—had been equally prominent in O'Malley's plans until January 28, when a Long Island car accident paralyzed him from the chest down.[1]

The Giants took the opposite tack. Their veterans had finished sixteen games below .500 in the final season in New York, so Manager Bill Rigney cleaned house. "We had definitely decided we were going with the young players when we got to San Francisco," he said. "It was going to be a new look." Willie Mays remained, of course, but he was surrounded by talented unknowns, ten of whom would be named to All-Star squads during their careers.[2]

The two clubs were given an immediate opportunity to rekindle their rivalry. The schedule sent the Dodgers to San Francisco for the initial three games of the 1958 season, directly followed by the Giants' first trip to Los Angeles. A sellout crowd of 23,448 jammed Seals Stadium for the opener on April 15. The two mayors provided a moment of inadvertent comedy during the pregame ceremony. George Christopher pitched to Norris Poulson, who tapped a dribbler to the infield and displayed the extent of his baseball knowledge by sprinting to third base. The Giants sent everybody home happy with an 8–0 victory.[3]

The whole thing seemed strange. Russ Hodges, the radio voice of the Giants, posted note cards in his booth on opening day, reminding him of the new names of both clubs. Yet he slipped in his very first seconds on the air, welcoming his listeners to "the Polo Grounds—I mean Seals Stadium."[4] The same problem afflicted a newsboy hawking special editions outside the ballpark after the game. "Giants beat the Brooklyn Dodgers," he kept shouting. The public-address announcer in Los Angeles fared no better a few days later. "Willie Mays and the New York Giants will play here again tomorrow," he intoned.[5]

The stars came out when the action shifted to Los Angeles. Popular singer Dinah Shore welcomed the Dodgers with a cheerful tune at a giant welcoming party on the evening of April 17:

All the Bums are older
So we used our common sense
Livened up the baseball
And shortened up the fence.[6]

That highly publicized left-field fence—the 40-foot screen towering just 250 feet from home plate—was as big an attraction as the game itself. A total of 78,672 fans streamed into the Coliseum on April 18, eager not only to watch a big-league game, but also to see how O'Malley possibly could have converted a football oval into a baseball diamond.

The reviews were overwhelmingly negative. Willie Mays ran into Dodgers slugger Duke Snider in the runway before the first game. Mays, who batted from the right side, pointed the left-handed Snider toward the 440-foot mark in right-center. "Look where that right-field fence is, Duke," Mays laughed. "And look what they gave me—250 feet. They sure fixed you up good. You couldn't reach it with a cannon."[7] Pitchers were caustic. Johnny Antonelli of the Giants called the screen "the biggest farce I ever heard of," and Don Drysdale of the Dodgers dismissed it as "nothing but a sideshow." The fans had it no better. Reporter Al Wolf ventured to the highest reaches of the Coliseum. "The game resembled a pantomime," he wrote. "You couldn't follow the ball, but the actions of the players told you what was happening."[8]

There was no point in complaining. O'Malley had drawn the line when a reporter asked how many Dodgers games would be shown on free television. "There won't be any," he replied. Anybody who wanted to see the Dodgers would have to buy a ticket, at least until the appropriate technology was developed. "As for pay television," O'Malley said, "I would welcome with open arms any pay-television company representatives who came in and put a contract in front of me."[9]

The Los Angeles City Council had given the go-ahead for pay TV on October 16, 1957, just a week after the Dodgers committed to moving. Skiatron and International Telemeter quickly announced plans to wire the city, though they cautioned that the process would not be simple or inexpensive.[10] The situation was the same in San Francisco, where Horace Stoneham had already reached a deal with Skiatron. "There won't be any free television at any time," the Giants owner decreed, though he held out hope that games might be available on the pay service before the end of the 1958 season.[11]

The movie studios and television networks vowed to resist, channeling their fury into California's referendum process. They easily secured the necessary signatures to send Los Angeles's pay-TV legislation to the voters on June 3, 1958, the same day that the fate of the Chavez Ravine land swap was to be decided.[12]

Early polls suggested a massive defeat for Skiatron and International Telemeter, causing each to raise a white flag by spring. Jerome Doff, a Skiatron vice president, blamed the studios and networks for a "heavily financed and misleading" campaign that prevented a "mature understanding of the real issues by the voters." Both companies forfeited their pay-TV franchises, forestalling the referendum.[13] California's big-league teams would not be seen on television anytime soon.

* * *

The general public knew virtually nothing about William Shea. He seemed, from a distance, to be just another white-shoe lawyer with wealthy corporate clients and powerful political connections. Why else would Mayor Wagner have picked him to chair New York's baseball committee?

Those on the inside knew better. "Shea is anything but one of those stuffy, pipe-smoking corporation attorneys. This is a guy who *knows*," wrote Jimmy Breslin, then a young sportswriter with the New York *Journal-American*.[14] Shea had done legal work for the Brooklyn Dodgers, and he and Ford Frick had crossed paths. The commissioner knew him to be "a gentleman of pleasing personality," but also attested to his iron will, his "tenacity of a pit bulldog when the chips were down."[15]

Shea was an affable man, a backslapper like Walter O'Malley. He was quick with a joke and eager to chat with everyone he encountered, Wall Street executives and shoeshine boys alike.[16] But he denied any similarity to O'Malley in their common field. "Walter was one lousy lawyer," Shea once told Roger Kahn. The author dissented, pointing to O'Malley's great success in baseball. "That's right," Shea replied. "O'Malley was the most brilliant businessman I've ever met, but we were talking law here, weren't we?"[17]

Yet Shea was no conventional lawyer himself. Litigation was not his strength. Colleagues joked that he didn't even know where the courthouse was located. He thrived as a power broker, a behind-the-scenes wizard who brought powerful men together, a go-between who quietly orchestrated multimillion-dollar deals. Shea's job plunged him into political intrigue, and he reveled in it. "We're not statesmen," he once said of his law firm. "We ain't white shoe."[18]

William Shea was a somewhat obscure lawyer tapped by Mayor Robert Wagner to lure a new big-league club to New York. "I started out to get a team," said Shea, "and it looked easy." It proved to be tougher than he expected [Library of Congress].

Shea was especially prized for his incisive intelligence, his ability to cut to the heart of a matter. He carefully analyzed the National League as the 1958 season began, determining that none of its existing clubs would move to New York—not in 1959, not in 1960, probably not ever. The only possible solution was to encourage the league to expand.

So he and Wagner traveled to Baltimore to make their pitch during the All-Star break in early July.[19] "We must get the promise of a franchise first," Shea told reporters. "If we do, we will promise the National League a ballpark. It's as simple as all that."[20] The league's owners didn't agree. They clung to the security of the status quo, preferring it to the uncertainty of expansion. Their midseason meeting yielded a vague promise to study Shea's proposal, but nothing more than that. Milwaukee's Lou Perini was typical. "I still favor expansion to a ten- or twelve-club league," he said, "but there's no telling when it will come."[21]

The owners, to be blunt, were starting to wonder if they even needed New York. The National League was prospering without it. Attendance soared by 15 percent in 1958 to the NL's best total in eleven seasons (and the second-best in its history). The Giants drew roughly the same number of fans to cramped Seals Stadium that year as to the spacious Polo Grounds in 1956 and 1957 combined. And the Dodgers broke their all-time Brooklyn attendance record in their very first season out west.[22]

New York had maintained a stranglehold over the majors to that point, with its teams taking nine of eleven World Series and seventeen of twenty-two league titles between 1947 and 1957. "These were, I believe, equally the most important and the most exciting years in the history of sport," contended Roger Kahn, who was, after all, a New Yorker himself.[23]

But the rest of America did not share his enthusiasm. The nation's heartland was suffering from New York fatigue, weary of the city's athletic dominance. Exhaustion was deepest in the American League, where the Yankees had won all but two of the pennants since 1947, greatly depressing public interest. AL attendance plummeted 11 percent as New York ran away with yet another title in 1958. Six of the eight clubs declined at the box office, with the Yankees surprisingly among them. Their attendance fell by 4.6 percent, despite their new monopoly in the nation's largest market.[24] Joe Cronin, who assumed the league presidency in 1959, fervently wished for some other club to push New York from center stage. "I'd like to see the Yankees drop to third place," he joked.[25]

This general indifference—or even hostility—toward New York was not the only reason for the National League's reluctance to expand. Front-office executives and scouts also warned that the on-field product would suffer if additional teams were created. "There is a scarcity of ballplayers," Dodgers vice president Fresco Thompson told Emanuel Celler's subcommittee in 1957. "It is difficult to find competent ballplayers to staff the present sixteen major-league clubs, sir."[26] Yankees co-owner Del Webb put a caustic twist on the same point. "The American League already showed the past season it has about five or six second-division clubs," he smirked. "Why add two more?"[27]

It was an old argument, dating back to the turn of the century. National League owners had asserted in 1901 that a dearth of talent made a second league impractical, yet Ban Johnson and his American League colleagues had persevered.[28] Attorney George Wharton Pepper had sounded the same alarm in the *Federal Baseball* case, which wound its way to the Supreme Court in 1922. Pepper denied that the Federal League had been victimized by a conspiracy of the American and National Leagues. He blamed the FL's demise on the supposedly poor quality of its product. "There were not enough recognized first-class players to supply both the then-existing leagues and also [the] Federal League," he said.[29]

This gospel, however, flew in the face of demographic fact. The United States had contained seventy-eight million residents in 1901, the first season with sixteen big-league teams. That translated to 4.9 million Americans per franchise. If the same ratio were applied in 1958, the national population of 175 million would have been sufficient to support 36 major-league ballclubs, 20 more than currently existed. There clearly was no shortage of potential players, nor of eager fans.[30]

Baseball's leaders failed to comprehend this basic equation, though two fading giants understood completely.

Sixty-eight-year-old Larry MacPhail, living in semi-retirement on a Maryland horse farm, called for immediate action. "Major-league baseball must be expanded to include all sections of the country," he wrote in *Life* magazine in February 1958. "The South and Southwest are not now represented in either major league. The Pacific Coast is not represented in the American League. The entire Eastern Seaboard has only one National League club. Canada, with two great metropolitan areas, has no major-league baseball at all. What can be done about it?" He proposed the creation of two additional major leagues.[31]

That was too extreme for Branch Rickey, though not by much. The seventy-six-year-old Mahatma was still technically involved in baseball as chairman of the Pirates. But he had been slowed by a heart attack in early 1958, and nobody in Pittsburgh evinced any interest in his opinions.[32] So Rickey took to the *Sporting News* in May to broadcast his call for one additional league. "It should be the creation of the present two leagues," he said. "It should be formed with their cooperation, if possible, and if not, then without their cooperation. That would result in a war, which should be avoided. But a third major is something we must have soon."[33]

Most of the current owners paid scant attention, dismissing MacPhail and Rickey as tired voices from the past. But one of the game's most influential men admitted some interest. He didn't want to create a third league—that would be too radical for his tastes—but he did believe it made sense to add teams. "I'm thinking of an expansion to ten clubs, rather than moving an existent National League franchise here," he said during a visit to New York. "I'd say it would be another club in Brooklyn and one perhaps in the twin cities of St. Paul and Minneapolis."

This emerging fan of expansion, this friendly advocate of New York baseball, was none other than Walter Francis O'Malley of Los Angeles, California.[34]

* * *

Bill Shea rarely experienced frustration. He was accustomed to satisfying his clients swiftly and completely, almost always delivering the results they desired. He prided himself on maintaining an even keel in the most troubled of waters. "I have no ulcers, don't take pills," he bragged.[35]

But this baseball case was different. Shea kept prodding the National League's owners to grant New York a franchise, yet they proved to be stunningly resistant. He had served as the city's chief recruiter for nearly a year, yet had made no progress whatsoever. The whole thing was—well, it was frustrating.

So Shea decided to raise the stakes. He called a press conference on November 13, 1958, at Toots Shor's Restaurant, a famous gathering place for athletes and sports executives in Midtown Manhattan. His announcement shocked the jaded reporters who attended. Shea and his committee declared that they would create a third major league themselves.[36] "Since it has now become apparent the National League means to do nothing about this," he said, "we have decided to go on this new tack." He suggested that the unnamed league might begin play as early as 1960.[37]

Reporters pressed for details. Had he conducted a feasibility study? Did he know which cities (other than New York) would receive teams? Where would he get his players? How would he pay the league's startup costs? Shea offered no solid answers. He opted for subtle threats instead of hard facts, hinting that he might slap the majors with an antitrust suit if they prevented New York from landing a second club.

The baseball establishment reacted with a mixture of annoyance and defiance. Ford Frick accused Shea of improper tactics. The commissioner insisted that a private meeting, not a press conference, would have been the best venue for discussions about a new league. "I was the man to whom they should have come," said Frick, who wasn't above issuing a vague threat of his own.[38] "A third league outside organized baseball is unthinkable," he warned.[39]

Frick eventually adopted a more conciliatory tone, undoubtedly at the behest of baseball's attorneys. Any attempt to intimidate the new league's organizers might be considered restraint of trade, a clear violation of the antitrust laws. But nothing required the commissioner or the owners to greet unexpected competitors with open arms. They reacted instead with an affected indifference that masked their fear, as Frick admitted fifteen years later. "Whether or not Mr. Shea was bluffing, no one will ever know," he wrote in his memoirs. "Baseball was scared. The nightmare of the Federal League war was common knowledge."[40]

Other people were excited. Wealthy fans in several cities seized on Shea's league as their best opportunity to join the ranks of major-league owners. Among the first to call was a brash forty-six-year-old Canadian entrepreneur. Jack Kent Cooke had dropped out of high school to peddle soap and encyclopedias door to door, discovering a natural talent for business. He became a millionaire by age thirty-one, purchasing companies in several fields, including Toronto's AAA baseball club. His ego was enormous, and so were his dreams. "Jack Kent Cooke wasn't a minor-league anything," as journalist Jim Murray once put it.[41] Cooke had fallen short in the 1956 auction for the Detroit Tigers, and he now wanted a big-league team for Toronto and its 1.9 million residents.[42]

Cooke appointed himself as Bill Shea's attack dog on the very day that the new league was announced. "Some owners of major-league clubs are dyed-in-the-world reactionaries," Cooke barked. "Perhaps this move will force them to realize the necessity of expansion through a third league."[43] Other prospective owners were quieter. George Kirksey was a former sportswriter who had assembled a group of twenty-eight men of greater means, uniting them in the aim of bringing big-league ball to Houston. He now placed a call to Shea, as did interested parties from Dallas, Denver, Minneapolis-St. Paul, and several other markets.[44]

New York, of course, was the key to Shea's entire enterprise. What he needed was an owner with deep pockets, an impeccable reputation, and an unshakable devotion to the city. He was willing to devote months to the search, taking all necessary precautions to avoid the reincarnation of Walter O'Malley. Shea never mentioned Brooklyn's wayward son, though he couldn't resist throwing an occasional jab, once suggesting that the new local franchise might be named the New York Dodgers. "I checked, and there's no law against using that name," he laughed.[45]

Shea had good reason to be lighthearted. His decision to create a third league had broken the logjam. "All I know," he said happily, "is that we were getting nowhere in our efforts to get another big-league baseball franchise for New York until the announcement was made the other day."[46] His campaign finally seemed to be on the right track.

23

Kefauver

Emanuel Celler was truly angry this time.

The Brooklyn congressman, renowned in Washington for his feistiness, had been surprisingly accommodating to baseball after his 1951 hearings, deigning to spare its beloved reserve clause. And his 1957 investigation had been milder than expected, failing to smoke out Walter O'Malley's intentions or block the eventual departure of the Dodgers. O'Malley had treated the powerful chairman as if he were a toothless backbencher, brushing aside many of his questions and speaking patronizingly of his intentions. "Manny is a friend of mine. He means well," the Dodgers president had assured his fellow owners.[1]

Not this time. Celler was determined to live up to his reputation for ferocity by pursuing legislative retribution. He introduced a bill in January 1958 to eliminate baseball's blanket immunity from antitrust regulations. All sports would henceforth be treated identically, receiving limited exemptions for "reasonably necessary" practices deemed essential for survival. "It would take care of Supreme Court decisions which are discriminatory in favor of baseball and against football," Celler said of his bill. "That's a barbarous situation."[2]

There was no doubt that Celler had the votes, at least in the early stages of the legislative process, thanks to his chairmanship of both the House Judiciary Committee and its Antitrust Subcommittee. The latter quickly gave its assent on January 30, though not before a brief debate about the bill's language. The subcommittee's senior Republican, Kenneth Keating, insisted that the phrase "reasonably necessary" raised more questions than it answered. Would the reserve clause be exempted from antitrust? How about player drafts and farm systems? Keating predicted that dozens of lawsuits would be filed if Celler's bill were passed.[3]

The two legislators sat next to each other on the dais and hailed from the same state, yet they had little in common. They belonged to opposite parties, and Keating's Rochester home was 250 miles distant from Celler's Brooklyn residence. Their prickly relationship had been evident from the start of the baseball hearings a year earlier. "I think it [is] unfortunate that the gentleman has not been objective," Celler had said of Keating in his opening statement. The latter shot back, "I differ with the gentleman, and everybody knows that we differ."[4]

Keating resumed his opposition in 1958, referring privately to "my efforts to save organized baseball from the antitrust zealots."[5] He announced his intention to draft a substitute bill, motivated partly by conservative beliefs and partly by personal ambition. Upstate politicians rarely won statewide elections in New York, but Keating hoped to buck the odds and secure a Senate seat in November. He had been insinuating himself whenever possible into New York City issues, such as the loss of the Giants and Dodgers, which he blamed on Robert Wagner's Democratic administration. "New York City might well have at least two and perhaps three big-league clubs today if the mayor had moved faster," Keating said in May 1958.[6]

Celler held the early momentum. He grabbed headlines with his passionate attacks on baseball owners—"they wish to be like feudal barons and to treat the public as serfs"—as he steered his legislation through the Judiciary Committee.[7] He objected heatedly whenever the wording of his bill was questioned. "The words 'reasonably necessary' are essential. Otherwise, the baseball magnates could go hog-wild," he insisted.[8] The reserve clause and farm systems would be protected, Celler promised, though the owners couldn't expect much more than that. "They cannot have a blank check to do whatever they want, reasonable or unreasonable," he said.[9]

The Judiciary Committee approved Celler's bill on April 17—nobody was surprised by that—but the vote was unexpectedly close. The final tally was seventeen to fifteen, with seven of the chairman's fellow Democrats defecting to Keating's side. The legislation now headed to the House floor, though its prospects were suddenly open to question.[10]

Paul Porter deserved much of the credit for this new uncertainty. His efforts had been decisive in saving the reserve clause after the 1951 hearings, and he was now back in the fray.[11] Ford Frick's marching orders were clear. Celler's bill "threatens the destruction of organized baseball," said the commissioner, who assigned Porter to kill it.[12] The intensity of the resulting campaign stunned Celler. "They came upon Washington like locusts," he said of Porter's army of lobbyists. "They were in every nook and cranny—baseball players, the owners, and their cohorts."[13]

And they were effective, as quickly became evident when Celler's bill, H.R. 10378, arrived on the floor of the House of Representatives on June 24, 1958. A young congressman from Massachusetts, Tip O'Neill, gave the initial speech in support of the legislation, though he conceded that its opponents were waiting to pounce. "I am aware of the fact that a substitute bill will be offered," he said, adding that Joe Cronin, Lou Perini, and Tom Yawkey had all asked him to endorse the switch. O'Neill's confession inspired Connecticut's Albert Morano to interrupt: "I, too, have been contacted by a baseball executive, George Weiss of the New York Yankees."[14] It soon became clear that Porter's army had gotten in touch with everybody.

The House rarely defied one of its committee chairmen, especially not if the only alternative was a bill sponsored by the minority party. But June 24 was an unusual day.[15] "The joker in H.R. 10378 is the phrase 'reasonably necessary,'" Ken Keating said as the debate heated up. He blasted Celler's legislation as an "anti-sports bill," then formally offered his substitute.[16] Keating's bill would remove Celler's offending phrase, replacing it with a list of activities specifically granted immunity from antitrust. Baseball would retain almost all of its current freedoms, including the right to use whatever language it wished in player contracts. "Why, it's no regulation at all," Celler exclaimed.[17] Yet Democrats and Republicans happily shouted "aye" when the switch was put to a voice vote. It passed easily, sending Keating's bill—not Celler's—to the Senate.

Celler ridiculed the new legislation as a "peanut substitute." It allowed owners to do virtually anything without antitrust ramifications, except maybe to "give concessions to sell peanuts," he snarled.[18] But his sarcasm could not diminish Keating's decisive victory. The baseball establishment flooded its new hero with congratulatory letters and telegrams. Ford Frick's gratitude was predictable—"I cannot refrain from thanking you on behalf of baseball"—but another message came as a complete surprise.[19] Walter O'Malley wrote on the letterhead of the Los Angeles Dodgers, not exactly a popular organization with the New York City voters whom Keating was trying to woo.

"I hope it will not jinx you to get a letter from the feller with the horns," O'Malley joked as he passed along his thanks.[20] Keating responded amiably, making no reference to the recent unpleasantness in Brooklyn, even wishing the Dodgers good luck in the future. The two men might never agree about the controversial move to California, but they were staunch allies in the battle against Manny Celler and his ilk.

* * *

The four-year-old Major League Baseball Players Association had endorsed Celler's legislation almost immediately after he submitted it. Player representatives still refused to call their group a union—they preferred to think of it as a fraternal organization—but they were increasingly acting like a labor guild. They unanimously supported Celler's bill during a meeting in Key West on February 8, 1958, putting them directly at odds with the men who signed their paychecks.[21]

The owners blamed the association's president, Bob Feller. The future Hall of Famer was no longer a player—he had retired from the Cleveland Indians after the 1956 season—yet he continued to run the MLBPA. Feller was the type of employee that management disliked—supremely confident, occasionally haughty, never willing to back down. The role of labor leader suited him perfectly.

Feller had displayed his backbone as far back as 1946, when Clark Griffith advertised a special promotion prior to Washington's game against Cleveland. The Senators owner brought in a "lumiline chronograph," a bulky device that measured the speed of flying objects. He announced that Feller, whose fastball reportedly exceeded one hundred miles per hour, would be officially timed during pregame festivities, an exciting prospect decades before the invention of the radar gun.

There was just one problem. Griffith waited until shortly before the game to ask Feller to participate. The pitcher, only twenty-seven years old, looked directly at the Old Fox, one of the game's preeminent figures, and demanded $1,000 ($13,200 in 2020 dollars).[22] "Bob, this kind of promotion is good for baseball," Griffith said soothingly, still hoping to pay nothing at all. Feller shook his head. He eventually settled for seven hundred dollars, though his anger at Griffith never abated. "It was like telling Fred Astaire he'd be doing his dance routines before the game," he said. "And the owner was going to make a lot of money, but he wasn't going to give Astaire anything."[23]

Feller alienated the rest of the baseball establishment with his testimony at Celler's 1957 hearings. "If the owners did not believe themselves immune from the ordinary laws that cover business organizations, they would never dare to disregard, as they do, the basic rules of collective bargaining," he said. And: "The owners basically do regard the players as pawns." And: "I am interested in the ballplayer being as independent as he possibly can be, and under the present conditions, he is not independent." And: "We [are] being treated like children by the owners."[24]

A firebrand like Bob Feller was definitely somebody to fear. But most of the sixteen player reps were compliant sorts, and they began to backtrack after being contacted by their owners. The two players who also served as leaguewide representatives, Robin Roberts and Eddie Yost, called for a formal reconsideration of the MLBPA's position in mid–March.[25] "Basically, we want what the owners want," they said in a joint statement. The endorsement of Celler's bill was withdrawn before the end of the month.[26]

Roberts accused the association's attorney, J. Norman Lewis, of encouraging the players to make their ill-fated stand.[27] "Lewis either made a mistake or gave us a poor lead," said Roberts, who tried, but failed, to get the lawyer fired in March 1958.[28] The Phillies pitcher persisted the following March, this time successfully forcing the issue. Lewis saw the fine hand of ownership behind his dismissal. "I am sure a lot of people on the other side of the fence are well pleased," he said bitterly.[29] The owners were even happier with his replacement, Robert Cannon, a Milwaukee judge who dreamed of becoming the commissioner of baseball. Cannon's new job was to represent the players, but he had no intention of angering the owners who would eventually select Ford Frick's successor. He made no waves.[30]

Baseball's other labor problem—the nagging matter of bonuses—was not so easily solved. Almost everybody disapproved of the reform instituted in 1952, which required any prospect who received a bonus larger than four thousand dollars to spend his first two seasons in the major leagues. Rosters were clogged with bonus babies who contributed nothing to their teams and had no opportunity to develop their skills. Fifty-nine bonus recipients whiled away their time between 1953 and 1957. Three of them—Al Kaline, Harmon Killebrew, and Sandy Koufax—would eventually reach the Hall of Fame. Most of the rest would disappear without a trace.[31]

Even worse, as far as baseball executives were concerned, was the rule's failure to restrain spending. Teams continued to compete for the best prospects, and bonuses kept rising. Owners saw no other option but to jettison the 1952 stipulations, which they did in December 1957. That put them back on square one, unable to agree on their next step, so they did nothing at all. "Bankrolls Now Only Limit on Bonus Bids," screamed a horrified headline in the *Sporting News*.[32]

The upward spiral accelerated. Paul Richards, who served as both the manager and general manager in Baltimore, set a new bonus record in January 1958, mere weeks after the repeal. He handed outfielder Dave Nicholson $135,000 ($1.2 million in 2020 terms), disturbing the Orioles' owners so greatly that they stripped Richards of his GM title. Counterparts joked that Baltimore had given Richards an unlimited budget, which he had somehow exceeded.[33]

Ford Frick was dismayed by the rampant fiscal intemperance. "I think some of these clubs have gone completely haywire," he groaned.[34] New milestones of extravagance would be reached in seasons to come. Infielder Bob Bailey pushed the mark up to $175,000 in 1961, inspiring speculation that the first $200,000 deal wasn't far away. It materialized in 1964, with University of Wisconsin outfielder Rick Reichardt the lucky recipient.[35]

Baseball's most powerful franchises, the Yankees and the Dodgers, found no fault with the bonus system. Their wealth and prestige enabled them to sign virtually any prospect they desired. But the Reichardt deal—at long last—proved to be the last straw for the other teams. They finally bowed to a basic rule of economics, agreeing to eliminate competition for young talent by implementing an amateur draft. It was hardly a new idea. The National Football League had initiated its draft (at Bert Bell's suggestion) in 1936, nearly three decades before baseball followed suit.[36]

This long-overdue change ended the annual bidding wars, since each prospect now negotiated solely with the team that drafted him. The highest bonus in 1965 went to the first player selected in the initial draft, Rick Monday, who received one hundred thousand dollars. Nobody would challenge Reichardt's record until 1979.[37]

Almost everybody was happy, except for the teams that had the greatest resources. The Yankees had won yet another American League pennant in 1964, so they drafted nineteenth in 1965. "All the known kids will be pretty well picked over when it comes our turn," groused Johnny Johnson, a Yankees vice president. But, a reporter asked, what about the big picture? Wouldn't the draft be good for the game overall? Johnson was in no mood to be magnanimous. "We don't like it," he snapped.[38]

* * *

Baseball had won the battle of wills in the House of Representatives in June 1958—Keating's legislation, not Celler's, had triumphed—yet its prospects in the Senate were cloudy at best. The bill was referred to the Subcommittee on Antitrust and Monopoly, which was chaired by Tennessee's Estes Kefauver, who was certain to be unsympathetic.[39]

Kefauver was one of America's most prominent politicians, a two-time presidential candidate who had been chosen as the Democratic Party's vice-presidential nominee in 1956. He was renowned as a dogged foe of big business and an inveterate publicity hound. "Senator Kefauver was not the usual type of legislator. Senator Kefauver was, in many respects, a public-relations senator," admitted the other senator from Tennessee, Albert Gore, Sr., the father of a future vice president.[40] Keating's bill was a legislative godsend, affording Kefauver an opportunity to grill the lords of baseball before a national audience.

The soft-spoken senator was an unlikely populist. He had been raised in an upper-middle-class household, held a degree from Yale Law School, and had once intended to become a corporation lawyer. But Kefauver's bland exterior masked a crusading spirit, which family members attributed to one of his grandfathers, a fiery Baptist minister. The young man detoured into politics, winning a seat in the House of Representatives in 1939 at the age of thirty-six.[41] "It might just lead to something," he said coolly on election night. His eye was already fixed on two prizes of greater magnitude—the Senate and the White House.[42]

Kefauver launched a Senate campaign in 1948 despite the opposition of the state's Democratic boss, who ridiculed the candidate as shifty and unreliable. Edward Crump likened him to a "pet coon that puts its foot in an open drawer in your room," to which Kefauver retorted, "I may be a pet coon, but I ain't Mr. Crump's pet coon." He donned a coonskin cap at campaign stops—unusual attire for a Yale grad—and attracted so much publicity that he scored an upset victory over Crump's handpicked candidate.[43]

His flair for the dramatic resurfaced in 1950, when Kefauver was installed as the head of the Senate's special committee on organized crime. The typical chairman would have conducted a few days of hearings in Washington, but that was too tame for the persistent Tennessean, who opted to hit the road. The panel, which eventually became known simply as the Kefauver Committee, traveled to fourteen cities, calling more than eight hundred politicians, law-enforcement officials, and criminals as witnesses. It generated front-page headlines everywhere it went.

And it did something even better for the future of Estes Kefauver: It attracted viewers. The hearings were telecast in two dozen cities along the Eastern Seaboard and across the Midwest, transfixing daytime audiences with a procession of gamblers, gangsters, and convicted felons to the witness table. Consolidated Edison had to add a generator to meet the increased demand for electricity when Kefauver hit the New York airwaves in March 1951. An estimated thirty million Americans watched the mild-mannered, crime-fighting senator go toe-to-toe with the shadowy figures of organized crime.[44] *Life* magazine wrote at the time: "Never before had the attention of the nation been riveted so completely on a single matter."[45]

Kefauver struck while the iron was hot. He ran for president the following year, even though the Democratic incumbent, Harry Truman, had not yet ruled out another term. The two men were not on speaking terms. Kefauver had conducted hearings in Kansas City, which was Truman's home turf. The senator declared that the city was "struggling out from under the rule of the law of the jungle," which infuriated the president.[46] Truman never referred to his opponent as anything but "Cow-fever," disparaging him as a "demagogic dumbbell."[47]

Kefauver stunned political pundits by defeating Truman in the 1952 New Hampshire primary, hastening the president's withdrawal from the race. Democratic bosses swiftly joined forces to deny the challenger the party's nomination that year, as they would again in 1956. Kefauver won twenty-one primary elections in his two national campaigns, yet he never had a realistic chance of becoming his party's presidential candidate.[48] "The boys in the smoke-filled rooms have never taken very well to me," he said in classic understatement.[49]

Their opposition stemmed partly from those televised hearings, which had exposed corruption in several states and cities controlled by Democratic administrations, including a link between Florida governor Fuller Warren and an associate of Al Capone, the late gangland kingpin. Warren spoke for dozens of enraged Democratic officeholders, lashing out at Kefauver as "an ambition-crazed Caesar." The senator gave as good as he got. "I've heard a stuck pig always squeals," he shot back.[50]

Party chieftains were also disturbed by Kefauver's populist leanings, his belief that the country was trapped in "an essentially feudal economic structure."[51] Most Democrats were rhetorically committed to the welfare of the common man, yet they stopped short of fanaticism. Not Kefauver. He pushed his egalitarian philosophy to the extreme, declaring his eagerness to battle "monopoly power held by a few companies which produce most of [an] industry's output." His antitrust subcommittee investigated a wide range of businesses—from steel, automobiles, and railroads to asphalt roofing, dairy products, and hearing aids.[52]

And now his gaze had settled on baseball. Nobody doubted that Kefauver would milk the upcoming hearings for every possible drop of publicity. Early polls suggested that he was a plausible candidate for president two years hence, running third behind Democratic frontrunners Adlai Stevenson and John Kennedy.[53] An attack on the plutocrats who controlled America's baseball monopoly would be certain to fire up his base and propel him back into the headlines.

The baseball establishment was understandably nervous as it awaited the first day of Senate hearings on July 9, 1958, a date that Kefauver had selected with care.

Estes Kefauver (waving) chaired a Senate subcommittee that was weighing baseball's antitrust fate. Nobody doubted that he would milk his hearings for every drop of publicity. "Senator Kefauver was, in many respects, a public-relations senator," said colleague Albert Gore, Sr. [National Archives and Records Administration].

The All-Star Game had been played the previous day in Baltimore, just forty miles northeast of the Capitol, and the chairman arranged for a bevy of superstars to visit his hearing room before they headed home. Mickey Mantle, Stan Musial, and Ted Williams were called as witnesses, not for any insight they might provide on antitrust jurisprudence, but for their documented ability to attract reporters and photographers. The same quality explained the presence of Casey Stengel, famed as much for his mangled syntax as for the six world titles he had won as manager of the Yankees.[54]

A standing-room crowd jammed the hearing room as the first witness took his seat. Kefauver asked Stengel to explain why baseball favored the Keating bill, eliciting a monologue that meandered from the future Hall of Famer's early days ("I had many years that I was not so successful as a ballplayer, as it is a game of skill") to his crowning glory as a manager ("if I have been in baseball for forty-eight years, there must be some good in it").[55] The senator interrupted to reiterate the matter at hand:

> **Kefauver:** Mr. Stengel, I am not sure that I made my question clear. [Laughter.]
> **Stengel:** Yes, sir. Well, that is all right. I am not sure I am going to answer yours perfectly either. [Laughter.]
> **Kefauver:** I was asking you, sir, why it is that baseball wants this bill passed.
> **Stengel:** I would say I do not know, but I would say the reason why they would want it passed is to keep baseball going as the highest-paid ball sport that has gone into baseball, and from the baseball angle, I am not going to speak of any other sport.[56]

The rest of the opening session was similarly uninformative, though highly productive in attracting publicity. Kefauver could only smile the next day as he perused the nation's leading newspapers, all carrying lengthy stories and large photographs, highlighted by a front-page package in the *New York Times*.[57]

Kefauver scheduled eleven more days of hearings as the dog days of July descended on Washington. They yielded a handful of interesting moments, like Robin Roberts once again siding with management ("the players are all for the reserve clause"), Calvin Griffith explaining why his Senators were always so bad ("lack of good ballplayers"), and Ford Frick stressing his attachment to the antitrust exemption ("very, very essential to baseball").[58] But it was all for show. Time was running out. Midterm elections were less than four months away, and the Senate would soon adjourn for the year.

Kefauver decided on August 1, 1958, to pull the plug, announcing that he simply wasn't able to draft "an acceptable substitute" for Keating's bill in the few legislative days that remained, though he promised to start the job from scratch in the coming year.[59] That was exactly what the owners feared.

Headlines: 1958

Williams blasts "space helmets"

Ted Williams hated the new rule requiring batters to wear protective headgear. "I don't like those space helmets," he said angrily, insisting that a plastic cap's weight threw off his timing. But what could he do? "If I have to wear them, I guess I will," said the Red Sox left fielder, who persevered to hit .328, winning his sixth American League batting crown at age forty.[60]

Musial lines 3,000th career hit

Stan Musial joined an exclusive club on May 13, becoming the eighth big leaguer with three thousand career hits. The Cardinals first baseman lined a double against the Cubs in Wrigley Field, making him the first player to reach three thousand since Paul Waner in 1942. Waner quickly extended congratulations, hailing Musial as "the best all-round ballplayer I've ever seen."[61]

Dodgers collapse in L.A. debut

The Dodgers notched ninety-three more victories than any other National League team during their final ten years in Brooklyn. But they struggled in their first Los Angeles season, languishing in last place as late as August 12 and finishing twelve games below .500. Losing Roy Campanella "was a terrible psychological blow," said catcher Rube Walker. Poor play by old-timers Pee Wee Reese (.224), Gil Hodges (.259), and Don Newcombe (7.86 ERA) also hurt.[62]

Yankees stage World Series comeback

The Braves were in a celebratory mood after surging to a World Series lead of three games to one. "I'd like to get the Yankees in the National League," hooted Milwaukee pitcher Lew Burdette. But New York roared back with victories in Games Five and Six, then broke a 2–2 tie with a four-run eighth inning in Game Seven. "I guess we can now play in the National League," snorted Casey Stengel after his Yanks secured their seventh title in ten years.[63]

24

Chavez

Walter O'Malley had grown accustomed to success. The Dodgers had won four National League pennants since he took control of the franchise in October 1950, a streak capped by 1955's gloriously unforgettable world championship. They finished at least fourteen games above .500 every season from 1951 through 1957, a record of elite consistency matched by just one other big-league club—the Yankees, of course.

There was every reason to expect O'Malley to be infuriated by the Dodgers' sudden deterioration in 1958. A six-game losing streak dropped Los Angeles to a record of nine wins and eighteen losses as of May 14, eight and a half games behind the surging Milwaukee Braves. The pennant race, at least as far as the Dodgers were concerned, had already come to an end.[1]

But O'Malley was surprisingly unruffled, taking consolation from the huge crowds streaming into the Coliseum. The season was only a month old, yet the Dodgers had already attracted seven crowds larger than thirty-two thousand fans, the capacity of old Ebbets Field. Total attendance in Los Angeles was already closing in on six hundred thousand, better than half of what the Dodgers had drawn during the entire 1957 season in Brooklyn and Jersey City.[2]

O'Malley was also distracted by off-field concerns, especially by the referendum that loomed on June 3. Los Angeles voters were being asked to decide the fate of Proposition B, which the ballot strangely described as a land agreement between the city and "the Brooklyn National League Baseball Club."[3] Political leaders told O'Malley not to worry. Petition drives, they said, forced referendums on all sorts of issues in California. "Los Angeles is probably America's softest touch for a guy clutching a petition," chuckled Norris Poulson, who predicted overwhelming approval.[4]

But O'Malley wasn't so sure. It was true that the referendum had caught him off guard—"we never had such a thing in New York"—yet his political antennae were usually well-tuned.[5] He sensed an ugliness in the air, an eagerness to repudiate an apparent gift of municipal land to a prominent private company. "The story is that this is a giveaway to the Dodgers," he thundered. "Giveaway, hell! We're buying the land."[6]

He was technically correct, though his point was flimsy at best. The Dodgers were deeding Wrigley Field to the city in exchange for 185 acres in Chavez Ravine, the city's "best efforts" to acquire an adjacent 130 acres, and at least $2 million in municipal funding "to place such property in proper condition."[7] The transaction was wildly imbalanced. Wrigley Field was more than thirty years old, almost devoid of parking, and virtually useless to the city. The county assessor placed its worth at one million dollars, a fraction of the potential value of the new stadium site.[8]

Yet the early polls showed Proposition B sailing to an easy victory with 70 percent support, just as Mayor Poulson had forecast.[9] The influential *Los Angeles Times* beat the drums in its favor, asking, "Do you, a citizen-voter, want Los Angeles to be a great city, with common interests and the civic unity which gives a great city character?"[10] The answer—initially, anyway—seemed to be yes.

But the opposition gathered strength as spring descended on Southern California. The owners of the Pacific Coast League's San Diego Padres, angered by the loss of the PCL's two dominant markets, pumped a substantial amount of money into the campaign against Proposition B. They were joined by real-estate interests who had their own plans for Chavez Ravine, conservatives who were offended by the Poulson administration's largesse, and non-fans who didn't care whether the Dodgers came or went.[11] "Political enemies of mine, O'Malley haters, baseball haters, crackpots, intelligent people feeling the city was being slickered, and groups with selfish motives seemed to emerge from the alcoves all at once," said Poulson.[12]

The Dodgers were shocked by this change of fortune. "We assumed everyone in Los Angeles wanted major-league baseball. We soon discovered otherwise," recalled Buzzie Bavasi.[13] Pollsters detected a virtual deadlock by late May, with roughly 40 percent of the electorate in favor, 40 percent opposed, and 20 percent undecided. The controversy divided the city. Heated arguments broke out everywhere from office water coolers to the chambers of the City Council.[14] "It got brutal during that fight," remembered Rosalind Wyman. "In fact, at one point, it got so bad I had to have policemen around the house and policemen around my chair [in the chambers]. My life was threatened."[15]

O'Malley reacted in predictable fashion, resorting to subtle threats similar to those he had floated in New York. He publicly expressed concern about the lack of local stadium options, vaguely hinting that he might have to look beyond Los Angeles if Chavez Ravine were unavailable.[16] National League president Warren Giles, undoubtedly acting at O'Malley's behest, accused the city of "reneging on its contract" by conducting the referendum. If Proposition B was defeated, Giles added, he intended to recommend that the Dodgers leave Los Angeles. Brooklyn seemed a likely destination, given that O'Malley still held the lease on Ebbets Field. "Dodger Return Here Possibility if Coast Voters Reject Contract," blared a headline in the *New York Times*.[17]

A group of high-profile fans decided that a positive approach was more likely to succeed. Movie and television stars banded together to stage a five-hour telethon—they called it a "Dodgerthon"—on Channel 11 two nights before the election. Jack Benny, Jerry Lewis, George Burns, Dean Martin, and Debbie Reynolds were among the dozens of luminaries who implored their fellow citizens to vote yes on Proposition B. Most appealed to local pride, equating major-league baseball with major-city status.[18] But the most persuasive pitch was delivered by an actor of lesser reputation, who stressed that the Dodgers and the city would both benefit from the land swap. "Sure, Walter O'Malley got a good deal when he was offered Chavez Ravine as a site for his ballpark," said Ronald Reagan. "Any deal, to be good, must be fair to both sides, not to one."[19]

Nobody knew who would win. The last-place Dodgers were playing the Reds at the Coliseum on the evening of June 3—a game that would end in yet another defeat—but O'Malley paid attention solely to the election results streaming from the county clerk's office. The race was nip and tuck for hours, though the pro-stadium side gradually secured a narrow lead. The final tally was 51.9 percent yes, 48.1 percent no. Proposition B snaked through with a dangerously thin advantage of 25,785 votes out of 677,581 cast.[20]

O'Malley reacted as if it were a landslide. "I don't regard the outcome as close, but rather as a very significant margin," he insisted.[21] He was finally free of politics, finally able to plan a groundbreaking ceremony for the ballpark of his dreams. The Dodgers' future in Los Angeles was secure—or so it seemed.

* * *

The glow of post-referendum optimism proved to be premature, much to O'Malley's unhappiness. The Dodgers owner announced on June 4 that stadium construction would begin in early July, though he soon backed off. Two significant barriers remained, and both had to be surmounted before any work could commence.[22]

The first hurdle was judicial. O'Malley had been served with a subpoena upon his arrival in Los Angeles the previous October, but the resulting lawsuit received little publicity. The initial courtroom jousting between the Dodgers and a taxpayer group was overshadowed by the massive excitement about the team's initial season in the Coliseum and the intense press coverage of Proposition B.

Conditions changed by early June. The Dodgers had entrenched themselves in their new home—in last place, too—and the referendum had been won. The legal battle now came into public focus. The opponents of the land swap persuaded a Superior Court judge to issue a temporary restraining order, preventing the city from conveying Chavez Ravine to O'Malley for the time being. The lawsuit itself—actually a merger of two similar suits—was placed on the docket for late June.[23]

The second impediment was the status of the property. The ravine had once been home to twelve hundred Mexican-American families. Most had been resettled in 1950, when the city decided to clear the land for public housing, a project eventually killed by intense political pressure. A few families—twenty or so—remained in their homes throughout that controversy and Norris Poulson's subsequent efforts to find a new use for the site. They would have to be cleared out before O'Malley's bulldozers could start moving earth.[24]

The court's decision came swiftly. Judge Arnold Praeger ruled on July 14, 1958— only forty-one days after the referendum—that Chavez Ravine could not be handed over to the Dodgers. His 32-page decision determined that the 315-acre tract had been earmarked for a "public purpose"—shades of Robert Moses—and hence could not be given to any private corporation, regardless of the outcome of Proposition B.[25]

O'Malley was defiant. "I am perhaps a stubborn man," he said. "But we were offered the Chavez Ravine site, accepted it, and came out with the intention of building a park on it. We are not abandoning the program."[26] Praeger's decision was far from the final word. Superior Court was the lowest rung in California's judicial system, which gave O'Malley at least two opportunities to appeal. But he had hoped to move the Dodgers into their new ballpark by July 1, 1959—less than twelve months away—and Praeger's ruling deferred that dream. It was obvious that 1959 was now out of the question, perhaps 1960 as well.

The delay offered a breather to municipal officials, who were unenthusiastic about the messy work of removing the final residents of Chavez Ravine. Eviction notices weren't sent out until March 9, 1959, granting a thirty-day window for compliance, soon extended to sixty days. Most of the families were resigned to leaving, though they complained that the compensation offered by the city was inadequate. A few homeowners refused to move under any circumstances.[27]

D-Day was May 8. An army of law-enforcement officers arrived in Chavez Ravine that morning, accompanied by several workmen driving large vehicles. They tackled their assignment with efficiency. Sheriff's deputies escorted recalcitrant family members outside—even carrying a stubborn few—before bulldozers demolished their homes.[28] A deputy negotiated in Spanish with an angry seventy-two-year-old woman, Avrana Arechiga, who shouted in the same language, "Why don't they play ball in Poulson's backyard, not ours?" She was eventually hauled out by four deputies, her furniture was loaded into a city van, power was cut to her small house, and the structure was flattened, all in less than two hours.[29]

Television cameras broadcast the entire operation to a wide audience, and the local papers followed with extensive photo spreads. White middle-class viewers and readers had little in common with the ousted Mexican-Americans. But the images of tiny homes reduced to sticks and rubble were heartbreaking, as were the pictures of small children living in tents and trailers with parents who refused to leave the ravine, presumably because they had nowhere else to go. Public opinion ran heavily against the evictions. It seemed that the city—and O'Malley—had overstepped in their zeal to build a ballpark.

The furor burned for several days. Hundreds of protesters jammed the City Council chambers on May 11, demanding assistance for the displaced and an investigation of the officials involved. But their indignation began to dissipate upon publication of a story about Avrana Arechiga and her family, who had organized the tent city after their house was seized. The Arechigas were far from homeless, according to the *Los Angeles Mirror-News*. They actually owned eleven houses outside the ravine, several of which were rental properties that generated steady income. Their holdings carried a total assessed value of $75,000 ($662,000 in 2020 dollars).

The irony was striking. Walter O'Malley had spent years wailing about inadequate government assistance in New York, and now his pet project in Los Angeles was being opposed by a family with precisely the same complaint. The Arechigas' beef with the city, it turned out, was not primarily about the demolition of their house, but rather about the $10,050 offered in compensation. They wanted seventeen thousand. Officials soon convinced them to strike their tents—they owned a vacant three-bedroom home nearby—but their battle against the city would continue in the courts.[30]

* * *

Judge Praeger's ruling in July 1958 had initiated a period of great frustration for O'Malley, who spent the next several months writing checks to lawyers and bemoaning the annihilation of his stadium timetable. The legal fight over Chavez Ravine would eventually cost him at least three million dollars and add more than two years to his construction calendar.[31] "I had hoped to get a bulldozer up in the ravine last month to begin shoving a pile of dirt around," he said wistfully in August, "even if it was simply pushing the same pile back and forth."[32]

His mood brightened in the new year. The taxpayer group's lawsuit wound its way to the California Supreme Court, which delivered an unexpectedly strong decision in O'Malley's favor on January 13, 1959. All seven justices agreed that the conveyance of Chavez Ravine to the Dodgers constituted a proper use of public funds.[33] "We must view the contract as a whole," wrote Chief Justice Phil Gibson, "and the fact that some of the provisions may be of benefit only to the baseball club is immaterial, provided the city receives benefits which serve legitimate public purposes."[34]

O'Malley immediately announced that construction would begin in February 1959—he apparently had forgotten about the people then still living in the ravine—but his opponents pledged to appeal the ruling. "This statement by O'Malley that he is going to start building in thirty days is ridiculous," scoffed Phill Silver, the lawyer for the taxpayers. "Any action taken before the U.S. Supreme Court acts will be entirely at his peril."[35]

City officials felt the same way, but the Dodgers owner pushed for action, which is why the eviction notices were mailed in March 1959 and the residents of Chavez Ravine were removed in May. O'Malley had no intention of dawdling while the justices in Washington pondered his case. He was desperate to move his team out of the Coliseum—partly because the temporary ballpark had become an object of national derision, more specifically because his contract stipulated a sizable rent increase if the Dodgers remained there after the 1959 season. He initially held out hope that the new stadium could be completed by 1960's opening day.[36] "I'm not ready to surrender on that yet," he told reporters with sunny optimism in February.[37] But 1961 seemed a better bet.

There was every reason to believe that Dodger Stadium would be a major hit, whenever it was finished. The Coliseum was a horrible venue for spectators, who baked in their uncovered seats under the midsummer California sun. "We were frying our customers alive in this stone skillet," recalled Harold Parrott, the team's ticket manager.[38] Most seats were so far from the action that it was difficult to follow the action, yet fans streamed to the football oval. The Dodgers drew 1,845,556 in their first season in Los Angeles—second only to Milwaukee in big-league attendance—and they vaulted to the top of the list with 2,071,045 in 1959. Who knew how much larger the crowds might be in a comfortable, modern stadium?[39]

Nothing dramatized the local enthusiasm for baseball more than an exhibition game on May 7, 1959, the night before the Chavez Ravine evictions. The Dodgers chose that evening to honor their disabled hero, Roy Campanella, scheduling the New York Yankees as their opposition. It was the first West Coast appearance by the vaunted world champions, and 93,103 jammed into the Coliseum to see them, establishing a single-game record that would endure for forty-nine years. Another fifteen thousand fans were turned away, and more than a hundred police officers were summoned to subdue what the Los Angeles Times described as a "near riot" at the ticket windows.[40]

Pee Wee Reese wheeled Campanella out between second base and the pitcher's mound before the Yankees came to bat in the sixth inning. The stadium lights were doused, and announcer Vin Scully asked everybody to strike a match or a cigarette lighter. "The flames winked like swarming fireflies in the darkness of the cavernous Coliseum," wrote reporter Frank Finch. Players on both teams would remember that silent minute as a highlight of their careers.[41]

The Los Angeles Memorial Coliseum had an absurd configuration for baseball, with a left-field screen looming 250 feet from home plate. But fans flocked to the Dodgers' temporary home. "No one can now question our moving out here from Brooklyn," crowed Walter O'Malley [National Baseball Hall of Fame and Museum].

The Dodgers donated their share of the night's box-office take—about sixty thousand dollars—to Campanella, but O'Malley couldn't help focusing on the bottom line. "This 93,103 is fantastic," he crowed. "No one can now question our moving out here from Brooklyn."[42] The remainder of the night's proceeds was given to Del Webb and Dan Topping, the co-owners of the Yankees. Frank Lane, the acerbic general manager of the Cleveland Indians, publicly speculated that the money "went to Webb and Topping's favorite charity, namely Webb and Topping."[43] Ford Frick ordered him to apologize.

The Chavez Ravine evictions came on the heels of the Campanella game, yet O'Malley remained unable to start construction. Months ticked by as city officials waded through "legal debris," as Los Angeles city attorney Roger Arnebergh described it.[44] There was another hearing before the California Supreme Court, new suits stemming from the removal of the Arechigas and other families, a City Council dispute over the closure of roads across the ravine, and always the looming specter of a definitive ruling by the U.S. Supreme Court.[45]

It wasn't until September 17, 1959, that O'Malley was allowed to proceed, and then only after promising to reimburse the city for any work done on the site if the case ended in judicial defeat. Five thousand people turned up for the Dodger Stadium groundbreaking. Those who brought their own shovels were given souvenir boxes to carry away some of the sacred soil. Seven large bulldozers did the real work, roaring to life to begin the lengthy process of grading the rugged tract.[46]

Local observers were surprised to note that the heavy equipment belonged to the Vinnell Company. It had been widely assumed that O'Malley would hand the lucrative Chavez Ravine contract to—who else?—the Del E. Webb Construction Company. Webb lived in Phoenix, but he was a native Californian with impeccable Los Angeles connections. O'Malley had relied on him two years earlier for advice about prospective stadium sites, and Webb had helped to pave the way for the subsequent move from Brooklyn.[47] "I think the city of Los Angeles should be quick to take advantage of the opportunity," he had urged local officials who were waffling in early 1957.[48]

The developer was renowned for his ability to land the most lucrative deals up and down the West Coast. "An ancestor of Del Webb's undoubtedly got the contract to build the Pyramids after elbowing the Pharaoh's favorite nephew out of position," laughed Bill Veeck.[49] Yet Webb failed in Chavez Ravine for two reasons. His bid proved to be considerably more expensive than Vinnell's. O'Malley believed that friends were friends, but a buck was a buck, too. Nor did it help that Webb was rumored to be plotting to bring an American League team to Los Angeles. O'Malley had no intention of sharing his paradise with anyone.[50]

Vinnell's earthmovers were rumbling up and down the ravine on the afternoon of October 19, when the big news finally arrived from Washington. The U.S. Supreme Court dismissed the taxpayer group's suit without comment. Phill Silver, the lawyer who had spearheaded the two-year battle, told reporters that he had raised every possible objection in his appeal, but it hadn't been good enough. The legal battle against Dodger Stadium, he sadly conceded, had reached its end.[51]

25

Continental

Creating a new league became Bill Shea's full-time job, pulling him away from his Manhattan law practice. He traveled around the United States and Canada in the spring of 1959, searching for investors who yearned to own big-league ballclubs. His days remained hectic after he returned to his seventeenth-floor office at the corner of Madison Avenue and Forty-Second Street. Shea spent hour after hour on the phone, forever talking baseball.[1] "I'll be glad when this is over," he told a visitor. "I wonder if I can ever get back to coming to work at nine and leaving at five?"[2]

The new impresario kept everything close to his vest—"we do not think it is in the best interests to issue any statements"—but owners of existing big-league teams began hearing rumors of steady progress.[3] Shea had lined up franchises in at least five cities, according to industry gossip, and as many as eleven other cities were interested. The third league was beginning to loom as a very real danger.[4]

The question was how to respond. Threats and coordinated financial pressure had brought the Federal League to its knees in 1915, but times had changed. Tactics so crude and heavy-handed would never be countenanced in an era of heightened antitrust awareness, especially not with legislative bulldogs like Manny Celler and Estes Kefauver keeping watch. A plan of greater subtlety was needed.

Ford Frick summoned the owners to a secret meeting on May 21 at John Galbreath's farm west of Columbus, Ohio. The new league was the sole item on the agenda. The commissioner spoke of the alarming rise in demographic pressure in recent years. The nation's population had grown rapidly—27 percent between the end of World War II and 1959—and the passion for big-league ball had ballooned at a corresponding rate.[5] It would be impossible to confine the majors to sixteen teams much longer. "I firmly believe we will have a third major league within five years," Frick said.[6]

Most owners considered this an unhappy prospect, though they conceded the accuracy of Frick's forecast. Their primary goal, they decided, was to retain control of the process. So they devised a two-pronged strategy. They would appease their lawyers by embracing Shea's league publicly, yet they would assert their dominance by tightening the screws whenever possible.

Their first step was to issue a surprisingly upbeat statement. "Since there is no existing plan to expand the present major leagues," they said, "the two major leagues declare they will favorably consider an application for major-league status within the present baseball structure by an acceptable group of eight clubs." But they appended ten stipulations, an initial attempt to bring Shea to heel. Among them: Every market in the new league must be larger than Kansas City, every ballpark must seat at least

25,000, the schedule must be 154 games, and proof must be supplied of the "financial ability and character" of all new owners.[7]

Shea was caught off guard—pleasantly so—by the announcement from Columbus. "We have been working for months, and I am sure they [American and National League owners] are aware of it," he said. "We are elated." His path suddenly seemed free of obstacles. He predicted that the third league would meet all ten requirements within two years.[8]

A similar drama was playing out in a second sport at the same time. National Football League commissioner Bert Bell had admitted two years earlier that the emergence of a competitor would not surprise him. "There is room for another [football] league in the country if it is operated properly and if its teams are located properly," he told Celler's subcommittee in 1957.[9] This vague speculation was destined to become reality by the summer of 1959.

Several young millionaires approached Bell with their NFL dreams. Among them was reedy, bespectacled Lamar Hunt, a twenty-six-year-old heir to one of the world's greatest oil fortunes. Hunt inquired about the possibility of securing a new team for Dallas, only to be told that the NFL had no plans to expand. Bell suggested that Hunt try to purchase the lowly Chicago Cardinals, advice the commissioner also dispensed to prospective owners from Denver, Houston, and Minneapolis.[10]

The Cardinals were a miserable franchise both on the field (winning only 33 of 120 games during the 1950s) and at the box office (drawing the fewest fans of any NFL team in the decade). Chicago had long ago given its heart to the Bears, the famed "Monsters of the Midway." The sole way for the city's other football team to survive, or so it seemed, was to seek greener pastures.

Yet the only two people whose opinion truly mattered, Cardinals owners Violet and Walter Wolfner, dissented from the conventional wisdom, hunkering down in Chicago and rebuffing all financial offers.[11] Hunt, their most ardent suitor, was flying back to Dallas in early 1959—weary from a typically unproductive meeting with the Wolfners—when an idea clicked. "It seemed to me a natural thing," Hunt recalled. "There had been an American and a National League in baseball, competing side by side for sixty years."[12] Why not do the same in football?

This brainstorm inspired him to contact another oilman, Houston's Bud Adams, a character as flamboyant as Hunt was reserved. "Bud," said Hunt, "I'm thinking about starting a new league. Would you be interested in joining me?" Adams was instantly excited. "Hell, yeah," he shot back, and with that, the American Football League was born.[13]

The Texas upstarts had no desire to buck the establishment. "I was at least intelligent enough to know that I did not want to start a war," said Hunt, who inquired if Bell might be willing to serve as commissioner of both football leagues simultaneously.[14] It wouldn't be possible, said Bell, though he wished Hunt luck. Bell, like Ford Frick, knew the importance of appearing to conform to antitrust regulations. He soon gave his public blessing to the AFL. "We are in favor of this league," he told a congressional panel.[15]

The new baseball and football leagues ran on parallel tracks in 1959. Shea and Hunt spent spring and early summer lining up owners and granting franchises, finally reaching critical mass during the hottest stretch of the year. Shea called a press conference at the Hotel Biltmore in New York on July 27, formally announcing the creation of the Continental League. The AFL followed suit seven days later in Houston.[16]

The Continental League named five charter members—New York, Denver, Houston, Minneapolis, and Toronto—with three additional franchises to be granted prior to its inaugural season in 1961. Shea kept things light at his press conference, stressing his eagerness to win the favor of the AL and NL. "I believe in the good faith of the major leagues," he said earnestly, adding that the Continental League intended to comply with all ten Columbus stipulations.[17] It most definitely did not want a war.

The investors he had recruited were an impressively wealthy bunch. Heading the list was the owner of the CL's New York franchise, Joan Whitney Payson, a lifelong baseball fan who still held a small stake in Horace Stoneham's Giants. Her representative on that team's board, Donald Grant, had cast the only vote against Stoneham's move to San Francisco. Payson was remarkably well-heeled, the beneficiary of a $120 million inheritance from her father's estate in 1927 (the equivalent of $1.78 billion in 2020).

Shea's other partners were unable to match Payson's financial firepower, though no one doubted their solvency or connections. Edwin Johnson, a former senator and governor of Colorado, took the lead in Denver. Texaco heir Craig Cullinan signed on in Houston. The heads of the Dayton-Hudson department-store chain and the Hamms Brewing Company invested in the new Minneapolis club. And Jack Kent Cooke snapped up the Toronto franchise.[18] "This is an historic occasion," Johnson told his new allies at the press conference. "I believe that each and every one of you here will always remember it as such."[19]

That, of course, depended on the baseball establishment's reaction. Ford Frick said all the right things, but several of his colleagues made no effort to hide their disdain. "Just branding a league 'major' doesn't make it one," scoffed American League president Joe Cronin. His National League counterpart, Warren Giles, called the CL a group, not a league, insisting that it didn't have enough teams to warrant the latter noun.

Yet Bill Shea denied there was any reason for concern. He pointed out that the major leagues had extended an olive branch in Columbus. "They will not go back on commitments they already have made," he said confidently.

A reporter expressed skepticism. What, he asked, if the majors secretly intended to go to war? Shea pondered the possibility for only a moment.

"We will go ahead, anyway," he said.[20]

* * *

Estes Kefauver doubted that Commissioner Frick and his colleagues were telling the truth. "I don't believe baseball will permit the formation of a third league," he said flatly.[21] The big problem, in Kefauver's opinion, was the monopoly on young talent held by the American and National Leagues. He saw no way for the Continental League to sign any decent players.

Shea was considerably more optimistic when the two men met on June 24, 1959. "If the major leagues cooperate with us," he said, "we won't have a bit of trouble getting players."[22] But Kefauver predicted that confrontation, not cooperation, lay ahead. He pointed out that the sixteen big-league teams controlled thousands of minor leaguers—a subsequent inventory would peg the number at 3,084—and every single one of those players would be off-limits to the CL.[23]

Kefauver intended to break this logjam with S. 886, his long-promised substitute for Ken Keating's 1958 legislation. The new bill was even tougher than the baseball establishment had feared. S. 886 pared down the game's antitrust exemption, trimmed each franchise's home territory to a thirty-five-mile radius, and imposed a cap on the number of players a given team could control. That last provision—limiting each club to eighty roster slots—drew the loudest wails. The Dodgers, for example, employed three hundred players on their Los Angeles and minor-league squads. If Kefauver's bill became law, they would be forced to set 220 free.[24]

Keating, who had been elected to the Senate the previous November, again stepped forward as baseball's legislative knight, urging his fellow senators to reject such heresies as territorial restrictions and roster limits. "The less that Congress has to do with organized baseball," he insisted, "the better baseball will be in the long run for both the fans and the players."[25]

The first skirmish in the new legislative battle occurred on July 28, 1959, the day after the Continental League's coming-out party. Kefauver had served in the Senate for a decade, and he understood the importance of slowly building support for his controversial bill, a need that would delay a roll-call vote until 1960. Yet his populist, publicity-loving side demanded a quick fix. His Subcommittee on Antitrust and Monopoly scheduled hearings for the final four days of July.[26]

Kefauver and Keating sparred amiably during the hearings, reserving their firepower for the floor debate a few months hence. The usual witnesses took the stand, including Ford Frick, who implored the Senate to abandon any thought of a roster limit. Frick offered the peculiar argument that most minor-league players were mediocre—"60 percent of them are not major-league caliber and never will be"—and therefore would be of no use to the Continental League. He did not explain why they were valued by their current employers.[27]

Senators were more interested in Frick's revelation that he and a committee of seven big-league owners intended to sit down with Shea and the Continental League's owners on August 18. "This meeting is on the level," said the commissioner, who proceeded to protest entirely too much. "It is a sincere meeting to help these people organize a third league to get [the] major leagues expanded. It is not a meeting that is being forced. It is not a coverup."[28]

Shea himself was one of two star witnesses slated for the final day of hearings, following Branch Rickey, the famed Mahatma. Rickey, languishing in semi-retirement as the chairman of the Pirates, emerged as the greatest cheerleader the Continental League could possibly desire. "I am third-major-league minded, completely so," he thundered. "It is a great need in the country. Twenty great cities in this country ought to have it."[29] He waved aside the critics who insisted that the talent base was insufficient for a third league. "The source of players has hardly been scratched," Rickey said excitedly, naming Japan, Central America, South America, Puerto Rico, Cuba, and South Africa as potential breeding grounds for future stars.[30]

The Continental League's official representative seemed subdued by comparison. "We have many obstacles to overcome, but none of them are insurmountable," Shea said quietly.[31] He sounded not like a soldier girding for a major battle, but a weary veteran who was ready to leave the field. "I am only a temporary chairman of this group for the simple purpose of getting a team back to my city, and my job is finished," he told the subcommittee. He revealed that a permanent leader would be taking charge of the Continental League before the August 18 meeting with Frick.[32]

Shea didn't name any names, but one obvious candidate jumped to everyone's mind.

* * *

One of Branch Rickey's greatest heroes was Ban Johnson, a Cincinnati sportswriter who left the press box in 1894 to become the head of baseball's Western League. Johnson elevated his minor league to major status seven years later, renaming it the American League. He remained its president until 1927, reigning as the sport's dominant force until being eclipsed by Kenesaw Mountain Landis.

Rickey hailed Johnson as "a new force on the baseball horizon," a man of unsurpassed creativity and dynamism who created America's second major league through sheer force of will. "He took conditions as he met them, face to face, as he marched headlong toward his objective," Rickey wrote admiringly. "He fought where he met the enemy."[33]

Rickey now faced an opportunity to duplicate his idol's feat. He listened with interest as Bill Shea secretly offered him the presidency of the Continental League in the summer of 1959. Both sides had much to gain. Rickey would instantly regain relevance, while the CL would immediately be elevated in the eyes of the existing leagues. Shea had read the May 1958 *Sporting News* interview in which the old man planted the seeds for a new league—"a third major is something we must have soon"—while flashing the feistiness that its presidency required.[34] "We knew we had to have a firebrand," Shea admitted.[35]

There were plenty of reasons for Rickey to say no. Ban Johnson was a youthful thirty-seven when he founded the American League. The seventy-seven-year-old Rickey, who had suffered a heart attack a year earlier, now relied on a cane.[36] He acknowledged three complicating factors: "One is health. One is inclination. And one, heaven knows, is age."[37] Yet he was intrigued. The owner of the Pirates, John Galbreath, tried to stop him, arguing that he and Rickey had "a reciprocal relationship which should be maintained." But Rickey was tired of serving as the team's figurehead chairman, his title since his 1955 dismissal as general manager. "You fired me from my present job, and you know it," he snapped as he handed his resignation letter to Galbreath.[38]

Rickey signed a Continental League contract on the morning of August 18, 1959. News of his hiring ricocheted around the country. "It was at that moment that the [AL and NL] owners knew that we were for real and that we meant business," recalled Craig Cullinan, who had been awarded the CL's Houston franchise.[39] Jimmy Cannon, the esteemed columnist for the *New York Journal-American*, also saw it as a turning point. "The baseball people ridiculed Shea," he wrote, "but they were shaken when he hired Branch Rickey."[40]

The new president immediately swung into action, heading to New York's Warwick Hotel for the previously scheduled meeting with Ford Frick. Rickey was at his evangelical best, preaching that baseball had reached a crossroads. It could expand into new markets, or it would fall behind other sports.[41] "I don't want football to supplant us," he roared. "I don't want anybody to supplant us."[42] Frick had been publicly supportive of the Continental League, but he waffled during this closed-door session, often speaking in the third person. "The commissioner will accept a third league if all the facts come in, and they show that it is an operable thing," he said, leaving himself plenty of wiggle room.[43]

A long debate ensued. Rickey and Shea kept pushing for reaffirmation of the endorsement that had been issued at Galbreath's farm in May. Frick dodged repeatedly before wearily submitting. "We will support a third-league movement," he said. "It is the consensus that we will stand by the Columbus resolution and stand by the third league."[44] Rickey, for his part, vowed that the Continental League would behave peacefully. "It is unthinkable that a third major league could come in and raid the old leagues," he said, even though Ban Johnson had been a ferocious raider of National League talent.[45]

The waiting reporters noted a change in Frick and the seven-member committee of big-league owners. They had entered the Warwick in a combative mood, but exited docilely. The Mahatma appeared to be the clear victor. "The magic, persuasive, convincing, highly respected Rickey won them over to his contention," concluded Dan Daniel in the *Sporting News*.[46]

It would prove to be a rash judgment. Resentment toward the Continental League smoldered among the AL and NL owners. Many had paid high prices for their teams, and all enjoyed the exclusive status of baseball ownership. They disdained the CL social climbers who bragged of the bargains they were obtaining. "A person couldn't buy a major-league franchise for less than seven million dollars. We can get this operation on the road much more economically than that," said J.W. Bateson, an investor who would soon land a Continental League team for Dallas.[47] And that was the problem, as far as the existing owners were concerned. An expansion team could be charged a handsome fee to join the American or National League. The CL teams were paying nothing.

Rickey moved briskly from the meeting at the Warwick. There was much to be done. It was up to him to determine the best locations for the league's three remaining franchises, then to make sure that all eight stadiums met the Columbus stipulations. "That's not a boy's job," he said.[48] He crisscrossed North America as his seventy-eighth birthday approached in December, eventually choosing Atlanta, Buffalo, and Dallas to fill out the Continental League.

The ballparks were a mixed bag. All had the necessary twenty-five thousand seats—or could be expanded to that capacity—though some were clearly inadequate. Rickey conceded that these stopgaps would have to suffice until new municipal stadiums could be built. The happy exception was New York, where the Board of Estimate voted on October 22 to initiate an engineering study for a fifty-five-thousand-seat palace at Robert Moses's preferred location, Flushing Meadow. Bill Shea and Joan Payson found this progress exciting, though Walter O'Malley issued a warning from the other coast.[49] "Before these well-meaning people put too much stock in what New York officials will do for them," O'Malley harrumphed, "let them recall what they did for me."[50]

Branch Rickey was a rock-ribbed conservative Republican, a strong believer in the status quo in most aspects of life, yet he morphed into a quasi-socialistic visionary in the fall of 1959. The transformation stunned all who knew him. It began with his bizarre suggestion to convert the World Series to a three-team round robin,

Buffalo's War Memorial Stadium was typical of the aging, midsized ballparks ticketed for the Continental League. Writer Brock Yates once suggested that the stadium "looks as if whatever war it was a memorial to had been fought within its confines" [Buffalo History Museum].

simultaneously matching the American, Continental, and National League champions.[51] Critics scoffed that such a series might bore the public by dragging on for as many as eleven games. "Bored? Why, the fans will devour it," Rickey boomed. "Baseball fever will run from one end of this great land to the other."[52]

Even more shocking was his proposal to pool the television and radio revenue of all eight Continental League teams. The same plan had been advanced by Bill Veeck in December 1952, causing O'Malley to blast him as "a damned communist" and inspiring his fellow owners to banish him from the St. Louis Browns the following year.[53] Rickey now adopted Veeck's logic that the two clubs participating in each game should share the profits. He suggested that 90 percent of each CL team's broadcast money be funneled to the pool. The league's owners were star-struck neophytes who generally did whatever Rickey recommended, but this was too outrageous even for them. They agreed only to 67 percent.[54]

Rickey's organizational work was hampered by periodic rumors. The American and National Leagues—still publicly supportive—were supposedly plotting to pull the rug from under him. He and Frick had a contentious meeting in mid–October. Rickey pounded the left side of his chest. "In here," he asked, "are you opposed to the organization of the third major league?" Frick assured Rickey that he intended to comply with the Columbus resolution, though he confessed a lack of enthusiasm. The commissioner admitted that he would prefer to simply add teams to the two existing leagues, rather than create a third.[55]

The American League briefly yielded to the same impulse on October 26, 1959, formally notifying Frick of its plans to expand, though it did not say when or how. The outcry was immediate.[56] Rickey blasted AL president Joe Cronin as an "obstructionist," and Shea angrily accused him of "just another move to harass us." Frick refused to intervene. "I'm not going to get into any controversy," he said. "I'm for expansion, and I don't care how it's done."[57] But the furor rattled Cronin, who quickly disavowed any immediate desire to add ballclubs.

Rickey had carefully positioned the Continental League as a partner, not a competitor, confining his franchises to markets that currently lacked big-league ball. (The sole exception, New York, had been declared an "open city" by Frick.) A group of California investors had already selected a name for the CL club it hoped to field—the Los Angeles Stars—yet Rickey resisted the temptation. He was certain that the nation's third-largest market could support a second team, but he did not want to antagonize Walter O'Malley. The Continental League, as a result, was not continental at all, containing only one franchise west of the central time zone.[58]

Frick's hesitance and Cronin's brief insurrection suggested that Rickey's strategy was not working. Estes Kefauver's prediction of major-league intransigence seemed to be coming true. Rickey and Shea were treated like interlopers when they attended baseball's winter meetings in early December 1959. Miami Beach was awash in rumors about expansion of the existing leagues.[59] The Continental League's prospects were almost universally disparaged, even by the normally cautious commissioner. "I can't organize for them," Frick said caustically. "I think the time has come for action and not alibis."[60]

Rickey channeled John Paul Jones in his rebuttal. "We have just begun to fight," he proclaimed to the reporters who gathered around him in the Hotel Fontainebleau, assuring them that the Continental League was "as inevitable as tomorrow morning."[61] They listened respectfully—Rickey, after all, was baseball's elder statesman—but they did not necessarily agree. Doubts about the third league were growing.

26

Comeback

Anybody younger than forty found it difficult to believe, yet the Chicago White Sox had once ranked among the strongest teams in the major leagues. The Sox won two world championships and four American League pennants in their first nineteen seasons. Charles Comiskey, who founded the franchise in 1901, was a pillar of the baseball establishment, widely respected by his peers for consistently fielding competitive clubs on a shoestring budget.

His employees took a different view, blasting Comiskey as a cheapskate. Eight of his players—bound for infamy as the "Black Sox"—supplemented their incomes by accepting payoffs from gamblers to throw the 1919 World Series. Kenesaw Mountain Landis barred all eight from organized baseball, thereby consigning Comiskey's team to a generation of ineptitude. The White Sox finished below .500 twenty-one times in the thirty seasons from 1921 through 1950. They never finished higher than third.[1]

The Black Sox scandal not only ruined Comiskey's franchise, it also destroyed his image. He had been esteemed as a man of high rectitude and dignity—frequently called the Old Roman in the nation's sports pages—but the widespread admiration vanished after 1919. Comiskey became an object of mockery, ridiculed for his miserly (and losing) ways. He died a brokenhearted man in 1931.[2]

The team stayed in the family, though son Louis lacked his father's dynamism. He allowed the White Sox to drift into irrelevance. Only 4.1 million fans wandered into Comiskey Park on Chicago's South Side between 1930 and 1939, dwarfed by the 8.8 million who flocked to Wrigley Field on the North Side to root for the Cubs. The sorry decade drew to a calamitous end in July 1939, when the younger Comiskey died at the age of fifty-three, throwing the franchise into chaos.[3]

Lou's wife, Grace, had never been involved in the team's management, and his only son, Chuck, was just thirteen years old. His will gave control of the White Sox to a trustee, the First National Bank, an arrangement that Grace found acceptable until bank officials suggested selling the family's stock.[4] "There must always be a Comiskey at the head of the White Sox," she insisted. She went to court, successfully convincing a judge to break the will.[5]

Grace Comiskey assumed the status of a regent, operating the Sox until Chuck came of age. The team played mediocre ball in the 1940s, and Chicago fans continued to favor the Cubs. "We have not yet recovered from the catastrophe which hit us in 1919," the new owner sighed.[6] But there were positive developments. Twenty-three-year-old Chuck took his first step toward control in 1948, joining the front office as a vice president. It was the same year that Grace finally found someone capable of elevating her club from the doldrums, hiring Frank Lane as general manager.[7]

Chuck Comiskey had hung around the White Sox since his childhood. He liked to put on a uniform as a teen and take infield practice before games. "He had pretty good hands, that kid," said Bill DeWitt, Sr., then an executive with the Browns.[8] Chuck was sitting in the dugout one day in 1942—still in uniform—when the players baited him into joining an argument on the field. Sox manager Jimmie Dykes was verbally lashing umpire John Quinn when the sixteen-year-old suddenly appeared beside him.

Dykes tried to make the best of it. "Meet Mr. Charles Comiskey, Mr. Quinn," he said. "Mr. Comiskey is going to own the Sox one day."

"I don't care if he owns the Tribune Tower right now!" shouted Quinn. "Get him off the field!"[9]

This episode put Chuck's dominant traits on display. He was impetuous, headstrong, and almost impossible to restrain. The same could be said of the new general manager.[10] Frank Lane, a protégé of the mercurial Larry MacPhail, absolutely loved to make trades. "If he didn't make a deal in a month, he'd be nasty, just like a smoker who needed a cigarette," recalled Bing Devine, who later worked with Lane in St. Louis.[11] There was no danger of withdrawal pangs in Chicago, where Lane swung 241 trades in 7 seasons.

The two White Sox executives were destined to come into conflict. Chuck grew increasingly impatient as he waited to assume control, chafing as Lane basked in public acclaim. The Sox suddenly emerged as the hot ticket in Chicago, drawing more than a million fans in 1951 for the first time ever. Lane built them into an annual contender—never winning a pennant, yet finishing second or third every season from 1952 to 1958. He and his handpicked manager, Paul Richards, got all the credit.

The inevitable break came in September 1955, after years of backroom arguments and sniping. "I have had fair and cooperative treatment from Mrs. Comiskey and the others, but Junior wants me out. Let's not pull any punches on that one," Lane told reporters. He demanded to be released from his contract. Grace conceded that Chuck could be difficult to work with. "He's my son, and when he was nine years old, I could tell

General Manager Frank Lane swung 241 trades during his 7 seasons with the White Sox. Lane built the club into a contender, but departed in 1955 after a long civil war with heir Chuck Comiskey. "Junior wants me out," Lane said [National Baseball Hall of Fame and Museum].

him to keep his mouth shut," she said. "But after all, he's twenty-nine now." She tried to reason with Lane, but eventually let him leave.[12]

The only apparent solution—or so it seemed—was to give Chuck the gift he most desired for his thirtieth birthday in November, the title of general manager. But Grace hesitated, still unconvinced that her son possessed the necessary gravitas to operate a big-league ballclub. She opted instead to split the duties between Chuck and John Rigney, a former White Sox pitcher who was married to Grace's daughter Dorothy.[13] "Under this arrangement," said Grace, "there is no necessity for hiring a general manager."[14] It was her intention to keep a close watch on her son. If he eventually showed signs of maturity, she might reconsider and hand him the reins—but only when she truly believed he could handle the job.

* * *

The morning of December 10, 1956, began as any other. Grace Comiskey woke up in her Lake Shore Drive apartment, retrieved the newspaper from the front door, and settled down with her coffee. The maid arrived soon thereafter, shocked to find her employer sprawled on the floor, with pages of the paper scattered about. The coroner determined that she had suffered a heart attack.[15]

Grace was the third White Sox owner to die in a quarter-century. The team's fate had been unclear following the demise of her husband, but there seemed no reason for doubt this time. The unsealing of Grace's will on December 21 was deemed a mere formality. "It hardly seems plausible that anyone but Chuck could be president," wrote Edgar Munzel in the *Sporting News*.[16]

But Grace had never overcome her doubts about Chuck's head for business. Her will designated her elder child, Dorothy Rigney, to serve as executor of her estate, and it further stipulated that Dorothy was to receive a majority of Grace's White Sox stock. The final allocation, including shares already held by the two siblings, would be 3,975 shares for Dorothy and 3,475 for Chuck. Dorothy Rigney, to everyone's amazement (including her own), had just become the new majority owner of the White Sox.[17]

Her first step was to promise continuity. "There will be no changes," she announced. "Charles and John [Rigney] will continue to run the ballclub together, just as they have the past year."[18] That was small solace to Chuck, who struggled for an explanation. His mother had promised in 1948 to eventually vacate the president's office for him—"both my husband and his father had planned for the team to be passed to my son"—but now she had snatched it away.[19] "She knew that, as a man, I always could work for a living if need be," he suggested weakly. "The larger stock interest was an extra insurance for Dorothy. That's the way mothers think of their daughters."[20]

He certainly had no intention of accepting Grace's decision. Chuck began to criticize and second-guess Dorothy with great frequency, first in private, then increasingly in public. He borrowed a page from his mother's playbook by heading to court, filing a pair of lawsuits to force changes in the administration of Grace's estate.[21] "Don't get alarmed," he told reporters. "It's a pure technicality."[22]

It also was the beginning of a nasty fight. Dorothy shot back that Chuck was guilty of "an unpardonable sin—ingratitude," and the war of words escalated.[23] Chicago's tabloids soon labeled the siblings the "Battling Comiskeys," trumpeting their disagreements in a string of bold headlines. Superior Court Judge Donald McKinlay issued a plea for goodwill when Chuck's third suit landed in his chambers in January

1958. "There is great public interest in the White Sox, and we hope to see them in the World Series," McKinlay said plaintively. "Continued disharmony might upset the team's chances in the upcoming pennant race."[24]

Dorothy seemed willing to heed his advice, offering in April to appoint Chuck as the team's new president if he suspended his legal action. But she undercut the gesture almost immediately, saying at a press conference that her thirty-two-year-old brother was "still very young and obviously very impetuous." If he hadn't run Frank Lane out of town, she added, "we would have had a pennant flying over the park today."[25] It came as no surprise when Chuck spurned her proposal, especially after Dorothy confirmed her intention to retain her stock.

The remedy was obvious. One Comiskey heir would have to buy out the other. Dorothy admitted in October 1958 that her brother's attacks were wearing on her, and she had begun thinking of selling her shares. "If it ever came up," she said, "I would sell to [Chuck] rather than somebody else."[26] Rumors of an imminent deal were soon in the air.

But Chuck miscalculated. He offered his sister less than two million dollars for her 54 percent stake in the White Sox, well below the commonly accepted value.[27] "It is certain that Charles will have to sweeten the pot to the extent of at least two million dollars and possibly more before Mrs. Rigney would step out," wrote Edgar Munzel in mid–November.[28] Dorothy grew weary as the talks dragged on—Chuck suggested it might take another three months to seal the deal—and she made a momentous decision. She quietly put the Sox on the open market.

That was Bill Veeck's cue. The Chicago native had been at loose ends since his 1953 ouster from St. Louis—scoping out Los Angeles for Phil Wrigley, bidding for the Athletics and Tigers, starting a public-relations firm, broadcasting an occasional ballgame. Here was his chance to reclaim center stage—and in his hometown, no less. He eagerly opened private negotiations with Dorothy's lawyers, paying one hundred dollars on December 20, 1958, for an option to purchase the White Sox.[29]

Several days passed before the story leaked. "This news about Veeck negotiating with my sister really came as a surprise," Chuck admitted.[30] He remained hopeful of striking his own deal, even as Veeck assembled an ownership group. Hank Greenberg signed on, as did Charlie Finley, the Indiana insurance broker who had been trying for years to purchase a franchise. But Veeck learned that Finley was pushing a separate bid for the White Sox on the sly. "Being rather narrow-minded about having people in my own syndicate working the other side of the street," Veeck later wrote, "I informed Finley that he had disqualified himself." Finley was unabashed. He immediately offered $250,000 for Veeck's $100 option.[31]

The answer, of course, was no. Veeck was too close to his goal. He lined up the necessary financing by March 10, 1959, handing Dorothy's lawyers a check for $2.7 million ($23.8 million in 2020 dollars).[32] The owners of other big-league teams were horrified. They had smirked at Veeck's 1953 pledge to launch a comeback—"like a bad penny, I'll probably turn up again somewhere"—and they had worked behind the scenes to guarantee that his bids in Philadelphia and Detroit were rejected.[33] His Chicago comeback blossomed without warning, catching them flat-footed. "It leaves them cold. In fact, it makes them shudder," wrote Arthur Daley in the *New York Times*.[34]

Chuck Comiskey predictably filed another lawsuit, asking the Cook County Probate Court to order Dorothy to keep the team in the family. "He was basing his action, as near as I could see, upon that ancient doctrine of divine right," Veeck said.[35] But the judicial system had grown tired of both Battling Comiskeys. "The litigants here are merely enjoying the fruits of their parents' and grandparents' industry," scoffed Judge Robert Jerome Dunne, who dismissed Chuck's latest motion.[36]

The new owner of the White Sox extended an olive branch. "We hope to sit down with Chuck and achieve an amicable and friendly working arrangement," Veeck told the press.[37] What he actually wanted was to buy Comiskey's 46 percent. If Veeck controlled at least 80 percent of the White Sox, federal regulations would allow him to reorganize the team as a new corporation, greatly reducing its tax burden. The savings might run as high as two million dollars in the next three years.[38]

Veeck launched a peace offensive on opening day, offering to share the limelight with Chuck during the gala ceremonies at Comiskey Park. They formed a battery—Veeck throwing out the first pitch, Chuck catching it. Photographers swarmed around them, and the crowd cheered the unexpected display of amity.[39] Veeck broke the magical mood by bouncing his pitch, skipping it past his hapless catcher. "I hadn't done it on purpose," he later wrote. "If anybody looked bad, it was yours truly. I got the ball over on the second attempt, though, which almost made me eligible for a fifty-thousand-dollar bonus."[40]

* * *

Veeck hit the ground running in Chicago. He had been exiled from baseball for five seasons, amassing a stockpile of ideas that he was eager to implement. He typically arrived at Comiskey Park before sunrise and stayed until midnight. His first step was to hire 150 workers to scrub and repaint the 49-year-old stadium.[41] "We may not be the most modern ballpark in the game," he said, "but we'll be the cleanest."[42] It was a metaphor for his broader plan to scour the franchise's mediocre reputation.

The promotions that had been so popular in Cleveland worked just as well in Chicago. Veeck staged a circus between games of a doubleheader against the Yankees, complete with clowns, jugglers, sword swallowers, and nine elephants. Lucky fans won strange prizes on a daily basis—five hundred cans of fried grasshoppers, a thousand pickles, ten thousand tickets to a minor-league game, free rental of five hundred tuxedos. The White Sox had drawn only 797,451 fans in 1958, their worst attendance since 1950. The 1959 team topped that figure before the end of July.[43]

Veeck's reputation was so strong that he received credit even for natural occurrences. A swarm of gnats descended on Baltimore pitcher Hoyt Wilhelm during a game in early June. Wilhelm would back off the mound, wave his arms to disperse the pests, restart his motion, suddenly stop, and repeat the process. The White Sox finally gave him a towel, then produced two cans of insecticide, and then handed rolled-up newspapers to the umpires, who ignited them as torches. Nothing worked, so Veeck summoned his fireworks crew, which constructed a small frame on the mound and set off a smoke bomb. The game resumed after a sixteen-minute delay.[44]

Sportswriters gazed suspiciously at Veeck when he entered the press box a few minutes later, and he decided to take full advantage. "It takes all winter to train them," he shouted, gesturing toward the field below. "And now—poof—one lousy bomb, and they're all blown up."[45]

The new owner did not expect success on the field in 1959. "Our pennant hopes are wishful thinking," he warned fans.[46] The White Sox were devoid of power. They would hit only ninety-seven home runs all season, the fewest in the majors. The team's star infielders—future Hall of Famers Luis Aparicio and Nellie Fox—combined for 348 hits, 124 walks, and 61 stolen bases, yet only 8 home runs. "We've got to get ourselves a couple of whackers," Veeck moaned. "We just don't score enough runs."[47] But the Sox had two countervailing strengths—speed and pitching. They stole more bases (113) and yielded fewer earned runs (3.29 per game) than any other big-league team that year.

It was a formula for the most improbable of pennants. The White Sox seized the American League lead on July 28 and refused to surrender it. Chuck Comiskey spent the summer claiming credit—"I brought in almost all the boys who are playing out there"—when he wasn't filing additional lawsuits.[48] His latest submission asked the courts to remove Veeck as president. "Let's say that this won't bring us any closer together," said Veeck, who told Hank Greenberg to handle any future negotiations for Comiskey's stock.[49] "Hank believes that if I had turned my boyish charm on Chuck, full force, I could have come to some kind of an understanding with him on the 80 percent," Veeck wrote. "But, I tell you, I have no patience with people who think everything is coming to them."[50]

The Sox had finished a distant second to the Yankees the previous two seasons, but something was different in 1959. Chicago sportswriters gave Veeck the credit. "His enthusiasm has infected a band of good ballplayers," wrote Dave Condon of the *Tribune*.[51] Bill Gleason of the *American* agreed: "There was never a Chicago team during the fifties—when they had very good ballclubs—that believed the team could win it. He changed that whole atmosphere."[52] The clincher came on the evening of September 22 in Cleveland, where the White Sox defeated the second-place Indians, 4–2, to secure their first pennant since 1919.

Pandemonium erupted in Chicago. The city's fire commissioner ordered all air-raid sirens and fire alarms to be sounded immediately after the final out—no matter that it was past ten o'clock—and they kept blaring for five long minutes. Police stations and newspapers were swamped with thousands of calls from citizens who feared a Russian attack or the second outbreak of the Chicago Fire. More than one hundred thousand fans jammed Midway Airport to greet their heroes, who didn't return from Cleveland until two in the morning.

The World Series still lay ahead, but Chicago couldn't wait to celebrate. The city staged a parade on September 24, attracting three-quarters of a million people to LaSalle Street. Veeck, Comiskey, and Mayor Richard Daley rode at the head of a long string of convertibles, virtually invisible in a fog of ticker tape and confetti.[53] "We're only halfway home," Veeck shouted to the vast throng in front of City Hall, though his words of caution fell on deaf ears.[54] He understood completely. White Sox fans had spent a long time in the wilderness, as indeed had Veeck. Now they were on top, and they intended to enjoy it.

Headlines: 1959

HADDIX LOSES GAME DESPITE PERFECTION

Pittsburgh's Harvey Haddix pitched one of history's greatest games, yet he took a loss on May 26. Haddix retired thirty-six straight Milwaukee batters—a twelve-inning perfect game—but the Braves eked out a 1–0 win in the thirteenth on an error, a sacrifice, a walk, and a double. Pirates outfielder Bill Virdon shook his head. "A pitcher does this once in a lifetime," he said, "and we can't win the game for him."[55]

Boston becomes last team to integrate

Pumpsie Green's big-league debut on July 21 was unexceptional at first glance. Green entered Boston's game against Chicago as a pinch runner, anchoring himself to first base as the next three batters made outs. But the color of his skin rendered his appearance historic. Green was the first black player for the Red Sox, the sixteenth and final team to integrate.[56]

Dodgers derail Braves' drive for third title

Milwaukee was a heavy favorite to win a third consecutive National League title, yet it finished the season in a first-place tie with the Dodgers. Braves slugger Henry Aaron saw no reason to worry. "We were sure—everybody in Milwaukee was sure—that we were the superior team," he recalled. But Los Angeles swept a best-of-three playoff to win the NL crown.[57]

Los Angeles unexpectedly prevails in World Series

Bill Veeck was right to be cautious about the World Series. His White Sox exploded for an 11–0 victory in Game One, then scored only twelve runs in the subsequent five games. The Dodgers rolled to an unlikely title, despite the weakest regular-season record (88–68) for any world champion between 1903 and 1974. "It was the worst club ever to win a World Series," admitted Buzzie Bavasi. "But it's also my favorite club. Those kids won on sheer courage."[58]

27

Outlaws

The census of 1890 marked a watershed in American history. Settlers had been pushing westward since the first Europeans set foot in the New World—ceaselessly seeking virgin land—but their options were dwindling as the nineteenth century drew toward a close. The Census Bureau detected a new demographic pattern in 1890, a generally continuous string of cities, towns, and villages between the Atlantic Ocean and the Pacific.[1] "People had settled throughout the Western territories," said analyst Ben Wattenberg, "and a clear frontier line could no longer be drawn."[2]

The federal government conducted a new census every decade, a total of seventeen between 1790 and 1950. Its 1890 report was widely considered the most significant of the lot, famed among historians for its careful documentation of the frontier's demise. None of the others came close in demographic esteem.

Not, that is, until the census of 1960, which showcased a force as powerful as the westward expansion of the previous century. The Census Bureau announced that the population of the United States had soared by 18.5 percent since 1950, an astounding gain of twenty-eight million people. Two-thirds of that increase—and this was the truly important point—occurred outside of the nation's major cities. The previous census had noted the first signs of a suburban exodus, but it was the 1960 report that fully exposed the dramatic evolution of the American landscape.[3] "From Boston to Los Angeles, vast new subdivisions and virtually new towns sprawled where, a generation earlier, nature held sway," wrote historian Kenneth Jackson.[4]

The time-honored hubs of major-league baseball—the urban centers of the East and Midwest—fared poorly in the new census. All but three of the fifteen cities with big-league franchises (the cities alone, not their metropolitan areas) suffered population losses during the 1950s. Several of the declines were dramatic: Boston and St. Louis down 13 percent in ten years, Pittsburgh down 11 percent, Detroit down 10 percent. The only places that bucked the negative wave were Los Angeles, not really a city in the classic sense, and Kansas City and Milwaukee, a pair of rare municipalities still on the rise.[5] "It marks the passage of the crest of the great city," author Theodore White wrote of the 1960 census, "the first turning of Americans decisively away from a community institution which has dominated our culture and politics for half a century."[6]

Major-league owners found this trend frightening, and they were equally concerned about two other patterns confirmed by the Census Bureau. America had become dramatically younger, with 30 percent of all residents under the age of fourteen, up from just 23 percent as recently as 1940. And cities had diversified, with blacks accounting for 54 percent of Washington's residents, making it the first majority-minority city in American history. Four other cities now had black populations greater than 25 percent: Cleveland, Detroit, Philadelphia, and St. Louis.[7]

The baseball establishment lacked proof, yet it strongly believed that youngsters, minorities, and suburbanites were less interested in ballgames than adults, whites, and city dwellers. The resulting sense of dismay was compounded by the Census Bureau's new population counts for metropolitan areas (the amalgams of cities and their suburbs), which suggested that the demand for big-league expansion would intensify in coming years, ratcheting up the pressure on owners. Seven markets outside of the majors—including five ticketed for the Continental League—now had more than one million residents, and another three were sure to pass that threshold during the early 1960s.[8]

Distance had always been the owners' primary defense against expansion. They had routinely rejected some cities, especially those on the West Coast, for being too difficult to reach. And they had rebuffed others, particularly those in the South, for being out of the loop, for existing on the fringe of the national consciousness. But neither excuse applied by 1960. Transportation had never been easier, and the country had never seemed smaller.

Air travel was a major reason for that. The number of domestic airline passengers had soared by 132 percent in just eight years—from twenty-five million in 1952 to fifty-eight million in 1960—attracted by aviation's combination of speed and convenience. Most flights were still propeller-driven, though jets had finally gone into transcontinental service on January 25, 1959, with Horace Stoneham among the passengers on the maiden trip. Eastbound travel from California to New York took as little as four and a half hours by jet.[9] "In net effect, the speed of the airplane moves Los Angeles about one thousand miles closer to our city," marveled C.R. Smith, the New York–based president of American Airlines.[10]

Ballclubs now did most of their traveling in the sky. "With the shifting of the two franchises to California, air travel has virtually become a necessity," admitted Fred Fleig, who drew up each season's National League schedule.[11] Players were not necessarily happy about that, especially if they found themselves stuck on a slow prop flight to the Pacific Coast, a frequent experience for NL teams. "Eight Mondays a season, we spend eight hours on an airplane," groused pitcher Jim Brosnan. "A hell of a way to enjoy an off-day."[12]

Air travel was accompanied by a disquieting element of danger. Eight players with Britain's famed Manchester United soccer team perished in a plane crash in February 1958, raising concerns that the same fate might befall a big-league club. The very first teams scheduled for western trips took off on April 21, 1958, the Cardinals heading to San Francisco, the Cubs to Los Angeles. They were en route when a United Airlines plane and an Air Force jet fighter collided near Las Vegas, killing forty-nine.[13] The players learned the news when they landed. Several were visibly shaken. "It looks like we're a lucky ballclub this year," sighed Cubs star Ernie Banks.[14]

Television also played a major role in bringing Americans closer together. The Census Bureau counted 46 million homes with TV sets in 1960, better than a tenfold increase from 1950's total of 3.9 million.[15] Distant corners of the United States now enjoyed immediate access to top-flight entertainment, including a wide range of athletic contests. "It is perfectly obvious that TV has hugely increased the nation's familiarity with, and interest in, sports of all sorts, from bowling to baseball to badminton,"

Sports Illustrated reported in December 1960. "There are old ladies in rocking chairs right this minute who can reel off the batting averages of the entire Yankee roster."[16]

Most owners continued to telecast as many games as possible—no matter the impact on their attendance—but Lou Perini and Walter O'Malley resisted. Perini relented on the two occasions when his Braves made the World Series, though he clung to his regular-season blackout, much to the irritation of Wisconsinites.[17] One malcontent sent the Braves owner a check for $1.70 in 1957. "The personal contribution to you is being made because I cheated last Saturday afternoon and watched the Braves play ball on television from an Illinois station," the fan wrote. "I am paying only for bleacher seats because reception was not good."[18]

Perini and O'Malley both had a temporary change of heart when their teams met in a playoff to break the tie for the 1959 National League title. The Braves had drawn a massive crowd of 48,642 for their final regular-season game on Sunday, September 27, setting the stage for the playoff opener the following day. Perini assumed a sellout was in store, so he authorized a local station to telecast the game. But Monday dawned cold and wet in Milwaukee, and most fans watched in homebound comfort. Only 18,297 clicked through the turnstiles.[19] "County Stadium wasn't even half full. It was weird," said Braves third baseman Eddie Mathews. "Maybe the fans were all waiting for us to play the World Series."[20]

The weather was considerably nicer in Los Angeles the next day, but the result was similar. O'Malley would long regret his decision to allow Southern Californians to see the network telecast of the second playoff game. Empty seats (56,500) outnumbered spectators (36,500) in the Coliseum as the Dodgers clinched the pennant, a disparity that reinforced O'Malley's disdain for free TV.[21] "I could, you know, pick up my telephone right now and arrange to get one million dollars more for television rights, but I won't do it," he once explained to a reporter. "I won't reach for it. Because I know that our radio rights would drop off and, soon, attendance in the park would fall, too."[22]

* * *

Everything about the evolution of modern America—the emergence of new metropolitan hubs, the initiation of jet travel, the pervasiveness of television—appeared to favor the Continental League. Markets that had been ignored for decades were clamoring for big-league ball, and Branch Rickey and Bill Shea were eager to fill the void.

Ford Frick's public support seemed to be another of the new league's assets. The commissioner continued to insist that he was rooting for the upstarts, even though he found their lack of progress a bit disappointing. "I hope the Continental League gets off the ground," Frick said flatly during a Senate subcommittee hearing.[23]

But Frick's position was not as steadfast or consistent as he pretended. His frustration with the CL had flared publicly in December 1959—"the time has come for action and not alibis"—and he had wavered badly in private meetings with Rickey prior to that.[24]

The two men got together again on February 2, 1960, and Frick laid his cards on the table. Serious problems might prevent the Continental League from ever playing an inning, said the commissioner, who urged Rickey to take three immediate steps: Appease the Yankees, who were irritated by the prospect of sharing New York with a competitor. Compensate the minor leagues for stealing several of their markets. And get some players.

"I don't know whether you can do it or not," said Frick.

"Don't try to scare me," Rickey replied.[25]

The Yankees were powerful, yet they didn't worry the Mahatma. He doubted that Del Webb and Dan Topping had the necessary muscle to block Joan Payson's new franchise. Frick had repeatedly proclaimed New York to be an "open city," lifting the territorial restriction that normally reserved a market for a single ballclub. But the commissioner's other two points were valid and imposing.

The Braves had established the pattern for indemnification in 1953. Lou Perini paid fifty thousand dollars for the rights to Milwaukee, making amends to the American Association for forcing its Brewers to relocate to Toledo. Payments for subsequent shifts grew larger, peaking at $473,000 apiece from the Dodgers and Giants to the Pacific Coast League, which moved three of its teams.[26]

Creation of the Continental League would compel relocation on a much larger scale. Seven AAA clubs would be affected—Buffalo and Toronto in the International League; Dallas-Fort Worth, Denver, Houston, Minneapolis, and St. Paul in the American Association. Atlanta's AA franchise would also require a new home. Rickey proposed a simple formula. Each team's home attendance for the past three years would be totaled, then multiplied by seven cents. The indemnity for Buffalo, for example, would be seventy-six thousand dollars.[27]

Frick refused to get involved. He ordered Rickey to negotiate directly with the minor leagues, whose presidents had no intention of accepting five-figure payments. "The Continental people claim they have millions. Well, they'd better get ready to spend some of it," barked the International League's Frank Shaughnessy.[28] His American Association counterpart, Edward Doherty, implied that no price could possibly be high enough. "If the Continental League begins operations in 1961," Doherty said unhappily, "it will mean the demise of the American Association, the most glorious of the higher minor leagues."[29]

Shaughnessy suggested $1.6 million ($13.9 million in 2020 dollars) as a fair indemnity for the IL, the equivalent of $800,000 for each of his two affected teams. Doherty went higher, proposing a fee of $1 million per club, a total of $5 million ($43.5 million in 2020) for his league.[30] Shea accused both presidents of highway robbery. He estimated that the actual value of a typical AAA team was in the range of $100,000 to $150,000. "Without trying to be facetious or anything like that," Shea sputtered, "I would say that you could almost buy the entire eight-club league for one million dollars."[31]

Shea and Rickey slowly began to suspect that Frick and the big-league owners were using Shaughnessy and Doherty for their own dilatory purposes. The indemnity negotiations stalemated, with neither side willing to budge. The minor leagues stuck to their demands, and the Continental League refused to pay. "We do not intend to be blackjacked into making exorbitant payments," Shea snapped.[32] Weeks and months passed, and the odds grew dimmer that the CL would be able to start play in April 1961.

And then there was the question of who would be taking the field. Rickey had initially been cavalier on the issue of talent. "Good lord, the world is full of baseball players," he had exclaimed upon taking command in August 1959.[33] But filling the new league's rosters wouldn't be quite that simple, especially since the sixteen existing clubs "have all the merchandise," as Shea put it.³⁴ Rickey had opposed Estes Kefauver's 1959 proposal to restrict the number of players under any team's control—"this limitation of forty or eighty or eight hundred takes away the enterprise, takes away the initiative"—but he became a convert as time grew short and pressure tightened.³⁵

Kefauver unveiled a modified bill in 1960, seeking to broaden its appeal. He now proposed to allow each big-league club to keep one hundred players, up from his previous limit of eighty. All others would become free agents, ensuring a stream of talent to the Continental League. Even better from the CL's perspective was Kefauver's provision for an annual draft. Each major-league team would protect forty of its players, exposing the remaining sixty to possible selection by other clubs in the American, National, and Continental Leagues.³⁶

Rickey jumped on board, oblivious to any contradiction with his previous position. "It will save the major leagues from themselves," he said of Kefauver's bill. "It will also provide equality in the distribution of player talent, defeat the irrational bonus system, guarantee merit advancements to players, and serve the public by paving the way for the Continental League."³⁷ Shea, as was his custom, spoke more directly. "The bill," he said, "is the only hope we have of getting players and going into business."³⁸ Frick agreed that the stakes were high, and he mobilized his forces in opposition.

"This measure is pernicious and vicious," the commissioner said with uncharacteristic bile, "the most dangerous bill yet introduced in the Congress."³⁹

The showdown was slated for June 28, 1960, though Kefauver was not present to see his bill, S. 3483, arrive on the Senate floor. His career took precedence. Kefauver was campaigning for reelection in Tennessee—where a primary election was imminent—while secretly angling for the Democratic presidential nomination. "He thought there was a possibility that they might have a Mexican standoff [at the convention] and go to voting. And several days might pass, and they might even send for him," recalled Paul Rand Dixon, a key aide. It proved to be wishful thinking. John Kennedy would win the nomination on July 13, driving the final stake into Kefauver's White House dreams. "Old Estes was fit to be tied," said Dixon.⁴⁰

Washington lobbyist Paul Porter is in his natural milieu, testifying before a congressional committee. Porter coordinated baseball's strategy during investigations by House and Senate panels in the 1950s [Harry S. Truman Library and Museum].

Paul Porter, baseball's lobbyist extraordinaire, assured his clients that the situation was firmly in hand. He predicted that S. 3483 would receive no more than twenty votes. But Porter's key ally in previous legislative fights, Ken Keating, backed away this time. Keating's constituents stood to gain teams in Buffalo and New York if the Continental League succeeded, so it seemed prudent for him to mute his opposition. His unlikely replacement was a liberal Democrat from Michigan, Phil Hart, who was married to one of the Briggs sisters who had sold the Detroit Tigers in 1956.[41] "In my book," said Hart, "when writing rules of baseball, Congress should stay in the grandstand."[42]

Kefauver's bill was divided into two parts. Title I offered relief to professional football, basketball, and hockey, providing each of those sports the limited antitrust exemptions they had sought for so long. Title II dealt only with baseball, imposing the 100-man limit and the annual draft.[43]

Hart questioned Kefauver's logic in loosening the restraints on three sports, while tightening them on the other. "A new imperative has developed—namely, the attempted emergence of a third major baseball league—and because of that fact, he has asked us to write bad law," said Hart.[44] Wisconsin senator Alexander Wiley jumped in with an amendment to appease the baseball establishment by eliminating Title II. "We should not be tinkering with every piece of human activity," Wiley lectured his colleagues.[45]

This was the crucial roll call for both sides. Nine of the ten senators from Continental League states (including Keating and Jacob Javits from New York) voted against the amendment—thereby siding with Kefauver—while thirteen of the fourteen senators from American and National League states (excluding New York) supported Wiley. The final margin—just four votes—was closer than Porter had anticipated. Wiley's amendment was approved, forty-five to forty-one, striking Kefauver's roster limit from the bill. S. 3483 was shipped back to committee, presumably to languish and die.[46]

The bill's sponsor was unbowed. "We've lost a skirmish, but not the battle," Kefauver declared from Tennessee.[47] But the Continental League's founders did not share his defiance. Their best source of players had just been snatched away, and their negotiations with the minor leagues were going nowhere. Branch Rickey, usually the most optimistic of men, was momentarily at a loss. The defeat in the Senate—and the establishment's role in securing it—had convinced him of one thing. "Negotiation with organized baseball," Rickey said, "is utterly futile."[48]

* * *

Rickey and Shea had invested their hopes in S. 3483. They had counted on Kefauver's bill to ease their admission to the baseball fraternity, granting them full and peaceful equality with the existing major leagues.

What would they do now?

Rickey was still pondering the options in early July when bold advice arrived from an unexpected quarter. Paul Rand Dixon, the counsel for Kefauver's subcommittee, mailed Rickey a long letter to urge decisive action. "I think the Continental League is now in the best position possible for publicly announcing that it intends to start operations whether it is accepted by baseball or not," Dixon wrote.[49]

The baseball establishment had a phrase for what he was suggesting—"going outlaw." If the Continental League chose such a course, it would essentially be declaring war against the American and National Leagues. Ford Frick would no longer take Rickey's phone calls. The sixteen existing clubs would never make any players available. Any dreams of participating in the World Series would fly out the window.

Dixon stressed that he was speaking for himself, not the subcommittee. He noted that the Continental League had traveled the two logical avenues toward its goal. It had approached the major leagues, then it had appealed to Congress. Both roads proved to be dead ends. The outlaw path was the remaining option.

Dixon saw advantages in going outlaw. The CL would no longer need to negotiate indemnities with minor leagues. The payments had been a necessary expense—an entrance fee—to join the family of organized baseball, but they were not legally required. If an entrepreneur opened a new hardware store in a promising neighborhood, he didn't send checks to his competitors, so why should the Continental League pay the International League and American Association? "The money saved at this point would go a long way toward starting the league," Dixon said.[50]

It would also be easier to attract players to an outlaw league. The CL could raid the existing leagues for talent, following the examples of Ban Johnson's American League in 1901 and the Federal League in 1914. The reserve clause, in Dixon's opinion, would never survive a legal challenge. "I am of the opinion that the Continental League could sign up any ballplayers they could persuade to sign a contract," Dixon wrote. "If this were done, I am convinced that because of the reserve clause in players' contracts as they exist today, no court would enforce such contracts."[51]

Rickey didn't need to look far to see Dixon's advice in action. Lamar Hunt had asked National Football League commissioner Bert Bell to fit the new American Football League under his umbrella, but Bell had declined. Hunt and his partners decided to push ahead, establishing the AFL as an outlaw operation. They negotiated a five-year television contract with ABC for $10.6 million, providing instant credibility and a steady stream of cash. NFL games were telecast on a crazy quilt of networks—nine teams on CBS, two on NBC, and the Cleveland Browns on their own system—and the TV payments to NFL clubs varied widely. But Hunt insisted that all eight teams in his league share their TV money equally, a concept he always credited to Rickey's Continental League pool.[52]

Relations between the NFL and AFL remained cordial until October 11, 1959, when two mediocre teams, the Pittsburgh Steelers and Philadelphia Eagles, squared off at Philadelphia's Franklin Field. Bert Bell was watching the final minutes of the game in the stands when he suddenly collapsed, the victim of a heart attack. Bell had understood the necessity of treating the new league fairly to avoid an antitrust lawsuit, but his death left a void that would be filled by the NFL's fire-eaters.[53]

George Halas, the hard-bitten owner of the Chicago Bears, took charge of the NFL until a new commissioner was chosen. Halas nursed bitter memories of the expensive war with the All-America Football Conference between 1946 and 1949, and he had no intention of reliving the experience. His first move was to offer Lamar Hunt and Bud Adams what they had long sought, NFL expansion franchises for Dallas and Houston. The AFL would surely die without its two linchpins.[54]

Hunt and Adams were tempted. Neither wanted a costly war with the NFL. Halas warned that everybody would suffer if the AAFC debacle were repeated—"it's going to be the same story, second verse"—and his two visitors knew he was right. They huddled at Chicago's Sherman Hotel after their meeting with the Bears owner, only to conclude that they had gone too far down the road with their AFL partners. They said no to the established league.[55]

Halas retaliated by granting an NFL team to Dallas, where the Cowboys would go head to head against Hunt's AFL Texans. And he lured away the AFL's Minneapolis-St. Paul franchise, which would become the NFL Vikings. The war was truly on. The AFL filed the inevitable antitrust lawsuit—the very claim that Bell had tried to avoid—before kicking off its inaugural season in Boston on September 9, 1960. The NFL's new commissioner promised a battle to the death.[56] "The two leagues will never be merged," said Pete Rozelle. "As for claims that we'll meet at some time in the near future in a World Series of Pro Football, that just won't be."[57]

Branch Rickey was preparing for a similar war. He was old enough at seventy-eight to recall the defiant stand taken by his hero, Ban Johnson, in 1901. "We have grown large and strong enough not to be dictated to," Johnson had declared in founding the American League.[58] Rickey was also aware that the AL's outlaw status had been critical to its success. Clark Griffith, the Old Fox himself, once admitted that the new league might have perished if not for its raids of National League rosters. "We could not have been a big league for quite some time," said Griffith. "You know, it takes time to develop ballplayers."[59]

Rickey said all the right things, pledging to go to extremes to establish the Continental League. He had been asked in November 1959 what might happen if the major leagues denied assistance. "It would be a case of survival or surrender," Rickey thundered, "and we propose to survive."[60] He went further with this promise in May 1960: "I am going to extend myself until my death."[61] Bill Shea was right there with him. "We can sign almost anybody you mention for fifty thousand dollars each, plus their present salary," he told a Washington reporter. "Do you think fellows like Bob Allison and Harmon Killebrew of the Senators wouldn't go for a deal like that?"[62] Didn't the reserve clause bind those players to their present club? Shea, himself a lawyer, scoffed at the very idea. "Those contracts," he said, "aren't worth the paper they're printed on."[63]

The owners of the sixteen existing teams greeted these declarations with a stony silence, but they were scared. "A baseball war would be a calamity beyond comprehension," Ford Frick admitted.[64] Everybody knew how clever Rickey was, and everybody knew he had scores to settle. Walter O'Malley had pushed him aside in Brooklyn, and John Galbreath had sidelined him in Pittsburgh. This was his chance to get even.

But Rickey was unsure that he had the stomach or the energy to face the gathering storm. He wasn't a young, wealthy outsider like Lamar Hunt. He was an elderly, conservative insider, a man who had spent his entire career in organized baseball. Would he be able to attack the very institution that had showered him with fame and fortune? He had his doubts.

Headlines: 1960

WILLIAMS CLIMBS TO THIRD IN HOMER STANDINGS

Ted Williams cleared the left-field fence in Cleveland's Municipal Stadium on June 17, becoming the fourth player to hit 500 home runs. "My goal now," the Boston left fielder announced, "is 512 homers," which would move him past Mel Ott into third place. He reached that mark on August 10, also in Cleveland, and retired on September 28. Williams's very last at-bat yielded his 521st homer. "I quit at the right time," he said. "There's nothing more that I can do."[65]

Managers swap jobs in bizarre trade

The Indians and Tigers made a strange trade on August 3, exchanging their managers. Joe Gordon went to Detroit, Jimmie Dykes to Cleveland. It was no surprise that Cleveland general manager Frank Lane, the ultimate trade addict, instigated the transaction. "I felt the change might loosen us," he said. Both managers posted losing records with their new clubs.[66]

Pirates beat the odds to win World Series

The Pirates won their first National League pennant in thirty-three years, but they seemed overmatched in the World Series. The Yankees easily outhit (91–60), outhomered (10–4), and outscored (55–27) them. Yet Pittsburgh eked out four tight victories to take the title, locking it down with Bill Mazeroski's ninth-inning homer in Game Seven. The glory of that moment was captured in a classic photograph, with Mazeroski rounding third base, his right arm high in triumph.[67]

Yankees clean house at season's end

The Yankees had qualified for eleven World Series since 1947—winning eight— yet Del Webb believed changes were needed. The team's co-owner forced Manager Casey Stengel and General Manager George Weiss to retire after the World Series. "I'll never make the mistake of being seventy again," Stengel said bitterly. The typically emotionless Weiss, who was sixty-six, cried at his farewell press conference.[68]

28

Uncertainty

The spate of franchise relocations in the 1950s appeared to have been the perfect remedy for baseball's box-office woes. Shifting five clubs to fresh, vibrant cities had jolted big-league attendance, elevating it from a nadir of 14.38 million in 1953 to 19.91 million in 1960, an impressive gain of 38 percent. Optimism was widespread.

Yet all was not well.

Total attendance for 1960—despite the steady progress in recent years—remained 5 percent below the majors' all-time record of 20.92 million, a mark that had been set way back in 1948. Several teams were still struggling, repeatedly failing to reach the time-honored benchmark of one million spectators per season. Seven of the sixteen clubs attracted fewer than 970,000 fans annually between 1956 and 1960. The three worst were mired below 900,000.[1]

At the very bottom were the Washington Senators, who drew just 544,600 fans per year during the half-decade. Turnout was so consistently anemic that Calvin Griffith once again began to waver, despite having declared lifelong fealty to his hometown in January 1958. He claimed six months later that his fellow owners were pushing him to relocate. "Some clubs are raising hell with us," he said. "They're sick and tired of playing to small crowds."[2]

The latter part was true, though it was incorrect to say that his counterparts were urging Griffith to move. They actually wanted him to do a better job in Washington, not run off to Minneapolis. Estes Kefauver's initial antitrust hearings were scheduled for July 1958, and the baseball establishment saw no reason to agitate him by vacating the nation's capital. "It is important that our game is identified with the important people of our country," said Del Webb, "and Washington is the best show-window that organized ball could possibly have." Webb and his colleagues ganged up on Griffith at an American League meeting in Baltimore, curtly informing him that they would prefer the Senators to stay put.[3]

This dust-up naturally came to the attention of Kefauver, who summoned the Senators owner before his subcommittee on July 15, 1958. Griffith was an evasive witness, insisting that the team's board of directors, not he, had spurred any talk of moving, even though he held majority control over the franchise. Wyoming senator Joseph O'Mahoney took him to task:

> O'MAHONEY: Do you think that the board of directors of the Washington team, or any member of the board, will bring the matter up again?
> GRIFFITH: This was just exploratory over there in Baltimore.
> O'MAHONEY: Are you through exploring, Mr. Griffith?
> GRIFFITH: Yes, sir. I am. [Laughter.][4]

28. Uncertainty

But he wasn't. Griffith flew to Minneapolis less than a week later. He gushed over Metropolitan Stadium in nearby Bloomington—"not until I saw it in person did I realize what you have here; it's terrific"—and spent four days touring the Twin Cities.[5] He reopened negotiations before the end of August, responding enthusiastically when Minnesota officials pledged nine million dollars to expand their ballpark to forty-two thousand seats. It was widely rumored that the Senators' move would be announced in early September 1958, yet Griffith again backed off, reiterating that the team would remain in the District of Columbia. His commitment, however, was not exactly solid.[6] "I would be a fool to say that we are going to play in Washington for the rest of my life," he said.[7]

Many of his fellow owners—several of whom were stuck in decaying ballparks of their own—considered Griffith a fool, anyway. The federal government had already committed $8.5 million ($75.8 million in 2020 terms) to build a modern stadium for the Senators and the football Redskins. Who would possibly turn his back on such a windfall?

But Griffith had three reasons for vacillating. The first (and most obvious) was the poor financial health of the Senators, who would almost certainly fare better in a new city. The second was an unhappy change that lay ahead. The Redskins were the Senators' tenants at Griffith Stadium, handing the baseball team as much as twenty-five thousand dollars in rental and concession profits after each football game. That money would be lost when both clubs became renters at Washington's government-funded ballpark.[8]

And then there was the racial issue, which Griffith bluntly addressed at a 1958 American League meeting. "The trend in Washington," he said, "is getting to be all colored."[9] More than half of the city's residents were black, a proportion that soared above 90 percent in the neighborhoods around Griffith Stadium and the site for the new field.[10] "Our ballpark was in a very black district," recalled Griffith's sister, Thelma Haynes. "People were afraid of getting their tires cut up all the time and things like that. Not that whites don't do the same thing, I don't mean that."[11] Calvin himself would be less circumspect in an infamous speech in 1978. "Black people don't go to ballgames," he said, "but they'll fill up a rassling ring and put up such a chant, it'll scare you to death."[12]

Griffith continued his flip-flopping throughout 1959 and into 1960—alternately defending Washington's honor and lamenting its lack of support. He steadfastly denied ever promising to remain in town—"sometimes those mistakes get in print"—even though he had made precisely such a pledge in the January 1958 *Washington Post* op-ed that carried his byline.[13] "Next year. The year after. Forever," he had written of his commitment to the nation's capital.[14] He no longer used such emphatic terms.

The other owners were exasperated by this never-ending soap opera. Their widespread annoyance extended even to Ford Frick, who usually spoke in the blandest possible terms. "If Griffith can't operate successfully in Washington, a fine baseball town," snapped the commissioner, "how can we assume he can operate well in Minneapolis after the novelty there wears off?"

The slow-witted Griffith occasionally found himself at a loss for words, but not this time. He let loose with an instant retort. "Frick doesn't have a vote," he spat. "We don't have to pay any attention to him."[15]

* * *

The lethargy that prevailed in a pair of new markets was unexpected. The excitement had already drained from Baltimore and Kansas City, even though each should have been lingering in a honeymoon phase.

The Orioles drew only 1.06 million fans in their inaugural season of 1954, ranking seventh in big-league attendance and embarrassing the civic leaders who had boasted that Baltimore would supplant front-running Milwaukee. Most of the subsequent years were worse. The Orioles averaged 968,000 fans annually between 1956 and 1960.

Kansas City had initially seemed to be a more promising market, as demonstrated by its home attendance of nearly 1.4 million in 1955. But the Athletics slipped to 1,015,154 the following year and dropped as low as 775,000 by 1960. Their five-year average of 916,000 was the fourth-worst among all sixteen big-league teams.[16]

Rumors began to circulate about the Athletics leaving Kansas City, though owner Arnold Johnson reiterated his commitment in late 1959, agreeing to a new short-term lease at Municipal Stadium. "We certainly do not plan to pay rent on two parks," he said, scotching any talk of a move to Los Angeles.[17] Johnson had promised that the A's would contend for a championship within five years of his 1954 purchase, only to post a miserable 313–456 record during that span. Yet his optimism did not waver. "We have the nucleus for a fine club," he assured Kansas City fans. "We're not too far away from our goal."[18]

Johnson remained confident after watching his Athletics practice in West Palm Beach, Florida, on March 9, 1960. "I think we'll fool somebody this year," he chuckled as he climbed into his car.[19] But a massive cerebral hemorrhage intervened, striking a few blocks from the ballpark. Johnson fell forward into the steering wheel—jamming the horn in a prolonged wail—and died at the age of fifty-four.[20]

His widow, Carmen, would remarry in less than four months, raising eyebrows throughout the baseball world. She vowed to retain control of the Athletics, but an army of potential buyers besieged her. Many of them, such as real-estate developers Kenneth and Leonard Berg, hoped to move the team. "We're going to be the first to present a major-league club that represents a state rather than a city," said Kenneth Berg. "We'll be known as the New Jersey Athletics."[21] A few Continental League owners made discreet inquiries, a St. Louis group submitted an offer, and the ubiquitous Charlie Finley started sniffing around. The impending loss of the franchise spurred the Kansas City Chamber of Commerce to begin recruiting local bidders.[22]

The contrast with Milwaukee could not have been sharper. The Braves were wildly successful both on the field and off, as proven by annual averages for the period from 1956 to 1960. Milwaukee notched 90.6 wins and drew 1,895,949 fans per season. The former was second only to the Yankees' 92.6 victories. The latter was far and way the best attendance in the majors, topping the runner-up Dodgers by 12.7 percent.[23]

Talk began to circulate that the Braves were *too* successful, that Lou Perini was getting bored. He stepped aside as the team's president in 1957—saying he would remain chairman "in an advisory capacity"—and he supposedly looked into selling the club a year later.[24] But Perini insisted that his competitive juices were still flowing, and he remained proud of the Braves' supremacy in attendance. "I'll bet a good bratwurst that we wind up ahead of Los Angeles," he said in July 1958.[25]

He was right. The Braves again topped the majors by attracting 1,971,101 fans to County Stadium that season, while the Dodgers drew 1,845,556 to the Coliseum. But there was no sense of triumph. Milwaukee's attendance had slipped 11 percent between 1957 and 1958, failing to reach two million for the first time in five years. The downward spiral would continue with another loss of 11 percent in 1959, then a slide of 14 percent in 1960. Milwaukee sold only 1,497,799 tickets during the latter season, dropping to sixth in the attendance derby. The golden years were definitely over.[26]

Various reasons were suggested—baseball was no longer a novelty, fans had been spoiled by championships, football's newly successful Green Bay Packers were stealing the Braves' thunder—but Perini accepted his share of the blame. He had never done anything but open his ticket windows and accept a flood of money. Now he would have to work. "There wasn't any need to promote when we were getting two million fans a year," he said, "but now there is."[27]

A young car dealer in suburban Milwaukee took a more jaundiced view. "The Braves were not aggressive marketers. And by saying that, I'm being kind. Very, very kind," Bud Selig said caustically.[28] His opinion was amplified by Bill Veeck, who detected a recurring pattern. "Either Boston and Milwaukee were bad baseball towns with a freak attendance during those good years," Veeck wrote, "or they were good baseball towns which were ruined by inept operation."[29] He inclined toward the latter. Attendance had plummeted 67 percent in the three seasons following the Boston Braves' World Series appearance in 1948. The three-year drop after Milwaukee's 1957 world title was not as precipitous—32 percent—but it was alarming nonetheless.[30]

Local observers agreed on one thing: Frederick Miller never would have allowed the Braves' situation to deteriorate so rapidly. The president of the Miller Brewing Company had masterminded Milwaukee's drive for a big-league team in the early 1950s, finally convincing Perini to make the frightening leap. The two men had ridden in the same convertible in the delirious parade that welcomed the Braves to town in 1953. "This could be the beginning of a championship," the brewer had shouted to the delighted owner, and he proved to be right.[31] Miller eased Perini's way, introducing him to local leaders, singing his praises in influential circles, and peppering him with upbeat notes. "I have always told everyone in Milwaukee who asked me, and thousands have, what a fine gentleman you are," he wrote to Perini in October 1954.[32]

But the forty-eight-year-old Miller died only two months later, one of four victims of a fiery plane crash near Milwaukee's General Mitchell Field on December 17, 1954. His funeral confirmed his outsized stature in Wisconsin and indeed all of the Midwest. More than three thousand mourners crowded into an ornate Catholic church, where the rites were conducted by no typical priest, but by the president of the University of Notre Dame.[33]

"In that crash," said Braves traveling secretary Donald Davidson, "Milwaukee lost its most sports-minded citizen, as well as a great man."[34] Lou Perini was deprived of his main champion and liaison to the community, as well as his possible successor. "Before his death, there was a lot of conversation that Miller might buy out Perini," recalled Braves manager Charlie Grimm, and there was no doubt that Miller had the necessary money and enthusiasm.[35] Perini might have turned to him in 1960, when the owner's energy began to wane. But that option was far in the past by then.

* * *

There was no formal ceremony. Matt Burns merely handed the keys to Seymour Goldsmith on New Year's Eve 1959, and that was that. The Dodgers' three-year lease had expired. They no longer had any claim on Ebbets Field.

Both men lived far north of Brooklyn in Yonkers, and they chatted ruefully about the distance they had driven to make a simple handoff of a decrepit ballpark. Burns, who served as the Dodgers' representative in New York, left with several packing cases of team memorabilia. Goldsmith, a vice president of the Kratter Corporation, took the keys back to his boss, Marvin Kratter, who had purchased the stadium from Walter O'Malley in 1956.[36]

The Dodgers' offices on Montague Street—where Branch Rickey first met Jackie Robinson and O'Malley hatched his plans for Los Angeles—had been demolished the previous June. Ebbets Field was slated for the same fate on February 23, 1960, an event that drew two hundred onlookers. Former Brooklyn stars Ralph Branca and Carl Erskine showed up, as did Roy Campanella in his wheelchair. A crane operator deployed a wrecking ball that was painted to look like a baseball.[37] "Men swung sledgehammers, the dugout crumbled, and an iron ball crashed like Pete Reiser against the wall," wrote Gay Talese, the young *New York Times* reporter assigned to the story.[38] Seven apartment buildings would rise on the site.

Twelve major-league stadiums had been constructed in a hectic flurry between 1909 and 1915. Braves Field was the first to face a demolition crew. Boston University had acquired it four months after Perini decamped for Milwaukee in 1953, tearing down everything but the administration building. Ebbets Field was the second to go. Nine others—all but the Polo Grounds, which would stand until 1964—were still hosting big-league games in 1960.[39] Most were in sad shape. "A lot of ballparks were built around 1910, and they look it," said Bill Veeck. "General Motors invests millions of dollars in a new model faster than some owners spend a couple of thousand to spruce up their old joints with a coat of paint."[40]

Only Cleveland and Milwaukee had constructed big-league stadiums since the onset of the Depression. (The projects in Baltimore and Kansas City, new as they may have seemed, were actually massive renovations.) But a fresh era was dawning, with modern ballparks soon to come in San Francisco, Los Angeles, and Washington.

Candlestick Park was the first to arrive. Horace Stoneham had hoped to move the Giants there in 1959, though he had to settle for April 12, 1960. The stadium's price tag was steep—$15 million (the equivalent of $130 million in 2020)—but the result was widely applauded.[41] "There has been nothing quite like it since the Romans, who had to struggle along by chariot, converged on the Colosseum," gushed *Time* magazine.[42]

Candlestick featured almost nine thousand parking spaces, the largest scoreboard in the world, and an innovative heating system designed to pump hot water through thirty-five thousand feet of pipe buried in the concrete slab. California governor Pat Brown enthused over the stadium's magnificence, revealing his baseball ignorance in the process. "I hope I'll be there to see the Giants and the Dodgers meet in the World Series next fall," he said excitedly at the park's dedication dinner.[43]

The only real drawback was the weather. Candlestick was routinely buffeted by bone-chilling gales that baffled even Willie Mays, the era's greatest fielder. "At times," Mays recalled, "the wind would blow the ball back as if it were a ping-pong ball."[44] The same frigid gusts from San Francisco Bay strained the endurance of Giants fans.

28. *Uncertainty* 247

San Francisco's Candlestick Park was hailed as the perfect modern stadium when it debuted in 1960. But its innovative heating system failed to work, and its gusty conditions exasperated players. "The wind would blow the ball back as if it were a ping-pong ball," said Willie Mays [Carol Highsmith Archive, Library of Congress].

Attending a game at Candlestick, in the opinion of author Roger Angell, was akin to "an Eskimo manhood ritual."[45]

The ballyhooed heating system—the great defense against the elements—was put to the test during the ballpark's first night game on April 14, 1960. It generated no warmth whatsoever. The estimated repair costs were so extreme that Stoneham and Mayor George Christopher eventually decided not to bother. The Giants and their fans were destined to suffer through four decades of wind, cold, and fog on Candlestick Point.[46]

Walter O'Malley gazed enviously upon Stoneham's new facility, even with its weather-related problems. Dodger Stadium—the first big-league park since Yankee Stadium to be built with private capital—had been slated to open in 1959, then in 1960, then in 1961, yet legal complications and construction delays kept extending the time frame. "I will not be happy until we overcome some of the inertia that exists here," O'Malley grumbled.[47] He was especially irritated that the Coliseum Commission had slapped the Dodgers with a sizable rent increase for the final two seasons in their makeshift home. "Whenever I see that left-field screen," he muttered, "I'd like to rip it down myself."[48]

But that wouldn't be possible until 1962, when O'Malley's club would finally make the six-mile trek from the Coliseum to Chavez Ravine. Milwaukee County Stadium was often cited as the nation's first modern ballpark, though it still had much in common with its ancient predecessors, with its austere bleachers and a second deck supported by massive posts. Dodger Stadium would have no uncomfortable seats and no pillars.[49] The structure taking shape in the ravine was pleasantly spacious and thoroughly contemporary—the complete opposite of Ebbets Field. It was, in the judgment of author Glenn Stout, "the first park designed with the comfort of the fan in mind."[50]

O'Malley's stadium was intended to blend in with its environment, offering a panoramic view of the San Gabriel Mountains beyond the outfield. But the proposed facility in Washington—a giant enclosed circle—would be completely walled off from its surroundings. Its multipurpose design—fitting the needs of both its baseball and football tenants—was something new. National Football League teams were accustomed to second-class status as renters of major-league ballparks. District of Columbia Stadium's vast playing surface would accommodate both the Senators and the Redskins.

The crotchety, racist owner of Washington's football team, George Marshall, signed a thirty-year lease to play in the new park.[51] "It won't be the biggest in the country," he said happily, "but it will be the most luxurious in spectator comfort." Marshall brought along the Redskins Band to supply music at the festive groundbreaking ceremony on July 8, 1960. Dwight Eisenhower sent a congratulatory telegram. "This fine structure," the president wrote, "will be a welcome addition."[52]

Calvin Griffith, however, remained unconvinced. The Senators owner had been badmouthing the project for years—disparaging its site near the National Armory, its design, even its necessity—but local leaders and the baseball establishment were pressuring him to submit. "I'm damned if I do and damned if I don't," he complained in October 1959, though he steadfastly refused to commit one way or the other.[53]

Hence the surprise when Griffith showed up for the groundbreaking. Reporters flocked to him after the ceremony. "I'm here," he said, "because this stadium is a good thing for the city of Washington." But was it a good thing for the Senators? Did his presence mean that the baseball team would be taking the field in D.C. Stadium in 1962? Griffith looked blankly at the questioner. "I wouldn't even comment on that," he said gloomily, and he headed back to his office.[54]

29

Expansion

The Continental League's owners gathered in New York on July 20, 1960, to plot their course. Branch Rickey laid out three options. The CL could declare war on the American and National Leagues, it could continue to seek their stamp of approval, or it could cease operations.[1]

The league's founder favored the middle route. "We have no thought of disbanding. We're going to break our necks trying to satisfy every possible demand made of us by the majors," Bill Shea assured reporters at the Warwick Hotel.[2] But the same daunting questions remained. Where would the Continental League get players? And how could it meet the minor leagues' financial demands? There were no new answers.

Sportswriters posed a fourth alternative. A few of baseball's titans—National League president Warren Giles among them—had begun hinting at a willingness to absorb CL franchises as expansion clubs. "If there isn't anything in the offing for the Continental League to go ahead," Giles had said two days earlier, "we're prepared to go ahead."[3] Wouldn't that be the easiest way for Shea to land a new team for New York? He shook his head vigorously. "That's impossible," he said. "We agreed long ago not to defect."[4]

The AL and NL proposed a joint meeting, and the CL's leaders decided to accept.[5] It would be the perfect opportunity, in Shea's words, to mount "an endeavor to persuade organized baseball to extend to the Continental League major-league status."[6] Rickey predicted that the third league might be welcomed under the commissioner's umbrella as soon as September. But not everyone shared their commitment or confidence. A co-owner of the CL's Minneapolis franchise, Wheelock Whitney, admitted that he and his partners had undergone "a complete reversal of opinion."[7] They now believed that expansion of the existing leagues was a real possibility—and perhaps a better bet than starting a league from scratch.

The critical meeting was slated for the Imperial Suite of Chicago's Conrad Hilton Hotel on August 2, with the American and National Leagues being represented by a panel of owners. Rickey immediately got down to business, submitting the CL's formal application for recognition as baseball's third major league. But the chairman of the committee had a different agenda entirely.[8]

"Gentlemen, I am against the soft-soap," said Walter O'Malley. "We are here to make serious decisions. Let us lay our cards on the table and face the facts without animosity and with a desire for the best things for baseball and this country." Rickey, Shea, and the CL's owners listened intently.

"There is only one move open," O'Malley went on. "We must compromise. We will take four of your cities and later add the rest."[9]

The Continental League's steely resolve dissolved at that moment. Its owners calmly requested a recess and filed into another room. Their raucous cheers could be heard through the closed doors. A smiling Rickey congratulated all eight teams on their impending admission to organized baseball. Several owners expressed concern about his abrupt unemployment, but he waved them off. "What happens to me makes no difference," he said, throwing his arms around Shea. "I may never see you again," Rickey told his closest ally with evident emotion. "But it was a great fight, a great fight."[10]

O'Malley had not offered a formal agreement, only a verbal assurance that four Continental League cities would join the majors quickly, followed by the other four at an undetermined date. His intent was similar to that of George Halas, who had unsuccessfully tried to kill the American Football League by co-opting two of its franchises. But the Dodgers owner acted with greater skill. O'Malley's genius was in dangling his offer before all eight CL teams, guaranteeing the embryonic league's demise.

New York's immediate selection was the lone certainty. The nation's largest market would obviously receive top priority in the first expansion, fulfilling the assignment that Bill Shea had undertaken in 1957. "It's been a lot of work," Shea said wearily, "but I set out to get a team for New York three years ago, and this is it."[11] Yet there was no official timetable, and the other seven CL clubs waited eagerly to learn if they would be chosen, too.

The National League moved with uncharacteristic haste to supply its part of the answer, granting teams to New York and Houston on October 17, 1960, after a formal motion by O'Malley. The irony was lost on no one. Both clubs were to begin play in 1962.[12] The American League, which had been eying Houston itself, was caught completely off guard. "They pulled a fast one on us," whined Del Webb.[13]

Joan Payson was awarded the New York franchise for a fee of $2.1 million ($18.3 million in 2020). She was hailed by a city that had been burned by O'Malley and Horace Stoneham.[14] "This is one who does not come to get contracts to build a ballpark or to maneuver for capital gains," Jimmy Breslin wrote of Payson. "This is a lady who comes for the sport of it."[15] The new owner wanted Rickey to run her club, but his demands were so grandiose—untrammeled authority and a five-million-dollar budget—that Payson eventually turned to another unemployed executive. George Weiss had been miserable since his forced retirement from the Yankees, and he was happy to return to baseball.[16] His wife was even happier to get him out of the house. "I married George for better or for worse," said Hazel Weiss, "but not for lunch."[17]

The immediate question was what to call the new club. "When you pick a name," said Payson, "you're stuck with it, and it better be a good one."[18] Fans were invited to submit nominations. Thousands responded, proposing 644 different nicknames. Payson was especially fond of Meadowlarks—the new ballpark would be located in Flushing Meadow—or Continentals.[19] But John Drebinger of the *New York Times* found the latter homage troublesome. "It is almost certain to be shortened to Cons or, worse yet, Con-men," he wrote. "And what about the players who later might be traded elsewhere? They'd have to be known as ex-Cons."[20] Payson finally settled on the prosaic option of Metropolitans, Mets for short.

New York's Board of Estimate approved a memorandum of understanding on January 27, 1961, paving the way for construction of the Mets' stadium.[21] Weiss, who had violently opposed the project as general manager of the Yankees, now became its

Joan Payson was favorably compared to Walter O'Malley and Horace Stoneham when she assumed control of New York's expansion team, soon to be named the Mets. "This is a lady who comes for the sport of it," wrote columnist Jimmy Breslin [National Baseball Hall of Fame and Museum].

biggest champion. "With the additional information I have received," he said with a straight face, "I think the new stadium is a good deal for both the city and the club."[22] Weiss inquired if the Mets might play in Yankee Stadium until their park was ready. "I'd suggest they try to get the Polo Grounds first," replied Del Webb.[23]

Thirteen men were initially listed as proprietors of Houston's new club, though billionaire oilman Bob Smith gradually amassed a majority of the stock. Smith preferred to remain in the shadows, so he yielded control to his flamboyant sidekick, former Harris County judge Roy Hofheinz, who quickly alienated the other partners.[24] Hofheinz's lust for power, thirst for publicity, and financial extravagance horrified Craig Cullinan, who still held a small stake in the franchise. "He'd make a dollar, then throw three out the window," said Cullinan. "It drove me nuts."[25]

Smith, Hofheinz, and the other owners weighed nicknames with a Texan flavor—Lone Stars, Rangers, Sheriffs—but publicist George Kirksey convinced them to leave the final choice to the fans. His motives were suspect, since he had already approached the Colt Firearms Company about using its name, yet he was allowed to proceed with his election. The public submitted twelve thousand ballots. Kirksey painstakingly tabulated the results, then announced Colt .45s as the surprise winner. The vote totals were never released.[26]

Houston did not have a stadium of big-league quality, not even an aging heap like the Polo Grounds. The Colt .45s intended to play in a temporary park while their future palace was erected on drained swampland south of downtown. Hofheinz carted around a thirty-five-thousand-dollar model of the new facility, which embodied Walter O'Malley's vision of a domed stadium. Local voters provided the necessary funds for the space-age concept, approving a twenty-two-million-dollar bond issue on January 31, 1961.[27]

American League owners were distressed by this flurry of activity. They had already been beaten to Los Angeles and San Francisco, and now they had lost Houston. "We've let the National League get too far out ahead," said AL president Joe Cronin. "They've been grabbing the big population centers, and now they're reentering New York." It appeared that his league would have to settle for the third- and fourth-best markets in the Continental League, most likely Minneapolis and Toronto.

But Cronin seemed unwilling to accept such a disheartening consolation prize. He hinted at a future surprise. "We can't go into the wrong towns when we expand," he said vaguely. "We already have ground to make up."[28]

* * *

American League owners finally decided to convene in New York on October 26, 1960, a week and a half after the National League welcomed its new members. The meeting was preceded by rumors about Calvin Griffith's renewed interest in moving the Senators. "That's a lot of baloney," Griffith snapped at the reporters who pestered him, though he left the door ajar.[29] He had allowed Los Angeles to slip through his fingers, and he worried about doing the same with Minnesota's Twin Cities. "The Minneapolis people are in New York," he admitted, "and I will listen if they seek me out."[30]

They did. Griffith and the Minneapolis delegation met for dinner on October 25 and kept talking until 3 a.m. The Minnesotans offered an enticing deal. They guaranteed attendance of one million per year for Griffith's first five seasons in Metropolitan Stadium—pledging to compensate him for any shortfalls—and they produced a radio-TV contract worth five hundred thousand dollars annually. The Senators hadn't drawn more than 750,000 fans since 1949, and their broadcasting deal in Washington was worth only $180,000.[31] Griffith recalled invoking his ancestor's spirit in those predawn hours. "Well, Unc, the time has come," he said to the ghost of Clark Griffith. "Something has to give."[32]

The men who ran the American League still wanted a team in the nation's capital, but they were tired of Calvin's annual flirtations. Del Webb got wind of the latest negotiations. He called the influential sports editor of the *Washington Post*, Shirley Povich, who was in New York to cover the expansion meeting. "What would you say," Webb asked, "if we let him go and put another major-league team in Washington?" Povich thought for only a second. "To hell with him. Let him go," he said.[33]

Washington's fans were getting a raw deal. The departing Senators had finally started to show promise. Outfielders Albie Pearson and Bob Allison had won consecutive Rookie of the Year awards in 1958 and 1959. Third baseman Harmon Killebrew had led the AL with forty-two home runs in 1959 at the age of twenty-three. This young talent propelled the Senators to fifth in 1960, up from three consecutive last-place finishes. Minnesota would enjoy the club's future rise to title contention, while Washington would slide back to the cellar with a new team of marginal competence.[34] "What [AL] leaders should have done was given [Griffith] the Minneapolis [expansion] franchise and made him start from the bottom," said Frank Lane.[35] But they didn't.

The American League's second expansion destination—presumably one of the five remaining Continental League cities—remained up in the air. Dan Topping, co-owner of the Yankees, urged his colleagues to look beyond the deal that O'Malley had struck. "If the National League puts a second team in New York," he said, "I see no reason why the American League can't put a second team in Los Angeles."[36] Topping's proposal would instantly extend the AL to the Pacific Coast and boost its population base. It would also serve as a rebuke to the National League for its perceived theft of Houston. The other owners were so enthusiastic that they voted to launch the new clubs in less than six months, a full year ahead of the NL.[37]

The remnants of the Continental League howled ineffectually at this violation of O'Malley's verbal compact. Bill Shea labeled it "one of the lowest blows below the belt in the history of sport."[38] Branch Rickey assumed the mien of an elderly tragedian. "The dictionary definition of perfidy has now been confirmed," he intoned.[39] But the ultimate fault, Rickey believed, lay with himself for not possessing Ban Johnson's internal strength. "If he had been the leader of the proposed Continental League," Rickey later wrote, "it would surely be in existence today as a third major league of eight clubs. He would never have accepted the promises of the American and National Leagues in Chicago."[40]

The AL's expansion meeting accomplished only half of its assignment. It chose the cities, but not the owners, and here Bill Veeck saw an opportunity. Veeck was tired of landing on the losing end of 7–1 league votes. He dreamed of assembling his own power bloc by installing friendly faces in the new front offices. His ownership candidates were renowned lawyer Edward Bennett Williams in Washington and White Sox partner Hank Greenberg in Los Angeles.[41] Both men—wealthy in their own right—were excited by the possibility. Williams ran into Joe DiMaggio shortly after talking with Veeck. "I'm going to buy a baseball club! Can I use your name?" Williams blurted out.[42] Greenberg quietly headed to California to scope out his prospects.

The baseball establishment was frightened. Veeck, despite his obnoxious tendencies, was politically impotent. If he gained allies, he might become dangerous. The Red Sox and Yankees recruited the retiring administrator of the Federal Aviation Agency, General Elwood Quesada, to block the charismatic Williams in Washington. The league sold the franchise to Quesada on November 17 for $2.1 million. His selection came on a split vote, after Calvin Griffith reneged on a pledge to support Williams. The new owner announced that his club would be known as the Senators, the same as its predecessor.[43]

The situation on the West Coast was considerably more complicated. Ford Frick had declared Los Angeles to be an open city, just like New York. "Any city with five million or more persons is entitled to continuous major-league baseball," the commissioner had ruled in August.[44] But Walter O'Malley bridled at the thought of sharing his lucrative new home. "I'd welcome the American League to the Pacific Coast," he said slyly. "I think both San Diego and Seattle are fine cities."[45]

Greenberg ignored the Dodgers owner as he reconnoitered the American League's newest market. "I'm not interested in O'Malley's opinions, but only those of the people of Los Angeles," he said.[46] The pieces quickly began falling in place. The

Coliseum Commission assured Greenberg that it could accommodate the AL club along with the Dodgers. Actor Gene Autry, the famed Singing Cowboy, expressed eagerness to broadcast the new team's games on his radio station. Locally influential partners signed up to help Greenberg carry the financial load, and there were persistent rumors that Veeck himself would sell the White Sox and come west.[47] "Los Angeles would have loved Veeck," Autry said.[48]

O'Malley had no desire to compete with anybody in Los Angeles, and most certainly not with the era's greatest promoter. The Dodgers owner placed an urgent call to Frick, pointing out that the unanimous approval of all clubs was required for the invasion of an existing team's territory, a rule the commissioner had somehow overlooked in making his open-city declaration. Frick backpedaled furiously.[49] "I'm not carrying any banner for O'Malley," he said, "but O'Malley has gone to great expense getting started in California. I think, in all fairness, he is entitled to another season to himself in the Coliseum."[50] Greenberg could read the signs. He soon dropped his bid.

The calendar flipped to December—leaving just four months until opening day—and the American League still lacked an owner in Los Angeles. Charlie Finley entered the competition, even asking Casey Stengel to be his manager, but he was too much of an unknown for O'Malley, who essentially held veto power over the AL's choice.[51] Mild-mannered Gene Autry seemed a better fit. "My interest in baseball was finding a client, not a franchise," Autry said, but he eventually realized that the best way to obtain the radio rights was to purchase the team, which he nicknamed the Angels.[52]

O'Malley drove a hard bargain. He required Autry's club to spend the 1961 season in dilapidated Wrigley Field, which had seventy-one thousand fewer seats than the Coliseum. The Angels would then move into Dodger Stadium as his tenants in 1962, paying $200,000 in annual rent ($1.7 million in 2020 dollars), giving all of their parking and concession revenue to the Dodgers, and covering 50 percent of the ballpark's expenses.[53] Autry knew it was a bad deal—"O'Malley was charging us for half the water and half the toilet paper"—but he saw no alternative.[54] The Dodgers owner, for his part, publicly lauded his own beneficence in allowing the AL to enter Los Angeles. "Old Mad Dog O'Malley wasn't really so bad after all," he chuckled, cigar in hand.[55]

It was shaping up as a chaotic winter for the American League. Calvin Griffith hastily relocated his operation from Washington to Minnesota, seeking to connect with a new fan base. He toyed with renaming his club the Griffs—the ultimate personal tribute—before settling on the Minnesota Twins, seeking to appease the rivalrous communities of Minneapolis and St. Paul. It was the first big-league franchise to carry the name of a state, not a city.[56]

At least the Twins possessed a full roster of players. The Angels and Senators didn't have any at all. They dispatched representatives to Boston on December 14, 1960, for something entirely new in American professional sports, an expansion draft. Each of the eight existing clubs was required to expose fifteen players from its forty-man roster. The new teams would dip into the resulting pool of 120 players, making 28 selections apiece.

Joe Cronin presided over the closed-door session in typically haphazard fashion. The rules stipulated that neither expansion club could pick more than four players from any existing team, yet the Angels chose six Tigers and five members of the Red Sox, Yankees, and White Sox, while the Senators took six Indians and five men from both the Athletics and Orioles. Cronin finally noticed the massive number of violations during the twenty-seventh round. He ordered a series of trades to cover his tracks. Future Cy Young Award winner Dean Chance was sent from Washington to Los Angeles as part of the corrective process.

The resulting squads were of dubious caliber. The 24 pitchers selected in the draft had won an average of 2.6 big-league games in 1960, and most of the position players were green rookies or creaky veterans.[57] A few owners of existing teams wondered if they had shortchanged the newcomers. "I think we could have been more generous," admitted Bill Veeck, whose White Sox surrendered seven marginal players to the expansion clubs.[58] Dick Young, an irascible columnist with the *New York Daily News*, scanned the rosters with disdain, envisioning doom for the new teams. "Neither L.A. nor Washington will win forty games," Young predicted. "No pitcher will win more than eight."[59]

* * *

The final months of 1960 did not go well for Veeck. "My modest little plan was to slip my own friends into the two new franchises, Washington and Los Angeles," he later wrote, "and there being little to gain by halfway measures, also to put a friend into the Kansas City franchise."[60] But the first two parts of his scheme had failed by mid–November, and the third turned sour shortly thereafter.

Veeck had encouraged one of his White Sox partners, investment broker Elliot Stein, to pursue a majority stake in the Kansas City Athletics. A probate judge ruled on November 15 that Arnold Johnson's widow could proceed with the sale, yet Stein backed off before signing the final papers a few days later. Explanations varied. Stein attributed his change of heart to a low-key meeting with Kansas City business leaders, who expressed their preference for a locally based owner.[61] But the former Mrs. Johnson, now Carmen Humes, contended that "tremendous political pressure"—she was vague about the source—forced Stein to capitulate. "He was so terribly upset when he telephoned to tell me about it that he could hardly talk," she said.[62]

Stein's withdrawal was the cue for Charlie Finley, whose recent application for the Los Angeles franchise had been rebuffed, and whose previous efforts to buy the Philadelphia Athletics, Detroit Tigers, and Chicago White Sox had gone for naught. Finley slapped down $1,975,000 (roughly $17 million in 2020 dollars) to outbid a group of Kansas City investors on December 20, obtaining 52 percent of the A's.[63]

The other American League owners knew little about their new colleague, though what they gleaned was positive. Finley's life story was truly inspiring. He had started at the bottom as an eighteen-year-old laborer in an Indiana steel mill, transferring to an ordnance plant after the army rejected his enlistment for medical reasons in 1941. Young Charlie was unusually energetic and ambitious, always looking for a way up. He began peddling insurance on the side, and soon was setting sales records for the Travelers Insurance Company.[64]

Finley never bought a policy himself—"I was a young guy and thought nothing would happen to me"—an oversight he would have cause to regret.[65] He developed a persistent cough after the war, the first sign of pneumonic tuberculosis. His weight plummeted from two hundred to ninety-six pounds, and his doctors gradually lost hope. They estimated Finley's odds of survival to be no better than 50–50. His wife and two children moved in with his parents while he wasted away in a sanitarium.

Finley's confinement gave him plenty of time for two activities—gaining weight and thinking. He pursued the former with his typical grit, undeterred by the constant vomiting induced by his illness. "I'd lose my food," he recalled, "and I'd push that button and get the nurse back with another tray."[66] His thoughts drifted increasingly to the insurance needs of the men and women who were treating him. Doctors and other medical professionals, ironically enough, were not covered by group plans at the time. "Suppose a surgeon loses a finger or gets crippled," Finley said. "His expenses go on, but his income dwindles." He devised a plan to sell insurance—if he survived, of course—through medical societies and associations.[67]

Finley did survive—thanks to sheer willpower—and he walked out of the sanitarium in 1948 after twenty-seven months. His new approach to insurance proved to be wildly successful, making him a millionaire by 1950 and freeing him to pursue his dream of owning a major-league baseball team. It required several years of dogged persistence, but he finally locked down the Athletics in the waning days of 1960.[68]

He said all the right things. "I have no intention of moving the club out of Kansas City," Finley announced.[69] He vowed to relocate his family from Indiana to Kansas City, hire "the best baseball brains available," and refrain from interfering in the club's operations. He lured the famed Frank Lane from Cleveland to be his general manager and veteran Joe Gordon to be his field manager. The minority stockholders in the Athletics were so impressed that they willingly sold Finley their 48 percent in February 1961, giving him complete control.[70]

It was unrealistic to expect such a driven man to sit back and watch. "As an executive," Roger Angell wrote of Finley, "he takes a personal hand in all the daily details of his club, including the most minute decisions on the field."[71] His meddling drove his employees crazy. Gordon became violently angry when Finley demanded a meeting at 1 a.m. during spring training. "You bought my contract, Mr. Finley, but you don't own me," shouted the manager, who would be fired by mid–June.[72] Lane received his pink slip two months later. "I have my pride, even though I have been working for a crackpot," he snapped on his way out.[73]

Finley never fulfilled his pledge to buy a home in Kansas City. He usually followed the Athletics by radio, listening to the signal on a telephone at his Chicago office or Indiana farm. He had not been Bill Veeck's candidate, yet he considered himself a disciple of the White Sox owner, frequently copying his promotions.[74] "If I ever run out of ideas," Veeck joked, "Finley is finished."[75] But Finley lacked Veeck's flair, and the early results were dismal. Attendance actually dropped 12 percent to 683,817 in Finley's first season, the worst annual total for the A's since their relocation from Philadelphia.

The new owner knew who to blame. "If you want to see the sunshine, you have to weather the storm," Finley said in August 1961. "We'll see that old sunshine in Kansas City or somewhere else. If they don't want us in Kansas City, I feel there are other places we might be wanted."[76]

Headlines: 1961

New clubs fade after promising starts

John Kennedy threw out the first pitch at Washington's opener on April 10. The field announcer sought a link with the young president's administration, known as the New Frontier. "Ladies and gentlemen," he boomed, "here come your New Frontier Senators!" Washington's expansion club lost that day, but the American League's other newcomers, Los Angeles and Minnesota, opened with wins. All three teams, however, would suffer at least ninety losses in 1961.[77]

Phillies suffer losing streak of epic proportions

The Phillies lost on July 29, again the next day, and again and again after that. They would not win until August 20, when a 7–4 victory in Milwaukee snapped a twenty-three-game losing streak. Two hundred fans welcomed the club at the Philadelphia airport that night, showering the players with confetti. "If we ever win twenty-three out of twenty-four," said Phillies manager Gene Mauch, "they'll have to build a bigger airport."[78]

Maris sets home-run record*

Americans watched eagerly as Yankees right fielder Roger Maris pursued Babe Ruth's single-year record of sixty home runs. But Ford Frick dampened the excitement. The American League lengthened its season to 162 games in 1961, and the commissioner, who had once been Ruth's ghostwriter, ruled that any new mark must be set within 154. If not, it would carry an asterisk in the record book. Maris did reach sixty-one homers, but not until the year's very last game.[79]

Yanks cruise to world title over Reds

The Yankees entered the World Series as heavy favorites over the Reds, the surprise champions of the National League. New York had posted sixteen more wins than Cincinnati in the regular season, and it swept to a five-game postseason triumph. "We were crushed," said Reds pitcher Jim Brosnan. "We didn't belong on the same field with the 1961 Yankees."[80]

30

Twilight

Jimmy Cannon was often hailed as the nation's most skillful and influential sports columnist—a prose stylist of uncommon grace and a social commentator of trenchant wit. No less an expert than Ernest Hemingway praised Cannon as "a very good writer." Colleagues occasionally suggested that he was squandering his prodigious talent in the rear pages of the *New York Journal-American*, though Cannon disagreed. "The people who write the pieces up front in the paper consider this a wasted life," he once said. "It's true that I have solved little of my country's dilemma, but the statesmen also have failed."[1]

Cannon was capable of tackling major issues. He had been the first white sports columnist in New York to bestow equal respect upon athletes of all races, once writing that heavyweight boxing champion Joe Louis was "a credit to his race—the human race."[2] But he was similarly happy as an advocate for smaller causes, and he adopted a new one in 1961, persistently urging the New York Mets to hire seventy-one-year-old Casey Stengel as their first manager. "I am not asking you to engage Casey for sentimental purposes," Cannon wrote in an open letter to Joan Payson. "Most of your players will be obscure kids or used-up old-timers. Casey's the most famous man in baseball. He's the only box-office manager in the game."[3]

Cannon's logic was undeniable. The Mets had already enlisted George Weiss, the front-office wizard who had assembled the Yankees' dynastic rosters in the late 1940s and 1950s. Why not add the manager who had directed those same squads to seven world titles in twelve seasons?

Payson and Weiss barraged Stengel with telephone calls, telegrams, and letters throughout the spring and summer of 1961, imploring him to return to New York from his home in suburban Los Angeles. But the old man hesitated. Stengel certainly had no need to work, having become wealthy through shrewd investments. And he had cause to worry about the daily grind, especially since he was at least nineteen years older than every current big-league manager. It wasn't until October 2 that he set aside his concerns and agreed to sign on.[4]

Stengel assured the expansion club instant credibility with the New York press. Sportswriters joyfully reported his peculiar advice to the youngest Mets ("spend carefully, take your shoes off when you come into the clubhouse, and play good") and his defiant defense of his new employer ("we're gonna win some games; we're not poor people").[5] His age and fractured English bothered some of his new players. "He was worthless," sputtered first baseman Ed Bouchee. "Worthless! A manager who falls asleep on the bench every day—and this is no exaggeration—should not be managing in the majors. Stengel couldn't even remember his players' names."[6] But the writers loved him. "I really thought he was a genius. I didn't think he was a blithering old man like a lot of people did," said Robert Lipsyte of the *New York Times*.[7]

Stengel signed his contract just a week prior to the National League's expansion draft on October 10, 1961. NL president Warren Giles sought to avoid a repeat of the American League's fiasco the year before. "I urge you to make available to the new clubs players whom they can use," Giles wrote in a secret memo to the existing teams.[8] But the pickings were predictably slim. Houston general manager Paul Richards, who had been a big-league catcher for eight seasons, was disgusted by the shallowness of the talent pool. "All I know," he said, "is that I could play on any team from this list." He was fifty-two at the time.[9]

Richards generally opted for young prospects, while Weiss favored older players. The Mets' first choice was catcher Hobie Landrith, who had been knocking around the majors since 1950 with a career batting average of .237.[10] Reporters asked Stengel if Landrith possessed special qualities that had escaped general notice. "You have to have a catcher," the manager replied, "or you'll have a lot of passed balls."[11] Subsequent picks brought pitcher Roger Craig, first baseman Gil Hodges, and utility infielder Don Zimmer to New York. All had once played for Brooklyn, and all were in their thirties, two qualities that somehow appealed to Weiss. Stengel was not as enthusiastic. "I want to thank all those generous owners for giving us those great players they did not want," he said sarcastically as the draft drew to a close.[12]

The makeshift nature of both rosters was matched by the inadequacy of the

Ground was broken in 1962 for the world's first indoor ballpark, Houston's Harris County Domed Stadium, eventually to be known as the Astrodome. Its roof would contain 4,796 Lucite panels [Library of Congress].

stadiums that awaited them. The Mets were consigned to the Polo Grounds as their new ballpark rose in Flushing Meadow. The ancient facility's only other tenant, the Titans of the American Football League, sent warnings about its filth and decay. "It really wasn't a good place to play football by the time we got there," said linebacker Larry Grantham. "There were rats in the locker room."[13]

The Colt .45s cobbled together a temporary ballpark, Colt Stadium, in just five months. Its thirty-three thousand seats were configured in a single tier that offered no protection from the merciless Texas sun. Most games were scheduled at night to reduce the misery, but visiting players quickly learned to hate trips to Houston.[14] "They played in a terrible stadium with bad lights and mosquitoes as big as half-dollars that would suck the blood out of your legs," Cincinnati pitcher Jim O'Toole recalled with a shudder.[15]

Colt Stadium's one saving grace was the anticipated brevity of its lifespan. Ground was broken on January 3, 1962, for the world's first indoor ballpark, Harris County Domed Stadium. The ceremony bordered on the bizarre. Houston officials spurned the traditional shovels, preferring to initiate the project by firing .45-caliber wax bullets into the earth. The blueprints for the massive structure inspired awe—its 208-foot-high roof would be tall enough to enclose an 18-story building—yet Warren Giles assured National League owners it would be completed within a year, give or take a few weeks.[16] "They still may be putting a few finishing touches on it when the 1963 season opens," he conceded.[17]

He turned out to be short by two years.

* * *

Chuck Comiskey appeared ready to surrender. He tentatively agreed to sell his 46 percent share of the White Sox to Bill Veeck on December 17, 1959. "All the papers were drawn and were ready for signing," recalled Arthur Allyn, Jr., a White Sox partner who had conducted the lengthy negotiations on Veeck's behalf.[18]

But the mercurial Comiskey changed his mind at the last minute, once again imploring the judicial system to invalidate Dorothy Rigney's sale. His latest plea landed in the Illinois Appellate Court, which rejected it on January 29, 1960, finally shutting the door on his campaign to regain control of the club that his grandfather had founded.[19] Veeck sought to resuscitate their previous deal—he needed Chuck's stock to reap a substantial tax benefit—but Comiskey surprised everyone by deciding to lay low as a minority partner. "It's comforting to know that for every dollar the White Sox earn, I'll be entitled to forty-six cents," he said.[20]

That was unhappy (and costly) news for Veeck, who turned his attention to the approaching season. He had big plans and bigger expectations for 1960. His twin goals were a second American League pennant and the Chicago attendance record of 1,485,166, which had been established by his father's Cubs in 1929.

Veeck greeted the new year with a pair of innovations. The first seemed harmless enough. The Sox added players' names to the backs of their uniforms, something no professional sports team had done. Other clubs immediately objected.[21] "They weren't quite sure what they were protesting," Veeck wrote. "All they knew was that the screwball out in Chicago was on the loose again."[22] The change cost the Sox only two hundred dollars, yet it brought a flood of positive publicity, especially when photographers noticed that slugger Ted Kluszewski's name was misspelled

KLUSZEWSXI—perhaps accidentally, perhaps not—with the Z backward and an X for the final K. The fledgling American Football League was so impressed that it decided to put names on its uniforms, too.

Veeck's second innovation was costlier—$325,000 (equal to $2.8 million in 2020)—and more controversial. He installed a massive scoreboard behind Comiskey Park's center-field fence. It was distinguished by ten vertical protrusions that appeared to be smokestacks, but actually were mortars that launched fireworks whenever a White Sox batter hit a home run. The scoreboard also marked the happy event by flashing strobe lights, sounding foghorns, and blasting the chorus of Handel's *Messiah*. Baseball had never seen (or heard) anything like it.[23]

The establishment absolutely hated Veeck's exploding scoreboard, as it came to be known. "To me, it was bush," groused Dan Daniel, the seventy-year-old correspondent for the *Sporting News*.[24] But Chicago fans couldn't get enough. "The scoreboard became such an attraction," Veeck wrote, "that it was the leading subject for questions as I wandered around the city making speeches."[25] Fans streamed to Comiskey Park to see the technological marvel in action, pushing attendance to a new Chicago record of 1,644,460 in 1960, even though the Sox slipped to third place.

Yet Veeck did not derive the expected satisfaction from his latest success. He had begun to experience blinding headaches, accompanied by coughing fits that occasionally rendered him unconscious. Doctors in Chicago suspected the worst—most likely brain cancer—but they could not pinpoint the cause. The White Sox owner, who was only forty-seven years old, fatalistically traveled to the Mayo Clinic in April 1961. "When I walked into the clinic," he admitted, "I literally did not expect to walk out again."[26]

The diagnosis was unexpectedly positive. Veeck did not have cancer, though smoking and excessive work had overtaxed his body. The only remedy was a lengthy rest. Veeck had no desire to be an absentee owner—"if I can't run a ballclub myself, I'm not interested in it"—so he sold the Sox to Art Allyn, Jr., on June 10, 1961, and moved his family to rural Maryland the following month.[27]

It was the start of a lengthy exile from baseball. Veeck spent the first year writing his autobiography, which soared up the best-seller list in 1962. The book closed with a defiant pledge. "Look for me under the arc-lights, boys," Veeck declared. "I'll be back."[28] He did indeed return for an encore with the White Sox, repurchasing them in December 1975, but the magic was gone. Veeck was old and undercapitalized. He sold the Sox for good in January 1981 and spent his final five years rooting for the club he had never stopped loving, the crosstown Cubs.[29]

Lou Perini, who had inadvertently teamed with Veeck to launch the era of franchise relocation in 1953, also drifted from baseball in the early 1960s. Perini had promised to work diligently to reverse the decline in Milwaukee, yet he did nothing. Attendance dropped to 1.1 million in 1961, then to 767,000 a year later. The man who had once been the toast of Wisconsin was now scorned by local fans as an absentee owner—and an ineffectual one, at that.[30]

"You can't compete in the market for players with clubs that consistently outdraw you," Perini moaned.[31] It was the same complaint that Walter O'Malley had uttered countless times in Brooklyn—always pointing with alarm at Milwaukee's runaway success—and Perini now landed on the same solution. He instructed Braves general manager John McHale to contact Furman Bisher, the sports editor of the

Atlanta Constitution. "Frankly, Mr. Perini is thinking about moving the Braves out of Milwaukee, and he has Atlanta in mind," McHale told the shocked journalist.[32]

But it didn't come to that. Perini chose the simpler path, selling the Braves to eleven Chicago businessmen on November 16, 1962. The departing owner, who was thirteen days short of his fifty-ninth birthday, admitted that his energy was waning. "It is a vital game," said Perini, "and needs vitality."[33] The leaders of the new ownership group, William Bartholomay and Thomas Reynolds, were both thirty-four. They had first drawn public attention eleven months earlier, when they somehow convinced Chuck Comiskey to sell his portion of the White Sox. But Bartholomay and his colleagues derived no thrills from their minority stake. They quietly sold out to Art Allyn, Jr., in May 1962, then began searching for a team to call their own.[34]

Milwaukee seemed to present the perfect opportunity. It was just ninety miles from Chicago, close enough that Bartholomay felt justified in characterizing his group as "local ownership." But Milwaukee residents had always been suspicious of monied entrepreneurs from the big city to their south, and they reacted with indifference to Perini's successors. Bartholomay sought to create a financial link, offering local investors an opportunity to buy 115,000 shares of Braves stock. Only thirteen thousand were sold.[35]

The new owners quickly shifted to Plan B. They held their first secret meeting with Atlanta officials on July 7, 1963, and eventually hammered out an agreement to relocate the Braves to the Georgia capital in 1965. (The move would be delayed a year by legal complications.) Franchise transfers had become commonplace in baseball—this would be the seventh in fourteen seasons—but the Milwaukee-Atlanta shift was the first to leave a city without a big-league team.[36]

Lou Perini had always insisted that the marriage between Milwaukee and baseball was unbreakable. "On a long-term basis," he told reporters in 1955, "there may be some leveling off in attendance, but it is not a novelty."[37] Milwaukee had successfully staged the All-Star Game that year, causing Walter O'Malley to express astonishment at the standing-room crowd. "There's no secret formula," Perini told him. "It's just the terrific enthusiasm."[38]

The Braves played their final game in County Stadium just ten years later, on the evening of September 22, 1965. Only 12,577 Milwaukee fans showed up.[39]

* * *

Other leading characters in baseball's postwar drama faded into the twilight during the 1960s and eventually vanished altogether.

The death of the Continental League on August 2, 1960, relieved the pressure in Washington to pass an antitrust bill. "This clears up the atmosphere," said baseball lobbyist Paul Porter, "and it means there can be realistic and orderly legislation."[40] His sunny forecast pleased the owners, who were even happier when Congress simply let the issue drop. Estes Kefauver began to investigate the pharmaceutical industry, then probed other businesses, never returning to baseball. He died after a heart attack in August 1963.[41]

Emanuel Celler remained bitter about the departure of the Brooklyn Dodgers, yet he too turned to other matters. The longtime chairman of the House Judiciary Committee was instrumental in passing such landmark bills as the Civil Rights Act of 1964 and the Voting Rights Act of 1965. He focused so intently on the big picture that he gradually lost sight of the Brooklyn constituency he had represented since 1923. "He never was present in any community meetings," said local lawyer Elizabeth Holtzman. "He was not involved in anything going on in the district. And I realized that he was vulnerable, so I decided to challenge him."[42] The thirty-one-year-old neophyte unseated the eighty-four-year-old Celler in a 1972 primary election.

Happy Chandler was afflicted with the same political disease as Celler, an inability to make a graceful exit. The ex-commissioner wrapped up his second term as governor of Kentucky in 1959 and turned his attention to the White House. He patronized frontrunner John Kennedy as "a nice young fellow" who lacked presidential stature, yet Chandler was incapable of snatching away the 1960 Democratic nomination.[43] Nor could he regain the governorship, though he mounted campaigns in 1963, 1967, and 1971.

Chandler's successor as commissioner, Ford Frick, retired in November 1965. He had presided timidly over a period of unprecedented change, dodging controversy whenever possible, especially when the Dodgers and Giants fled New York. "I am going to have very little to say from this time on. I'll give a good imitation of a clam," he had joked in the midst of that transcontinental furor, voicing the philosophy that guided his entire fourteen-year tenure.[44] Frick was replaced as commissioner by William Eckert, an obscure air force general who was totally unsuited for the job.

Horace Stoneham and Calvin Griffith proved to be equally inept. Both had inherited big-league teams that they were unqualified to run, both had flopped in their hometowns, and both had fled to fresh markets. Their fortunes would be buoyed by early pennants in their new homes—the Giants in 1962, the Twins in 1965—but both owners slipped toward irrelevance because of another common trait, laziness.

Stoneham had failed in New York because of his unwillingness to promote his club, and he remained inert after moving. "It will eventually catch up to him again in San Francisco," Bill Veeck correctly predicted in 1965.[45] Attendance at Candlestick Park plummeted to 520,000 by 1974. The second-lowest figure that season was 662,400 in Minnesota, clear proof of Griffith's lassitude. Both men eventually had no choice but to sell—Stoneham in 1976, Griffith in 1984.[46]

Del Webb was their polar opposite, commonly considered the most influential man in the American League—and perhaps all of baseball—throughout the 1950s. But his interest gradually waned. The Yankees won ten world championships during his co-ownership with Dan Topping. The prospect of an eleventh title held no thrill.

Webb branched into a promising new field in 1960, creating a retirement community on twenty thousand acres outside of Phoenix. He hoped that ten thousand visitors might tour his model homes on the day that Sun City opened—certainly an aggressive goal—but the actual number was ten times greater. His agents sold so many houses that they ran out of contracts, forcing them to run to a nearby store for blank receipts. Webb had always been a developer first and foremost, and he found the blossoming of Sun City more exciting than the endless run of championships in New York.[47] He and Topping sold the Yankees to the Columbia Broadcasting System in August 1964. Each partner received $8.4 million ($69.8 million in 2020 terms) for his half of the team. Webb pronounced it "the best deal I ever made."[48]

Few executives in baseball history were more influential than Webb in his prime, but Branch Rickey was an obvious exception. The Mahatma exuded authority through his physical presence and erudition. "Branch Rickey was an impressive-looking man," wrote Jackie Robinson. "He had a classic face, an air of command, a deep, booming voice, and a way of cutting through red tape and getting down to basics."[49] Rickey's pioneering role in integration and his invention of the farm system were sufficient to assure his baseball immortality. But his legend was enhanced by the artistic and financial strength of the clubs he assembled in St. Louis and Brooklyn, winning eight National League pennants and four world titles between 1926 and 1949.

The Continental League was commonly believed to be Rickey's swan song. He disagreed. "I mean to have another fling," he said after the CL folded, though his confidence initially seemed misplaced.[50] The Mets job slipped through his fingers in 1961, and he suffered another heart attack shortly before his eightieth birthday. But an opportunity presented itself in 1962, when Gussie Busch decided that the Cardinals' young general manager, Bing Devine, would benefit from a seasoned adviser. Who better to fill the role than the greatest St. Louis GM of all time?[51]

Rickey eagerly rejoined his old club—promising "a pennant at the earliest possible date"—though he almost immediately made a false step.[52] He outraged players and fans alike by proposing the immediate retirement of Stan Musial, despite the fact that the Cardinals' brightest star had batted a robust .330 in 1962. "I know I'm forty-two," Musial said, "but it seems strange to have Mr. Rickey recommend my retirement when he's almost twice my age."[53]

Controversy dogged the Cardinals for the next two years. Devine and Rickey engaged in a power struggle, which escalated into a squabble between Devine and Busch. The outcome appeared to favor the Mahatma. Devine was fired in the midst of the 1964 season, the Cardinals improbably rallied to win the World Series that October, and the press awaited Rickey's official appointment as the club's new leader. The stage was set for a glorious final act.

But Busch opted to clean house instead, and he unexpectedly asked Rickey to resign. The old man's departure from the Cardinals—and from organized baseball—was announced on October 19, 1964. Rickey slipped into the retirement he had always dreaded, emerging on rare occasions to answer a reporter's call or accept accolades for his distinguished career.[54]

He was especially pleased by his election to the Missouri Sports Hall of Fame, an honor that recognized his lengthy record of success (and ignored his recent failure) in St. Louis. Rickey appeared to be in fine form at the induction banquet on November 13, 1965. He happily acknowledged the applause and began to deliver one of his patented stemwinders, only to slump suddenly to the floor, the victim of yet another heart attack. "I don't believe I'm going to be able to speak any longer," he said brokenly before being rushed to the hospital. He slipped into a coma and died on December 9.[55]

Baseball's most eloquent voice had been stilled.

Headlines: 1962

Senators open D.C. Stadium
in fine style

Washington christened its new ballpark on April 9. "Nearly everything about the District of Columbia Stadium is a thing of beauty," marveled the *New York Times*.

The expansion Senators, who had been imprisoned in decaying Griffith Stadium the previous year, adapted quickly to their new surroundings. They spanked the Detroit Tigers, 4–1, before a crowd of 44,383, including President John Kennedy.[56]

Mets stumble to 120 losses in inaugural season

The Mets were routed 11–4 by the Cardinals in their opener on April 11. Losing became a habit for New York's new club, which suffered 120 defeats and finished 60½ games out of first place. Bill Veeck had always insisted that his St. Louis Browns were the worst team in big-league history, but he ceded that distinction to the Mets. "They achieved total incompetence in a single year," he admitted.[57]

Giants swipe NL title from faltering Dodgers

Shortstop Maury Wills did his best to propel the Dodgers to the National League pennant. He set a major-league record by stealing 104 bases, sparking Los Angeles to a four-game lead over San Francisco by mid–September. But the Dodgers lost ten of their final thirteen games, ending the season in a first-place tie with the Giants. San Francisco prevailed in a three-game playoff.[58]

Yankees eke out victory in World Series

The Giants generated more runs (21–20), hits (51–44), and homers (5–3) in the World Series, yet the Yankees took the title with a nail-biting 1–0 triumph in Game Seven. San Francisco advanced runners to second and third with two outs in the ninth. Willie McCovey smashed a line drive toward right field, but second baseman Bobby Richardson speared the ball to save the day—and the championship—for New York.[59]

Epilogue: Beyond

Major-league owners longed for a breather after the 1962 season, and who could blame them? Their equilibrium had been shaken by eighteen years of dizzying change. Phil Wrigley once bemoaned the game's resistance to progress—"the heads of organized ball move slowly"—but he no longer had cause for complaint.[1] Baseball had evolved from a nineteenth-century relic to a continental, multiracial, modern sport in less than two decades.

The most evident change was geographic. Six clubs had relocated since the war, and four had joined through expansion, freeing the game from its traditional lineup of sixteen teams in ten Northeastern and Midwestern cities. Baseball's new footprint encompassed twenty clubs in seventeen markets from sea to sea. It was already difficult to recall the musty days when St. Louis served as the sport's western outpost. Six current ballclubs were located farther west: Minnesota, Kansas City, Houston, and the three on the Pacific Coast.

Nor could baseball's racial progress be denied. Only fifteen seasons had passed since Jackie Robinson's debut, yet every roster had been integrated by black stars. Robinson himself was inducted into the National Baseball Hall of Fame in July 1962, breaking the monochromatic monopoly in Cooperstown. Maury Wills was voted the National League's Most Valuable Player that year, the award's ninth black winner in ten seasons. Other black players dominated 1962's statistics. Major-league leaders included Tommy Davis with a .346 batting average and 153 runs batted in, Willie Mays with 49 homers, and Frank Robinson with 92 extra-base hits.[2]

Baseball had caught up with the times in other ways, too. Most of 1945's stadiums were old and poorly maintained, with only the Yankees and Indians playing in ballparks that were less than thirty years old. But seven of 1962's teams boasted facilities that had been built within the past decade (Houston, Milwaukee, Minnesota, San Francisco, Washington, and both Los Angeles clubs), while another pair of stadiums had been extensively remodeled in recent years (Baltimore and Kansas City). Other examples of modernity in the early 1960s would have been almost impossible to imagine back in 1945: Teams now traveled by jet, most games were broadcast on television, and the players—much to the owners' unhappiness—had established a union.[3]

Ford Frick pondered most of these developments—all, really, but the Major League Baseball Players Association—with a sense of satisfaction. He recalled the baseball establishment's desperation when Emanuel Celler had gaveled his first congressional hearings to order. "When we appeared before the committees in

Washington in 1951, there was not one question on expansion that they asked that we could answer," the commissioner said in 1962. "We had no plan, no thinking on it. The reality of today and the prospect for the future comprise excellent progress in a brief period of ten years."[4]

Frick may have sounded smug, but he considered himself justified. The major leagues drew 21,375,215 fans in 1962, finally busting the attendance ceiling of 20,920,842 that had stood since 1948. The new record should have been accompanied by one of the commissioner's famed asterisks—it had been achieved only after the expansion by four clubs and the addition of eight games to the regular-season schedule—but he brooked no negativity. Baseball, he insisted, had never been stronger.[5]

Frick's tone of self-satisfaction, however, wasn't of much importance. What was truly significant about his worldview in 1962 was the four-word admission buried in its midst: *We had no plan.*

Baseball's postwar evolution had been influenced at key points by the intervention of strong-willed owners. It was impossible to imagine integration occurring in 1947 without Branch Rickey, or franchise relocation in 1953 without Bill Veeck, or expansion in 1960 without Walter O'Malley. But Frick was right. There had been no master plan, no coordinated effort, no mandate from the commissioner to grow the sport in an orderly, rational fashion.

The upheaval from 1945 to 1962 would broaden baseball's appeal in the long run, setting the stage for tremendous growth in the half-century to follow. Yet a close study of that chaotic eighteen-year span leads to only one conclusion: The game's postwar progress was almost entirely accidental, shaped not by careful planning, but by three external forces—fear, greed, and incompetence.

Fear was universal in the 1940s and 1950s. The owners were afraid of unknown markets, racial integration, unions, modern technology such as television and jet travel, outside competition, and change of any kind. They dragged their heels whenever possible, even when action was clearly necessary. But their greatest fear was of being left behind, a dread that inspired sudden and inexplicable decisions. Horace Stoneham professed his loyalty to New York for decades, then abruptly shifted his club to San Francisco. "If we don't move now," he said with a note of panic, "there won't be any good cities left."[6]

Greed was evident in the tight grip that the owners maintained on every dollar. They slashed player salaries to 22 percent of team expenses by 1950, a huge reduction from 35 percent a generation earlier. Yet they did not skimp on themselves, especially not Rickey, who paid a far greater salary to himself than to any of his greatest stars.[7] O'Malley elevated greed to an art by inciting a bidding war between Brooklyn and Los Angeles for the Dodgers. "O'Malley showed his colleagues how it was possible to use the ballclub as a lever to extract real estate," Bill Veeck said with a touch of admiration.[8]

Incompetence, of course, was everywhere. The owners made mistake after mistake. They elected two commissioners—the irrepressible Happy Chandler and the inert Frick—who were far from ideal. They allowed their aging stadiums to decay. They integrated the game at a fitful pace, with several teams resisting until the mid-1950s. They long ignored the Pacific Coast's population explosion. They spurned several cities that were clearly ready for major-league ball, only to suddenly scramble to relocate to those same markets. They opposed expansion until 1960, when they hastily approved it. They patronized their players, even after the latter had unionized. They turned a blind eye to football's growing power. And on and on.

Yet Frick believed that most things—somehow, some way—had turned out for the best, despite the disagreement of Danny Gardella, Robert Murphy, Earl Toolson, Pants Rowland, hundreds of underpaid players, and dedicated fans of the Boston Braves, St. Louis Browns, Philadelphia Athletics, Brooklyn Dodgers, and New York Giants.

The commissioner was not troubled by even the most controversial action of the previous eighteen years, the relocation of the Dodgers and Giants. New York now had the Mets, so where was the harm? "What is done is done, and most fans, I am sure, realize that baseball is better off today because these moves were made," said Frick. "Maybe the methods were wrong. Maybe the motives of the persons involved were selfish and inspired by personal gain and profit, but the results were beneficial."[9]

Nothing could shake the equanimity of baseball's supreme leader, who envisioned smooth sailing ahead. Frick exulted in the postwar transformation of his beloved game—its Atlantic-to-Pacific reach, its sparkling ballparks, its stars of all races, and, of course, its new attendance record.

His optimism was best expressed in one of the sport's oldest clichés. Baseball truly had emerged from the postwar chaos as a brand new ballgame.

* * *

The dawn of baseball's modern age—the successor to the postwar era—was heralded by the rapid-fire completion of three architectural marvels in the early 1960s.

Dodger Stadium was the first. A decade of scheming, negotiating, and engineering finally produced the ballpark of Walter O'Malley's dreams. Fifty-two thousand spectators streamed into Chavez Ravine on April 10, 1962, to admire his stadium's cantilevered design, bright color scheme, and breathtaking views of the San Gabriel Mountains. The *New York Times* likened it to the Taj Mahal. Only two flaws marred the festive opener: The Reds defeated the Dodgers, 6–3, and critics noted the complete absence of drinking fountains. A simple oversight, said O'Malley. A cheap ploy to increase beverage sales, said his critics. Thirteen fountains were soon installed.[10]

New York's massive five-tiered palace debuted in 1964 on the very site that O'Malley and Robert Moses visited in April 1957. The Dodgers owner had rejected Flushing Meadow back then—he insisted it was too swampy and unstable to support a stadium—but he became a fan after visiting the fifty-five-thousand-seat showpiece.[11] "I was wrong as hell about that," O'Malley said of his original verdict.[12]

Most ballpark names fit into one of two categories. They either honored past or present team owners (Comiskey Park, Wrigley Field, Crosley Field) or reflected the limited imaginations of local bureaucrats (County Stadium, Memorial Stadium, Municipal Stadium). Branch Rickey urged New York to buck both trends. "Without Shea, there is nothing," Rickey barked. "Without him, there is no National League in New York."[13] So the Mets' new home was named after Bill Shea, who had been an obscure lawyer as recently as 1957. Fans were enchanted by Shea

Stadium's scoreboard, which displayed photos and showed movies, two skills that were unique in 1964. "Lovely, just lovely," said Casey Stengel. "The park is lovelier than my team."[14]

But the most awe-inspiring new facility was Houston's gigantic Harris County Domed Stadium, which finally opened for business in 1965. Colt .45s owner Roy Hofheinz had always hated his club's nickname, which he finally jettisoned on December 1, 1964. Hofheinz rebranded his team as the Astros, and its ballpark inevitably became known as the Astrodome. Sunlight passed through 4,796 Lucite panels on the roof, allowing grass to grow inside. Fielders were blinded by the resulting glare, so the Astros eventually painted the panels white, causing the grass to die. The Monsanto Company came to the rescue by inventing artificial grass, which attained worldwide fame as AstroTurf.[15]

The new stadiums were considerably more impressive than the clubs that joined the major-league family in the early 1960s. The Mets were especially pathetic, suffering at least 109 losses in each of their first four seasons. They didn't climb above .500 until 1969, when they won a wildly improbable world championship. But New York fans had inexplicably taken a shine to their new heroes years earlier. The last-place Mets outdrew the AL champion Yankees by 427,000 spectators in 1964, a margin that widened to 808,000 by 1966.[16] George Weiss, the staid president of the Mets, was baffled by his club's popularity. "I'm grateful," he said, "but I don't understand it."[17]

The other expansion teams struggled badly. The Angels chafed under their onerous lease with the Dodgers.[18] "We had endlessly petty arguments with our landlord," recalled owner Gene Autry, whose club fled to a new stadium in suburban Anaheim in 1966.[19] The Angels would not qualify for the World Series until 2002.

Autry provided stable ownership at least, contrasting with the other expansion clubs. Former aviator Elwood Quesada operated Washington's franchise "about as effectively as I would run an air force," joked Bill Veeck.[20] The new version of the Senators, who never drew more than 920,000 fans in a season, escaped to Dallas-Fort Worth in 1972. Their first World Series as the Texas Rangers wouldn't come until 2010.

The Astros were more successful at the gate—attracting 2.15 million fans during the Astrodome's inaugural year—but they flopped on the field and in the front office. They didn't host a World Series until their forty-fourth season, 2005. Roy Hofheinz was long gone by then, but his reputation for bumbling, officious management still shadowed the franchise. "He was the dumbest genius I've ever known. He did what he thought he had to do, and he didn't really care whose toes he stepped on," said Houston broadcaster Gene Elston.[21] General Manager Paul Richards battled Hofheinz for four seasons before being fired in 1965. A sportswriter suggested that the Houston owner was sometimes his own worst enemy. "Not while I'm alive," Richards replied grimly.[22]

Big-league owners had resisted expansion throughout the 1940s and 1950s, but they subsequently came to appreciate the process. They enjoyed divvying up the $8.4 million in fees paid by the four newcomers in 1960—the 2020 equivalent of $73 million—and they loved beating up on the expansion squads, which averaged ninety-three losses per season in the 1960s.[23] "I am certain that within the next few years, the two leagues will expand to twelve clubs," said Ford Frick.[24]

Charlie Finley helped the process along. He announced on January 6, 1964, that he was relocating the Athletics from Kansas City to Louisville. "We have these caps that have KC on the front, and we don't want to throw them away," Finley said, "so I think we'll call ourselves the Kentucky Colonels."[25] His fellow owners were contemptuous. "Finley is a fool," scoffed White Sox owner Art Allyn.[26] The American League rejected the Louisville move by a 9–1 vote, then rebuffed Finley's effort a month later to take the A's to Oakland.[27]

But the Athletics kept losing, and Finley kept agitating for relocation. Attendance inevitably spiraled downward in Kansas City, bottoming out at 528,000 in 1965, the worst total in the majors that year. American League owners grew weary of the whole mess, finally voting in October 1967 to allow Finley to shift to Oakland. But they failed to account for the anger of Stuart Symington, a powerful Missouri senator who immediately threatened an antitrust lawsuit and a congressional investigation. The league mollified him by hastily expanding to Kansas City and Seattle, effective in 1969.[28] Symington expressed double gratitude, both for Kansas City's new team and the departure of Finley. "Oakland is the luckiest city since Hiroshima," the senator snorted.[29]

The AL's panicky maneuver caught the National League off guard. It responded methodically, granting franchises to Montreal and San Diego, thereby bringing the total number of expansion teams to eight.

Walter O'Malley had pledged on August 2, 1960, that Continental League markets would be favored with the first eight bids—"we will take four of your cities and later add the rest"—yet only Houston and New York were chosen as expansion sites.[30] Two others, Atlanta and Minneapolis-St. Paul, lured existing clubs from other cities. But four CL markets—Dallas-Fort Worth, Denver, Toronto, and Buffalo—remained on the outside as of 1969. The first three would be welcomed to the big-league fraternity between 1972 and 1993. Buffalo was the only Continental League city that never received the promised call.

Charlie Finley tried to transfer the Kansas City Athletics in 1964, first to Louisville and then to Oakland. The American League blocked both moves. Finley finally obtained approval in October 1967 for an Oakland relocation, triggering a new round of expansion [Kansas City Public Library].

* * *

The structure of major-league baseball was supported by a pair of strong pillars in the 1960s, or so the owners believed.

Television was one of those essential buttresses. Even Lou Perini had come to understand its importance. He had barred regular-season telecasts of Milwaukee Braves games for nine years, but finally relented in 1962, happily accepting the additional revenue.[31] A key factor in the club's departure for Atlanta four years later was the lure of a multimillion-dollar contract to beam games to eight Southern states. "We moved south in the first place because of TV," admitted Braves spokesman Tom Bennett.[32]

Most owners had become totally reliant on television money by the mid–1960s. They knew that free TV coverage depressed attendance, yet their survival depended on the rights payment that arrived at the beginning of each season. "It is a matter of life or death, that's all," admitted Calvin Griffith. "We could not function without it."[33]

A solution seemed to be at hand in 1964, when another of Walter O'Malley's longtime dreams came to fruition. Pay television arrived in California that summer, and the Dodgers became the first sports franchise to climb aboard. The price was $1.50 per game, with 48 cents going to the ballclub. Only 2,500 households were wired when the service debuted with the Dodgers-Cubs game on July 17, though O'Malley envisioned a bright and prosperous future.[34] "The compensation from [pay TV] should more than make up for the drop [in stadium attendance]," he said. Theater owners and movie producers threatened to force a referendum to illegalize pay television, but the Dodgers owner laughed at the very idea. "I don't think they have a chance of stopping us," he said.[35]

O'Malley had misjudged a California referendum before, and he was wrong again. Nearly 70 percent of the state's voters supported Proposition 15 in November 1964, prohibiting all pay–TV services. The company that was wiring the Los Angeles and San Francisco markets, Subscription Television, filed a lawsuit to invalidate the referendum. It emerged victorious two years later, not that it mattered.[36] "The immediate practical effect is none," said John Nelson Steele, a company official, "because at the present time we do not have funds to reactivate our cable system."[37] Pay television would eventually become supremely successful, but not in the lifetime of Walter O'Malley, who died in 1979.

The other pillar revered by the owners was the reserve clause, which somehow remained intact throughout the 1960s. Nobody had been more of a stalwart in its defense than Branch Rickey. "I think everybody wants baseball to continue, and I think everybody realizes it couldn't without the reserve clause," he had declared in 1949.[38] But Rickey possessed a law degree, and he came to harbor grave doubts several years before his death in 1965. "The attorneys for the commissioner and the leagues are not hesitant to say that the reserve clause in players' contracts will no longer hold up," he admitted in a private report to Continental League owners in 1959.[39]

The moment of reckoning finally seemed at hand in October 1969, when the Cardinals traded center fielder Curt Flood to Philadelphia, and Flood refused to go. His lawsuit wound its way by 1972 to the United States Supreme Court, evolving into a rerun of the *Toolson* case. The baseball establishment again braced itself for the worst—and again was shocked by a favorable verdict.[40] The court allowed baseball's antitrust exemption to stand, a luxury afforded no other sport. "If there is any inconsistency or illogic in all this," wrote Justice Harry Blackmun, "it is an inconsistency and illogic of long standing that is to be remedied by Congress and not this court."[41]

Congress paid no heed to this latest judicial recommendation, and the owners sighed with relief. They happily embraced the status quo, only vaguely aware that a new foe was scheming to disrupt their complacence.

Marvin Miller, the executive director of the Major League Baseball Players Association since 1966, was considerably more imaginative and energetic than predecessors J. Norman Lewis and Robert Cannon. The union had been a toothless irritant to ownership between its 1954 founding and Miller's hiring, even when the fiery Bob Feller served as president in the late 1950s.[42] Feller's habitual militance somehow vanished when confrontation with the owners was suggested. "You cannot carry collective bargaining into baseball," the future Hall of Famer said docilely, and his fellow players readily agreed.[43]

That was pure nonsense to Miller, who came to baseball from one of the nation's most powerful unions, the United Steelworkers of America. He was horrified by the MLBPA's meekness and disorganization. "The closest thing to headquarters they had," he recalled, "was a filing cabinet in the office of a players' licensing agent named Frank Scott." Miller quickly established a base of operations, negotiated an improvement to the players' pension fund, and won the loyalty of his constituents.[44]

The union leader had a bigger objective in mind. He pushed in 1970 for arbitration, a concept initially proposed in 1946 by Robert Murphy's American Baseball Guild. If a player and his club disputed the terms of a contract, Miller suggested that an independent arbitrator could settle the matter. Owners had always rejected arbitration out of hand. Happy Chandler's sympathy for the process was just another reason for his ouster by Fred Saigh, Del Webb, and their cabal in 1951. But Bowie Kuhn, the commissioner in 1970, saw no way to reject Miller's proposal.[45] "I reluctantly went along," Kuhn recalled. "Provisions of this kind were commonplace in American collective-bargaining agreements and could not realistically be resisted by sports managements."[46]

Miller now had a tool to destroy the reserve clause. The MLBPA no longer needed congressional legislation or a Supreme Court ruling to pave the way for free agency. It was Miller's contention that the clause bound a player to his team for a single season after the expiration of his contract, not for a lifetime. He searched for a player who was willing to put this interpretation to the test. A pair of pitchers, Andy Messersmith of the Los Angeles Dodgers and Dave McNally of the Montreal Expos, stepped forward in 1975. They completed the season without contracts, then appealed to an arbitrator for free agency.[47]

The ruling in their favor was handed down on December 23, 1975, a landmark day for American professional sports. "I am enormously disturbed," said Kuhn. "It is just inconceivable that after nearly one hundred years of developing this system for the overall good of the game, it should be obliterated in this way."[48] McNally had always intended to retire, but Messersmith readily signed a three-year deal with the Atlanta Braves for $1 million ($4.8 million in 2020 dollars), more than three times what the Dodgers had been paying him.

The baseball establishment had always predicted that the death of the reserve clause—and the consequent birth of free agency—would spell the sport's doom. Stars would inevitably flock to the biggest cities, and the clubs in smaller markets would wither and die. But that's not what happened. Talent actually became more evenly dispersed, making the game more competitive. Three franchises—the Yankees, Dodgers, and Charlie Finley's Athletics—had won at least three world championships during the twenty seasons prior to free agency. No team earned more than two titles in the twenty years that followed.

Salaries skyrocketed in this new era, as every sports fan knows, but so did revenue. Big-league games had attracted 29.8 million fans in 1975. The total climbed above 40 million three years later, passed 50 million in 1987, and reached 70 million by 1993. Franchise values kept pace. Walter O'Malley had invested roughly twenty million dollars to obtain control of the Dodgers and build their stadium. His son, Peter, sold the whole package in 1997 for $311 million (the equivalent of $499 million in 2020). The value of the Los Angeles franchise skyrocketed to $3.3 billion by the beginning of the 2019 season.[49]

Such broad-based prosperity made it difficult for later generations to understand the owners' desperate attachment to the reserve clause prior to 1975. "They have been forced to share a bigger piece of the revenue pie," economist Michael Haupert wrote in 2016, "but the pie has grown exponentially since Marvin Miller arrived on the scene, allowing both sides to grow rich far beyond anything they could have imagined a half-century ago."[50]

* * *

A popular joke made the rounds after the Dodgers departed for Los Angeles. An armed Brooklynite was placed in the same room with Adolf Hitler, Joseph Stalin, and Walter O'Malley. It seemed a golden opportunity, yet the outsider found himself in a quandary. He was inadequately armed, having only two bullets in his gun. Which of these notorious villains should he shoot?

The same answer erupted from millions of baseball fans—*O'Malley! twice!*—followed by the sad laughter of disillusionment. It was commonly believed in the late 1950s and early 1960s that America's national pastime, a game of purity and joy, was suddenly being corrupted by money. O'Malley's decision to relocate one of baseball's most storied franchises was viewed as the tipping point—the moment when avarice triumphed over virtue, when the nation's favorite sport was sold to the highest bidder.[51]

"The only word that fits the Dodgers is greed," Arthur Daley proclaimed in the *New York Times* in late 1957.[52] Manny Celler blasted O'Malley on the floor of the House of Representatives: "His greed was so great that he moved his club elsewhere, where he thought he could make even more money."[53] Critics of a more thoughtful bent also gravitated to the G-word when discussing O'Malley's relocation. "I think greed was a factor," said Brooklyn-born author Pete Hamill, "but I think he was also a visionary."[54]

The whole sport would be tarred with the same brush. "Baseball is music played on an adding machine," complained columnist Jimmy Cannon as the 1960s drew to a close. "The grass is being pulled up, and in some places they play on green carpet. It should be a boy's dream, but it has become a fast-dollar hustle." Cannon died in 1973, two years prior to the advent of free agency, but he was already convinced that the game was changing for the worse. He believed the players had come to be overpaid, though he reserved his greatest scorn for their bosses. "The crack of the bat striking the ball in modern baseball," he wrote, "is drowned out by the noises of the owners yelling about money."[55]

Cannon was the rare sportswriter who possessed a broad base of knowledge. He understood human nature, and he had a solid grasp of history. If anyone in the press box was equipped to debunk the pervasive myth of baseball's innocence, it was Jimmy Cannon. Yet he sided with the majority. He agreed that a newfound lust for cash was ruining the game.

It was all nonsense. Money had been one of baseball's driving forces since the dawn of the twentieth century. Several early owners were notorious penny-pinchers, the original Charles Comiskey foremost among them. Contemporary stars, especially Babe Ruth, always demanded top dollar. The nefarious activities of the Black Sox in 1919 clinched the argument, proving that baseball had never been immaculate. Anybody familiar with the postwar era—as Cannon certainly was—had seen consistent and compelling evidence of selfishness throughout the 1940s and 1950s, long before the Dodgers moved or the players gained free agency. It could not be denied that greed had propelled the sport's evolution between 1945 and 1962.

Sportswriters traditionally portrayed the owners as civic-minded philanthropists. Profits or losses were supposedly meaningless to these benefactors, who simply enjoyed bringing the national pastime to the masses. "My hobby is baseball," a smiling Lou Perini told reporters in 1952. He expressed no concern about the recent decline in the Boston Braves' attendance. "That doesn't discourage me," he said. "I expect we'll have good years and bad ones."[56]

Perini was playing his role as a "sportsman," a term used by columnists to describe well-heeled industrialists who operated baseball teams on the side. Yet Perini had his limits. He fled to Milwaukee the following year, pursuing the profits that had eluded him in his hometown. He came to view himself not as a traitor to Boston, but as a trailblazer who led the sport to greater prosperity. "Moving is one of the greatest contributions to modern baseball," he said proudly.[57]

It was impossible to name a postwar baseball executive who wasn't heavily motivated by money. Connie Mack and Bill Veeck looked to be exceptions. Mack was frequently portrayed as an idealist, a man who truly devoted his life to the game. Veeck seemed to be motivated by something more basic than money, a simple desire to astound the fans. "You get them to say *aaaah* and you get them to say *ohhhhh*," he said, "but the real success comes when you can get them to gasp and bulge out their eyes and say, 'Ho-ly smoke!'"[58]

Yet both men kept a close watch on the bottom line. "I feel that I've been a failure," Mack once said, a curious statement from someone whose Philadelphia Athletics had secured five world titles and nine American League pennants before their descent to irrelevance. But his self-analysis was entirely financial. "Any man who can't make ends meet must be a failure," Mack explained. "And I didn't make ends meet for the Athletics."[59]

Veeck could appear altruistic. He waved off any discussion of the profit he derived from selling the St. Louis Browns in 1953. "What I take out isn't important," he said. "The fact that I failed in this assignment, lost prestige as well, is important."[60] But financial considerations were in the forefront a decade later, when he attempted to purchase the Washington franchise in 1963. "The reason I tried to buy the

Senators," Veeck wrote, "is that I am pure of heart and noble of spirit, and I believed I could make a barrelful of money."[61]

Branch Rickey passed into history as the greatest baseball executive of all time, an innovative genius who assembled dynasties in St. Louis and Brooklyn, a visionary who created the farm system and integrated the game. Happy Chandler, who had his share of disagreements with Rickey, nonetheless saluted him as "probably the most knowledgeable baseball fellow that ever was."[62] Buzzie Bavasi agreed: "He was the finest baseball man I ever met. Everyone who knew him will tell you the same thing."[63] Bill Veeck recalled Rickey as the only man in baseball "who could simply outtalk you, outgeneral you, and outmaneuver you."[64]

It became unfashionable after Rickey's death to allude to his fascination with money. Bavasi, who worked for both men, drew a sharp distinction between the Mahatma and O'Malley in his 1987 memoirs. "When it came to money, Walter was shrewd," Bavasi wrote. "When it came to business, he was without peer."[65] Rickey's brilliance, by implication, was confined to the diamond, while O'Malley was the supreme administrator.

Yet that wasn't necessarily true. Rickey was an astute businessman in his own right, always keeping a tight rein on salaries. "He had all the players and all the money," said Ralph Kiner, "and he never let the two get together."[66] He not only won eight pennants with the Cardinals and Dodgers, but he also banked substantial profits for those clubs. Nothing else could explain the Dodgers' willingness to bless him with enormous salaries and bonuses throughout the late 1940s.[67]

Where Rickey truly outclassed his contemporaries was in his ability to envision baseball's future—not only as a game, but also as a business. He was the first executive to acquire a string of farm clubs, sign black players, establish a permanent complex for spring training, embrace statistical analysis, require players to wear batting helmets, transport teams almost exclusively by air, and advocate expansion.[68] Red Barber was fully justified in asserting that Rickey "changed the game more than any other single man."[69]

There was a single-minded purpose behind every one of his innovations—a desire to get more. More victories, more pennants, more world titles, more fans, more money. Most owners believed in the sanctity of the status quo, but Rickey knew that any business that refused to evolve would eventually die. He warned as early as 1943 that the National Football League might eventually supplant major-league baseball as America's favorite sport. Skeptics chuckled. "Whether professional football ever can challenge baseball is open to question," wrote Arthur Daley.[70]

The numbers were on Daley's side. Thirty-nine percent of Americans identified baseball as their favorite sport in a 1948 Gallup poll, dwarfing the 17 percent who picked football, a gap of twenty-two percentage points. The margin shrank by 1960, though baseball's lead remained a comfortable thirteen points.[71] The NFL started play each September, yet its young commissioner, Pete Rozelle, always waited until the mid–October conclusion of the World Series to pop the cork on a bottle of champagne. "Here's to the beginning of football season," he would say.[72]

Rickey was the rare leader in either sport who envisioned the lines crossing on the graph, who imagined football surpassing baseball in America's heart. "Right now, baseball is on its way out as the national sport," he warned in 1959, even though Gallup's numbers remained fairly strong.[73] He proposed further expansion as early as

1963 to retain the advantage. "We must beat football into the new areas," he said, "in order to control the stadiums."[74] Nobody in the baseball establishment shared his urgency.

But that had always been true. Rickey believed devoutly in the importance of planning. "Luck is a residue of design," he famously said.[75] Most of the other owners preferred to wing it.

Rickey had exhorted his counterparts to face the future at the very start of the postwar era. "The center of population in this country has shifted," he warned them in 1945. Attitudes on civil rights were changing. New modes of transportation "will destroy remoteness in the United States."[76] The strategies that he devised—expansion, integration, air travel—did not motivate the other owners to act, not at first. They preferred to lurch from crisis to crisis, reshaping the national pastime with makeshift remedies and ad hoc solutions.

Yet Rickey—even as a feeble man in his eighties—refused to stop pushing. He urged the baseball establishment to get with the times, to meet the new challenges of the 1960s. "Baseball must advance," he kept saying to the end.[77]

The miracle, perhaps, is that it advanced as far as it did.

Chapter Notes

Abbreviations

BR—Baseball Reference
CT—*Chicago Tribune*
FRBM—Federal Reserve Bank of Minneapolis
FRBSL—Federal Reserve Bank of St. Louis
HOF—National Baseball Hall of Fame and Museum
JFK—John F. Kennedy Presidential Library and Museum
LAT—*Los Angeles Times*
LOC—Library of Congress
NYT—*New York Times*
NYTM—*New York Times Magazine*
OH—Oral History
OSP—O'Malley Seidler Partners LLC
SABR—Society for American Baseball Research
SEP—*Saturday Evening Post*
SI—*Sports Illustrated*
SN—*Sporting News*
UCB—University of California at Berkeley
UCLA—University of California at Los Angeles
UKY—University of Kentucky
UM—University of Michigan
UNC—University of North Carolina
UR—University of Rochester
USCB—U.S. Census Bureau
USHR—U.S. House of Representatives
USS—U.S. Senate
WOHD—Walter O'Malley Historic Documents
WP—*Washington Post*

Preface

1. Thomas, *The Pursuit of the White House*, pp. 127–29; Smith, *Thomas E. Dewey and His Times*, p. 546.
2. Richard Puerzer, "Engineering Baseball: Branch Rickey's Innovative Approach to Baseball Management," *Nine* (Fall 2003), pp. 82–83.
3. *Report of the Major League Steering Committee for Submission to the National and American Leagues, August 27, 1946*, Albert "Happy" Chandler Collection, UKY, p. 18; Chandler OH, UKY.
4. Durocher, *The Dodgers and Me*, p. 226.
5. Sewell OH, UKY.
6. *Minutes of the Annual Meeting of the National League, December 10–11, 1945*, National League Meetings, Conferences, Minutes, and Financial Ledgers, HOF, p. 118.
7. *Brooklyn Eagle* (May 8, 1953).
8. *NYT* (March 15, 1953).
9. *Brooklyn Eagle* (August 4, 1954).
10. Parrott, *The Lords of Baseball*, p. 241.
11. Joe Cronin to Philip Hart, telegram, June 3, 1960, Philip Hart Papers, UM.
12. *NYT* (December 9, 1959).

Prologue: Inertia

1. FRBSL website.
2. *LAT* (January 2, 1942); SABR website.
3. *LAT* (January 2, 1942); *SN* (December 4, 1957).
4. Mead, *Even the Browns*, p. 66.
5. DeWitt OH, UKY.
6. *NYT* (January 14, 1942); FRBM website.
7. USCB, *Census of Population: 1940, Volume I*, p. 32.
8. *NYT* (March 24, 1940).
9. *LAT* (August 25, 1932); USHR Subcommittee on the Study of Monopoly Power, *Organized Baseball, Hearings, July 30-October 24, 1951*, pp. 80–81.
10. Steve Treder, "Open Classification: The Pacific Coast League's Drive to Turn Major," *Nine* (Fall 2006), pp. 91–92.
11. *St. Louis Star-Times* (August 1, 1939).
12. *SN* (December 4, 1957).
13. *Ibid.*
14. Mead, *Even the Browns*, p. 34; *SN* (December 4, 1957).
15. Golenbock, *The Spirit of St. Louis*, pp. 280–81.
16. DeWitt OH, UKY.
17. *St. Louis Post-Dispatch* (December 9, 1941); *NYT* (January 14, 1942); *SN* (August 29, 1951).
18. *SN* (December 18, 1941).
19. USCB, *Census of Population: 1950, Volume I*, p. 65.
20. USCB, *Historical Statistics of the United States*, pp. 8, 11.

21. USCB, *Census of Population: 1950, Volume I*, p. 65; Dominion Bureau of Statistics, *Eighth Census of Canada, 1941, Bulletin A-13*, p. 18.
22. SABR website.
23. L. Jon Wertheim, "Remembering the Pathetics," *SI* (June 6, 2016), p. 54.
24. Marshall, *Baseball's Pivotal Era*, pp. 195–96; *NYT* (June 12, 1949, and December 11, 1956).
25. *Congressional Record, 85th Congress, 2nd Session* (June 24, 1958), p. 12082.
26. USHR Antitrust Subcommittee, *Organized Professional Team Sports, Hearings, June 17-August 8, 1957*, p. 1828.
27. Bob Considine and Shirley Povich, "The Old Fox Turns Magnate," *SEP* (April 20, 1940), p. 98.
28. Boxerman and Boxerman, *Ebbets to Veeck to Busch*, pp. 91–92.
29. Kerr, *Calvin*, p. 39.
30. *NYT* (August 24, 1933).
31. Boxerman and Boxerman, *Ebbets to Veeck to Busch*, pp. 91–92; *NYT* (July 2, 1954); Jeff Obermeyer, "War Games: The Business of Major League Baseball During World War II," *Nine* (Fall 2010), p. 5.
32. Tygiel, *Baseball's Great Experiment*, pp. 33–34.
33. *SN* (July 24, 1957).
34. *SN* (April 11, 1951).
35. Pietrusza, *Judge and Jury*, pp. 39–40; *SN* (November 30, 1944).
36. Voigt, *American Baseball, Volume II*, pp. 141–42; FRBM website; Helyar, *Lords of the Realm*, pp. 7–8; Pietrusza, *Judge and Jury*, pp. 52, 62–63.
37. Helyar, *Lords of the Realm*, pp. 7–8.
38. Pietrusza, *Judge and Jury*, p. 67.
39. Voigt, *American Baseball, Volume II*, pp. 141–42; Pietrusza, *Judge and Jury*, pp. 84–86, 88–89.
40. Zimbalist, *Baseball and Billions*, pp. 8–10; Helyar, *Lords of the Realm*, p. 6.
41. Pietrusza, *Judge and Jury*, p. 157.
42. *Ibid.*, p. 156.
43. Banner, *The Baseball Trust*, p. 60.
44. *Federal League of Professional Baseball Clubs v. National League of Professional Baseball Clubs et. al.*, U.S. Circuit Court, Northern District of Illinois, February 7, 1916, August Herrmann Papers, HOF, p. 3.
45. Voigt, *American Baseball, Volume II*, pp. 126–27, 139–40; Tygiel, *Baseball's Great Experiment*, p. 31.
46. *SN* (November 30, 1944).
47. Lowenfish and Lupien, *The Imperfect Diamond*, p. 113.
48. Pietrusza, *Judge and Jury*, p. 388.
49. Voigt, *American Baseball, Volume II*, p. 257; McKelvey, *Mexican Raiders in the Major Leagues*, p. 20; Jeff Obermeyer, "War Games: The Business of Major League Baseball During World War II," *Nine* (Fall 2010), pp. 6–7.
50. Golenbock, *The Spirit of St. Louis*, pp. 293, 303.
51. Mead, *Even the Browns*, pp. 178–79.
52. *SN* (August 23, 1945).
53. USHR Subcommittee on the Study of Monopoly Power, *Organized Baseball, Hearings, July 30-October 24, 1951*, pp. 1035–36; *St. Louis Post-Dispatch* (March 28, 1935); *Detroit Free Press* (March 29, 1935).
54. *St. Louis Star-Times* (March 28, 1935).
55. *Minutes of the Joint Meeting of the Major Leagues, July 11, 1944*, Major League Agreements Collection, HOF.
56. J.A. Zeller to William Harridge, letter, August 25, 1944, Major League Agreements Collection, HOF.
57. *SN* (August 29, 1951).
58. *NYT* (August 11, 1945).

Chapter 1

1. Gilbert, *They Also Served*, pp. 189–90.
2. *SN* (November 30, 1944).
3. Pietrusza, *Judge and July*, pp. 449–50; *SN* (October 5, 1944, and November 23, 1944).
4. *SN* (October 19, 1944).
5. *SN* (November 23, 1944).
6. *SN* (November 30, 1944).
7. *Ibid.*
8. Voigt, *American Baseball, Volume II*, pp. 149–50, 295; *SN* (November 30, 1944).
9. SABR website; *SN* (February 8, 1945, and May 3, 1945).
10. *Minutes of the Joint Meeting of the Major Leagues, April 24, 1945*, Joint Major League Meetings, 1915–1951, HOF, pp. 38–41.
11. Branch Rickey, memorandum, April 25, 1945, Branch Rickey Papers, LOC.
12. *Ibid.*; *SN* (May 3, 1945); Marshall, *Baseball's Pivotal Era*, pp. 18–19.
13. Goldstein, *Superstars and Screwballs*, p. 194.
14. Smith OH, UKY.
15. *SN* (January 15, 1947).
16. Smith OH, UKY.
17. Chandler OH, UKY.
18. Durocher and Linn, *Nice Guys Finish Last*, pp. 118–19.
19. Graham, *The Brooklyn Dodgers*, pp. 152–53; Goldstein, *Superstars and Screwballs*, p. 193; Gerald Holland, "Who in the World But Larry?" *SI* (August 17, 1959), p. 65.
20. Warfield, *The Roaring Redhead*, pp. 24–27, 31–32.
21. Graham, *The Brooklyn Dodgers*, p. 233; Gerald Holland, "Feuds, Finale, and a Fairy Tale," *SI* (August 30, 1959), pp. 60–61.
22. Warfield, *The Roaring Redhead*, p. 45.
23. Graham, *The Brooklyn Dodgers*, p. 155.
24. Warfield, *The Roaring Redhead*, p. 72.
25. Barber and Creamer, *Rhubarb in the Catbird Seat*, p. 25.
26. Goldblatt, *The Giants and the Dodgers*, pp. 77–79; Kahn, *The Era*, p. 18.

27. Durocher, *The Dodgers and Me*, p. 106.
28. Graham, *The Brooklyn Dodgers*, p. 229.
29. *SN* (February 1, 1945, and February 24, 1954); Sullivan, *The Diamond in the Bronx*, p. 77.
30. *NYT* (January 27, 1945); *SN* (February 1, 1945); FRBM website.
31. *SN* (February 1, 1945).
32. Branch Rickey, memorandum, April 25, 1945, Branch Rickey Papers, LOC; Marshall, *Baseball's Pivotal Era*, pp. 18–19; *SN* (May 3, 1945).
33. Branch Rickey, memorandum, April 25, 1945, Branch Rickey Papers, LOC; Marshall, *Baseball's Pivotal Era*, p. 19.
34. Marshall, *Baseball's Pivotal Era*, pp. 25–27.
35. USS Subcommittee on S. 1396, *Broadcasting and Televising Baseball Games, Hearings, May 6–12, 1953*, p. 144.
36. *SN* (February 1, 1945).
37. *SN* (March 22, 1945).
38. *SN* (May 3, 1945).
39. Marshall, *Baseball's Pivotal Era*, p. 20.
40. *Ibid.*, pp. 19–20; *NYT* (April 25, 1945).
41. *SN* (May 3, 1945).
42. *Minutes of the Joint Meeting of the Major Leagues, April 24, 1945*, Joint Major League Meetings, 1915–1951, HOF, p. 41.
43. Earl Ruby, "Baseball's Traveling Salesman," *Esquire* (August 1945), p. 77.
44. Chandler OH, UKY.
45. *Ibid.*
46. *SN* (May 3, 1945).
47. *Ibid.*
48. Chandler OH, UKY.
49. *SN* (May 24, 1945, and June 7, 1945).
50. *SN* (July 5, 1945); Goldstein, *Spartan Seasons*, p. 259.
51. Halberstam, *Summer of '49*, pp. 19–20; *SN* (August 30, 1945); Gilbert, *They Also Served*, pp. 204–5.
52. *SN* (October 4, 1945, and October 11, 1945).

Chapter 2

1. *SN* (September 4, 1946).
2. *SN* (August 16, 1945).
3. *SN* (September 4, 1946).
4. James Gould, "What Makes Rickey Tick?" *Esquire* (March 1943), p. 168.
5. Bavasi, *Off the Record*, p. 42.
6. Mack, *My 66 Years in the Big Leagues*, pp. 201–2.
7. Rickey and Riger, *The American Diamond*, p. 157; Polner, *Branch Rickey*, pp. 45–46.
8. Mann, *Branch Rickey*, pp. 49–52.
9. Richard Puerzer, "Engineering Baseball: Branch Rickey's Innovative Approach to Baseball Management," *Nine* (Fall 2003), pp. 76–77; McCue, *Mover and Shaker*, p. 39.
10. Sullivan, *The Minors*, pp. 95–97; James Gould, "What Makes Rickey Tick?" *Esquire* (March 1943), p. 169.
11. J. Roy Stockton, "From Rags to Riches," *SEP* (March 9, 1935), pp. 89–90; James Gould, "What Makes Rickey Tick?" *Esquire* (March 1943), pp. 168–69; *NYT* (May 11, 1949).
12. Polner, *Branch Rickey*, p. 90; Kahn, *The Boys of Summer*, pp. 93–94.
13. Hornsby and Surface, *My War With Baseball*, pp. 105–6.
14. White, *Creating the National Pastime*, pp. 286–88.
15. Frank Graham, Jr., "Branch Rickey Rides Again," *SEP* (March 9, 1963), p. 68.
16. Breslin, *Branch Rickey*, p. 45; Richard Puerzer, "Engineering Baseball: Branch Rickey's Innovative Approach to Baseball Management," *Nine* (Fall 2003), pp. 77–78; J. Roy Stockton, "From Rags to Riches," *SEP* (March 9, 1935), pp. 89–90; White, *Creating the National Pastime*, pp. 286–88.
17. USHR Subcommittee on the Study of Monopoly Power, *Organized Baseball, Report*, pp. 63–64.
18. SABR website.
19. Mann, *Branch Rickey*, p. 154.
20. Sullivan, *The Minors*, pp. 112–13; Polner, *Branch Rickey*, p. 113; Mann, *Branch Rickey*, p. 209.
21. Sullivan, *The Minors*, p. 99; Mann, *Branch Rickey*, pp. 172–73.
22. J. Roy Stockton, "A Brain Comes to Brooklyn," *SEP* (February 13, 1943). pp. 24, 57; FRBM website.
23. *NYT* (September 15, 1942).
24. *NYT* (September 24, 1942); Durocher, *The Dodgers and Me*, pp. 132–33.
25. *SN* (February 19, 1958).
26. J. Roy Stockton, "A Brain Comes to Brooklyn," *SEP* (February 13, 1943), p. 24; *SN* (October 29, 1947); *NYT* (December 10, 1965).
27. Polner, *Branch Rickey*, p. 42.
28. Dickson, *Leo Durocher*, p. 58.
29. J. Roy Stockton, "A Brain Comes to Brooklyn," *SEP* (February 13, 1943), p. 59; *NYT* (February 12, 1943); Halberstam, *October 1964*, p. 32; Durocher and Linn, *Nice Guys Finish Last*, p. 217.
30. Barber and Creamer, *Rhubarb in the Catbird Seat*, p. 247.
31. Galbreath OH, UKY.
32. Chandler OH, UKY.
33. Smith OH, UKY.
34. Durocher and Linn, *Nice Guys Finish Last*, p. 271.
35. Prince, *Brooklyn's Dodgers*, p. 65.
36. Lopez OH, HOF.
37. *NYT* (October 30, 1942); Lee Lowenfish, "When All Heaven Rejoiced: Branch Rickey and the Origins of the Breaking of the Color Line," *Nine* (Fall 2002), pp. 4–5; SABR website.
38. Lee Lowenfish, "When All Heaven Rejoiced: Branch Rickey and the Origins of the Breaking of the Color Line," *Nine* (Fall 2002), p. 1; *NYT* (February 12, 1943).
39. *SN* (March 15, 1950).

40. *NYT* (August 10, 1943).
41. D'Antonio, *Forever Blue*, pp. 73–74; Andy McCue, "Two Out of Three Ain't Bad: Branch Rickey, Walter O'Malley, and the Man in the Middle of the Dodger Owners' Partnership," *Nine* (Fall 2005), pp. 43–44; *NYT* (November 2, 1944); Mann, *Branch Rickey*, p. 230.
42. D'Antonio, *Forever Blue*, p. 79; *NYT* (August 14, 1945); McCue, *Mover and Shaker*, pp. 47–48.
43. J. Roy Stockton, "A Brain Comes to Brooklyn," *SEP* (February 13, 1943), p. 60.
44. Tygiel, *Baseball's Great Experiment*, p. 27.
45. Lemon OH, HOF.
46. Tygiel, *Baseball's Great Experiment*, p. 30.
47. Norman Macht, "Does Baseball Deserve This Black Eye?" *Baseball Research Journal* (Summer 2009), pp. 28–29.
48. Breslin, *Branch Rickey*, pp. 27–28; Lee Lowenfish, "When All Heaven Rejoiced: Branch Rickey and the Origins of the Breaking of the Color Line," *Nine* (Fall 2002), p. 10.
49. *SN* (November 1, 1945).
50. Parrott, *The Lords of Baseball*, pp. 187–88.
51. Durocher, *The Dodgers and Me*, p. 226.
52. Mann, *Branch Rickey*, pp. 215–17.
53. Lee Lowenfish, "When All Heaven Rejoiced: Branch Rickey and the Origins of the Breaking of the Color Line," *Nine* (Fall 2002), p. 9.
54. Schwartz, *Trends in White Attitudes Toward Negroes*, pp. 8–10, 84–85.
55. *Report of the Major League Steering Committee for Submission to the National and American Leagues, August 27, 1946*, Albert "Happy" Chandler Collection, UKY, p. 18.
56. Chandler OH, UKY.
57. SABR website; *NYT* (October 24, 1945); Gilbert, *They Also Served*, pp. 222–23.
58. SABR website.
59. Peary, *Jackie Robinson in Quotes*, p. 86.
60. *NYT* (October 24, 1945); *SN* (November 1, 1945).

Chapter 3

1. *SN* (February 21, 1946); Ron Briley, "Danny Gardella and Baseball's Reserve Clause: A Working-Class Stiff Blacklisted in Cold War America," *Nine* (Fall 2010), p. 54.
2. Virtue, *South of the Color Barrier*, pp. 125–27; McKelvey, *Mexican Raiders in the Major Leagues*, pp. 86–87.
3. Virtue, *South of the Color Barrier*, pp. 125–27; Marshall, *Baseball's Pivotal Era*, pp. 46–47; Testa, *Sal Maglie*, pp. 52–53.
4. McKelvey, *Mexican Raiders in the Major Leagues*, p. 45; *NYT* (April 5, 1946); David Mandell, "Danny Gardella and the Reserve Clause," *National Pastime* (2006), p. 41; FRBM website.
5. Virtue, *South of the Color Barrier*, pp. 88, 119.
6. David Mandell, "Danny Gardella and the Reserve Clause," *National Pastime* (2006), pp. 41–42; Lowenfish and Lupien, *The Imperfect Diamond*, p. 157; *NYT* (February 13, 1946).
7. *NYT* (February 14, 1946).
8. *NYT* (February 19, 1946).
9. Frank Graham, Jr., "The Great Mexican War of 1946," *SI* (September 19, 1966), pp. 118–19; Ron Briley, "Danny Gardella and Baseball's Reserve Clause: A Working-Class Stiff Blacklisted in Cold War America," *Nine* (Fall 2010), p. 55.
10. McKelvey, *Mexican Raiders in the Major Leagues*, p. 62; Ron Briley, "Danny Gardella and Baseball's Reserve Clause: A Working-Class Stiff Blacklisted in Cold War America," *Nine* (Fall 2010), pp. 56–57; Testa, *Sal Maglie*, pp. 56–57; SABR website; Marshall, *Baseball's Pivotal Era*, pp. 50–52.
11. McKelvey, *Mexican Raiders in the Major Leagues*, pp. 98–101; Frank Graham, Jr., "The Great Mexican War of 1946," *SI* (September 19, 1966), p. 124.
12. Oakley, *Baseball's Last Golden Age*, p. 36.
13. Owen OH, UKY.
14. Golenbock, *The Spirit of St. Louis*, p. 369.
15. *SN* (March 21, 1946).
16. Marshall, *Baseball's Pivotal Era*, pp. 49–50, 55; *SN* (March 14, 1946, and March 21, 1946).
17. Vecsey, *Stan Musial*, pp. 120–22.
18. *SN* (March 14, 1946).
19. Chandler OH, UKY.
20. *NYT* (August 6, 1946, and August 7, 1946).
21. Owen OH, UKY.
22. *NYT* (March 22, 1946); SABR website.
23. Ron Briley, "Danny Gardella and Baseball's Reserve Clause: A Working-Class Stiff Blacklisted in Cold War America," *Nine* (Fall 2010), pp. 64–65.
24. *NYT* (March 20, 1946).
25. Durocher, *The Dodgers and Me*, p. 231.
26. Miller, *A Whole Different Ball Game*, pp. 177–78; Simon Rottenberg, "The Baseball Players' Labor Market," *Journal of Political Economy* (June 1956), pp. 255–58.
27. *SN* (November 13, 1946).
28. *NYT* (February 11, 1949).
29. *NYT* (April 14, 1949); Ron Briley, "Danny Gardella and Baseball's Reserve Clause: A Working-Class Stiff Blacklisted in Cold War America," *Nine* (Fall 2010), pp. 63–64.
30. Simon Rottenberg, "The Baseball Players' Labor Market," *Journal of Political Economy* (June 1956), p. 247.
31. Banner, *The Baseball Trust*, pp. 4–5.
32. Dworkin, *Owners Versus Players*, pp. 44–46; Ross Davies, "Along Comes the Players Association: The Roots and Rise of Organized Labor in Major League Baseball," *Journal of Legislation and Public Policy* (2013), pp. 324–26; Quirk and Fort, *Pay Dirt*, pp. 181–82.
33. Lowenfish and Lupien, *The Imperfect Diamond*, p. 31.
34. Duquette, *Regulating the National Pastime*, p. 7; Dworkin, *Owners Versus Players*, p. 49.

35. Banner, *The Baseball Trust*, p. 16.
36. Quirk and Fort, *Pay Dirt*, p. 183; Dworkin, *Owners Versus Players*, pp. 51–52; Banner, *The Baseball Trust*, pp. 20–22.
37. *SN* (February 15, 1956).
38. Bob Considine and Shirley Povich, "Old Fox," *SEP* (April 13, 1940), pp. 130–31.
39. Banner, *The Baseball Trust*, pp. 27, 36.
40. Mack, *My 66 Years in the Big Leagues*, p. 36.
41. USHR Subcommittee on the Study of Monopoly Power, *Organized Baseball, Hearings, July 30-October 24, 1951*, pp. 527–28.
42. Lowenfish and Lupien, *The Imperfect Diamond*, p. 88; Freedman, *Professional Sports and Antitrust*, p. 33.
43. Dworkin, *Owners Versus Players*, pp. 55–56; Freedman, *Professional Sports and Antitrust*, p. 32.
44. Justia website; Banner, *The Baseball Trust*, pp. 86–87.
45. USHR Subcommittee on the Study of Monopoly Power, *Organized Baseball, Report*, p. 109.
46. D'Antonio, *Forever Blue*, p. 89.
47. Chandler OH, UKY.
48. Dallek, *Harry S. Truman*, pp. 39–40; Manchester, *The Glory and the Dream*, p. 400.
49. *SN* (June 5, 1946); Lowenfish and Lupien, *The Imperfect Diamond*, pp. 139–40.
50. *SN* (June 5, 1946).
51. Ross Davies, "Along Comes the Players Association: The Roots and Rise of Organized Labor in Major League Baseball," *Journal of Legislation and Public Policy* (2013), pp. 329–31.
52. Dworkin, *Owners Versus Players*, p. 19.
53. *Pittsburgh Post-Gazette* (April 18, 1946).
54. *SN* (April 25, 1946).
55. Ibid.; *SN* (May 9, 1946); FRBM website.
56. *SN* (April 25, 1946).
57. *SN* (May 9, 1946).
58. Chandler OH, UKY.
59. Oakley, *Baseball's Last Golden Age*, p. 37.
60. Marshall, *Baseball's Pivotal Era*, pp. 65–68; *SN* (May 23, 1946).
61. Kiner and Peary, *Baseball Forever*, pp. 93–99.
62. Lowenfish and Lupien, *The Imperfect Diamond*, p. 145.
63. *Pittsburgh Press* (June 6, 1946).
64. *Pittsburgh Press* (June 7, 1946).
65. Lowenfish and Lupien, *The Imperfect Diamond*, pp. 146–47.
66. Sewell OH, UKY.
67. *SN* (June 19, 1946).
68. Ibid.; Kiner and Peary, *Baseball Forever*, pp. 93–99; *NYT* (December 2, 2012).
69. Sewell OH, UKY.
70. *SN* (June 19, 1946); *Pittsburgh Post-Gazette* (June 8, 1946).
71. Kiner and Peary, *Baseball Forever*, pp. 93–99.
72. *Pittsburgh Press* (June 8, 1946).
73. Marshall, *Baseball's Pivotal Era*, pp. 64–65.
74. Paul Gould, "Unionism's Bid in Baseball," *New Republic* (August 5, 1946), p. 136.
75. *SN* (July 17, 1946).
76. USHR Subcommittee on the Study of Monopoly Power, *Organized Baseball, Hearings, July 30-October 24, 1951*, pp. 1062–66; *SN* (July 24, 1946, and July 31, 1946); Warfield, *The Roaring Redhead*, pp. 203–5.
77. Marshall, *Baseball's Pivotal Era*, pp. 74–78.
78. Povich OH, UKY.
79. *SN* (October 24, 1951); Dworkin, *Owners Versus Players*, p. 19.
80. Chandler OH, UKY.
81. *Pittsburgh Press* (August 21, 1946).
82. *Report of the Major League Steering Committee for Submission to the National and American Leagues, August 27, 1946*, Albert "Happy" Chandler Collection, UKY, pp. 12–13.
83. *SN* (October 24, 1951); Marshall, *Baseball's Pivotal Era*, pp. 79–82.
84. Oakley, *Baseball's Last Golden Age*, p. 102; D'Antonio, *Forever Blue*, p. 90.
85. Marshall, *Baseball's Pivotal Era*, p. 82; Oakley, *Baseball's Last Golden Age*, p. 38.
86. *NYT* (December 2, 2012).
87. Chandler and Trimble, *Heroes, Plain Folks, and Skunks*, p. 194.
88. Virtue, *South of the Color Barrier*, p. 183; Testa, *Sal Maglie*, pp. 77–78; McKelvey, *Mexican Raiders in the Major Leagues*, p. 172; *NYT* (March 12, 1947).
89. McKelvey, *Mexican Raiders in the Major Leagues*, pp. 167–69.
90. Virtue, *South of the Color Barrier*, pp. 195–200.
91. Paul Gould, "Unionism's Bid in Baseball," *New Republic* (August 5, 1946), p. 136.
92. *SN* (November 1, 1945); John Burbridge, "The Brooklyn Dodgers in Jersey City," *Baseball Research Journal* (Summer 2010), p. 21.
93. *SN* (May 9, 1946).
94. *SN* (October 9, 1946).
95. *SN* (October 23, 1946).

Chapter 4

1. *NYT* (April 15, 1943).
2. Manchester, *The Glory and the Dream*, pp. 396–97.
3. *LAT* (June 5, 1942, and January 3, 1945).
4. FRBSL website.
5. *NYT* (August 8, 1949).
6. USCB website; USCB, *Historical Statistics of the United States*, pp. 46–53.
7. *SN* (October 17, 1951).
8. Philip Wrigley to Warren Giles, letter, January 7, 1952, Radio and Television Broadcasting Collection, HOF.
9. USCB, *Forecasts of the Population of the United States*, p. 39.
10. Teaford, *The Twentieth-Century American City*, pp. 15, 19, 74–75.

11. Charles Edmundson, "St. Louis: A City in Decay," *Forum and Century* (November 1939), pp. 200–201.
12. George Sessions Perry, "Cincinnati," *SEP* (April 20, 1946), p. 101; George Sessions Perry, "Pittsburgh," *SEP* (August 3, 1946), pp. 14–15.
13. USCB, *Census of Population: 1940, Volume I*, pp. 32, 61–65.
14. Thomas, *The United States of Suburbia*, pp. 35–37; Manchester, *The Glory and the Dream*, pp. 431–32; Lewis, *Divided Highways*, pp. 75–76; Teaford, *The Twentieth-Century American City*, p. 101.
15. White, *Theodore H. White at Large*, pp. 511–12; Gibson and Jung, *Historical Census Statistics on Population Totals by Race*, pp. 26–113.
16. USHR Antitrust Subcommittee, *Organized Professional Team Sports, Hearings, June 17-August 8, 1957*, p. 1945.
17. Bernard and Rice, *Sunbelt Cities*, p. 12; Teaford, *The Twentieth-Century American City*, pp. 91–92; Zingg and Medeiros, *Runs, Hits, and an Era*, pp. 107–8.
18. USCB, *Census of Population: 1950, Volume I*, p. 10; Hobbs and Stoops, *Demographic Trends in the 20th Century*, pp. 26–29; USCB website.
19. *SN* (August 23, 1945).
20. *NYT* (December 17, 1945, and January 13, 1946); *Akron Beacon Journal* (January 13, 1946); Halas, Morgan, and Veysey, *Halas by Halas*, p. 237.
21. MacCambridge, *America's Game*, p. 16.
22. Horrigan, *NFL Century*, p. 85; Littlewood, *Arch*, pp. 149–51; Quirk and Fort, *Pay Dirt*, pp. 341–42; Halas, Morgan, and Veysey, *Halas by Halas*, pp. 205–6; *LAT* (June 19, 1943).
23. Holtzman and Vass, *Baseball, Chicago Style*, pp. 99–100.
24. Davis, *Papa Bear*, p. 196.
25. Littlewood, *Arch*, pp. 155–56.
26. Dan Endsley, "West Coast Baseball: Too Big For Its Britches," *Harper's* (October 1946), p. 375.
27. Steve Treder, "Open Classification: The Pacific Coast League's Drive to Turn Major," *Nine* (Fall 2006), pp. 89–90; USHR Subcommittee on the Study of Monopoly Power, *Organized Baseball, Hearings, July 30-October 24, 1951*, p. 1622; *NYT* (November 13, 1947); Zingg and Medeiros, *Runs, Hits, and an Era*, pp. 73–75, 91–92.
28. Vincent, *We Would Have Played for Nothing*, p. 39.
29. *LAT* (November 19, 1954); Steve Treder, "Open Classification: The Pacific Coast League's Drive to Turn Major," *Nine* (Fall 2006), pp. 93–94; Sullivan, *The Minors*, p. 217.
30. USCB, *Census of Population: 1950, Volume I*, p. 74.
31. *Minutes of the Annual Meeting of the National League, December 10–11, 1945*, National League Meetings, Conferences, Minutes, and Financial Ledgers, HOF, pp. 86, 118.
32. *Ibid.*, p. 133.
33. *NYT* (December 12, 1945).
34. Zingg and Medeiros, *Runs, Hits, and an Era*, pp. 110–12.
35. *Minutes of the Annual Meeting of the National League, December 5–7, 1946*, National League Meetings, Conferences, Minutes, and Financial Ledgers, HOF, p. 176.
36. Zingg and Medeiros, *Runs, Hits, and an Era*, pp. 110–12; James Gordon, "Los Angeles' Wrigley Field: 'The Finest Edifice in the United States,'" *National Pastime* (2011), p. 110; USHR Subcommittee on the Study of Monopoly Power, *Organized Baseball, Hearings, July 30-October 24, 1951*, pp. 1618–22.
37. *Minutes of the Meeting of the National League, July 7, 1947*, National League Meetings, Conferences, Minutes, and Financial Ledgers, HOF, pp. 4–5.
38. Halas, Morgan, and Veysey, *Halas by Halas*, p. 237.
39. Pro Football Reference website.
40. *Minutes of the Annual Meeting of the National League, December 10–11, 1945*, National League Meetings, Conferences, Minutes, and Financial Ledgers, HOF, p. 133.
41. White, *Creating the National Pastime*, p. 308.
42. *NYT* (August 30, 1947).
43. Frick, *Games, Asterisks, and People*, pp. 121–22.
44. USHR Subcommittee on the Study of Monopoly Power, *Organized Baseball, Hearings, July 30-October 24, 1951*, pp. 88–91.
45. *Ibid.*, pp. 88–89.
46. *Ibid.*
47. *NYT* (August 30, 1947).
48. Sullivan, *The Minors*, p. 219; *NYT* (December 12, 1947).
49. *SN* (December 17, 1947).
50. *NYT* (August 26, 1948); *SN* (September 1, 1948).
51. *NYT* (December 23, 1947).
52. *SN* (April 25, 1951).
53. *SN* (August 18, 1948).
54. *Ibid.*
55. *SN* (April 23, 1947); BR website.
56. SABR website; *SN* (September 24, 1947); *NYT* (September 29, 1947).
57. *SN* (October 15, 1947).
58. BR website; *Boston Globe* (July 23, 2002).

Chapter 5

1. Goldstein, *Spartan Seasons*, pp. 263–67.
2. *NYT* (August 12, 1945).
3. Yarnell, *Democrats and Progressives*, pp. 34–35, 44; Clifford and Holbrooke, *Counsel to the President*, p. 203.
4. Irvin OH, HOF.
5. *NYT* (May 16, 1945).
6. Boxerman and Boxerman, *Ebbets to Veeck to Busch*, p. 95.

7. Macht, *The Grand Old Man of Baseball*, p. 355.
8. Jordan, *The Athletics of Philadelphia*, p. 146; Mack, *My 66 Years in the Big Leagues*, p. 133.
9. Barber and Creamer, *Rhubarb in the Catbird Seat*, pp. 269–71.
10. Eig, *Opening Day*, p. 43.
11. SABR website; *NYT* (October 24, 1945, and April 10, 2010).
12. Eig, *Opening Day*, pp. 43–44.
13. SABR website.
14. *NYT* (April 10, 1947); *SN* (April 9, 1947, and April 16, 1947).
15. Chandler and Trimble, *Heroes, Plain Folks, and Skunks*, p. 203.
16. Barber and Creamer, *Rhubarb in the Catbird Seat*, p. 83.
17. McCue, *Mover and Shaker*, p. 64; *SN* (April 16, 1947).
18. Threston, *The Integration of Baseball in Philadelphia*, pp. 72–74.
19. SABR website.
20. Marshall, *Baseball's Pivotal Era*, pp. 130–31.
21. *SN* (January 14, 1948).
22. Chandler and Trimble, *Heroes, Plain Folks, and Skunks*, p. 229.
23. Peary, *We Played the Game*, p. 324.
24. Jack Bales, "'It Was His Fairness that Caught Wrigley's Eye': William L. Veeck's Journalism Career and His Hiring by the Chicago Cubs," *Nine* (Spring 2012), p. 1.
25. Veeck and Linn, *Veeck—As in Wreck*, pp. 24–25.
26. SABR website; Jack Bales, "Baseball's First Bill Veeck," *Baseball Research Journal* (Fall 2013), pp. 7–13.
27. Eskenazi, *Bill Veeck*, pp. 6–12; Veeck and Linn, *Veeck—As in Wreck*, pp. 25–26; Fleder, *Great Baseball Writing*, p. 225.
28. Veeck and Linn, *Veeck—As in Wreck*, p. 36.
29. *NYT* (November 15, 1940).
30. Robert Yoder and James Kearns, "Boy Magnate," *SEP* (August 28, 1943), pp. 19, 81; Stanley Frank and Edgar Munzel, "A Visit With Bill Veeck," *SEP* (June 6, 1959), pp. 93–94; *NYT* (June 24, 1941).
31. Veeck and Linn, *Veeck—As in Wreck*, pp. 48–49.
32. Grimm and Prell, *Jolly Cholly's Story*, p. 142.
33. *NYT* (May 9, 1943, and December 22, 1955); Grimm and Prell, *Jolly Cholly's Story*, p. 147.
34. John Hoffman, "Squirrel Night at the Brewers," *Esquire* (September 1943), p. 141.
35. *Ibid.*, p. 53.
36. Veeck and Linn, *Veeck—As in Wreck*, p. 80.
37. *Ibid.*, pp. 171–72; Norman Macht and Robert Warrington, "The Veracity of Veeck," *Baseball Research Journal* (Fall 2013), pp. 17–20.
38. Jules Tygiel, "Revisiting Bill Veeck and the 1943 Phillies," *Baseball Research Journal* (2006), p. 109.
39. Fleder, *Great Baseball Writing*, p. 226; *NYT* (November 28, 1943, and November 2, 1946); *SN* (March 4, 1959); SABR website.
40. Sievers OH, HOF.
41. SABR website; *NYT* (June 22, 1946, and June 23, 1946).
42. *SN* (July 10, 1946).
43. Veeck and Linn, *Veeck—As in Wreck*, p. 102.
44. *Ibid.*, p. 61.
45. Bill Veeck and Gordon Cobbledick, "So You Want to Run a Ball Club?" *SEP* (April 23, 1949), pp. 144–46.
46. Golenbock, *The Spirit of St. Louis*, pp. 352–53; *SN* (February 23, 1949).
47. *NYT* (July 4, 1947).
48. Boudreau and Schneider, *Covering All the Bases*, p. 95.
49. Veeck and Linn, *The Hustler's Handbook*, p. 22.
50. *SN* (October 17, 1951).
51. Caplow, Hicks, and Wattenberg, *The First Measured Century*, pp. 100–101; Robert Bellamy, Jr., and James Walker, "Did Televised Baseball Kill the 'Golden Age' of the Minor Leagues? A Reassessment," *Nine* (Fall 2004), pp. 59–61.
52. Mack, *My 66 Years in the Big Leagues*, p. 188.
53. USHR Subcommittee on the Study of Monopoly Power, *Organized Baseball, Hearings, July 30–October 24, 1951*, pp. 1599–1600; FRBM website.
54. Kahn, *The Era*, pp. 144–45; Marshall, *Baseball's Pivotal Era*, p. 164; *SN* (October 15, 1947).
55. *NYT* (October 7, 1947); *SN* (October 15, 1947).
56. Warfield, *The Roaring Redhead*, p. 220; Kahn, *The Era*, pp. 139–43; Sullivan, *The Diamond in the Bronx*, p. 79.
57. *SN* (October 15, 1947).
58. Golenbock, *Amazin'*, pp. 94–95.
59. *NYT* (October 8, 1947).
60. Gerald Holland, "Who in the World But Larry?" *SI* (August 17, 1959), pp. 62–64.
61. *SN* (June 2, 1948, and June 30, 1948).
62. Durocher and Linn, *Nice Guys Finish Last*, pp. 282–83.
63. *NYT* (October 5, 1948); *SN* (October 13, 1948).
64. *NYT* (October 13, 1948); SABR website; Veeck and Linn, *Veeck—As in Wreck*, pp. 207–8.

Chapter 6

1. *SN* (June 2, 1948).
2. *Ibid.*
3. Gallup website.
4. *NYT* (January 5, 1944).
5. Davis, *Papa Bear*, p. 229; Littlewood, *Arch*, p. 173; *SN* (December 14, 1949).
6. *NYT* (January 7, 1948).

7. D'Antonio, *Forever Blue*, pp. 108–9; McCue, *Mover and Shaker*, p. 73.
8. *NYT* (August 20, 1959).
9. Quirk and Fort, *Pay Dirt*, p. 156; Kuklick, *To Every Thing a Season*, pp. 25–26.
10. Voigt, *American Baseball, Volume II*, p. 206; Teaford, *The Rough Road to Renaissance*, p. 15; Thomas, *The United States of Suburbia*, pp. 35–37; Thorn, Palmer, Gershman, and Pietrusza, *Total Baseball*, p. 2186.
11. Bob Ruzzo, "Braves Field: An Imperfect History of the Perfect Ballpark," *Baseball Research Journal* (Fall 2012), pp. 50–54; Thorn, Palmer, Gershman, and Pietrusza, *Total Baseball*, p. 88.
12. Mathews and Buege, *Eddie Mathews and the National Pastime*, p. 66.
13. *Wall Street Journal* (September 28, 1955).
14. Peary, *We Played the Game*, p. 104.
15. Giles OH, SABR.
16. Peary, *We Played the Game*, p. 73.
17. USCB, *Historical Statistics of the United States*, p. 716; White, *Creating the National Pastime*, pp. 21–24.
18. *NYT* (July 5, 1950); David Pincus, "A Man Was Once Shot at an MLB Game and Play Went On," *SI* (April 7, 2014).
19. Robert James, "Field of Liens: Real-Property Development in Baseball," *Baseball Research Journal* (Fall 2010), pp. 116–17.
20. Barber and Creamer, *Rhubarb in the Catbird Seat*, p. 290.
21. Kowet, *The Rich Who Own Sports*, p. 63.
22. *Minutes of the Board of Directors of Brooklyn Baseball Club Inc., October 22, 1946*, Branch Rickey Papers, LOC.
23. White, *Creating the National Pastime*, p. 214.
24. *SN* (April 27, 1922).
25. James Walker, "The Baseball-Radio War," *Nine* (Spring 2011), p. 53; Rader, *In Its Own Image*, p. 26; Zimbalist, *Baseball and Billions*, p. 149.
26. James Walker, "The Baseball-Radio War," *Nine* (Spring 2011), p. 56.
27. White, *Creating the National Pastime*, pp. 224–25.
28. Powers, *Supertube*, pp. 33–34; James Walker and Robert Bellamy, Jr., "Baseball on Television: The Formative Years, 1939–51," *Nine* (Spring 2003), pp. 2–3; Robert Warrington, "The First Televised Baseball Interview," *Baseball Research Journal* (Fall 2015), pp. 37–39.
29. *NYT* (February 21, 1937).
30. *NYT* (May 21, 1939); James Walker and Robert Bellamy, Jr., "Baseball on Television: The Formative Years, 1939–51," *Nine* (Spring 2003), pp. 3–4.
31. Johnson, *Super Spectator and the Electric Lilliputians*, pp. 34–36.
32. *NYT* (May 21, 1939).
33. James Walker and Robert Bellamy, Jr., "Baseball on Television: The Formative Years, 1939–51," *Nine* (Spring 2003), pp. 5–6.
34. Larry MacPhail, "A Pulmotor for Baseball," *Life* (February 24, 1958), p. 119.
35. DeWitt OH, UKY.
36. *Minutes of the Board of Directors of Brooklyn Baseball Club Inc., September 16, 1946*, Branch Rickey Papers, LOC.
37. Robert Bellamy, Jr., and James Walker, "Did Televised Baseball Kill the 'Golden Age' of the Minor Leagues? A Reassessment," *Nine* (Fall 2004), p. 59.
38. *NYT* (September 14, 1934); White, *Creating the National Pastime*, pp. 218–19; FRBM website.
39. James Walker and Robert Bellamy, Jr., "Baseball on Television: The Formative Years, 1939–51," *Nine* (Spring 2003), p. 8.
40. *Minutes of the Board of Directors of Brooklyn Baseball Club Inc., October 16, 1947*, Branch Rickey Papers, LOC.
41. James Walker and Robert Bellamy, Jr., "Baseball on Television: The Formative Years, 1939–51," *Nine* (Spring 2003), pp. 9–10; *SN* (October 18, 1950).
42. *SN* (January 3, 1951); Oakley, *Baseball's Last Golden Age*, p. 114.
43. Armour, *Joe Cronin*, pp. 201–3; FRBM website; Kelley, *Baseball's Biggest Blunder*, pp. 2–3.
44. *SN* (October 23, 1946, and February 24, 1954).
45. Kelley, *Baseball's Biggest Blunder*, pp. 4–7; *SN* (March 8, 1950).
46. *SN* (March 9, 1955).
47. Marshall, *Baseball's Pivotal Era*, p. 49.
48. David Mandell, "Danny Gardella and the Reserve Clause," *National Pastime* (2006), pp. 42–43; Testa, *Sal Maglie*, pp. 80–83; McKelvey, *Mexican Raiders in the Major Leagues*, pp. 191–92; Ron Briley, "Danny Gardella and Baseball's Reserve Clause: A Working-Class Stiff Blacklisted in Cold War America," *Nine* (Fall 2010), pp. 58–59; *NYT* (April 19, 1949).
49. Testa, *Sal Maglie*, pp. 88–89.
50. Ron Briley, "Danny Gardella and Baseball's Reserve Clause: A Working-Class Stiff Blacklisted in Cold War America," *Nine* (Fall 2010), pp. 59–60; *SN* (July 21, 1948); *NYT* (February 10, 1949); Lowenfish and Lupien, *The Imperfect Diamond*, p. 164.
51. *NYT* (February 10, 1949).
52. Ron Briley, "Danny Gardella and Baseball's Reserve Clause: A Working-Class Stiff Blacklisted in Cold War America," *Nine* (Fall 2010), pp. 60–61.
53. *SN* (February 16, 1949).
54. USHR Subcommittee on the Study of Monopoly Power, *Organized Baseball, Hearings, July 30–October 24, 1951*, pp. 290–91.
55. Ron Briley, "Danny Gardella and Baseball's Reserve Clause: A Working-Class Stiff Blacklisted in Cold War America," *Nine* (Fall 2010), pp. 62–63; *NYT* (February 10, 1949).
56. *NYT* (June 6, 1949).
57. USHR Subcommittee on the Study of

Monopoly Power, *Organized Baseball, Hearings, July 30–October 24, 1951*, p. 288.
58. *SN* (September 28, 1949); *NYT* (September 20, 1949); Ron Briley, "Danny Gardella and Baseball's Reserve Clause: A Working-Class Stiff Blacklisted in Cold War America," *Nine* (Fall 2010), pp. 63–64.
59. *NYT* (September 20, 1949).
60. Marshall, *Baseball's Pivotal Era*, pp. 245–47; J. Roy Stockton, "Baseball's Amazing Amateur," *SEP* (May 27, 1950), p. 142.
61. Saigh OH, UKY.
62. *NYT* (February 10, 1949).
63. Ron Briley, "Danny Gardella and Baseball's Reserve Clause: A Working-Class Stiff Blacklisted in Cold War America," *Nine* (Fall 2010), p. 64; McKelvey, *Mexican Raiders in the Major Leagues*, pp. 186–87; FRBM website.
64. *NYT* (November 10, 1953).
65. *SN* (August 15, 1951).
66. David Mandell, "Danny Gardella and the Reserve Clause," *National Pastime* (2006), p. 44.
67. Gardella OH, UKY.
68. *SN* (June 22, 1949); Rich Cohen, "The Chilling Story of Eddie Waitkus and His Encounter with an Obsessed Cubs Fan," *SI* (September 13, 2017).
69. *SN* (October 12, 1949).
70. Ibid.
71. Peary, *We Played the Game*, p. 110.

Chapter 7

1. Eskenazi, *Bill Veeck*, p. 17.
2. *SN* (October 27, 1948).
3. Greenberg and Berkow, *Hank Greenberg*, p. 205.
4. Ibid., pp. 199–200; *SN* (April 7, 1948); Kurlansky, *Hank Greenberg*, pp. 92–94.
5. Greenberg and Berkow, *Hank Greenberg*, p. 116.
6. Kurlansky, *Hank Greenberg*, p. 121.
7. Greenberg and Berkow, *Hank Greenberg*, p. 198.
8. Ibid., p. 205.
9. *NYT* (October 30, 1949); *SN* (November 9, 1949, and November 23, 1949).
10. Veeck and Linn, *Veeck—As in Wreck*, pp. 208–9.
11. Eskenazi, *Bill Veeck*, p. 86.
12. *SN* (September 21, 1949).
13. *SN* (October 27, 1948).
14. *NYT* (August 1, 1948, and February 3, 1949); Golenbock, *The Spirit of St. Louis*, p. 321.
15. *NYT* (February 3, 1949).
16. Sievers OH, HOF.
17. *NYT* (June 23, 1950).
18. *NYT* (November 26, 1947).
19. Ibid.; *NYT* (January 28, 1949); *SN* (February 4, 1953); J. Roy Stockton, "Baseball's Amazing Amateur," *SEP* (May 27, 1950), pp. 38–39, 136–40.
20. Musial and Broeg, *Stan Musial*, p. 155.
21. J. Roy Stockton, "Baseball's Amazing Amateur," *SEP* (May 27, 1950), pp. 38–39; *NYT* (January 28, 1949, and October 7, 1949).
22. Broeg OH, UKY.
23. J. Roy Stockton, "Baseball's Amazing Amateur," *SEP* (May 27, 1950), p. 142.
24. *SN* (April 1, 1953).
25. Bob Ruzzo, "Braves Field: An Imperfect History of the Perfect Ballpark," *Baseball Research Journal* (Fall 2012), pp. 57–58; Bryant, *The Last Hero*, pp. 85–86; *NYT* (January 22, 1944, and April 17, 1972).
26. Davidson and Outlar, *Caught Short*, p. 86.
27. Irey, *The Tax Dodgers*, pp. 204–9.
28. *NYT* (May 14, 1947).
29. Meany, *Milwaukee's Miracle Braves*, p. 4.
30. Creamer, *Stengel*, p. 195.
31. Kaese, *The Boston Braves*, pp. 261–62; SABR website.
32. *NYT* (August 30, 1946).
33. *SN* (January 28, 1948).
34. Kaese, *The Boston Braves*, p. 273.
35. Peary, *We Played the Game*, pp. 86–87.
36. Kaese, *The Boston Braves*, p. 278; SABR website.
37. MacCambridge, *America's Game*, p. 68; Nowlin, *Tom Yawkey*, p. 134; *NYT* (March 19, 1953).
38. Mort Bloomberg, "Roland Hemond: If You Can't Take Part in a Sport, Be One Anyway, Will You?" *Baseball Research Journal* (2008), pp. 12–13.
39. *Boston Globe* (April 17, 1972).
40. SABR website; William Weart, "Then and Now," *NYTM* (December 2, 1951), p. 12; *SN* (November 10, 1954, and February 15, 1956).
41. *NYT* (October 28, 1955); Joel Rippel, "Clark Griffith," *National Pastime* (2009), pp. 112–13; Bob Considine and Shirley Povich, "Old Fox," *SEP* (April 13, 1940), pp. 14–15, 127, 129; Deveaux, *The Washington Senators*, pp. 29–31.
42. *SN* (July 30, 1952).
43. William Kashatus, "Cobb's Last Stand," *American History* (June 1999), p. 40; *NYT* (February 9, 1956); L. Jon Wertheim, "Remembering the Pathetics," *SI* (June 6, 2016), p. 54.
44. Mack, *My 66 Years in the Big Leagues*, p. 36.
45. Fleder, *Great Baseball Writing*, pp. 344–45.
46. Bob Considine and Shirley Povich, "The Old Fox Turns Magnate," *SEP* (April 20, 1940), pp. 92–96; Deveaux, *The Washington Senators*, pp. 80–81.
47. Povich, *All These Mornings*, p. 81.
48. *SN* (December 1, 1948).
49. *SN* (February 29, 1956).
50. Ritter, *The Glory of Their Times*, p. 113.
51. Gary Smith, "A Lingering Vestige of Yesterday," *SI* (April 4, 1983), p. 107.
52. SABR website; Deveaux, *The Washington Senators*, p. 156.
53. Veeck and Linn, *Veeck—As in Wreck*, pp. 138–39.
54. Robert Warrington, "Departure Without Dignity: The Athletics Leave Philadelphia,"

Baseball Research Journal (Fall 2010), pp. 98–99; Macht, *The Grand Old Man of Baseball*, pp. 333–35; Kuklick, *To Every Thing a Season*, p. 113.

55. Robert Warrington, "Departure Without Dignity: The Athletics Leave Philadelphia," *Baseball Research Journal* (Fall 2010), pp. 97–100; Harry Paxton, "The Philadelphia A's Last Stand," *SEP* (June 12, 1954), p. 133.

56. Rosenthal, *The 10 Best Years of Baseball*, p. 15.

57. Mack, *My 66 Years in the Big Leagues*, p. 5.

58. Macht, *The Grand Old Man of Baseball*, p. 90.

59. Jordan, *The Athletics of Philadelphia*, pp. 135–36.

60. Robert Warrington, "Departure Without Dignity: The Athletics Leave Philadelphia," *Baseball Research Journal* (Fall 2010), pp. 100–101; Harry Paxton, "The Philadelphia A's Last Stand," *SEP* (June 12, 1954), pp. 133–34; *NYT* (August 1, 1950).

61. *NYT* (October 19, 1950).

62. *SN* (November 15, 1950).

63. Louis Carroll to A.B. Chandler, letter, April 24, 1950, Chandler Reserve Clause Suits Collection, HOF; *NYT* (April 26, 1950).

64. BR website; Jon Tayler, "30–3: Rangers and Orioles Players From MLB's Biggest Blowout Recall History-Making Game," *SI* (August 22, 2017); *NYT* (August 1, 2018).

65. *SN* (October 11, 1950); SABR website.

66. Peary, *We Played the Game*, p. 140.

Chapter 8

1. USCB, *Provisional Revision of the Projections of the Total Population of the United States, July 1, 1953, to 1960*, pp. 1–2; Hobbs and Stoops, *Demographic Trends in the 20th Century*, p. 13; USCB website.

2. USCB, *Census of Population: 1950, Volume I*, p. 65; *NYT* (October 22, 1950).

3. *NYT* (July 30, 1950).

4. Teaford, *The Twentieth-Century American City*, p. 115; Gibson and Jung, *Historical Census Statistics on Population Totals by Race*, pp. 26–113.

5. Teaford, *The Twentieth-Century American City*, p. 117.

6. Manchester, *The Glory and the Dream*, pp. 777–78.

7. Thomas, *The United States of Suburbia*, p. 40.

8. USCB website; USCB, *Census of Population: 1950, Volume I*, pp. 69–73.

9. Sullivan, *The Diamond in the Bronx*, pp. 112–13.

10. Teaford, *The Rough Road to Renaissance*, pp. 97–98.

11. Jackson, *Crabgrass Frontier*, p. 167; *CT* (February 17, 1940); Teaford, *The Rough Road to Renaissance*, p. 120.

12. Thomas, *The United States of Suburbia*, pp. 37–38.

13. USCB website.

14. USCB, *Census of Population: 1950, Volume I*, p. 74.

15. USCB, *Census of Population: 1960, Volume I*, pp. 100–105; Hobbs and Stoops, *Demographic Trends in the 20th Century*, pp. 18–19.

16. *SN* (May 31, 1950).

17. Fishman, *Bourgeois Utopias*, pp. 116–17.

18. Weil, *A History of New York*, p. 98.

19. USCB, *Census of Population: 1940, Volume I*, p. 32.

20. Weil, *A History of New York*, pp. 166–67; *Brooklyn Eagle* (November 7, 1894, and November 9, 1894); *NYT* (November 9, 1894).

21. Burrows and Wallace, *Gotham*, p. 1235; *Brooklyn Eagle* (December 31, 1897); *NYT* (January 1, 1898).

22. *NYT* (January 1, 1898).

23. Gunther, *Inside U.S.A.*, p. 554.

24. Delsohn, *True Blue*, p. 10.

25. Barber and Creamer, *Rhubarb in the Catbird Seat*, pp. 16–17.

26. *Census of Population: 1950, Volume I*, p. 37; *NYT* (November 22, 1954); Gibson and Jung, *Historical Census Statistics on Population Totals by Race*, pp. 26–113.

27. Golenbock, *Bums*, p. 429.

28. Ibid., p. 428.

29. Erskine OH, HOF.

30. Boxerman and Boxerman, *Ebbets to Veeck to Busch*, p. 13.

31. Delsohn, *True Blue*, p. 12.

32. Paul Hirsch, "Walter O'Malley Was Right," *National Pastime* (2011), p. 81.

33. Walter O'Malley to George McLaughlin, letter, June 18, 1953, WOHD, OSP.

34. Murray, *Jim Murray*, pp. 54–55.

35. Lee Lowenfish, "Forever Blue," *Nine* (Spring 2010), p. 184; Robert Moss, "Triple Play," *Nine* (Fall 2010), p. 97; Murphy, *After Many a Summer*, pp. 34–35; *NYT* (April 12, 1953).

36. Melvin Durslag, "A Visit With Walter O'Malley," *SEP* (May 14, 1960), p. 105.

37. Murphy, *After Many a Summer*, pp. 55–56; D'Antonio, *Forever Blue*, pp. 31–33; Shapiro, *The Last Good Season*, pp. 24–27.

38. Boxerman and Boxerman, *Ebbets to Veeck to Busch*, p. 100.

39. Kahn, *The Era*, pp. 263–64.

40. SABR website.

41. Garvey, Gurnick, and Garvey, *My Bat Boy Days*, pp. 65–66.

42. Kuhn, *Hardball*, p. 23.

43. McCue, *Mover and Shaker*, p. xiii.

44. *LAT* (May 19, 1957).

45. D'Antonio, *Forever Blue*, p. 160.

46. McCue, *Mover and Shaker*, pp. 24–25; Murphy, *After Many a Summer*, pp. 52–53.

47. Kahn, *The Era*, p. 261.

48. Barber and Creamer, *Rhubarb in the Catbird Seat*, p. 279.

49. DeWitt OH, UKY.
50. Parrott, *The Lords of Baseball*, pp. 20–21.
51. D'Antonio, *Forever Blue*, pp. 108–9; *NYT* (November 8, 1951); SABR website; FRBM website.
52. *NYT* (January 9, 1978).
53. Sullivan, *The Dodgers Move West*, pp. 29–31; Breslin, *Branch Rickey*, p. 119.
54. *NYT* (July 11, 1950); D'Antonio, *Forever Blue*, pp. 123–25; Andy McCue, "Two Out of Three Ain't Bad: Branch Rickey, Walter O'Malley, and the Man in the Middle of the Dodger Owners' Partnership," *Nine* (Fall 2005), pp. 41, 45–46.
55. *NYT* (April 11, 1956).
56. Goldstein, *Superstars and Screwballs*, p. 286; Delsohn, *True Blue*, pp. 4–5; *NYT* (September 24, 1950); FRBM website.
57. Jack Mann, "The King of the Jungle," *SI* (April 18, 1966), p. 116.
58. O'Toole, *Branch Rickey in Pittsburgh*, p. 9; Barber and Creamer, *Rhubarb in the Catbird Seat*, p. 281; *NYT* (September 24, 1950).
59. McCue, *Mover and Shaker*, pp. 81–82.
60. Barber and Creamer, *Rhubarb in the Catbird Seat*, p. 281; *NYT* (September 24, 1950).
61. *NYT* (October 27, 1950).
62. *Transcript of Comments by the Board of Directors of Brooklyn Baseball Club Inc.*, undated [1950], Branch Rickey Papers, LOC.
63. Parrott, *The Lords of Baseball*, pp. 30–32.
64. *NYT* (October 25, 1950).
65. Bavasi, *Off the Record*, pp. 40–41.

Chapter 9

1. *SN* (October 19, 1949).
2. Chandler and Trimble, *Heroes, Plain Folks, and Skunks*, p. 238.
3. Dickson, *Leo Durocher*, p. 204.
4. Povich OH, UKY.
5. Chandler and Trimble, *Heroes, Plain Folks, and Skunks*, p. 187.
6. Virtue, *South of the Color Barrier*, p. 175.
7. Golenbock, *The Spirit of St. Louis*, p. 393.
8. *SN* (December 20, 1950, and February 4, 1953); *NYT* (March 13, 1951); Saigh OH, UKY.
9. Marshall, *Baseball's Pivotal Era*, pp. 378–79.
10. Robert Boyle, *Re: Ownership of St. Louis Cardinals, Fred M. Saigh Jr.*, undated [1949], Albert "Happy" Chandler Collection, UKY.
11. Golenbock, *The Spirit of St. Louis*, p. 393.
12. Shapiro, *Bottom of the Ninth*, pp. 70–73; *SN* (February 1, 1945); *NYT* (September 19, 1964).
13. *NYT* (July 9, 1961); Arelo Sederberg and John Lawrence, "Del Webb, the Bashful Barnum," *West* (September 14, 1969), p. 17; SABR website; Sullivan, *The Diamond in the Bronx*, pp. 80–83; Freedman, *Prime Time*, pp. 55–58.
14. Finnerty, *Del Webb*, pp. 33–34, 41–46, 64–66; *SN* (February 1, 1945, and December 3, 1952); "Modern Living: Man on the Cover," *Time* (August 3, 1962).
15. *NYT* (January 27, 1945, and July 9, 1961).
16. *SN* (June 19, 1946).
17. *SN* (November 19, 1952).
18. Shapiro, *Bottom of the Ninth*, pp. 73–75; Denton and Morris, *The Money and the Power*, p. 53; Finnerty, *Del Webb*, pp. 128–29.
19. Arelo Sederberg and John Lawrence, "Del Webb, the Bashful Barnum," *West* (September 14, 1969), p. 19.
20. *SN* (July 16, 1947); Finnerty, *Del Webb*, pp. 130–31; Denton and Morris, *The Money and the Power*, pp. 233–34.
21. Chandler and Trimble, *Heroes, Plain Folks, and Skunks*, pp. 199–201.
22. *NYT* (December 12, 1950).
23. *SN* (February 14, 1951).
24. *NYT* (March 13, 1951).
25. USHR Subcommittee on the Study of Monopoly Power, *Organized Baseball, Hearings, July 30-October 24, 1951*, p. 253.
26. Chandler and Trimble, *Heroes, Plain Folks, and Skunks*, p. 3.
27. Marshall, *Baseball's Pivotal Era*, p. 380.
28. Shapiro, *Bottom of the Ninth*, pp. 74–75.
29. *NYT* (July 6, 1951); *SN* (July 18, 1951).
30. Chandler OH, UKY.
31. Helyar, *Lords of the Realm*, p. 234.
32. *NYT* (July 4, 1951).
33. Dickson, *Bill Veeck*, p. 187.
34. Veeck and Linn, *Veeck—As in Wreck*, p. 219.
35. Fleder, *Great Baseball Writing*, p. 221.
36. *SN* (November 14, 1951).
37. *SN* (July 4, 1951).
38. *SN* (June 27, 1951).
39. *Ibid.*
40. Veeck and Linn, *Veeck—As in Wreck*, pp. 221–22.
41. Eric Robinson, "The Peculiar Professional Baseball Career of Eddie Gaedel," *National Pastime* (2015), pp. 72–73; Dickson, *Bill Veeck*, pp. 191–93.
42. Golenbock, *The Spirit of St. Louis*, p. 330.
43. Veeck and Linn, *Veeck—As in Wreck*, p. 14.
44. *NYT* (August 20, 1951); Dickson, *Bill Veeck*, p. 193.
45. Veeck and Linn, *Veeck—As in Wreck*, p. 23.
46. *NYT* (August 25, 1951); Veeck and Linn, *Veeck—As in Wreck*, pp. 219–21.
47. Veeck and Linn, *Veeck—As in Wreck*, p. 216.
48. *Ibid.*, p. 223.
49. *NYT* (October 9, 1951, and November 30, 1951).
50. *NYT* (October 9, 1951).
51. SABR website.
52. Veeck and Linn, *Veeck—As in Wreck*, p. 231.
53. *NYT* (December 15, 1950); *SN* (April 18, 1951).
54. *NYT* (September 7, 1951).

55. SABR website; *SN* (June 16, 1948, and January 26, 1949).
56. Smith OH, UKY.
57. *NYT* (September 21, 1951); *SN* (September 26, 1951).
58. *NYT* (September 21, 1951, April 15, 1956, and June 20, 1957); *SN* (January 25, 1945); Holtzman, *No Cheering in the Press Box*, pp. 210–11.
59. Holtzman, *No Cheering in the Press Box*, p. 199.
60. *SN* (November 7, 1951).
61. *SN* (October 1, 1952).
62. Veeck and Linn, *Veeck—As in Wreck*, p. 240.
63. Marshall, *Baseball's Pivotal Era*, p. 426.
64. *SN* (April 4, 1951, and June 6, 1951).
65. *SN* (October 10, 1951); Tom Harris, "But the Polo Grounds Belonged to the Giants," *National Pastime* (2008), pp. 70–71.
66. Peary, *We Played the Game*, p. 177.
67. *SN* (December 19, 1951).

Chapter 10

1. Dandridge OH, HOF; Dandridge OH, UKY; *NYT* (May 10, 1987); Ron Briley, "Danny Gardella and Baseball's Reserve Clause: A Working-Class Stiff Blacklisted in Cold War America," *Nine* (Fall 2010), p. 57.
2. *NYT* (May 10, 1987).
3. Ibid.
4. *Minutes of the Joint Meeting of the Major Leagues, December 14, 1949*, Joint Major League Meetings, HOF, pp. 34–36.
5. *NYT* (April 4, 1950, and August 30, 1951); Simon Rottenberg, "The Baseball Players' Labor Market," *Journal of Political Economy* (June 1956), pp. 248–49; White, *Creating the National Pastime*, p. 282; Sullivan, *The Dodgers Move West*, pp. 91–93.
6. *LAT* (November 17, 1950).
7. Wunderlin, *The Papers of Robert A. Taft*, p. 398.
8. Tom Wicker, "Anatomy of the Goldwater Boom," *NYTM* (August 11, 1963), p. 28.
9. *NYT* (November 2, 1950).
10. W. Graham Claytor, Jr., *Preliminary Notes for Commissioner of Baseball Re: Pacific Coast League Proposals*, undated, Albert "Happy" Chandler Collection, UKY.
11. Clarence Rowland and the Presidents of Pacific Coast League teams to Albert Chandler, letter, April 14, 1950, Branch Rickey Papers, LOC.
12. *Minutes of the Joint Meeting of the Major Leagues, July 10, 1950*, Joint Major League Meetings, HOF, pp. 53–58.
13. Ibid., pp. 35–36.
14. *SN* (April 11, 1951).
15. *SN* (May 2, 1951, and August 22, 1951).
16. Quirk and Fort, *Pay Dirt*, p. 157.
17. *Milwaukee Journal* (April 8, 1953).
18. Povletich, *Milwaukee Braves*, pp. 4–5; *SN* (July 13, 1955); *Milwaukee Journal* (October 19, 1951, and May 3, 1952).
19. *Milwaukee Journal* (June 16, 1950).
20. Greater Milwaukee Committee, *Progress Report 1952*, Ballparks and Stadiums Collection, HOF, p. 2.
21. *SN* (November 26, 1952).
22. *Boston Globe* (July 6, 1951).
23. *SN* (May 9, 1951).
24. USHR Antitrust Subcommittee, *Organized Professional Team Sports, Hearings, June 17-August 8, 1957*, p. 1207.
25. *SN* (May 9, 1951); Buhite, *The Continental League*, pp. 79–80; Justia website.
26. Lowe, *The Kid on the Sandlot*, p. 15; Celler, *You Never Leave Brooklyn*, pp. 147–52, 165–66.
27. *NYT* (May 5, 1951).
28. Celler, *You Never Leave Brooklyn*, pp. 30–31, 141–42.
29. *NYT* (March 19, 1960).
30. Stevens, *The Making of a Justice*, pp. 77–78.
31. Lait and Mortimer, *Washington Confidential*, pp. 158–59; Arnold, *Fair Fights and Foul*, pp. 190–91; Kalman, *Abe Fortas*, pp. 184–85.
32. Paul Porter to Ford Frick, Louis Carroll, Ben Fiery, and Herman Tingley, memorandum, January 2, 1952, Celler Antitrust Hearings Collection, HOF.
33. Paul Porter to Emanuel Celler, letter, January 29, 1952, Celler Antitrust Hearings Collection, HOF.
34. *NYT* (July 31, 1951).
35. USHR Subcommittee on the Study of Monopoly Power, *Organized Baseball, Report*, pp. 208–10.
36. *NYT* (July 31, 1951).
37. USHR Subcommittee on the Study of Monopoly Power, *Organized Baseball, Report*, pp. 201–2.
38. *NYT* (October 16, 1951); *SN* (October 24, 1951); *Report of the Major League Steering Committee for Submission to the National and American Leagues, August 27, 1946*, Albert "Happy" Chandler Collection, UKY, pp. 10–13.
39. USHR Subcommittee on the Study of Monopoly Power, *Organized Baseball, Hearings, July 30-October 24, 1951*, p. 1069.
40. Ibid., p. 735.
41. Golenbock, *The Spirit of St. Louis*, p. 337; *NYT* (November 14, 1951); Dickson, *Bill Veeck*, p. 196; FRBM website.
42. *SN* (January 23, 1952).
43. *SN* (August 8, 1951).
44. *SN* (August 15, 1951).
45. *NYT* (August 7, 1951).
46. USHR Subcommittee on the Study of Monopoly Power, *Organized Baseball, Hearings, July 30-October 24, 1951*, p. 531.
47. Ibid.
48. Ibid., p. 1090.
49. Celler, *You Never Leave Brooklyn*, pp. 165–66.
50. Lowe, *The Kid on the Sandlot*, p. 24; *SN*

(May 28, 1952); Ross Davies, "Along Comes the Players Association: The Roots and Rise of Organized Labor in Major League Baseball," *Journal of Legislation and Public Policy* (2013), p. 335.

51. USHR Subcommittee on the Study of Monopoly Power, *Organized Baseball, Report*, pp. 231–32.
52. Banner, *The Baseball Trust*, pp. 110–11.
53. USHR Subcommittee on the Study of Monopoly Power, *Organized Baseball, Report*, p. 84.
54. *SN* (May 28, 1952).
55. Charles Johnson, "The Little Corporation: Professional Baseball in San Francisco, 1953–1955," *Baseball Research Journal* (Summer 2009), p. 106; Steve Treder, "Open Classification: The Pacific Coast League's Drive to Turn Major," *Nine* (Fall 2006), pp. 95–96; *Oakland Tribune* (August 30, 1951); *NYT* (August 30, 1951).
56. *NYT* (November 15, 1951); Steve Treder, "Open Classification: The Pacific Coast League's Drive to Turn Major," *Nine* (Fall 2006), pp. 96–97.
57. *SN* (November 21, 1951).
58. *SN* (December 5, 1951).
59. *Oakland Tribune* (November 15, 1951).
60. *SN* (November 21, 1951).
61. Ford Frick to All Major League Clubs, memorandum, November 5, 1952, American League Papers, HOF; *Minutes of the Joint Meeting of the Major Leagues, December 7, 1952*, Joint Major League Meetings, HOF, p. 74; *NYT* (December 8, 1952).
62. *SN* (December 17, 1952).
63. *Milwaukee Journal* (December 12, 1952).
64. *SN* (December 24, 1952).
65. Louis Perini to Joe Barnes, letter, December 29, 1952, Louis Perini Papers, HOF.

Chapter 11

1. *NYT* (June 24, 1951); USCB, *Historical Statistics of the United States*, p. 796.
2. White, *The Making of the President 1960*, pp. 279–80.
3. MacCambridge, *America's Game*, p. 103.
4. Marc and Thompson, *Prime Time, Prime Movers*, p. 120.
5. Murphy, *After Many a Summer*, p. 97.
6. Manchester, *The Glory and the Dream*, pp. 425, 589–90.
7. *NYT* (June 24, 1951).
8. *NYT* (June 26, 1951); Rader, *In Its Own Image*, pp. 37–39.
9. Manchester, *The Glory and the Dream*, pp. 484–85.
10. Johnson, *Super Spectator and the Electric Lilliputians*, p. 93.
11. *SN* (January 31, 1951).
12. *SN* (December 10, 1952).
13. *LAT* (September 4, 1951, and October 2, 1951); *NYT* (September 5, 1951); MacCambridge, *America's Game*, pp. 70–74.
14. *NYT* (June 6, 1951, and June 16, 1951).
15. *SN* (June 27, 1951).
16. *NYT* (March 4, 1952).
17. Zenith Radio Corporation, *Zenith Presents Facts About Phonevision*, December 1951, American League Papers, HOF; *NYT* (January 2, 1950, February 27, 1952, and June 14, 1953).
18. *NYT* (February 19, 1950, January 2, 1951, and May 20, 1951); FRBM website.
19. *NYT* (January 2, 1951).
20. *NYT* (May 20, 1951).
21. *NYT* (February 27, 1952, and June 14, 1953).
22. *NYT* (June 6, 1955).
23. "O'Malley Favors Pay TV at Both Ends," *Broadcasting Telecasting* (June 20, 1955), p. 87.
24. *SN* (January 28, 1953).
25. *Brooklyn Eagle* (May 8, 1953).
26. Rader, *In Its Own Image*, p. 86; Wilson and Wiggins, *LA Sports*, p. 120; Pro Football Reference website.
27. MacCambridge, *America's Game*, pp. 70–74; Davis, *Papa Bear*, pp. 270–71; FRBM website; Pro Football Reference website.
28. Dale Cressman and Lisa Swenson, "The Pigskin and the Picture Tube: The National Football League's First Full Season on the CBS Television Network," *Journal of Broadcasting and Electronic Media* (September 2007), pp. 486–87; Davis, *Papa Bear*, p. 271.
29. Robert Bellamy, Jr., and James Walker, "Baseball and Television Origins: The Case of the Cubs," *Nine* (Fall 2001), pp. 37–39; James Walker and Robert Bellamy, Jr., "Baseball on Television: The Formative Years, 1939–51," *Nine* (Spring 2003), pp. 8–11; *NYT* (June 26, 1951).
30. *NYT* (February 28, 1951).
31. Al Hirshberg, "He Calls the Signals for Pro Football," *NYTM* (November 23, 1958), pp. 28, 35, 37; Davis, *Rozelle*, pp. 47–49; *NYT* (January 15, 1946).
32. Al Hirshberg, "He Calls the Signals for Pro Football," *NYTM* (November 23, 1958), p. 37; Davis, *Papa Bear*, pp. 199–200.
33. Al Hirshberg, "He Calls the Signals for Pro Football," *NYTM* (November 23, 1958), p. 28.
34. Veeck and Linn, *Veeck—As in Wreck*, pp. 243–44.
35. *NYT* (November 13, 1953); Banner, *The Baseball Trust*, pp. 160–61.
36. *NYT* (November 13, 1953).
37. Herb Graffis, "The Sporting Scene," *Esquire* (September 1944), p. 91; Fenton, *In Your Opinion*, p. 39; Bilstein, *Flight in America*, p. 233.
38. Bilstein, *Flight in America*, pp. 94, 171–72; *NYT* (May 28, 1950).
39. Crouch, *Wings*, pp. 592–94.
40. Bernard DeVoto, "The Easy Chair: Transcontinental Flight," *Harper's* (July 1952), p. 49.
41. Crouch, *Wings*, p. 451.
42. Bilstein, *Flight in America*, pp. 179–80; Crouch, *Wings*, pp. 452–53; *NYT* (October 11, 1953).
43. *NYT* (April 5, 1953, and October 11, 1953).

44. Bavasi, *Off the Record*, pp. 61–62; Snider and Gilbert, *The Duke of Flatbush*, pp. 115–16.
45. Peary, *We Played the Game*, p. 411.
46. Thompson and Rice, *Every Diamond Doesn't Sparkle*, pp. 175–76.
47. Zimniuch, *Baseball's New Frontier*, p. 1; Bilstein, *Flight in America*, pp. 234–35; *SN* (March 31, 1954).
48. *Boston Globe* (June 9, 1957).
49. Oakley, *Baseball's Last Golden Age*, pp. 39–40; *NYT* (March 27, 1954); *SN* (March 31, 1954); O'Toole, *Branch Rickey in Pittsburgh*, pp. 127–28.
50. *NYT* (March 27, 1954).
51. Peary, *We Played the Game*, p. 284.
52. Cerv OH, HOF.
53. *LAT* (February 18, 1954).
54. BR website.
55. *SN* (May 7, 1952).
56. Golenbock, *Dynasty*, pp. 139–42; *SN* (October 15, 1952).
57. Lowry, *Green Cathedrals*, pp. 117–20; *SN* (October 15, 1952).

Chapter 12

1. *SN* (March 25, 1953); Lowry, *Green Cathedrals*, pp. 228–29.
2. Hornsby and Surface, *My War With Baseball*, p. 248.
3. Paige and Lipman, *Maybe I'll Pitch Forever*, p. 252.
4. Dickson, *Bill Veeck*, p. 199.
5. *SN* (June 18, 1952).
6. *NYT* (June 11, 1952).
7. *NYT* (June 12, 1952).
8. Veeck and Linn, *Veeck—As in Wreck*, p. 231.
9. *SN* (March 4, 1959).
10. *SN* (March 25, 1953).
11. Eskenazi, *Bill Veeck*, p. 112.
12. Meany, *Milwaukee's Miracle Braves*, pp. 21–23; *Milwaukee Journal* (March 3, 1953).
13. *NYT* (September 23, 1952).
14. Kaese, *The Boston Braves*, p. 283; *Boston Globe* (November 14, 1952); *SN* (December 10, 1952).
15. *SN* (December 3, 1952).
16. USHR Antitrust Subcommittee, *Organized Professional Team Sports, Hearings, June 17-August 8, 1957*, p. 353; FRBM website.
17. *Boston Globe* (September 22, 1952); *SN* (October 1, 1952).
18. Povletich, *Milwaukee Braves*, pp. 3–4.
19. *Boston Globe* (March 19, 1953).
20. Zimbalist, *Baseball and Billions*, p. 57; David Surdam, "A Tale of Two Gate-Sharing Plans: The National Football League and the National League, 1952–1956," *Southern Economic Journal* (April 2007), pp. 932–36; Stanley Frank and Edgar Munzel, "A Visit With Bill Veeck," *SEP* (June 6, 1959), p. 94; *SN* (February 11, 1953).
21. *SN* (December 17, 1952).
22. Ibid.
23. USHR Antitrust Subcommittee, *Organized Professional Team Sports, Hearings, June 17-August 8, 1957*, p. 353; FRBM website.
24. *NYT* (December 8, 1952).
25. Stanley Frank and Edgar Munzel, "A Visit With Bill Veeck," *SEP* (June 6, 1959), p. 94; Dickson, *Bill Veeck*, p. 207.
26. *SN* (May 16, 1951).
27. Dickson, *Bill Veeck*, p. 207.
28. Veeck and Linn, *Veeck—As in Wreck*, p. 278.
29. *NYT* (December 6, 1952); Veeck and Linn, *Veeck—As in Wreck*, pp. 276–77.
30. *NYT* (December 9, 1952).
31. *NYT* (January 9, 1953, and January 31, 1953); *SN* (February 25, 1953).
32. Veeck and Linn, *Veeck—As in Wreck*, pp. 276–77.
33. Ibid., pp. 271–73.
34. *NYT* (April 23, 1952).
35. *NYT* (April 24, 1952).
36. Saigh OH, UKY.
37. *St. Louis Post-Dispatch* (January 29, 1953).
38. Saigh OH, UKY.
39. Broeg OH, UKY; Saigh OH, UKY.
40. *NYT* (October 25, 1952, January 29, 1953, and February 21, 1953); *SN* (November 5, 1952, November 19, 1952, and March 4, 1953).
41. *St. Louis Post-Dispatch* (February 20, 1953); *SN* (March 4, 1953).
42. Harold Martin, "The Cardinals Strike It Rich," *SEP* (June 27, 1953), pp. 22–23; Boxerman and Boxerman, *Ebbets to Veeck to Busch*, p. 180.
43. Harold Martin, "The Cardinals Strike It Rich," *SEP* (June 27, 1953), pp. 77–78.
44. Halberstam, *October 1964*, p. 19; Helyar, *Lords of the Realm*, pp. 97–98; Harold Martin, "The Cardinals Strike It Rich," *SEP* (June 27, 1953), pp. 22–23.
45. Golenbock, *The Spirit of St. Louis*, p. 399.
46. USS Subcommittee on Antitrust and Monopoly, *Subjecting Professional Baseball Clubs to the Antitrust Laws, Hearings, March 18-May 25, 1954*, p. 104.
47. *St. Louis Post-Dispatch* (February 20, 1953); *NYT* (February 21, 1953); *SN* (February 25, 1953); FRBM website.
48. Golenbock, *The Spirit of St. Louis*, p. 397.
49. *SN* (May 13, 1953).
50. Warren Giles to Louis Perini, telegram, February 21, 1953, Louis Perini Papers, HOF.
51. Meany, *Milwaukee's Miracle Braves*, pp. 26–28; Veeck and Linn, *Veeck—As in Wreck*, p. 280.
52. R.G. Lynch to Emanuel Celler, letter, March 6, 1953, Emanuel Celler Papers, LOC.
53. Marion OH, HOF.
54. Meany, *Milwaukee's Miracle Braves*, pp. 26–28.
55. Veeck and Linn, *Veeck—As in Wreck*, p. 228.
56. *Milwaukee Journal* (March 3, 1953); *Boston Globe* (March 4, 1953); Veeck and Linn, *Veeck—As in Wreck*, p. 280; *SN* (March 11, 1953).

57. *Milwaukee Journal* (March 3, 1953).
58. *St. Louis Post-Dispatch* (March 3, 1953).
59. *Boston Globe* (March 5, 1953).
60. *NYT* (March 5, 1953, and March 6, 1953); *Milwaukee Journal* (March 6, 1953).
61. Kaese, *The Boston Braves*, p. 285.
62. Veeck and Linn, *Veeck—As in Wreck*, pp. 280–81; Lowry, *Green Cathedrals*, pp. 103–4; *Baltimore Sun* (March 17, 1953); Dickson, *Bill Veeck*, p. 209.
63. *NYT* (March 13, 1953).
64. Meany, *Milwaukee's Miracle Braves*, pp. 35–37; *Boston Globe* (March 20, 1953).
65. *NYT* (March 15, 1953).
66. *Boston Globe* (March 16, 1953).
67. *NYT* (March 15, 1953, and March 16, 1953).
68. *Baltimore Sun* (March 14, 1953).
69. *Minutes of the Meeting of the American League, March 16, 1953*, American League Papers, HOF, pp. 1–2.
70. Veeck and Linn, *Veeck—As in Wreck*, pp. 285–86.
71. *Minutes of the Meeting of the American League, March 16, 1953*, American League Papers, HOF, p. 2.
72. *Ibid.*, p. 4.
73. *SN* (March 25, 1953).
74. *NYT* (March 18, 1953).
75. *NYT* (March 19, 1953).
76. Bob Ruzzo, "Braves Field: An Imperfect History of the Perfect Ballpark," *Baseball Research Journal* (Fall 2012), p. 59.
77. Hemond OH, SABR.
78. Povletich, *Milwaukee Braves*, p. 11.
79. *NYT* (April 9, 1953).
80. Peary, *We Played the Game*, p. 214.
81. Mathews and Buege, *Eddie Mathews and the National Pastime*, p. 82.
82. *NYT* (April 9, 1953).
83. Povletich, *Milwaukee Braves*, pp. 15–17; *NYT* (April 15, 1953); Grimm and Prell, *Jolly Cholly's Story*, pp. 198–99.
84. *SN* (April 23, 1953).
85. *SN* (May 13, 1953); SABR website.
86. Peary, *We Played the Game*, p. 243.

Chapter 13

1. Povletich, *Milwaukee Braves*, p. 25.
2. BR website; Gilbert Millstein, "More Brooklyn Than Brooklyn," *NYTM* (July 5, 1953), p. 10.
3. Gilbert Millstein, "More Brooklyn Than Brooklyn," *NYTM* (July 5, 1953), pp. 10, 28.
4. Louis Perini to Walter O'Malley, letter, April 21, 1953, Louis Perini Papers, HOF.
5. *Boston Globe* (August 5, 1954).
6. Louis Perini to Walt Munson, letter, June 1, 1953, Louis Perini Papers, HOF.
7. *NYT* (June 28, 1953, September 24, 1954, and October 29, 1954).
8. BR website; *NYT* (September 28, 1953).
9. *Brooklyn Eagle* (August 27, 1953).
10. Mehl, *The Kansas City Athletics*, p. 26; *NYT* (August 9, 1953).
11. Veeck and Linn, *Veeck—As in Wreck*, p. 292.
12. *Ibid.*, p. 216.
13. *NYT* (April 10, 1953); Golenbock, *The Spirit of St. Louis*, p. 405.
14. *SN* (August 12, 1953); Fleder, *Great Baseball Writing*, p. 228; BR website.
15. *SN* (April 8, 1953).
16. Dickson, *Bill Veeck*, p. 212.
17. USHR Antitrust Subcommittee, *Organized Professional Team Sports, Hearings, June 17-August 8, 1957*, p. 353; FRBM website.
18. Golenbock, *The Spirit of St. Louis*, p. 356.
19. *NYT* (June 10, 1953); *Baltimore Sun* (May 15, 1953).
20. *Baltimore Sun* (June 7, 1953).
21. Dickson, *Bill Veeck*, p. 214; *NYT* (August 19, 1953, and September 10, 1953).
22. *SN* (August 5, 1953).
23. *NYT* (September 16, 1953).
24. *NYT* (September 17, 1953).
25. BR website.
26. Melvin Durslag, "A Visit With Walter O'Malley," *SEP* (May 14, 1960), p. 104.
27. Stout, *The Dodgers*, pp. 224–25; *NYT* (February 28, 1951).
28. Kahn, *The Era*, p. 285.
29. Arthur Daley, "Wait 'Til—This Year," *NYTM* (September 7, 1952), p. 23.
30. *SN* (March 7, 1951).
31. *SN* (May 7, 1952).
32. *SN* (October 29, 1952).
33. Kahn, *The Era*, pp. 311–12.
34. *NYT* (March 6, 1952); Peter Ellsworth, "The Brooklyn Dodgers' Move to Los Angeles: Was Walter O'Malley Solely Responsible?" *Nine* (Fall 2005), pp. 24–25.
35. *Brooklyn Eagle* (December 11, 1953).
36. Robert James, "Field of Liens: Real-Property Development in Baseball," *Baseball Research Journal* (Fall 2010), pp. 116–17; Boxerman and Boxerman, *Ebbets to Veeck to Busch*, pp. 13–14; Peter Ellsworth, "The Brooklyn Dodgers' Move to Los Angeles: Was Walter O'Malley Solely Responsible?" *Nine* (Fall 2005), pp. 25–29.
37. Walter O'Malley to Robert Moses, letter, June 18, 1953, WOHD, OSP.
38. Walter O'Malley to George McLaughlin, letter, June 18, 1953, WOHD, OSP.
39. George McLaughlin to Walter O'Malley, letter, June 22, 1953, WOHD, OSP.
40. Robert Moses to Walter O'Malley, letter, June 22, 1953, WOHD, OSP.
41. Walter O'Malley to Robert Moses, letter, October 28, 1953, WOHD, OSP.
42. Robert Moses to Walter O'Malley, letter, November 2, 1953, WOHD, OSP.
43. Walter O'Malley to Frank Schroth, letter, February 11, 1954, WOHD, OSP.
44. BR website; Stout, *The Dodgers*, p. 197.

45. *Brooklyn Eagle* (August 4, 1954).
46. *NYT* (September 28, 1953); Dickson, *Bill Veeck*, p. 214.
47. Veeck and Linn, *Veeck—As in Wreck*, p. 299.
48. *Baltimore Sun* (September 27, 1953).
49. *Baltimore Sun* (September 28, 1953); *NYT* (September 28, 1953).
50. *Baltimore Sun* (September 28, 1953).
51. Ibid.
52. *NYT* (September 28, 1953).
53. Veeck and Linn, *Veeck—As in Wreck*, pp. 300–301.
54. *Minutes of the Meeting of the American League, September 29, 1953*, American League Papers, HOF, pp. 1–2.
55. *LAT* (September 29, 1953, and September 30, 1953); *SN* (October 7, 1953); *NYT* (September 30, 1953).
56. Dickson, *Bill Veeck*, p. 216; *NYT* (September 30, 1953); FRBM website; *Baltimore Sun* (September 30, 1953).
57. Veeck and Linn, *Veeck—As in Wreck*, pp. 304–5.
58. *SN* (October 7, 1953).
59. Dickson, *Bill Veeck*, p. 209; *SN* (October 21, 1953); *NYT* (December 11, 1953).
60. *NYT* (September 30, 1953).
61. Joseph Cairnes to Louis Perini, letter, November 4, 1953, Louis Perini Papers, HOF.
62. Gilbert Millstein, "Let's Back Up Them Birds," *NYTM* (May 9, 1954), p. 37; Lowry, *Green Cathedrals*, pp. 103–5.
63. Thompson and Beard, *Ain't the Beer Cold!*, p. 173.
64. Peary, *We Played the Game*, p. 610.
65. Ibid., p. 271.
66. Thorn, Palmer, Gershman, and Pietrusza, *Total Baseball*, p. 2208; BR website.
67. Gilbert Millstein, "Let's Back Up Them Birds," *NYTM* (May 9, 1954), p. 34.

Chapter 14

1. Kelley, *Baseball's Biggest Blunder*, pp. 9–11; *SN* (February 8, 1950); *LAT* (May 10, 2019).
2. *SN* (February 8, 1950).
3. *LAT* (May 10, 2019).
4. Kelley, *Baseball's Biggest Blunder*, pp. 9–11.
5. Peary, *We Played the Game*, p. 123.
6. *SN* (November 11, 1953).
7. Armour, *Joe Cronin*, pp. 203–5; Nowlin, *Tom Yawkey*, p. 157; *SN* (June 25, 1952).
8. *SN* (June 11, 1952).
9. *SN* (December 17, 1952); Armour, *Joe Cronin*, pp. 205–7.
10. *SN* (March 11, 1953, and July 8, 1953).
11. *SN* (March 11, 1953).
12. Kelley, *Baseball's Biggest Blunder*, pp. 27–30.
13. Ibid., pp. 34–36.
14. Tom Verducci, "Vin Scully," *SI* (May 16, 2016), pp. 53–54.
15. Koufax and Linn, *Koufax*, p. 89.
16. Brown OH, SABR.
17. *NYT* (August 29, 1946); *SN* (September 2, 1953, and December 9, 1953); FRBM website.
18. *NYT* (August 23, 1953).
19. Ross Davies, "Along Comes the Players Association: The Roots and Rise of Organized Labor in Major League Baseball," *Journal of Legislation and Public Policy* (2013), p. 336.
20. Voigt, *American Baseball, Volume III*, p. 207; *SN* (December 9, 1953).
21. *SN* (December 16, 1953).
22. Lowenfish and Lupien, *The Imperfect Diamond*, p. 188; *SN* (February 24, 1954, March 31, 1954, and April 21, 1954); Miller, *A Whole Different Ball Game*, p. 8.
23. *SN* (February 13, 1957).
24. USHR Antitrust Subcommittee, *Organized Professional Team Sports, Hearings, June 17-August 8, 1957*, pp. 1311–12.
25. Dworkin, *Owners Versus Players*, p. 27; Duquette, *Regulating the National Pastime*, p. 55; Zimbalist, *Baseball and Billions*, pp. 17–18; Ross Davies, "Along Comes the Players Association: The Roots and Rise of Organized Labor in Major League Baseball," *Journal of Legislation and Public Policy* (2013), p. 337.
26. *SN* (July 21, 1954).
27. *SN* (April 20, 1955).
28. Dworkin, *Owners Versus Players*, p. 28.
29. USHR Antitrust Subcommittee, *Organized Professional Team Sports, Hearings, June 17-August 8, 1957*, pp. 1252–53.
30. Marshall, *Baseball's Pivotal Era*, pp. 64–65.
31. Holtzman, *No Cheering in the Press Box*, p. 203.
32. McCue, *Mover and Shaker*, p. 59.
33. USHR Subcommittee on the Study of Monopoly Power, *Organized Baseball, Hearings, July 30–October 24, 1951*, p. 1023.
34. Emanuel Celler to J.G. Taylor Spink, letter, August 28, 1953, Emanuel Celler Papers, LOC.
35. *SN* (June 20, 1951, December 17, 1952, and March 4, 1953).
36. *SN* (November 14, 1951).
37. Justia website; *NYT* (November 10, 1953); *SN* (October 3, 1951, October 14, 1953, and October 21, 1953).
38. Kuhn, *Hardball*, pp. 19–20.
39. Banner, *The Baseball Trust*, p. 114.
40. *SN* (October 21, 1953).
41. Warren Giles to All National League Clubs, memorandum, October 15, 1953, Louis Perini Papers, HOF.
42. *NYT* (November 10, 1953); *SN* (November 18, 1953); Lowe, *The Kid on the Sandlot*, p. 29.
43. Justia website.
44. *NYT* (November 10, 1953).
45. USS Subcommittee on Antitrust and Monopoly, *Organized Professional Team Sports, Hearings, July 9–31, 1958*, p. 177.
46. USS Subcommittee on Antitrust and

Monopoly, *Organized Professional Team Sports, Hearings, July 28–31, 1959*, p. 69.
   47. *SN* (March 4, 1953).
   48. USS Subcommittee on Antitrust and Monopoly, *Organized Professional Team Sports, Hearings, July 9–31, 1958*, p. 296.
   49. *SN* (April 3, 1957).
   50. Bryant, *The Last Hero*, p. 63; BR website.
   51. BR website.
   52. *SN* (April 21, 1954); Peary, *We Played the Game*, p. 283.
   53. Steve Treder, "Paul Richards: The Wizard of Waxahachie," *Nine* (Spring 2007), pp. 5–8; SABR website; *SN* (September 22, 1954, and November 24, 1954); *Baltimore Sun* (October 29, 2003).

Chapter 15

   1. *SN* (September 8, 1954); BR website.
   2. Povletich, *Milwaukee Braves*, p. 50.
   3. *NYT* (March 15, 1953).
   4. *Boston Globe* (April 17, 1972).
   5. *SN* (July 13, 1955).
   6. BR website.
   7. Harry Paxton, "The Philadelphia A's Last Stand," *SEP* (June 12, 1954), p. 133; Robert Warrington, "Departure Without Dignity: The Athletics Leave Philadelphia," *Baseball Research Journal* (Fall 2010), pp. 100–101; Peterson, *The Kansas City Athletics*, p. 25.
   8. Harry Paxton, "The Philadelphia A's Last Stand," *SEP* (June 12, 1954), p. 31.
   9. Dykes and Dexter, *You Can't Steal First Base*, p. 109.
   10. *Philadelphia Inquirer* (July 9, 1954).
   11. *SN* (August 11, 1954).
   12. *SN* (August 4, 1954).
   13. *SN* (August 11, 1954).
   14. Mehl, *The Kansas City Athletics*, p. 69.
   15. Peterson, *The Kansas City Athletics*, pp. 8–9; Robert Warrington, "Departure Without Dignity: The Athletics Leave Philadelphia," *Baseball Research Journal* (Fall 2010), p. 103; Arthur Mann, "How to Buy a Ball Club for Peanuts," *SEP* (April 9, 1955), pp. 25, 106–7; *SN* (November 17, 1954).
   16. USHR Antitrust Subcommittee, *Organized Professional Team Sports, Hearings, June 17-August 8, 1957*, pp. 2084–85; Topping Family Archives, HOF; *NYT* (December 18, 1953).
   17. Arthur Mann, "How to Buy a Ball Club for Peanuts," *SEP* (April 9, 1955), p. 106; *NYT* (December 18, 1953).
   18. Peterson, *The Kansas City Athletics*, pp. 10–11.
   19. *NYT* (March 10, 1960).
   20. Mehl, *The Kansas City Athletics*, pp. 48–50; *NYT* (August 4, 1954, and October 13, 1954); Veeck and Linn, *Veeck—As in Wreck*, p. 267; Peterson, *The Kansas City Athletics*, p. 38.
   21. "Philadelphia Story," *SI* (October 25, 1954), p. 13.
   22. *NYT* (September 28, 1954, and September 29, 1954).
   23. Robert Warrington, "Departure Without Dignity: The Athletics Leave Philadelphia," *Baseball Research Journal* (Fall 2010), pp. 103–4.
   24. USCB, *Census of Population: 1950, Volume I*, p. 74; Robinson, *Canadian Urban Growth Trends*, p. 35.
   25. *Philadelphia Inquirer* (September 29, 1954).
   26. *SN* (November 17, 1954).
   27. *Minutes of the Meeting of the American League, October 12, 1954*, American League Papers, HOF, pp. 1–3.
   28. *Kansas City Times* (October 13, 1954).
   29. *Minutes of the Meeting of the American League, October 12, 1954*, American League Papers, HOF, pp. 4–5.
   30. *NYT* (October 14, 1954); Veeck and Linn, *The Hustler's Handbook*, p. 70; Robert Warrington, "Departure Without Dignity: The Athletics Leave Philadelphia," *Baseball Research Journal* (Fall 2010), pp. 103–5.
   31. *Minutes of the Meeting of the American League, October 12, 1954*, American League Papers, HOF, p. 11.
   32. *Kansas City Times* (October 13, 1954).
   33. *Philadelphia Inquirer* (October 15, 1954).
   34. *Philadelphia Inquirer* (October 18, 1954); *NYT* (October 18, 1954).
   35. *Philadelphia Inquirer* (October 19, 1954).
   36. *NYT* (October 18, 1954).
   37. Robert Warrington, "Departure Without Dignity: The Athletics Leave Philadelphia," *Baseball Research Journal* (Fall 2010), pp. 106–7; Macht, *The Grand Old Man of Baseball*, pp. 557–59; *Philadelphia Inquirer* (October 29, 1954).
   38. *Philadelphia Inquirer* (October 28, 1954).
   39. *Kansas City Times* (October 29, 1954).
   40. Robert Warrington, "Departure Without Dignity: The Athletics Leave Philadelphia," *Baseball Research Journal* (Fall 2010), p. 108.
   41. *Philadelphia Inquirer* (October 31, 1954).
   42. *Philadelphia Inquirer* (November 5, 1954); *NYT* (November 5, 1954).
   43. *NYT* (November 9, 1954); *Philadelphia Inquirer* (November 9, 1954).
   44. USHR Antitrust Subcommittee, *Organized Professional Team Sports, Hearings, June 17-August 8, 1957*, p. 2085.
   45. *Philadelphia Inquirer* (November 9, 1954).
   46. *SN* (February 2, 1955); *NYT* (January 21, 1955).
   47. *SN* (February 2, 1955).
   48. Thorn, Palmer, Gershman, and Pietrusza, *Total Baseball*, pp. 99–100, 2204; Kuklick, *To Every Thing a Season*, p. 124; Peterson, *The Kansas City Athletics*, p. 28; *NYT* (December 11, 1954).
   49. *NYT* (November 9, 1954).
   50. Mehl, *The Kansas City Athletics*, p. 132; Peterson, *The Kansas City Athletics*, pp. 45–47.
   51. Peterson, *The Kansas City Athletics*, p. 61.

52. *NYT* (April 12, 1955, June 27, 1955, July 21, 1955, and February 9, 1956).
53. Peterson, *The Kansas City Athletics*, p. 50.
54. *NYT* (March 23, 1955); Sullivan, *The Diamond in the Bronx*, p. 87; *SN* (March 30, 1955).
55. USHR Antitrust Subcommittee, *Organized Professional Team Sports, Hearings, June 17-August 8, 1957*, pp. 2089–90.
56. *Ibid.*, p. 2099.
57. Robert Warrington, "Departure Without Dignity: The Athletics Leave Philadelphia," *Baseball Research Journal* (Fall 2010), pp. 111–12; Sullivan, *The Diamond in the Bronx*, pp. 88–89.
58. Boudreau and Schneider, *Covering All the Bases*, p. 165.
59. USHR Antitrust Subcommittee, *Organized Professional Team Sports, Hearings, June 17-August 8, 1957*, p. 2082.
60. BR website; SABR website.
61. *Kansas City Times* (December 12, 1959).
62. BR website; *NYT* (October 21, 1959); *LAT* (September 25, 1957).
63. *SN* (July 8, 1959).

Chapter 16

1. Veeck and Linn, *The Hustler's Handbook*, p. 304.
2. *NYT* (November 10, 1954).
3. USCB, *Census of Population: 1960, Volume I*, pp. 105, 117; Statistics Canada website; Robinson, *Canadian Urban Growth Trends*, p. 35.
4. American League Realignment Committee, *Is a Ten-Club League Practicable?*, January 30, 1955, American League Papers, HOF.
5. *NYT* (December 9, 1954).
6. *SN* (November 21, 1951).
7. Steve Treder, "Open Classification: The Pacific Coast League's Drive to Turn Major," *Nine* (Fall 2006), pp. 97–99.
8. *LAT* (September 15, 1950).
9. *LAT* (October 18, 1953).
10. Holtzman and Vass, *Baseball, Chicago Style*, pp. 252–54; Golenbock, *Wrigleyville*, p. 269.
11. Golenbock, *Wrigleyville*, pp. 174–75.
12. William Barry Furlong, "P.K.," *Chicago Tribune Magazine* (October 12, 1969), p. 27.
13. *Ibid.*
14. Golenbock, *Wrigleyville*, pp. 239–40.
15. William Barry Furlong, "P.K.," *Chicago Tribune Magazine* (October 12, 1969), p. 28.
16. SABR website; *NYT* (January 21, 1942).
17. *SN* (February 20, 1952).
18. Chandler OH, UKY.
19. *NYT* (July 19, 1953).
20. *NYT* (April 4, 1950); *SN* (December 5, 1951); Zingg and Medeiros, *Runs, Hits, and an Era*, p. 142.
21. *LAT* (October 28, 1953).
22. *SN* (October 28, 1953); *LAT* (October 8, 1953, and October 18, 1953).
23. *SN* (October 28, 1953).
24. *SN* (November 4, 1953); USCB, *Census of Population: 1950, Volume I*, p. 74.
25. *SN* (November 4, 1953); *LAT* (November 17, 1953).
26. *LAT* (October 31, 1953).
27. *LAT* (October 27, 1953).
28. *NYT* (October 20, 1953).
29. Marshall, *Baseball's Pivotal Era*, p. 261; *LAT* (December 1, 1953).
30. *LAT* (February 7, 1954).
31. Dewey and Acocella, *The Ball Clubs*, p. 110; Lowry, *Green Cathedrals*, pp. 172–73; *LAT* (November 29, 1953).
32. *SN* (December 29, 1954).
33. James Gordon, "Los Angeles' Wrigley Field: 'The Finest Edifice in the United States,'" *National Pastime* (2011), p. 111; *NYT* (December 17, 1954); FRBM website; *LAT* (December 2, 1953).
34. *LAT* (February 5, 1954, and February 7, 1954); FRBM website.
35. *LAT* (February 5, 1954).
36. Stanley Frank and Edgar Munzel, "A Visit With Bill Veeck," *SEP* (June 6, 1959), p. 94.
37. *NYT* (August 2, 1953); Kevin Nelson, "Los Angeles Dodgers vs. San Francisco Giants, April 1958," *California History* (Winter 2005), p. 49.
38. *NYT* (October 28, 1954); *SN* (November 10, 1954); *San Francisco Chronicle* (September 22, 2000).
39. *SN* (November 10, 1954).
40. *NYT* (November 4, 1954).
41. *SN* (November 10, 1954).
42. *NYT* (November 16, 1954).
43. Zingg and Medeiros, *Runs, Hits, and an Era*, pp. 110–12; *LAT* (September 20, 1954, and September 21, 1954); Charles Johnson, "The Little Corporation: Professional Baseball in San Francisco, 1953–1955," *Baseball Research Journal* (Summer 2009), pp. 108–10.
44. *LAT* (November 19, 1954).
45. *LAT* (February 6, 1955).
46. D'Antonio, *Forever Blue*, pp. 190–91; Dickson, *Bill Veeck*, p. 220.
47. Dickson, *Bill Veeck*, p. 220.
48. *LAT* (February 4, 1955); *SN* (February 9, 1955).
49. *LAT* (February 4, 1955).
50. *LAT* (September 22, 1954).
51. *LAT* (February 6, 1955).
52. Charles Johnson, "The Little Corporation: Professional Baseball in San Francisco, 1953–1955," *Baseball Research Journal* (Summer 2009), pp. 109–10; *LAT* (December 3, 1953, and December 4, 1953).
53. Veeck and Linn, *Veeck—As in Wreck*, p. 372.
54. *LAT* (December 17, 1954, and June 1, 1955); *NYT* (June 2, 1955).
55. *LAT* (December 17, 1954).
56. *Baltimore Sun* (September 28, 1953).
57. *LAT* (September 30, 1953).
58. *LAT* (December 9, 1954).
59. Peary, *We Played the Game*, p. 241; *SN* (April 6, 1955).

60. BR website; Koufax and Linn, *Koufax*, p. 89.
61. *SN* (October 12, 1955); Goodwin, *Wait Till Next Year*, pp. 212–14.
62. *NYT* (October 20, 1955); *SN* (January 24, 1951); Branch Rickey, memorandum, undated [1959], Branch Rickey Papers, LOC.

Chapter 17

1. Halberstam, *October 1964*, pp. 57–58.
2. Mark Armour, "The Effects of Integration, 1947–1986," *Baseball Research Journal* (Fall 2007), pp. 53–57; SABR website; BR website.
3. Golenbock, *Dynasty*, p. 206.
4. D'Antonio, *Forever Blue*, p. 105.
5. Halberstam, *October 1964*, pp. 54–55.
6. SABR website; Nowlin, *Tom Yawkey*, p. 112; BR website.
7. Nowlin, *Tom Yawkey*, p. 184.
8. SABR website; The Undefeated website; *SN* (July 28, 1954); Rudd and Fischler, *The Sporting Life*, p. 123.
9. Peary, *We Played the Game*, p. 91.
10. Drysdale and Verdi, *Once a Bum, Always a Dodger*, pp. 3–4.
11. Roseboro and Libby, *Glory Days With the Dodgers and Other Days With Others*, p. 98.
12. BR website; Peter Ellsworth, "The Brooklyn Dodgers' Move to Los Angeles: Was Walter O'Malley Solely Responsible?" *Nine* (Fall 2005), p. 23.
13. Thompson and Rice, *Every Diamond Doesn't Sparkle*, pp. 144–45.
14. *Brooklyn Eagle* (January 18, 1955).
15. Breslin, *Branch Rickey*, p. 63; Goldblatt, *The Giants and the Dodgers*, p. 136.
16. Bavasi, *Off the Record*, p. 77.
17. Kahn, *The Era*, p. 328.
18. USCB, *Census of Population: 1950, Volume III*; USCB, *Census of Population: 1960, Series PHC(1)*; USCB, *Census of Population: 1970, Series PHC(1)*.
19. Rickey and Riger, *The American Diamond*, p. 166.
20. *Brooklyn Eagle* (January 28, 1955).
21. Goldstein, *Superstars and Screwballs*, pp. 322–23.
22. "Walter in Wonderland," *Time* (April 28, 1958).
23. Walter O'Malley to Robert Moses, letter, December 17, 1953, WOHD, OSP.
24. Walter O'Malley, memorandum, April 19, 1955, WOHD, OSP.
25. Walter O'Malley to Frank Schroth, letter, February 11, 1954, WOHD, OSP.
26. *NYT* (November 17, 1954).
27. *LAT* (November 23, 1954).
28. Bavasi, *Off the Record*, p. 78.
29. Walter O'Malley to Buckminster Fuller, letter, May 26, 1955, WOHD, OSP.
30. Walter O'Malley to Frank Schroth, letter, June 17, 1952, WOHD, OSP.
31. Caro, *The Power Broker*, p. 830.
32. Weil, *A History of New York*, p. 196; Shapiro, *The Last Good Season*, p. 33; Podair, *City of Dreams*, pp. 13–14.
33. Caro, *Working*, pp. 31–34.
34. Caro, *The Power Broker*, p. 1136; McCue, *Mover and Shaker*, pp. 130–31; Murphy, *After Many a Summer*, p. 58.
35. Caro, *The Power Broker*, p. 1023.
36. *NYT* (November 6, 1957, and February 13, 1991); Teaford, *The Rough Road to Renaissance*, p. 138.
37. Murphy, *After Many a Summer*, pp. 131–32.
38. *NYT* (February 13, 1991).
39. Caro, *The Power Broker*, p. 799.
40. *Ibid.*, p. 804.
41. Sullivan, *The Dodgers Move West*, pp. 50–51; Peter Ellsworth, "The Brooklyn Dodgers' Move to Los Angeles: Was Walter O'Malley Solely Responsible?" *Nine* (Fall 2005), pp. 25–29; Robert James, "Field of Liens: Real-Property Development in Baseball," *Baseball Research Journal* (Fall 2010), p. 118.
42. Robert Moses to Walter O'Malley, letter, June 22, 1953, WOHD, OSP.
43. Robert Moses to Walter O'Malley, letter, November 2, 1953, WOHD, OSP.
44. Peter Ellsworth, "The Brooklyn Dodgers' Move to Los Angeles: Was Walter O'Malley Solely Responsible?" *Nine* (Fall 2005), p. 29.
45. Shapiro, *The Last Good Season*, p. 71; Sullivan, *The Dodgers Move West*, pp. 47–48.
46. Robert Moses to Walter O'Malley, letter, August 15, 1955, WOHD, OSP.
47. *NYT* (August 17, 1955); John Burbridge, "The Brooklyn Dodgers in Jersey City," *Baseball Research Journal* (Summer 2010), pp. 19–20.
48. Thorn, Palmer, Gershman, and Pietrusza, *Total Baseball*, p. 94; Lowry, *Green Cathedrals*, pp. 162–63; John Burbridge, "The Brooklyn Dodgers in Jersey City," *Baseball Research Journal* (Summer 2010), pp. 21–22; *NYT* (August 23, 1955).
49. USHR Antitrust Subcommittee, *Organized Professional Team Sports, Hearings, June 17–August 8, 1957*, p. 1857.
50. *SN* (January 4, 1956).
51. Koppett, *The New York Mets*, p. 17.
52. *NYT* (August 18, 1955).
53. *Ibid.*
54. *NYT* (August 20, 1955).
55. *NYT* (August 20, 1955, and August 25, 1955).
56. *NYT* (November 2, 1955).
57. Shapiro, *The Last Good Season*, pp. 74–75; *NYT* (August 23, 1955).
58. *NYT* (August 23, 1955).
59. *LAT* (May 27, 1953, May 28, 1953, April 7, 1957, and May 14, 2016); D'Antonio, *Forever Blue*, p. 192.
60. *LAT* (May 28, 1953).
61. Wyman OH, UCB.
62. Shapiro, *The Last Good Season*, pp. 307–8.

63. *LAT* (April 7, 1957).
64. *NYT* (August 23, 1955); Wyman OH, UCB; *LAT* (May 14, 2016).
65. Rosalind Wyman to Walter O'Malley, letter, September 1, 1955, WOHD, OSP.
66. Walter O'Malley to Rosalind Wyman, letter, September 7, 1955, WOHD, OSP.
67. Charles Johnson, "The Little Corporation: Professional Baseball in San Francisco, 1953–1955," *Baseball Research Journal* (Summer 2009), pp. 113–15; *LAT* (November 29, 1955); *Boston Globe* (December 4, 1955).
68. *Boston Globe* (December 1, 1955).
69. Nowlin, *Tom Yawkey*, p. 188.
70. USHR Subcommittee on the Study of Monopoly Power, *Organized Baseball, Hearings, July 30-October 24, 1951*, p. 531.
71. *NYT* (October 29, 1955).
72. *SN* (November 2, 1955); BR website; Deveaux, *The Washington Senators*, p. 192.
73. *SN* (May 30, 1956).
74. Kerr, *Calvin*, pp. 47–48.
75. Rudd and Fischler, *The Sporting Life*, pp. 138–39.
76. *NYT* (October 1, 1955, and November 2, 1955); Stout, *The Dodgers*, pp. 215–17; "Dodgers' Dome (Cont.)," *SI* (November 28, 1955), p. 16.
77. *SN* (December 7, 1955).
78. *NYT* (October 6, 1955).

Chapter 18

1. BR website.
2. *NYT* (August 19, 1955).
3. *NYT* (April 20, 1956); BR website.
4. Hodges and Hirshberg, *My Giants*, p. 135.
5. Hirsch, *Willie Mays*, p. 257.
6. Angell, *Five Seasons*, p. 262; *NYT* (July 18, 1957); Robert Shaplen, "The Lonely, Loyal Mr. Stoneham," *SI* (May 5, 1958), p. 72; Dewey and Acocella, *The Ball Clubs*, pp. 353–62; Graham, *The New York Giants*, pp. 220–21.
7. Graham, *The New York Giants*, pp. 108–9.
8. Marshall, *Baseball's Pivotal Era*, p. 190; Robert Shaplen, "The Lonely, Loyal Mr. Stoneham," *SI* (May 5, 1958), p. 75; Steve Treder, "A Legacy of What-Ifs: Horace Stoneham and the Integration of the Giants," *Nine* (Spring 2002), pp. 71–72.
9. Schott and Peters, *The Giants Encyclopedia*, p. 91.
10. Graham, *The New York Giants*, pp. 222–23; Durocher and Linn, *Nice Guys Finish Last*, p. 297; Angell, *Five Seasons*, p. 265; Dark and Underwood, *When in Doubt, Fire the Manager*, p. 72.
11. Hirsch, *Willie Mays*, p. 84.
12. Angell, *Five Seasons*, p. 271.
13. Veeck and Linn, *The Hustler's Handbook*, p. 96.
14. Durocher and Linn, *Nice Guys Finish Last*, pp. 288–89.
15. *SN* (December 10, 1952), emphasis added.
16. Robert Shaplen, "The Lonely, Loyal Mr. Stoneham," *SI* (May 5, 1958), p. 76.
17. USHR Antitrust Subcommittee, *Organized Professional Team Sports, Hearings, June 17-August 8, 1957*, p. 353.
18. *NYT* (August 19, 1955, and March 2, 1958).
19. Veeck and Linn, *Veeck—As in Wreck*, p. 104.
20. Mann, *Branch Rickey*, p. 286; FRBM website; O'Toole, *Branch Rickey in Pittsburgh*, p. 166; *NYT* (October 20, 1955).
21. *NYT* (August 23, 1954).
22. *NYT* (June 4, 1956).
23. *SN* (August 11, 1954).
24. *NYT* (January 15, 1954); O'Toole, *Branch Rickey in Pittsburgh*, p. 156.
25. Shapiro, *Bottom of the Ninth*, pp. 31–33; *SN* (December 1, 1954); Holtzman, *The Jerome Holtzman Baseball Reader*, pp. 19–20; O'Toole, *Branch Rickey in Pittsburgh*, p. 75.
26. Polner, *Branch Rickey*, p. 232.
27. Peary, *We Played the Game*, p. 226.
28. Thomas OH, HOF.
29. Kiner and Peary, *Baseball Forever*, p. 106; *NYT* (March 16, 1953, and June 5, 1953).
30. O'Toole, *Branch Rickey in Pittsburgh*, p. 97.
31. *NYT* (June 5, 1953).
32. Polner, *Branch Rickey*, p. 240.
33. Veeck and Linn, *Veeck—As in Wreck*, p. 307.
34. Dickson, *Bill Veeck*, p. 221; *SN* (January 11, 1956, and April 25, 1956).
35. *SN* (August 14, 1957).
36. SABR website; *Detroit News* (September 1, 2018); *NYT* (October 27, 1955); *Detroit Free Press* (July 12, 1956).
37. *Detroit Free Press* (July 1, 1956).
38. *Detroit Free Press* (July 4, 1956, and July 10, 1956); *NYT* (October 27, 1955, and July 4, 1956).
39. *Detroit Free Press* (July 17, 1956); *NYT* (July 17, 1956); *SN* (February 4, 1959).
40. *SN* (July 25, 1956).
41. Veeck and Linn, *Veeck—As in Wreck*, p. 313.
42. Dickson, *Bill Veeck*, p. 223.
43. *SN* (August 14, 1957); SABR website; Steve Treder, "A Legacy of What-Ifs: Horace Stoneham and the Integration of the Giants," *Nine* (Spring 2002), pp. 71–72.
44. Angell, *Five Seasons*, p. 269.
45. Thorn, Palmer, Gershman, and Pietrusza, *Total Baseball*, pp. 97–98; Lowry, *Green Cathedrals*, pp. 195–201; BR website.
46. Pro Football Reference website; FRBM website; *SN* (February 8, 1956).
47. *NYT* (January 28, 1956); *SN* (February 8, 1956).
48. *NYT* (January 28, 1956).
49. *NYT* (November 23, 1955).
50. *NYT* (November 26, 1955, and January 31, 1956); *SN* (February 8, 1956, and February 22, 1956).
51. Murphy, *After Many a Summer*, p. 148;

NYT (March 5, 1956, March 6, 1956, and April 5, 1956).
52. NYT (April 11, 1956).
53. NYT (May 13, 1956, May 15, 1956, and May 23, 1956).
54. NYT (May 23, 1956).
55. *Minneapolis Star* (April 24, 1956, and April 25, 1956); NYT (April 13, 1946); BR website.
56. *Minneapolis Star* (April 24, 1956).
57. *Minneapolis Star* (May 19, 1956); SN (May 30, 1956).
58. SN (June 6, 1956).
59. BR website; SN (October 10, 1956); Povletich, *Milwaukee Braves*, pp. 61–63.
60. SN (October 17, 1956, and October 24, 1956).
61. Walter O'Malley to Jackie Robinson and Rachel Robinson, letter, December 14, 1956, Jackie Robinson Papers, LOC.

Chapter 19

1. NYT (January 12, 1956, and February 6, 1956); Sullivan, *The Dodgers Move West*, p. 72.
2. Walter O'Malley, press statement, February 2, 1956, WOHD, OSP.
3. NYT (February 29, 1956).
4. NYT (February 7, 1956).
5. *Minutes of the Stockholders Meeting of Brooklyn Baseball Club Inc., January 16, 1956*, WOHD, OSP.
6. NYT (April 22, 1956).
7. John Lardner, "Would It Still Be Brooklyn?" *NYTM* (February 26, 1956), p. 78.
8. NYT (April 20, 1956); BR website.
9. John Burbridge, "The Brooklyn Dodgers in Jersey City," *Baseball Research Journal* (Summer 2010), p. 21; Lowry, *Green Cathedrals*, pp. 162–63.
10. John Burbridge, "The Brooklyn Dodgers in Jersey City," *Baseball Research Journal* (Summer 2010), p. 22.
11. NYT (February 7, 1956).
12. Peter Ellsworth, "The Brooklyn Dodgers' Move to Los Angeles: Was Walter O'Malley Solely Responsible?" *Nine* (Fall 2005), pp. 27–29; D'Antonio, *Forever Blue*, p. 247.
13. NYT (January 12, 1956); Podair, *City of Dreams*, p. 16.
14. NYT (March 9, 1956).
15. Peter Ellsworth, "The Brooklyn Dodgers' Move to Los Angeles: Was Walter O'Malley Solely Responsible?" *Nine* (Fall 2005), pp. 30–32; D'Antonio, *Forever Blue*, p. 228; NYT (December 29, 1956).
16. Shapiro, *The Last Good Season*, p. 193.
17. NYT (December 29, 1956).
18. NYT (July 25, 1956); FRBM website; Sullivan, *The Dodgers Move West*, p. 75.
19. Sullivan, *The Dodgers Move West*, pp. 78–79.
20. SN (October 17, 1956).
21. USS Subcommittee on Fiscal Affairs, *Construction, Maintenance, and Operation by the Armory Board of the District of Columbia of a Stadium in the District of Columbia, Hearings, July 1, 1957*, pp. 4–9; SN (August 15, 1956).
22. SN (August 15, 1956).
23. SN (September 26, 1956); LAT (October 5, 1956, and October 6, 1956).
24. LAT (October 5, 1956).
25. SN (October 17, 1956); NYT (September 5, 1958).
26. American Presidency Project of the University of California-Santa Barbara website.
27. Holtzman, *The Jerome Holtzman Baseball Reader*, p. 1.
28. Kevin Hennessy, "Calvin Griffith: The Ups and Downs of the Last Family-Owned Baseball Team," *National Pastime* (2012), p. 63; SABR website; SN (August 13, 1952).
29. Holtzman, *The Jerome Holtzman Baseball Reader*, p. 2; Gary Smith, "A Lingering Vestige of Yesterday," *SI* (April 4, 1983), p. 107; Paul Levy, "The Late Innings of Calvin Griffith," *Minneapolis Star and Tribune Sunday Magazine* (July 12, 1987), p. 7.
30. Gary Smith, "A Lingering Vestage of Yesterday," *SI* (April 4, 1983), p. 107.
31. Veeck and Linn, *The Hustler's Handbook*, p. 144.
32. Kerr, *Calvin*, pp. 47–48.
33. Ibid., p. 48.
34. LAT (October 6, 1956, and October 7, 1956); Shapiro, *The Last Good Season*, p. 309; Deveaux, *The Washington Senators*, p. 198; *Louisville Courier-Journal* (October 7, 1956); *Minneapolis Star* (October 18, 1956).
35. USS Subcommittee on Antitrust and Monopoly, *Organized Professional Team Sports, Hearings, July 9–31, 1958*, pp. 86–87.
36. WP (October 17, 1956).
37. SABR website; Dewey and Acocella, *The Ball Clubs*, pp. 585–88; NYT (October 12, 1956).
38. NYT (October 18, 1956).
39. SN (October 31, 1956).
40. Ibid.
41. LAT (October 20, 1956).
42. SN (October 31, 1956).
43. NYT (March 6, 1956, April 6, 1956, and May 23, 1956).
44. NYT (May 30, 1957).
45. NYT (October 13, 1956); Shapiro, *The Last Good Season*, pp. 309–10; Delsohn, *True Blue*, p. 17; Golenbock, *Bums*, p. 439; Sullivan, *The Dodgers Move West*, p. 87.
46. Peter Ellsworth, "The Brooklyn Dodgers' Move to Los Angeles: Was Walter O'Malley Solely Responsible?" *Nine* (Fall 2005), p. 33; SN (November 7, 1956).
47. USHR Antitrust Subcommittee, *Organized Professional Team Sports, Hearings, June 17–August 8, 1957*, pp. 1856–57.
48. John Burbridge, "The Brooklyn Dodgers in Jersey City," *Baseball Research Journal* (Summer

2010), p. 22; Kevin Nelson, "Los Angeles Dodgers vs. San Francisco Giants, April 1958," *California History* (Winter 2005), pp. 44–47; *NYT* (October 13, 1956).
49. *LAT* (October 12, 1956).
50. Sullivan, *The Dodgers Move West*, p. 87; Golenbock, *Bums*, p. 439.
51. Peter Ellsworth, "The Brooklyn Dodgers' Move to Los Angeles: Was Walter O'Malley Solely Responsible?" *Nine* (Fall 2005), p. 33; McCue, *Mover and Shaker*, p. 139; *SN* (November 7, 1956).
52. *SN* (November 7, 1956).
53. Walter O'Malley to John Cashmore, letter, January 13, 1955, WOHD, OSP.
54. Walter O'Malley to John Cashmore, letter, December 7, 1956, WOHD, OSP.
55. Walter O'Malley to John Cashmore, letter, January 11, 1957, WOHD, OSP.
56. *NYT* (January 5, 1957).
57. *SN* (January 16, 1957).
58. Murphy, *After Many a Summer*, pp. 183–84.
59. Peter Ellsworth, "The Brooklyn Dodgers' Move to Los Angeles: Was Walter O'Malley Solely Responsible?" *Nine* (Fall 2005), pp. 33–34.
60. *NYT* (February 22, 1957); *SN* (February 27, 1957); *LAT* (February 22, 1957).
61. *NYT* (February 22, 1957).
62. *NYT* (March 2, 1957).
63. Thompson and Rice, *Every Diamond Doesn't Sparkle*, p. 151.
64. *NYT* (March 7, 1957); *LAT* (March 7, 1957).
65. *LAT* (March 7, 1957).
66. Walter O'Malley to Frank Schroth, letter, March 11, 1957, WOHD, OSP.

Chapter 20

1. Quirk and Fort, *Pay Dirt*, pp. 189–90; Pro Football Reference website; *NYT* (October 21, 1949, and February 26, 1957).
2. Banner, *The Baseball Trust*, p. 134.
3. Duquette, *Regulating the National Pastime*, p. 49; Freedman, *Professional Sports and Antitrust*, pp. 44–45.
4. Banner, *The Baseball Trust*, pp. 130–31.
5. *SN* (May 29, 1957).
6. *SN* (February 9, 1955).
7. *NYT* (February 26, 1957); Banner, *The Baseball Trust*, p. 143.
8. Justia website.
9. *SN* (March 20, 1957).
10. *LAT* (February 23, 1957).
11. *Minneapolis Star* (October 4, 1956).
12. *SN* (March 6, 1957).
13. Sullivan, *The Dodgers Move West*, p. 116; FRBM website.
14. D'Antonio, *Forever Blue*, p. 239; Melvin Durslag, "A Visit With Walter O'Malley," *SEP* (May 14, 1960), p. 104; Murphy, *After Many a Summer*, pp. 189–90.
15. Golenbock, *Amazin',* p. 57.
16. Walter O'Malley, memorandum, March 23, 1957, WOHD, OSP.
17. Kowet, *The Rich Who Own Sports*, p. 71.
18. Kevin Nelson, "Los Angeles Dodgers vs. San Francisco Giants, April 1958," *California History* (Winter 2005), pp. 49–50; Hirsch, *Willie Mays*, p. 260; Thompson and Rice, *Every Diamond Doesn't Sparkle*, p. 158; *San Francisco Chronicle* (September 15, 2000); USCB, *Census of Population: 1960, Volume I*, pp. 105, 117.
19. Walter O'Malley to Frank Schroth, letter, March 31, 1957, WOHD, OSP.
20. Walter O'Malley, memorandum, April 15, 1957, WOHD, OSP.
21. Murphy, *After Many a Summer*, p. 197; USCB, *Census of Population: 1960, Volume I*, p. 58.
22. D'Antonio, *Forever Blue*, pp. 240–41; *NYT* (April 19, 1957).
23. Thompson and Rice, *Every Diamond Doesn't Sparkle*, p. 147.
24. Melvin Durslag, "A Visit With Walter O'Malley," *SEP* (May 14, 1960), p. 104.
25. Smith, *Pull Up a Chair*, p. 47; Fleder, *Great Baseball Writing*, p. 185.
26. Robert Moses, "Robert Moses on the Battle of Brooklyn," *SI* (July 22, 1957), p. 49.
27. *NYT* (April 30, 1957); D'Antonio, *Forever Blue*, p. 241; *LAT* (May 3, 1957, and May 4, 1957); *SN* (May 15, 1957); Robert James, "Field of Liens: Real-Property Development in Baseball," *Baseball Research Journal* (Fall 2010), pp. 118–19.
28. Andy McCue, "Barrio, Bulldozers, and Baseball: The Destruction of Chavez Ravine," *Nine* (Fall 2012), pp. 48–49.
29. Poulson OH, UCLA.
30. *LAT* (June 13, 1957).
31. *NYT* (May 11, 1957); Kowet, *The Rich Who Own Sports*, p. 71; Thompson and Rice, *Every Diamond Doesn't Sparkle*, pp. 158–59; Kevin Nelson, "Los Angeles Dodgers vs. San Francisco Giants, April 1958," *California History* (Winter 2005), pp. 49–50.
32. USHR Antitrust Subcommittee, *Organized Professional Team Sports, Hearings, June 17–August 8, 1957*, pp. 1404–6; *NYT* (May 29, 1957).
33. *NYT* (May 29, 1957).
34. Sullivan, *The Dodgers Move West*, p. 113; *NYT* (May 30, 1957, and June 5, 1957).
35. *NYT* (May 30, 1957).
36. *NYT* (June 5, 1957).
37. *NYT* (February 27, 1957).
38. Lowe, *The Kid on the Sandlot*, p. 30; *NYT* (June 2, 1957).
39. *NYT* (June 2, 1957); *LAT* (June 2, 1957).
40. Emanuel Celler to Richard Akagi, letter, May 29, 1957, Emanuel Celler Papers, LOC.
41. *SN* (June 19, 1957).
42. Frick, *Games, Asterisks, and People*, p. 127.
43. USHR Antitrust Subcommittee, *Organized Professional Team Sports, Hearings, June 17–August 8, 1957*, p. 100.
44. *Ibid.*, p. 98.

45. *Ibid.*, p. 165.
46. *Ibid.*, p. 1850.
47. *Ibid.*, p. 1866.
48. *Ibid.*, p. 1872.
49. *Ibid.*, p. 1866.
50. *LAT* (June 28, 1957).
51. USHR Antitrust Subcommittee, *Organized Professional Team Sports, Hearings, June 17-August 8, 1957*, p. 1947.
52. *Ibid.*, p. 1948.
53. *NYT* (February 12, 1955, and June 10, 1955); Shapiro, *Bottom of the Ninth*, p. 111.
54. USHR Antitrust Subcommittee, *Organized Professional Team Sports, Hearings, June 17-August 8, 1957*, p. 1952.
55. *SN* (July 24, 1957); *LAT* (June 7, 1957); *NYT* (July 20, 1957).
56. USHR Antitrust Subcommittee, *Organized Professional Team Sports, Hearings, June 17-August 8, 1957*, p. 1954; *SN* (July 24, 1957).
57. *SN* (August 14, 1957).
58. *NYT* (August 20, 1957).
59. *SN* (August 28, 1957).
60. *NYT* (August 20, 1957).
61. *SN* (March 27, 1957, and May 15, 1957); BR website.
62. *SN* (July 10, 1957); SABR website.
63. Povletich, *Milwaukee Braves*, pp. 71–74; Bryant, *The Last Hero*, p. 205.
64. *SN* (October 16, 1957); Povletich, *Milwaukee Braves*, pp. 85–88; *NYT* (October 11, 1957); Davidson and Outlar, *Caught Short*, p. 61.

Chapter 21

1. BR website; *NYT* (August 23, 1957).
2. *SN* (September 4, 1957).
3. *NYT* (August 23, 1957).
4. *NYT* (August 27, 1957); FRBM website.
5. *NYT* (August 27, 1957).
6. *NYT* (May 30, 1957).
7. *NYT* (June 4, 1957).
8. Robert Moses, "Robert Moses on the Battle of Brooklyn," *SI* (July 22, 1957), p. 27.
9. Robert Moses to Peter Campbell Brown, letter, August 28, 1957, WOHD, OSP.
10. *NYT* (October 14, 1957); Shapiro, *The Last Good Season*, p. 314.
11. *NYT* (September 30, 2007).
12. Drysdale and Verdi, *Once a Bum, Always a Dodger*, p. 70.
13. Snider and Gilbert, *The Duke of Flatbush*, p. 198.
14. Koufax and Linn, *Koufax*, pp. 122–23.
15. *LAT* (September 22, 1957).
16. *NYT* (September 11, 1957).
17. *NYT* (September 11, 1957).
18. Smith, *Thomas E. Dewey and His Times*, p. 624.
19. Smith, *On His Own Terms*, pp. 271–72.
20. Reich, *The Life of Nelson A. Rockefeller*, p. 690.
21. *NYT* (September 19, 1957).
22. *NYT* (September 11, 1957, September 19, 1957, and September 20, 1957).
23. *LAT* (September 20, 1957).
24. SABR website; Shapiro, *Bottom of the Ninth*, pp. 24–25.
25. *NYT* (September 30, 1957).
26. Angell, *Five Seasons*, p. 272.
27. Hirsch, *Willie Mays*, p. 265.
28. Kevin Nelson, "Los Angeles Dodgers vs. San Francisco Giants, April 1958," *California History* (Winter 2005), p. 51; *LAT* (September 30, 1957, and October 2, 1957); *NYT* (October 2, 1957, and October 8, 1957).
29. *LAT* (October 8, 1957).
30. Podair, *City of Dreams*, pp. 27–29; Sullivan, *The Dodgers Move West*, p. 104; Shapiro, *The Last Good Season*, p. 321; *LAT* (October 8, 1957); *NYT* (October 8, 1957).
31. D'Antonio, *Forever Blue*, pp. 251–52.
32. *LAT* (October 9, 1957); *NYT* (October 9, 1957).
33. Brooklyn Dodgers, press release, October 8, 1957, WOHD, OSP.
34. *LAT* (October 9, 1957).
35. *LAT* (October 10, 1957).
36. Koppett, *The New York Mets*, p. 19; *NYT* (September 27, 1957).
37. *NYT* (October 17, 1957).
38. *NYT* (November 6, 1957, and November 7, 1957); Paul Hirsch, "Walter O'Malley Was Right," *National Pastime* (2011), p. 82.
39. *SN* (July 31, 1957, and August 14, 1957).
40. *SN* (August 28, 1957).
41. *SN* (July 31, 1957).
42. *NYT* (October 18, 1957).
43. *SN* (October 30, 1957); Statistics Canada website; USCB, *Census of Population: 1960, Volume I*, p. 117.
44. *NYT* (August 23, 1957); *Minneapolis Morning Tribune* (September 26, 1957, and October 22, 1957); *Minneapolis Star* (October 21, 1957); *NYT* (October 22, 1957).
45. *Minneapolis Morning Tribune* (August 15, 1957).
46. *WP* (January 15, 1958).
47. Kerr, *Calvin*, p. 50.
48. BR website; *SN* (July 24, 1957, and November 26, 1958); *NYT* (October 17, 1957).
49. Greenberg and Berkow, *Hank Greenberg*, pp. 213–14.
50. *NYT* (November 30, 1957); *SN* (December 11, 1957, and December 18, 1957).
51. *SN* (December 18, 1957).
52. Breslin, *Can't Anybody Here Play This Game?*, pp. 45–46.
53. *NYT* (February 1, 1958).
54. *NYT* (December 29, 1957).
55. *Pittsburgh Press* (August 25, 1957).
56. *Cincinnati Enquirer* (January 14, 1958, and January 15, 1958); *Pittsburgh Post-Gazette* (April 2, 1958); *Philadelphia Inquirer* (April 16, 1959).
57. Breslin, *Can't Anybody Here Play This Game?*, p. 46.

58. *NYT* (December 3, 1957, and January 14, 1958); *LAT* (December 3, 1957); SABR website; FRBM website; Zingg and Medeiros, *Runs, Hits, and an Era*, p. 142.
59. *SN* (October 30, 1957).
60. *NYT* (October 16, 1957, and November 7, 1957).
61. *SN* (July 2, 1958).
62. *SN* (September 4, 1957).
63. Lowry, *Green Cathedrals*, pp. 233–34; *NYT* (February 5, 1958).
64. Robert Shaplen, "The Lonely, Loyal Mr. Stoneham," *SI* (May 5, 1958), p. 72.
65. Hirsch, *Willie Mays*, pp. 274–80.
66. Podair, *City of Dreams*, p. 84.
67. *NYT* (October 24, 1957); Podair, *City of Dreams*, pp. 52–54.
68. *NYT* (November 18, 1957, November 23, 1957, and December 31, 1957); *SN* (November 6, 1957); Robert James, "Field of Liens: Real-Property Development in Baseball," *Baseball Research Journal* (Fall 2010), p. 119; Podair, *City of Dreams*, pp. 88–89; Melvin Durslag, "A Visit With Walter O'Malley," *SEP* (May 14, 1960), pp. 31, 104.
69. Boxerman and Boxerman, *Ebbets to Veeck to Busch*, p. 114.
70. James Gordon, "Los Angeles' Wrigley Field: 'The Finest Edifice in the United States,'" *National Pastime* (2011), pp. 111–12; Melvin Durslag, "A Visit With Walter O'Malley," *SEP* (May 14, 1960), p. 105; Lowry, *Green Cathedrals*, pp. 172–73.
71. *NYT* (December 19, 1957, and December 21, 1957); SABR website.
72. *SN* (January 8, 1958).
73. *NYT* (January 14, 1958); *SN* (January 22, 1958).
74. *NYT* (December 7, 1957).
75. *SN* (January 22, 1958).
76. *NYT* (January 18, 1958).
77. *NYT* (January 18, 1958, and January 19, 1958); Thorn, Palmer, Gershman, and Pietrusza, *Total Baseball*, pp. 94–95; Lowry, *Green Cathedrals*, pp. 168–71.
78. Parrott, *The Lords of Baseball*, p. 243.
79. Ibid., p. 241.

Chapter 22

1. Kevin Nelson, "Los Angeles Dodgers vs. San Francisco Giants, April 1958," *California History* (Winter 2005), pp. 55–58; *NYT* (January 29, 1958); SABR website.
2. Steve Treder, "A Legacy of What-Ifs: Horace Stoneham and the Integration of the Giants," *Nine* (Spring 2002), p. 78; Cepeda and Fagen, *Baby Bull*, p. 35.
3. Goldblatt, *The Giants and the Dodgers*, p. 162; Hirsch, *Willie Mays*, pp. 285–86.
4. Hodges and Hirshberg, *My Giants*, p. 149.
5. Arthur Daley, "Will the Dodger-Giant Gold Rush Pan Out?" *NYTM* (May 11, 1958), p. 34.
6. *NYT* (April 20, 1958).
7. Snider and Gilbert, *The Duke of Flatbush*, pp. 201–2.
8. Don Zminda, "A Home Like No Other: The Dodgers in L.A. Memorial Coliseum," *National Pastime* (2011), p. 84.
9. *NYT* (January 22, 1958).
10. *LAT* (October 17, 1957); *NYT* (September 6, 1957); *SN* (November 23, 1960).
11. *NYT* (January 24, 1958).
12. Sullivan, *The Dodgers Move West*, pp. 142–44; *NYT* (February 23, 1958, and February 25, 1958).
13. *NYT* (February 23, 1958).
14. Breslin, *Can't Anybody Here Play This Game?*, p. 44.
15. Frick, *Games, Asterisks, and People*, p. 127.
16. *NYT* (April 18, 1964, and October 4, 1991); Shecter, *Once Upon the Polo Grounds*, p. 19; Shapiro, *Bottom of the Ninth*, pp. 26–27.
17. Kahn, *The Era*, p. 30.
18. *NYT* (October 4, 1991).
19. *SN* (July 16, 1958); *NYT* (July 8, 1958).
20. *NYT* (July 7, 1958).
21. *NYT* (July 8, 1958).
22. BR website.
23. Kahn, *The Era*, pp. 1–2.
24. BR website; Jason Winfree, "Fan Substitution and Market Definition in Professional Sports Leagues," *Antitrust Bulletin* (Winter 2009), p. 805.
25. Armour, *Joe Cronin*, p. 264.
26. USHR Antitrust Subcommittee, *Organized Professional Team Sports, Hearings, June 17–August 8, 1957*, p. 2459.
27. *NYT* (October 13, 1957).
28. F.C. Lane, "Is There Room for a Third Big League?" *Baseball Magazine* (June 1914), p. 48.
29. USHR Subcommittee on the Study of Monopoly Power, *Organized Baseball, Report*, pp. 197–98.
30. USCB, *Historical Statistics of the United States*, p. 8; USCB website.
31. Larry MacPhail, "A Pulmotor for Baseball," *Life* (February 24, 1958), pp. 120, 122.
32. *NYT* (March 13, 1958).
33. *SN* (May 21, 1958).
34. *NYT* (January 22, 1958).
35. *NYT* (April 18, 1964).
36. *NYT* (November 14, 1958, and November 15, 1958); *SN* (November 19, 1958).
37. *NYT* (November 14, 1958).
38. *SN* (November 26, 1958).
39. *SN* (November 19, 1958).
40. Frick, *Games, Asterisks, and People*, pp. 128–29.
41. Murray, *Jim Murray*, pp. 115–16.
42. Kowet, *The Rich Who Own Sports*, pp. 193–95; Harris, *The League*, pp. 143–45; *Detroit Free Press* (July 10, 1956); Robinson, *Canadian Urban Growth Trends*, p. 35.
43. *NYT* (November 15, 1958).
44. Reed, *A Six-Gun Salute*, pp. 16–20; Shapiro, *Bottom of the Ninth*, pp. 45–46, 114–15; Andy McCue and Eric Thompson, "Mis-management

101: The American League Expansion for 1961," *National Pastime* (2011), pp. 42–43.
 45. *NYT* (June 28, 1959).
 46. *NYT* (November 18, 1958).

Chapter 23

 1. *SN* (June 12, 1957).
 2. *NYT* (January 12, 1958).
 3. *SN* (February 12, 1958, and March 12, 1958); *NYT* (January 28, 1958, and March 7, 1958).
 4. USHR Antitrust Subcommittee, *Organized Professional Team Sports, Hearings, June 17-August 8, 1957*, p. 8.
 5. Kenneth Keating to Alfred Joiner, letter, July 13, 1959, Kenneth Keating Papers, UR.
 6. Kenneth Keating, prepared statement, May 15, 1958, Kenneth Keating Papers, UR.
 7. USS Subcommittee on Antitrust and Monopoly Legislation, *Organized Professional Team Sports, Hearings, July 9–31, 1958*, p. 379.
 8. *SN* (March 12, 1958).
 9. *NYT* (May 15, 1958).
 10. *NYT* (April 18, 1958); *SN* (May 28, 1958).
 11. *SN* (June 25, 1958); *Congressional Record, 85th Congress, 2nd Session* (June 24, 1958), p. 12081.
 12. *NYT* (May 15, 1958).
 13. USS Subcommittee on Antitrust and Monopoly Legislation, *Organized Professional Team Sports, Hearings, July 9–31, 1958*, pp. 378–79.
 14. *Congressional Record, 85th Congress, 2nd Session* (June 24, 1958), p. 12073.
 15. Lowe, *The Kid on the Sandlot*, pp. 32–34; *NYT* (June 25, 1958); *SN* (July 2, 1958).
 16. *Congressional Record, 85th Congress, 2nd Session* (June 24, 1958), pp. 12084–85.
 17. *SN* (June 25, 1958).
 18. *NYT* (June 25, 1958).
 19. Ford Frick to Kenneth Keating, letter, May 21, 1958, Kenneth Keating Papers, UR.
 20. Walter O'Malley to Kenneth Keating, letter, June 25, 1958, Kenneth Keating Papers, UR.
 21. *NYT* (February 9, 1958).
 22. Sickels, *Bob Feller*, pp. 143–44; FRBM website.
 23. Sickels, *Bob Feller*, p. 144.
 24. USHR Antitrust Subcommittee, *Organized Professional Team Sports, Hearings, June 17-August 8, 1957*, pp. 1311–28.
 25. *SN* (March 19, 1958, and March 26, 1958); *NYT* (March 31, 1958).
 26. *SN* (March 19, 1958).
 27. *NYT* (March 31, 1958); *SN* (April 16, 1958, and April 1, 1959).
 28. *SN* (April 16, 1958).
 29. *SN* (April 1, 1959).
 30. Helyar, *Lords of the Realm*, p. 14; Voigt, *American Baseball, Volume III*, p. 207; Dworkin, *Owners Versus Players*, p. 31; Lowenfish and Lupien, *The Imperfect Diamond*, p. 191.
 31. Armour, *Joe Cronin*, p. 207.
 32. *SN* (December 18, 1957).
 33. Warren Corbett, "The Oriole Way: The Founding Fathers," *National Pastime* (2009), pp. 90–92; Kelley, *Baseball's Biggest Blunder*, p. 175; FRBM website; Steve Treder, "Paul Richards: The Wizard of Waxahachie," *Nine* (Spring 2007), pp. 11–12.
 34. USS Subcommittee on Antitrust and Monopoly, *Organized Professional Team Sports, Hearings, July 9–31, 1958*, p. 153.
 35. Kelley, *Baseball's Biggest Blunder*, pp. 177–83; *SN* (July 4, 1964).
 36. Al Hirshberg, "He Calls the Signals for Pro Football," *NYTM* (November 23, 1958), p. 28; Davis, *Rozelle*, pp. 47–49.
 37. SABR website.
 38. *SN* (April 17, 1965).
 39. *SN* (July 9, 1958).
 40. Gore OH, UNC.
 41. Gorman, *Kefauver*, pp. 299–300; Fontenay, *Estes Kefauver*, p. 111.
 42. Fontenay, *Estes Kefauver*, p. 97.
 43. Ibid., pp. 137–38; Thomas, *The Pursuit of the White House*, p. 244.
 44. Fontenay, *Estes Kefauver*, pp. 164–70, 182; Gorman, *Kefauver*, pp. 78–81; Peter Carlson, "Costello Meets Kefauver," *American History* (October 2016), p. 14.
 45. Gorman, *Kefauver*, p. 92.
 46. Fontenay, *Estes Kefauver*, p. 177.
 47. *WP* (November 2, 1980).
 48. Thomas, *The Pursuit of the White House*, pp. 129–33, 325; Peter Carlson, "Costello Meets Kefauver," *American History* (October 2016), p. 16.
 49. Thomas, *The Pursuit of the White House*, p. 130.
 50. Gorman, *Kefauver*, pp. 80–81.
 51. Kefauver, *In a Few Hands*, pp. 190–91.
 52. Fontenay, *Estes Kefauver*, pp. 362–63.
 53. Gorman, *Kefauver*, pp. 285, 334–35.
 54. Peter Carlson, "Casey Stengel Filibusters Estes Kefauver," *American History* (June 2014), pp. 30–31; *NYT* (July 9, 1958, and July 10, 1958); Creamer, *Stengel*, pp. 278–79.
 55. USS Subcommittee on Antitrust and Monopoly Legislation, *Organized Professional Team Sports, Hearings, July 9–31, 1958*, p. 11.
 56. Ibid., p. 13.
 57. *NYT* (July 10, 1958).
 58. USS Subcommittee on Antitrust and Monopoly Legislation, *Organized Professional Team Sports, Hearings, July 9-31, 1958*, pp. 45, 101, 156.
 59. Lowe, *The Kid on the Sandlot*, p. 36; *SN* (July 9, 1958, and August 13, 1958); *NYT* (August 2, 1958).
 60. *SN* (March 19, 1958).
 61. *SN* (May 14, 1958, and May 21, 1958).
 62. BR website; Peary, *We Played the Game*, p. 390.
 63. *SN* (October 15, 1958).

Chapter 24

1. BR website.
2. Lowry, *Green Cathedrals*, pp. 117–20; BR website.
3. Podair, *City of Dreams*, p. 62.
4. Poulson OH, UCLA.
5. Boxerman and Boxerman, *Ebbets to Veeck to Busch*, p. 114.
6. Melvin Durslag, "A Visit With Walter O'Malley," *SEP* (May 14, 1960), p. 105.
7. Online Archive of California website.
8. *Ibid.*; *NYT* (May 18, 1958); Thorn, Palmer, Gershman, and Pietrusza, *Total Baseball*, p. 95; Dewey and Acocella, *The Ball Clubs*, pp. 287–89.
9. Kevin Nelson, "Los Angeles Dodgers vs. San Francisco Giants, April 1958," *California History* (Winter 2005), pp. 58–59; Sullivan, *The Dodgers Move West*, p. 153.
10. *LAT* (June 1, 1958).
11. Goldblatt, *The Giants and the Dodgers*, pp. 160–61; Kevin Nelson, "Los Angeles Dodgers vs. San Francisco Giants, April 1958," *California History* (Winter 2005), pp. 58–61.
12. Poulson OH, UCLA.
13. Bavasi, *Off the Record*, p. 87.
14. Podair, *City of Dreams*, p. 109; *NYT* (June 1, 1958).
15. Wyman OH, UCB.
16. *NYT* (May 24, 1958, May 27, 1958, and June 1, 1958).
17. *NYT* (May 24, 1958).
18. *LAT* (June 2, 1958); Sullivan, *The Dodgers Move West*, pp. 159–61; *SN* (June 11, 1958); *Daily Variety* (June 20, 2008).
19. Podair, *City of Dreams*, p. 117.
20. *NYT* (June 5, 1958, and June 6, 1958); Podair, *City of Dreams*, p. 120.
21. Sullivan, *The Dodgers Move West*, pp. 160–61.
22. *NYT* (June 5, 1958).
23. *NYT* (June 5, 1958, and July 15, 1958).
24. Podair, *City of Dreams*, pp. 19, 163; Andy McCue, "Barrio, Bulldozers, and Baseball: The Destruction of Chavez Ravine," *Nine* (Fall 2012), p. 51; *LAT* (May 27, 1953); Kevin Nelson, "Los Angeles Dodgers vs. San Francisco Giants, April 1958," *California History* (Winter 2005), pp. 44–47.
25. *NYT* (June 5, 1958, and July 15, 1958); Podair, *City of Dreams*, pp. 133–34.
26. *NYT* (July 15, 1958).
27. Podair, *City of Dreams*, p. 163; Andy McCue, "Barrio, Bulldozers, and Baseball: The Destruction of Chavez Ravine," *Nine* (Fall 2012), p. 51.
28. *LAT* (May 9, 1959, and May 9, 2017); Andy McCue, "Barrio, Bulldozers, and Baseball: The Destruction of Chavez Ravine," *Nine* (Fall 2012), pp. 47–52.
29. Podair, *City of Dreams*, pp. 181–82.
30. *NYT* (May 17, 1959); Sullivan, *The Dodgers Move West*, p. 180; Andy McCue, "Barrio, Bulldozers, and Baseball: The Destruction of Chavez Ravine," *Nine* (Fall 2012), p. 47; FRBM website.
31. Goldblatt, *The Giants and the Dodgers*, pp. 176–77.
32. *SN* (August 27, 1958).
33. *NYT* (January 14, 1959); *LAT* (January 14, 1959).
34. Podair, *City of Dreams*, pp. 146–47.
35. *SN* (January 21, 1959).
36. Andy McCue, "Barrio, Bulldozers, and Baseball: The Destruction of Chavez Ravine," *Nine* (Fall 2012), pp. 51–52; *SN* (February 11, 1959).
37. *SN* (February 11, 1959).
38. Parrott, *The Lords of Baseball*, p. 243.
39. Don Zminda, "A Home Like No Other: The Dodgers in L.A. Memorial Coliseum," *National Pastime* (2011), pp. 84–86; BR website.
40. Oakley, *Baseball's Last Golden Age*, p. 292; HOF website; *LAT* (May 8, 1959); Peary, *We Played the Game*, p. 429.
41. *LAT* (May 8, 1959).
42. Oakley, *Baseball's Last Golden Age*, p. 292.
43. *SN* (June 10, 1959).
44. *SN* (January 21, 1959).
45. *SN* (April 29, 1959, May 20, 1959, and September 2, 1959).
46. *NYT* (September 18, 1959); *SN* (September 23, 1959).
47. Shapiro, *Bottom of the Ninth*, p. 127; *SN* (February 25, 1959, and August 12, 1959); Freedman, *Prime Time*, pp. 55–58; *LAT* (May 3, 1957, and October 29, 1957); *NYT* (December 8, 1957).
48. *LAT* (May 4, 1957).
49. Veeck and Linn, *Veeck—As in Wreck*, p. 266.
50. McCue, *Mover and Shaker*, p. 259; Podair, *City of Dreams*, p. 224.
51. *NYT* (October 20, 1959); *SN* (October 28, 1959).

Chapter 25

1. *NYT* (April 14, 1959).
2. *NYT* (June 28, 1959).
3. *NYT* (April 14, 1959).
4. *NYT* (August 2, 1959).
5. *SN* (May 27, 1959); *NYT* (May 22, 1959); USCB website.
6. *SN* (May 27, 1959).
7. *NYT* (May 22, 1959).
8. *Ibid.*
9. USHR Antitrust Subcommittee, *Organized Professional Team Sports, Hearings, June 17–August 8, 1957*, pp. 2526–27.
10. Bryan Burrough, "Game Changers: How Two Texas Oilmen Invented the Super Bowl," *Texas Monthly* (February 2009), pp. 70–71; Harris, *The League*, pp. 102–4; MacCambridge, *America's Game*, pp. 119–22.
11. Pro Football Reference website; Davis, *Papa Bear*, p. 343; MacCambridge, *America's Game*, pp. 119–22.

12. Horrigan and Rathet, *The Other League*, p. 15.
13. Bryan Burrough, "Game Changers: How Two Texas Oilmen Invented the Super Bowl," *Texas Monthly* (February 2009), pp. 71, 95.
14. MacCambridge, *America's Game*, p. 123.
15. USS Subcommittee on Antitrust and Monopoly, *Organized Professional Team Sports, Hearings, July 28–31, 1959*, pp. 40–41.
16. *NYT* (July 28, 1959); Bryan Burrough, "Game Changers: How Two Texas Oilmen Invented the Super Bowl," *Texas Monthly* (February 2009), p. 95.
17. *NYT* (July 28, 1959).
18. Andy McCue and Eric Thompson, "Mis-management 101: The American League Expansion for 1961," *National Pastime* (2011), pp. 42–43; *NYT* (June 10, 1959, July 28, 1959, and October 18, 1960); Hirsch, *Willie Mays*, pp. 261–62; FRBM website.
19. *NYT* (July 28, 1959).
20. *Ibid.*
21. *NYT* (July 2, 1959).
22. *NYT* (July 28, 1959).
23. *NYT* (July 2, 1959, and May 6, 1960).
24. Lowe, *The Kid on the Sandlot*, pp. 36–37; *NYT* (February 4, 1959, and May 6, 1960); *SN* (February 11, 1959).
25. Kenneth Keating, speech draft, June 27, 1961, Kenneth Keating Papers, UR.
26. USS Subcommittee on Antitrust and Monopoly, *Organized Professional Team Sports, Hearings, July 28–31, 1959*, p. 27.
27. *Ibid.*, p. 82.
28. *Ibid.*, p. 75.
29. *Ibid.*, p. 157.
30. *Ibid.*, p. 161.
31. *Ibid.*, p. 170.
32. *Ibid.*, p. 172.
33. Rickey and Riger, *The American Diamond*, pp. 20–21.
34. *SN* (May 21, 1958).
35. *Minutes of the Meeting of the Commissioner of the American and National Leagues with the Continental League, August 18, 1959*, Branch Rickey Papers, LOC, p. 11.
36. SABR website; Buhite, *The Continental League*, pp. 56, 167; *NYT* (March 13, 1958, and August 19, 1959).
37. *SN* (February 3, 1960).
38. Branch Rickey, memorandum, undated [1959], Branch Rickey Papers, LOC.
39. Reed, *A Six-Gun Salute*, p. 28.
40. Zimniuch, *Baseball's New Frontier*, p. 36.
41. *NYT* (August 19, 1959).
42. *Minutes of the Meeting of the Commissioner of the American and National Leagues with the Continental League, August 18, 1959*, Branch Rickey Papers, LOC, p. 43.
43. *Ibid.*, p. 21.
44. *Ibid.*, p. 61.
45. *Ibid.*, p. 141.
46. *SN* (August 26, 1959).
47. *Minneapolis Star* (January 7, 1960).
48. *SN* (January 13, 1960).
49. *NYT* (October 23, 1959); *SN* (January 13, 1960).
50. *NYT* (August 10, 1959).
51. Buhite, *The Continental League*, p. 2; *NYT* (August 23, 1959).
52. *NYT* (August 23, 1959).
53. MacCambridge, *America's Game*, pp. 130–31.
54. Shapiro, *Bottom of the Ninth*, pp. 36–37, 179–80; *NYT* (January 30, 1960); Veeck and Linn, *Veeck—As in Wreck*, pp. 275–76.
55. Branch Rickey, memorandum, October 12, 1959, Arthur Mann Papers, LOC.
56. Shapiro, *Bottom of the Ninth*, p. 141; *NYT* (October 27, 1959, and October 28, 1959).
57. *NYT* (October 27, 1959).
58. Buhite, *The Continental League*, pp. 60, 96–97; *NYT* (November 11, 1959); Stanley Brown, statement, November 4, 1959, Arthur Mann Papers, LOC.
59. *NYT* (December 8, 1959, and December 11, 1959); *SN* (December 16, 1959).
60. *SN* (December 16, 1959).
61. *NYT* (December 9, 1959).

Chapter 26

1. BR website; SABR website; Thorn, Palmer, Gershman, and Pietrusza, *Total Baseball*, pp. 22–24.
2. Holtzman and Vass, *Baseball, Chicago Style*, pp. 86–87; Eskenazi, *Bill Veeck*, p. 120.
3. Holtzman and Vass, *Baseball, Chicago Style*, pp. 250–51; BR website.
4. *SN* (December 19, 1956).
5. Holtzman and Vass, *Baseball, Chicago Style*, p. 94.
6. *SN* (June 15, 1949).
7. *SN* (November 24, 1948); *NYT* (September 23, 1959, and August 28, 2007).
8. DeWitt OH, UKY.
9. Dykes and Dexter, *You Can't Steal First Base*, pp. 87–88.
10. *SN* (November 24, 1948, and November 26, 1952); Peterson, *The Kansas City Athletics*, pp. 125–26; Holtzman and Vass, *Baseball, Chicago Style*, p. 104.
11. Devine and Wheatley, *The Memoirs of Bing Devine*, pp. 81–82.
12. *SN* (September 21, 1955).
13. *CT* (November 17, 1955); *NYT* (November 17, 1955); *SN* (November 23, 1955).
14. *CT* (November 17, 1955).
15. CT (December 11, 1956).
16. *SN* (December 19, 1956).
17. *CT* (December 22, 1956); *NYT* (December 22, 1956); *SN* (January 2, 1957).
18. *CT* (December 22, 1956).
19. *SN* (November 24, 1948).
20. *SN* (June 22, 1960).

21. *CT* (December 12, 1957, and December 17, 1957).
22. *CT* (December 11, 1957).
23. *CT* (December 19, 1957).
24. *SN* (January 29, 1958).
25. *SN* (April 30, 1958).
26. *CT* (October 17, 1958).
27. *SN* (November 12, 1958); Veeck and Linn, *Veeck—As in Wreck*, pp. 319–22.
28. *SN* (November 12, 1958).
29. *NYT* (March 13, 1957, and February 9, 1959).
30. *SN* (December 31, 1958).
31. Veeck and Linn, *Veeck—As in Wreck*, p. 324.
32. *NYT* (February 8, 1959, and February 18, 1959); *CT* (March 11, 1959); FRBM website.
33. *NYT* (September 30, 1953).
34. *NYT* (February 12, 1959).
35. Veeck and Linn, *Veeck—As in Wreck*, p. 323.
36. *CT* (March 6, 1959).
37. *NYT* (March 11, 1959).
38. Veeck and Linn, *Veeck—As in Wreck*, p. 331; Quirk and Fort, *Pay Dirt*, pp. 91–93; Peterson, *The Kansas City Athletics*, pp. 32–33; *SN* (February 10, 1960).
39. *CT* (April 15, 1959); Dickson, *Bill Veeck*, p. 230.
40. Veeck and Linn, *Veeck—As in Wreck*, p. 339.
41. *SN* (April 8, 1959); *CT* (April 7, 1959).
42. *SN* (August 19, 1959).
43. Dickson, *Bill Veeck*, p. 231; *NYT* (June 28, 1959); *SN* (July 8, 1959); BR website.
44. Dickson, *Bill Veeck*, p. 232; *NYT* (June 3, 1959).
45. Veeck and Linn, *Veeck—As in Wreck*, pp. 111–12.
46. Stanley Frank and Edgar Munzel, "A Visit With Bill Veeck," *SEP* (June 6, 1959), p. 31.
47. *SN* (May 13, 1959).
48. *CT* (September 19, 1959).
49. *CT* (June 1, 1959).
50. Veeck and Linn, *Veeck—As in Wreck*, p. 331.
51. *SN* (August 19, 1959).
52. Eskenazi, *Bill Veeck*, p. 124.
53. Holtzman and Vass, *Baseball, Chicago Style*, pp. 115–16; Dickson, *Bill Veeck*, pp. 233–34; *CT* (September 23, 1959).
54. *NYT* (September 25, 1959).
55. *SN* (June 3, 1959).
56. Dewey and Acocella, *The Ball Clubs*, pp. 61–62; *SN* (July 29, 1959).
57. Aaron and Wheeler, *I Had a Hammer*, pp. 141–42; *SN* (October 7, 1959).
58. BR website; Delsohn, *True Blue*, p. 33.

Chapter 27

1. Thomas, *A New World to Be Won*, pp. 93–94; USCB website.
2. Public Broadcasting Service website.
3. Thomas, *The United States of Suburbia*, pp. 47–48; *NYT* (June 21, 1960); USCB, *Census of Population: 1960, Volume I*, pp. 3–4.
4. Jackson, *Crabgrass Frontier*, p. 243.
5. USCB, *Census of Population: 1960, Volume I*, p. 66; USCB website.
6. White, *Theodore H. White at Large*, pp. 290–91.
7. USCB, *Historical Statistics of the United States*, p. 10; *NYT* (March 15, 1961); Gibson and Jung, *Historical Census Statistics on Population Totals by Race*, pp. 26–113.
8. USCB, *Census of Population: 1960, Volume I*, pp. 100–105, 117.
9. Crouch, *Wings*, pp. 596–97; *NYT* (January 21, 1959, and January 26, 1959).
10. *NYT* (January 26, 1959).
11. *SN* (November 13, 1957).
12. Brosnan, *The Long Season*, pp. 87–88.
13. *NYT* (February 7, 1958, February 21, 1958, and April 22, 1958).
14. *SN* (April 30, 1958).
15. USCB, *Historical Statistics of the United States*, p. 796; Thomas, *A New World to Be Won*, pp. 68–69.
16. M.R. Werner, Henry Romney, Margot Marek, and Eugenia Frangos, "The $6,000,000,000 Question," *SI* (December 26, 1960), p. 82.
17. Rader, *In Its Own Image*, p. 60.
18. Johnson, *Super Spectator and the Electric Lilliputians*, pp. 100–101.
19. *Milwaukee Sentinel* (September 28, 1959); *NYT* (September 28, 1959, and September 29, 1959).
20. Mathews and Buege, *Eddie Mathews and the National Pastime*, p. 186.
21. Povletich, *Milwaukee Braves*, pp. 114–17; M.R. Werner, Henry Romney, Margot Marek, and Eugenia Frangos, "The $6,000,000,000 Question," *SI* (December 26, 1960), p. 83.
22. Johnson, *Super Spectator and the Electric Lilliputians*, pp. 28–29.
23. USS Subcommittee on Antitrust and Monopoly, *Organized Professional Team Sports, Hearings, May 19–20, 1960*, p. 104.
24. *SN* (December 16, 1959).
25. Buhite, *The Continental League*, pp. 96–97.
26. Ford Frick to Philip Hart, letter, May 25, 1960, Philip Hart Papers, UM.
27. BR website; Buhite, *The Continental League*, pp. 93–94.
28. *SN* (August 26, 1959).
29. Edward Doherty, Jr., to Branch Rickey, letter, March 4, 1960, Branch Rickey Papers, LOC.
30. Frank Shaughnessy to Branch Rickey, letter, March 1, 1960, Branch Rickey Papers, LOC; *NYT* (June 7, 1960); FRBM website; *SN* (August 10, 1960).
31. USS Subcommittee on Antitrust and Monopoly, *Organized Professional Team Sports, Hearings, May 19–20, 1960*, p. 21.
32. *NYT* (January 30, 1960).

33. *NYT* (August 23, 1959).
34. USS Subcommittee on Antitrust and Monopoly, *Organized Professional Team Sports, Hearings, May 19–20, 1960*, p. 35.
35. USS Subcommittee on Antitrust and Monopoly, *Organized Professional Team Sports, Hearings, July 28–31, 1959*, pp. 152–54.
36. Lowe, *The Kid on the Sandlot*, p. 40; *NYT* (May 5, 1960, and June 7, 1960).
37. *NYT* (June 7, 1960).
38. *NYT* (May 13, 1960).
39. *SN* (May 18, 1960).
40. Dixon OH, JFK.
41. Polner, *Branch Rickey*, p. 260; Lowe, *The Kid on the Sandlot*, pp. 41–45; Veeck and Linn, *The Hustler's Handbook*, pp. 79–80.
42. Philip Hart, typescript of notes, undated [1960], Philip Hart Papers, UM.
43. *Congressional Record, 86th Congress, 2nd Session* (June 28, 1960), pp. 14728–33; Lowe, *The Kid on the Sandlot*, p. 40.
44. *Congressional Record, 86th Congress, 2nd Session* (June 28, 1960), pp. 14741–42.
45. *Ibid.*, pp. 14740–41.
46. *Ibid.*, pp. 14748–49.
47. *SN* (July 6, 1960).
48. *NYT* (June 30, 1960).
49. Paul Rand Dixon to Branch Rickey, letter, July 5, 1960, Branch Rickey Papers, LOC.
50. *Ibid.*
51. *Ibid.*
52. Davis, *Rozelle*, pp. 68, 105; Helyar, *Lords of the Realm*, pp. 64–65; Dale Cressman and Lisa Swenson, "The Pigskin and the Picture Tube: The National Football League's First Full Season on the CBS Television Network," *Journal of Broadcasting and Electronic Media* (September 2007), pp. 485–86; Shapiro, *Bottom of the Ninth*, pp. 274–75; Buhite, *The Continental League*, p. 149.
53. *NYT* (October 12, 1959); Davis, *Rozelle*, pp. 90–91.
54. Quirk and Fort, *Pay Dirt*, pp. 344–46; Miller, *Going Long*, p. 6; Shapiro, *Bottom of the Ninth*, pp. 151–52.
55. Miller, *Going Long*, p. 6.
56. Shapiro, *Bottom of the Ninth*, pp. 219–20; Horrigan and Rathet, *The Other League*, pp. 66–67; Bryan Burrough, "Game Changers: How Two Texas Oilmen Invented the Super Bowl," *Texas Monthly* (February 2009), pp. 71, 95; Kowet, *The Rich Who Own Sports*, p. 80.
57. Shapiro, *Bottom of the Ninth*, p. 220.
58. Eugene Murdock, "The Tragedy of Ban Johnson," *Journal of Sport History* (Spring 1974), p. 27.
59. USHR Subcommittee on the Study of Monopoly Power, *Organized Baseball, Hearings, July 30-October 24, 1951*, p. 519.
60. *SN* (November 25, 1959).
61. USS Subcommittee on Antitrust and Monopoly, *Organized Professional Team Sports, Hearings, May 19–20, 1960*, p. 79.
62. *SN* (June 1, 1960).
63. Shapiro, *Bottom of the Ninth*, pp. 188–89.
64. Frick, *Games, Asterisks, and People*, pp. 128–29.
65. *SN* (June 29, 1960, and October 5, 1960); BR website.
66. *SN* (August 10, 1960); BR website.
67. Thomas, *The Best (and Worst) of Baseball's Modern Era*, pp. 15–17.
68. Golenbock, *Dynasty*, pp. 386, 402; Thomas, *The Best (and Worst) of Baseball's Modern Era*, pp. 17–18.

Chapter 28

1. BR website.
2. *Minneapolis Morning Tribune* (July 7, 1958).
3. *SN* (July 30, 1958).
4. USS Subcommittee on Antitrust and Monopoly, *Organized Professional Team Sports, Hearings, July 9–31, 1958*, p. 90.
5. *Minneapolis Star* (July 22, 1958).
6. *Minneapolis Morning Tribune* (August 28, 1958); *Minneapolis Star* (August 29, 1958, and September 2, 1958); *SN* (September 10, 1958).
7. *Minneapolis Morning Tribune* (September 8, 1958).
8. *NYT* (September 5, 1958); FRBM website; *WP* (October 26, 1960).
9. *Minneapolis Star* (September 9, 1958).
10. *NYT* (March 15, 1961); USCB, *Census of Population: 1950, Volume III*; USCB, *Census of Population: 1960, Series PHC(1)*; USCB, *Census of Population: 1970, Series PHC(1)*.
11. Kerr, *Calvin*, p. 49.
12. Kevin Hennessy, "Calvin Griffith: The Ups and Downs of the Last Family-Owned Baseball Team," *National Pastime* (2012), pp. 66–67.
13. *Minneapolis Morning Tribune* (May 1, 1959).
14. *WP* (January 15, 1958).
15. *SN* (October 14, 1959).
16. BR website; Joseph Cairnes to Louis Perini, letter, November 4, 1953, Louis Perini Papers, HOF; *NYT* (December 11, 1953).
17. *SN* (October 28, 1959).
18. *SN* (August 5, 1959).
19. *SN* (March 16, 1960).
20. *NYT* (March 10, 1960); *SN* (March 16, 1960); SABR website.
21. *NYT* (March 24, 1960).
22. *NYT* (March 15, 1960, May 26, 1960, and June 29, 1960); Peterson, *The Kansas City Athletics*, pp. 109–14.
23. BR website.
24. *NYT* (January 27, 1957); *Boston Globe* (July 8, 1958).
25. *Boston Globe* (July 27, 1958).
26. BR website; Povletich, *Milwaukee Braves*, p. 125.
27. *Boston Globe* (March 10, 1961).
28. Aaron and Wheeler, *I Had a Hammer*, p. 177.

29. Veeck and Linn, *The Hustler's Handbook*, p. 304.
30. BR website.
31. *NYT* (April 9, 1953).
32. Frederick Miller to Louis Perini, letter, October 1, 1954, Louis Perini Papers, HOF.
33. *Milwaukee Journal* (December 18, 1954, and December 20, 1954).
34. Davidson and Outlar, *Caught Short*, p. 88.
35. Grimm and Prell, *Jolly Cholly's Story*, p. 207.
36. *NYT* (January 1, 1960).
37. *NYT* (June 7, 1959, February 24, 1960, and January 6, 2008); Rory Costello, "Twilight at Ebbets Field," *National Pastime* (2006), pp. 104–9; D'Antonio, *Forever Blue*, p. 285; Sam Anderson, "Exorcising the Dodgers," *New York* (September 24, 2007), p. 38.
38. *NYT* (February 24, 1960).
39. Quirk and Fort, *Pay Dirt*, pp. 156–58; Kuklick, *To Every Thing a Season*, pp. 25–26; Bob Ruzzo, "Braves Field: An Imperfect History of the Perfect Ballpark," *Baseball Research Journal* (Fall 2012), p. 59; *NYT* (May 31, 1964).
40. Stanley Frank and Edgar Munzel, "A Visit With Bill Veeck," *SEP* (June 6, 1959), p. 93.
41. *NYT* (July 31, 1958, August 16, 1959, and April 13, 1960); FRBM website; Hirsch, *Willie Mays*, pp. 317–18.
42. "Lighting the Candlestick," *Time* (April 25, 1960).
43. Goldblatt, *The Giants and the Dodgers*, p. 175.
44. Mays and Sahadi, *Say Hey*, pp. 156–57.
45. Angell, *Five Seasons*, p. 263.
46. Hirsch, *Willie Mays*, p. 319; Goldblatt, *The Giants and the Dodgers*, p. 174; Lowry, *Green Cathedrals*, pp. 83–86.
47. Melvin Durslag, "A Visit With Walter O'Malley," *SEP* (May 14, 1960), p. 104.
48. *NYT* (September 24, 1961).
49. Podair, *City of Dreams*, pp. 250–51; *SN* (October 6, 1962).
50. Stout, *The Dodgers*, pp. 256–60.
51. Povich, *All These Mornings*, p. 86; *WP* (December 23, 1959).
52. *WP* (July 9, 1960).
53. *WP* (October 14, 1959).
54. *SN* (July 20, 1960).

Chapter 29

1. *NYT* (July 19, 1960, and July 21, 1960).
2. *NYT* (July 21, 1960).
3. *NYT* (July 19, 1960).
4. *NYT* (July 21, 1960).
5. *NYT* (July 22, 1960).
6. William Shea to Kenneth Keating, telegram, July 29, 1960, Kenneth Keating Papers, UR.
7. Shapiro, *Bottom of the Ninth*, p. 211.
8. *NYT* (August 3, 1960); *SN* (August 10, 1960).
9. Shapiro, *Bottom of the Ninth*, pp. 213–14.
10. *SN* (August 10, 1960).
11. *Ibid.*
12. *NYT* (October 18, 1960).
13. *SN* (November 2, 1960).
14. SABR website; FRBM website.
15. Breslin, *Can't Anybody Here Play This Game?*, p. 51.
16. Creamer, *Stengel*, pp. 295–96; *NYT* (January 7, 1961); Golenbock, *Dynasty*, p. 412.
17. Fleder, *Great Baseball Writing*, p. 336.
18. *NYT* (January 8, 1961).
19. Koppett, *The New York Mets*, pp. 26–27; *NYT* (May 9, 1961).
20. *NYT* (January 8, 1961).
21. *NYT* (January 28, 1961).
22. Koppett, *The New York Mets*, p. 30.
23. *NYT* (March 20, 1961).
24. Reed, *A Six-Gun Salute*, pp. 28–30, 39, 204–5.
25. *Ibid.*, pp. 50–51.
26. *Ibid.*, pp. 46–47.
27. Ron Briley, "Baseball's Other Expansion Team of 1962," *Nine* (Spring 2013), pp. 141–42; SABR website; *SN* (February 8, 1961); Reed, *A Six-Gun Salute*, p. 42.
28. Armour, *Joe Cronin*, pp. 266–67.
29. *SN* (October 26, 1960).
30. *WP* (October 26, 1960).
31. *Minneapolis Star* (October 27, 1960); *SN* (November 2, 1960); BR website.
32. Kerr, *Calvin*, pp. 59–60.
33. Povich, *All These Mornings*, pp. 160–62.
34. Deveaux, *The Washington Senators*, pp. 203–4; BR website.
35. Armour, *Joe Cronin*, p. 268.
36. *NYT* (August 14, 1960).
37. Zimniuch, *Baseball's New Frontier*, p. 42; *NYT* (October 27, 1960).
38. *NYT* (October 27, 1960).
39. Roy Terrell, "The Damndest Mess Baseball Has Ever Seen," *SI* (December 19, 1960), p. 18.
40. Rickey and Riger, *The American Diamond*, p. 23.
41. *NYT* (October 27, 1960); Veeck and Linn, *Veeck—As in Wreck*, pp. 353–56; Harris, *The League*, pp. 140–41; *SN* (November 2, 1960).
42. Thomas, *The Man to See*, pp. 166–69.
43. Gerald Astor, "Almost Like Baseball," *SI* (September 4, 1961), p. M8; *NYT* (November 18, 1960); Veeck and Linn, *Veeck—As in Wreck*, pp. 357–59; Thomas, *The Man to See*, p. 169; Kerr, *Calvin*, p. 58.
44. *NYT* (August 14, 1960).
45. *NYT* (October 24, 1960).
46. *SN* (November 2, 1960).
47. *NYT* (October 27, 1960); Veeck and Linn, *Veeck—As in Wreck*, pp. 356, 359–62; Kowet, *The Rich Who Own Sports*, pp. 231–34.
48. Autry and Herskowitz, *Back in the Saddle Again*, pp. 147–48.
49. *NYT* (November 18, 1960); *SN* (November 23, 1960); Roy Terrell, "The Damndest Mess Baseball Has Ever Seen," *SI* (December 19, 1960), pp. 19, 61.

50. *NYT* (November 24, 1960).
51. *NYT* (November 19, 1960); Veeck and Linn, *Veeck—As in Wreck*, p. 363; Steve Treder, "Baseball's New Frontier: The Expansion of 1961–62," *Nine* (Spring 2004), p. 31; *LAT* (December 7, 1960).
52. Autry and Herskowitz, *Back in the Saddle Again*, pp. 146–47.
53. Roy Terrell, "The Damndest Mess Baseball Has Ever Seen," *SI* (December 19, 1960), p. 16; Shapiro, *Bottom of the Ninth*, p. 272; FRBM website.
54. Autry and Herskowitz, *Back in the Saddle Again*, p. 156.
55. Roy Terrell, "The Damndest Mess Baseball Has Ever Seen," *SI* (December 19, 1960), p. 61.
56. *NYT* (November 5, 1960); *SN* (December 7, 1960); Rex Hamann, "Baseball's Twin Towers in the Twin Cities," *National Pastime* (2012), pp. 29–37; Jackson, *Crabgrass Frontier*, p. 274.
57. Andy McCue and Eric Thompson, "Mis-management 101: The American League Expansion for 1961," *National Pastime* (2011), pp. 43–44; BR website; *SN* (December 28, 1960).
58. *NYT* (November 18, 1960).
59. *SN* (December 28, 1960).
60. Veeck and Linn, *Veeck—As in Wreck*, pp. 353–55.
61. Peterson, *The Kansas City Athletics*, pp. 113–14; *NYT* (November 16, 1960, and November 19, 1960).
62. *NYT* (November 19, 1960).
63. Peterson, *The Kansas City Athletics*, pp. 116–17; *NYT* (December 17, 1960, and December 20, 1960); FRBM website.
64. Libby, *Charlie O. and the Angry A's*, pp. 40–43; Peterson, *The Kansas City Athletics*, pp. 118–20; William Barry Furlong, "Charlie Finley: Triumph and Turmoil," *SEP* (October 1975), pp. 31–32.
65. Libby, *Charlie O. and the Angry A's*, p. 41.
66. Peterson, *The Kansas City Athletics*, pp. 119–20.
67. Libby, *Charlie O. and the Angry A's*, pp. 42–43.
68. William Barry Furlong, "Charlie Finley: Triumph and Turmoil," *SEP* (October 1975), pp. 31–32; Boxerman and Boxerman, *Ebbets to Veeck to Busch*, pp. 153–54; Peterson, *The Kansas City Athletics*, pp. 119–20.
69. *NYT* (December 20, 1960).
70. Libby, *Charlie O. and the Angry A's*, pp. 51–52; *SN* (December 28, 1960, and May 17, 1961); Peterson, *The Kansas City Athletics*, pp. 123–28; SABR website; *NYT* (August 23, 1961).
71. Angell, *Five Seasons*, pp. 264–65.
72. Peterson, *The Kansas City Athletics*, p. 137.
73. *NYT* (August 24, 1961).
74. SABR website; Angell, *Five Seasons*, p. 265; BR website.
75. Libby, *Charlie O. and the Angry A's*, p. 55.
76. *NYT* (August 19, 1961).
77. Walter Bingham, "A Change After 60 Years," *SI* (April 24, 1961), pp. 23–24; Hartley, *Washington's Expansion Senators*, pp. 5–6; Autry and Herskowitz, *Back in the Saddle Again*, p. 153.
78. BR website; *SN* (August 30, 1961).
79. *NYT* (July 18, 1961); *SN* (October 11, 1961).
80. BR website; Peary, *We Played the Game*, p. 530.

Chapter 30

1. *NYT* (December 6, 1973).
2. *Ibid.*
3. Shapiro, *Bottom of the Ninth*, p. 262.
4. Steve Treder, "Baseball's New Frontier: The Expansion of 1961–62," *Nine* (Spring 2004), pp. 46–47.
5. Shecter, *Once Upon the Polo Grounds*, p. 28.
6. Peary, *We Played the Game*, p. 541.
7. Golenbock, *Amazin',* p. 110.
8. Warren Giles to All National League Clubs, memorandum, August 24, 1961, National League Papers, HOF.
9. Reed, *A Six-Gun Salute*, p. 57.
10. Stephen Boren and Eric Thompson, "The Colt .45s and the 1961 Expansion Draft," *National Pastime* (2014), pp. 28–33; Steve Treder, "Baseball's New Frontier: The Expansion of 1961–62," *Nine* (Spring 2004), pp. 42–43; Koppett, *The New York Mets*, p. 37; BR website.
11. Creamer, *Stengel*, p. 297.
12. Breslin, *Can't Anybody Here Play This Game?*, p. 62.
13. Miller, *Going Long*, p. 36.
14. Reed, *A Six-Gun Salute*, pp. 72, 108; Lowry, *Green Cathedrals*, p. 158; *NYT* (June 6, 1961).
15. Peary, *We Played the Game*, p. 546.
16. *NYT* (January 4, 1962, and May 26, 1964).
17. *NYT* (June 6, 1961).
18. *CT* (January 15, 1960).
19. *SN* (December 16, 1959, and February 10, 1960).
20. *SN* (February 10, 1960).
21. *NYT* (April 10, 1960, and May 9, 1960); Dickson, *Bill Veeck*, p. 241.
22. Veeck and Linn, *Veeck—As in Wreck*, p. 253.
23. *NYT* (May 21, 1960); *SN* (June 1, 1960); Golenbock, *Dynasty*, p. 376; FRBM website; Veeck and Linn, *Veeck—As in Wreck*, pp. 342–44; BR website.
24. *SN* (June 1, 1960).
25. Veeck and Linn, *Veeck—As in Wreck*, p. 344.
26. Dickson, *Bill Veeck*, p. 245.
27. SABR website; *NYT* (June 6, 1961, and June 11, 1961); *SN* (June 21, 1961); Dickson, *Bill Veeck*, pp. 248–50.
28. Veeck and Linn, *Veeck—As in Wreck*, p. 380.
29. *SN* (February 21, 1962); Dickson, *Bill Veeck*, p. 253; *CT* (February 9, 2014); SABR website; HOF website.

30. Povletich, *Milwaukee Braves*, p. 133; BR website; *SN* (April 29, 1972).
31. Walter Bingham, "No More Joy in Beertown," *SI* (July 23, 1962), p. 41.
32. Bisher, *Miracle in Atlanta*, p. 20.
33. *NYT* (November 17, 1962).
34. Francis Kinlaw, "The Franchise Transfer that Fostered a Broadcasting Revolution," *National Pastime* (2010), pp. 140–41; *NYT* (December 16, 1961, and November 17, 1962); Povletich, *Milwaukee Braves*, pp. 141–43; *CT* (December 16, 1961, and May 5, 1962).
35. Bryant, *The Last Hero*, p. 301; Bisher, *Miracle in Atlanta*, p. 25.
36. Bisher, *Miracle in Atlanta*, pp. 31–32; Francis Kinlaw, "The Franchise Transfer that Fostered a Broadcasting Revolution," *National Pastime* (2010), pp. 140–41.
37. Povletich, *Milwaukee Braves*, pp. 52–53.
38. *Ibid.*, p. 50.
39. SABR website.
40. *NYT* (August 4, 1960).
41. Fontenay, *Estes Kefauver*, pp. 288–90, 362–63.
42. Holtzman OH, USHR Office of the Historian.
43. SABR website.
44. *SN* (April 3, 1957).
45. Veeck and Linn, *The Hustler's Handbook*, p. 108.
46. Voigt, *American Baseball, Volume III*, p. 87; Goldblatt, *The Giants and the Dodgers*, pp. 221–25; Kevin Hennessy, "Calvin Griffith: The Ups and Downs of the Last Family-Owned Baseball Team," *National Pastime* (2012), p. 63; BR website.
47. Freedman, *Prime Time*, pp. 32–37; Marc Freedman, "Coming of Age," *American Prospect* (November 23, 1999), p. 66; Kim Shetter, "Sun City Holds On," *Planning* (January 1996), p. 16; *NYT* (July 9, 1961, August 14, 1964, and March 2, 1965); Golenbock, *Dynasty*, p. 415; FRBM website.
48. Shapiro, *Bottom of the Ninth*, p. 270.
49. Robinson, *I Never Had It Made*, p. 30.
50. Branch Rickey to Wheelock Whitney, letter, August 2, 1960, Branch Rickey Papers, LOC.
51. Creamer, *Stengel*, pp. 295–96; *NYT* (June 28, 1961); Halberstam, *October 1964*, pp. 30–31; Frank Graham, Jr., "Branch Rickey Rides Again," *SEP* (March 9, 1963), p. 66.
52. *NYT* (October 30, 1962).
53. *NYT* (March 20, 1963).
54. Devine and Wheatley, *The Memoirs of Bing Devine*, p. 23; Golenbock, *The Spirit of St. Louis*, pp. 459–60; *NYT* (October 20, 1964).
55. *NYT* (December 10, 1965).
56. *NYT* (April 10, 1962).
57. Koppett, *The New York Mets*, pp. 45–46; Breslin, *Can't Anybody Here Play This Game?*, p. 12.
58. *SN* (October 6, 1962, and October 13, 1962); BR website.
59. *SN* (October 27, 1962).

Epilogue: Beyond

1. *SN* (April 11, 1951).
2. HOF website; BR website.
3. Thorn, Palmer, Gershman, and Pietrusza, *Total Baseball*, p. 2186; Voigt, *American Baseball, Volume III*, pp. 118–19; Rader, *In Its Own Image*, p. 63.
4. *SN* (April 25, 1962).
5. BR website.
6. *SN* (August 14, 1957).
7. USHR Subcommittee on the Study of Monopoly Power, *Organized Baseball, Report*, p. 109; Andy McCue, "Two Out of Three Ain't Bad: Branch Rickey, Walter O'Malley, and the Man in the Middle of the Dodger Owners' Partnership," *Nine* (Fall 2005), pp. 45–46.
8. Veeck and Linn, *The Hustler's Handbook*, p. 306.
9. Frick, *Games, Asterisks, and People*, p. 123.
10. Matt Jaffe, "Why Dodger Stadium Is One of a Kind," *Los Angeles Magazine* (March 7, 2018); *NYT* (April 1, 1962, and April 11, 1962); *SN* (April 25, 1962).
11. *NYT* (March 29, 1964, and April 18, 1964); Lowry, *Green Cathedrals*, pp. 69–71.
12. Jack Mann, "The King of the Jungle," *SI* (April 18, 1966), p. 127.
13. *NYT* (November 9, 1962).
14. Creamer, *Stengel*, p. 305.
15. Boorstin, *The Americans*, pp. 357–58; Reed, *A Six-Gun Salute*, p. 208; Thorn, Palmer, Gershman, and Pietrusza, *Total Baseball*, p. 78; Lowry, *Green Cathedrals*, pp. 46–48.
16. Koppett, *The New York Mets*, p. 79; Steve Treder, "Baseball's New Frontier: The Expansion of 1961–62," *Nine* (Spring 2004), pp. 42–48; BR website.
17. Shecter, *Once Upon the Polo Grounds*, p. 79.
18. *SN* (December 27, 1961); *NYT* (April 11, 1964).
19. Autry and Herskowitz, *Back in the Saddle Again*, p. 156.
20. Bill Veeck and Edward Linn, "How I Didn't Buy a Ball Club," *SEP* (September 7, 1963), p. 80.
21. Steve Treder, "Baseball's New Frontier: The Expansion of 1961–62," *Nine* (Spring 2004), p. 39.
22. Steve Treder, "Paul Richards: The Wizard of Waxahachie," *Nine* (Spring 2007), p. 16.
23. FRBM website; BR website.
24. *NYT* (December 9, 1960).
25. Peterson, *The Kansas City Athletics*, p. 184.
26. *NYT* (January 7, 1964).
27. *Louisville Courier-Journal* (January 7, 1964); *NYT* (January 7, 1964, and January 17, 1964); Peterson, *The Kansas City Athletics*, pp. 186–87.
28. BR website; *NYT* (October 19, 1967).
29. Peterson, *The Kansas City Athletics*, pp. 261–62.
30. Shapiro, *Bottom of the Ninth*, pp. 213–14.

31. Povletich, *Milwaukee Braves*, pp. 136, 161–62.
32. Johnson, *Super Spectator and the Electric Lilliputians*, p. 102.
33. *Ibid.*, p. 58.
34. *NYT* (March 8, 1964, June 14, 1964, and July 18, 1964); *SN* (August 1, 1964).
35. *SN* (April 4, 1964).
36. *NYT* (November 5, 1964, March 3, 1966, and October 11, 1966).
37. *NYT* (October 11, 1966).
38. *NYT* (February 14, 1949).
39. Buhite, *The Continental League*, p. 83.
40. Andrew Zimbalist, "Baseball's Antitrust Exemption: Why It Still Matters," *Nine* (Fall 2004), p. 6; Freedman, *Professional Sports and Antitrust*, pp. 34–35; SABR website.
41. Freedman, *Professional Sports and Antitrust*, p. 34.
42. Dworkin, *Owners Versus Players*, p. 31; SABR website.
43. Ross Davies, "Along Comes the Players Association: The Roots and Rise of Organized Labor in Major League Baseball," *Journal of Legislation and Public Policy* (2013), p. 337.
44. Miller, *A Whole Different Ball Game*, p. 7.
45. *SN* (April 25, 1946); Dworkin, *Owners Versus Players*, p. 141; SABR website.
46. Banner, *The Baseball Trust*, p. 220.
47. *Ibid.*, pp. 221–24; Lowenfish and Lupien, *The Imperfect Diamond*, pp. 20–22; FRBM website.
48. Banner, *The Baseball Trust*, pp. 230–31.
49. BR website; Goldblatt, *The Giants and the Dodgers*, pp. 255–56; FRBM website; Mike Ozanian and Kurt Badenhausen, "Baseball Team Values 2019: Yankees Lead League at $4.6 Billion," *Forbes* (April 10, 2019).
50. SABR website.
51. *NYT* (April 25, 1960); Sam Anderson, "Exorcising the Dodgers," *New York* (September 24, 2007), pp. 34–39.
52. *NYT* (October 14, 1957).
53. *Congressional Record, 85th Congress, 2nd Session* (June 24, 1958), p. 12082.
54. Delsohn, *True Blue*, p. 14.
55. Cannon, *Nobody Asked Me, But...*, pp. 72–73.
56. *SN* (May 28, 1952).
57. *Boston Globe* (April 17, 1972).
58. Veeck and Linn, *Veeck—As in Wreck*, p. 344.
59. Norman Macht, "Connie Mack's Income," *Baseball Research Journal* (Fall 2015), p. 115.
60. *SN* (October 7, 1953).
61. Bill Veeck and Edward Linn, "How I Didn't Buy a Ball Club," *SEP* (September 7, 1963), p. 79.
62. Chandler OH, UKY.
63. Bavasi, *Off the Record*, p. 42.
64. Veeck and Linn, *The Hustler's Handbook*, p. 135.
65. Bavasi, *Off the Record*, pp. 46–47.
66. Kiner OH, UKY.
67. Andy McCue, "Two Out of Three Ain't Bad: Branch Rickey, Walter O'Malley, and the Man in the Middle of the Dodger Owners' Partnership," *Nine* (Fall 2005), pp. 45–46.
68. Richard Puerzer, "Engineering Baseball: Branch Rickey's Innovative Approach to Baseball Management," *Nine* (Fall 2003), pp. 72–87; Jack Brodsky, "Keep Your Head On," *NYTM* (July 31, 1955), p. 46; Oakley, *Baseball's Last Golden Age*, pp. 202–3.
69. Barber OH, UKY.
70. *NYT* (January 5, 1944).
71. Gallup website.
72. MacCambridge, *America's Game*, p. 192.
73. *NYT* (October 15, 1959).
74. Frank Graham, Jr., "Branch Rickey Rides Again," *SEP* (March 9, 1963), p. 66.
75. Richard Puerzer, "Engineering Baseball: Branch Rickey's Innovative Approach to Baseball Management," *Nine* (Fall 2003), p. 73.
76. *SN* (August 23, 1945).
77. *NYT* (August 20, 1959).

Bibliography

Archival Materials

Library of Congress (Washington, D.C.):
- Emanuel Celler Papers
- Arthur Mann Papers
- Branch Rickey Papers
- Jackie Robinson Papers

National Baseball Hall of Fame and Museum (Cooperstown, New York):
- American League Papers, 1930–1990
- Ballparks and Stadiums Collection
- Celler Antitrust Hearings Collection
- Chandler Reserve Clause Suits Collection
- August Herrmann Papers
- Joint Major League Meetings, 1915–1951
- Major League Agreements Collection
- National League Meetings, Conferences, Minutes, and Financial Ledgers, 1899–1995
- National League Papers, 1883–1985
- Louis Perini Papers
- Radio and Television Broadcasting Collection
- Topping Family Archives

O'Malley Seidler Partners LLC (Los Angeles, California):
- Walter O'Malley Historic Documents

University of Kentucky, Special Collections Research Center (Lexington, Kentucky):
- Albert "Happy" Chandler Collection

University of Michigan, Bentley Historical Library (Ann Arbor, Michigan):
- Philip Hart Papers

University of Rochester, Rush Rhees Library (Rochester, New York):
- Kenneth Keating Papers

Congressional Documents

U.S. Congress. *Congressional Record, 85th Congress, 2nd Session (1958)*. Washington, D.C.: U.S. Government Printing Office, 1958.

_____. *Congressional Record, 86th Congress, 2nd Session (1960)*. Washington, D.C.: U.S. Government Printing Office, 1960.

U.S. Congress. House of Representatives. Committee on the Judiciary. Antitrust Subcommittee. *Organized Professional Team Sports, Hearings, June 17–August 8, 1957*. Washington, D.C.: U.S. Government Printing Office, 1957.

U.S. Congress. House of Representatives. Committee on the Judiciary. Subcommittee on the Study of Monopoly Power. *Organized Baseball, Hearings, July 30–October 24, 1951*. Washington, D.C.: U.S. Government Printing Office, 1952.

_____. *Organized Baseball, Report*. Washington, D.C.: U.S. Government Printing Office, 1952.

U.S. Congress. Senate. Committee on Interstate and Foreign Commerce. Subcommittee on S. 1396. *Broadcasting and Televising Baseball Games, Hearings, May 6–12, 1953*. Washington, D.C.: U.S. Government Printing Office, 1953.

U.S. Congress. Senate. Committee on the District of Columbia. Subcommittee on Fiscal Affairs. *Construction, Maintenance, and Operation by the Armory Board of the District of Columbia of a Stadium in the District of Columbia, Hearings, July 1, 1957*. Washington, D.C.: Ward & Paul, 1957.

U.S. Congress. Senate. Committee on the Judiciary. Subcommittee on Antitrust and Monopoly. *Organized Professional Team Sports, Hearings, July 9–31, 1958*. Washington, D.C.: U.S. Government Printing Office, 1958.

_____. *Organized Professional Team Sports, Hearings, July 28–31, 1959*. Washington, D.C.: U.S. Government Printing Office, 1959.

_____. *Organized Professional Team Sports, Hearings, May 19–20, 1960*. Washington, D.C.: U.S. Government Printing Office, 1960.

_____. *Subjecting Professional Baseball Clubs to the Antitrust Laws, Hearings, March 18–May 25, 1954*. Washington, D.C.: U.S. Government Printing Office, 1954.

Demographic Documents

Dominion Bureau of Statistics. *Eighth Census of Canada, 1941, Bulletin A-13: Population of the Greater Cities*. Ottawa: Ministry of Trade and Commerce, 1941.

Gibson, Campbell, and Kay Jung. *Historical Census Statistics on Population Totals by Race, 1790 to 1990, and by Hispanic Origin, 1970 to*

1990, for Large Cities and Other Urban Places in the United States. Washington, D.C.: U.S. Government Printing Office, 2005.
Hobbs, Frank, and Nicole Stoops. *Demographic Trends in the 20th Century.* Washington, D.C.: U.S. Government Printing Office, 2002.
U.S. Census Bureau. *Census of Population: 1940, Volume I: Number of Inhabitants.* Washington, D.C.: U.S. Government Printing Office, 1942.
_____. *Census of Population: 1950, Volume I: Number of Inhabitants.* Washington, D.C.: U.S. Government Printing Office, 1952.
_____. *Census of Population: 1950, Volume III: Census Tract Statistics.* Washington, D.C.: U.S. Government Printing Office, 1953.
_____. *Census of Population: 1960, Series PHC(1): Census Tracts.* Washington, D.C.: U.S. Government Printing Office, 1962.
_____. *Census of Population: 1960, Volume I: Characteristics of the Population.* Washington, D.C.: U.S. Government Printing Office, 1961.
_____. *Census of Population: 1970, Series PHC(1): Census Tracts.* Washington, D.C.: U.S. Government Printing Office, 1972.
_____. *Forecasts of the Population of the United States, 1945–1975.* Washington, D.C.: U.S. Government Printing Office, 1947.
_____. *Historical Statistics of the United States: Colonial Times to 1970.* Washington, D.C.: U.S. Government Printing Office, 1975.
_____. *Provisional Revision of the Projections of the Total Population of the United States: July 1, 1953, to 1960.* Washington, D.C.: U.S. Government Printing Office, 1952.

Oral Histories

John F. Kennedy Presidential Library and Museum (Boston, Massachusetts):
- Paul Rand Dixon

National Baseball Hall of Fame and Museum (Cooperstown, New York):
- Bob Cerv
- Ray Dandridge
- Carl Erskine
- Monte Irvin
- Bob Lemon
- Al Lopez
- Marty Marion
- Roy Sievers
- Frank Thomas

Society for American Baseball Research (Phoenix, Arizona):
- Joe L. Brown
- Warren Giles
- Roland Hemond

U.S. House of Representatives, Office of the Historian (Washington, D.C.):
- Elizabeth Holtzman

University of California at Berkeley, Bancroft Library (Berkeley, California):
- Rosalind Wiener Wyman

University of California at Los Angeles, Charles Young Research Library (Los Angeles, California):
- Norris Poulson

University of Kentucky, Special Collections Research Center (Lexington, Kentucky):
- Red Barber
- Bob Broeg
- Albert "Happy" Chandler
- Ray Dandridge
- Bill DeWitt, Sr.
- John Galbreath
- Danny Gardella
- Ralph Kiner
- Mickey Owen
- Shirley Povich
- Fred Saigh
- Rip Sewell
- Red Smith

University of North Carolina, Louis Round Wilson Library (Chapel Hill, North Carolina):
- Albert Gore

Published Oral History Collections

Delsohn, Steve. *True Blue: The Dramatic History of the Los Angeles Dodgers, Told by the Men Who Lived It.* New York: William Morrow, 2001.
Golenbock, Peter. *Amazin': The Miraculous Story of New York's Most Beloved Baseball Team.* New York: St. Martin's, 2002.
_____. *Bums: An Oral History of the Brooklyn Dodgers.* New York: G.P. Putnam's Sons, 1984.
_____. *The Spirit of St. Louis: A History of the St. Louis Cardinals and Browns.* New York: Avon, 2000.
_____. *Wrigleyville: A Magical History Tour of the Chicago Cubs.* New York: St. Martin's, 1996.
Holtzman, Jerome. *No Cheering in the Press Box: Recollections—Personal and Professional—By Eighteen Veteran American Sportswriters.* New York: Holt, Rinehart, and Winston, 1974.
Miller, Jeff. *Going Long: The Wild 10-Year Saga of the Renegade American Football League in the Words of Those Who Lived It.* Chicago: Contemporary, 2003.
Peary, Danny. *We Played the Game: 65 Players Remember Baseball's Greatest Era, 1947–1964.* New York: Hyperion, 1994.
Ritter, Lawrence. *The Glory of Their Times: The Story of the Early Days of Baseball Told by the Men Who Played It.* New York: Macmillan, 1966.
Vincent, Fay. *We Would Have Played for Nothing: Baseball Stars of the 1950s and 1960s Talk About the Game They Loved.* New York: Simon & Schuster, 2008.

Memoirs and Autobiographies

Aaron, Henry, and Lonnie Wheeler. *I Had a Hammer: The Hank Aaron Story.* New York: HarperCollins, 1991.

Arnold, Thurman. *Fair Fights and Foul: A Dissenting Lawyer's Life*. New York: Harcourt, Brace, and World, 1965.

Autry, Gene, and Mickey Herskowitz. *Back in the Saddle Again*. Garden City, NY: Doubleday, 1978.

Barber, Red, and Robert Creamer. *Rhubarb in the Catbird Seat*. Garden City, NY: Doubleday, 1968.

Bavasi, Buzzie. *Off the Record*. Chicago: Contemporary, 1987.

Boudreau, Lou, and Russell Schneider. *Covering All the Bases*. Champaign, IL: Sagamore, 1993.

Brosnan, Jim. *The Long Season*. Chicago: Ivan R. Dee, 2002 reprint.

Caro, Robert. *Working: Researching, Interviewing, Writing*. New York: Alfred A. Knopf, 2019.

Celler, Emanuel. *You Never Leave Brooklyn: The Autobiography of Emanuel Celler*. New York: John Day, 1953.

Cepeda, Orlando, and Herb Fagen. *Baby Bull: From Hardball to Hard Time and Back*. Dallas: Taylor, 1998.

Chandler, Albert, and Vance Trimble. *Heroes, Plain Folks, and Skunks: The Life and Times of Happy Chandler*. Chicago: Bonus, 1989.

Clifford, Clark, and Richard Holbrooke. *Counsel to the President*. New York: Random House, 1991.

Dark, Alvin, and John Underwood. *When in Doubt, Fire the Manager: My Life and Times in Baseball*. New York: Dutton, 1980.

Davidson, Donald, and Jesse Outlar. *Caught Short*. New York: Atheneum, 1972.

Devine, Bing, and Tom Wheatley, *The Memoirs of Bing Devine: Stealing Lou Brock and Other Winning Moves by a Master GM*. Champaign, IL: Sports Publishing, 2004.

Drysdale, Don, and Bob Verdi. *Once a Bum, Always a Dodger: My Life in Baseball from Brooklyn to Los Angeles*. New York: St. Martin's, 1990.

Durocher, Leo. *The Dodgers and Me: The Inside Story*. Chicago: Ziff-Davis, 1948.

Durocher, Leo, and Ed Linn. *Nice Guys Finish Last*. New York: Simon & Schuster, 1975.

Dykes, Jimmie, and Charles Dexter. *You Can't Steal First Base*. Philadelphia: J.B. Lippincott, 1967.

Frick, Ford. *Games, Asterisks, and People: Memoirs of a Lucky Fan*. New York: Crown, 1973.

Garvey, Steve, Ken Gurnick, and Candace Garvey. *My Bat Boy Days: Lessons I Learned from the Boys of Summer*. New York: Scribner's, 2008.

Goodwin, Doris Kearns. *Wait Till Next Year: A Memoir*. New York: Simon & Schuster, 1997.

Greenberg, Hank, and Ira Berkow. *Hank Greenberg: The Story of My Life*. New York: Times, 1989.

Grimm, Charlie, and Ed Prell. *Jolly Cholly's Story: Baseball, I Love You!* Chicago: Henry Regnery, 1968.

Halas, George, Gwen Morgan, and Arthur Veysey. *Halas by Halas: The Autobiography of George Halas*. New York: McGraw-Hill, 1979.

Hodges, Russ, and Al Hirshberg. *My Giants: The Story of the Giants in San Francisco and New York*. Garden City, NY: Doubleday, 1963.

Hornsby, Rogers, and Bill Surface. *My War With Baseball*. New York: Coward-McCann, 1962.

Kahn, Roger. *The Boys of Summer*. New York: Harper & Row, 1987 reprint.

Kiner, Ralph, and Danny Peary. *Baseball Forever: Reflections on 60 Years in the Game*. Chicago: Triumph, 2004.

Koufax, Sandy, and Ed Linn. *Koufax*. New York: Viking, 1966.

Kuhn, Bowie. *Hardball: The Education of a Baseball Commissioner*. New York: Times, 1987.

Mack, Connie. *My 66 Years in the Big Leagues: The Great Story of America's National Game*. Philadelphia: John C. Winston, 1950.

Mathews, Eddie, and Bob Buege. *Eddie Mathews and the National Pastime*. Milwaukee: Douglas American Sports Publications, 1994.

Mays, Willie, and Lou Sahadi. *Say Hey: The Autobiography of Willie Mays*. New York: Simon & Schuster, 1988.

Miller, Marvin. *A Whole Different Ball Game: The Sport and Business of Baseball*. New York: Birch Lane, 1991.

Murray, Jim. *Jim Murray: An Autobiography*. New York: Macmillan, 1993.

Musial, Stan, and Bob Broeg. *Stan Musial: The Man's Own Story*. Garden City, NY: Doubleday, 1964.

Paige, LeRoy, and David Lipman. *Maybe I'll Pitch Forever: A Great Baseball Player Tells the Hilarious Story Behind the Legend*. Lincoln: University of Nebraska Press, 1993.

Parrott, Harold. *The Lords of Baseball: A Wry Look at a Side of the Game the Fan Seldom Sees—The Front Office*. New York: Praeger, 1976.

Povich, Shirley. *All These Mornings*. Englewood Cliffs, NJ: Prentice-Hall, 1969.

Rickey, Branch, and Robert Riger. *The American Diamond: A Documentary of the Game of Baseball*. New York: Simon & Schuster, 1965.

Robinson, Jackie. *I Never Had It Made: The Autobiography of Jackie Robinson*. Hopewell, NJ: Ecco, 1995.

Roseboro, John, and Bill Libby. *Glory Days With the Dodgers and Other Days With Others*. New York: Atheneum, 1978.

Rudd, Irving, and Stan Fischler. *The Sporting Life: The Duke and Jackie, Pee Wee, Razor, Phil, Ali, Mushky Jackson, and Me*. New York: St. Martin's, 1990.

Snider, Duke, and Bill Gilbert. *The Duke of Flatbush*. New York: Zebra, 1988.

Stevens, John Paul. *The Making of a Justice: Reflections on My First 94 Years*. New York: Little, Brown, and Co., 2019.

Thompson, Chuck, and Gordon Beard. *Ain't the Beer Cold!* South Bend, IN: Diamond, 1996.

Thompson, Fresco, and Cy Rice. *Every Diamond Doesn't Sparkle: Behind the Scenes With the Dodgers*. New York: David McKay Co., 1964.

Veeck, Bill, and Ed Linn. *The Hustler's Handbook*. New York: G.P. Putnam's Sons, 1965.

_____. *Veeck—As in Wreck: The Autobiography of Bill Veeck*. New York: G.P. Putnam's Sons, 1962.

Baseball Histories and Biographies

Angell, Roger. *Five Seasons: A Baseball Companion*. New York: Simon & Schuster, 1977.

Armour, Mark. *Joe Cronin: A Life in Baseball*. Lincoln: University of Nebraska Press, 2010.

Banner, Stuart. *The Baseball Trust: A History of Baseball's Antitrust Exemption*. New York: Oxford University Press, 2013.

Bisher, Furman. *Miracle in Atlanta: The Atlanta Braves Story*. Cleveland: World Publishing Co., 1966.

Boxerman, Burton, and Benita Boxerman. *Ebbets to Veeck to Busch: Eight Owners Who Shaped Baseball*. Jefferson, NC: McFarland, 2003.

Breslin, Jimmy. *Branch Rickey*. New York: Viking, 2011.

_____. *Can't Anybody Here Play This Game?* Chicago: Ivan R. Dee, 2003 reprint.

Bryant, Howard. *The Last Hero: A Life of Henry Aaron*. New York: Pantheon, 2010.

Buhite, Russell. *The Continental League: A Personal History*. Lincoln: University of Nebraska Press, 2014.

Cannon, Jimmy. *Nobody Asked Me, But...: The World of Jimmy Cannon*. New York: Holt, Rinehart, and Winston, 1978.

Creamer, Robert. *Stengel: His Life and Times*. New York: Simon & Schuster, 1984.

D'Antonio, Michael. *Forever Blue: The True Story of Walter O'Malley, Baseball's Most Controversial Owner, and the Dodgers of Brooklyn and Los Angeles*. New York: Riverhead, 2009.

Deveaux, Tom. *The Washington Senators, 1901–1971*. Jefferson, NC: McFarland, 2001.

Dewey, Donald, and Nicholas Acocella. *The Ball Clubs: Every Franchise, Past and Present, Officially Recognized by Major League Baseball*. New York: HarperCollins, 1996.

Dickson, Paul. *Bill Veeck: Baseball's Greatest Maverick*. New York: Walker & Co., 2012.

_____. *Leo Durocher: Baseball's Prodigal Son*. New York: Bloomsbury, 2017.

Duquette, Jerold. *Regulating the National Pastime: Baseball and Antitrust*. Westport, CT: Praeger, 1999.

Dworkin, James. *Owners Versus Players: Baseball and Collective Bargaining*. Boston: Auburn House, 1981.

Eig, Jonathan. *Opening Day: The Story of Jackie Robinson's First Season*. New York: Simon & Schuster, 2007.

Eskenazi, Gerald. *Bill Veeck: A Baseball Legend*. New York: McGraw-Hill, 1988.

Fleder, Rob, editor. *Great Baseball Writing: Sports Illustrated, 1954–2004*. New York: Sports Illustrated, 2005.

Gilbert, Bill. *They Also Served: Baseball and the Home Front, 1941–1945*. New York: Crown, 1992.

Goldblatt, Andrew. *The Giants and the Dodgers: Four Cities, Two Teams, One Rivalry*. Jefferson, NC: McFarland, 2003.

Goldstein, Richard. *Spartan Seasons: How Baseball Survived the Second World War*. New York: Macmillan, 1980.

_____. *Superstars and Screwballs: 100 Years of Brooklyn Baseball*. New York: Dutton, 1991.

Golenbock, Peter. *Dynasty: The New York Yankees, 1949–1964*. New York: Berkley, 1985.

Graham, Frank. *The Brooklyn Dodgers: An Informal History*. New York: G.P. Putnam's Sons, 1945.

_____. *The New York Giants: An Informal History*. New York: G.P. Putnam's Sons, 1952.

Halberstam, David. *October 1964*. New York: Villard, 1994.

_____. *Summer of '49*. New York: William Morrow, 1989.

Hartley, James. *Washington's Expansion Senators: 1961–1971*. Germantown, MD: Corduroy, 1997.

Helyar, John. *Lords of the Realm: The Real History of Baseball*. New York: Villard, 1994.

Hirsch, James. *Willie Mays: The Life, The Legend*. New York: Scribner's, 2010.

Holtzman, Jerome. *The Jerome Holtzman Baseball Reader: A Treasury of Award-Winning Writing from the Official Historian of Major League Baseball*. Chicago: Triumph, 2003.

Holtzman, Jerome, and George Vass. *Baseball, Chicago Style: A Tale of Two Teams, One City*. Chicago: Bonus, 2001.

Jordan, David. *The Athletics of Philadelphia: Connie Mack's White Elephants, 1901–1954*. Jefferson, NC: McFarland, 1999.

Kaese, Harold. *The Boston Braves, 1871–1953*. Boston: Northeastern University Press, 2004 reprint.

Kahn, Roger. *The Era: 1947–1957, When the Yankees, the Giants, and the Dodgers Ruled the World*. New York: Ticknor & Fields, 1993.

Kelley, Brent. *Baseball's Biggest Blunder: The Bonus Rule of 1953–1957*. Lanham, MD: Scarecrow, 1997.

Kerr, Jon. *Calvin: Baseball's Last Dinosaur*. Dubuque, IA: Wm. C. Brown, 1990.

Koppett, Leonard. *The New York Mets: The Whole Story*. New York: Macmillan, 1970.

Kuklick, Bruce. *To Every Thing a Season: Shibe Park and Urban Philadelphia, 1909–1976*. Princeton, NJ: Princeton University Press, 1991.

Kurlansky, Mark. *Hank Greenberg: The Hero Who Didn't Want to Be One*. New Haven, CT: Yale University Press, 2011.

Libby, Bill. *Charlie O. and the Angry A's: The Low and Inside Story of Charlie O. Finley and*

Baseball's Most Colorful Team. Garden City, NY: Doubleday, 1975.

Lowenfish, Lee, and Tony Lupien. *The Imperfect Diamond: The Story of Baseball's Reserve System and the Men Who Fought to Change It.* New York: Stein and Day, 1980.

Lowry, Philip. *Green Cathedrals: The Ultimate Celebration of All 273 Major League and Negro League Ballparks.* Reading, MA: Addison-Wesley, 1992.

Macht, Norman. *The Grand Old Man of Baseball: Connie Mack in His Final Years, 1932–1956.* Lincoln: University of Nebraska Press, 2015.

Mann, Arthur. *Branch Rickey: American in Action.* Boston: Houghton Mifflin, 1957.

Marshall, William. *Baseball's Pivotal Era, 1945–1951.* Lexington: University Press of Kentucky, 1999.

McCue, Andy. *Mover and Shaker: Walter O'Malley, the Dodgers, and Baseball's Westward Expansion.* Lincoln: University of Nebraska Press, 2014.

McKelvey, G. Richard. *Mexican Raiders in the Major Leagues, 1946.* Jefferson, NC: McFarland, 2006.

Mead, William. *Even the Browns: The Zany, True Story of Baseball in the Early Forties.* Chicago: Contemporary, 1978.

Meany, Tom. *Milwaukee's Miracle Braves.* New York: Grosset & Dunlap, 1956.

Mehl, Ernest. *The Kansas City Athletics.* New York: Henry Holt and Co., 1956.

Murphy, Robert. *After Many a Summer: The Passing of the Giants and Dodgers and a Golden Age in New York Baseball.* New York: Union Square, 2009.

Nowlin, Bill. *Tom Yawkey: Patriarch of the Boston Red Sox.* Lincoln: University of Nebraska Press, 2018.

Oakley, J. Ronald. *Baseball's Last Golden Age, 1946–1960: The National Pastime in a Time of Glory and Change.* Jefferson, NC: McFarland, 1994.

O'Toole, Andrew. *Branch Rickey in Pittsburgh: Baseball's Trailblazing General Manager for the Pirates, 1950–1955.* Jefferson, NC: McFarland, 2000.

Peary, Danny. *Jackie Robinson in Quotes: The Remarkable Life of Baseball's Most Significant Player.* Salem, MA: Page Street, 2016.

Peterson, John. *The Kansas City Athletics: A Baseball History, 1954–1967.* Jefferson, NC: McFarland, 2003.

Pietrusza, David. *Judge and Jury: The Life and Times of Judge Kenesaw Mountain Landis.* South Bend, IN: Diamond, 1998.

Podair, Jerald. *City of Dreams: Dodger Stadium and the Birth of Modern Los Angeles.* Princeton, NJ: Princeton University Press, 2017.

Polner, Murray. *Branch Rickey: A Biography.* New York: Atheneum, 1982.

Povletich, William. *Milwaukee Braves: Heroes and Heartbreak.* Madison: Wisconsin Historical Society Press, 2009.

Prince, Carl. *Brooklyn's Dodgers: The Bums, the Borough, and the Best of Baseball, 1947–1957.* New York: Oxford University Press, 1996.

Reed, Robert. *A Six-Gun Salute: An Illustrated History of the Houston Colt .45s.* Houston: Lone Star, 1999.

Rosenthal, Harold. *The 10 Best Years of Baseball: An Informal History of the Fifties.* Chicago: Contemporary, 1979.

Schott, Tom, and Nick Peters. *The Giants Encyclopedia.* Champaign, IL: Sports Publishing, 2003.

Shapiro, Michael. *Bottom of the Ninth: Branch Rickey, Casey Stengel, and the Daring Scheme to Save Baseball from Itself.* New York: Times, 2009.

_____. *The Last Good Season: Brooklyn, the Dodgers, and Their Final Pennant Race Together.* New York: Doubleday, 2003.

Shecter, Leonard. *Once Upon the Polo Grounds: The Mets That Were.* New York: Dial, 1970.

Sickels, John. *Bob Feller: Ace of the Greatest Generation.* Washington, D.C.: Brassey's, 2004.

Smith, Curt. *Pull Up a Chair: The Vin Scully Story.* Washington, D.C.: Potomac, 2009.

Stout, Glenn. *The Dodgers: 120 Years of Dodgers Baseball.* Boston: Houghton Mifflin, 2004.

Sullivan, Neil. *The Diamond in the Bronx: Yankee Stadium and the Politics of New York.* New York: Oxford University Press, 2001.

_____. *The Dodgers Move West.* New York: Oxford University Press, 1987.

_____. *The Minors: The Struggles and the Triumph of Baseball's Poor Relation from 1876 to the Present.* New York: St. Martin's, 1990.

Testa, Judith. *Sal Maglie: Baseball's Demon Barber.* DeKalb, IL: Northern Illinois University Press, 2007.

Thomas, G Scott. *The Best (and Worst) of Baseball's Modern Era: The Top (and Bottom) Teams and Players From 1961 Through 2016.* Buffalo: Niawanda, 2016.

_____. *Leveling the Field: An Encyclopedia of Baseball's All-Time Great Performances as Revealed Through Adjusted Statistics.* New York: Black Dog & Leventhal, 2002.

Thorn, John, Pete Palmer, Michael Gershman, and David Pietrusza, editors. *Total Baseball: The Official Encyclopedia of Major League Baseball.* 6th ed. New York: Total Sports, 1999.

Threston, Christopher. *The Integration of Baseball in Philadelphia.* Jefferson, NC: McFarland, 2003.

Tygiel, Jules. *Baseball's Great Experiment: Jackie Robinson and His Legacy.* New York: Oxford University Press, 1997.

Vecsey, George. *Stan Musial: An American Life.* New York: Ballantine, 2011.

Virtue, John. *South of the Color Barrier: How Jorge Pasquel and the Mexican League Pushed Baseball Toward Racial Integration.* Jefferson, NC: McFarland, 2008.

Voigt, David Quentin. *American Baseball, Volume II: From the Commissioners to Continental*

Expansion. University Park: Pennsylvania State University Press, 1983.

_____. *American Baseball, Volume III: From Postwar Expansion to the Electronic Age*. University Park: Pennsylvania State University Press, 1983.

Warfield, Don. *The Roaring Redhead: Larry MacPhail—Baseball's Great Innovator*. South Bend, IN: Diamond, 1987.

White, G. Edward. *Creating the National Pastime: Baseball Transforms Itself, 1903–1953*. Princeton, NJ: Princeton University Press, 1996.

Zimbalist, Andrew. *Baseball and Billions: A Probing Look Inside the Big Business of Our National Pastime*. New York: Basic, 1992.

Zimniuch, Fran. *Baseball's New Frontier: A History of Expansion, 1961–1998*. Lincoln: University of Nebraska Press, 2013.

Zingg, Paul, and Mark Medeiros. *Runs, Hits, and an Era: The Pacific Coast League, 1903–58*. Urbana: University of Illinois Press, 1994.

Other Books

Bernard, Richard, and Bradley Rice, editors. *Sunbelt Cities: Politics and Growth Since World War II*. Austin: University of Texas Press, 1983.

Bilstein, Roger. *Flight in America: 1900–1983, From the Wrights to the Astronauts*. Baltimore: Johns Hopkins University Press, 1984.

Boorstin, Daniel. *The Americans: The Democratic Experience*. New York: Random House, 1973.

Burrows, Edwin, and Mike Wallace. *Gotham: A History of New York City to 1898*. New York: Oxford University Press, 1999.

Caplow, Theodore, Louis Hicks, and Ben Wattenberg, *The First Measured Century: An Illustrated Guide to Trends in America, 1900–2000*. Washington, D.C.: AEI Press, 2001.

Caro, Robert. *The Power Broker: Robert Moses and the Fall of New York*. New York: Vintage, 1974.

Crouch, Tom. *Wings: A History of Aviation from Kites to the Space Age*. New York: W.W. Norton & Co., 2003.

Dallek, Robert. *Harry S. Truman*. New York: Times, 2008.

Davis, Jeff. *Papa Bear: The Life and Legacy of George Halas*. New York: McGraw-Hill, 2005.

_____. *Rozelle: Czar of the NFL*. New York: McGraw-Hill, 2008.

Denton, Sally, and Roger Morris. *The Money and the Power: The Making of Las Vegas and Its Hold on America, 1947–2000*. New York: Alfred A. Knopf, 2001.

Fenton, John. *In Your Opinion: The Managing Editor of the Gallup Poll Looks at Polls, Politics, and the People from 1945 to 1960*. Boston: Little, Brown, and Co., 1960.

Finnerty, Margaret. *Del Webb: A Man, A Company*. Flagstaff, AZ: Heritage, 1991.

Fishman, Robert. *Bourgeois Utopias: The Rise and Fall of Suburbia*. New York: Basic, 1987.

Fontenay, Charles. *Estes Kefauver: A Biography*. Knoxville: University of Tennessee Press, 1980.

Freedman, Marc. *Prime Time: How Baby Boomers Will Revolutionize Retirement and Transform America*. New York: Public Affairs, 1999.

Freedman, Warren. *Professional Sports and Antitrust*. New York: Quorum, 1987.

Gorman, Joseph Bruce. *Kefauver: A Political Biography*. New York: Oxford University Press, 1971.

Gunther, John. *Inside U.S.A.* London: Hamish Hamilton, 1948.

Harris, David. *The League: The Rise and Decline of the NFL*. New York: Bantam, 1986.

Horrigan, Jack, and Mike Rathet. *The Other League: The Fabulous Story of the American Football League*. Chicago: Follett, 1970.

Horrigan, Joe. *NFL Century: The One-Hundred-Year Rise of America's Greatest Sports League*. New York: Crown, 2019.

Irey, Elmer. *The Tax Dodgers: The Inside Story of the T-Men's War With America's Political and Underworld Hoodlums*. New York: Greenberg, 1948.

Jackson, Kenneth. *Crabgrass Frontier: The Suburbanization of the United States*. New York: Oxford University Press, 1985.

Johnson, William Jr. *Super Spectator and the Electric Lilliputians*. Boston: Little, Brown, and Co., 1971.

Kalman, Laura. *Abe Fortas: A Biography*. New Haven, CT: Yale University Press, 1990.

Kefauver, Estes. *In a Few Hands: Monopoly Power in America*. New York: Pantheon, 1965.

Kowet, Don. *The Rich Who Own Sports*. New York: Random House, 1977.

Lait, Jack, and Lee Mortimer. *Washington Confidential: The Lowdown on the Big Town*. New York: Crown, 1951.

Lewis, Tom. *Divided Highways: Building the Interstate Highways, Transforming American Life*. New York: Viking, 1997.

Littlewood, Thomas. *Arch: A Promoter, Not a Poet—The Story of Arch Ward*. Ames: Iowa State University Press, 1990.

Lowe, Stephen. *The Kid on the Sandlot: Congress and Professional Sports, 1910–1992*. Bowling Green, OH: Bowling Green State University Popular Press, 1995.

MacCambridge, Michael. *America's Game: The Epic Story of How Pro Football Captured a Nation*. New York: Random House, 2004.

Manchester, William. *The Glory and the Dream: A Narrative History of America, 1932–1972*. Boston: Little, Brown, and Co., 1974.

Marc, David, and Robert Thompson. *Prime Time, Prime Movers: From I Love Lucy to L.A. Law—America's Greatest TV Shows and the People Who Created Them*. Boston: Little, Brown, and Co., 1992.

Powers, Ron. *Supertube: The Rise of Television Sports*. New York: Coward-McCann, 1984.

Quirk, James, and Rodney Fort. *Pay Dirt: The*

Business of Professional Team Sports. Princeton, NJ: Princeton University Press, 1992.

Rader, Benjamin. *In Its Own Image: How Television Has Transformed Sports*. New York: Free Press, 1984.

Reich, Cary. *The Life of Nelson A. Rockefeller: Worlds to Conquer, 1908–1958*. New York: Doubleday, 1996.

Robinson, Ira. *Canadian Urban Growth Trends: Implications for a National Settlement Policy*. Vancouver: University of British Columbia Press, 1981.

Schwartz, Mildred. *Trends in White Attitudes Toward Negroes*. Chicago: National Opinion Research Center, 1967.

Smith, Richard Norton. *On His Own Terms: A Life of Nelson Rockefeller*. New York: Random House, 2014.

_____. *Thomas E. Dewey and His Times*. New York: Simon & Schuster, 1982.

Teaford, Jon. *The Rough Road to Renaissance: Urban Revitalization in America, 1940–1985*. Baltimore: Johns Hopkins University Press, 1990.

_____. *The Twentieth-Century American City: Problem, Promise, and Reality*. Baltimore: Johns Hopkins University Press, 1986.

Thomas, Evan. *The Man to See: Edward Bennett Williams—Legendary Lawyer, Ultimate Insider*. New York: Touchstone, 1992.

Thomas, G. Scott. *A New World to Be Won: John Kennedy, Richard Nixon, and the Tumultuous Year of 1960*. Santa Barbara, CA: Praeger, 2011.

_____. *The Pursuit of the White House: A Handbook of Presidential Election Statistics and History*. New York: Greenwood, 1987.

_____. *The United States of Suburbia: How the Suburbs Took Control of America and What They Plan to Do With It*. Amherst, NY: Prometheus, 1998.

Weil, Francois. *A History of New York*. New York: Columbia University Press, 2004.

White, Theodore. *The Making of the President 1960*. New York: Atheneum, 1961.

_____. *Theodore H. White at Large: The Best of His Magazine Writing, 1939–1986*. New York: Pantheon, 1992.

Wilson, Wayne, and David Wiggins, editors. *LA Sports: Play, Games, and Community in the City of Angels*. Fayetteville: University of Arkansas Press, 2018.

Wunderlin, Clarence Jr., editor. *The Papers of Robert A. Taft: Volume 4, 1949–1953*. Kent, OH: Kent State University Press, 2006.

Yarnell, Allen. *Democrats and Progressives: The 1948 Presidential Election as a Test of Postwar Liberalism*. Berkeley: University of California Press, 1974.

Newspapers

Akron Beacon Journal
Baltimore Sun
Boston Globe
Brooklyn Eagle
Chicago Tribune
Cincinnati Enquirer
Daily Variety
Detroit Free Press
Detroit News
Kansas City Times
Los Angeles Times
Louisville Courier-Journal
Milwaukee Journal
Milwaukee Sentinel
Minneapolis Morning Tribune
Minneapolis Star
New York Times
Oakland Tribune
Philadelphia Inquirer
Pittsburgh Post-Gazette
Pittsburgh Press
St. Louis Post-Dispatch
St. Louis Star-Times
San Francisco Chronicle
Sporting News
Wall Street Journal
Washington Post

Magazines and Journals

American History
American Prospect
Antitrust Bulletin
Baseball Magazine
Baseball Research Journal
Broadcasting Telecasting
California History
Chicago Tribune Magazine
Esquire
Forbes
Forum and Century
Harper's
Journal of Broadcasting and Electronic Media
Journal of Legislation and Public Policy
Journal of Political Economy
Journal of Sport History
Life
Los Angeles Magazine
Minneapolis Star and Tribune Sunday Magazine
National Pastime
New Republic
New York
New York Times Magazine
Nine
Planning
Saturday Evening Post
Southern Economic Journal
Sports Illustrated
Texas Monthly
Time
West

Websites

American Presidency Project of the University of California–Santa Barbara, https://www.presidency.ucsb.edu
Baseball Reference, https://www.baseball-reference.com
Federal Reserve Bank of Minneapolis, https://www.minneapolisfed.org
Federal Reserve Bank of St. Louis, https://fred.stlouisfed.org
Gallup, https://www.gallup.com
Justia, https://supreme.justia.com
National Baseball Hall of Fame and Museum, https://baseballhall.org
O'Malley Seidler Partners LLC, https://www.walteromalley.com
Online Archive of California, https://oac.cdlib.org
Pro Football Reference, https://www.pro-football-reference.com
Public Broadcasting Service, https://www.pbs.org
Society for American Baseball Research, https://www.sabr.org
Statistics Canada, https://www.statcan.gc.ca
The Undefeated, https://www.theundefeated.com
U.S. Census Bureau, https://www.census.gov

Index

Numbers in ***bold italics*** refer to pages with illustrations

Aaron, Henry 135, 185, 232
Ackerman, Carl ***167***
Adams, Bud 219, 239
air transportation 6, 109–11, 175, 234–35
All-America Football Conference 47, 49, 61–62, 107, 177, 239
Allison, Bob 240, 252
Allyn, Arthur, Jr. 260–62, 271
Alston, Tom 152
Ameche, Don 47
American Association 47, 51, 97, 167, 236, 239
American Baseball Guild 39–41, 87, 273
American Football League 219–20, 239–40, 250, 260–61
Amoros, Sandy 153
Anderson, Dave 3, 126–27
Angell, Roger 247, 256
antitrust hearings 9, 98, 99–102, 171, 182–84, 202–4, 206–9, 221, 242, 267–68
antitrust laws 11, 37–38, 67–68, 98, 100–101, 109, 119, 133–35, 177–78, 182–83, 201–3, 206–9, 218–19, 221, 238–40, 242, 262, 271–73
Antonelli, Johnny 67, 197
Aparicio, Luis 231
Arechiga, Avrana 214
Arnebergh, Roger 216
Astrodome (Houston) *see* Harris County Domed Stadium (Houston)
Atlanta, Georgia 131, 144, 223, 236, 262, 271–73
Autry, Gene 254, 270

Bailey, Bob 205
Baker, Home Run 141
Ball, Philip 26
Baltimore, Maryland 7–8, 51, 91, 101, 113, 119–20, 124, 127–28, 144, 164, 198, 208, 242, 244, 246, 267
Baltimore Orioles 77, 128, 136, 205, 244, 254
Bankhead, Dan 153
Banks, Ernie 135, 234
Barber, Red 19, 21, 29, 54, 63, 82, 84, 276

Barnes, Donald 5–9, 14, 47, 51, 71
Barnes, Joe 103
Barnes, Robert 169
Barrow, Edward 21
Bartholomay, William 262
Bateson, J.W. 223
Baumann, Frank 130
Bavasi, Buzzie 25, 82, 105, 125, 153, 155, 188, 212, 232, 276
Bearden, Gene 60
Becker, Bill 187
Bel Geddes, Norman 125
Bell, Bert 107, ***108***, 109, 206, 219, 239–40
Bennett, Tom 272
Benny, Jack 212
Benswanger, William 40
Berg, Kenneth 244
Berg, Leonard 244
Berger, Victor 11
Bevens, Bill 52, 59
Bisher, Furman 261
Blackmun, Harry 273
Blues Stadium (Kansas City) 139
Blume, Clinton 192
bonus babies 67, 75, 129–30, 150, 164, 205–6, 237
Boston, Massachusetts 6–7, 233, 240, 245
Boston Braves 3, 10, 39, 56, 60, 72–73, 97, 102–3, 105, 115, 119, 122, 245, 269
Boston Red Sox 43, 60, 61, 69, 72, 73, 77, 116, 119, 130, 152, 153, 159, 184, 232
Bouchee, Ed 258
Boudreau, Lou 142–43
Bowman, Joe 25
Boyer, Clete 143
Boyle, Robert 88
Branca, Ralph 246
Braves Field (Boston) 62, 73, 142, 246
Breadon, Sam 6, 14, 17, 23, 26–30, 71
Breslin, Jimmy 198, 250–51
Briggs, Walter "Spike," Jr. 140–41, 164–65
Briggs, Walter, Sr. 164
Briggs Stadium (Detroit) 24
broadcasting 3, 21, 56, 58,
 64–66, 68, 73, 83, 88, 91, 104–9, 111, 115–16, 122, 125, 131, 137, 145, 163, 179–80, 183–84, 197, 224, 234–35, 239, 252, 254, 272
Broeg, Bob 72
Brooklyn, New York 7, 81–83, 125, 153–54, 183, 246, 274
Brooklyn Dodgers 1, 3, 7, 21, 28–32, 35, 42–43, 51–55, 59, 60, 63–66, 69, 82–86, 94, 106, 111, 121, 123, 125–26, 137, 150, 153–55, 157–62, 168–70, 174–76, 179, 180, 181–83, 187–90
Brooklyn Sports Center Authority 169–71, 173–74, 181, 187
Brosnan, Jim 234, 257
Brown, Jimmy 40
Brown, Joe L. 130
Brown, Pat 246
Bruton, Bill 121
Buffalo, New York 8, 37, 47, 144, 191, 223–24, 236, 238, 271
Buhl, Bob 110, 120
Burdette, Lew 185, 210
Burns, George 212
Burns, Matt 246
Busch, August "Gussie," Jr. 117–18, 124, 135, 144, 152, 264
Busch Memorial Stadium (St. Louis) 124, 127
Bush, Donie 58

Camilli, Dolph 29
Campanella, Roy 84, 95, 153, 196, 210, 215–16, 246
Candlestick Park (San Francisco) 193, 246, ***247***, 263
Cannon, Jimmy 222, 258, 274–75
Cannon, Robert 205, 273
Capone, Al 207
Caray, Harry 117
Carleton, Will 81
Caro, Robert 155
Carpenter, Robert, Jr. 9, 40, 141–42, 144, 193
Carroll, Louis 77
Carson, Jack 106
Cashmore, John 154–55, 158, 169, 175
Celler, Emanuel 9, 98, ***99***,

321

Index

100–102, 127, 132–34, 142, 171, 178, 182–83, 199, 202–6, 218–19, 262–63, 267, 274
census of 1890 233
census of 1900 7–8
census of 1940 6, 8
census of 1950 48, 79–81, 96
census of 1960 144, 233–34
Cerv, Bob 110
Chance, Dean 255
Chandler, Albert "Happy" 2, 19, 22–25, 29, 31, 34–35, 38–39, 41–42, 50–51, 54–55, 66–69, 87–89, **90**, 93–94, 96, 100, 102, 108, 117, 146, 173, 263, 268, 273, 276
Chapman, Ben 55
Chase, Hal 37
Chavez Ravine (Los Angeles) 175, 181, 190, 194–95, 197, 211–17, 269
Cherne, Leo 44
Chicago, Illinois 6–7, 46, 79–81, 96, 106, 109–10, 219, 260–61
Chicago Cubs 24, 47, 49, 56, 65, 71, 96, 107, 135, 145–46, 149, 164, 209, 226, 234, 260–61
Chicago White Sox 12, 37, 47–48, 51–52, 62, 71, 74, 76, 105, 113, 122, 127, 136, 142, 149, 226–32, 255, 260–62
Christenberry, Robert 191
Christopher, George 179, 181, 187, 196, 247
Cicotte, Eddie **48**
Cincinnati, Ohio 8, 45, 80, 110
Cincinnati Reds 9, 13, 20–22, 65, 110, 126, 152, 154, 184–85, 192, 212, 257, 269
Clark, Joseph, Jr. 138
Clark, Tom 178
Claytor, Graham, Jr. 96
Clemente, Roberto 164
Cleveland, Ohio 8, 45, 46–47, 49, 62, 79–80, 97, 192, 234, 246
Cleveland Indians 24, 42, 55, 57–58, 60, 70–71, 73, 76, 90, 116, 135, 184, 192, 231, 241, 254, 267
Clifford, Clark 53
Cobb, Ty 99
Cobo, Albert 80
Colt Stadium (Houston) 260
Comiskey, Charles 226, 275
Comiskey, Charles "Chuck," II 62, 226–31, 260, 262
Comiskey, Grace 9, 226–28
Comiskey, Louis 226
Comiskey Park (Chicago) 7, 31, 62–63, 226, 230, 261, 269
Condon, Dave 231
Connie Mack Stadium (Philadelphia) 141
Connors, Chuck 29
Consolo, Billy 130
Continental League 3, 219–25,

234–40, 244, 249–50, 252–53, 262, 264, 271
Coogan, James 166
Cooke, Jack Kent 165, 201, 220
Corbett, Jack 98, 101, 132–34
Corum, Bill 89
Coveleski, Stan 76
Cox, Billy 111
Cox, John 142
Craig, Roger 259
Creamer, Robert 82
Cronin, Joe 3, 29, 153, 199, 203, 220, 225, 252, 254
Crosley, Powel 192
Crosley Field (Cincinnati) 20, 62, 116, 192, 269
Crump, Edward 206
Cullinan, Craig 220, 222, 251

D'Alesandro, Thomas, Jr. 119, 124
Daley, Arthur 17, 35, 61, 71, 87, 90, 116, 125, 144, 191, 229, 274, 276
Daley, Bill 192
Daley, Richard 231
Dallas, Texas 144, 147, 201, 219, 223, 236, 239–40, 270–71
Dandridge, Ray 95
Daniel, Dan 25, 87, 102, 150, 223, 261
Davidson, Donald 72, 185, 245
Davis, Tommy 267
Day, Laraine 54
Dean, Dizzy 30, 51–52, 164
Denver, Colorado 147, 201, 219–20, 236, 271
Detroit, Michigan 14, 79–80, 233–34
Detroit Tigers 14, 24, 61, 65, 67, 70, 91, 124, 130, 142, 146, 152, 164–65, 241, 265
Devine, Bing 227, 264
DeVoto, Bernard 109
Dewey, Thomas 1, 19, 22, 188
DeWitt, Bill, Sr. 6–7, 66, 71, 84, 227
DeWitt, Charley 71
Dickens, Charles 81
Dickson, Paul 57
DiMaggio, Joe 47, 52, 58, 84, 94, 253
District of Columbia Stadium (Washington) 171, 243, 248, 264–65
Ditmar, Art 143
Dixon, Paul Rand 134, 237–39
Doby, Larry 58
Dodger Stadium (Los Angeles) 215–17, 247–48, 254, 269
Doerr, Bobby 60, 72–73, 77
Doff, Jerome 197
Doherty, Edward 236
Donargo, Anthony **167**
Doyle, Bernard 63
Drebinger, John 250
Dropo, Walt 77
Drysdale, Don 153, 188, 197
Dunlap, Orrin, Jr. 65

Dunn, Jack 119
Dunne, Robert Jerome 230
Duren, Ryne 143
Durocher, Leo 2, 19, 21, 29, 31, 54, 55, 60, 87, 135, 148, 162
Dykes, Jimmie 138, 227, 241

Ebbets, Charles 63–64, 82, 126
Ebbets Field (Brooklyn) 21, 30, 63, **64**, 65–66, 82–83, 111, 125–26, 153–54, 158, 169–70, 174–75, 180, 189, 192, 194, 212, 246
Eckert, William 263
Ehlers, Art 120
Eisenhower, Dwight 171–72, 191, 248
Elliott, Bob 40
Elston, Gene 270
Erskine, Carl 82, 246
expansion 1, 8–10, 50–51, 100, 127–28, 144, 148, 150, 199–201, 223, 225, 234, 249–55, 267–68, 270–71

Face, Roy 164
Farley, James 2, 192
Federal Baseball Club v. National League (1922) 37–38, 133, 178, 199
Federal League 11–12, 36–38, 74, 199, 218, 239
Federoff, Anthony 40
Feeney, Charles 161
Feller, Bob 24, 34, 42, 131–32, 184, 204, 273
Fenway Park (Boston) 62, 63, 73, 111
Fetzer, John 165
Finch, Frank 215
Finley, Charles 140, 165, 229, 244, 254–56, 270, **271**, 274
Fleig, Fred 234
Flood, Curt 272
football, professional 46–47, 49–50, 61–62, 64, 106–9, 128, 159, 166, 177–78, 182, 202, 219–20, 222, 238–40, 248, 269, 276–77
Ford, Whitey 78
Fox, Nellie 231
Foxx, Jimmie 141, 166
Frank, Jerome 68
free agency 27, 35, 100, 134–35, 237, 273–75
Frick, Ford 10, 50, 93–94, 99, 102, 108, 117–18, 131–32, 134–35, 144, 146, 171, 178, 182–83, 185, 191–92, 198, 201, 203–5, 209, 216, 218–25, 235–37, 239–40, 243, 253–54, 257, 263, 267–70
Frisch, Frankie 40
Fuller, Buckminster 160
Furillo, Carl 196

Gaedel, Eddie 91–92
Galbreath, John 27, 29, 85, 131, 164, 192, 218, 222–23, 240

Index

Gallagher, James 56
Gandhi, Mohandas 27
Gardella, Danny 33–35, 38, 67–69, 77, 87–88, 95, 98, 132–33, 269
Garner, John Nance *90*
Garver, Ned 91, 100, 113
Garvey, Steve 84
Gehrig, Lou 74
Gerlach, Larry 57
Gibson, Phil 215
Gilbert, Tookie 67
Giles, Warren 22, 45, 58, 63, 66, 93, 118, 120, 131, 134, 212, 220, 249, 259–60
Gilliam, Jim 153
Gimbel, Bernard 192
Gleason, Bill 231
Glickman, Marty 82
Goldsmith, Seymour 246
Goldstein, Ernest 99–100
Goldwater, Barry 96
Goodding, Gladys 189
Goodwin, Doris Kearns 150
Gordon, Joe 241, 256
Gore, Albert, Sr. 206, 208
Gould, Paul 42
Graff, Milt 143
Graham, Charlie 2, 49
Grant, M. Donald 184, 220
Grantham, Larry 260
Gray, Pete 13, 24
Green, Pumpsie 232
Greenberg, Hank 8, 24, 70–71, 131, 140, 192, 229, 231, 253–54
Greenwade, Tom 31–32
Griffith, Ann Robertson 173
Griffith, Calvin 3, 76, 120, 159–60, 171, *172*, 173–74, 191–92, 209, 242–43, 248, 252–54, 263, 272
Griffith, Clark 9–10, 17–18, 37, 39–40, 53, 74, *75*, 76, 100–101, 121, 132, 159–60, 172–73, 204, 240, 252
Griffith Stadium (Washington) 53, 75, 243, 265
Grim, Allan 109
Grimm, Charlie 56, 58, 121, 135, 245
Grove, Lefty 141
Gunther, John 81

Haddix, Harvey 231–32
Hahn, Kenneth 173–76
Halas, George 47, 49, 108, 239–40, 250
Hamberger, Babe 35
Hamey, Roy 129
Hamill, Pete 82, 274
Haney, Fred 163
Hannegan, Robert 22–23, 71–72
Harper, Roy 117
Harridge, Will 6, 140, 171
Harriman, Averell 169–70, 174
Harris County Domed Stadium (Houston) *259*, 260, 270

Hart, Philip 238
Haupert, Michael 274
Havana, Cuba 191
Haynes, Joe 76, 171
Haynes, Thelma 76, 172, 243
Hemingway, Ernest 258
Hemond, Roland 73, 120
Henie, Sonja 21, 88
Higbe, Kirby 54
Hillings, Patrick 100, 182
Hirshberg, Al 72, 108
Hodges, Gil 196, 210, 259
Hodges, Russ 161, 196
Hofheinz, Roy 251–52, 270
Holland, John 181, 190
Holloman, Bobo 121
Holmes, Oliver Wendell 38, 68, 101, 109, 133–34, 178
Holtzman, Elizabeth 263
Hoover, J. Edgar 18–19, 22
Hope, Bob 57
Hornsby, Rogers 25, 26, 92, 113
Houston, Texas 26, 51, 117, 124, 144, 147, 201, 219, 220, 222, 236, 239
Houston Colt .45s 250–52, 260, 270
Howard, Elston 150, 152
Hughes, Howard 127
Hulbert, William 35–36
Humes, Carmen *see* Johnson, Carmen
Hunt, Lamar 219, 239–40
Hurley, Ed 91
Hutchinson, Fred 99
Hylan, John 83

integration 2, 10, 23, 30–33, 42, 46, 51, 53–55, 57–58, 79–80, 82, 95, 150, 152–54, 164, 193–94, 232–34, 243, 264, 267–68, 277
International League 47, 51, 191, 236, 239
Irvin, Monte 33, 53, 95
Isaminger, James 76

Jack, Hulan 166, *167*, 173–74
Jackson, Kenneth 233
Jackson, Robert 134
James, Jesse 74
Jamieson, Frank 188–89
Javits, Jacob 238
Jersey City, New Jersey 157–58, 160–61, 170, 175, 191
Johnson, Arnold 138, *139*, 140–43, 244, 255
Johnson, Ban 39, 199, 222–23, 239–40, 253
Johnson, Carmen 244, 255
Johnson, Edwin 220
Johnson, Frederic 67–68, 98, 133
Johnson, Johnny 206
Jonas, Paul 105
Jones, Jesse 44
Jordan, David 57
Jorgensen, Spider 69

Kaese, Harold 122, 159
Kahn, Joseph 155
Kahn, Roger 84, 153–54, 198–99
Kaline, Al 130, 205
Kansas City, Missouri 123–24, 127, 139–41, 144, 147, 233, 244
Kansas City Athletics 141–44, 244, 255–56, 271
Keating, Kenneth 182, 202–4, 206, 209, 221, 238
Kefauver, Estes 206–7, *208*, 209, 218, 220–21, 225, 237–38, 242, 262
Kennedy, John 207, 237, 256, 263, 265
Keough, Marty 130
Kessler, Gene 18
Killebrew, Harmon 130, 205, 240, 252
Kiner, Ralph 39–40, 129–31, 164, 276
Kirksey, George 201, 251
Kluszewski, Ted 260–61
Knorr, Fred 165
Konstanty, Jim 77–78, 153
Koufax, Sandy 130, 150, 188, 205
Kowalski, Walter 133–34
Kratter, Marvin 175, 246
Kryhoski, Dick 143
Kuhn, Bowie 84, 133, 273

La Guardia, Fiorello 53
Lajoie, Napoleon 37
Landis, Kenesaw Mountain 9–11, *12*, 13–14, 17–18, 23–24, 27, 30–31, 55, 57, 87, 92, 132, 222, 226
Landrith, Hobie 259
Lane, Clem 106
Lane, Frank 138, 216, *227*, 228–29, 241, 253, 256
Lanier, Max 34, 95
Lardner, John 12–13, 105, 170
Larsen, Don 136, 168
Lasorda, Tommy 150
Lausche, Frank 22–23
Lavagetto, Cookie 52, 59
Laws, Brick 96, 146
Leiser, Bill 47
Lemon, Bob 30
Levitt, William 45, 79
Lewis, Franklin 71
Lewis, J. Norman 130–32, 205, 273
Lewis, Jerry 212
Lieb, Fred 24
Lipsyte, Robert 259
Lockman, Whitey 161
Lopez, Al 29, 40
Lopez, Hector 143
Los Angeles, California 2, 6–9, 15, 46–48, 50–51, 80–81, 91, 96–97, 101, 106–7, 109, 123–24, 127, 143–50, 154–55, 158–60, 171, 173–76, 180–84, 187–90, 212–13, 233, 253–54
Los Angeles Angels (American League) 254–55, 270

Index

Los Angeles Angels (Pacific Coast League) 6, 49, 145, 147, 148, 149, 175, 193, 194
Los Angeles Dodgers 190–91, 193–97, 199, 204, 210–17, 232, 235–36, 244–45, 247, 254, 265, 268–70, 272–75
Los Angeles Memorial Coliseum (Los Angeles) 50, 107, 147–48, 181, 194–95, 197, 211, 215, *216*, 235, 245, 247–48, 254
Louis, Joe 105, 258
Louisville, Kentucky 173, 271
Lynch, Russ 118–19
Lyons, James 189

MacArthur, Douglas 18–19, 93
Mack, Connie 8–9, 25, 37, 51, 53–54, 58, 74, *75*, 76–77, 111, 137–38, 141–42, 275
Mack, Connie, Jr. 77
Mack, Earle 76–77, 137–41
Mack, Katherine 76, 141
Mack, Roy 76–77, 137–41
MacPhail, Larry 19, *20*, 21–23, 25, 28, 31, 39–41, 59–60, 63, 65–66, 82, 89, 99–100, 110, 200, 227
Maglie, Sal 67
Major League Baseball Players Association 131–32, 204–5, 267, 273
Malamud, Bernard 69
Malzone, Frank 110
Maney, Joe 72
Mann, Arthur 31
Mantle, Mickey 94, 111, 121, 168, 208
Mara, Jack 166
Mara, Tim 166
Marc, David 104
Marion, Marty 92, 118, 121, 124
Maris, Roger 143, 257
Marshall, George *108*, 248
Martin, Dean 212
Mathews, Eddie 62, 120, 122, 235
Mauch, Gene 257
Mays, Willie 94, 135, 163, 166, 185, 189–90, 193–94, 196–97, 246–47, 267
Mazeroski, Bill 241
McAuley, Ed 23
McCabe, Thomas 44
McCarty, Francis 148
McCovey, Willie 265
McCue, Andy 84
McGillicuddy, Cornelius *see* Mack, Connie
McGraw, Blanche 189
McGraw, John 189
McHale, John 261–62
McKechnie, Bill 25
McKinlay, Donald 228–29
McKinney, Frank 50
McLaughlin, George 83, 126
McNally, Dave 273
Meany, Tom 23, 27

Medwick, Joe 29
Mehl, Ernest 139
Melton, Rube 25
Memorial Stadium (Baltimore) 119, 128, 269
Mendelson, Frederic 114
Messersmith, Andy 273
metropolitan areas 48, 80, 144, 147, 179, 234
Metropolitan Stadium (Bloomington, Minnesota) 167, 243, 252
Mexican League 33–35, 38, 41–42, 87–88, 95
Mexico City, Mexico 51
Miami, Florida 164, 191
Miles, Clarence 128
Miller, Damon 100
Miller, Frederick 117, 121, 245
Miller, Marvin 273–74
Millstein, Gilbert 128
Milwaukee, Wisconsin 7–8, 56–57, 73, 91, 97, 114–15, 117–19, 233, 244–45, 261–62
Milwaukee Braves 119–23, 125, 128, 135, 137, 142, 144, 168, 185, 192, 210–11, 232, 235–36, 244–45, 261–62, 272
Milwaukee County Stadium (Milwaukee) 97, 114, 119, 121–22, *123*, 125, 137, 235, 245, 247–48, 262, 269
Minneapolis, Minnesota 8, 124, 127, 144, 147, 167, 173, 178–79, 191–92, 200–1, 219–20, 236, 240, 242–43, 249, 252, 271
Minnesota Twins 254, 263
Monday, Rick 206
Montreal, Quebec 8, 14, 32, 42, 51, 101, 124, 127, 144, 191, 271
Morano, Albert 203
Moses, Robert 126, 155, *156*, 157–58, 160, 170–71, 174–75, 180–81, 187, 194, 213, 223, 269
Moss, Les 63
Muckerman, Richard 15, 71
Municipal Stadium (Cleveland) 60, 62, 97, 240
Municipal Stadium (Kansas City) 142–43, 244
Munzel, Edgar 228–29
Murphy, Gabriel 173
Murphy, Robert 39–42, 87, 269, 273
Murray, Jim 83, 201
Musial, Stan 34, 72, 135, 208–9, 264
Mylod, Charles 170

National Football League 7, 21, 46–47, 49–50, 61, 106–9, 128, 166, 177–78, 206, 219, 239–40, 248, 276
Necciai, Ron 164
New Orleans, Louisiana 8, 67, 129
New York, New York 6–7, 21, 35, 53, 65, 80–82, 96, 155–57, 199, 238
New York Giants 1, 7, 33–37, 40, 60, 63, 67–68, 75, 77, 94–95, 106, 126, 135, 148–49, 161–68, 174, 179, 181–84, 189–90
New York Mets 250–51, 258–60, 264–65, 269–70
New York Yankees 14, 21–22, 24, 35, 42, 52, 58–61, 66, 69, 74, 78, 89–90, 93–94, 98, 110–11, 116, 121, 133, 135–36, 138, 141–43, 150, 152–53, 161, 168, 183, 185, 199, 205–6, 210, 215–16, 230–31, 235–36, 241, 244, 253, 257, 263, 265, 267, 270
Newcombe, Don 55, 153, 210
Newfield, Jack 82
Nicholson, Dave 205
Nuxhall, Joe 13

O'Connor, Leslie 9, 132
Olmo, Luis 69
O'Mahoney, Joseph 134, 242
O'Malley, Edwin 83
O'Malley, Peter 274
O'Malley, Walter 1, 3, 30, 38, 63–64, 66, 83–84, *85*, 86, 102, 106–7, 111, 116, 120, 122–23, 125–26, 131, 137, 153–55, 157–61, 163, 168–71, 174–76, 179–84, 187–88, 190, 194–98, 200–202, 204, 211–17, 223–25, 235, 240, 246–54, 261–62, 268–69, 271–72, 274, 276
O'Neill, Steve 24
O'Neill, Tip 203
O'Toole, Jim 260
Ott, Mel 33, 165–66, 241
Owen, Mickey 34, 67–68

Pacific Coast League 2, 47–51, 95–98, 100–102, 144–49, 159, 175, 193, 212, 236
Page, Joe 59
Paige, Satchel 30, 113
Parke, Howard 133–34
Parrott, Harold 3, 31, 86, 195, 215
Pasquel, Alfonso 34
Pasquel, Bernardo 42
Pasquel, Jorge 33–35, 38, 42, 67, 87
Passarella, Art 127
Patterson, Chuck 115
Patterson, Red 175, 190
Patterson, Robert 21
Pauley, Edwin 147–48
pay television 3, 106, 183–84, 197, 272
Payson, Joan Whitney 220, 223, 236, 250, *251*, 258
Pearson, Albie 252
Peer, William 187
pension plan 41–42, 130–31, 135, 273
Pepper, George Wharton 199
Perini, Louis 3, 10, 40, 51, 72–73,

97, 102–3, 105, *114*, 115, 118–25, 137, 199, 203, 235–36, 244–46, 261–62, 272, 275
Peters, Hank 113
Pettit, Paul 129
Philadelphia, Pennsylvania 6–7, 45, 63, 79–81, 137–41, 234
Philadelphia Athletics 37, 60, 74–77, 92, 111, 121, 129, 137–41
Philadelphia Phillies 9, 37, 40, 55, 57, 67, 69, 76–78, 130, 137–38, 141–42, 152, 170, 192–93, 257
Pierce, Billy 63
Pilarcik, Al 143
Pittsburgh, Pennsylvania 64, 79, 192, 233
Pittsburgh Pirates 2, 39–41, 61, 66, 70, 110–11, 126, 129, 151, 163–64, 189, 192, 231–32, 241
Polo Grounds (New York) 31, 62–63, 105, 149, 161–63, 165–66, 179, 184, 189, 193, 196, 199, 246, 251–52, 260
Porter, Paul 98–101, 203, *237*, 238, 262
Portland, Oregon 50, 146–47, 149
Poulson, Norris 176, 181, 188, 190, 194, 196, 211–14
Povich, Shirley 41, 74–75, 87, 120, 173, 252
Power, Vic 150
Praeger, Arnold 213–14
Prendergast, Jim 98, 101, 133

Qualters, Tommy 130
Quesada, Elwood 253, 270
Quinn, John (Braves general manager) *114*, 120
Quinn, John (umpire) 227

radio *see* broadcasting
Radovich, Bill 177–78, 182
Radovich v. National Football League (1957) 178, 182
rail transportation 6, 109–11
Raisdek, Cecilia 164
Reagan, Ronald 212
Reese, Pee Wee 99, 196, 210, 215
Reeves, Dan 46–47, 49–50, 107
Rehnquist, William 134
Reichardt, Rick 205–6
Reiser, Pete 246
reserve clause 35–41, 67–68, 96, 98–102, 132–35, 177–78, 182, 202–3, 209, 239–40, 272–74
Reynolds, Allie 130, 131
Reynolds, Debbie 212
Reynolds, Thomas 262
Rice, Bob 40
Richards, Paul 136, 205, 227, 259, 270
Richardson, Bobby 265
Richardson, William 75
Richmond, Virginia 191
Rickey, Branch 1–3, 14, 19–20, 25–26, *27*, 28–32, 35, 38, 42, 46, 53–55, 60–64, 67, 82, 84–86, 91, 96, 110–11, 129, 132, 151, 153–54, 162–64, 200, 221–25, 235–40, 246, 249–50, 253, 263–64, 268–69, 272, 276–77
Rickey, Branch "Twig," Jr. 32
Rigney, Bill 47, 94, 196
Rigney, Dorothy Comiskey 228–29, 260
Rigney, John 228
Rizzuto, Phil 34
Roberts, Robin 205, 209
Robinson, Brooks 128
Robinson, Frank 267
Robinson, Jackie 1–2, 32, 42, 51, 53–55, 66, 70–71, 88, 95, 111, 135, 152–53, 168, 246, 264, 267
Rochester, New York 191, 202
Rockefeller, John D. 11
Rockefeller, Nelson 188, *189*
Rolfe, Red 91
Roosevelt, Franklin 20, 65, 192
Roosevelt, Theodore 10
Roosevelt Stadium (Jersey City, New Jersey) 157–58, 160, 170, 194
Rose Bowl (Pasadena, California) 194
Roseboro, John 153
Rossi, John 57
Rottenberg, Simon 35
Rowland, Clarence "Pants" 47, *48*, 49–51, 96, 102, 144, 146, 149, 193, 269
Roybal, Edward 159
Rozelle, Pete 240, 276
Rudd, Irving 160
Ruel, Muddy 75
Ruppert, Jacob 21
Ruth, Babe 13, 70, 74, 93, 163, 165, 257, 275

Sacramento, California 48, 50, 146, 149
Saigh, Fred 68, 71–72, 77, 88–89, 91–92, 115–18, 273
Sain, Johnny 73
St. Louis, Missouri 5–7, 14, 45, 71, 79–80, 91, 233–34
St. Louis Browns 2, 5–7, 9–10, 13–15, 24, 26, 31, 34, 49, 51–52, 56, 71–72, 77, 90–92, 100, 102, 105, 113–21, 124, 127–28, 147, 265, 275
St. Louis Cardinals 5–6, 13–14, 20, 26–28, 30–31, 34, 43, 69, 71–73, 77, 91–92, 113–18, 135, 152, 185, 192, 209, 234, 264–65, 272
St. Paul, Minnesota 140, 144, 147, 179, 200–201, 236, 240, 254, 271
Salomon, Sidney, Jr. 114
San Diego, California 48, 50, 81, 144, 146–47, 175, 212, 253, 271
San Francisco, California 8, 47–51, 81, 100–102, 109–10, 124, 127, 144, 146–50, 154, 159, 171, 173, 179, 181–84, 194, 246–47, 252, 263, 265, 267–68, 272
San Francisco Giants 184, 187, 193–94, 196–97, 199, 220, 236, 246–47, 263, 265
Sarnoff, David 106
Savold, Lee 105
Schaffer, Rudie 70, 124
Schramm, Tex 104
Schroth, Frank 126, 154, 176, 180
Score, Herb 184
Scott, Frank 273
Scully, Vin 130, 215
Seals Stadium (San Francisco) 50, 193, 196, 199
Seattle, Washington 48, 50, 144, 146–47, 253, 271
Selig, Bud 245
Sewell, Luke 14, 24
Sewell, Rip 2, 40
Shantz, Bobby 143
Shaughnessy, Frank 191, 236
Shea, William 192–93, 197, *198*, 199–201, 218–23, 225, 235–38, 240, 249–50, 253, 269
Shea Stadium (New York) 269–70
Shibe Park (Philadelphia) 63, 77, 138, 141
Shore, Dinah 196
Sick, Emil 146–47
Siegel, Bugsy 89
Siegel, Morrie 173
Sievers, Roy 57, 71
Silver, Phill 215, 217
Simmons, Curt 67
Singman, Julius 132
Sisler, Dick 77
Slaughter, Enos 43
Sleater, Lou 143
Smith, Bob 251
Smith, C.R. 234
Smith, John 30, 84
Smith, Mary Louise 84
Smith, Red 19, 29, 87, 93
Snider, Duke 69, 111, 188, 197
Southworth, Billy 73
Spahn, Warren 122, 168
Sportsman's Park (St. Louis) 5, 14, 31, 63, 71, 91–92, 113, 115, 118, 124
stadiums 62–64, 97, 125–26, 142, 146–50, 154, 157, 160, 166–71, 173–75, 187–88, 191–95, 211–17, 223–24, 243, 246–48, 250–52, 259–60, 264–65, 269–70
Stanton, Frank 106
Steele, John Nelson 272
Stein, Elliot 255
Steinhagen, Ruth Ann 69
Stengel, Casey 69, 72–73, 150, 208–10, 241, 254, 258–59, 270
Stephens, Vern 34
Stern, Bill 65

Stevens, John Paul 98
Stevenson, Adlai 207
Stoneham, Charles 161–62
Stoneham, Horace 9, 46, 49, 106, 148, 149, 161–67, 174, 178, *179*, 181–84, 187, 189, 191, 193, 197, 220, 234, 246–47, 250–51, 263, 268
Stout, Glenn 248
Surkont, Max 122
Swift, Bob 91–92
Symington, Stuart 271

Taft, Robert 96
Talese, Gay 246
Taylor, Zack 91–92
television *see* broadcasting
Terry, Ralph 143
Theobald, John 187
Thomas, Charlie 31
Thomas, Frank 164
Thompson, Chuck 128
Thompson, Fresco 110, 153, 176, 199
Thompson, Robert 104
Thomson, Bobby 94, 105, 166
Throneberry, Marv 143
Toolson, Earl 98, 101, 132, *133*, 134, 177–78, 269, 272
Toolson v. New York Yankees Inc. (1953) 133–34, 177–78, 272
Topping, Dan 21, 59, 88–89, 116, 127, 138–41, 216, 236, 253, 263
Toronto, Ontario 8, 124, 140, 144, 160, 173, 191, 201, 220, 236, 252, 271
Trout, Dizzy 111
Truman, Harry 1, 53, 71, 93, 105, *108*, 109, 117, 207
Turley, Bob 128, 136
Tyson, Ty 65

Veeck, Bill 1, 55–56, *57*, 58–61, 70–71, 73, 76, 90–94, 102, 109, 113–20, 124, 127–28, 130, 140, 145–50, 162–65, 172, 192, 217, 224, 229–32, 245–46, 253–56, 260–61, 263, 265, 268, 270, 275–76
Veeck, Mary Frances 90, 164
Veeck, William, Sr. 55–56, 58, 65, 92
Vinson, Fred 22
Virdon, Bill 232

Waddell, Rube 141
Wagner, Honus 37
Wagner, Robert, Jr. 155, *156*, 157–58, 160, 166–67, 169–71, 175–76, 181, 187–88, 190–92, 198, 203
Waitkus, Eddie 69
Wakefield, Dick 67
Walker, Fred "Dixie" 54
Walker, Harry 43
Walker, Rube 210
Waner, Paul 209
War Memorial Stadium (Buffalo) *224*
Ward, Arch 47
Ward, John Montgomery *36*, 37, 39
Warren, Earl 134, 173, 177
Warren, Fuller 207
Washington, D.C. 8, 79–80, 108, 171, 233–34, 243, 248, 252, 264–65
Washington Senators (first franchise) 3, 10, 26, 53, 59, 74–76, 121, 130, 152, 159, 168, 171–74, 191–92, 204, 209, 240, 242–43, 248, 252
Washington Senators (second franchise) 253–54, 257, 264–65, 270, 276
Wattenberg, Ben 233
Webb, Del 21, 59, 88–90, 93, 96–97, 116, 127–28, 138–39, 143–44, 150, 199, 216–17, 236, 241–42, 250–52, 263, 273
Weber, Boots 56
Weiss, George 28, 30, 58–59, 116, 120, 143, 152, 203, 241, 250–51, 258–59, 270
Weiss, Hazel 59, 250
Wertz, Vic 135, 166
Wheaton, Woody 77
White, Theodore 104, 233
Whitney, Wheelock 249
Wiley, Alexander 238
Wilhelm, Hoyt 230
Wilkinson, J.L. 55
Williams, Edward Bennett 253
Williams, Ted 34, 47, 52, 72–73, 77, 84, 111, 208–9, 240–41
Wills, Maury 265, 267
Wolf, Al 145, 147, 197
Wolfner, Violet 219
Wolfner, Walter 219
Wolters, Larry 106
Woodling, Gene 78, 121
Wrigley, Phil 6, 9–10, 45, 49–50, 56, 65, 71, 93, 96, 100, 127–28, *145*, 146–49, 161, 175, 191, 193, 229, 267
Wrigley, William, Jr. 55–56, 65, 145–47
Wrigley Field (Chicago) 56, 62, 65, 146, 209, 226, 269
Wrigley Field (Los Angeles) 6, 147–48, 181, 194, 211, 254
Wyman, Rosalind 158–59, 190, 212
Wynn, Early 76

Yankee Stadium (New York) 31, 53, 59, 62–63, 115–16, 138, 141–42, 166, 168, 185, 247, 251
Yates, Brock 224
Yawkey, Tom 9, 110, 116, 119, 130, 144, 159, 203
Yost, Eddie 205
Young, Dick 255

Zanuck, Darryl 104
Zeckendorf, William 85–86
Zeidler, Frank 119, 122
Zeller, Jack 14
Zimmer, Don 259

www.ingramcontent.com/pod-product-compliance
Lightning Source LLC
Chambersburg PA
CBHW060335010526
44117CB00017B/2841